SIR ROBERT PEEL

The Life of Sir Robert Peel after 1830

SIR ROBERT PEEL

The Life of Sir Robert Peel after 1830

Second Edition
NORMAN GASH

'How miserable is all worldly business, take it for a course of time, that is not carried on by men who make a conscience of what they do in it.'

SPEAKER ONSLOW

LONGMAN
London and New York

Longman Group Limited
Longman House, Burnt Mill, Harlow
Essex CM20 2JE, England
Associated companies throughout the world

Published in the United States of America
by Longman Inc., New York

British Library Cataloguing in Publication Data

Gash, Norman
  Sir Robert Peel: the life of Sir Robert Peel
  after 1830.—2nd ed.
  1. Peel, *Sir* Robert, *bart.*   2. Prime ministers
  —Great Britain—Biography
  I. Title
  941'.081'092'4   DA536.P3

  ISBN 0-582-49722-1

Library of Congress Cataloging in Publication Data

Gash, Norman.
  Sir Robert Peel: the life of Sir Robert Peel after 1830.

  Bibliography: p.
  Includes index.
  1. Peel, Robert, Sir, 1788–1850.   2. Prime ministers—
Great Britain—Biography.   3. Great Britain—Politics
and government—1830–1837.   4. Great Britain—Politics
and government—1837–1901.   I. Title.
DA536.P3G32   1986   941.081'092'4 [B]   85-23934
ISBN 0-582-49722-1

Produced by Longman Group (FE) Limited
Printed in Hong Kong

CONTENTS

ACKNOWLEDGEMENTS

I wish to express my humble thanks for the gracious permission of Her Majesty The Queen to use material in the Royal Archives. I am also greatly indebted to the following for their courtesy in allowing me to read and quote from papers in their possession or of which they hold the copyright: His Grace the Duke of Wellington, the late Earl Stanhope, the Rt. Hon. the Earl of Clarendon, Lord Brabourne, Sir Fergus Graham, Bt., the late Sir William Dugdale, Maj. Gen. E. H. Goulburn, George F. Peel esq., Robert Bright esq., and the Trustees of the Newcastle Estate.

Other personal acknowledgements will be found in the footnotes, but this is the only place where I can record my gratitude for the assistance I have received from Dr. George Kitson Clark, Professor W. O. Aydelotte, Dr. F. A. Dreyer, Mr. Aubrey Newman, Mr. Francis Needham, Mr. Robert Mackworth-Young and the staff of the Archives Department at Windsor Castle, Miss W. D. Coates and the staff of the National Register of Archives, the staff of the University Library of St. Andrews, and from my old friend Dr. A. J. Taylor. It is proper also for me to mention my obligation to the University Court of St. Andrews for their travel and research grants which make the business of writing history in a northern university less difficult than might be supposed.

St. Salvator's College NORMAN GASH
St. Andrews
March 1971

The publishers are indebted to John Murray (Publishers) Limited for permission to use copyright material from *The Private Letters of Sir John Peel* edited by G. Peel.

FOREWORD

As in the first volume of this new edition of the life of Sir Robert Peel, I have amended a few misprints and stylistic defects and added a bibliographical note on subsequent publications. I have also taken the opportunity in Part II of this Foreword to give a brief sketch of the later Peel family in order to round off the account in the text which halts in 1850.

A feature of the new bibliographical material is the number of books and articles on the Conservative Party in the first twenty years of its existence. This is clearly useful for the biography of a politician of whom it could be said (with a certain amount of compression) that his career after 1832 consisted of leading the party in opposition, splitting it when in office, and repudiating it thereafter. As a historian, however, one may regret that the same amount of attention has not been given to the rival party. The process of bringing together Whigs, Liberals and radicals in one coherent organisation is just as important a field for investigation as the parallel movement among Conservatives. Indeed, a comparison of the two might well illuminate both. In this pioneer phase of party evolution the problems were similar. The position of the leader, responsibility for policy, tactics in opposition, maintenance of discipline, the permissible latitudes of dissent, the role of public opinion in a limited electoral system—all these were important matters for which there were few accepted rules. The whole question of party as distinct from parliamentary authority was still viewed with a certain objectivity. As late as 1851 G. C. Lewis wrote that 'my attachment to party is the result more of reason than of feeling. I believe it to be the only means of government in our political system and it is impossible for a party to continue if everybody insists on his own opinion to its full extent.'[1] That one intelligent politician writing to another should feel it necessary to enunciate such a basic principle argues a certain slowness in the acceptance of party as an object of supreme political loyalty.

SIR ROBERT PEEL

In the controversies which attended the emergence of the party system one central issue was the question of 'ministerial responsibility'. The concept was old enough; it was the circumstances under which it operated which had changed. To whom were ministers responsible? To the monarch whose servants they professed to be? To parliament on which their practical ability to govern depended? To the party which sustained them in office? To the country which they governed? Or, embodying but transcending all these claims, to a personal concept of public duty? After his defeat on the sugar duties in June 1844 Peel said in cabinet that his personal honour would not permit him to accept the victorious resolution or, alternatively, to take refuge in a mere renewal of the old duties for another year. Both he and Sir James Graham talked of the incapacity of disgraced men to serve their party or their country. This was not an argument taken up just for the occasion. Graham wrote privately to the Lord Lieutenant of Ireland that after the opposition of some of their own party to the measures of the ministry, he was 'at a loss to discover how, with honor or advantage to the country, we can be made responsible for the administration of affairs'.[2] Much the same attitude had been displayed by Peel, Graham and Stanley over the ministerial defeat on the factory bill a few months earlier. Their young colleague Gladstone was moved to reflect that ministers were clearly not men of expediency, as often portrayed, but on the contrary 'they act upon a strong, rigid, and jealous sense of honour, and they are perpetually dwelling on principle as apart from expediency'.[3] Similar language was used by the future Lord Salisbury over twenty years later. 'It has been well understood', he wrote in 1867, that a parliamentary leader would not endure to be overruled on any important point of policy; and that he could not concede this claim without a loss of personal honour.'[4] If the use of the word 'honour' was old-fashioned at the time of the second Reform Act, it was certainly not so a generation earlier.

The obverse of this notion of ministerial honour was an unflattering (and in Peel's case an occasionally contemptuous) opinion of the parliamentary parties as either reliable channels of public feeling or as depositories of higher statesmanship. For Peel there was a world of difference between government through party and government by party. It would, he wrote in 1846, be an 'odious servitude' if a prime minister, in addition to leading his cabinet, directing his administration, securing harmony between the sovereign, the Lords and the Commons, had also to act as the tool of a party: 'that is to say, to adopt the opinions of men who have not access to your knowledge, and could not profit by it if they had'. The weakness of party, he thought, was that the tail always wanted to control the head. 'As heads see, and tails are blind, I think heads are the best judges as to the course to be taken.' It is true that these, and even more scathing words about Conservative M.P.s who spent their time in 'eating and drinking, and hunting, shooting, gambling, horse-racing and so forth', were written after his fall from office.[5] But there is more than enough evidence to suggest that his language after 1846 was no more than the candid utterance of long-held feelings. In office he accepted the need for compromises between his views and the opinions of the rank and file of the party. On the general direction of his policy, however, he was not prepared to compromise; and once he was in office, the underlying divergences between himself and many of his parliamentary followers were soon exposed. As Charles Greville wrote, in what is still the best short essay on Peel's career, when he came to power in 1841: 'there was no real community of sentiment between him and his party, except in respect to certain great principles, which had ceased to be in jeopardy, and which therefore required no united efforts to defend them'. Between Peel and a large number of the Conservative members, he concluded, 'there was an unexpressed but complete difference in their understanding and his of the obligations by which the Government and the party were mutually connected'.[6]

Any consideration of the disruption of the Conservative Party in 1846 ought therefore to begin with the years before 1841. It has been argued indeed that Peel's attempt to inspire and lead a Conservative opposition party between 1832 and 1841 was a failure in the sense that he was unable to animate his party with the Tamworth Manifesto principles which informed his own actions and unable to secure sufficient support from other classes in the electorate to change the nature of his party. Failure is a relative term. Most political leaders would gladly compound for a 'failure' which gave them a majority of eighty in the Commons and made possible five years of epoch-making legislation. Over the truth of the underlying proposition, however, there can be no dispute; though it is scarcely a novel discovery. Nobody has ever contended that Peel moulded an entire party in his own image. It would be difficult, in fact, to name any outstanding party leader who has. That large political parties are coalitions, in a state of uneasy equilibrium, is one of the commonplaces of political observation. As far as the Conservatives of 1841 are concerned, a tentative assessment which I put forward over twenty years ago was that the Peelite section numbered only between a third and a quarter of the parliamentary party. Nor has it commonly been contended that Peel alone was responsible for the strength of the party in the 1841 general election. The real issue is whether Peel's leadership produced the margin of victory. Party politicians today measure success in terms of 5 per cent or 10 per cent swings in electoral support. Did Peel's presence make the difference between victory and defeat? It cannot be proved; though many contemporaries believed so in 1841. The fact remains, however, that for all its natural strength in the rural constituencies, this was the only occasion on which the party obtained a parliamentary majority in the whole period between the first and second reform acts; and that, despite the weaknesses and divisions among their opponents after 1847.

II

After 1846 there was frequent speculation that Peel might lead a new Peelite party or that the Conservative Party would reunite. Peel made it clear that he had no intention of pursuing either object. The only realistic possibility was that he might be persuaded to return to office as head of a coalition government. Given the bitterness of the 1846 disruption, that coalition could only be composed of Peelites and Liberals. Such an administration actually came about two and a half years after his death. It cannot, however, be taken for granted that a junction with the formidable Peel instead of the amiable Aberdeen would have been equally attractive to the Whigs. Certainly it would not have been so to Lord John Russell who entered the ministry in 1852 with the firm expectation that Aberdeen would be little more than a caretaker premier. It would have been difficult even for Lord John to believe that Peel would allow himself to be cast for such a limited role. We cannot even be sure that Peel would have agreed to become prime minister again even if invited. It would not have been an easy choice. On the one side there would have been his sense of duty, his attachment to Victoria and Albert, and a wish to safeguard his own policies. On the other, a distaste for party acrimony, disillusionment with politics, and doubts about his own health. The last was not so much a matter of age—he was only sixty-two when he died—as of stamina. Like Pitt and Liverpool, unlike Melbourne and Palmerston, he over-worked himself when in office. The five years from 1841 to 1846 had undoubtedly taken a great deal out of him. To assume the burden of government once more, he wrote to his old friend Hardinge in 1846, 'requires more youth, more ambition, more love of official power and official occupation, than I can pretend to'.[7] That was not conclusive. Six or seven years of comparative leisure might have produced a change of heart; but it was an attitude which would have had to be overcome.

There were other considerations. Lady Peel's wishes were strongly against a return to office and he had more than one reason to consider her feelings. In the fifth decade of her life (a difficult period for many women) her emotional nervousness had visibly increased. Any personal strain—the assassination of her husband's private secretary in 1843 (probably in mistake for the prime minister himself), her youngest daughter's serious illness in 1844, her eldest daughter's illness in 1845, the bitter abuse of her husband during the corn law crisis in 1846—made her ill with agitation.[8] There was gossip in fact that her temperamental sensitivity amounted almost to mental instability. Baron Rothschild, talking about her to John Bright in 1853, told him that 'during her husband's lifetime she was often excited almost to insanity, and that her husband only could quiet her. His looking into the room where she was had the immediate effect of subduing the disturbance of mind under which she at times laboured'.[9] Stories like this usually lose little in the telling and as evidence it is too slender to carry much weight. Greville, who became a great friend of Lady Peel after 1850, found her 'very pleasing' but thought her a little peculiar and unpredictable in her emotional reactions.[10] Certainly she had been very dependent on her husband, even in little things. Her dressmaker told Lady Shelley that he always accompanied her when she was choosing a dress and 'entered into all the details, the ornaments she was to wear, etc.'.[11] Peel's fatal accident in 1850 was a shock from which she took a long time to recover. Over the next two years, most of which she spent travelling abroad, she was still pouring out her grief and desolation in highly-strung language to intimate friends like Graham and Goulburn. She had never been used to containing her feelings and it was an age which did not find the expression of fervid emotions unnatural especially in a bereaved widow. But there is nothing in those letters which suggest that her mind was unbalanced. They are remarkably similar to those in which Victoria relieved her feelings after the death of Albert in 1861, and nobody has suggested that Victoria was mentally unstable.

For all that it seems probable that Julia Floyd had introduced a new quirkish strain into the next generation of Peels. The tragedy was that it appeared in her eldest boy, the heir to the title and estate. Her own favourite among her sons was the serious, dependable Frederick just as Peel's had been his active, sailor-son William who served with the Naval Brigade in the Crimea, fought with the Guards at Inkerman, carried the first ladder at the storming of the Redan, and won the V.C. Robert, on the other hand, was a continual source of anxiety to his parents and after his father's death an unpleasant rift opened up between him and his mother. There was a dispute over the disposal of property (Julia had been left the townhouse in Whitehall Gardens for her lifetime); she felt neglected and slighted; and in October 1851 she was writing to Goulburn that 'most of my sorrow lies at his door'.[12] For his part the new Sir Robert nourished a cordial dislike of his mother which he was at no pains to conceal. Lady Peel died at her house in London in 1859, her last years further clouded by the death of her son William during the Indian Mutiny. He was wounded at the relief of Lucknow and died of small-pox while convalescing at Cawnpore in 1858.

It was a peculiar irony, therefore, that more than one observer traced the eccentricities of the 3rd baronet to his mother's heredity. 'Alike in his character and in his aspect', wrote G. W. E. Russell, the Victorian politician and author, who knew the family well, 'the Creole blood which he had inherited from his maternal descent triumphed over the robust and serviceable commonplace which was the characteristic quality of the Peels.'[13] The term Creole (usually confined to persons born or naturalised in the West Indies, with no implication of mixed race) is a reference to Julia's mother who was the daughter of a Madras merchant. Robert was undoubtedly a genetic oddity in the Peel family. Short, slight, dapper and moustachioed, he was an amusing, debonair, faun-like figure in mid-Victorian society. Yet with all the advantages of birth, wealth and influence behind him, he lacked powers of application and had no judgement. As a politician his chief assets were a melodious voice and a witty, sometimes rabelaisian, tongue. Appointed junior lord of the Admiralty by Palmerston in 1855, he was sent to Russia the following year as a member of Granville's diplomatic mission. On his return he scandalised the Court and parliamentary world by giving a disrespectful account of his experiences, to a public audience in Birmingham, which according to his late chief Lord Granville, was 'a marvellous specimen of everything that ought not to have been said'.[14] As Chief Secretary in Ireland in 1861 his racy style at first gained him popularity in that unconventional country but his indiscreet political utterances eventually earned him a challenge to a duel from a hot-tempered Irishman and a recall by Russell in 1865. Having previously supported the Liberals he moved over to the side of Disraeli's ministry in the 1880s in disapproval of Gladstone's foreign policies—only to become a Home Ruler in 1886 and shock the Victorian public once more with a profane attack on the ladies of the Primrose League.

In his personal affairs he was equally reckless. Of the three classic methods of getting rid of a fortune, he chose the most certain—horse-racing. He set up a training establishment at Bonehill on the Drayton estate and from about 1856 raced under the not very original alias of Robinson. The slow but remorseless draining of his finances which followed caused him in 1871 to sell off his father's great collection of pictures to the National Gallery for £75,000. Even this was not enough and in 1884 came the first big sale of the Peel estate—shops, offices and houses in Tamworth, covering a large part of the centre of the town, together with pastures, orchards, and more houses on the outskirts of the borough, bringing in a total rental of £3,000 per annum. In 1893 the rest of the settled estate was sold, comprising nearly 10,000 acres with a rental of £20,000.

The 3rd baronet died in 1895. He had married in 1856 Lady Emily Hay, daughter of the 8th Marquess of Tweeddale, a socially distinguished alliance though (according to one old friend of the family) it contributed a further streak of irresponsibility to the senior line of Peels. Their son and heir, born in 1867, was another Robert and like his father a lively, engaging man. He also followed his father's downward financial course. He went bankrupt in 1893 and when he succeeded as baronet promptly and illegally sold Lawrence's famous portrait of his grandmother to a dealer in Paris from where it eventually found its way to its present resting-place in the Frick Museum in New York. This action brought down on him a court injunction, obtained at the instance of his uncle Viscount Peel, which was followed by Chancery proceedings in 1899–1900 to restrain him from selling off any more of the family heirlooms.

The rest of the story can soon be told. The 4th Sir Robert married in 1897 Baroness Mercedes von Graffenried, his residence in 1908 being described as unfixed, though his mother was by that time living in Geneva. The 5th baronet, offspring of this exotic union, married Beatrice Lillie, the actress. Their son, the 6th baronet, died on active service in HMS *Hermes* in April 1942. The baronetcy then passed to his cousin, the 2nd Earl Peel, and thus fell into abeyance. The spectacular decline of the elder branch did not affect the rest of the family. Of the prime minister's other sons all had respectable careers, William's was brief but brilliant, and that of Arthur the youngest was long and distinguished. A tall, commanding figure (also, like many Peels, a shy man) he was one of the more authoritative Speakers of the House of Commons during the stormy Home Rule period of Gladstone's final administrations. When on retirement he was offered a viscountcy, he consulted his brother, the 3rd baronet. Sir Robert Peel reminded him that their father had left an injunction at his death that none of his children should accept a title for his public services and said that he himself had refused an earldom from Gladstone. The Speaker, sensibly dissenting from this perverse view of their father's intentions, took the viscountcy—to the indignation of his elder brother who never spoke to him again. Viscount Peel's son William, Unionist politician, junior minister, and twice Secretary of State for India in the 1920s, obtained in 1929 the earldom which his uncle had allegedly rejected half a century before. The coolness between the two branches of the Peels seems to have carried over into the next generation. There is a tradition that his wife, Eleanor Williamson, was intended by her father, the wealthy textile and linoleum manufacturer Lord Ashton, for the 4th baronet but she jilted that rather wild young man in favour of his more dependable cousin, grandfather of the present Earl Peel.[15]

In 1818 the first Sir Robert spoke of Tamworth as the place 'where ourselves and offspring may be expected to reside for a century to come'. In the event the direct family connection with the borough lasted only another sixty years. After 1878 the great house at Drayton, built by the prime minister in the 1830s, remained unoccupied. The house and grounds were finally sold to Tamworth Corporation in 1926. Most of the buildings were taken down and the park turned into a pleasure-ground. In little over a century, since the first Sir Robert had set himself up as a Staffordshire landowner in 1790, the Peels of Tamworth had come and gone. The prime minister's other architectural legacy, his house in Whitehall Gardens, survived only a few years longer. Reverting to the Crown when the lease ran out in the 1920s, it was used for a time as government offices. After the last war it was pulled down to make way for the great concrete blocks which constitute the modern Whitehall. The visitor to Drayton today who may be tempted to moralise on the vicissitudes of family fortunes, can reflect on the curious circumstance that the three great houses built by the Peels at the height of their power and prosperity (Drayton Old Hall, Drayton Manor, and Whitehall Gardens) have all disappeared. Only Peel Fold, the primitive little Jacobean farmhouse at Oswaldtwistle in Lancashire, which was their first recorded family home, still stands.

October 1985   *Norman Gash*

[1] Netherby Papers, to Graham 27 Jan. 1851.

[2] *ibid.* to de Grey, 15 June 1844.

[3] *Prime Ministers Papers: W. E. Gladstone, Autobiographical Memoranda*, p. 254.

[4] *Lord Salisbury on Politics*, ed. Paul Smith (1972), p. 276.

[5] *Peel*, III, 474.

[6] *Greville*, 6 July 1850.

[7] *Peel*, III, 474.

[8] For Julia's nervousness see e.g. *Peel, Private Letters*, pp. 268–70, 274–5. It may be noted here that some of these letters were misdated by the editor. Her letter dated 20 June 1845 seems from internal evidence to be more likely 27 June 1846. The succeeding letter dated 15 Sept. 1845 is obviously 15 Dec. 1845 in reply to Peel's of 13 Dec. and answered by him on 16 Dec. (pp. 272–4).

[9] *Diaries of John Bright*, ed. R. A. J. Walling (1930), p. 138.

[10] *Letters of Charles Greville and Henry Reeve*, ed. A. G. Johnson, (1924), pp. 251, 263.

[11] *Diary of Lady Shelley*, ed. R. Edgcumbe (1912–13) II, 292.

[12] Goulburn Papers, 7 Oct. 1851.

[13] *Collections and Recollections* (n.d. ?1904) p. 131.

[14] Lord Edmond Fitzmaurice, *Life of 2nd Earl Granville* (1905) 1, 225.

[15] The more anecdotal parts of the preceding two paragraphs are based on conversations a quarter of a century ago with the late Mrs Helen Soames, youngest daughter of the 3rd Sir Robert Peel (Gladstone peerage) and the late Sir William Dugdale of Merevale Hall, close friend and protégé of Frederick Peel, the prime minister's second son. (the Hay and Williamson marriages).

1831	1st reform bill defeated in H. of C.	*general election*
	2nd reform bill defeated in H. of L.	*rioting in country*
1832	3rd reform bill amended in H. of L.	
	Peel refuses office	*Reform Act passes: general election*
1833	Irish Church debates	
1834	Oxford Chancellor's election	*Appropriation disputes*
		Grey resigns
	Peel and Wellington refuse coalition	*Melbourne forms ministry*
	Peel recalled from Italy to become prime minister	*king dismisses Whigs*
	Tamworth Manifesto	
	Mansion House speech	
1835	Ecclesiastical Commission	*general election*
		Lichfield House Compact
	Peel's resignation	
	City banquet speech	*English Municipal Corporations Act*
1836	Drayton Manor completed	*Irish Corporations and Irish Church bills abandoned*
	Peel elected Rector of Glasgow University	
1837	Glasgow speech	*Irish Corporations bill postponed*
		Accession of Queen Victoria
	Townshend affair	*general election*
	Peel's visit to Germany and France	*Canadian rebellion*
1838		*Irish poor law and tithes bills pass: Irish Municipal Corporations bill abandoned*
	Merchant Taylor's Hall speech	*People's Charter published*
		Anti-Corn Law Association founded
1839		*Jamaican crisis*
	Peel invited to form an	*Melbourne resigns*

	defeat and resignation of government	*Oregon treaty*
1847	budget talks with Wood	*general election*
	further talks with Wood	*financial crisis*
1848	West Indian legislation	*Chartist demonstration*
	Peelites disagree on Pakington amendment	*Revolutions in Europe*
1849	Peel's speeches on Ireland and Free Trade	*Repeal of the Navigation Acts*
1850	Peel appointed to Commission on Great Exhibition	*British naval demonstration in Dardanelles*
	Peelites disagree on agricultural distress motion	*Blockade of Piraeus*
	29 June–2 July Peel's accident and death	*Don Pacifico debate*

THE FAMILY OF THE PRIME MINISTER

Sir Robert Peel 1st Bt.

(see genealogical table in Mr Secretary Peel)

Children of Sir Robert Peel 1st Bt.:

- **Mary** b. 1785 m. Geo. Dawson M.P.
- **Elizabeth** b. 1786 m. Rev. Wm. Cockburn Dean of York
- **William Yates** b. 1789 M.P. m. Jane d. of E. of Mountcashel
- **Edmund** b. 1791 M.P. m. Emily Swinfen
- **John** b. 1798 m. Augusta Swinfen
- **Jonathan** b. 1799 M.P. soldier and racehorse owner m. Alice d. of M. of Ailsa Maj. Gen. 1859 secretary for war 1858–59, 1866–67
- **Lawrence** b. 1801 m. Jane d. of D. of Richmond
- **Harriet** b. 1803 m. Robert Eden later Lord Henley

ROBERT 2nd Bt. b. 5 Feb. 1788 Prime Minister 1834–35, 1841–46
m. **JULIA FLOYD** b. 1795 d. of Gen. Sir John Floyd

Children of Robert 2nd Bt. and Julia Floyd:

- **Julia** b. 1821 m. Vt. Villiers later E. of Jersey
- **Robert** 3rd Bt b. 1822 politician and diplomat m. Lady Emily Hay d. of M. of Tweeddale P.C., G.C.B. Chief Secretary for Ireland
- **Frederick** b. 1823 M.P. barrister at law P.C., K.C.M.G. financial secretary to Treasury 1859–65 chief railway
- **William** b. 1824 capt. R.N. K.C.B., V.C. served in Crimean War comd. Naval Brigade in Indian Mutiny d. of fever in India 1858
- **John Floyd** b. 1827 capt. Scots Fusilier Guards
- **Arthur Wellesley** b. 1829 M.P. secretary Poor Law Board Board of Trade and Treasury Speaker of House of Commons 1884–95 cr. Vt. Peel 1895
- **Eliza** b. 1832 m. Hon. Francis Stonor s. of Lord Camoys

xx

PRELUDE

For Robert Peel the year 1830 in which he reached his forty-second birthday was like a second coming of age; it brought him, both privately and politically, his final independence. In May had come the death of his father, the first baronet. His passing brought Peel the title, the ownership of Drayton Manor and a large estate, a fortune in invested wealth, the patronage of the borough of Tamworth, and the freedom to use this wealth and influence as he wished. After more than twenty years of paternal assistance, the purchased support of pocket boroughs or the unbought but more demanding suffrages of his late constituents of Oxford University, he was now head of his family, squire of Drayton, a leading Staffordshire landowner, a rich man in his own right and secure in the possession of a parliamentary seat almost within sight of his park gates. A few months later he reached the great divide of his political career. When Peel retired from the Home Office on the resignation of Wellington's ministry in November 1830, he came to the end of a long homogeneous phase in his public life. From that point the pattern underwent an abrupt transformation. Never again was he merely a departmental minister; never again did he serve under another man; never again did he hold any office as long as he had held the Irish secretaryship or the seals of the Home Department. All but five of his previous twenty-one years in politics had been in harness; of the remaining twenty all but five were out of office. Before 1830 Peel had never been in opposition to the government of the day; after 1830 he rallied and led to victory the first modern opposition party in British parliamentary history. The energy which he had been able in his early career to devote almost continuously to tasks of government, in his later years was dammed back for over a decade until the eruption of legislation in his last great ministry. Something of this fundamental shift in his political position could already be discerned at the end of 1830. In the previous few years Peel had reached that stage in a man's life when the ranks of the preceding generation suddenly give way and his own moves inexorably to the front. The eighteen-twenties had seen the almost total disappearance from the political stage of the great names which dominated the scene during Peel's parliamentary apprenticeship. Castlereagh had gone early and by his own hand in 1822. Then in 1827 came Liverpool's stroke followed by nearly two years of physical imbecility before the final release in December 1828. Canning, just when he had achieved the premiership, collapsed and died an agonising death in August 1827. All three had gone while still in their fifties, younger by several years than Grey was when he first became prime minister in November 1830. Of Peel's other cabinet colleagues of the Liverpool period, Sidmouth and Eldon lingered on as old men into the next decade but never held office again. For Bathurst and Melville resignation in 1830 was the closing event in political careers which had started under the younger Pitt. Vansittart held his last post under Canning and Goderich in 1827, though he survived into the middle of the century, an aged and forgotten figure. Among his more recent colleagues under Wellington, Dudley's eccentricities were about to degenerate into madness and death; Huskisson had been killed by one of Stephenson's new locomotives at the opening of the Manchester–Liverpool railway; Palmerston, Grant, Melbourne and Goderich had transferred their allegiance to Grey. Not only had Peel reached the top, but all other possible House of Commons rivals on his side of politics seemed to have disappeared.

Yet what coloured Peel's outlook at this stage in his career was less the distant prospect than the immediate background: the disillusionment left by the closing months of Wellington's administration, the personal coolness between himself and his former chief, and an exaggerated sense of his own unpopularity and lack of political support. The summit of power he had achieved under Wellington, as second-in-command and leader of the House of Commons, had proved a bleak and wind-swept eminence. That Peel in the end had been glad to quit it was a measure of his impotence. The real charge against the duke's ministry, despite its integrity, its reforms, and its economies, was its parliamentary weakness. Peel had recognised this and parted with office without regret, ready to support Lord Grey if that veteran Whig aristocrat could provide a more stable government. Unable to control events, he reacted by discarding responsibility for them. It was an attitude which his followers found hard to understand and it further weakened the already divided opposition. Peel was a man who throve on power, responsibility and action. The sudden deprivation of all three brought him in the years 1831–32 to the lowest point of his political life.

Yet the man had not altered; and in the winter of 1830–31, at this dead-point in his career, Peel faced the future with the training and temperament of the past. Though he could not change the vulnerable temperament and quick pride which was already his when he entered politics in 1809, he now had the great deposit of administrative experience laid down by nearly two decades in office. To a sympathetic observer at the end of 1830 two separate elements might have been detectable in the composition of the ex-Home Secretary. One was a product of his temperament; the other of his intellect and training. The one was moral and strategic; the other utilitarian and tactical. Together they formed the basis for his whole later career. Fundamentally Peel was an idealist in politics. From the start of his public life he had consciously set up, too consciously indeed for his own reputation, his private altars of honour and duty. His ambition had been not just for power but for the right use of power. For success and fame he was as eager as any ambitious and talented politician; perhaps more than most, since he had a sense of posterity as well as of the present. But for Peel there was always the antecedent question; how should he act to deserve that success and fame? It was this ethical scrupulousness which marked him out from the throng of mere politicians and earned him some of his unpopularity. Yet it would not have occurred to many people at the time to regard him either as an idealist or as impractical. Even those, and they included many on his own side of politics, who thought him priggish and egotistic, had to admit his parliamentary skill. For the other great attribute of Peel in 1830 was twenty years' experience in the art of getting things done; an asset which idealists do not usually acquire. Upon the groundwork of his intellect, his industry, and his ambition to deserve well of his country, had been built up a career which by early middle-age had given him more practice in the handling of affairs than many politicians get in a lifetime. For sheer administrative and debating talent he would always have to be reckoned with as long as he remained in parliament.

Embedded in that success, however, was a certain penalty. He had always been close to the working-face of politics; too close to take long views and form abstract principles. The responsibilities of office had forced him to concentrate on what was possible within the political system of his day; and though he lacked neither imagination nor courage, the daily habits of the first twenty years of his career had fostered his instinct for what was immediately necessary and attainable rather than for what was ideally or ultimately desirable. By temperament bold and creative, by hard experience he was cautious and realistic. Yet even in the authoritarian administrative structure in which Peel had served since 1810, policies could not be completely divorced from politics. Within the shelter of Liverpool's fifteen-year ministry (the last of the old eighteenth-century governments in form and spirit if not in its problems), he had been able to absorb himself in departmental duties and build up his reputation as an administrator. But in the years after Liverpool's fatal illness, he had taken two major political decisions which had large consequences for his own career. The first in 1827 was to break with Canning over the Catholic question and so, in the event, to place himself under the political leadership of that most unpolitical leader the Duke of Wellington. The other was to support and ultimately to direct the passing of Catholic emancipation in 1829. For these contradictory decisions there had been good, almost compelling reasons; but their results for Peel personally had been disastrous. They not only inflicted deep damage on his reputation but brought about in the end the collapse of the administration of which he was the ablest member and his own retirement from office. It was a collapse which was attended by peculiar bitterness, for it was caused not so much by the efforts of the opposition as by the desertion of former supporters and the misjudgement of his own chief. Estranged from a section of his own party, mortified by the ignominious end of the administration, Peel faced the future with more uncertain prospects and more resentful feelings than he had ever known before.

Even that did not exhaust the catalogue of mistakes and failures. For the circumstances of the fall of Wellington's government had public as well as personal consequences. It brought up parliamentary reform as a pressing political issue at the same time as it inhibited Peel from making any constructive approach to that fundamental problem. Of all questions this was one on which Peel found it difficult to make up his mind. For parliament and especially the House of Commons he had a deep respect. It was an institution as small, intimate and historic as the little cramped chapel of St. Stephen's in which it met; it was an institution which worked; one in which he had grown up and to the understanding of which he devoted much thought. Whatever the method of producing the House of Commons (and he never denied the absurdities and abuses of the system), it resulted in an assembly with as much commonsense and talent as a representative body of over six hundred men is likely to possess under any system of selection. Reared in this close political society, he was reluctant to acknowledge any authority other than parliament on specific issues of policy; and still more reluctant to accept a radical reform of parliament which would change its independent character and reduce it to a mere delegacy of the electorate. He did not think the representative system sacrosanct in its details but any reform to which he could assent would have to preserve the traditional nature of the House of Commons. The kind of reform which the extreme radicals were advocating, however, threatened to destroy the actual principles of the parliamentary constitution as he knew it. His own deep instincts, therefore, collided with the popular pressures of the day. Moreover, even though he recognised, along with most politicians at the end of 1830, that some reform would have to come, he did not think that Wellington's ministry was the one to propose it. After Catholic emancipation another great retreat from principle to expediency would have been intolerable. 'Peel was for Parliamentary Reform,' wrote Wellington sourly to Mrs. Arbuthnot on 26 December, 'provided it was not carried by *us* in Office.'[1]

What characterised his attitude on parliamentary reform was true in a larger sense of his general views. He was not an unthinking defender, either from birth or interest, of the old order. A zealot for efficiency and justice, a tart critic of corruption and privilege, he always found the selfish aristocrat, the job-hunting politician,

[1] *Wellington and His Friends*, p. 91.

the conscienceless cleric, as distasteful in practice as they were to the radical reformers in principle. But the social aristocracy which produced these, as well as better men, was one which he knew from within and at close quarters. His own family background was Pittite and Anglican; he had grown up during the Revolutionary and Napoleonic Wars; he entered politics six years before Waterloo. It was not surprising that he possessed some of the emotional heritage of the war period and felt himself in a measure identified with the maintenance of the aristocratic constitution in Church and State against Jacobinism, radical democracy, Irish Catholic nationalism, and the class struggle of an emerging industrial proletariat. Yet he was never a reactionary. That requires an element of stupidity or panic, and Peel had neither; he was too level-headed and intelligent. The paradox of his position lay precisely in this. He was the defender of a system of which he was the intellectual critic and active reformer; which he upheld in principle and amended in detail. To be either a mere reactionary or a mere radical was foreign to his nature. Everything depended therefore on how far he could make a synthesis of these different strains in his nature; and how far he could impose that synthesis on his followers—if indeed he was to have any followers after 1830. He cared for and respected the great institutions of the state; and because he cared for them for their own sake, as distinct from seeing in them only the interest of his class or party, he wished to remove their abuses, restore their energies, and enable them to survive in a changed and changing world. Stated as an abstract proposition, this was simple enough. In the circumstances of the time it needed great delicacy, perception and judgement to carry out; above all, courage to undertake actions which seemed to be against the very interests which he claimed to be preserving. At the close of 1830 all the omens seemed to be against him.

Yet misfortune is often as deceptive as success. Peel had encountered many things in his career but not until then failure and defeat. This hardening element was now added to his political education. The wreckage of his political world, and the new climate of politics which the coming to power of Lord Grey was to create, forced him to make a fresh point of departure. Where the next landfall would be could not be predicted; but men of forty-two with intelligence and ambition do not easily despair.

THE CRISIS OF REFORM

When Lord Grey was summoned on 16 November 1830 to form a
ministry, it was also to meet a crisis: one that had blown up suddenly like a summer storm, and was as fierce and inexplicable.
Afterwards, as men looked back on the events of that autumn, they
tended sometimes to ascribe the astonishing collapse of Wellington's
ministry to adventitious factors, such as the coincidence of the July
revolution in France with the general election in Britain. But the
causes ran deeper than that; for what had happened was the end of
an order. The illness and resignation of Lord Liverpool in 1827 had
started the disintegration; and the cracks which he had pinned
together at once opened into yawning gaps under Canning,
Goderich and Wellington. Once the political system over which
Liverpool had presided for fifteen years lost its cohesion and
momentum, it was seen how little support it had from without.

There should have been little for surprise in that. For two generations or more there had been a steady erosion of confidence in the
country's institutions which only the national mood of patriotism
during the Napoleonic Wars had contrived temporarily to halt.
The growth of this profound distrust started at least as far back as
the War of American Independence and after the coming of peace
in 1815 it mounted with slow but unceasing pressure. It was fed
from many social sources: the spreading towns of the north and
midlands with their millocracies and industrial proletariats; the
middle-class and predominantly urban educated public with growing wealth and growing political articulateness; the militant trade
unions; the radical societies; the press, both national and provincial;
the economists and social philosophers; the active body of English
dissent. These were elements to which the classic eighteenth-century

structure of Church and State, monarchy and aristocracy, offered at best only partial status and satisfaction. A society that liked to call itself one of intellect and industry was growing up inside the institutional shell of another and older society based on land and privilege; and the shell was cracking with each passing year. The aristocracy, at no point divorced from the larger society it ruled, was itself increasingly affected by the social and intellectual changes after the Napoleonic War. Its chief economic interest, the land, was as hardly hit as industry by the postwar depression; and the government's currency and Corn Law reforms were a constant source of grievance. Spokesmen of liberal views were to be found in both houses of parliament; the Whigs had their own antique tradition of civil and religious liberty; and, greatest eccentricity of all, after the enforced passage by the executive government of Catholic emancipation in 1829, some ultra-Protestant Tories momentarily turned their thoughts to reform of a kind that would restore the independence of the legislature. The events of 1830—the revolutions in France and Belgium, the renewal of radical agitation in London and the north, the rioting of the agricultural labourers of the south (the most depressed and unpolitical of the English social classes)—formed only a backcloth against which forces long stirring in British society suddenly came together.

The defeat of Wellington's ministry in November 1830 was in many respects a technical defeat, due to loss of flexibility by a ministry which was too weak to manœuvre, and a prime minister who risked everything on a tight defensive battle at a time when his troops were still restive and mutinous from the events of 1829. But in a larger sense the defeat of the government was only a spectacular and extreme symptom of a permanent weakness which had been afflicting the machine of government for a quarter of a century. When men talked, as they were beginning to do, of government by public opinion, they meant in effect that the time had gone when there could be a government of influence and interest. The authority of the crown, the control of the legislature by the executive, the cement of patronage, the loyalty of the country gentry, had all been slowly diminishing since the end of the eighteenth century; and more important than the physical decline in the means of controlling parliament was the intellectual acceptance by rulers and ruled alike that these were not defensible means of carrying on administration. Authoritative systems of government are notoriously vulnerable when they begin to reform themselves. Not only had the outworks of the eighteenth-century constitution been surrendered—some without a shot like the Test and Corporation Acts, others after a bitter struggle like Catholic disabilities—but a longer and more subtle process of sapping and mining had undermined the central keep. Wellington's ministry was weak because it came at the end of a long line of ministries which had successively whittled away the instruments of power. It was unpopular because the image of government that had been imprinted on the public mind by two generations of radical agitation was the corrupt face of the old eighteenth-century rather than the reforming neo-aristocratic countenances of Liverpool, Canning, Huskisson and Peel. The public had turned decisively against venality, extravagance and nepotism; but in turning it failed to observe that the Wellington ministry was scarcely characterised by any of these things.

The fact that the unreformed parliament had worked in practice and that able men were produced to govern the country, was now irrelevant in the face of a public opinion which thought the system socially repugnant and intellectually absurd. No system could work efficiently if it did not have a degree at least of general acceptance; and by 1830 the system of representation was no longer acceptable. It was true that Wellington's ministry was one of the most economical of the century; its conduct of affairs as upright and disinterested as the conduct of politics can ever be. But only a small section of the public was prepared to recognise its merits. For the most part the general radical picture of swollen pension lists, jobbery and inefficiency, of an indolent and avaricious Church and a grasping borough-mongering aristocracy, was accepted in gross even when discounted in detail. For years every great institution and many great political personalities had been remorselessly and indecently pilloried in countless broadsheets, prints and pamphlets. What Hone, Cruikshank, Cobbett and Carlile, and numerous editions of *Red Books*, *Black Books*, and *People's Books* had portrayed in coarse and savage exaggeration, was reflected in paler tones by more influential and respectable journals. George IV, as regent and king, had immeasurably added to the discredit into which all the great institutions of the state seemed to have fallen. Only the arrival of a virtually unknown sailor-king, coinciding, after a brief interval, with a reforming ministry, had retrieved for the throne a specious and sentimental popularity. That Church and State, rather than the monarchy, were in disrepute if not actual danger in 1830–31, was only an accident of date.

Against this the government was powerless. With all its merits, Wellington's ministry had one great demerit. It had failed to establish a firm link with either parliament, press or the public. Publicity and propaganda were almost entirely in the hands of critics and enemies. By the end of 1830 hardly one newspaper of substance could be found to give it wholehearted support. With much will to do good, and some potentiality for achieving it, it lacked the talisman of public strength which alone could compensate for the intrinsic weakness of the parliamentary system. The crowning disaster of Wellington's brief career as prime minister was that he contrived to identify his administration with the distorted image drawn by radical propaganda. Two issues in November 1830 had brought down his government, one directly, the other indirectly. The first was the refusal to submit the new Civil List to the scrutiny of a parliamentary committee; the second was the duke's uncompromising declaration against parliamentary reform. One was taken as evidence of extravagance; the other of reaction.

When, therefore, Grey took office he was not merely confronted with a crisis; he was provided with a programme. It was incumbent on him to provide proof of parsimony and integrity; it was imperative for him to carry through some kind of reform of the representation. The technical fact that the opposition had defeated the government over the Civil List meant that the new ministers would have to concede what had been refused by the old. Even the outgoing cabinet, with the solitary and recalcitrant exception of the Duke of Wellington, told the king when they took their leave of him that something must be done about parliamentary reform. The Civil List was essentially an administrative matter and as such was clogged by those brute facts which (as Bagehot once observed) seem to reside permanently in office to subdue the spirits and policies of successive politicians. In the event the new ministry could do little with the Civil List except to divide and rearrange it in order to exhibit more plainly its essential necessity. Without manifest hardship to individuals no great reduction in its charges could be made for several years. But parliamentary reform was a legislative matter and this was from the start the cardinal issue on which the fate of the ministry hung. That some reform must come was certain. How great that reform should be largely depended on the character of the prime minister and the force of public opinion. Party organisation and party policy were at this juncture almost meaningless. Indeed it was only for the sake of brevity that Grey's government and the majority on which it rested could be described as Whig. His ministry, like that of nearly all his predecessors, was a coalition and it faced the same heterogeneous and indisciplined House of Commons which had pulled down Wellington and harried Liverpool and Canning. It was inevitable that the new government should reflect the variegated complexion of the old opposition. The Whigs, reunited after their internal disagreement over Canning, provided the bulk of the new team; but after a quarter of a century of almost continuous isolation, they were depressingly deficient in men with administrative practice. The Canningites, who made up in experience what they lacked in numbers, secured all three secretaryships of state and the Presidency of the Board of Control. Tories like Anglesey, Wynn, Wellesley and Richmond accepted office and approaches were even made to the ultra-Protestant Knatchbull and Wellington's Irish Secretary, Hardinge.[1] As the *Courier*, in the process of dexterously shifting its allegiance from the outgoing to the incoming administration, comfortingly observed: 'the majority, in number and character, are Whigs; but there is a happy mixture of Toryism and independence'.[2]

There was an equal if less happy mixture of independence in the House of Commons. When after a long Christmas recess it reassembled early in February, the disappointed grumbling over the new Civil List arrangements and the rough handling of Althorp's budget showed with painful clarity that Grey's government had little more control over the legislature than Wellington's. It was obvious that the ministers held their places only as the midwives of reform and that their tenure would depend on what tender infant

[1] Aspinall, *Diaries*, p. xxvii.
[2] 20 Nov. 1830.

they would eventually deliver. On taking office in November, Grey had announced in the Lords that the government intended to introduce a plan of moderate reform; and after the first buzz of speculation, the country settled down to wait. During the midwinter months the labourers' riots and their judicial aftermath, the activities of O'Connell in Ireland, and the disturbed state of France and the Netherlands, crowded reform from the columns of the press. But if speculation died down, reform remained the iron test for both the government and the country. Behind the temporary lull the question of the day was brief and simple. What would the Whigs do? But there could be no simple answer. Ever since Peterloo in 1819 had shocked liberal minds, individual Whigs in the Commons had intermittently put forward reform proposals, notably Lord Durham (Grey's son-in-law) in an extreme, and Lord John Russell in a milder form. But they could not speak for a party and most Whigs had been ready in 1827 to join Canning who had flanked his advocacy of Catholic emancipation with an equally constant condemnation of parliamentary reform. Grey himself, though he had held aloof from the Canning coalition, had after Waterloo made Catholic emancipation and not reform the *sine qua non* of taking office.

At the age of sixty-six the new prime minister could look back across the gulf of a third of a century to the time when, as friend and disciple of Fox, he had seen his own reform bill extinguished in a Pittite House of Commons at the height of the wartime reaction. Since those distant days, disappointment and constant exclusion from power had left their mark on this proud, ageing aristocrat. As early as 1810 he had reconciled himself to an indefinite postponement of reform in the face of royal opposition and public indifference. As late as February 1830 he had warned his son Howick against involvement in an issue that still lacked the prerequisite of popular support. Yet in the remote and patriarchal domesticity of his Northumberland home, Grey had long ago decided that only a radical measure of reform would rally public opinion round a Whig government; only public opinion could provide a basis on which a Whig government could stand. The events of 1830 transformed that detached and abstract opinion of 1820 into a practical decision. The death of George IV had removed a personal obstacle to his taking office. The weakness of the government had brought the Whigs for the first time since the death of Pitt to the threshold of power on their own terms. Above all, Grey reached the conviction that a perpetuation of the old regime under Wellington's stubborn and unrealistic leadership was beginning to imperil the aristocratic order to which they both belonged. He took office, therefore, not in response to popular clamour, still less from desire for power, but from an innate feeling that the survival of the social and political structure of the country depended on passing a measure of parliamentary reform generous enough to restore the confidence of the country in its own institutions. His own fundamentally aristocratic nature led him towards a solution that was apparently radical but, as he believed, essentially conservative. In defence of his order he was prepared to be a revolutionary. It was a paradox which few outside the cabinet could discern at the close of the eventful year of 1830.

II

After the new ministers had met both Houses in December, parliament was adjourned until 3 February to allow time for their measures to be concocted. In the interval the government embarked on prosecutions of Carlile and Cobbett; Melbourne at the Home Office faced a series of strikes in the cotton industry; and the Committee of Four (Durham, Russell, Graham and Duncannon) began their deliberations on parliamentary reform. Free from all such cares, Peel spent a pleasant rural Christmas in Staffordshire which was marred only by his wife's ill-health. With the assistance of Smirke, the well-known architect, and Gilpin, the fashionable landscape gardener of the time, he had already started to plan a new mansion at Drayton. Meanwhile the old square-built house erected by his father thirty-five years earlier, which Mrs. Arbuthnot dismissed as 'frightful', accommodated within its few spare bedrooms a succession of political guests. The Arbuthnots were there for Christmas; Charles Ross, the assistant whip, and Sir George Clerk came early in January; Croker, Twiss, and Sir Alexander Grant in the second week; Murray, Herries, and Holmes, the chief whip, were asked for the middle of the month. Peel refused an invitation from Wellington to join a rather more distinguished political gathering at Stratfield Saye, pleading Julia's illness and his domestic affairs. The excuses were genuine but perhaps he was glad that he had excuses to offer. Yet it was clear that for his own part he was keeping in touch with the subalterns of the party and as newly succeeded master of Drayton was taking an early opportunity of establishing his position in his own locality. With his guests he attended the Tamworth Ball on 11 January, where politicians and landowners rubbed shoulders with farriers, farmers and their wives. At the end of the month a number of neighbouring squires trundled over the snowy roads for an all-male dinner at Drayton at which Sir Robert laid himself out to be agreeable and told anecdotes of his experiences at the Home Office.[1]

Despite the weather, the strikes, and the activity of reform clubs and political unions, there seemed little cause for immediate alarm. Everyone remembered that Grey had promised to stand by his order and any measure of reform would have to face the judgement of a House of Commons in which he was far from possessing a firm majority. It was evident that reform of some sort must come, and that it would be more than the enfranchisement of Manchester, Leeds and Birmingham proposed by Lord John Russell the previous session. Many Tories themselves thought a reform was desirable; others had their electors to consider. The real question for the opposition was tactical: whether to admit a moderate measure because it could not be defeated and because it would be an inoculation against radicalism, or to oppose it however mild its details because it embodied a pernicious principle. But tactics demanded party unity and party leadership. In the absence of either, the Tory country-house conversations of January 1831 could only be discussions without decisions. If Wellington was still the nominal chief, his authority had been severely shaken by his actions the previous autumn; and though Peel was disliked and distrusted by many on both personal and political grounds, there were others who saw in his outstanding House of Commons ability the only rallying-point for the future. What Peel would do personally was no more clear than what the party could do collectively. Croker tried at Drayton to extract from him a pledge against any parliamentary reform, but though cheerful and friendly, Peel was not to be drawn.

[1] *Croker*, II, 97, 105; *Dyott*, II, 101, 104.

He was sick of eating pledges, he said good-humouredly, and though he would oppose anything, he would pledge nothing.[1]

When parliament reassembled in February it was announced that 1 March had been fixed by the government as the date for the introduction of their reform proposals, and in the intervening weeks all that Peel did seemed to consolidate his reputation as the most eminent individual member of the House of Commons. His speech of 8 February on Irish affairs was a notable contribution to one of the best debates in the House for many years. In a measured criticism of the budget on 11 February he appealed to Althorp to withdraw the proposed tax on exchanges of funded property which had attracted general hostility in parliament and the City. Three days later it was in fact withdrawn. When an attempt was made to reduce the West Indian sugar duties he came to Althorp's rescue and induced Lord Chandos to abandon his resolution. Yet though in these early tentative weeks he was by common consent the arbiter of the House, an air of unreality hung over the political scene. Nothing was important until the ministers' intentions were revealed on 1 March, and until then no one could take the responsibility of unseating them.[2]

In the meantime the question of opposition tactics had still to be decided. Nothing had leaked out on the details of the government's plan, and the old dilemma remained. It is probable that Peel's instinct was to oppose at the outset, or at least that he was not persuaded of the wisdom of any other course. But many of his followers, for the sake of their consciences or their constituents, were reluctant to block the mere introduction of a reform bill. A ministerial defeat on such an issue would probably bring about a dissolution and at a general election anti-reformers would be marked men. Lord Granville Somerset, one of the party managers, was even reported to have told Peel that he would if necessary have to vote against his leader in order to save his electoral position in Monmouthshire. On Sunday, 20 February, there was a meeting of House of Commons members at Peel's house in Whitehall Gardens. While there were some, not otherwise classed as ultras, who favoured the bolder course, the general conclusion was that the party could not sufficiently rely on its followers to vote against reform at the outset.

[1] *Croker*, II, 101.
[2] *ibid.*, 108; *Greville*, 12, 13, 24 Feb. 1831.

A week later there was a joint meeting of leading peers and commoners at Apsley House to settle the matter. Though the duke still hankered for resistance, Peel expressed the view of the House of Commons men that opposition should be reserved until the details of the bill were known and this became the final party decision.[1] In all the circumstances it seemed a sensible as well as a necessary course.

Two days later the bandage of ignorance and miscalculation was ripped from their eyes. Tuesday, 1 March 1831, saw the staging of a parliamentary occasion in the old chapel of St. Stephen's which recalled the opening night of the great Catholic debate in 1829. But now it was not Peel but Lord John Russell, small, sharp-featured and intellectual, who was in the centre of the stage. Though not a cabinet minister he had been chosen to introduce the bill rather than Althorp, the leader of the House, because he was a better orator, despite his thin reedy voice, and as a member of the drafting committee conversant with all its details. Members had gone early to reserve places and when the public gallery was opened at 5 p.m. there was a rush of visitors with much noise, trampling and confusion, while the benches below steadily filled up. At six o'clock Russell entered the House to the cheering of his supporters.

A few minutes later his name was called and in a deep silence he began his first low-toned sentences. The occasion was greater than his speech; but there was no need for eloquence. He was heard with profound attention, punctuated by cheering and counter-cheering that grew in volume and violence as the government's plan was disclosed section by section to his astonished audience: the total disfranchisement of all boroughs with less than 2,000 inhabitants; the partial disfranchisement of those with less than 4,000; the institution of a common borough franchise for £10 householders; twenty-seven new boroughs; 168 M.P.s to lose their seats; half a million to be added to the electorate. The noise and temper of the House reached a climax when he read out the list of sixty boroughs, old and honoured—or dishonoured—in parliamentary history, which were to be swept away and ('more yet', said Russell mockingly) a second schedule of forty-seven to be reduced to one member. There were screams of wild ironical laughter from the opposition

[1] *Croker*, II, 108, 110; *Greville*, 13 Dec. 1831; Aspinall, *Diaries*, p. 13 n. 2; *Courier*, 28 Feb. 1831.

benches as each name was pronounced and even government supporters sat appalled at the holocaust they had brought upon themselves. In the early stages of the speech Peel had sat looking half-angry, half-contemptuous; but as the staggering scope of the measure was revealed, the colour came and went in his handsome florid countenance. In the end, while his colleagues around exulted at what seemed the suicide of the government, he put his hands before his face. With his quick political sagacity perhaps he already realised that there was now no room for compromise or moderation. The government had made a bid for popular support which they could never withdraw. The old parliamentary constitution in which he had lived for twenty-one years was dead.

When Russell sat down there was prolonged cheering and a rush of members from the House. Groups of M.P.s gathered in lobbies, ante-chambers and passages to form the most excited and vivid scene known at Westminster for many years, and Inglis, the first opposition speaker, could not be heard for several minutes in the general hubbub. Twiss, Althorp, and Leveson Gower carried on the debate until Hume secured the adjournment at half-past twelve, but all the time Peel sat virtually silent on the opposition front bench. Once when Althorp said that the bill gave to the people of England an 'overpowering influence' in the choice of their representatives, he uttered a sarcastic 'hear, hear!' But this was a minor riposte to the hammer-blow of the bill itself. Next day members pulled their wits together after the shock and confusion of the night before, and on the Liberal side men even began to think that the government's plan, instead of being an audacious and preposterous speculation, might after all prove a political feasibility. But there was still considerable hesitation and in London and the City opinion showed no immediate rallying to the government. Parliamentary curiosity about the line Peel would adopt began to intensify and many thought that his attitude might decide the fate of the measure.

The second night was marked by brilliance from Macaulay and buffoonery from Wetherell. On the third, Peel rose to make his opening contribution to the great reform debate. It was a good speech, able, eloquent, and measured; and he received tremendous acclamation when he sat down. Some people said ('as usual', observed Greville with his mordant commonsense) that it was the finest oration they had ever heard in parliament. Moreover he timed it well, rising after a weak speech by the ex-Canningite and reluctant reformer Palmerston, against whom Peel was able to recall with formidable effect the authority of his dead master. The body of his text was filled out with a number of arguments that were to be worn threadbare by innumerable speakers in the succeeding months: the arbitrary and ultimately untenable line of the £10 franchise; the wanton abolition of the old democratic franchises; the value of the rotten boroughs as a door for young talent and a refuge for elder statesmen; the need to strengthen rather than weaken the already diminished influence of executive government. But he went to the root of the reform issue when he enquired scornfully what practical advantages were claimed in compensation for the acknowledged risks, other than conciliating public opinion.

> Why, no doubt, you cannot propose to share your power with half a million men without gaining some popularity—without purchasing by such a bribe some portion of good-will. But these are vulgar arts of government; others will outbid you, not now, but at no remote period—they will offer votes and power to a million of men, will quote your precedent for the concession, and will carry your principles to their legitimate and natural consequences.

It was a warning that began to become true even in his own lifetime.

There were three points in particular, however, which stood out from his speech. He made it clear that he was opposing, not reform, but the particular reform proposed by the government. When last in office, he said, he had been unable as a minister of the crown to bring forward a reform measure. As a private member, balancing the danger of reform against the danger of executive instability, 'I do not hesitate to avow, that there might have been proposed certain alterations in our representative system, founded on safe principles, abjuring all confiscation, and limited in their degree, to which I would have assented.' Secondly, the ministerial proposals, entailing as they did a literal reconstruction of the House of Commons, were so extensive that they could not be changed in detail and he would therefore have to oppose them in their entirety. Lastly, by bringing forward this plan at a time of national excitement, the government had abdicated from their executive responsibility and provoked a crisis of which it was impossible to foresee the outcome. 'They have sent through the land the firebrand of agitation and no one can now recall it.'

It was a strong speech which concealed a delicately balanced position. He had committed himself against the bill without joining those committed against reform; and he had implicitly admitted the success of Grey's appeal to the country over the heads of the politicians. Already opinion in the provinces, especially the large towns, was showing itself overwhelmingly behind the government. In turn the enthusiasm out of doors was consolidating Whigs, reformers, radicals and waverers within the House of Commons. Grey had carried the crown and caught the country; it remained to be seen whether he could complete his success with the Commons and the peers. By 10 March, when leave was given to bring in the bill, political opinion was already beginning to reckon on a probable majority for a measure on which hardly an M.P. would have laid odds the week before. As the balance swung, the opposition backbenchers, their derision turned to dismay, began to look back at the rapid slide of events since the fatal evening of 1 March and wonder why they had not rejected the measure when the House was still in a state of wonder and shock. It was easy now, with the perspicacity that follows behind events, for men to believe that had Peel immediately moved the negative, he would have had a majority; and easy to blame him for not having done so. In the end the charge was repeated so often that it became a minor parliamentary legend. But Russell himself did not accept it. Talking with Greville in 1842 he pointed out that nothing Peel could have done would have prevented some debate from taking place; and once the plan was known, public opinion would have carried it through.[1] There was also the other consideration. If the ministers had been beaten, they would probably have dissolved parliament and won the general election. But if they had in fact merely resigned, what stable government could have been formed with a House of Commons which in less than six months had got rid of one Tory ministry and one Whig? The notion that a quick piece of parliamentary tactics on

[1] *Greville*, 22 Nov. 1842.

the evening of 1 March could have averted reform is scarcely credible.

Nevertheless the imputation of bad tactics persisted and in proportion as Peel's leadership was criticised, the slight tendency visible in January for the various sections of the opposition to unite, dwindled once more. His declaration in favour of some reform had annoyed the ultras—it was noticed that Wetherell abruptly ceased to applaud at that point in the speech; and Peel on his side withheld any gesture of conciliation to the extremists of the party. A meeting he called at his house on 19 March to decide what to do on the second reading of the bill showed the old fearfulness of members to risk their seats at a dissolution by voting against reform; and his spirits were not made more cheerful by reports that a meeting called by Sir Edward Knatchbull was better attended than his own.[1] That meetings were being called by three independent persons—Peel, Knatchbull and Wetherell—was in itself a sufficient advertisement of the state of the opposition. In effect the old line of division between the former ministerialists and the ultras who had broken with them in 1829-30, was now intersected by another line of cleavage over parliamentary reform. Meanwhile, with mounting popular excitement, the reform bill proper was introduced and had its second reading on 21 March. The protracted seven-day contest earlier in the month seemed to have temporarily exhausted parliamentary energies and after only two nights of undistinguished discussion the first trial of strength was taken. In the largest division ever known in the history of the House of Commons 603 members with their four tellers cast their votes; 302 stayed in their seats to be counted for the bill; and when the opposition streamed back from the lobby confident of success they were found to be only 301.

But though parts of London were illuminated and the mob smashed a few darkened windows, for the ministry it was success rather than victory. A fragile majority of one would hardly stand up to heavy pounding in committee. The task of the opposition now was to find some point of substance, not contradicted by previous declarations or likely to hamper future attitudes, on which their deeply divided groupings could unite. Under the shock of defeat there was a renewed attempt at conciliation, though Peel

[1] Aspinall, *Diaries*, pp. 14, 70.

was still too depressed and uncertain of his course to have much enthusiasm for pasting paper over cracks. He thought matters had gone too far for reform of some sort to be withheld, and he had no intention himself of returning to office with the support of the ultra-Tories. When Herries by request went to him to express the desire of Wetherell and Stormont to join under his leadership, he observed chillingly that 'these were the fellows who turned us out three months ago', and expressed a complete indifference to office under such conditions.[1] This was the kind of behaviour which kept alive the old criticisms of his caution and his coldness. But part of the difficulty for Peel was that his mind was always one stage ahead of most of the other members of the party (already in a speech of 24 March he had brought up the problem of the House of Lords); and part, his reluctance to accept political allies who would almost certainly become political liabilities.

Yet his tactical skill which made him indispensable, however exasperating, to his followers once more supplied their immediate needs. On 13 April he raised the question of the reduction of the total number of English M.P.s envisaged by the bill, and extracted a promise from Althorp that there would be a division on the issue. 'I think we shall beat them on that question,' he wrote to Croker, and in his confidence over the tactical success he allowed himself a momentary illusion of optimism. 'Give us another month, and there is an end of the bill, positively an end to it. It never could be carried except by the dread of physical force'; and he toyed with the notion of an alliance between the aristocracy and the disfranchised population.[2] General Gascoyne, M.P. for Liverpool, was put up to make the motion and on 19 April, after the Easter recess, when the House went into committee on the bill, the government were beaten by eight votes after a two-day debate.[3] Peel spoke on the second night, briefly and confidently, though he repeated his readiness to support the ministers in some moderate change of the parliamentary system. There was no cheering from the opposition over a not unexpected result, and any rejoicing at this major reverse to the ministers was soon cut short. Peel had asked for one month; he was only given one week. Lord Grey, deceived in his original

<hr>

[1] *Arbuthnot Journal*, II, 415–16.   [2] *Croker*, II, 114.
[3] *Broughton*, IV, 101.

expectation of passing the bill through the existing House of Commons, had already been preparing his reluctant royal master for a dissolution. After hesitating for twenty-four critical hours, William now gave way; and once he had turned on a new tack he acted characteristically and energetically in support of his ministers. It was in many ways the real crisis of reform. On the 21st Althorp announced the withdrawal of the bill but was beaten on the adjournment when he tried to bring in the Ordnance estimates. The ministers decided on immediate action and to prevent an anticipated majority in the Lords for Wharncliffe's motion against a dissolution, the king agreed to come in person for the prorogation.

When the Commons met the following afternoon, full of anger and excitement, the eccentric Cornish M.P. Vyvyan started a wild speech against the ministers in the middle of which the guns signalling the king's arrival began to boom and rattle through the little chamber. When he sat down Burdett, Peel and Althorp all rose simultaneously in a clamour that prevented any of them from being heard. All semblance of order was lost; members left their seats and invaded the floor of the House; Peel spoke at the top of his voice but was inaudible in the tumult. The Speaker, in a passion of fury himself, at length gained a temporary respite and called up Peel. Completely carried away by the tempestuous atmosphere, scarlet and shaking with temper, he plunged into an incoherent denunciation of the ministers to a running accompaniment of groans, cheers and calls to order, while the guns continued to thunder outside. Even to a House half-mad with emotion and physical excitement it was a startling revelation of the depths of passion which lay beneath Peel's tightly disciplined nature. He spoke of the despotism of demagogues; the despotism of journalists; and declared violently that the ministry was more unfit to rule than any which had previously held power in England. But in a few minutes he was cut short by the arrival of Black Rod to summon them for the prorogation and by the time the group of M.P.s following the Speaker arrived in the House of Lords, he had recovered his self-possession. Indeed, he even contrived to make a mild joke to the Whig lawyer Campbell who had his watch-glass broken in the crush as they went through the narrow passages. It was a clear case, observed Peel, for a compensation clause in the reform bill, whatever became of the proprietors of the Schedule A boroughs. Yet Campbell wrote to his brother afterwards that it had been worth a few thousand pounds to be present as member in the Commons when Peel had been interrupted by Black Rod and that he now had a much livelier notion of various other episodes in English history.[1]

The country faced the general election with little doubt of the result. In London the dissolution was greeted with an official illumination and mobbing in the West End. A bishop, a prince of the blood, many peers and most of the clubs in St. James's had their windows smashed, and only a strong body of police from the A division stationed in Whitehall Gardens prevented damage to Peel's house.[2] The excitement was not confined to the populace. In an extravagant speech to his electors at Westminster J. C. Hobhouse was reported in the press as having referred to Peel's exhibition at the prorogation as 'human nature in its lowest and most debased state' and accused him of subscribing vast election sums 'for the purpose of deceiving and defrauding the people of England'. Peel reacted sharply to the insult and travelled up to London to confer with his ex-military colleague Hardinge, who broke off his Cornish election campaign to answer the summons. Taking a cooler view of the offensiveness of the speech than his hot-tempered chief, he helped Peel to compose a stiff but carefully moderated letter which he then delivered in person. For the astonished Hobhouse it was the formal opening move in an affair which might have had serious consequences. But the two seconds, Lord Dacre and Hardinge, prudently adjusted matters on behalf of their principals. Some of the offending words were explained away; others disavowed; and a letter of apology signed by Dacre and approved by Hobhouse ended the incident without publicity.[3]

On the only slightly less murderous field of the hustings, however, the month of May saw the anti-reformers unmistakably worsted. The election of 1831 was not a landslide; no general election under the old system could produce that. Of the 658 members of the old House of Commons, 510 were returned again, the great majority for the same constituencies as before. But to a public accustomed to

[1] *Broughton*, IV, 105; *Campbell*, I, 511; *Liverpool Mercury*, 29 Apr. 1831.
[2] C. Reith, *British Police* (1943), p. 93.
[3] 40313 fos. 145–8; 40402 fos. 21–31; *Peel*, II, 182–4; *Broughton*, IV, 110–12.

estimate political tendencies as much by the straws of particular constituencies as by the aggregate of results, the temper and outcome of the election were decisive. There was much excitement and violence. In some popular constituencies reform candidates running as unfancied second-strings to more reputable colleagues found themselves unexpectedly hoisted to victory. Elsewhere old and respected anti-reform members saw their traditional support slide inexorably from under them. Of the eighty-two English county members, over a third were new men; and seventy-six of them came to Westminster pledged to support the bill. Peel in his own borough of Tamworth was safe enough and had the satisfaction of seeing his brother William and his close friend Goulburn returned (and Palmerston evicted) by Cambridge University. But outside the universities and the close boroughs the election returns offered little comfort to the opposition.

> I never doubted [Peel wrote pessimistically to his old Home Office confidant Henry Hobhouse on 9 May] that when such an extraordinary event in the history of this country should take place, as that the King of England should be proclaimed by his ministers a Radical Reformer and that the Royal name and authority should be suddenly transferred from one scale to another (between which scales it was difficult enough before to maintain an equipoise)—that Royalty and Physical Strength combined must carry all before them.[1]

He could see no hope that the king would appeal to his former ministers or that such an appeal could be answered. There was no analogy here with Catholic emancipation. Then it was the whole bill or nothing; now it was a question of more or less. But the limited amount of reform he could approve would not be enough for the new House of Commons, and he was likely therefore to continue to enjoy the unaccustomed luxury of acting as a private politician. Meanwhile he recruited his health in the country air of Drayton in preparation for what promised to be a long and arduous session.

The new parliament met on Tuesday, 14 June, and Peel did not put in an appearance in town until the previous Saturday. He had excused himself from the Pitt dinner at the end of May, deprecated

[1] 40402 f. 43.

the project of a Tory dinner on the eve of session designed to facilitate reunion with the ultras, and flatly declined to have his name used in the party circulars sent out to ensure early attendance.[1] It was a discouraging attitude for a leader to adopt, but Peel had made up his mind not to come forward as leader if by that was meant he should angle for the support of men with whom personally and politically he had almost nothing in common. He had disagreed with the ultra-Tories in the twenties over currency reform, Catholic emancipation and the Corn Law; and though he differed only in degree over parliamentary reform, that degree was important. Writing confidentially to Goulburn on all these matters, moreover, he showed a remarkable sensitivity to the repeated suggestions in the press that his tactics over reform were merely designed to ensure his early return to office.[2] The sensitivity was significant; it was precisely this question of taking office that was occupying his mind, though not in the sense the newspapers ascribed. With a foreboding which was in striking contrast to the simple party loyalties of Herries and Goulburn, he could not rid himself of the fear that the occasion might suddenly arise when he and Wellington would be asked to form a ministry and pass a modified reform act as the only way of unseating the Whigs. It was a contingency he was determined to avoid. To forfeit his public reputation once again, only to find himself permanently saddled with a ministry of Wetherells, Vyvyans and Knatchbulls—inflationists and agriculturalists—was to commit murder in order to put himself into gaol. With a firmness which bordered on frigidity, therefore, he held aloof from any attempt to unite on the sole ground of opposing the bill. He would continue to oppose it, but only on his own terms. 'I have no wish to *slight* the offers of *new* party adherents,' he ended his letter of 5 June to Goulburn, 'or to offend those who make them, but I shall be very cautious in contracting any new party engagements.'

It was not surprising, consequently, that the struggle over the second reform bill in 1831, with a diminished, divided and headless opposition, was of the nature of a sham battle, despite the eloquence

---

[1] Goulburn, II/18 (Peel to Goulburn, 24 May 1831); 40402 f. 89; Aspinall, *Diaries*, xl; *Herries*, II, 120.

[2] Goulburn, II/18 (5 June 1831), ptly. pr. in *Peel*, II, 187, to which the undated fragment on p. 170 should be added as the concluding section of the letter.

and invective it engendered. Peel spoke on appropriate occasions and on 6 July, at the second reading, he delivered a grand set oration, recapitulating his own attitude and mocking the hasty ministerial second-thoughts embodied in the new bill—'you have been administering prussic acid and you forgot to look at the prescription'. He repeated that in view of the impossibility of forming an anti-reform administration he had been prepared to support any safe measure of reform introduced by his opponents rather than risk a change of government. But he answered any taunts of inconsistency by asserting that he had been uniformly opposed to reform on principle because, in a memorable phrase, 'I was unwilling to open a door which I saw no prospect of being able to close'. He ended with an appeal for delay, deliberation, and a return to the good sense and reason of the people of England. With a majority of nearly one hundred and forty, however, the ministers could afford to admit blemishes in their original bill; and the prospect of any anti-reform reaction in the country was as yet little more than the wishful thinking of Tory politicians. Moreover, as Rickman the clerk-assistant of the House noted, Peel's opposition while the session wore on grew more and more measured, and his position more isolated. Indeed he hardly troubled at times to conceal his indifference. In a debate on wine duties in July he annoyed his party by walking out in the middle of a speech by Herries. A messenger sent to recall him from Whitehall Gardens found he had already gone to bed. Next evening, when an absurd wrangle broke out over the adjournment, he went off at midnight, leaving a couple of dozen hotheads to fight it out against the weight of the government benches.[1] It remained for Croker, with a wealth of tenacious detail, and Wetherell with his peculiar mixture of the violent and the ludicrous, to attempt to fill the vacuum in the Tory leadership. The inevitable result was that bitter, continuous complaint was made of Peel's coldness and neglect. Doubts were even cast on the genuineness of his opposition to the bill. 'Peel was equable and plausible,' wrote Campbell in a subsequent review of the session, 'but if he did believe, as he pretended, that the measure was death to the Constitution, he never opposed it with that energy and depth of feeling that might have been expected from the first man in the

[1] *Greville*, 13, 14, 31 July 1831; O. Williams, *Life of J. Rickman* (1911), pp. 285, 289.

House of Commons, standing forward to save it from destruction.'[1]

All through July and early August, however, Peel stuck to his chosen and unpopular path, moving without success one amendment after another, while the bill slowly inched its way through committee. It seemed an interminable session. On and off parliament had been sitting ever since the previous October, and everyone's temper was tried by the heat and the endless debates in the crowded, stuffy chamber. Peel's lassitude was increased by his physical loneliness. Julia and the children had gone off to Drayton for the summer and all his letters to her spoke of his depression at their 'unusual and unnatural separation' and his detestation of 'that infernal place' which claimed his nights and days. As he came back at two or three o'clock each morning to a darkened house and a bedroom where Julia's little belongings mutely proclaimed her absence, he found it almost more than he could bear. By the time the committee reached the £10 franchise clause, his patience had run out.

> I went this morning to Charles Street [he wrote to Julia on 23 August] and told the persons assembled there that I could not undertake to continue in town—that in my opinion there is very little use in protracting the debates on the Reform Bill from night to night, and that I could not undertake to remain here to conduct the battle. I found several people, such as Lord Chandos, Sir C. Wetherell, and Lord Stormont, dissatisfied with this and prepared to go on interminably on the present system. Others were disposed to agree with me and seemed anxious to bring the business to a close. We parted not in very good humour. I said I should stay a few days longer, and would then go into the country, and come back for the Third Reading of the bill, but that if their view was to continue debating the Bill in the same way much longer, they must make some arrangements to dispense with my attendance.[2]

His clear intention to abandon the bill to its fate had its effect. Three days later at another meeting at Charles Street, where the party headquarters had been established after the general election, it was agreed not to divide again until the third reading. Peel joyfully arranged a party at Drayton for Hardinge, Murray, Clerk, and Goulburn, and made his escape as soon as he could to find peace,

---

[1] *Campbell*, I, 526   [2] Peel, *Letters*, p. 134.

pleasure, and partridges in Staffordshire.[1] Once at Drayton there were fears that he would stay there, and his loyal friend Hardinge wrote on 12 September, earnestly pleading for his return for the last three weeks of the bill's progress through the Commons.

> Your absence gives rise to a thousand reports—disperse and crush them to atoms as you always do when you appear—give us confidence and unity of action by your presence, and admitting as I do the personal sacrifice, make it at a moment when all right-thinking men acknowledge that upon you in our House and the Duke in the Upper the salvation of the country depends.[2]

Return he did and on 21 September delivered one last great speech against the bill. 'He cut Macaulay to ribbons', noted Greville approvingly; and even Campbell the Whig admitted privately to his brother that it 'would have made you hesitate about carrying *this Bill* into a law'. But the time had long passed when debating could effect anything. The decision now lay with the peers.

In the early hours of Saturday, 8 October, the House of Lords rejected the reform bill by 199 to 158. Twenty-one bishops cast their vote against the bill who would have ensured its success had they been on the other side. The numerical coincidence was too good not to attract attention and in the succeeding weeks radical orators and journalists raved against the 'mitred Iscariots' who had sold their country. The question now was not what would the Lords do, but what would the government do with the Lords. An adverse majority of forty-one seemed beyond the reach of any practicable creation of new peers, even if the king had been prepared for coercion. William begged his ministers to stay in office, however, and the Commons fortified them by a vote of confidence in the government and the bill. With much misgiving and internal friction the cabinet decided to introduce a third reform bill, rather than hand over responsibility to their opponents. Grey had miscalculated the peers as he had miscalculated the Commons. But after extorting a dissolution to deal with the one, he and most of his colleagues flinched from the only means open to them of dealing with the other. Yet in the furious state of the country to abandon office seemed even more dangerous

[1] Peel, *Letters*, pp. 131–7; Goulburn, II/18 (Peel to Goulburn, 26 Aug. 1831).
[2] 40313 f. 159.

than to essay another reform bill. In London there were vast meetings and demonstrations, and though Peel's metropolitan police confined the pent-up anger of the capital to the breaking of windows, at several points in the provinces the national mood of indignation and alarm overflowed into riot and blood. There were widespread disturbances in the west country. At Derby the reform mob began by attacking the houses of opponents of the bill, later rescued from imprisonment those of their number who had been committed to custody in the early stages of the riot, and finally launched an attack on the county gaol. Only the arrival of troops, the resort to firearms, and the loss of several lives ended the disturbance. At Nottingham the crowd stormed the Castle, the property of the Tory Duke of Newcastle, and burnt it to the ground. Though a detachment of hussars prevented further damage to the town, various groups roamed round the neighbourhood attacking the country houses of anti-reform gentry. The house of Mr. Musters was pillaged and his invalid wife, forced to take hiding in the grounds on a cold and rainy autumn night, subsequently died of shock and exposure. Behind the movement for political reform was now raised the spectre of class war; and for the first time since the Civil War English country houses were put in a state of armed defence.

Peel, whose children were in Staffordshire, left London on 12 October to see to their safety. Wedged into the heart of the midland industrial area, Drayton Manor was peculiarly open to attack. Nottingham was thirty miles to the north-east; Derby about twenty miles north; Birmingham—where the Political Union had just held a mass-meeting and was about to plan the organisation of an armed national guard—was only about ten miles to the south-west; and Coventry, another industrial trouble-spot, about twenty miles south-east. The next great outburst of violence, however, came in another quarter. Parliament was prorogued on 20 October and a week later Sir Charles Wetherell, who was recorder of Bristol, arrived in the city for the customary gaol-delivery. The appearance of such a notorious figure started a riot which, as a result of civic timidity and local military incompetence, degenerated into a saturnalia of destruction. For three days the mob ruled the city and when their rule ended the Mansion House, the bishop's palace, three gaols, the Customs and Excise Houses, and many private dwellings were in smoking ruins, while in the gutters lay the charred corpses of drunken rioters. To Peel, brooding over the state of England as he walked the stubble-fields of Drayton after his neglected partridges, the only consolation was that violence might produce its own antidote.

> There is yet a hope [he wrote to Henry Hobhouse on 30 November] that by diligently reading the lessons which have been written in blood at Bristol . . . that class of the People which has either Property or sense may learn the risk or rather the certain price of revolutions. How you must be disgusted at seeing the influence which is now exercised on the councils and destinies of old England by the whole reptile tribe of spouters at public meetings, newspaper editors, Attwoods, O'Connells, Edmonds and Lord Durhams. It is quite sickening . . . I wish you could come and see us here and watch the tardy progress of my new house. I am just importing carbines, as I mean to defend my old one as long as I can. [1]

He was not the only landowner to turn his thoughts to the arming and garrisoning of his house that winter. At Clumber, the Duke of Newcastle's country house, the great rooms were stripped of their furniture, paintings, and ornaments, and a force of two hundred men with ten three-pounder cannon installed in readiness for an attack. The Duke of Rutland at Belvoir ordered powder and shot from Woolwich and set an artillery sergeant to drill his servants and labourers daily in the handling of the castle guns. [2] Hobhouse himself, who on the news of the Bristol riots had hastened home to Somerset, 'not knowing what might be the fate of my house and family', commented bitterly on this new phenomenon in English social life. 'Look at any country house which has been built in England for three hundred years,' he wrote to Peel on 11 December, 'and you will see that the owners have never dreamed of being obliged to provide against the attack of a Mob.' [3]

But while taking precautions against popular violence and advising his friends to do the same, [4] Peel was faced with a new turn in the political crisis. Through the initiative of Palmerston, one of the more conservative members of Grey's sorely divided cabinet,

---

[1] 40402 f. 140.   [2] *Shelley Diary*, II, 214.   [3] 40402 f. 144.
[4] *Croker*, II, 136–9, where Peel's letter of 12 should read 10 November (cf. *Peel*, II, 190–1).

an approach was made to Lords Wharncliffe and Harrowby to explore the possibility of mutual concessions over the bill. Wharncliffe called on Grey in the middle of November and though nothing definite was decided, it seemed that there might be a chance of compromise. On the 21st Wharncliffe wrote to both Peel and Wellington to sound their attitude. Peel, who had already heard from more than one quarter what was in the wind, replied discouragingly. He said he must keep himself unfettered until he could go to London and talk with others of the party, and expressed considerable doubt on the probability of any major concessions by the government. Wellington, to whom he sent the correspondence, replied in similar vein; and Herries and Holmes, on behalf of the party men in London, sent immediate approval for Peel's letter. The mere talk of concessions, coming on top of the rumoured divisions in the cabinet and the ministers' known anxieties at the state of the country, put new heart in the opposition. Peel told Holmes to send off letters for a good attendance when parliament met on 6 December and he himself travelled to town on 3 December to have some preliminary talks on union and tactics. Out of this new access of spirit came a not unimportant development. The Charles Street office, small and debt-ridden, had for some time been unsatisfactory and mainly through the efforts of Holmes a move was now set on foot to form a new meeting-place for the party. Peel and Wellington supported the project and after various discussions in January 1832 the Carlton Club was founded at a meeting under Lord Salisbury's chairmanship in March. Some five hundred persons, mainly peers and M.P.s, put their names down as members; and the club, designed as both a social and political centre of activity—the first of its kind in party history—flourished from the start.

The significance of the Carlton, however, was for the future; the present lay with the Whigs. When the third reform bill was introduced in December it passed its second reading by a two to one majority. It was true that various concessions had been made, including the maintenance of the existing numbers in the House, for which the opposition had formerly fought in vain; and many ministerial supporters had been sobered by the bloodshed and violence of the autumn. But the essentials of the bill remained, and the knowledge that an increasing number of waverers on his own side were now prepared to support it probably infused a greater bitterness into Peel's speech at the opening of the debate than he realised.[1] Much of his speech on the second reading five days later was devoted to a long and unnecessary refutation of Macaulay, who in most of his reform speeches had contrived to remind Peel of his recantation over Catholic emancipation. On the previous evening (still nettled perhaps by his drubbing in September) he had come down to the House, as Peel put it, 'with all the sweltering venom collected in the interval', to launch another attack. Peel himself had been touched on the raw, for he gave a more elaborate explanation than the Commons had yet heard, of the circumstances which led him as minister to advocate and ultimately introduce the Catholic bill in 1829. But he ended with a solemn vindication of his position.

> I am satisfied with the constitution under which I have lived hitherto, which I believe is adapted to the wants and habits of the people. . . . I will continue my opposition to the last, believing as I do, that this is the first step, not directly to revolution, but to a series of changes which will affect the property, and totally change the character, of the mixed constitution of this country. I will oppose it to the last, convinced that though my opposition will be unavailing, it will not be fruitless, because the opposition now made will oppose a bar to further concessions hereafter. . . . On this ground I take my stand, not opposed to a well-considered reform of any of our institutions which need reform, but opposed to this reform.[2]

It was a concise summary of the views he had maintained in public and private throughout the protracted contest, and it was the basis of his attitude towards waverers like Wharncliffe and Harrowby, who were assuming an increasingly important middle position between the two sides.

The size of the ministerial majority in December made nonsense in Peel's view of various schemes being put forward by independent opposition members for a new compromise bill. In any case he recoiled from the odium and responsibility which would be theirs if they actually initiated a reform measure. It must be the government bill or nothing. The task of the opposition was to amend it as

---

[1] *Wharncliffe*, II, 101–3; *Greville*, 13 Dec. 1831.
[2] *Speeches*, II, 433 (17 Dec. 1831).

much as they could in committee so that the Lords could give it a second reading and amend it still further. If this was impossible, and he knew that it was improbable, then the only course was rejection. The House met again after Christmas and on 20 January resumed the familiar grind in committee which lasted up to March. But more important than the succession of amendments which Peel unsuccessfully moved during these weeks was the prospective struggle in the Lords. What was passing in the lower House was little more than a tedious formality before the real collision of power took place above. Holmes, who had close contacts with the other party, assured Peel early in January that a sufficient number of peers would be created to pass the bill and that the king would do all he was asked.[1] This, within limits, was reasonably correct intelligence but it made no difference to Peel. When Harrowby on 4 February wrote to him suggesting that the best course of action was for the Lords to give a second reading to the bill and subsequently amend it in committee, Peel advised resistance. In the abstract he agreed that, since the measure was inevitable, it would be better to yield gracefully rather than suffer the indignity of a massive influx of new reforming peers. But after the events of 1831 it was impossible for any yielding to be graceful. The upper House would vindicate its honour and dignity more by compelling the government to carry its measure by the brute force of a peerage creation than by a tame surrender. He thought that no important concessions could now be wrested in committee, where the rules of the upper House forbade the use of proxy votes. In those circumstances the only prize to play for was such drastic and unpalatable action by the government as would deter them or their successors from any further inroads on the constitution. He insisted that he had no desire for office and no desire to obstruct the settlement of the reform question. But his fundamental conviction was clear. Victory could not be denied to the government; but it could be made a Pyrrhic victory. In that lay their last and only defence.

The bill passed its third reading in the Commons on 22 March, when Peel made one final elegiac speech on reform, admitting the need but opposing the extent to which the ministers had gone in answering that need; and his last vote like his first was cast against

[1] 43061 f. 142. Holmes' informant was Ellice, the Whig whip.

it. When it went up to the Lords, despite his counsel from without and the example of Wellington within, the growing body of waverers was sufficient to give it a second reading by the slender majority of nine votes; and it was ordered to go into committee after the Easter recess. In this new situation Peel was obliged to retreat to the second line of defence, whatever his private views were on its tenability. To Croker, who at Haddington's request had drawn up a modified scheme of reform which was privately printed and circulated, he wrote later in April that he approved its general tenor and since Lords and Commons had now both accepted the principle of reform, all that was left was to try to lessen the effects of the inevitable evil. He felt a certain scruple at interfering in the affairs of the upper House, but in conversation with Harrowby he privately advocated much the same kind of amendments as were being hatched in the interval by Ellenborough, Lyndhurst, Wellington and a few other moderate peers. The basis of this new plan was the reduction in the number of both enfranchisements and disfranchisements, limitations on the £10 householder qualification, and the exclusion of borough properties from the county vote. To Ellenborough, who explained the details to him on 4 May, Peel showed himself helpful and sympathetic; and he stressed the tactical need to win over the Harrowby group and to explain at the earliest possible moment exactly how far they were prepared to go in reform.[1]

Three days later came the trial of strength in the House of Lords. On 7 May Lyndhurst carried an amendment against the government to postpone the disfranchising clauses, after which Ellenborough snatched the opportunity to outline the proposals which they intended to bring forward. Grey now faced the final challenge. Angry at the defection of the Waverers at what seemed the first test of their sincerity, and convinced that the opposition meant to take complete charge of the bill, the prime minister made up his mind to play the last card remaining to him. If that failed he was prepared to go out and leave the bill to his opponents. The following afternoon he and Brougham saw the king at Windsor and informed him that the cabinet would resign unless they were empowered to make at least fifty new peers. In January William had agreed to

[1] Aspinall, *Diaries*, pp. 236–40; *Peel*, II, 198–203; *Croker*, II, 171–6.

make sufficient peers to carry the bill if need arose; but in his subsequent uneasy communications with the cabinet he had made it plain that the numbers asked for must not be unreasonable. At no point had he talked in terms of more than forty creations. Now that he was faced with the large and naked figure of fifty, all his doubts and fears crystallised into stubborn decision. He could feel, with some justice, that from the start of the reform crisis he had been consistently deceived by his ministers—or they had deceived themselves—on the strength of parliamentary support for the measure they proposed. He had been asked for one concession after another, and it was time to call a halt. In a letter written the next day he accepted his ministers' resignation and asked them to stay in office until their successors were appointed. The contingency which Peel had foreseen for over a year had arrived.

In the famous Days of May which followed, England came nearer to a national popular resistance than at any other time during the reform crisis. Countless meetings, processions, and petitions were organised all over the country; factories and shops were closed; several of the large industrial towns in the north virtually suspended business; the Common Council of the City followed by hundreds of other bodies petitioned the Commons to stop supplies; there was an organised run on the banks; there were public declarations to withhold taxes; and lower down in the ranks of the radical movement, talk of pikes and barricades. The most impressive aspect of the demonstration, however, was not the contingent threat of violence but the social solidity that lay behind it. At the centre of this angry vortex were the twenty or thirty opposition peers and politicians into whose hands the king had thrown the initiative. They were not particularly intimidated by the political excitement which was shaking the country; or if they were, they did not admit it. They were hardened to the turbulent habits of their countrymen; they had good nerves and were accustomed to the exercise of authority. Whatever faults were possessed by the governing class of early-nineteenth-century England, cowardice was not one. Divided and doubtful as most of them were on their course of action, the motives which prompted them were those of loyalty, political expediency, and in some cases at least, of statesmanlike principle. In the last resort it was the House of Commons and not the mob in the streets or the radicals of the Rotunda to whom they finally deferred.

On 9 May Lyndhurst on behalf of the king came to Peel and asked whether he would be prepared to take office. He had already been to Wellington who had expressed a readiness in or out of office to assist the formation of a new government. Peel understood that he was being asked to become prime minister on condition of honouring the king's commitment to pass a wide measure of reform. He had no need to reflect on a decision which had long been present in his mind. He said at once that he could not take office on those terms. He was pledged against the bill and had made it clear to everyone that he was personally precluded from taking part in the kind of ministry now contemplated. If a mediator was wanted, he was not the man. The following morning there was a meeting of opposition M.P.s at Lord Stormont's to consider how they should meet a motion of confidence in the outgoing ministry of which Lord Ebrington had given notice. Wellington and Lyndhurst called on Peel beforehand and it was agreed that they should confer again later in the day. After the party meeting Peel went to Apsley House taking Croker with him, and when Croker had the situation explained to him, he asked the crucial question: 'Whom do you mean to put at the head?' Lyndhurst gestured to Peel who replied in what Croker described as a tone of 'concentrated resolution' that he could not and would not have anything to do with a settlement of the reform question and that it was evident that it must be settled, and on the basis of the existing bill. Lyndhurst was unable to explain exactly what the king had in mind, but it was clear at least that he was committed to an 'extensive' reform. This for Peel was enough. He would not, he declared, go through the performance of 1829 over again.

There remained the question whether any more appropriate and mediating minister could be found. Croker mentioned the name of Harrowby, which was not received with enthusiasm by the duke. Walking back with Croker afterwards Peel suggested Manners Sutton, the Speaker. Croker paid little attention to this since, although he was adamant against taking office himself in a reform ministry, he thought with peculiar illogic that Peel should; and the next day, 11 May, composed a long letter designed to persuade him to do so. But it is possible that Peel made the same suggestion to others—Baring, Fitzgerald, and Manners Sutton himself. He would not form a government personally; he did not think that the duke, even more heavily committed against reform, should attempt it; but Manners Sutton was in the unique position of a conservative politician who by reason of his office was publicly uncommitted on reform. In the meantime, however, the duke received the backing of the ultra-Tory peers for a Tory ministry which would at least unseat the Whigs, even if it had regrettably to pass their measure; and thus encouraged he went forward with the task of finding suitable timber for building a cabinet. He met discouragingly small response from the leading men of the party whom he approached; and the odd circumstance that it was not yet settled who was to be the head of the new ministry hardly assisted his efforts.

On Saturday, 12 May, Peel had an interview with the king, who invited him to take office though he did not specify in what capacity. Peel, who had just come from a long and acrimonious argument on the subject with Croker, shortly and firmly refused. His example probably weighed with others, for Goulburn, Herries, C. W. Wynn, Manners Sutton, and Alexander Baring all declined to serve with the duke, though the last was ready to take office if Manners Sutton would. Finally Wellington on Sunday evening sent for the Speaker once more and invited him to take the premiership. Sutton was hesitant and nervously voluble. Without giving a definite answer he treated Wellington, Lyndhurst and Baring to a two-hour description of his situation and feelings which made the coarse, impatient Lyndhurst swear afterwards that he would have nothing to do with such 'a damned tiresome old bitch'. However, Manners Sutton had asked for a day's grace in which to consider the matter and when he consulted Peel and Fitzgerald the next morning they both advised him to accept. By this time both Lyndhurst and the duke were beginning to regret their offer and it was doubtful in any case how far the ultra-Tory peers would welcome the Speaker in place of the duke as their commander. Yet as Hardinge pointed out, with more truth than kindness, Manners Sutton was 'not to be estimated by his real ability but by the reunion of many advantages, which no other man can possess'.[1] He had the respect of the House, had heard all

[1] *W.N.D.*, VIII, 312.

the reform debates, and was the only uncommitted man in the Commons. The comedy, however, was by this time nearly over. Manners Sutton took the chair as usual on Monday, 14 May, and he had for obvious reasons asked that nothing should be known in parliament of his readiness to take office. The House of Commons assumed therefore that the Duke of Wellington was premier-designate and since Saturday it was also being confidently asserted that the new ministry would be pledged to pass an extensive measure of reform. The unnatural combination produced a bitter and pro-longed scene in the House. Violent attacks were made on the duke from the Whig benches but what completed the ruin of his cause in the lower House were two statements from the Tory side. Baring, who had agreed to serve under Manners Sutton and was considered as a possible leader of the House, had little chance to assert his powers of leadership. Appalled by the rain of attacks on the duke he finally suggested a compromise on the basis of the retention of Schedule A in return for the abandonment of peerage creations; and agreed that it would be a calamity if the Whig ministers left office. The rout of the duke was completed by Inglis, spokesman of the high-principled Tory Anglicans, who denounced Wellington's behaviour as a fatal violation of public confidence.

Peel tried briefly to moderate the tone of the debate. While not contradicting the explicit assumption made by Russell that he would not join and could not support the new ministry, he went out of his way to pay a compliment to the courage and honour of the duke, whatever decision he might ultimately adopt.[1] He left the House before the debate ended and over dinner at Whitehall Gardens with Hardinge, Dawson, Goulburn, Croker, Lord Stormont, and his brother, William Peel, he forcibly expressed his opinion that the game was up and that the return of the Whigs was infinitely prefer-able to a Wellingtonian or indeed any anti-reform ministry which merely took office in order to carry reform. Hardinge, who shared his views, was anxious that he should go at once to Wellington. In view of the divergent attitudes they had taken, Peel was reluctant to do so unless the duke should express a wish to confer with him. A hurried note from Hardinge to Apsley House brought a few lines from a somewhat surprised duke who had been under the impression

[1] For the debate, see *Hansard*, XII, 905-80.

that the debate was going well. However, he replied that he would be delighted to meet Peel or anybody else from the House of Commons. Since the Speaker had promised to give Wellington his final decision that night as soon as the House rose, he took Peel, Hardinge, and Croker along in his coach at midnight to call on the waiting duke. All talk of a Manners Sutton administration was silently dropped; the only consideration of importance was the attitude of the House of Commons. After much argument it was at last agreed, on Peel's proposal, that Wellington should inform the king that it was impossible to form a Tory administration and that in order to save him as far as possible from the painful necessity of creating fresh peers, the duke would withdraw his opposition to the bill.[1]

The Days of May thus ended in a day of dupes. But when Peel rose the next morning he felt pleased and relieved at the night's work. Between them all they had saved Wellington from an immense blunder. Manners Sutton had been a respectable candidate as 'mediating minister', but Peel had probably only put him forward as the lesser evil. It is unlikely that he seriously thought he had much chance of success. An attempt by the duke to form a government, however, would have meant not only failure but ignominy. To Ellenborough, who was one of Peel's first visitors, he observed pungently that 'the Tory party would have been disgraced by accepting office to carry the Reform bill after all that had been said by them against it'.[2] Yet the fact remained that the two leaders of the party, one in the upper and the other in the lower House, with identical views on reform, had differed diametrically on policy. The duke's motives in consenting to form an administration were simple. He was ready to respond with direct and disarming military duty to any call from the crown for his services; and he thought that since reform was inevitable, it was better done by ministers who would not need to subvert the House of Lords in order to carry it. Peel on the other hand thought that the constitution, and that party

[1] For the events of 7–14 May see *W.N.D.*, VIII, 30–32; *Croker*, II, 153–69, 177–81; Aspinall, *Diaries*, pp. 247–58. Cf. also *Greville*, 12, 14, 17 May. The subsequent additions under 26 Oct. 1832 and 3 Jan. 1833 besides being contradictory in some particulars are coloured by time and the prejudices of his informants, Arbuthnot and Lyndhurst.

[2] Aspinall, *Diaries*, p. 256.

which stood for the conservation of the constitution, would best be served by an uncompromising resistance which would force their opponents into open coercion. To endure coercion would subvert the House of Lords less than a dishonourable connivance at reform. What mattered was not the physical but the moral degradation of the peers. In the final analysis his stubborn and negative attitude was the primary factor in bringing about the result he desired. He might not have been able to control the House of Commons had he become prime minister; but it was obvious that without him no one else could. As Wellington wrote that same day to the Duke of Buckingham, 'there was an end to it when I found that I could neither form a government nor find support for the government in the House of Commons'. To William IV it was self-evident where the attempt had failed. In the next few doubtful days when he was negotiating with Grey he still kept in mind the possibility of one last appeal to the recalcitrant leader of the opposition in the lower House. Writing to Wellington from Court on 16 May the Earl of Munster (the king's eldest son by Mrs. Jordan) emphasised 'for God's sake, be sure, if the King is driven to the wall, of *Peel*. An appeal to him and his countrymen could not be disregarded. Unless you have *Peel*, the House of Commons *cannot* be managed.'[1]

Yet Peel himself did not come through the Days of May without blame. He was accused of want of moral courage, of selfishness, and of disloyalty to the duke. It was insinuated that he had put forward Manners Sutton as his stalking-horse, to play Addington to his Pitt, so that he could later reap the reward of office without the price of apostasy. The worst slash of all, whether intended or not, came from Wellington. In his explanatory speech to the Lords he drew an acid comparison between his own behaviour and that of prudent men who had ulterior considerations in mind and looked only at consistency. All the world took this as a reference to Peel and the wounds of 1830 were visibly opened once more. Forced now into an explanation of his own, Peel the following evening took pains in the Commons to acknowledge the honourable motives of those who had differed from him and to deplore his temporary separation 'from that man whom I chiefly honour'. But he riposted sharply by saying that Wellington's feelings of shame had he not consented to

[1] *W.N.D.*, VIII, 322, 326, 329.

assist the king in his difficulty would have been his if he had consented. In the circumstances it was perhaps impossible for either to vindicate himself without implicitly condemning the other. But it was this final episode rather than November 1830 which turned coolness into separation. In the summer of 1831 when alone in town, Peel had called each day on either Aberdeen or the duke. After May 1832 came a gradual freezing of relations which was to last for another two years.[1]

III

It was the end of the crisis, though this was not obvious until 18 May when the king at last pledged himself irrevocably to make enough peers to pass the bill. Wellington and Lyndhurst had already agreed to abandon their personal opposition and the other Tory peers, privately warned by Taylor, the king's secretary, generally abstained from attendance. Passing rapidly through committee, the bill was given a third reading on 4 June and became law three days later. In the House of Commons the rest of the session was taken up with the Scottish and Irish reform bills, Althorp's belated budget, and attempts by the government, consistently supported by Peel, to meet the immediate consequences of the tithe war in Ireland and devise some permanent solution for that intractable problem. The more mundane politicians of the party turned their thoughts to electioneering. Though Croker swore he would never sit in a reformed parliament (and kept his word), and the duke saw the future with a matter-of-fact pessimism which seemed to take into account every possible disaster, an election committee was set up at the end of May to obtain information about the new boroughs. After the fever of excitement in which the country had lived for eighteen months, it was a relief for some to return to the normalities of party management.

Parliament was prorogued on 16 August. Peel had already departed to Drayton earlier that month and he read the newspaper accounts of the last weeks of debate with the detached contentment of one who had finished with such matters for a long time to come. His great new house was now rising before the windows of the old,

[1] Cf. *Peel*, II, 236; Peel, *Letters*, p. 136.

and politics were consciously put aside as he corresponded with Croker on the rival merits of battlements and parapets, or took his Staffordshire neighbours to admire his stables and farmyard and the flower-gardens which Gilpin had laid out around the half-built mansion.[1] His brother Lawrence with Lady Jane took refuge at Drayton from the cholera scare in Worcestershire, but otherwise August passed quietly. For September he invited Henry Baring, Holmes and Bonham. Since all three belonged to the inner group of politicians who carried out the detailed work of party management, the choice was not perhaps accidental even though Holmes had to cry off till later in the autumn. Bonham was a recent acquisition to the party. A middle-aged bachelor of Anglo-Irish family, an Oxonian and a member of Lincoln's Inn, he had some private means and in 1830, probably through the influence of Planta, then treasury secretary, he entered parliament as member for Rye. Though he lost his seat in 1831, he remained active as one of the party's unofficial managers and his obvious taste and talent for electioneering made him even in 1832 one of the most useful and indefatigable members of the election committee. Rough, discreet and loyal, he attached himself to Peel from the start. The two men were much of an age (Bonham was forty-seven to Peel's forty-four) and between them there soon developed a close friendship which was to survive all the vicissitudes of politics in the next twenty years.

In October, Herries, Goulburn, Croker and Holmes spent a week at Drayton. They found their host in unusually good spirits and in no way disposed to take a gloomy view of the political future of the country. Croker grumpily ascribed this to his sanguine temper rather than to his judgement; but if so, it was not a sudden mood. Other observers during the year had noticed the contrast between Wellington's irritable pessimism and Peel's calmness over the probable effects of the reform act. Princess Lieven, who listened to both men over her dinner table in February, explained the difference as one between a man of forty and one of seventy.[2] Even apart from the unkind addition of seven years to the duke's age which this physiological explanation involved, there were perhaps other

---

[1] *Croker*, II, 188; *Dyott*, II, 136.
[2] *The Lieven–Palmerston Correspondence 1828–1856*, ed. Lord Sudley (1943), p. 35; *Croker*, II, 140, 151, 153, 192.

reasons. Peel had foreseen for so long the certain victory of reform that by 1832 it no longer had the terror of novelty, even though intellectually he might agree with much of Wellington's more emotional reaction. Moreover he drew a distinction between the crude political attempts of the ultra-Tories to evict Grey's ministry at all costs and with any kind of ally, and the growth in the country of a wider feeling on behalf of law, order, and government, ready (as he wrote to Croker in 1831) 'to support monarchy, property and public faith, wherever attacked'.[1] Both called themselves Conservative, in the new phrase borrowed from continental politics and becoming increasingly popular since the *Quarterly* had used it in January 1830;[2] but the essence of conservatism to Peel's mind was an attitude to politics, not party tactics—an ethic rather than an interest. It was to give time for this attitude to develop and strengthen that he wished the battle over reform to be fought to the last. From this point of view the interminable sessions of 1831 and 1832 had not been in vain, and he could look back at his own part in them with some satisfaction.

From the day when the Whig ministry first exposed their intentions, Peel's views had been consistent and logical. He had been appalled by Grey's radicalism and angered by what seemed a violation of the constitution. In his judgement the prime minister had first invited disorder and violence by putting forward an extreme measure at a time of popular excitement; and having secured his democratic backing had then proceeded to a course of arbitrary government, coercing in turn the House of Commons, the crown, and the House of Lords. Looking to Grey's actions, rather than to his motives, Peel was neither unreasonable nor alone in holding this view. Grey never expected his bill to raise the opposition it did. Had he or most of his cabinet been able to anticipate the enforced dissolution of parliament, the quarrel with the king, and the coercion of the Lords, the reform bill which Russell introduced in March 1831 would have been much more moderate. Grey had been right in estimating the popularity of his measure; but he had

[1] *Peel*, II, 186.
[2] The article (Internal Policy) which contained the phrase 'the Conservative Party' was apparently *not* written, as commonly believed, by Croker. See M. F. Brightfield, *J. W. Croker* (1940), p. 403 n.

profoundly miscalculated the temper of the three elements of the political constitution—king, lords and commons—which alone could give legal sanction to his proposals.[1] Once committed, he could not turn back; but he only won through to the end after precipitating the most prolonged and dangerous crisis in the country's history since the Revolution of 1688. It was not merely what the Reform Act was, but how it had been passed, that provided the danger to the constitution. It was true that the two aspects could not be divorced. The extremism of the bill provoked the extremism of the opposition; and his opponents bore their share of responsibility for the excitement raised in the country at large.

Peel, almost from the start and certainly after the dissolution, realised the inevitable success of the bill. The nature of its provisions made it in effect an appeal to the country. The general election of 1831 merely registered in the court of the lower House a judgement delivered by the people outside. Granted the certain victory of reform, the only way of limiting its dangerous effects was to ensure that its passage to the statute book was made as painful as possible. Instead of being an inspiration, it should be a warning to future reformers. As he wrote to Harrowby in February 1832,

> Why have we been struggling against the Reform Bill in the House of Commons? Not in the hope of resisting its final success in that House, but because we look beyond the Bill, because we know the nature of popular concessions, their tendency to propagate the necessity for further and more extensive compliances. We want to make the 'descensus' as 'difficilis' as we can—to teach young inexperienced men charged with the trust of the government that, though they may be backed by popular clamour, they shall not override on the first springtide of excitement every barrier and breakwater raised against popular impulses; that the carrying of extensive changes in the Constitution without previous deliberation shall not be a holiday task; that there shall be just what has happened—the House sick of the question, the Ministers repenting they brought it forward, the country paying the penalty for the folly and incapacity of its rulers. All these are salutary sufferings, that may I trust make people hereafter distinguish between the amendment, and the overturning of their institutions.[2]

[1] See M. G. Brock, 'The Reform Act of 1832' in *Britain and the Netherlands* (1960), pp. 174 et seq.   [2] *Peel*, II, 201–2.

Admitting the premiss, it was a justifiable policy. In 1832 it was still not certain that the Reform Act would fail to produce the destructive effects which its opponents prophesied.

Yet in maintaining this attitude, Peel had been obliged to thread a narrow path between alternating dangers; to oppose reform in detail without opposing in principle; to admit the certainty of the reform victory while trying to mitigate its results; to criticise the Whigs while refusing to take their place; to join the ultra-Tories in opposition but not in office. As the battle of reform swirled backwards and forwards, and his own moods inevitably fluctuated with it, he had to defend first one and then the other flank of his entrenched position. In the heat and dust of the conflict, it was not surprising that his shifts of emphasis to conform with a constantly shifting situation seemed to many people evasive, half-hearted, and opportunistic. By looking to the future he forfeited much of the present; and the reform crisis left him more unpopular and more estranged from his party than he had been even in November 1830. There was, however, this substantial consolation. He had come through the crisis with his character uncompromised, and his future policy uncommitted. If one of the secrets of politics is to preserve freedom of action, that he had secured. If there was, as he believed, a large potential conservative feeling in the country which could be rallied in defence of government in the post-reform era, then the future was not without hope. Despite all his parliamentary miscalculations, Grey had succeeded in satisfying a deep national demand and a new alignment of forces was now possible. Peel in the end owed more to Grey's courage and imagination than it was possible for him to admit in the autumn of 1832. For Grey's work was ended; Peel's about to begin.

CHAPTER

2

CONSERVATIVE OPPOSITION

After some delay, caused by the preliminary registration of electors prescribed by the Reform Act, parliament was dissolved early in December. With the crisis behind them, the Conservative opposition faced the contest of the polls with equanimity. They could not expect to win, but they thought at least that the disaster of 1831 would be partially retrieved. At a house dinner at the Carlton in November, attended by Peel, Manners Sutton, Scarlett, Herries, Bonham, Holmes and other good party men, there was a festive and optimistic atmosphere. Electioneering had already started and the reports coming in were remarkably sanguine. Holmes, the veteran expert, though abandoning on score of expense any attempt to get himself returned, assured Peel that the party would do well in England and Ireland, though not in whiggish Scotland where reform had worked a greater electoral revolution than in the other two kingdoms. Hardinge's forecast was that the opposition would muster 250. Bonham's calculations put the figure even higher, though Ellice, the rival Whig manager, was only prepared to concede them 136.[1] Peel at Tamworth, sharing an uncontested return with Lord Charles Townshend, had little more to do than give a banquet to his supporters; but he assiduously went round his constituency (now enlarged under the act into a semi-rural district), canvassing nearly 600 electors and only meeting three refusals.[2] Since he had successfully fought for the retention of Tamworth's two members and at his election dinner promised to support the abolition of slavery and declared his acceptance of the Reform Act, his return passed off in a more cordial atmosphere than in 1831.

[1] 40403 fos. 71, 98; 40313 f. 165; *Raikes*, I, 110.
[2] Goulburn II/18 (Peel to Goulburn 14 Dec. 1832).

It was a different story elsewhere; and as the general election continued, the opposition saw the fool's paradise in which they had been lingering collapse like pasteboard around them. With many new constituencies, an enlarged franchise, and the disappearance of old strongholds, electoral prognostication was bound in any case to be a hazardous business. What ruined the estimates of the opposition managers were incalculable factors: the strong tide of excitement still running in the country, the expectations which parliamentary reform had raised, and the anti-Tory animus resulting from the passions of the past eighteen months. In the event they suffered a smash worse than that of 1831. When all the returns were in, Ellice's estimate of the previous November, which had then been taken as cheerful partisan bluff, was seen to be only a degree short of the truth. As reported to Peel early in January, the prospective state of the new House was Conservatives 150, ministerialists about 320, radicals and Irish repealers not less than 190. Some estimates put the Conservative total even lower. In any case they were now the third and smallest party in the legislature, alongside the Whigs and the radical monster they had engendered. The Conservative revival, which was easy to credit in the club-rooms of the Carlton, patently lacked impetus and organisation, perhaps any real existence, in the constituencies. More than ever the Reform Act appeared not the end but the beginning of a new radical era.

Among the laments, excuses and recriminations that swelled Peel's postbag were some outright counsels of despair. Lord Mahon suggested that the Conservatives should yield to the radicals the customary opposition benches to the left of the Speaker and take their place near the gangway as a visible confession that 'we as a party are suspended; or at least that from our weakness we must be umpires rather than parties in the great struggle which the new House is so shortly to witness'.[1] To Aberdeen it seemed that Peel would be placed 'in a new and, I fear, painful situation in the House of Commons'. Peel, however, as he shot partridges at Drayton or made his round of the great country houses after Christmas, saw no cause for panic. Writing to condole with Sir George Clerk on his defeat in Midlothian, he spoke sympathetically of his 'despair of any effectual struggle against the new voters—particularly the residents

[1] 40403 f. 167, pr. Peel, 210-11.

41

in Towns and Villages' and of the miscalculations of 'our too confident friends in Carlton Terrace'.[1] Yet bad as the situation was, it was not hopeless and he was clear in his own mind how he should meet it. The function of the Conservative party, however small, must be to resist the further encroachments of radical democracy which could be expected from the verdict of the polls. Their policy should be to observe the reaction of the government before taking action themselves. If ministers and radicals combined, they must be resisted. If ministers resisted the radicals, they should be supported.

To Goulburn, who wrote advocating a union of all the forces of the right as the only means of forming a strong party, he showed a discouraging caution and scepticism; and beneath his temperate language Goulburn sensed a marked unwillingness still to enter into any combination with the ultra-Tories. He did not think discussion on general topics would be much help; he was not prepared to make concessions on policy merely to obtain followers. As for what the Conservative party stood for, other than the general principle of order and authority:

> I suppose the 140 members of whom you speak will agree as to the strict appropriation of Church property to purposes *bona fide* connected with the interests of the established religion, and to purposes for which in principle it was originally designed; as to the resistance of all such schemes as excluding the Church from the House of Lords; as to protection to agriculture, the maintenance of public faith to the public creditor, and generally, resistance to the real tyranny which mobs and newspapers, if aided by a popularity-hunting Government, will infallibly establish. I think such a party acting with temperance and firmness and avoiding a Union with Radicals for the mere purpose of annoyance to the Government will soon find in circumstances a bond of Union and will ultimately gain the confidence of the Property and good sense of the Country.[2]

If this rough draft of Conservative strategy was deliberately left vague, it at least allowed him flexibility in tactics and room, should

[1] Clerk (27 Dec. 1832).

[2] Goulburn, undated but postmarked 3 Jan. 1833. Ptly. pr. in *Peel*, II, 212. What Parker describes as the 'wanting' section is written inside the wrapping of the letter and is here reproduced in full. For Goulburn's reaction and also a similar expression of Peel's views to Herries, see *Herries* II, 163-6.

he ever come to power, for writing in the details of policy according to circumstances. Though it contained a kernel of political philosophy, it was a politician's and not a philosopher's programme of action. Socially, moreover, he lent himself to party purposes, joining a Tory shooting party organised by the Duke of Cumberland at Kew which included Wellington, Chandos and Holmes, and attending a party dinner at the Carlton on the eve of session. Indeed it was at Peel's suggestion that the decision was taken to serve late suppers at the club so that members could go there after the evening's debates in the Commons.[1] If the party was diminished, under the impact of disaster it was showing some signs of consolidation; and dinners were perhaps as important as discussions for bringing men together again.

Parliament opened on 29 January and the first week was occupied in electing a new Speaker and taking the prescribed oaths. In the House of Commons it was a strange and disorderly assembly. Not much more than half of them had sat in the preceding parliament and many new members seemed ill at ease in their environment, like boys at the start of the first term at school. There were some unusual characters among them: Attwood, the currency crusader, who had come in for Birmingham; Gully, the prizefighter and racehorse owner; and the stout figure of Cobbett, white-haired and ruddy-complexioned, with rustic accent and equalitarian manners, who at first plumped himself down on the Treasury bench on the principle that the House knew no distinction of seating. The Conservative members found themselves sitting pellmell with radicals and Irish, who even invaded the front bench and drove Peel out of his usual place to one nearer the Speaker, while O'Connell swaggered about the floor of the House attended by his tail of obsequious followers, talking and gesticulating to other members of his party on the benches in a conscious pose of authority. To Peel it seemed a House different in tone and character from any he had seen: asperity, rudeness and self-assertive independence within, mixed with fawning references to the power of the public without.[2] The real feature of the 1833 House of Commons, however, was not the individual eccentrics thrown up by the first election under the Reform Act nor

[1] G. M. Willis, *Duke of Cumberland* (1954), pp. 225–7.
[2] *Raikes*, I, 157.

the relatively small left wing of extreme radicals, but the lack of purpose and discipline on all sides of the House. The task of government, difficult enough before, was going to be even more difficult in future.

Conscious of the unruly nature of the new assembly, the government invited Manners Sutton, who had retired from the Speakership at the close of the previous session, to stand again for the Chair. This gesture to an opponent was prompted not only by genuine respect for his abilities but, as Althorp wrote to him, 'still more from the peculiar circumstances of the ensuing meeting of Parliament, where above all other times to have a Speaker whose experience is so great and whose authority will be so unbounded with all the old Members at least is an object of the greatest and most essential importance'.[1] It was a popular as well as a sensible choice; and though Hume and O'Connell demonstrated their anti-Tory sentiments by putting forward Littleton as a reluctant Liberal candidate, they could only muster thirty-one votes in his favour. This was satisfactory as far as it went; but it was clear where trouble could be expected, and there were issues more controversial than the Speakership on which additional support could be obtained. The king's speech the following month unfolded some of them: foreign affairs, new charters for the Bank of England and the East India Company, reform of Church revenues, and repression of Irish disorders. The prospect of yet another Irish coercion act provoked an immediate onslaught from O'Connell on what with his habitual vocabulary he called 'a bloody, brutal unconstitutional address'; and a series of amendments from the Irish and radicals prolonged the debate over four nights. Stanley, the Irish Secretary, on whom much of the invective was centred, returned the fire of his attackers with skill and venom. But he received remarkably little support from his colleagues and on the Liberal benches as a whole there was some embarrassment at inaugurating a reform session with a measure which in the past they had liked to associate solely with their opponents.

On the third night Peel intervened. It was precisely the kind of situation he had anticipated and he used it with immense effect. He spoke for two hours, with what his late antagonist J. C. Hobhouse

[1] Manners Sutton, 29 Dec. 1832.

described as good sense, good feeling and great eloquence; and was cheered repeatedly on both sides of the House. From the start he obtained complete mastery over his audience and to the many new members who had never heard him before it was a consummate demonstration of the talents to which he owed his commanding position. 'That is a *handy fellow*, that leader of yours', old Cobbett exclaimed to Holmes afterwards. 'If he would place himself at the head of the Movement we would turn these fellows out in twenty-four hours.'[1] He gained the sympathy of his audience by a brief, unsentimental reference to the changed position of himself and his party in the new House. He carefully reserved his position on the appropriation of Church funds for other than religious purposes. He paid a neat and loudly applauded compliment to Stanley—'I rather think I should hear fewer complaints . . . if the right hon. gentleman were a less powerful opponent in debate'—and he dealt trenchantly with O'Connell's campaign for the repeal of the Union. But what men remembered most about the speech was his attitude to the government and future legislation. It was his duty, he declared, to support the crown in the measures proposed for Ireland, not because he wished or hoped to return to office, nor because he felt increased confidence in the government, but on grounds of public interest.

The great change that had recently taken place in the constitution of the House, justified and required from public men a different course of action. Formerly there were two great parties in the state, each confident in the justice of its own views, each prepared to undertake the government upon the principles which it espoused. All the tactics of party were then resorted to, and justifiably resorted to, for the purpose of effecting the main object,—that of displacing the government. He doubted whether the old system of party tactics were applicable to the present state of things—whether it did not become men to look rather to the maintenance of order, of law, and of property, than to the best mode of annoying and disquieting the government. He saw principles in operation, the prevalence of which he dreaded as fatal to the well-being of society; and whenever the king's government should evince a disposition to resist those principles, they should have his support; when they encouraged them, his decided opposition.

[1] Aspinall, *Diaries*, p. 298.

As for the rage for reforming legislation evident in the House, as though everything in the past had been wrong and a remodelled legislature would set everything in future right, he flatly denied that he had ever been an enemy to gradual and temperate reform.

> He was for reforming every institution that really required reform; but he was for doing it gradually, dispassionately, and deliberately, in order that reform might be lasting.... The king's government had abstained from all unseemly triumph in the king's speech respecting the measure of reform. He would profit by their example, and would say nothing upon that head, but consider that question as finally and irrevocably disposed of. He was now determined to look forward to the future alone, and considering the constitution as it existed, to take his stand on main and essential matters.

His purpose was clear. In a confused political situation and a frothy, indisciplined legislature, he held up the standard not of reaction but of sense, firmness and moderation. It was a rallying-call to which a surprisingly large number of the House of Commons responded. Without compromising himself with the Whigs, at one stroke he had re-established his stature as a national leader. As Greville acutely observed, he had 'contrived to transfer to himself personally much of the weight and authority which he had previously held as the organ and head of a great and powerful party'. In that case there was a further implicit conclusion of some consequence for the future. If his party were ever to become great and powerful again, it would only be by accepting his leadership and his principles. What remained to be seen was how fast and how far they would travel down the road which he opened up for them that evening.

Whatever lay ahead, however, the effect on the House of Commons, as Croker noted, was 'instantaneous and prodigious'. The uneasy Liberal members were brought to their senses, the debate moderated, and the following night handsome majorities of eight and ten to one demonstrated the numerical insignificance of the extreme radical and Irish groups when thrown back on their own resources. Nevertheless, when the Irish coercion bill, first introduced in the upper House, came down to the Commons at the end of February, it contained strong meat for tender Liberal stomachs: powers to proclaim disturbed districts, curfew regulations, a species of military law, and special courts-martial to try offences under the act. After a preliminary and successful delaying motion, the debate even on the first reading lasted five nights. Althorp, opening the proceedings, made a weak speech; there was considerable opposition; and only Stanley with his aristocratic and scornful oratory seemed a match for the bitter onslaughts of the Irish and radicals. Once more, on 1 March, Peel came to the rescue of the government with a speech that even Arbuthnot described as 'magnificent', reading new members a brief lecture on the different functions of the first reading, committee stage, and second reading of a bill, and reinforcing Stanley's catalogue of crime with fresh evidence of his own. He emphasised, as he had done for years, that the root of Ireland's trouble was social—poverty, over-population and under-employment—to which the only checks had been the failure of the potato crop, famine and disease. He admitted that for these evils repression was no relief; but what remedies could be applied as long as anarchy remained? 'Coercion is not a cure; but continued insurrection is positive death.' Then, inspired to passion and eloquence by his own dark memories of Ireland, he denounced the political agitation which encouraged the terrible continuance of crime—196 murders, 194 burnings, 1,827 burglaries and attacks on houses in a single province in a single year—and the 'load of agony' inflicted by Irishmen on Irishmen, unchecked by ordinary law or human pity. If, in his earlier great speech of the session, he had been the Peel of political sense and high principle, this was another person less often shown to the House: the Peel of sensibility and indignation. It was none the less effective; and the bill passed its first reading by a triumphant majority of 466 to 89, the most emphatic support it was destined to receive. Despite concessions from the government, it was still sharply criticised in committee and abstentions by discontented Liberals and disappointed Conservatives at times reduced the ministerial majority to little more than a hundred before it safely passed its third reading and returned to the Lords. When it was through Stanley, between whom and O'Connell an almost personal vendetta had developed, retired to the Colonial Office and J. C. Hobhouse took his uncomfortable place as Irish Secretary.

Long before this, however, the government had given notice of a bill for Irish Church reform on which collaboration between ministers and conservative opposition was immeasurably less easy to obtain. Though religion was not the touchstone of politics, it came nearer to being so than most other issues. Yet if it could unite the Conservatives, it could equally effectively split the Liberals. For the leaders on both sides, therefore, the reconciliation of tactics and principles was not simple. The repeal of the Test and Corporation Acts in 1828 and Catholic emancipation in 1829 had not so much disarmed the critics of the established Church as exposed to them its weaknesses. The third chapter of the revolutionary trilogy, the Reform Act of 1832, further encouraged the formidable alliance of political radicalism and religious dissent. There was a widespread demand for the abolition of tithes, church rates, and the Establishment's monopoly of baptismal, marriage and funeral ceremonies; there was a jealous and exaggerated impression of its wealth; and in the background lurked the ultimate threat of disestablishment. If another attack on the Church was to be launched in the guise of liberal reform, there were many Conservatives (led by the two university representatives, Inglis for Oxford and Peel's close friend, Goulburn, for Cambridge) ready to oppose at the outset any concessions. In this they were only reflecting the opinions of a growing body of churchmen throughout the country who, after the catastrophic events of the past five years, were beginning to view the issue in the fundamental terms of an erastian State set against a spiritual Church. That July, in a famous assize sermon, Keble denounced the Irish Church bill as an act of national apostasy and the first year of the reformed parliament saw the foundation of the Oxford Movement. Peel was not so apprehensive nor so intransigent as his High Church colleagues. He accepted the need for administrative reform in both the English and Irish Churches and perhaps for some concessions of expediency to Dissenters and Roman Catholics. He thought that the best preliminary defence of the Establishment was its reorganisation and reform. Yet he was not prepared to see its position weakened and its property impounded by a legislature which had constitutionally ceased to be even a Protestant, let alone an Anglican assembly, and openly numbered in its ranks Catholics, Dissenters, Unitarians and free-thinkers.

The Irish Church bill announced by Althorp early in the session neither proclaimed nor rejected the controversial principle of lay

48

appropriation. A tax was imposed on bishoprics and ordinary benefices in place of the old church cess for the upkeep of church buildings and other church purposes; ten redundant bishoprics were to be abolished; and the estates which formed the ordinary episcopal endowments were to be leased on new principles under the superintendence of a board of commissioners. This last device was expected to yield an increased revenue and the increase was to be regarded as the property of the State, to be appropriated for any purpose approved by parliament. The distinction between ordinary revenue and the 'increase' was a compromise designed to cover a divided cabinet. It was too subtle for a House of Commons in which both sides promptly claimed the bill as a vindication of their own principles. The ambiguity of the bill was not improved by the mismanagement of its opening stages. After the first reading on 11 March Althorp refused Peel's plea for a month's interval between the circulation of the printed bill and the second reading; but in the end there was almost eight weeks' delay because of the government's failure to observe the formalities incidental to a money bill. In the meantime the indefatigable Duke of Cumberland endeavoured without much success to stir up opposition among the Irish bishops. When the debate on the second reading finally took place in May, Shaw (the member for Dublin University) moved the outright rejection of the bill, supported by Estcourt and Inglis, his colleagues for Oxford University.

Peel, who had been arguing privately with Goulburn against the extreme Anglican attitudes proclaimed in the high Tory press, gave them carefully moderated assistance. As he had said in earlier discussions on the bill and emphasised once more, he was not opposed to a reform of the Irish Church or to parliamentary legislation. He did not hold, with the high Anglicans, that the coronation oath precluded the crown from assenting to alterations in the constitution of the Church nor that the Irish Act of Union involved the maintenance of that constitution in all its details. Yet he was not satisfied that evidence had been brought forward which justified the abolition of ten bishoprics; he objected to certain of the financial arrangements; and above all, he objected to the proposition that church property, when improved by an act of the legislature, could be diverted to secular purposes. It was this issue, as he made clear in an almost personal appeal to Stanley, which was the real stumbling-block. All other objections could be removed by discussion, but not that. To Cumberland, listening impatiently in the gallery, it seemed a shuffling speech. Nevertheless, if not inspiring, it was a clear enunciation of his position and it may have helped to resolve the tactics of a harassed and uncomfortable cabinet. The government gained an easy majority on the second reading but when the appropriation clause (no. 147) was reached in committee, Stanley announced that the ministers had decided to abandon it. In this the cabinet were thinking more of the prospective opposition in the Lords than immediate tactics in the Commons. But it was clear that on a principle where even Peel had declared his unalterable opposition, there was little chance of compromise with the Tory peers.

Not surprisingly the *volte-face* over clause 147 depressed the Liberals and enraged the Irish. It also surprised the Conservative opposition and for Peel it brought yet another complication. Behind the scenes he had been talking with the Archbishop of Canterbury, interviewing the agents of Irish episcopal estates, and labouring to get agreement with men like Goulburn on the wider issue of church endowment in Ireland. As always he looked to facts and consequences. The disordered state of Irish church finances, which bore most hardly on the lower clergy, had not been set right by the government's compulsory Tithe Commutation Act of 1832. For the sake of the Church itself some further reorganisation of its other sources of revenue seemed necessary if the full social benefits of tithe commutation were to be realised. The financial provisions of the Irish Church bill, though not entirely unobjectionable, offered as good a practical arrangement as was likely to be secured under existing circumstances. 'The great question, then, is this,' he wrote to Goulburn on 24 June. 'Is it best for the Church to submit to this Bill, or to speculate upon the chance of a better?'

There were also personal issues involved. In the preceding two years his relationship with Stanley had developed by small, almost imperceptible, but by no means unimportant degrees. They had served together on the select committee appointed in December 1831 to enquire into the collection and payment of Irish tithe. In April 1832, with Lord Grey's assent, Stanley had confidentially submitted for Peel's criticism (observing in his covering note that 'there is no very great difference in the views which we entertain') a memorandum on which he proposed to found the Committee's report.[1] In February 1833 came Peel's public compliment in the debate on the Address, for which Stanley sent him a private note of thanks the following day.[2] In May there was further correspondence on the Irish Church bill, which Peel passed on to Goulburn. It was evident that the ministry was divided on the principle of appropriation but Peel suspected that only a threat of resignation from Stanley had prevented a cabinet decision in its favour. Stanley, grandson of the Earl of Derby, a product of Eton and Christ Church, scholar, sportsman and orator, was at the age of thirty-three already an ornament to his party and a future candidate for the premiership. Less popular but infinitely more talented than Althorp, he had consistently overshadowed his nominal leader in the Commons. It was already a matter of curiosity whether he and his friends, Graham and Richmond, would remain content with current Whig policy or break away on a line of their own, particularly if Grey abandoned office. It was therefore obviously in Peel's interest to encourage him, and through him the Church party in the cabinet. It was better tactics to draw together the conservative elements in government and opposition on an agreed measure of moderate reform, than be left in the ungrateful position of mediator between upper and lower Houses should the Lords reject the bill.

The remainder of the Irish Church bill had a relatively easy passage through committee and a number of minor amendments proposed by Peel were accepted without demur. Though he voted in the minority against the third reading in July, this was probably a merely formal act since there was no danger that the bill would be defeated. The real crisis would come in the Lords and it was to this that Peel now turned his thoughts and influence. More than the fate of the bill was in question. Though Wellington had so far refrained from any organised effort in the upper House against the government, there was mutual antipathy between him and Grey. In June the duke had carried a resolution on Portuguese policy against the ministry and in July the peers threw out Brougham's local courts bill in the teeth of a savage warning from *The Times*,[3]

[1] 40403 f. 25.   [2] *ibid.*, f. 177.   [3] 9 July 1833.

aimed particularly at the bishops, reminding them of their vulnerable position as heads of 'the temporal church, with all its abuses, grievances, and administrative abominations'. This was a disquieting prelude to the Irish Church bill and even before it went up to the Lords, there was a buzz of speculation whether the government would resort to fresh peerage creations to force through the measure; whether they would resign if defeated; and what kind of ministry could be formed if they did. The withdrawal of clause 147 later in the month seemed to weaken the ministry rather than mollify the peers; and excitable Tory Bourbons, who had forgotten nothing and learned nothing from the events of 1832, already spoke of a possible new ministry under Manners Sutton. Equally excitable politicians on the other side of the House took fright as the day for the second reading in the Lords drew near. One of them, Sir John Wrottesley (Peel's neighbour in Staffordshire), moved for a call of the House so that the Commons could be ready to support the government. Early in July Peel had been in touch with Wellington and was satisfied that he would not vote against the second reading;[1] but the duke faced difficulties with his unruly followers and was himself apt to talk more violently than he acted. In the end he voted for the second reading, though he indicated that he would wish to make changes in committee; and the bill passed after a three-day debate by the not unhandsome majority of 59.

The following day (20 July) Peel took the unusual step of writing a long letter to the duke, the mere act of doing so marking his sense of the urgency of the occasion.

> I am confident (even if you should not agree with me) that you will excuse me, for pressing upon your notice the following considerations before you enter upon the Committee of the Bill. First, is it possible to form a Government which shall command a Majority in the present House of Commons—or which shall either in this or any future House of Commons pass those Bills which are essential for the maintenance of the Church in Ireland? I allude particularly to the provision of a substitute for Church Cess, and also to the infinitely more important question, the provision of a substitute for Tithe. Unless the latter substitute be immediately found, there is an end in my opinion both of Tithe and any equivalent for it. I mention

[1] Aspinall, *Diaries*, p. 347.

this the more, because I find that some Peers who are most bent on throwing out the Church Bill, have never considered the position of the Irish Church with respect to Tithe. But I will not trouble you with details. I will only mention those points which should, I think, be considered before the present Government has a fair cause given to it for escaping from its difficulties by resignation. Can thirty seats be vacated as they must be to enable the King to form a Government? Can the present Parliament be dissolved without the remaining estimates having been voted, and is there a chance that the present Parliament will vote them? In case the King should fail in forming a Government, or having formed one, that Government should be unable to maintain itself, will not the democratic party in the Country be greatly strengthened? Looking at the influence given to the dissenting interest in elections, is not a Church Question and particularly one connected with the Church in Ireland, a very unfavourable one for a General Election? Does not the present state of the West India Question present in itself alone, a very serious difficulty in the way of the formation of a Government? Both Houses of Parliament have pledged themselves to resolutions which it is equally difficult now, either to enforce or to abandon, and yet the promise of immediate Emancipation has gone forth to the West Indies. I have so strong an opinion on these points, and I differ so much from many of our friends as to the prospects and as to the advantages of gaining the support of Radicals for a Government acting on really Conservative principles, that I could not help writing to you, though I have little doubt that everything I have said has already occurred to your own mind.[1]

The duke replied on the 23rd. On the main issue he expressed complete agreement, though he was not hopeful of being able to make much improvement to the bill and was certain of incurring the indignation of many of his followers. 'But it is better', he added characteristically, 'to displease them than to increase and aggravate the confusion of the times.' In the event the agreed policy of the two Conservative leaders carried the day against the ultra-Tories and a handful of recalcitrant bishops. Though the government was pressed to the limit of concession in committee, the bill passed and in August the Commons accepted the revised text. The most dangerous crisis of the session was over and the ministry was still intact.

[1] Wellington.

The remaining business of the Commons mainly revolved round the budget. In this field not only could Peel speak with the authority of an acknowledged expert, but he found himself in the more congenial role of assisting the government against the currency heresies and irresponsible economies demanded by radicals and agriculturalists. Early warning of the direction and spirit of the attack came in March, when Thomas Attwood moved for a select committee on distress among the labouring population. His motion was defeated, though only by thirty-four votes. The debate, however, enabled him to ride his hobby-horse of the iniquities of the return to gold in 1819 and the need to devalue the currency; and he was supported not only by English and Irish radicals but by a number of influential Tory agriculturalists, including Knatchbull and Chandos. A month later his kinsman Matthias Attwood renewed the proposal for a select committee, coupling it with a specific instruction to consider how far the existing monetary system had contributed to national distress. Althorp, while leaving open the question of enquiry, prepared to meet the resolution on currency with a direct negative. Nevertheless he was sufficiently alarmed to communicate with Peel beforehand on the question of tactics.[1] Peel answered his call for assistance by coming down to the House and delivering a long and intricate speech, reviewing the whole course of financial policy since the war and its effects on industry and the working population.[2] He ended his defence of the 1819 act by appealing to members to vote from a sense of national policy rather than of local interests. But neither his arguments nor his eloquence convinced the extreme agriculturalists of his party who followed Attwood into the lobby. However, the danger had been foreseen; the problem was large and technical; and on 24 April, after three nights of debate, the government received a comfortable majority.

Meanwhile, on 19 April, Althorp had introduced his budget. With an estimated revenue of £46½ million and an expenditure of £45, he was able to make a number of miscellaneous tax reductions which would leave him with a surplus of £500,000. Since the revenue was showing a tendency to fall rather than rise, Peel thought this was too fine a margin for safety. That, however, was not the general view of the House and attacks were promptly mounted

[1] 40403 f. 231.   [2] 23 Apr. 1833.

against the two most unpopular items of revenue, the malt tax and the house and window tax. The first, which yielded nearly £5 million, Althorp had left intact; the second he had reduced only for shops and warehouses. On 26 April Chandos brought in a motion asking for relief for the agricultural interest which was defeated by less than thirty votes in a thin House. The same evening, with the House dispersing for the weekend, the government whips were caught napping and Sir William Ingilby, one of the four Whig members for Lincolnshire, carried by ten votes a motion for halving the malt tax. Althorp, surprised and discomfited, foolishly uttered words which seemed to imply that the government would defer to the will of the House. But the loss of £2½ million which the reduction entailed would clearly wreck his budget and the cabinet were thrown into complete confusion. Grey wished to resign, and perhaps would have done so had any alternative ministry been possible. Once again support came to them from the opposition front bench. Over the weekend, through the well-tried channel of communication between Holmes and Ellice, Peel sent a message assuring Althorp of his support if the government proposed to rescind the malt tax vote. On Sunday Althorp informed him in reply of the cabinet's decision. Using the occasion of a motion on the house and window tax on the following Tuesday, the ministers put forward an amendment to the effect that a reduction in either that or the malt tax could only be effected by a property and incomes tax at present inexpedient.[1] Not all the opposition were pleased at this. They thought that the government could be unseated on the issue and they resented the way in which the income tax was dragged in as a threat. But Holmes, who at Ellenborough's suggestion spoke to Peel on the possibility of a different amendment, found no encouragement from his leader for any wrecking tactics.[2] When the debate came on, Peel briefly supported the government on the grounds that the malt tax vote was an error which ought to be rescinded, and that in present circumstances he thought it impolitic to resort to an income tax. By a majority of more than two to one the House endorsed Althorp's resolution, though the manner in which he tried to explain away his words of the previous Friday was strangely uncharacteristic of his plain and honest nature.

[1] 40403 f. 239, cf. *Peel*, II, 216.   [2] Aspinall, *Diaries*, pp. 321–2.

The ministry had won the day and saved the budget; but in doing so they had alienated many of their Liberal and radical supporters. Outside the House the reaction was more violent. The window tax relief motion had been moved by Sir John Key, one of the City members, and in the metropolitan constituencies generally there was strong feeling on the issue. Hobhouse, the Irish Secretary, who had pledged himself on the Westminster hustings against the tax, resigned his seat and was beaten when he offered himself for re-election. Resolutions were passed against the tax at parish meetings all over London; there were threats to withhold payment; and the Birmingham Political Union joined the agitation. On 13 May, despite a prohibition from the Home Office, the Political Unions staged a large public protest in Cold Bath Fields and when the police broke up the meeting one constable was stabbed to death and another seriously wounded in the fighting which broke out. The popular agitation was mainly directed against the ministry. But in the long running battle over national distress, currency, and taxes which filled so many columns of *Hansard* during the session, Peel also attracted his share of unpopularity. As chairman of the currency committee of 1819, and its last surviving senior member in the House of Commons, he had become so identified with the return to gold under the 1819 Act that it was now habitually styled Peel's Act; and in the financial debates of 1833 he had been as decided and influential a defender of orthodox finance as any of the occupants of the treasury bench. To the inflationary economists in the House, who numbered agriculturalists as well as radicals among their supporters, he was a living symbol of official policy. Three days after the Cold Bath riots, Cobbett moved a series of verbose and complicated resolutions condemning his connection with the currency acts of 1819, 1822 and 1826, and demanding his dismissal from the Privy Council. The attack, seconded by John Fielden, Cobbett's radical colleague for Oldham, was a fiasco. In a cool, contemptuous speech Peel cut his two opponents to ribbons and then left the House to a storm of cheers. When Cobbett attempted to reply he was shouted down and only four members were found to support the motion. By a similarly overwhelming vote the House approved Althorp's proposal that the defeated resolution should not be entered in the minutes of their proceedings.

The first session of the 1833 parliament, one of the longest and most arduous in parliamentary recollection, ended on 29 August. Its labours had not been altogether unproductive. In addition to the Irish legislation it had abolished slavery, continued the work of legal reform, passed a factory regulation act, and renewed the charters of the Bank of England and East India Company. Reforms had been expected of a reformed legislature; and there was enough put on the statute book to justify the issue of a Whig party pamphlet on *The Reform Ministry and the Reformed Parliament*. Nevertheless this unusual piece of official propaganda was a mark of self-defence rather than of self-congratulation. No party and few personalities had come through the session with enhanced credit. Greville, while noting cynically that the reformed parliament had turned out to be much like any other, thought it less talented though more industrious than its predecessors. He singled out Peel and Stanley as the only two men who gained in reputation as the session advanced. Peel, with whom he accidentally got into conversation one day in July while riding in the Park, shared his views to the extent of speaking well of Stanley and ill of the rest of the cabinet.[1] He had been irritated on a number of occasions by the blunders and ineptitude of the ministers; and though he personally found the new House a good and receptive audience, perhaps for the same reason it was a volatile and unpredictable assembly. As the greatest parliamentary practitioner of his day, sitting on the opposition bench night after night while honest, blundering, good-natured Althorp struggled to guide the House, he was conscious that there were occasions when he could easily have swept a majority against the government had he so chosen. He had not done so, but his restraint towards the ministers in public found relief in a certain contempt for them in private.

My belief is [he wrote to Croker in March] that the Reform Bill has worked for three weeks solely from this, that the Conservatives have been too honest to unite with the Radicals. . . . What are we doing at this moment? We are making the Reform Bill work; we are falsifying our own predictions. . . . We are protecting the authors of the evil from the work of their own hands. It is right we should do this, but I must say it was expecting more than human institutions,

[1] *Greville*, 18 July, 3 Sept. 1833.

57

intended to govern the unruly passions and corrupt natures of human beings, ought to calculate upon.[1]

A number of incidents in the succeeding weeks did nothing to improve his opinion of the reform ministry. One was a scandal over Sir John Key, the radical M.P. given a baronetcy by the Whigs and later discovered not only to be holding an illegal contract with the government but to have procured the appointment of his son, under age, as government inspector of his father's contract with the stationery office. Another was the shuffling attempts of the Home Office to repudiate responsibility for the police action at the Cold Bath Fields riots, which he was able to observe at close hand as member of the committee of enquiry. To Croker, who undertook to answer the Whig pamphlet with an article in the *Quarterly Review*, aided by contributions from Peel and Wellington, he wrote acidly that he could see little cause for triumph on the part of the promoters of the reform bill. The business of the House was got through but only

> because that which we prophesied took place; namely, that the popular assembly exercised tacitly supreme power, that the House of Lords—to avoid the consequences of collision—declined acting upon that which was notoriously the deliberate judgement and conviction of a majority. I allude particularly to the Irish Church bill. With respect to that Bill, it is quite clear that the course taken was in spite of the opinions of two out of three branches of the legislature.[2]

But with Peel there was always the contrast between the sharp contemptuous sentiments which he gave himself the satisfaction of uttering in private, and the cautious sagacity which controlled his public actions. Throughout the session he was guided by one dominating consideration. Weak as it was, there was no substitute for Lord Grey's ministry and as long as this situation lasted, the duty of a Conservative opposition was not to oppose but conserve.

Not all the angry and indisciplined right-wing critics of the government accepted or even comprehended conservatism in this sense. As Melville wrote in the course of a sympathetic correspondence with Peel during the summer:

[1] *Croker*, II, 204.
[2] *ibid.*, 214-15 (29 Sept. 1833).

I am shocked and provoked at the radical doctrines and language of some of our ultra-Conservative Newspapers both in London and in Edinburgh, from no other apparent motive than hostility to the present Ministers, and totally forgetting that all those Doctrines and anti-*governmental* principles (I use the word advisedly as opposed to anti-Administration) are much more at variance with our sound principles than with those of our Whig ministers. In short, if our ultra-friends push matters to such extremities, they will disgust all really loyal and well-intentioned conservatives, who look only to the stability of the Monarchy and preservation of the Constitution.[1]

These divisions in the party not merely created difficulties of leadership; they raised the question whether a single leadership actually existed. Party understrappers like Holmes and Ross might look to Peel for direction, but this counted for little with some of the proud and self-willed country gentlemen. The disunion in the ranks of the opposition was so evident indeed that early in the session attempts were made to procure some overt recognition of Peel's authority. There was a gathering at Lord Rosslyn's at the end of February at which it was decided that Herries and others should use their influence with Inglis, Knatchbull, Vyvyan, Stormont and other malcontents to get their consent to a general party meeting at which Peel would be formally elected leader. When approached, however, they exhibited an attitude more suitable to independent partners in a potential coalition than to dissidents within a single party. Knatchbull and Vyvyan, before they would agree to Peel's election, asked that 'places should be fixed *d'avance*' in, presumably, any future Conservative ministry. Vyvyan was idiot enough to call on Peel and inform him that they would make him 'their minister' if they succeeded in repealing the 1819 Act. Condescension from Vyvyan combined with debasement of the currency was something more than Peel's temper could stand.[2] It was true that there was no open breach and at the traditional fish dinner at Greenwich in June, attended by some thirty or forty of the leading members of the opposition, the old *corps* of the party—Wellington, Aberdeen, Lyndhurst, Ellenborough among the peers, Peel, Manners Sutton, Hardinge, Granville Somerset, Scarlett and Sir Alexander Grant from the Commons—was joined for the first

---

[1] 40403 f. 252 (20 May 1833).   [2] Aspinall, *Diaries*, pp. 308, 316, 324.

time by such ultras as Stormont, Vyvyan and Knatchbull, even if the harmony was post-prandial rather than political. Nevertheless, the session ended with the question of leadership undecided; and since it was undecided, it was not surprising that the pathetic and faintly ludicrous ghost of 1832—a conservative ministry with Manners Sutton as interim prime minister—still hovered on the outskirts of party discussions. But it was talk without action and the Whig Le Marchant was able to note in July with partisan malice that though the Tories were full of activity, 'they were more active than united', and that Peel was keeping well clear of their plans.[1]

II

Autumn came and with it the annual lull in the cycle of parliamentary warfare during which politicians could recuperate from the strains of the past campaign and hatch strategems for the new. In the latter Peel had little interest. The Long Vacation for him meant Drayton with his estate, his farms, his new house, shooting over his fields and coverts, dining with neighbours, talking with tenants, above all the company of his wife and his seven children from whom the House of Commons exiled him for half the year. Julia was now recovering her health and his youngest child, Eliza, had entered her second year. The eldest of them, Julia the second, was twelve years old and beginning to grow into a handsome young lady. Bobby, her junior by one year, was already experiencing the modified rigours of boarding-school life at a private establishment at Brighton, and the joys of returning home for the holidays. Later in the season came the familiar round of visits—to Alexander Baring's Norfolk seat at Buckenham in November, to Lord Exeter at Burghley and the duke of Rutland at Belvoir in January. At Buckenham Peel found himself in the company of Greville, the diarist, and from this first prolonged contact between the two men was born an odd relationship, halfway between friendship and acquaintance. On Greville's side it was not without an element of interest and respect, whatever other reservations his observant and sardonic intellect was careful to make. His first discovery, like that of others before him, was that Peel could be very good company—

[1] Aspinall, *Diaries*, p. 361.

'it is a toss-up whether he talks or not, but if he thaws, and is in good humour and spirit, he is lively, entertaining, and abounding in anecdotes which he tells extremely well'.[1] Greville himself went to Belvoir early in January and while there he met 'Gosh' Arbuthnot, the Duke of Wellington's crony, who assured him that Peel and the duke were always on good terms and no large question was ever decided without Peel's coming to the duke and discussing it with him. Of their formal political collaboration this was perhaps correct; but the absence of any personal warmth between the two Conservative leaders was still obvious. An episode in the winter of 1833–34 brought the temperature of their relationship even lower.

In November 1833 old Lord Grenville was dying. He had been Chancellor of Oxford University since 1809 and academic politicians, no less thoughtful than their parliamentary tribesmen, were already looking round for a successor. The Whigs, few in number but fortified by government influence, were canvassing for the Earl of Carlisle. Christ Church, large enough if united to rank as a separate party, approached without success Lord Mansfield and Lord Talbot. The High Church ultra-Tory party, headed by St. John's College, made overtures to Wellington. The fourth and last group of Oxford politicians, the Liberal-Conservatives, were left to view with some distaste the prospect before them. Carlisle, the minority candidate, was personally the most impressive. Talbot, who under family pressure subsequently withdrew his earlier refusal, was a good-hearted blundering nonentity. Wellington was an even greater oddity as candidate for the Chancellorship. He was not an Oxonian; he was not even a university graduate; and as prime minister he had passed Catholic emancipation and removed his sons from Oxford to Cambridge. He himself showed no eagerness for the distinction and in default of Lord Talbot, he advised his St. John's supporters in mid-December to agree with the heads of the larger houses and the more influential conservatives in the university on some more suitable Oxford man. It was customary to elect a peer, but there was at least one commoner whose distinction might justify a breach with convention. It was true that Peel had lost his university seat in 1829 because of his support for Catholic emancipation; but if this was a disqualification, it also applied to

[1] *Greville*, 13 Nov. 1833, 14 Mar. 1834.

Wellington. Otherwise the intervening years had merely strengthened his claims as the most eminent Oxford man in public life. His old Christ Church tutor, Bishop Lloyd, had several years before his death sounded him on the possibility of succeeding Grenville. Peel had discouraged the notion then and after the rupture over emancipation he was too proud to make any gesture of conciliation. To Henry Hobhouse, who urged him in December to mediate between the conflicting candidatures of Wellington and Talbot, he merely observed that since 1829 he had abstained as much as possible from any interference in university affairs.

Yet to others he seemed the obvious candidate and he could not have been unmoved by his sister Mary's affectionate urgings that 'it would be complete atonement for the disappointment we all experienced at Oxford in the year 1829 and . . . the most desirable honor and testimony of public approbation which could be conferred upon you'. Yet he would not lift a finger to obtain that solace, and information which Bonham had obtained on the state of parties in the university made it clear that there was no chance of success unless the St. John's party joined in his support. Of this there was never any prospect. When Lord Grenville died early in the new year, Talbot told Christ Church that he could not come forward in opposition to the Duke of Wellington; and the duke himself under renewed pressure from his supporters on 16 January finally accepted an invitation to stand. A private appeal from Oxford to retire in favour of Peel received the reply that it was in effect too late. The Peelite party, joined now by the Whigs, had in fact allowed themselves to be overtaken by events. Though on the news of Grenville's death a requisition was immediately drawn up and taken to Drayton by the Warden of Merton and the Principal of New Inn Hall, Peel declined it in terms which left no hope that he could be induced to change his mind. All was now over and the duke, left in possession of the empty field, proceeded to an uncontested election.[1]

[1] For the history of the Chancellor's election of 1834 see *Peel*, II, 227–39; 40403 fos. 281–93; 40313 fos. 176–80; Wellington (corr. with Bathurst, Dr. Wintle, Talbot, Hardinge and others Nov. 1833–Jan. 1834); *H. M. C. Bathurst MSS.* (1923), pp. 663–5. An account of the internal manœuvring in the university is given in my article 'Oxford politics in the Chancellor's election of 1834' (*Oxford Magazine*, 28 Apr., 5 May 1938), where Mary Dawson's letter was wrongly attributed to her husband.

Throughout the affair, Peel's behaviour had been correct to the point of unnecessary circumspection. But he had been hurt, and the cause of his hurt was the attitude of Wellington. Though Peel had consistently said that he had made up his mind not to stand for the Chancellorship, he felt—naturally if unreasonably—that he had for some time been openly spoken of as an obvious candidate, that he had strong personal and academic ties with Oxford which the duke conspicuously lacked, and that a large and respectable requisition had been made to him. If the objection to him was his conduct over Catholic emancipation, that conduct had been largely owing, as he told Aberdeen afterwards, to 'fidelity at a trying time to the Duke of Wellington'. Yet the very party which had secured his defeat in 1829 had been the duke's chief backers in 1834 and Wellington had allowed himself to be nominated 'without one word of communication with me direct or indirect' to ascertain whether Peel might not wish to stand. He did not even know of the duke's decision until he received a letter from Hardinge on 18 January, the day after his own formal refusal to the Warden of Merton. In all this Peel was less than just; for the duke had not entirely ignored his claims. Hardinge assured Peel that when the St. John's delegation came to Stratfield Saye early in December, the duke had urged them to force the office upon Peel by a junction of all parties in his favour. This was certainly consonant with the terms of the duke's letter of 14 December, urging the principal colleges of the University to unite behind some fit candidate who had been educated at Oxford. Publicly the duke could hardly have done more, other than to decline outright an honour for which he admitted he was not qualified. But he could have told Peel privately what he had said to the Oxford dons. Wellington had acted honourably, as he always did; what he lacked was the imagination which would have enabled him to understand the susceptibilities of his prickly colleague.

As it was, the circumstances of the Chancellor's election in 1834 following on the unhealed breach of 1832, put a constraint upon the relationship between the two men which began to disturb their closest adherents. Peel would make no move to explain or end the coolness. Wellington, misinterpreting his attitude, thought that Peel disliked him personally. In the session of 1834 the separation was so marked that Arbuthnot went out of his way to bring them together at a dinner on 1 May, the duke's birthday. But scarcely a word passed between the two principals, to the distress and concern not only of their host but of the other guests, Hardinge and Fitzgerald. Next day Arbuthnot sent an appeal to the good-natured and pacific Lord Aberdeen, a close friend of both men, to use his efforts to bring the duke and Peel together again. Aberdeen, the soul of uprightness and candour, wrote to Peel enclosing Arbuthnot's letter and adding a few sympathetic lines of his own, admitting that the duke had in great measure himself been responsible for the situation which their friends were deploring. Peel did not care to write on such a subject but he saw Aberdeen at his house in London a few days later and had a long conversation with him on the matter. The breach had gone too deep for this conciliatory diplomacy to produce an immediate effect. Nevertheless it did something to clear the air, and Aberdeen told Peel frankly that he did not think him entirely blameless. Moreover, in their anxiety over the superficial coldness, the lieutenants of the party tended to overlook more permanent things. Between Peel and Wellington there was great mutual respect; neither was disposed to undervalue the political importance of the other; and when left to themselves, they usually came to very similar conclusions.

Nevertheless, it was as well for the slow growth of Conservative recovery that the main events of the 1834 session hinged not on the personal difficulties of the opposition but on the political differences within the government. From the start the Whigs ran into trouble with the independent Irish group. A dispute in February over the Irish Coercion Act, in which the personal integrity of some Irish M.P.s was impugned, ended in Althorp and Sheil being placed in the protective custody of the sergeant-at-arms. The same month Littleton outlined the government's proposals for an Irish tithe settlement. They were at once violently attacked by O'Connell, Sheil, and other Irish members, who in turn were equally strongly attacked by Lord John Russell. In April O'Connell's motion for an enquiry into the legislative union between Great Britain and Ireland was answered by the government with a call of the House and a formal amendment by Spring Rice for an address to the crown in favour of maintaining the Union. Against the extreme Irish wing the ministers could rely on massive majorities drawn from both sides of the House. But the occasions that necessitated them enabled Peel once again to come forward as the disinterested supporter of government authority and a policy of moderation. In the debate on the repeal of the Union Greville observed that only two men made good speeches, Spring Rice and Peel, 'the latter super-eminently so'. Though Peel reserved his main effort on Irish tithe for the committee stage, the Conservatives generally supported the measure which passed the second reading by a large majority early in May.

Yet at the same time he took several opportunities to speak in defence of the great interests, social, political, and economic, for which conservatism stood. In February, on Chandos's motion on agricultural distress, he made an appeal for some relief for agriculture. Then in March came three notable speeches. The first, on 17 March, was a smart and effective attack on Palmerston's Turkish policy. Two days later, in a free trade debate brought on by Ewart, the member for Liverpool, he defended agricultural protection. A week afterwards, in a debate on the Cambridge petitions, he upheld the exclusion of Dissenters from Oxford and Cambridge. He spoke well and strongly; and he attracted the more attention because not everyone had expected him to speak at all on that issue, or if he did, to say anything which might offend dissenting susceptibilities. Yet even in these partisan, or what might be considered partisan efforts, he chose his arguments carefully. Greville noted, for example, that on the Cambridge petitions he did not attack the principle of toleration but grounded his case on the inherent character of the two ancient universities as seats of religious instruction and on the damage to the constitutional connection between Church and State if the claims of Dissenters to be admitted were considered as claims of right.[1] Similarly, on the issue of free trade, he took his stand on facts rather than principles. Agriculturists, he argued, were no more monopolists than any other producers. The whole British fiscal system was based on protection for domestic industry, whether agricultural or manufacturing. Even if protection for manufactured goods were removed, there would still remain the secondary question of the special burdens on the land—malt tax, land tax, tithe, and county rate—which justified some equivalent advantage.

[1] *Greville*, 29 Mar. 1834.

In private moreover he vented to Croker his dislike of the more far-reaching protectionist arguments used in debate: the appeal *ad misericordiam* because of agricultural distress, and 'the invidious and startling argument' that the landed interest, as the most important, should be a favoured class for the benefit of which the rest of the community should be taxed.[1]

While he was developing in these various directions his conception of rational and moderate conservative policy, the explosive elements of Ireland and the Church—the most lethal material in contemporary British politics—fused together after the Easter recess in a series of detonations which in the end brought Grey's reform ministry to the ground. The mild Irish tithe bill introduced by Littleton had evaded the two fundamental questions: whether the Church of Ireland was over-endowed; and if so, whether part of its revenues should be diverted elsewhere. In the debate on the second reading on 6 May, Russell, who had been taunted with inconsistency, admitted the differences within the cabinet on appropriation. Speaking for himself, however, he promised that when the problem came for solution, he would stand by his previous opinion that the revenues of the Irish Church were too large either for its spiritual functions or its political stability; and he added that if any nation had a right to complain, it was the people of Ireland of the Church of Ireland. This was upsetting enough for an already disturbed cabinet; but what brought on the real crisis was a notice promptly given by Ward, an independent liberal M.P. (probably instigated by Lord Durham), that he would move a resolution pledging the House to a reduction of the temporalities of the Church of Ireland and asserting the right of the state to apply surplus ecclesiastical revenues to such purposes as parliament might determine. The cabinet thought it would be impossible to meet Ward's motion with a direct negative; and as a compromise it was decided to offer a commission of enquiry into Irish Church revenues. Stanley refused to be mollified. The discussions in the cabinet clearly showed what little support he had and the device of a commission merely demonstrated, in his view, that the government was virtually prepared to accept the principle of appropriation. On 27 May, the day of Ward's motion and the government announcement of the

[1] *Croker*, II, 222.

enquiry commission, he resigned with three of his cabinet colleagues—his close friend Sir James Graham, the ex-Tory Duke of Richmond, and the ex-Canningite Earl of Ripon, better known as Peel's old colleague Robinson or by his intermediate title of Viscount Goderich.

It was the first great crack in the reform cabinet; but it was not unexpected. For several weeks rumours had been going round of internal dissensions in the administration. Indeed, it was a perhaps exaggerated impression of the shakiness of the government and the likelihood of a complete collapse, which had prompted Arbuthnot's peace-making dinner party at the beginning of the month. 'In what state would our Party be,' he wrote next day to Aberdeen, 'if the king had to seek us while the duke and Peel were hardly on speaking terms! (This is too strongly expressed.)'[1] In an effort to avoid such a situation he followed up Aberdeen's mediation with a letter of his own to Peel on 12 May, giving him a summary of Wellington's thoughts on the crisis. The duke felt strongly that they might at any moment be sent for; he thought the minister chosen must be in the House of Commons; and he would aid the formation of such a government in any capacity, though his preference would be to go to the Horse Guards, leaving Aberdeen as leader of the House of Lords. This, reinforced as it was by Arbuthnot's not unreasonable explanation of the duke's behaviour in 1832, could hardly have failed to bring satisfaction to Peel. Though he and the duke were not men who found it easy to make personal approaches, he for his part had already made a gesture of conciliation. In his speech in the Union debate on 25 April, he had paid a warm tribute to Wellington's role as saviour of the country in the Napoleonic Wars; and he told Aberdeen when they were talking on 9 May that there was no misunderstanding between the duke and himself, and even the admitted lessening of social intercourse had not been to the extent imagined by Arbuthnot. The real problem for the opposition, in his view, was the circumstances in which they might be called to office. He was absent at Drayton in the latter part of May when Ward's resolution came on and Goulburn, with some misgivings as to his own skill as parliamentary tactician, was left to manage the opposition front bench. Both to him and to Arbuthnot, who wrote

[1] 40312 f. 178 (omitted from version in *Peel*, II, 232).

again with gossip gleaned from Lord Tavistock of the gloomy government prospects, Peel returned the same reply. Abstractly he would prefer to meet Ward's motion by a direct negative; but if the government preferred for tactical purposes to move the previous question, it would be wrong to join with radicals and Irish in opposing them. The policy for a Conservative opposition was not petty manœuvring to inflict technical defeats, but a broad and consistent line of conduct which would conciliate, or at least lessen the hostility of, the more moderate and respectable government supporters. If, despite this, the government broke up from its own disunity, there would then be good grounds for an appeal to the country by their successors; but not otherwise. What was clearly in his mind was that any thought of a Conservative administration was premature unless, both among parliamentary politicians and in the electorate, there could be some detachment of men who had previously supported Grey's ministry. Already, at the end of March, Greville had been hearing encomiums from some of the Whigs on Peel's parliamentary superiority and his fair and prudent conduct towards the government. Charles Grey had even told him that if his father resigned, he himself and others would be willing to support Peel.[1] The secession of the Stanleyites made this kind of language seem something more than dinner-table conversation.

After the ministerial reconstruction at the beginning of June the temper of parliamentary politics noticeably hardened. Stanley's departure inevitably meant a slight but perceptible veer to the left in government policy and this in turn widened the gap between the two front benches. Towards the end of the month discussions were renewed on the Irish tithe bill. O'Connell tried to get an instruction to committee that after any funds raised in lieu of tithe had been suitably applied, the remainder should be used for public purposes. The motion was defeated, but both Russell and Althorp agreed that when the results of the commission of enquiry were known, it would be proper to consider whether any surplus should be devoted to more beneficial objects. Peel, who had opposed the commission and doubted whether there was any surplus to discover, criticised the ministry for evading the issue and trying to cover up their own uncertainty. The extensive changes made in the bill before it went

[1] *Greville*, 25 Mar. 1834.

into committee seemed to justify what he said and drew from Stanley on 4 July a bitter and unfortunate attack on his late colleagues whom he compared to thimble-rigging cheats on a race-course. Nevertheless the government went on, though with decreased majorities. When they offered only a token resistance to a successful O'Connell amendment at the end of the month, Irish criticism gradually ceased and the bill passed rapidly through its later stages. Long before the third reading, however, a second crisis shattered the government. The tithe war and the general disorder in Ireland had made it necessary to renew the Coercion Act due to expire in August. Wellesley, the Lord Lieutenant, during the spring and early summer agreed in principle with this decision though with confusing and contradictory expressions of opinion on the more severe clauses. It was the kind of exasperating behaviour which Peel had experienced from him in the same office ten years earlier;[1] but Grey, taking a firm line, introduced a bill on the more drastic lines originally sanctioned by Wellesley.

Meanwhile the Irish Secretary Littleton, unknown to Grey, tried to conciliate O'Connell by revealing to him the more wavering second thoughts of the Irish government, on the assumption that these would in fact be accepted by the cabinet. When O'Connell discovered his error, he thought he had been hoodwinked and promptly revealed the whole story in the House of Commons. O'Connell and Littleton gave the lie to each other across the floor of the House and the Irish Secretary could only with difficulty be restrained from resignation. A few days later, when the coercion bill was about to come down to the Commons, Althorp as a preparatory measure laid before the House papers relating to the state of Ireland. O'Connell at once moved that they should be referred to a select committee. Peel, while opposing this, sharply criticised the government's handling of the affair and supported a suggestion made by Lord Stormont that Wellesley should be asked to sanction publication of the correspondence with Littleton which might bear on his alleged change of opinion. When his first motion was rejected, O'Connell took up this point and gave notice that he would move for the production of the relevant part of the Lord Lieutenant's correspondence. Althorp, who had fought against the

[1] See *Mr. Secretary Peel*, ch. 11.

more rigorous clauses of the Act and was partially inculpated in Littleton's disclosures to O'Connell, refused to be dragged any further through the dirt and that evening (7 July) sent in his resignation. But Grey also had had enough. Sick and angry at the wrangling in cabinet and the radical proclivities of some of his colleagues, he resigned from his own office the next day. The great reform ministry was at an end and Peel, without conscious intention, had played a part in its downfall.

He had not anticipated the abrupt collapse of Grey's administration. He could not have wanted it unless he felt that it was possible to form a Conservative government; and this was still very doubtful. It was true that the steady drift of ministerial opinion towards a more radical Church policy had stiffened his own reactions. At a dinner at the Carlton Club on 18 June, Waterloo Day, he had made a speech of half an hour to which the political gossips attached much importance. Reports differed, but according to one account he had declared that he had supported the government as long as he could, but seeing them bent on attacking the Church, he was determined to oppose them in company with other defenders of the Establishment.[1] It was unlikely that he said more, but it pleased ultras like Chandos and Falmouth; and it was in any case an issue on which the opposition could cheerfully unite. As Wellington observed somewhat cynically to Peel the following month, 'there is nothing that people care so much about as the Church, excepting always their own Properties'.[2] It was important moreover that Peel was in communication with the duke once more. On 4 July he consulted him about a message from the Irish primate, brought to him by Shaw, the member for Dublin University, about the desire of the Irish bishops to present an address to the king on Irish Church policy. He was disinclined to encourage this; but he asked Wellington's advice and as usual found him in agreement. The duke in fact had discouraged a similar overture from one of the English bishops only a few days earlier. It was equally important that he was in contact with Stanley and Graham, the Whig seceders. The previous day Graham had talked with him about the Irish tithe bill and assured him that Stanley and himself would support the original terms of the bill which the government had now materially altered.

[1] *Greville*, 20 June 1834.   [2] 40309 f. 268.

On his side, as Graham reported to his chief, Peel showed himself easy, communicative, and anxious to work in harmony with them.[1] The shadow of a Conservative alliance was taking shape. But it was not yet a reality; nor was there yet any actual prospect of power.

The end of Grey's ministry, however, did bring up, if only fleetingly, the possibility of a political regrouping. When the king summoned Melbourne on 9 July, it was not to request him to carry on the Whig government but to attempt a coalition with Wellington, Peel and Stanley. Melbourne declined the commission in a reasoned statement based chiefly on their opposition to measures, notably the Irish tithe bill and the Irish Church Commission of Enquiry, which Melbourne thought 'vital and essential'. He was directed to send them copies of his letter so that they would at least be apprised of William's views. Peel and Wellington, struck by the oddity of a document which presented them not with the king's sentiments but with Melbourne's reply, did not feel called on to make an explanation of their own position and returned only formal acknowledgements. William was not to be baulked so easily and expressed a desire through Melbourne that the two Conservative leaders should make explicit observations on Melbourne's letter. In response to this direct command, Peel wrote a memorandum for the king, concurring generally in Melbourne's view that the suggested union of parties could not in existing circumstances hold out the prospect of 'an efficient and vigorous administration'. If Lord Grey and his colleagues were divided, he pointed out, it was unlikely that unity would be secured by a junction with their opponents. Yet he made it clear that it was not the attitude of the Conservative leaders but Melbourne's express statement which had made a coalition impossible from the start. Wellington replied in similar terms. Indeed, throughout the episode, the two men acted in concert. On 11 July, the date of their first formal reply, Peel had called on Wellington at Apsley House and was closeted with him for a considerable time; and though they drew up their second and fuller letters separately, they showed them to each other beforehand. Their private attitudes were clear and identical. Melbourne had himself killed any chance of a coalition both by his own refusal to

[1] Wellington (Peel to Wellington, 4 July 1834); *Graham*, I, 206.

the king and his determination to go through with the Irish Church measures. The opposition leaders had not refused, and would not refuse, to serve the king if they could do so without stipulations as to coalitions or limitations on their freedom of action. They had no desire for office in the unfavourable circumstances confronting them; but they would not have rejected it and would have been ready if necessary to appeal to the electorate on behalf of a Conservative administration offering, as Peel put it, 'cautious and well-digested reforms' and 'the redress of proved grievances'.[1]

Indeed, Peel took one small but significant action to prepare for such an event. On 14 July, the day after his second letter to the king, he asked Knatchbull in the House of Commons to call on him next morning. When he came, he showed him the correspondence with Melbourne and expressed a wish to consult Knatchbull should he ever be required to form a ministry. It was the first overt move by Peel to renew formal contact with the ultra-Tories who had defected from Wellington's ministry in 1829 and helped to defeat it in 1830. The choice of recipient for this olive-sprig was judicious and certainly deliberate. Sir Edward Knatchbull, ninth baronet, M.P. for East Kent, was one of the most respected and respectable of the independent county members. High-minded, mediocre, diffident and dull, he was free from either the vanity of Chandos or the hysteria of Vyvyan, the other two Conservative politicians in the House of Commons who might lay claim to the leadership of the country party. In such company Knatchbull stood out as eminently sensible and moderate. Though he had regarded himself as deceived by Peel over Catholic emancipation, he had never allowed himself to become identified with the extremism of Cumberland nor had he ever entirely broken with Wellington.[2] For his character and influence, if not his intellect and ability, he was of some value on the right flank of the political chessboard, if the loose pieces assembled there were ever to be organised as a cohesive force.

But the curtain dropped on this faint vista of the future almost immediately. After a futile attempt to lay down conditions as to men and measures, the king finally followed the only course open

[1] 40302 fos. 1–5; 40404 fos. 197–222. Most of this is in *Peel Memoirs*, II, 1–13. See also T. Martin, *Life of Lyndhurst* (1883), pp. 316–18; *Greville*, 12 July 1834.

[2] *Knatchbull*, p. 213.

72

to him and on 16 July Melbourne took office as first minister. Althorp returned to provide what seemed the indispensable basis in the lower House, and the liberal progress of the ministry was resumed. The Coercion Act, shorn of its more drastic clauses, was renewed and the recast Irish tithe bill sent up to the Lords. With House of Commons business virtually over, Peel thankfully returned to Julia and his family at Drayton on the last day of July. It had been another long and laborious session. In addition to his customary activities on and behind the parliamentary political scene, he had also been busy as chairman of a sub-committee on county rates to which were referred all questions relating to the expenses of administering justice. With his usual industry and command of detail he had gone thoroughly into the question with advisers like Henry Hobhouse, his old Home Office permanent official, and a mass of documents and statistics from all parts of the country had piled up on his desk as the summer wore on. That task was now over, however, and early in July he was able to present an advance copy of the committee's report to his Staffordshire neighbour, General Dyott.[1]

Nevertheless, the session was not finished yet. The government's weakness had been stripped bare by the events of the summer, and with the consciousness that both crown and church were on their side, the Tory peers were waiting in the upper House. Even before he left London, Peel had been alarmed by Wellington's formal amendment in the Lords for the reinsertion of the omitted clauses in the Coercion Act. Peel himself was present in the House of Lords at the time and as he wrote to Julia next day:

> the Opposition mustered very strong, the friends of Government were comparatively few, and I have not a doubt that, if the Duke had divided the House, the clause would have been introduced, and whether the Government broke up or not, my departure from Town tomorrow would have been impossible. However, the Duke did not divide, and my horses are, thank God, ordered for tomorrow to carry me to my own dear Love.[2]

But though the coercion bill was allowed to pass under protest, it was otherwise with the measure for Irish tithes. Though the problem was pressing and the Irish clergy themselves were likely to suffer

---

[1] *Dyott*, II, 179. For the county rates committee see 40404 *passim*.
[2] Peel, *Letters*, p. 149.

from any postponement of a solution, the reframed government measure seemed to many Conservatives to come near to appropriation by diverting from the Church of Ireland part of its revenues without even the consolation of providing a final scheme of redemption. When the bill came before the Lords on 11 August the Tory peers, rejecting the sensible advice of Richmond and Ripon to vote for a second reading and then restore in committee its original character, threw out the bill by a large majority. The duke, in the face of the intransigent confidence of his party in the House, had promised to be guided by the sentiments of the bishops. In the end he spoke and voted for rejection. It was late in the session; tempers were impatient; and even the moderate Bishop of London spoke against the bill. Nevertheless, it was not so much victory as defiance: Tory opposition as Cumberland, Kenyon, Londonderry and Buckingham understood it rather than the prudent Peelite formula which Wellington had followed the previous session. If in some respects moderate conservatism had consolidated its forces during 1834, so also had the less manageable diehards of the right. It was painfully clear that political co-ordination between the Conservative parties in the two Houses was still the exception rather than the rule.

The odd feature of Peel's behaviour during the events of August was that he did nothing. He may have said all he had to say to the duke before he left London; he may have been reluctant to overstrain his credit by intervening on an issue less vital than the Irish Church bill of 1833; he may not have realised that Wellington's mood was perceptibly hardening towards the end of the session. The duke's threat to the coercion bill had clearly surprised him, though to some of the ultra-Tory peers it had been evident for some time that Wellington was more ready for battle than in the preceding session. Some observers connected this with his new role as Chancellor of Oxford University and the great demonstration he had received at his installation in June. Certainly he had encouraged the peers to stay on in London after the successful rejection of the universities admission bill on 1 August and at a party meeting of peers next day, when pressed by Cumberland and Kenyon to throw out the tithes bill before going into committee, he had said enough to satisfy the ultras. Yet if Peel was unaware of the duke's change of attitude, it argued a dangerous lack of contact; since Peel could hardly have given a wholehearted approval to the action of the Tory peers. For the first time since 1832 a hostile party in the Lords had contemptuously and unconditionally rejected a major government measure. By any long-term calculation it was a hazardous step.

Four days later came the end of the session. Except for the Poor Law Amendment Act, which Peel approved in principle though he took little or no part in debate, it had not been a constructive session in legislation. One notable casualty had been the ministerial programme of relief measures for Dissenters. Under pressure from the central dissenting organisation, the United Committee formed in London in the previous year, the government in 1834 had introduced a universities admission bill, a Dissenters marriage bill, and church rates bill. The first had been defeated in the Lords, the second was abandoned as an unsatisfactory compromise, and the third, which transferred the burden of church rates to the land tax, was successfully opposed in the Commons by both radicals and Dissenters. The failure of all three had raised dissenting agitation to its highest pitch since 1828. Politically, however, the second session of the reformed parliament had seen the first noticeable shift towards a redefinition of party, not in terms of the Reform Act but in terms of what the Reform Act would mean in future policy. After the preliminary sparring of the first session, the lines of battle were beginning to appear more clearly. The Dissenters were angry and resentful at the strength of Anglican opposition to the redress of their public grievances. The radicals and Irish nationalists were beginning to realise that the opposition of the House of Lords was a formidable barrier to the progress of reform. Realism was breaking in on the optimistic assumptions which the passage of the Reform Act had trailed in its wake, and tempers were not improved. But for Peel all this was temporarily in abeyance. He knew what he would do if ever summoned to office; but when that would be seemed as far off as ever. After the momentary flutter of hope at the time of Grey's retirement, some of what one observer called the 'high and foolish' Tories were sulky and disappointed. Peel, however, was perfectly content. Even without office his position in public life had its rewards and satisfactions.

Greville, who was growing increasingly interested in Peel's career, wrote in February an eloquent description of how golden these years of independent opposition appeared to a detached and friendly observer.

> Peel's is an enviable position; in the prime of life, with an immense fortune, *facile princeps* in the House of Commons, unshackled by party connections and prejudices, universally regarded as the ablest man, and with (on the whole) a very high character, free from the cares of office, able to devote himself to literature, to politics, or idleness, as the fancy takes him. No matter how unruly the House, how impatient or fatigued, the moment he rises, all is silence, and he is sure of being heard with profound attention and respect. This is the enjoyable period of his life, and he must make the best of it, for when time and the hour shall bring about his return to power, his cares and anxieties will begin, and with whatever success his ambition may hereafter be crowned, he will hardly fail to look back with regret to this holiday time of his political career.

Greville's more pensive reflections could be left to the future. For Peel in August 1834 it was holiday-time even from politics. At the end of the month he was organising, as he expressed it to Goulburn, a small conspiracy against the Drayton partridges, timed to explode on 8 September, to which he invited Hardinge, Goulburn, Sugden, Rosslyn, 'Chin' Grant, Scarlett, and the duke. After that he planned an even greater diversion, a visit to Italy with his wife and eldest daughter. Neither he nor Julia had ever been there, and after her illness of the previous year a winter in the Mediterranean promised a pleasant relief from Staffordshire weather and state affairs.

Leaving England in mid-October they travelled in easy stages via Calais, Paris, Genoa and Turin, reaching Milan at the end of the month. Then, by a circuitous route through Venice, Bologna and Florence, they made their way in mid-November to Rome. Here they settled down in the Hôtel de l'Europe for a leisurely two weeks of shopping, sightseeing and entertainment. An amateur of the fine arts, Peel took the opportunity of buying three statues: one by the great Thorwaldsen, and two others by British sculptors in the fashionable Roman artists' colony, R. J. Wyatt and John Gibson. On 24 November, in company with Lord Stanhope, he paid a courtesy call on the Pope who thanked him warmly for having granted Catholic emancipation, which (as Stanhope amusedly observed to his son afterwards) might have been thought a somewhat tender point to touch on.[1] But after this momentary political tactlessness, the greater part of the interview was taken up by the Pope in showing his visitors what Peel later described with good Protestant scorn as 'a trumpery illuminated model of some excavations he had been making (I think) at Tivoli, which he regarded with childish admiration . . . I was almost tempted to send him a dark lantern and some coloured figures as a present from London, seeing the delight he had in the inferior phantasmagoria which he exhibited to me'.[2] Afterwards the Peels proposed to go to Naples for a short time and then return to Genoa or Marseilles by steam boat before coming back through France, where the Duchesse de Dino had invited them to Talleyrand's country house at Valençay. Towards the end of their Roman fortnight Peel read in the papers of the death of Althorp's father, Earl Spencer. Though it was obvious that Althorp's elevation to the upper House would involve some reshuffle of the government front bench, he did not otherwise attach much importance to it. There seemed no reason for haste. Croker, who heard of their continental tour and characteristically showered them with advice on how to get to Italy and what to do when they got there, told Peel before he left home that there was no need to exert himself to return for the opening of the new session in February; Easter would be early enough. But he had one afterthought. 'Who will know where to send letters to you? One *might* have occasion to write to you.'[3]

[1] Stanhope (Stanhope to Mahon, 26 Nov. 1834).
[2] 40455 f. 226. The Pope in question was Gregory XVI.
[3] 40321 fos. 18, 20.

THE HUNDRED DAYS

Earl Spencer had died on the afternoon of 10 November. Two days later Melbourne wrote to the king asking for an interview to discuss the arrangements necessitated by Althorp's elevation to the upper House. His mood was dispassionate to the point of indifference. Four months' experience of the premiership had confirmed his fundamentally pessimistic attitude to politics. Since the end of the session the complaints of the Dissenters, the public extravagances of Brougham, the attacks of O'Connell, a threatened resignation from Lansdowne, the quarrels of Durham with Brougham and Russell, had endeared to him neither the colleagues he had inherited from Grey nor the political allies forced upon him by circumstances. On 16 October, two days after the Peels left England, a destructive fire in the rambling palace of Westminster had gutted the House of Lords and burnt down the ancient chapel of St. Stephen's which had been the meeting-place of the lower House since the reign of Henry VIII. The old House of Commons had gone the way of its old constitution and to the prime minister's nostalgic and melancholy mind it seemed, as he watched the flames, to symbolise the passing of the old order of politics to which he belonged.

In his letter to the king four weeks later he reminded him that in its existing form the government had been chiefly founded on Althorp's weight and influence in the Commons and asked whether he should proceed with fresh arrangements to carry on the business of the government, or whether the king wished to follow some other course. He added that no personal consideration for Melbourne should deter the king from taking any action that was in the interests of the public service. Privately he was disturbed not so much by Althorp's removal from the Commons, which was inevitable and long foreseen, as by his known wish to leave office altogether; and it is more than possible that the phrasing of his letter to the king was designed to open the way for the new Earl Spencer to succeed him as prime minister. For the king, however, who had brooded during the autumn over the state of politics and the onward march of reform, it seemed that a way had opened for an even more salutary change. Though, when Melbourne arrived at Brighton on 13 November, he disappointed his royal master by refraining from any mention of resignation or indeed from any suggestion that the ministry could not carry on, William's mind was made up. What alarmed him above all was the attitude of the government towards Irish Church reform, further plans for which had been indiscreetly communicated to him by Duncannon. Melbourne's only important proposal—the appointment of Russell as leader of the House of Commons in place of Althorp—seemed proof that his ministers were now firmly committed to the extreme policy which had provoked the resignation of the Stanleyites in the summer. Melbourne pointed out that neither he nor the king was pledged to any Irish Church measure, and the king could always refuse consent to any proposal made to him. But William, not without commonsense, rejected this somewhat sophisticated argument and after sleeping on the decision, gave Melbourne a note of dismissal the following day. As originally drafted it made the ground of his action the proposed appointment in the Commons, but this was softened at Melbourne's suggestion to avoid any personal offence. The final version made it appear that it was simply Althorp's departure to the upper House which had prompted the king's action. Piqued, momentarily angered, but too proud to protest, Melbourne returned to London on the evening of 14 November, carrying with him a sealed packet for delivery at St. James's Palace which with sardonic humour he realised must contain a message for the Duke of Wellington. For the last time in British history a monarch had dismissed his political servants; and Melbourne's first ministry was over before it had barely started.

The king's summons reached Wellington at Stratfield Saye early on the morning of Saturday, 15 November, just as he was about to go hunting. Setting off within a couple of hours he arrived at Brighton about five o'clock and was at once invited by the king to form a ministry. The duke was neither optimistic nor overawed and he spoke bluntly of the parliamentary difficulties. But the king's mind was clearly set firm and the dismissal of the Whigs was a *fait accompli* for which Wellington did not feel that the opposition had any responsibility. On the matter of a new government he told the king that he must have his prime minister in the Commons and that the only possible man was Sir Robert Peel. For the time being, however, Wellington consented to take office as First Lord and Secretary of State; and he suggested that to prevent any folly from Brougham, the Great Seal should be put in commission under Lyndhurst. To all this the king cheerfully consented. Only Peel's absence in Italy, he observed, had prevented his being summoned in the first place. The same evening the king and Wellington each wrote letters to Peel, while a young official of the queen's household named Hudson, who had been acting as assistant to Sir Herbert Taylor, made ready to start abroad in search of the missing member for Tamworth. After he had been despatched the king and the duke turned to the task of establishing an interim administration. Neither of them believed in allowing cashiered officers to linger in their commands, and in view of Peel's absence it seemed to Wellington essential 'to take possession of the Government' on his behalf. At a Council precipitately assembled on Monday, 17 November, the Whig ministers were unceremoniously deprived of their commissions and Wellington was formally installed as First Lord and Secretary of State for the Home Department with provisional custody of the seals of the other two secretaryships. The change of government, which on its first premature announcement in *The Times* and *Morning Chronicle* of the previous Saturday had been greeted by the public with astonished scepticism, was now a demonstrated fact; and the country settled down to wait under the singular constitutional rule of the Duke of Wellington. Fixing his headquarters in the Home Office, from which he made periodic descents on the other departments, the duke was unperturbed. The king's government must go on and he was indifferent to ridicule encountered in the line of duty. Everything would be regularised when Peel arrived; though when that would be no one could say, since no one knew exactly where Peel was. The opening scene of the new *Hamlet* had to be played without the prince.[1]

II

The twenty-four-year-old gentleman usher whom fate had entrusted with the task of locating the unconscious prime minister-elect had a frustrating time. In London he could get neither information on Peel's whereabouts from his household nor money for the journey from the Keeper of the Privy Purse. It was Sunday; the banks were closed; and only the intervention of a clerk in Herries' Bank eventually secured him the £500 he wanted for travel expenses. Reaching Dover the same evening he found that the last steam boat for that day had already left. He therefore hired a rowing boat, some oarsmen and a pilot who landed him at Boulogne after a four-hour crossing. Arriving by post-chaise in Paris at noon on Monday, he called at the British Embassy where nothing was known of Peel's movements further than that he was believed to be in Italy. Travelling by diligence via Dijon and Mont Cenis Hudson reached Turin still to find no trace of the Peels. He decided to go west to Milan, but there was no British legation or consulate there to assist his efforts and after a fruitless round of the hotels, he was delayed a further eighteen hours before he could recover the passport impounded by the police on his arrival. Striking south-west to Bologna, where he hoped to discover whether his quarry had gone south to Rome or west to Venice, he at last picked up the trail and followed it to Florence, only to be told that the Peels had left for Rome. Bribing his way past the Papal frontier guards he next found himself blocked by the floodwaters of the Trasimene at Casa Piano, and was forced to abandon his luggage while he proceeded at snail's pace on an ox-wagon as far as Perugia. There he found horses but no carriages except a disused rattle-trap which conveyed him precariously to Rome, where he arrived wet, mud-spattered, tired, and clad in huge borrowed postilion-boots, on the evening of Tuesday, 25 November. At his hotel he learned that Peel was at a

[1] For the change of ministry see esp. the king's memorandum (40302 fos. 194 et seq.); Ellenborough, 19 Nov. 1834; *Peel Memoirs*, II, 14 et seq.; *Melbourne Papers*, ed. L. C. Sanders (1889), pp. 219 seq.; *Greville*, 16–19 Nov. 1834.

ball given by the Duchess of Torlonia and was due to leave for Naples the next day. After a bath, a change of clothes lent by his landlord, and a warm meal, he completed his odyssey by taking his despatches to Peel's hotel to await his return from the ball. If he expected the great man's congratulations he was possibly disappointed. According to a Foreign Office tradition which if true could only have originated with Hudson, Peel unkindly observed, on being told his somewhat erratic itinerary, that he could have done the journey in one day less.[1]

Time in fact must have been weighing heavily on Peel's mind. Already it was eleven days since Melbourne had been dismissed; at least as many would be needed for the return journey. It was an aggravation of fate that the summons to power had come at a moment when he was further from London than he had ever been before or would be again. The packet which had been delivered to him contained six documents: an introduction for Hudson from Sir Herbert Taylor, two letters from Wellington briefly outlining the situation and giving his own view of the royal action, copies of Melbourne's letter of 12 November and the king's dismissal note of 14 November, and lastly an official summons from William dated 15 November to return to England and 'put himself at the head of the administration of the country'. In the city of the popes and emperors, destiny had caught up with Peel at last. Two replies, a brief one to the king and a longer, cordial one to Wellington, were hastily written and given to Hudson, who after twenty-four hours' rest set out once again on the evening of 26 November. Travelling more directly than on his outward journey he arrived at Boulogne again too late for the regular steam-packet. After another hazardous crossing in a small fishing boat, he eventually arrived at London in the small hours of Friday, 5 December, to put an end to three long weeks of ignorance and speculation. Even before he had left Rome the Peels were on the road. Starting soon after midday they travelled via Genoa, Turin, Mont Cenis, and Lyons over bad roads and Alpine snows which made necessary the frequent hiring of extra horses and postilions. They stopped only four nights: at Massa to

[1] For Hudson's journey see *Lecture in commemoration of Sir James Hudson* by Gustavo Dalgas (private, London 1887); W. M. Torrens, *Memoirs of Viscount Melbourne* (1890), pp. 316–17; A. West, *Recollections* (1899), I, 49; *Peel Memoirs*, II, 24–5.

avoid a night ferry across a swollen river, at Susa before the ascent of the Mont Cenis pass, at Lyons where the town was under emergency law and their passports had to receive a visa, and finally at Paris to deal with correspondence and see the British ambassador. Outside Mâcon they were met by a special messenger carrying various communications from the duke, including a memorandum on offices and possible candidates, together with the first few scattered letters requesting employment and patronage that heralded the shoal of applications ready to pour in on him after his arrival. At Calais they found the steam-packet *Ferret* waiting expressly for them, and late on the evening of 8 December they landed at Dover. Leaving his wife and daughter behind him Peel posted on through the night and by eight o'clock the following morning he was at his desk at Whitehall Gardens writing to the king.[1]

In his letters to William and the duke from Rome Peel had committed himself to nothing except his immediate return to England. Since then twelve days had been allowed him for reflection. As the long miles passed and the wintry landscape of southern Europe slowly receded across his carriage windows, it had become increasingly clear to him that on two essential points at least a decision was virtually taken. He would have to take office and there would have to be a dissolution of parliament. By taking office, whatever the duke might think, he would be accepting responsibility for the king's dismissal of the Whigs. The justification of that dismissal, on the scanty information conveyed to him, he was inclined to doubt. Even from a purely political point of view it would have been better both for the king and for the Conservative opposition to have waited until Melbourne's ministry broke up from its own dissensions. Yet to refuse the king's commission, after a three-weeks' interval during which a provisional government had already been formed, would be to inflict an unthinkable humiliation on the crown. Equally clearly no Conservative ministry could hope to maintain itself in a House of Commons which numbered only 150 Conservative supporters; and to take office without being ready to meet the electorate would be almost as ignominious as refusing to take office

---

[1] For Peel's return from Rome, see Wellington (Peel to Wellington, 4 Dec. 1834); Ellenborough, 5, 9 Dec. 1834; Goulburn, memorandum book on travel expense, Italian visit, 1834; *Peel Memoirs*, II, 26–32; *Raikes*, I, 308–10.

at all. The only question was one of timing. Pitt in 1784 had braved and half won over a hostile House of Commons before making his successful appeal to the country. But 1834 was not 1784; the reformed lower House was more impervious to management and more partisan in its views than its eighteenth-century predecessor; and an initial and noisy conflict between the crown, the executive, and the House of Lords on the one side, and the Commons on the other, would inflict irreparable public damage on the Conservative cause. In any case, a general election could not long be staved off, and it might therefore be impossible at the outset to find twenty or thirty members of the Commons ready to face the prospect of two elections in quick succession, one on appointment and another at a dissolution. The letters Peel had received from Wellington at Mâcon had already spoken of the activities of the party's election committee and on his arrival in London he found that not only was an immediate general election taken for granted but that candidates were already in the field. Peel would probably have decided on an immediate dissolution, had he been left to choose; but in fact the choice was scarcely his to make.

On one point, however, his mind was firm. His ministry would not be a mere repetition of Wellington's ministry of 1830. Tactics and statesmanship both demanded an infusion of greater talent and greater liberality. The reconstruction on a wider basis which had been mismanaged by the duke four years earlier would have to be carried out by his former lieutenant if the new government was to have a reasonable chance of survival; and the men whom he would invite to office before any others were Stanley and Graham.[1] Even this, however, was a predictable reaction to the difficult situation into which he had been thrust. It would have been more surprising had he not tried to enlist Stanley's support. From the day the dismissal of the Whig government was made public, there had been newspaper speculation on Stanley's future; and the interest was not confined to the columns of the press. The prospect of office combined with a consciousness of parliamentary weakness had an agreeably liberalising effect on many leading Tories; and the chances of a coalition were already being discussed by them with affectionate anticipation. The impetuous Ellenborough, who had been assisting

[1] *Peel Memoirs*, II, 30-3, 43-8.

Wellington at the Treasury, was pressing for some approach to the Whig seceders even before Peel arrived. In the list of potential ministers which Peel had received from the duke at Mâcon, the names of Stanley, Graham, Richmond and Ripon had all been put down; and though Wellington had made no comment on the policy of including them in the new government, he had written laconically that 'I think it is expected, and will give satisfaction'.

Within a few hours of Peel's arrival the duke called on him and the two men were closeted together for about sixty minutes. There was another briefer conversation with Lord Granville Somerset, the chief of the party's small staff of organisers, and at two o'clock Peel went off to St. James's for his audience with the king. At the interview William considerately enquired whether he would prefer to reflect further on the offer made to him by letter and confer with others before making his decision. But Peel needed no further deliberation on his course of action. He told the king that the prospects of success for a new administration at that time were doubtful enough and that they would be even more doubtful if there were any appearance of delay or hesitation on his part. It was essential that when he began negotiations, it should be with the authority of a prime minister. He accepted therefore without condition or further discussion the office of First Lord of the Treasury and Chancellor of the Exchequer. All he asked was permission to invite Stanley and Graham to join the cabinet. The letters went off the same day. Time was pressing and in any case a direct approach seemed preferable to negotiations through a third party. But what the outcome would be was doubtful. Greville, who had learned a little from his racing intimate, Lord George Bentinck, told the duke at the end of November that Stanley, though not averse to serving under Peel, was sensitive to accusations of abandoning his political principles and in any case would only take office on the promise of a liberal policy and in the company of his friends. Early in December Greville repeated the warning to another sporting friend, Colonel Jonathan Peel, who passed the letter to his brother. Similar reports came to Peel from other quarters. In his invitation to Stanley he did what he could to meet these scruples. He said that all practical questions at issue between them had been settled, that he could not foresee any disagreement on future policy, and that he would be happy to discuss privately any point on which Stanley might seek clarification. In the interval a Council was held on 10 December and Peel formally appointed First Lord of the Treasury. At a dinner party given the same evening in Apsley House for some two dozen leading Conservative peers, commoners and party officials, the new prime minister made a short explanatory speech to his followers. He said that if the duke had formed an administration during his absence, he would have supported it; that he had told the king that the issue was no longer one between parties, but whether the monarchy and ancient institutions of the country should be preserved; and for that purpose it was necessary to form a government on as broad a base as possible. He had therefore invited Stanley and Graham to join a coalition. The only men appointed so far, besides himself, were the duke as Foreign Secretary, and Lyndhurst as Lord Chancellor; and no more offices would be filled until the result of his overture was known. The news gave general satisfaction to the assembled company and Peel himself, despite the fatigues of his recent journey, was lively and in good spirits.[1]

Two days later came the first blow. In a long explanatory letter Stanley categorically refused to join the new ministry. His attitude was courteous and he held out the prospect of an independent support. But he referred to the general opposition that had existed between them on all points except the Irish Church; he mentioned with some asperity the attacks of the Duke of Wellington on Grey's ministry; and he concluded that a sudden coalition between himself and Peel's administration would ruin the character of the one without adding strength to the other. The sense of the letter was so explicit that Peel did not renew the suggestion of a private meeting; and he discouraged Sir Herbert Taylor when he proposed next day that the king should write to Stanley to obtain his general support for the government.[2] Graham, though equally firm in declining office, was more conciliatory. To show his appreciation of the offer he made the long journey from Netherby to London and in a friendly interview on 13 December assured Peel of his desire to support the government and his own personal regard. He tried to give some

[1] *Peel Memoirs*, II, 28–35; 40404 fos. 266, 340; 40318 f. 7; 40309 f. 380; Ellenborough, 9–10 Dec. 1834; *Greville*, 29 Nov. 1834.
[2] 40302 fos. 14–42.

comfort to his refusal, moreover, by arguing that if he and Stanley remained independent, they would be able to prevent a junction of Whigs and radicals, and possibly even bring some Whigs over to the side of the ministry. The unpalatable truth remained, however, that neither Stanley nor Graham and presumably therefore none of their friends would take office. It was more than a disappointment; it was a foretaste of failure. Yet in fact the issue had been decided before Peel's letters had been written. In expectation of such an invitation, Stanley and his friends had already conferred at Knowsley and decided against a junction. They had little personally against Peel, but there was considerable animosity against Wellington; and this in the end was perhaps the decisive factor. The duke had been the first person summoned by the king to form a government; he had administered the country for the first three weeks of its existence. 'This circumstance alone', Stanley wrote in his letter to Peel, 'must stamp upon the administration about to be formed the impress of his name and principles.' The chance of securing Stanley had been at most a slender one; but if there had been a chance at all, it had been destroyed by the fatality of Peel's absence from the country at the start of the crisis. The Stanleyites turned to a consideration of the proper tactics for a third party which they hoped would hold the scales between government and opposition in the new parliament; and Peel to the formation of a ministry out of the diminished resources at his disposal.

The first problem was the cabinet. For himself Peel took both the Treasury and the Exchequer while his old friend and loyal colleague Henry Goulburn, who had been Chancellor in 1830, made the reciprocal transfer to Peel's former post at the Home Office. Aberdeen, the former Foreign Secretary now displaced by Wellington, was at first designed for the Admiralty but cheerfully offered to move to the Colonies in order to accommodate the slightly imperious de Grey, who had refused both that post and the Lord Lieutenancy of Ireland. Other survivors of the duke's 1830 ministry reappeared. Ellenborough became President of the Board of Control; Rosslyn, President of the Council; Herries, Secretary at War; Wellington's military crony, Sir George Murray, Master-General of the Ordnance; and Hardinge, Chief Secretary for Ireland. There were a few notable absentees among the old brigade.

Fitzgerald turned down an offer on the score of health; Melville had made up his mind not to return to active politics; and Croker, to whom Peel made an overture within a few days of his return from Italy, resolutely declined to enter a reformed House of Commons. The prime minister, who had just received the refusal of Stanley, thought this political prudery a trifle excessive and observed a little sharply that if men would not help in such a crisis, he would be left with only the duke's old cabinet. Nevertheless, the work of construction was effected with commendable despatch. By 13 December the nucleus of the cabinet was settled and that evening nine new ministers dined with their leader at Whitehall Gardens. Outside the cabinet, however, there continued to be difficulties and disappointments. One of Peel's first acts was to offer the Lord Lieutenancy of Ireland to the Duke of Northumberland who had won his unqualified respect when occupying that position in 1829–30. He refused the post on grounds of ill-health; it was also turned down by de Grey; and only at the third attempt was a new viceroy found in the person of Lord Haddington. The bestowal of the legal offices also presented embarrassment. The old Tory Wetherell, dangerous if left out and awkward if brought in, was originally destined for the judicial neutrality of the vice-chancellorship; but when the holder of that office refused promotion to the Chancellorship of Ireland, Wetherell was offered with some misgivings his old office of Attorney-General. This, to the private delight of the cabinet, he declined; but Scarlett, who might otherwise have taken it, preferred the greater but non-political eminence of Chief Baron with a seat in the Lords.[1] Pollock finally became Attorney-General and a new man, Follett, of whose professional talents both Lyndhurst and Peel had a high opinion, was advanced to Solicitor-General though not yet a silk. By 20 December, after ten days of incessant interviews and interminable correspondence, at the end of which Peel was hardly able to hold a pen in his hand, the arrangements for the government were largely concluded.

The most tedious and time-consuming negotiations were over minor posts and with lesser men. To all earlier claims for office, promotion and preferment, the duke had replied concisely that they

[1] Campbell claimed to have dissuaded his father-in-law from accepting the attorney-generalship (*Campbell*, II, 59).

must wait until Sir Robert returned. This, though it kept Peel clear of all commitments, also resulted in a mass of delicate and tiresome correspondence with suitors who had had three or four weeks in which to compose their applications and whose prolixity seemed to vary inversely with their importance. The Household appointments, because of the aristocratic susceptibilities of the candidates, the stubborn claims based on previous service, and the likes and dislikes of the monarch, needed much personal correspondence and an interview with William IV himself before they could finally be settled. But there were difficulties everywhere. The Duke of New-castle wanted the Garter for the Duke of Hamilton; the Duke of Buckingham conceived that he had a right to the cabinet in 1834 because he would have been in the cabinet if Wellington had formed a government in 1832; the undistinguished claims of H. Corry found distinguished advocates in his father-in-law, the Earl of Shaftesbury, and his aunt, the Countess of Sandwich; Lord Orford wanted a diplomatic post at The Hague; and the Duchess of Gordon had to be informed that Peel had no appointment at his disposal suitable for a gentleman, other than those which required personal attendance to the duties attached to them. Human nature did not always appear very amiable in these transactions. Peel's old Irish friend and shooting companion, James Daly, who had missed a peerage in 1829 because the government was unwilling to risk another Irish county by-election after the Clare catastrophe, had promptly renewed his claim. When this was refused, he wrote an angry, insolent and abusive letter to Peel, followed on reflection by two more that were full of apology and fulsome protestations of old friendship and affection. 'Mr. James Daly', wrote the prime minister dryly on the docket of the last of these missives. 'Some compunction, a great deal of mortified vanity, and ending with symptoms of not entire disinterestedness.'[1] Even from relatives and ministers came suggestions which Peel was not disposed to enter-tain. The Marquess of Ailsa, father-in-law to Jonathan Peel, wrote that the latter had been 'pained to the core' not to receive an offer of a post; an assertion which Peel, in view of his brother's tastes and habits, found hard to credit. The new Home Secretary, Henry Goulburn, pressed the claims of his own brother for a judgeship.

[1] 40407 fos. 16, 65.

'I will say to you', replied the prime minister, not altogether to the liking of his colleague, 'what I should say if my own brother were a candidate, that I think the judicial office ought always to be filled without reference to any personal considerations whatever.' In this welter of depressingly similar letters, invariably beginning with congratulations and ending with a request, the offer from Lord Exeter of a safe seat at Stamford for any candidate the government chose to nominate, was a rare and welcome gleam. 'I never guessed', wrote Peel to his old friend Hobhouse on Christmas Day, when the flood of correspondence was at last subsiding, 'and doubt whether the most vivid fancy could form a guess of what it is "to form a government".'[1]

Yet formed it was, within a fortnight of his arrival at Dover, and it was something more than 'the duke's old cabinet'. Despite the failure to win over Stanley, the new government displayed perceptible differences from Wellington's administration of 1830. Alexander Baring, the financier and member for Essex, who had left the Whigs during the reform crisis, entered the cabinet as president of the Board of Trade. Lord Wharncliffe, one of the leading Waverers of 1831–32 and a supporter of the reform bill, was also in the cabinet as Lord Privy Seal, his obvious pleasure at the invitation to join the ministry being indicative perhaps of his uncertainty whether he would receive it. Not the least of Hadding-ton's qualifications for Ireland was that, as Ellenborough put it, he was 'a half-liberal Canningite'; and early in the New Year an offer was made to Lady Canning of a post in the Treasury for her son which made a flattering impression even if it was not taken up. J. E. Denison, a son-in-law of the Duke of Portland and a follower of Stanley, declined office, but some sort of contact with the reluctant Stanleyites was established through de Grey, who though a brisk and strong-minded Tory, and an old acquaintance of Peel, was also brother to Lord Ripon. Of the former Grenvillites C. W. Wynn, who had served successively Liverpool, Canning and Grey, received the chancellorship of the duchy of Lancaster with a seat in the cabinet; and Fremantle became one of the secretaries to the Treasury.

The chief representatives of that group, however, were the Duke of Buckingham and his son Lord Chandos; and these two provided

[1] 40407 f. 229.

Peel with one of his most difficult personal and party problems. Their importance lay not in their political talents which were negligible but in Buckingham's ducal pretentiousness and Chandos's self-assumed leadership of the agricultural party among the country gentry. Peel had not neglected that interest in making up the pattern of his ministry. Besides Baring another hostage from the country party had been secured in the person of Sir Edward Knatch-bull, who as early as 13 December had accepted the Paymastership of the Forces. Chandos and his father, however, were made of vainer and less manageable material. Denied the cabinet, the Duke of Buckingham had next refused the ornamental office of Lord Steward and then made an unsolicited offer of his services as Lord Lieutenant; and his sulky attitude towards the ministry had delayed and almost prevented the appointment of Fremantle who was dependent for his seat at Buckingham on the duke's goodwill. The difficulty with Chandos, who had cast himself for the role in and out of parliament of 'the farmers' friend', was chiefly over the malt tax. On 13 December, a remorselessly long Saturday full of inter-views and letter-writing, Peel had explained to Chandos his views on malt and the same day sent him a memorandum on the subject with the expressed hope that it would be no obstacle to his entering the ministry. The memorandum offered explanations rather than concessions. Peel argued that it would be difficult to abolish the malt tax without reimposing a property tax which might be regarded as an even greater burden on agriculture; and he refused to pledge himself even to partial repeal or the substitution of a portion of the tax by, for example, one on beer. Nevertheless as late as 19 December he wrote to Chandos to say that the final arrangements for the cabinet had been postponed up to that point in case he changed his mind about taking office. Chandos replied cordially enough that he hoped that this one difference over malt would not prevent his joining the cabinet but he conveyed clearly that it was for Peel to give way and not himself. An open breach was avoided and Chandos's desire to be put on the Privy Council was promptly acceded to by the prime minister. All the same the equivocal position of the Buckinghams and its possible effect on the county elections created much uneasiness among party whips. Bonham (whom Peel had given minor office as storekeeper to the

Ordnance) told him that Chandos's power of 'doing mischief *at this moment* is immense'.[1]

If prejudice, pique and principle offered the familiar difficulties among the more senior members of the party, there was some promise for the future among the younger men. 'All my experience in public life', Peel observed to Wellington in 1829, 'is in favour of the employment of what the world would call young men instead of old ones.'[2] His first essay in constructing a ministry gave practical witness of this belief; and the 1834 administration provided several youthful politicians with their first experience of office. At the time perhaps the best-known of them was the brilliant young Cambridge barrister, W. M. Praed, who at the age of thirty-two had a reputation for parliamentary debate and polemical journalism which made some regard him as the Tory answer to the Whig Macaulay. First elected at the end of 1830 he had helped fight the battle of the reform bill and as early as 1832 Peel had told people that he liked him better than any other of his young recruits. As prime minister two years later he showed that the compliment had not been an idle one by appointing Praed secretary of the Board of Control and in effect the government's spokesman on Indian affairs in the House of Commons.[3] Praed's untimely death from consumption in 1839 robbed this promise of its fruit; but there were others who were to stay longer on the stage. W. E. Gladstone, an Oxford double-first and son of the great Liverpool merchant and Canningite supporter, had brought himself under the approving eye of his leader during the 1834 session and was now at the age of twenty-five placed in the Treasury. The graceful and aristocratic Sidney Herbert, a year younger, less distinguished in debate but on more intimate terms with Peel, was given the second secretaryship of the Board of Control refused by Denison. The third member of the youthful triumvirate, all friends and fellow-Oxonians who had been new members in the first reformed parliament, was Lord Lincoln, son and heir of the Duke of Newcastle. He like Gladstone was put to an apprenticeship in the Treasury. Under-secretaryships were found for two other aristocratic Christ Church men: Lord

[1] 40405 fos. 116, 166, 235; 40406 fos. 158, 160, 234; 40407 f. 61.
[2] *W.N.D.*, VI, 287.
[3] D. Hudson, *Poet in Parliament* (1939), pp. 184–208.

Mahon, at the age of twenty-nine, at the Foreign Office and Lord Eliot, seven years his senior and a member of parliament 1824–32, at the Home Office. There were of course grumbles from the disappointed and the onlookers over these and other appointments. Peel was criticised for taking too many old hands, for favouring friends such as Aberdeen and Goulburn, for taking young untried men like Herbert or old reactionary men like Knatchbull. Yet it is hard to see how Peel could have done much better with the available material; and he might have done much worse. As in all ministries, party claims had to be balanced against administrative performance, seniority against youth, influence and connection against past services and future promise. The critics themselves were singularly reticent in naming anyone of importance likely to accept office to whom offers had not been made. There were some, however, not unsympathetic to Peel, who nevertheless felt that the composition of the government would not by itself rouse much national enthusiasm. Here at least their instinct was right. More important than the details of ministerial appointments was the impression made by the new ministry on the country at large. The shrewdest distribution of office and the most energetic electioneering efforts of Granville Somerset, Bonham and Ross, would be unavailing unless public opinion in general and the electorate in particular could be persuaded that the new administration had something to offer.

Here again Peel was faced with the fact that the circumstances in which the 1834 ministry came into existence hindered its chances of survival. From the day he arrived he found enough evidence in his correspondence and in the columns of the press to confirm what his own judgement might in any case have led him to fear: that the arbitrary dismissal of the Whigs and the Duke of Wellington's three weeks of power had alienated many who might otherwise have been won over. As an Essex correspondent of Baring wrote in November, in a letter which found its way into Peel's hands, there was 'a great horror of Radicals and of Lord Durham, an earnest desire to support moderate councils, a disposition to confide in Sir Robert Peel. But with certain reservations as to the composition of his government.'[1] It was true that valuable support from new quarters was already coming forward. An offer of the services of the *Standard* had been

[1] 40333 f. 185.

made by its editor Giffard; and largely through the instrumentality of Greville and Scarlett there had been friendly communications between *The Times* and the new government even before Peel returned from Italy. Yet publicity was of limited value unless there was something to publicise; and Barnes, the editor of *The Times*, had made it clear that he could only support the new ministry if it was prepared to show a liberal attitude towards measures already accepted by the House of Commons. After Peel's arrival several correspondents in different parts of the country emphasised the widespread distrust of the Duke of Wellington and the need to dispel this by an early statement of the government's policy. Colonel Lindsay of Balcarres, writing from Fife on 8 December, told Peel that in Scotland the duke's name was still associated with the cry of *No Reform* but even moderate Whigs would accept Peel if he made some reforming declaration. Sir Thomas Lethbridge wrote from Taunton four days later that he could see no change in the general desire of the country for a reform of abuses in church and state. There was, however, an expectation that Peel would see the wisdom and necessity of liberal concessions and a feeling that he was the man to carry out 'the right and proper degree' of reform. 'Should you dissolve Parliament,' he concluded, 'I do not anticipate any great alteration of Men, in the new House. But I should anticipate a vast alteration of *sentiment* among those returned, if before the Dissolution, the Country should be apprised of something like the Principles by which your Government will be ruled.' Scarlett, who among other things was legal adviser to *The Times*, sent Peel a letter from John Walter, its proprietor, which was even more outspoken. Walter, recently Liberal M.P. for Berkshire and now contesting the county as a Liberal-Conservative, reported that among his former supporters there was an 'unreasonably angry hostility to the Duke of Wellington' and a rooted objection to what they called 'the return of the Tories to office'. But Peel was by no means regarded with the same distrust and Walter urged consequently that an attempt should be made to reassure the moderates and win over the unattached voters by 'some frank explanation, some popular declaration, *previous* to a Dissolution of Parliament'.[1]

Neither Peel nor the cabinet needed much persuading that it

[1] 40404 f. 312, ptly. pr. *Peel*, II, 261; 40405 fos. 24, 89.

would be advisable to make a public announcement of the government's general policy before encountering the hazards of a general election. It was unusual, almost unprecedented; but so too were the circumstances of the new ministry. Even before Hudson reached Rome, it had occurred to the fertile mind of Ellenborough that Peel might take advantage of the traditional Lord Mayor's banquet to deliver a speech dealing with the principles of his administration. At the first cabinet dinner on 13 December Peel raised the subject himself and it was agreed that Hardinge should discuss details with the Lord Mayor. Further reflection produced alternative suggestions. Ellenborough, anxious for as little delay as possible, proposed next day that Peel should write a letter to his supporters in the House of Commons which could be published before the dinner and give greater point to his speech. At the same time a scheme was hatched out, apparently in the office of *The Times*, for a letter to be addressed to Peel by a number of Conservative M.P.s which would enable the prime minister to make a statement of principles in his reply. Barnes sent Scarlett a copy of the proposed address with emendations of his own; but Scarlett, sceptical whether Walter had enough standing to attract many signatures, prudently forwarded it to his principal without any commitment. By 16 December Peel had made up his mind for himself. Though parliament had not yet been dissolved, by accepting office he had vacated his seat at Tamworth. There would be no impropriety therefore in beginning his own election campaign. The need for prompt action would be met and all embarrassment avoided, by issuing an address to his constituents in which he could outline his general policy. 'My answer to the enclosed, therefore,' he replied to Scarlett, 'would be in substance contained in that Address, and I had rather give it in that form.' The document was drafted at once and read to the cabinet after dinner on 17 December. When they had approved it ('very good but very long' noted Ellenborough) it was copied out at midnight and a messenger sent to warn *The Times*, *Morning Herald* and *Morning Post* of its coming. Between three and four in the morning it was inserted in the waiting presses and on 18 December the *Tamworth Manifesto* appeared before the public.[1]

[1] For the genesis of the *Tamworth Manifesto* see 40405 fos. 202, 325, 327; Ellenborough, 13, 14, 16–19 Dec. 1834; *Greville*, 20 Dec. 1834; *History of 'The Times'*, I, 340–4.

It made, as Greville recorded, 'a prodigious sensation, and nobody talks of anything else'. If some Whigs affected to despise it as an artful but clever production, and some ultra-Tories growled at its liberalism, 'all the moderate people are satisfied with it'. Both the sensation and the satisfaction were understandable. In form an address to Peel's constituents, in fact a statement to the country of the principles of the new administration, the *Tamworth Manifesto* was an electioneering document on a grand and unprecedented scale. Beginning with a brief reference to the circumstances of his taking office and his intention to stand once more for Tamworth, Peel made it clear that he was also taking the opportunity of making through his constituents a wider appeal 'to that great and intelligent class of society . . . which is far less interested in the contentions of party, than in the maintenance of order and the cause of good government'. In the seven pages of print which followed he stated his present position and future intentions. He could not accept that past opposition to the reform bill disqualified either him from office or the crown from seeking an alternative to the Whigs. His own record in public life proved that he had never been a defender of abuses or an enemy of judicious reform. He had already declared in parliament that he considered the reform bill 'a final and irrevocable settlement of a great Constitutional question'. If to govern in the spirit of the reform bill meant following every popular whim, promising instant redress of every alleged abuse, abandoning respect for ancient rights and prescriptive authority, he could not promise to do so. But if it meant 'a careful review of institutions, both civil and ecclesiastical' and 'the correction of proved abuses and the redress of real grievances', then 'I can for myself and colleagues undertake to act in such a spirit'. More explicitly he would continue the enquiry into municipal corporations instituted by his predecessors; he would endeavour to relieve Dissenters of the burden of Church rates and enforced Anglican marriage rites; and though he still opposed their admission to Oxford and Cambridge as 'a claim of right' he would support their entry into the legal and medical professions on terms of equality with Anglicans. On the great question of Church reform he could not consent to the alienation of ecclesiastical property, but he would support a reorganisation of church revenues and a reform of tithes, and he would himself initiate a full enquiry into the general structure of the Establishment. A few brief but not uncalculated references to purity in the administration of pensions, a peaceful foreign policy, the maintenance of public credit, and the enforcement of governmental economy, rounded off the body of the letter.

As a political document it was destined to be waved from innumerable hustings and to be cited as an authority by countless party candidates. Its posthumous fame has obscured both its character and purpose. Peel wrote the *Tamworth Manifesto* at short notice not for posterity but for the public and the electorate of 1834. It was not primarily a statement of the principles of the new Conservatism. It was not a programme of governmental action. Elements of both could be found in it, but only incidentally or by inference. Above all, it was not an announcement of a sudden political conversion. On the reform bill itself, Peel was only restating what he said in the first session of the reformed parliament; and on reform in the abstract, he was only declaring the beliefs and practice of his whole previous career. Fundamentally the *Tamworth Manifesto* was no more than a considered statement of the attitude of the new government towards the main political issues of the moment: a statement designed to reassure the timid, conciliate the neutrals, and attract the moderates in the forthcoming election, without committing Peel to policies in which he did not believe or promises which he might not be able to keep. When Croker in January submitted to him the proofs of a review of the *Manifesto* for the *Quarterly Magazine*, Peel made the criticism that it ascribed the Tamworth address too much to the necessities imposed by the Reform Act. 'I think', he added practically, 'the necessities rather arose from the abruptness of the change in the Government, and, to say the truth, from the policy of aiding our friends at the election.'[1] What gave the *Manifesto* its importance were the circumstances in which it was issued; what gave it its character was that it was written by Peel. But if the ideas and language were typically Peelite, the authority behind it was that of a prime minister. It was this conjunction of an old attitude with a new power that made the *Manifesto* the significant document it was.

At the Mansion House dinner five days later before an audience of ministers and their wives, a selection of the Tory aristocracy, the

[1] *Croker*, II, 256.

Speaker, the Archbishop of Canterbury, the Bishop of London, bankers and merchants of the City, seated in the palatial splendour of the Egyptian Hall, his speech was a firm and straightforward repetition with variations of the Tamworth theme. In addition he appealed for the confidence of the country in his administration. 'No Government', he said, 'can stand unless it be supported by public opinion'; and this was a question not merely of approval for specific measures but of personal trust in the men in charge of government. Mention of men led him to pay a brief but eloquent tribute, as he had often done in the past, to the Duke of Wellington, 'one magic and immortal name'. He ended with what was perhaps as much a warning to the hotheads of his own party as a reassurance to the public at large. He would commit himself to no precipitate and ill-conceived action. 'I will not, by pledging myself to relieve particular burdens or hastily to adopt particular remedies, debar the Government from affording that fair consideration which is due to the claims of all interests, or put out of our power a deliberate application of the most efficacious remedies.'[1]

Meanwhile copies of the *Manifesto* had been going off to all sorts of probable and improbable recipients: to the king, to Tamworth, to his native town of Bury in Lancashire; to that cynical, corpse-like figure from the past, the Prince de Talleyrand, who had seen the *ancien régime*, the Terror, the Empire, the Restoration and the July Monarchy, and now survived, a little incredibly, to witness the beginning of the Victorian party system. One made its way to the Princess Lieven in distant St. Petersburg with a personal note in which the author wryly described himself as one 'who has had to travel from Rome, form a Government and publish a Manifesto in less than three weeks' and now sent a copy of the last 'as a very unromantic proof' of his sincere regard. The replies he received were not surprisingly flattering and sometimes hyperbolic. The king, who said he had read every word in the press before he received his own copy, expressed a practical hope that it would be given the widest circulation. Bishop Phillpotts of Exeter, the great Tory controversialist, described it as 'an Address than which a more important document hardly ever issued from the pen of man'.[2] But neither

[1] *The Times*, 24 Dec. 1834; *Greville*, same date.
[2] 40406 fos. 148, 165, 173, 196; 40302 f. 69.

William IV nor Henry of Exeter were very representative members of the British public; and it was on the elections that much—if not everything—now depended. The day after the Mansion House dinner it was settled in cabinet to dissolve the old parliament on 30 December and summon the new for 19 February. With that the die was cast. The government had precisely eight weeks in which to fight an election and prepare their measures. If the *Tamworth Manifesto* had done something to efface the Wellingtonian image of the new administration, it remained to be proved how far it had succeeded in attracting new support. In some quarters and among certain classes the opposition was still inveterate. The Whigs had been dismissed because of their Irish Church policy and the emergence of Lord John Russell as their new spokesman in the House of Commons. It was not to be expected that they would accept either loss of power or the defeat of their policy. Here then was a formidable nucleus of resistance and outside the ranks of the Whigs were many potential parliamentary and electoral allies. To many radicals the action of the crown seemed an attempt to rescue the House of Lords by dissolving the Commons; to many Dissenters it seemed an attempt to rescue the Church by evicting the Whigs. A powerful irritant had been added to the excited feelings left over from the last session and against sectional and sectarian passions the pacific wording of the *Manifesto* had little effect. Already the United Committee of the Dissenters in London had publicly deplored the change of government and called on their coreligionists in the country to show 'decided and uncompromising opposition' to ministerial candidates. The leading dissenting periodicals entered the political fray; and a central Dissenters' Parliamentary Committee was set up to stimulate electioneering activity in the constituencies.

It seemed to Peel probable from the start that the fate of his ministry would be decided largely by religious issues. A reforming ministry in 1835 could not avoid making ecclesiastical reform one of its primary objectives. Indeed he had already committed the cabinet by the *Tamworth Manifesto* to an immediate consideration of Church reorganisation and dissenting grievances. Here if anywhere would come the test of the Conservative claim to constitute a genuine reforming party. In this violent and prejudiced arena there was at least one advantage to offset the hostility of organised Dissent. The Church might yield to Conservative persuasion what had been refused to Whig coercion. The Archbishop of Canterbury had said to the Speaker early in December that more concessions could be made to the new government than to its predecessors; and at a cabinet on 27 December Peel told his colleagues that because of their confidence in the administration, the leaders of the Church were prepared to go to the extreme limit in accepting changes.[1] What the Establishment needed was not merely a stimulus to reform. This had already been given by the radical and dissenting attacks and by its own consciousness of long-entrenched defects and abuses. Even before the reform bill had passed into law, Peel's brother-in-law, Lord Henley, had startled the Anglican and rejoiced the dissenting world by his bold pamphlet, *A Plan for Church Reform*; and the Whig commission of enquiry into church revenues set up in 1832 had further prepared the ground. Two great episcopal advocates of reform, Archbishop Howley of Canterbury, and Bishop Blomfield of London, had already joined forces; and the notion of a mixed ecclesiastical and lay commission to formulate and propose specific measures was finding advocacy. The occasion, as Peel with his instinctive sense of timing realised, was ripe for action. What was needed was sympathetic leadership which the Church would trust and follow. To provide this was the first great act of policy to which Peel turned his attention. To the Bishop of Exeter he had replied on 22 December that 'the Church should avail itself of this, possibly the last, opportunity of aiding its true friends in the course of judicious reform'. Conversations with Church leaders in London in the succeeding days provided assurance that they would be willing both to initiate internal reform and to support conciliatory legislation for the Dissenters. Under Peel's impetus the ministers found themselves both individually and as a body joining in the work. The duke was commissioned to use his influence at Oxford to procure the abolition of the subscription to the Thirty-Nine Articles at matriculation; Goulburn to collect opinions at the other university constituency of Cambridge on the general matter of Church reform and dissenting grievances. In the last days of the old year the cabinet was turning its thoughts to the refractory problems

[1] Ellenborough, II, 27 Dec. 1834.

of church rates and Irish tithe, and a committee consisting of Goulburn, Rosslyn, Wharncliffe and Ellenborough was set up to enquire into the question of dissenting marriages. Gregson, the barrister who had assisted Peel in his legal reforms at the Home Office six years before, was recruited as under-secretary to Goulburn, and early in January Peel was sending in a collection of letters and memoranda to assist him in drafting a bill for marriage registration.[1]

In the middle of all this cabinet and departmental activity came the general election. Starting in the first week of January and straggling over the next fortnight, it engaged the interest of the public and the calculations of the whips for the greater part of the month. At Christmas Hardinge had reported 365 Conservative candidates in the field. Allowing for fifty to be beaten, this would mean 315 government supporters in the new House: a method of estimation which Peel did not think very safe. It was obvious that an outright majority in a House of 658 members was out of the question; but 315 supporters, if they could be got, might prove adequate in view of the divisions to be expected among the rest. When the results began to come in from 7 January onwards, however, this optimistic prospect slowly receded. Since Hardinge's provisional report, some forty more Conservative candidates had entered the lists. Even so, the party was only contesting about three-fifths of the parliamentary seats and many of these were hopeless from the start. Expected gains were balanced only too often by unexpected losses, and within a few days Ellenborough was resigning himself to a parliamentary stalemate with the chance of another dissolution at Easter. By 20 January the Conservative whips counted 265 supporters elected, 251 opponents, and 49 doubtful, with a further hundred seats still to be decided. At the end of the month the final analysis ran: government 290, radicals 150, Whigs and Stanleyites 218, of whom 40 or 50 were regarded as doubtful.[2] It was not victory; it was not exactly defeat. With improvised organisation and hastily collected candidates the party had won over two-thirds of the seats they contested. In the English counties, with their large electorates, they had done particularly well, winning 29 seats and losing none. Their

---

[1] ibid.; 40333 fos. 206, 216, 232, 238, 241; Goulburn, II/18 (Peel to Goulburn, 1 Jan. 1835).

[2] 40302 f. 241; Ellenborough, 24 Dec. 1834, 7, 21, 30 Jan. 1835.

highest rational expectation had been to return 300 members and this they had come near to achieving. They had nearly doubled their numbers; they were the largest single party in the House. If the opposition remained as divided as Whigs and radicals had been in the 1833–34 Commons; if the Stanleyites proved friendly; if some moderate Whigs could be won over; if some or all of these things happened, then the ministry would stand.

Peel himself was unperturbed by the election results, because he had never assumed that the election in itself would give him an absolute majority. His hopes lay elsewhere. As he wrote to Herries on 11 January:

> in spite of returns, and occasional mishaps, I have a confidence in our success which arises mainly from this reflection: If what we shall propose to the House of Commons will not satisfy, who are the men that will propose that something which is to satisfy? I do not hesitate to say that I feel that I can do more than any other man can who means his reforms to work practically, and who respects, and wishes to preserve, the British Constitution. I think this must ultimately prevail, and attract for us more support than we at present calculate upon.[1]

Notwithstanding four weeks of ceaseless activity in which even Christmas Day afforded no break, the prime minister was noticeably sanguine and energetic. On 9 January he betook himself briefly to Staffordshire for his own election festivities and a few days relaxation. Though he had not got to bed the previous night till two in the morning, he was up again at four, travelled the 115 miles of wintry road to Drayton, and attended a ball with Lady Peel and Julia the same evening. Next day he was out shooting and brought back eleven wild ducks, twelve pheasants and uncounted lesser game to prove that his eye and hand had lost nothing of their cunning. His election for Tamworth during his absence had gone smoothly. The extension of the borough boundaries in 1832 weakened the Townshend interest and in 1835 Peel was given the luxury of an unopposed return along with his brother William, now a junior lord of the Treasury. What little electioneering excitement there was for Peel personally had come immediately after his return from Italy when he had taken stiff exception to some words of Stephen Lushington,

[1] *Herries*, II, 173.

the radical member for Tower Hamlets. In a speech reported in the *Morning Chronicle* he had thought fit to compare Peel and Wellington to a pair of convicted swindlers or street prostitutes. When called upon to explain himself, however, Dr. Lushington, with the prudence of a trained lawyer, made a suitable apology and Peel satisfied himself with sending the correspondence to the *Chronicle* with a request, duly complied with, for publication.[1] It was a trivial and unnecessary incident, but Peel was always oversensitive to anything that seemed to impugn the integrity of his motives and on this, as on many other occasions, refused to let even the smallest affront pass unchallenged.

After less than a week's respite he was back in London on 17 January to superintend the last stages of policy-making before parliament met. One important success was already achieved. The day before he left for Staffordshire he had a long conference at Lambeth with the Archbishop and Blomfield at which it was agreed that a royal commission should be set up to carry out in the first place a reorganisation of episcopal and diocesan responsibilities and more generally to review church patronage with the object of ending clerical sinecures, improving small livings and making preferment depend on efficiency. On 19 January the plan was unfolded to the cabinet: on 4 February the commission was issued; and on 9 February the commissioners had their first meeting. It was the essence of Peel's policy not merely to reconcile the Church to reform, but to make the Church the instrument of its own regeneration. The membership of the Commission (the two archbishops, the bishops of London, Lincoln and Gloucester, the Lord Chancellor and six other laymen of known Anglican loyalties,[2] headed by Peel himself) offered a guarantee that the work of review would be carried through in a sympathetic spirit: and the responsibility placed on the Commissioners not only for enquiring into abuses but for recommending remedies, ensured that the initiative would remain in their hands. As the prime minister made it clear in personal correspondence both with the men invited to serve on the Commission and

---

[1] 40405 fos. 92–7, 150; *Morning Chronicle*, 13 Dec. 1835. *Annual Register* 1834, p. 177.

[2] The other five were Lord Harrowby, Goulburn, C. W. W. Wynn, Henry Hobhouse, Sir Herbert Jenner.

with others like the bishops of Exeter and Durham who regarded the project with latent hostility, the whole purpose was to lay 'the safe foundations' of 'progressive reform in the Church'. No reasonable politician could doubt that the Establishment would sooner or later undergo reformation. What Peel feared was that resistance to change within the Establishment would in the end provoke the extreme penalties prescribed by its opponents. Clerical reaction rather than the antagonism of Dissenters and radicals was the real danger: and that reaction was likely to increase as soon as the first measures of reform were actually introduced. The Church had to be saved from itself as well as from its enemies. Of this Peel soon had early proof. From the start the members of the Commission and the crown agreed to delay appointments to clerical sinecures until the posts themselves could be brought under review. When the Archbishop of Canterbury, under pressure from his unregenerate lower clergy, wavered over the application of a vacant stall at Westminster to endow a living at St. Margaret's, Peel replied with some asperity. To his intimates he was even more outspoken. 'Every post', he wrote to Goulburn at the end of January, 'brings me statements which, if they are true, convince me that the deepest responsibility attaches to the Church, or at least to authorities connected with the Church, for the present state of this country in regard to the progress of Dissent.'[1] When Croker reported a few days later the fears and criticisms of the ultra-Tories, Peel asked sharply whether the function of the Church was to make provision for men of birth and learning, or the worship of God according to the doctrines of the reformed faith. 'For God's sake don't let pretended friends of the Church provoke the statement of the case which can be made out in favour of a temperate review of the present state of the Establishment.'[2]

The prospect of serious Church reform was accompanied by the promise of legislation to meet dissenting grievances. As early as 24 December Peel had told his colleagues that while the Establishment had to be maintained, everything else must be granted to Dissenters and clearly set out in the king's speech. In the succeeding

[1] Goulburn, II/18, 29 Jan. 1835. See generally for the origin of the Ecclesiastical Commission 40302 fos. 166, 307; Ellenborough, 19 Jan. 1835; *Peel Memoirs*, II, 69–85; *Peel*, II, 282–5; O. J. Brose, *Church and Parliament* (1959), pp. 125–30.
[2] *Peel*, II, 285.

weeks cabinet committees busied themselves with the problems of English and Irish tithes, church rates, dissenting marriages, and the registration of births, marriages and deaths. The question of dissenting marriages evoked much correspondence and memoranda-writing. Russell's bill of the previous session had linked a legal marriage service in licensed dissenting chapels with calling of banns in the Anglican parish church. This had been rejected by the Dissenters themselves on various grounds and some new solution was therefore necessary. Peel's own thoughts on the matter were simple and practical. Dissenters should be allowed to arrange their own marriage rites. There should be a compulsory civil ceremony in the shape of a declaration before a magistrate, who should keep a register of such marriages. It was on these principles, in fact, with the one exception that responsibility for the register was transferred to the Anglican parish minister, that the bill was finally drawn up. Even so not all Anglicans could be satisfied with this breach with the past. Croker, who compensated for his abstention from office by considerable indulgence in gratuitous advice, sent the prime minister in March an enormous letter of twenty-four sides of quarto, criticising the substitution of a civil for a sacramental marriage-bond.[1] Time did not allow the full list of ministerial measures to be ready before the session opened. Irish tithe, for example, proved as always a long and exhausting topic. It was not until the middle of February that it was remitted to a committee consisting of Hardinge, Shaw (the leader of the Irish Conservatives) and Ellenborough; and not until mid-March after many changes that the bill was approved in cabinet. Meanwhile, as the moment of engagement drew near, with all the bustle of ministerial preparation still going on below deck, Peel trimmed his ship for action. Instructions had already been sent to all departments for rigid economy in their estimates and a plea made to the Irish government not to risk any political prosecutions until after the election and then only if there was a strong case. At a final meeting on 16 February the cabinet discussed for three hours finance, agriculture and Irish tithe; and Peel made a preliminary statement on the revenue position from which it could be inferred that their surplus might be a bare £260,000.[2]

[1] 40321 fos. 42, 103; Ellenborough, 24 Dec. 1834.
[2] *Knatchbull*, p. 220; Ellenborough, 19 Jan., 13, 16 Feb., 17, 18 Mar. 1835.

III

Parliament met on 19 February among the fire-damaged buildings of Westminster. The Commons were commodiously housed in the old peers' chamber, reroofed and furnished with a reporters' gallery; while the peers themselves took up rather more uncomfortable quarters in the Painted Chamber. The first business of the House of Commons was to elect a Speaker. Manners Sutton had been the servant of the House for eighteen years; he had been pressed by the Whig government in 1833 to continue to preside over the reformed Commons; his tact and impartiality were generally recognised. Yet for weeks past the opposition journals had been alleging that he had been party to a 'plot' to overthrow the Melbourne ministry and that he had himself advised the dissolution of parliament. All this was partisan malice arising from the heated feelings of the moment and when the damage had been done it was publicly disowned by Lord John Russell. It was true, however, that Sutton was a Tory; he had been mentioned as a possible prime minister, if only one of convenience, at various times between 1832 and 1834; and Peel had actually sounded him on the possibility of joining the new government. Moreover, he had attended a few formal meetings of the Privy Council after the change of ministry in November. This to the minds of the Whigs was enough to mark him out for slaughter. What the opposition wanted was to unite their heterogeneous elements, emphasise their control of the House, and inflict an early defeat on the government. The speakership election offered the opportunity and by the end of January it was known to the cabinet that the Whigs intended to contest the Chair. The government remained optimistic. Loyalty to an old and popular Speaker and the factious nature of the opposition to him would, they thought, attract enough neutrals or deter enough opponents to make Sutton's re-election safe if not spectacular.

But the Whigs too had not been idle. The events of the past three months had been a chastening experience and after the election their whips had worked on their own initiative for closer co-operation with the Radicals and O'Connell. Despite the protests of party grandees and the coolness of his nominal leader, Russell was ready in the last resort to accept uncongenial allies in the pursuit of a line of policy which might return him to office. A joint meeting of Whigs, radicals and O'Connellites at Lichfield House the day before parliament assembled formally united the forces of the left for the purpose of evicting the government. The following evening they carried the election of Abercromby as Speaker in opposition to Manners Sutton by 316 votes to 306. There was some cross-voting; Stanley spoke and voted for Sutton; it was not a direct test of government strength; and the result was closer than the Whigs had expected. Ellenborough was told that Peel dismissed the defeat on the Speakership as a fleabite. In one sense this attitude was practical enough; it did not matter much who occupied the Chair. What did matter, however, was the way in which it had been decided. Over an issue where certain general advantages were on their side, the government had been unable to carry the House with them; and the narrowness of the opposition majority reinforced rather than weakened the solidarity of the Lichfield House compact. The small crowd outside the House cheered when the result was known; and though Peel preserved his composure, his colleagues on the front bench showed their discomfiture. For the prime minister himself, however, as well as for some of his colleagues, it must have been a premonition of ultimate failure. It was noted that Peel did not put in an appearance at the ministerial dinner at Lord Salisbury's house which followed the debate.

Yet one battle did not make a campaign. The more revealing test would come over the king's speech in which the ministerial pro-gramme of legislation would be unfolded. Peel had staked his real hopes on attracting independent support by a fair offer of fair reforms. The cabinet was satisfied that for this purpose the speech could hardly be bettered. Ellenborough, indeed, thought the danger was that they had not said enough in it to please their agricultural backbenchers. What was of more concern to Peel was whether it would be enough to please the Stanleyites. Despite their refusal to join the government in December, the delicate threads of contact between them had not been broken. Sir Herbert Taylor, who had private information through his niece, Lady Stanley, told Peel in January that Stanley had expressed approval of the *Tamworth Manifesto*; and it was unlikely that Lady Stanley was writing without her husband's knowledge. Graham had been considered as a possible governor-general for India in the discussions which preceded the appointment of Lord Heytesbury; and the ministers would have been ready to offer him the post, had they been sure of his acceptance. When sounded by the Court of Directors, Graham declined. But he was flattered by the overture and by the approval of Peel and Wellington for his nomination. After the election there was a friendly exchange of letters between Graham and Peel on certain legislative reforms of a non-party nature; and Graham later called at Whitehall Gardens for a private discussion. In February the prime minister put forward Graham's name to be a director of the National Gallery and would have been ready to do the same for Stanley had it not appeared to the prudent politician of Knowsley that a sinister interpretation might be placed on such a double nomination. Yet though Graham was showing himself the more approachable of the Third Party, he was still under the influence of the other's dominant personality; and when the session commenced, Stanley was clearly hoping to play a decisive role in the new balance of forces. While ready to back many of Peel's measures, he wanted their success to be attributable to his support. Ultimately perhaps he looked to a coalition in which Peel would have to come to him as much as he to Peel. His neutrality therefore was more calculating and guarded. An offer by Peel through Graham to send him an advance copy of the king's speech was declined; though the request was made that he should be given an authentic copy in time for the meeting of his followers which he proposed to hold immediately after it had been read in parliament.[1]

The king's speech and the formal opening of the session took place on 24 February. The address, moved by Lord Sandon, a former supporter of the reform bill, was answered by an opposition amendment regretting the dissolution of parliament. Russell did not venture on a direct censure of the crown or a vote of no confidence, having no confidence himself that either could be carried. The main point of attack was not the action of the king in dismissing the Whigs but the policy and character of the men called in to replace them. The debate was dull, the Speaker put the question; and everything seemed about to peter out on the first evening when

---

[1] 40318 f. 31 ptly pr. *Peel*, II, 289; see also fos. 15, 20, 22, 27, 33; 40302 f. 224; *Graham*, I, 222–7.

Peel's tall figure was seen to rise. The effect on the House was instantaneous. The uproar died down, and members pushed and scrambled back into their places until all was quiet and the House sat expectant. Speaking for over two hours, firmly and with dignity, Peel made it clear that he had been no party to the king's act. Formally, however, he took responsibility for the change of government and offered justification for both that and the dissolution. His defence concluded, he launched into a vigorous exposition of the policy of the new administration and appealed as a minister of the crown for a fair trial in 'the trust, which I did not seek, but which I could not decline. . . . I make great offers, which should not lightly be rejected. . . . I offer you these specific measures, and I offer also to advance, soberly and cautiously, it is true, in the path of progressive improvement.' He ended with a warning and a prophecy. His offers might be refused; his opponents might prefer to travel the same road by more violent means. If they did, they would find in the end that moderate opinion would withdraw from them, and they would be forced either to replace power in the hands of those from which they now wished to remove it, or to evoke the forces of violence and compulsion from below. It was a good and effective speech, calculated (observed Greville, who was present) 'to make an impression on all who were impressible'.

It remained to be seen how many politicians fell into that limited category. Immediately after the king's speech Stanley had held his first party meeting. About forty were present but as it seemed probable that the debate would last over until the next day, it was decided to meet again the following afternoon. At the second meeting, joined by a small squad of moderate Whigs under Sir Oswald Mosley, such lack of confidence in the government was expressed on all sides, that it almost certainly influenced Stanley's speech later the same day. He declared that he wished to give Peel a fair trial and would vote against the amendment. But he said he could put no trust in the ministry as a whole and regretted that no pledge had been given on municipal reform. It was a grudging and unpleasant speech which annoyed many government and especially Wellingtonian supporters. Lady Stanley wrote apologetically to her uncle to explain that it had been more anti-ministerial than her husband had wished but he was obliged to take the line he did because of his followers. Had he shown more cordiality towards the ministers 'or led his friends to imagine there was the least appearance of understanding with the Government, he could not have attained his ends, and carried their vote'.[1] In fact, though he carried some votes to the side of the ministry, he did not carry enough. On 26 February, after three days of debate, a division in which 611 members voted yielded a majority of seven for the opposition amendment. For the government this was a crushing blow. It had not been expected and it came after the prime minister had made a personal appeal to the House to suspend judgement on the new administration. There was little more that he could do now, except to offer separately what the House had rejected in bulk. At cabinet next day he was noticeably depressed. 'If he lose heart', wrote Ellenborough in his journal, 'we are lost, but I trust he will fight to the last.'

Though the odds had lengthened alarmingly, however, there was no question of immediate surrender. Peel had said in the debate that an unfavourable division would not lead him to resign; and some of those who had voted against him had expressed a similar hope. His own followers at least were showing better discipline than in the last House, and early in March the cabinet had a few tactical successes to give them heart. A threat by Hume to limit supplies to three months was subsequently watered down to a motion to refer the navy estimates to a select committee and this in turn was overwhelmingly defeated in a thin House. An independent move by Lord Chandos to abolish the malt tax profoundly disturbed and irritated Peel but it was countered by a large and successful party meeting at which leading agriculturalists promised to abandon their pledges to constituents rather than risk the fall of the government. The incipient country party revolt collapsed on 10 March with a cross-bench vote of 350 to 192 against Chandos's motion. But malt was not the only internal irritant. Sugden, the Irish Lord Chancellor, sent in his resignation because his wife, by whom he had had several children before their marriage, was not received by the Lord Lieutenant at the Castle. Only late in March, after his son-in-law had gone across to plead with him, did he agree to remain in office. On 13 March there was a concerted opposition attack on the nomination as ambassador to St. Petersburg of Lord Londonderry,

[1] 40303 fos. 23, 29.

who had publicly and provocatively supported Russian policy against Turkey and the rebellious Poles. The appointment had been Wellington's and his motive had been the human but not very defensible one of putting an unpopular and intriguing Tory peer in a position where he could do no mischief. The deed had been done, however, and Peel refused to sacrifice the government's first diplomatic appointment to the House of Commons or even privately advise resignation. Fortunately Londonderry himself recognised the dilemma and handsomely gave up his post. Nevertheless, it had been a damaging attack, despite Peel's speech of defence in the House. Stanley, who rarely missed an opportunity of showing his dislike of the duke, joined the critics and the cabinet did not trust even their own supporters to vote solidly with the government if a formal motion were put down. It had been an attack on the weakest aspect of the ministry, the individual appointments to offices. Knatchbull, from his unfamiliar and slightly uncomfortable seat on the front bench, felt that for the first time the government had actually lost ground in the House.[1]

Equally irritating, and as the session continued, even more depressing than those specific reverses, was the daily inability of the front bench to control the ordinary business of the House. On no issue could they be sure beforehand of a majority. On many minor matters Peel could not depend on either impromptu debating support or even regular attendance from his followers. While the impecunious, clubless, radical and Irish members spent their whole days in and around the House, the country squires and professional men of his own party showed a distressing tendency to allow social and personal interests to distract them from their nightly duty on the benches behind him. Some of the peers in the cabinet—Ellenborough, Wharncliffe and Wellington—were inclined to blame this defective support on the defective qualities of the government whip, Sir George Clerk, and his two assistants, Bonham and Ross. This olympian judgement offered perhaps too simple and personal an explanation. With few sanctions to enforce attendance, the success of the whips depended to a great extent on the morale of their troops, and this ebbed perceptibly during March. It was not pleasant always to be beaten. A peculiarly disastrous day on 25 March,

[1] *Knatchbull*, pp. 221–2; Ellenborough, 9 Dec. 1834, 14 Mar. 1835.

however, when the government were defeated in three out of four divisions, helped to emphasise the danger and bring about a temporary improvement. Three days later a large meeting of Conservative M.P.s under the chairmanship of Lord Francis Egerton gave renewed pledges of support to the government and promised better attendance in the House for the future.[1]

While his backbenchers were belatedly recognising the extent to which the government was imperilled, Peel knew that it was doomed. From the tone of his remarks in cabinet after the disastrous Londonderry debate it was apparent that he thought they could not go on much longer. The only question was to find some distinct and satisfactory issue on which to resign. This was the difficulty. It seemed the tactics of the opposition not to risk a major encounter but to harry the government at every conceivable point in a protracted campaign of attrition. On several occasions in March and again in early April, Peel invited Russell, if he thought the ministry should retire, to proceed to a straightforward vote of no confidence as the only manly and constitutional course. The challenge was evaded. Instead, whether with or without the consent of their leader, individual members of the opposition resorted to all the time-wasting and obstructive devices which the lax rules of the House allowed. With the financial year ending on 1 April and the Mutiny Act due to expire on 25 April, there were constant motions and amendments either to postpone the days set aside for the committee of supply or to drown discussion of government business in irrelevant topics. 'Never was there more noise and violence, and less business done, than in this session,' noted Greville on 26 March. In the absence of effective government control, the behaviour of the House, never notably decorous, steadily deteriorated. Shouting, hooting, groaning, stamping of feet and beating of sticks on the floor became a regular feature of proceedings. Greville was told by one Whig that there was a set of men on his side of the House who made it their practice to start up these vocal adornments to debate in an endeavour to 'bellow Peel down'.

In these circumstances the legislative programme of the ministry from which so much had been expected made singularly little impact. The introduction of the dissenting marriage bill on 17 March

[1] Ellenborough, 4, 27, 28 Mar. 1835; 40419 fos. 186–96; *Knatchbull*, pp. 222–3.

met with some criticism from Dissenters but general approval. A motion a few days later to bring in a bill for English tithe commutation was agreed unanimously. On 19 March the first epoch-making report of the Ecclesiastical Commission was laid before the House containing recommendations for diocesan and parochial reorganisation and the creation of two new bishoprics. These were not issues, however, on which Russell wished to fight because they were not issues which would unite his followers. Even the Irish tithe bill, brought forward by Hardinge on 20 March, had a degree of success. His motion did no more than pledge the House to abolish tithe in Ireland and substitute a redeemable rent charge on the land; and in the debate which followed the prime minister was in his best House of Commons form, bowling down his antagonists (as Greville said) like so many ninepins. The opposition was confused and disjointed, contradictory resolutions being moved by Hume and Spring Rice, and in the division the ministers had a majority of fifteen. The tithe debate, however, raised the acrimonious question of the Irish Church in which Lord John Russell had played so prominent a part in the previous session and which at bottom had been the reason for Melbourne's dismissal. The Irish Church commission set up as a face-saving device at the time of Stanley's resignation had not yet issued its report and for a while Russell hesitated in his tactics. It was obvious, however, that he was only looking for a favourable opportunity to renew the struggle and finally, without waiting for the commission's findings, he gave notice of a motion for 30 March. Three days before, in response to pressure from Peel, he announced that it would take the form of a motion to go into committee to consider the application of the surplus revenues of the Church of Ireland to the 'religious and moral instruction of all classes of the community'.

With this explicit renewal of the appropriation conflict, the climax of the session had arrived. Peel had asked for a fair trial. He was given a pitched battle on ground of his opponent's choice and on an issue which would unite Whigs, Liberals, Dissenters and O'Connell's Irish party. Inevitably it would throw Stanley to the side of the government but the famous Third Party had perceptibly thinned as the session went on. It was unlikely now that Stanley would be able to bring to Peel's assistance enough troops to win the day, even if they were still rather more than was suggested by O'Connell's gibe at the start of the session—'the Derby Dilly with his six insides'. The ministers themselves were under no delusion. They expected, just as much as the opposition, that Russell would carry his motion; the only difference of opinion was by how many. But whether by twenty or forty made little difference. For Peel the issue was not whether he would be defeated but when he should resign. On 25 March he circulated a memorandum to the cabinet arguing strongly in favour of retirement. Since the start of the session, he pointed out, the government had endured a succession of defeats; they had made no progress even in ordinary business; they had been subjected to frivolous and vexatious obstruction; they stood every chance of being beaten on the great issue of policy which had brought about Stanley's resignation the previous year. No further evidence was needed of their inability to control the House; and there was no longer any rational hope of attracting additional support or of converting their minority into a majority. To continue in office, if beaten on Russell's motion, would be to throw away a good and intelligible ground for resignation with no certainty that they would get a better and every prospect that they would in the end have to be content with a worse. That night, at a cabinet dinner in Rosslyn's house, there was some discussion of the memorandum. But Peel did not force a decision and there was some reluctance, especially among ministerial peers insulated from the realities of the House of Commons, to face resignation. In any case, it was still in a sense a hypothetical question and during the next few days the cabinet devoted itself to the more limited task of preparing for the great debate. Peel drew up an amendment to Russell's resolution, disapproving of any appropriation other than for Church purposes; Stanley and Graham were informed of the cabinet's decision to make no compromise; and it was arranged that Graham should speak early in the debate. On 29 March a final cabinet, meeting exceptionally on a Sunday, put the last touches to these preparations. It was evident by then that the weight of Peel's arguments was beginning to sink into the minds of his colleagues. Nevertheless it was agreed to take no irrevocable step until the result of the debate was known.[1]

[1] Ellenborough, 25–9 Mar. 1835; *Knatchbull*, pp. 222–3; *Peel Memoirs*, II, 87–93.

For the next four days the centre of political interest shifted to the House of Commons. In the country at large there was little overt public interest. But within the parliamentary arena it was recognised that the existence of the ministry was now at stake and both sides called up their full panoply of debate. Russell, trying to reconcile support for an established Church in principle with criticism of the Irish Church in detail, did not make an impressive speech. He was answered by Knatchbull, who for a man never reckoned among the oratorical ornaments of the House acquitted himself better than his colleagues had expected; by Graham, who spoke impressively and at length; by Gladstone and Praed among the younger men; by Follett, the Solicitor-General, in another outstanding speech; and by Hardinge, who, though no debater, on this occasion rose above his ordinary level. Against them were ranged Lord Howick, Sheil, J. C. Hobhouse, Littleton the former Irish Secretary, Spring Rice, and O'Connell. Stanley, making his intervention on 1 April, gave a characteristic speech: able and effective from a partisan point of view, but hard and provocative towards his late colleagues. He denounced the alliance with O'Connell and held up to ridicule the divided councils and heterogeneous composition of any government that could conceivably be formed by the Liberal opposition. It pleased his supporters but was unlikely to have made converts; and it widened the gap between himself and his former party. The protracted debate, except for a few concluding remarks by Russell, was wound up by Peel. Whether because he was tired from the strains of the preceding months, or hampered (as Knatchbull thought) by recollections of Catholic emancipation, or (as is more likely) dispirited by the certainty of defeat, he spoke less well than usual. The tactical strength of the government case was that the opposition were discussing the appropriation of a surplus which had not yet been proved to exist: and Peel made play with the attempt to assert, as he put it, 'an unprofitable right to apply an imaginary surplus to an unexplained purpose'. But in outlining the various methods open to the government in dealing with the Irish Church, and in answering *seriatim* the arguments of the previous opposition speakers, he allowed himself to be led off into long and detailed discussions of subordinate topics. He reasoned with great power and tact, as he almost always did, and he had some impressive passages. But the speech as a whole lacked fire and in his peroration he virtually admitted the inevitability of defeat. When, about three in the morning, the House divided, the Whig amendment was carried by 322 to 289, a majority of 33. The government whips calculated afterwards that the total available strength on their side was 304, the difference being accounted for by the two tellers, eight pairs, one vacancy and four absentees.[1] It was not enough, even with the further addition of some ten Stanleyites who were ready to support the ministry on all but the church question: the only one, as Ellenborough sardonically observed, on which their support was needed. For the moment the government was powerless. Peel was unable to prevent the House from going into committee on the state of the Irish Church the very next day; and although the debate was adjourned until the following Monday, it was a foregone conclusion that a second defeat would be inflicted on the ministers.

When the cabinet met on the afternoon of Saturday, 4 April, there was a general acceptance that resignation was now only a matter of days. Peel spoke of the discredit into which both the influence of the executive government and the authority of the crown were falling as a consequence of the control which the House of Commons was exercising over the ministers; and he turned down flatly a suggestion by Wharncliffe that they should struggle on in the hope of a successful dissolution. Even if a second general election could be justified, Peel doubted whether it would prove as favourable as the last. The return of a Whig government was in his view a certainty. At the start of the session the king had said he would grant a second dissolution if advised. But what the king would do was now irrelevant except in so far as his difficult position would become even more difficult if the ministers of his choice clung to office long after their impotence had been demonstrated. Both verbally and by letter Peel had tried to prepare the king's mind for the inevitable; and though on 30 March William had sent him a despairing appeal not to be abandoned to the opposition, the only remedy which the king himself could suggest was a coalition with moderate Whigs such as Grey, Melbourne and Stanley.[2] This in the circumstances was hardly worth serious discussion. There were certainly those, both in the party and in the cabinet, who wished to

[1] Ellenborough, 4 Apr. 1835.   [2] 40303 f. 112; Peel, II, 298.

fight on. Ellenborough, who exhibited at times the political judgement as well as the dashing temperament of a cavalry subaltern, even had the fanciful notion of replacing Peel if he persisted in his determination to resign. At a dinner at de Grey's, when only the cabinet peers were present, he suggested that the existing ministry should be reconstructed under Stanley. This evoked no enthusiasm from his colleagues. Wellington, who on 25 March had privately urged Peel to carry on the battle, was increasingly influenced by the prime minister's argument that the assumption by the opposition of executive powers was injuring the authority of the legal government in the eyes of foreign powers such as France.[1] Meanwhile Russell and his triumphant majority were giving the final twists to the parliamentary screw. On 6 April they carried their resolution in committee. On the 7th Russell moved that no tithe settlement for Ireland should be deemed satisfactory unless it embodied the principle of the resolution. As a final sanction he announced his intention to move if necessary an address to the crown to the same effect. With this the end of the road had been reached. The latest resolution completely blocked any progress on the government's Irish tithe bill; an address to the crown would circumvent the House of Lords and bring direct pressure on the king. In the interval the mere passage of declaratory resolutions was enough to paralyse the tardy collection of tithes in Ireland which in some parts were already three or four years in arrears. On 7 April the cabinet finally agreed to resign if beaten on Russell's new resolution and the same evening Peel made one last fighting speech. Perhaps because the decision to go out was already made, he was more spirited, more defiant, and evoked more enthusiasm than on 2 April. But the time had long passed when speeches could affect the outcome. In the division the ministers were beaten by a majority of twenty-seven, for the fourth time in less than a week.

At cabinet the following morning the only question was what they should do if the king asked them to join a coalition. Peel was clear and uncompromising. He would never accept any post but that of prime minister; he thought the Duke of Wellington essential to government; he could not ask any man who had joined him in office in December to sacrifice it now for political convenience. Others

[1] Ellenborough, 27 Mar., 1, 4 Apr. 1835; *Peel*, II, 294.

were less adamant. The duke said that if it were a matter of only some resignations, a selection could be made; and Hardinge, Ellenborough and Rosslyn offered to give up their posts to facilitate arrangements.[1] Until the king's intentions were known, however, all this was idle speculation. The same day Peel presented his resignation to the king and informed the Commons of the retirement of the ministry. He spoke briefly and practically. The votes of the House had implied clear lack of confidence and had raised an insuperable barrier to the efficient conduct of Irish administration. Ministers could not, therefore, consistently with their duty continue in office. He made a graceful reference to the disinterested support of the Stanleyites and towards the end added one personal touch, designed perhaps to answer the rumours already circulating of his permanent retirement from politics. He had tried to make his short explanation as free from offence as possible, he said, and then went on:

> For himself, the whole of his political life had been spent in the House of Commons—the remainder of it would be spent in the House of Commons, and, whatever might be the conflict of parties, he, for one, should always wish, whether in a majority or in a minority, to stand well with the House of Commons.

He was cheered at this, and again for several minutes at the conclusion of his speech, with an enthusiasm which derived from something more than the easy magnanimity of a majority relaxing in the sunlight of victory. The House adjourned; the ministry was effectively at an end. From 9 December when Peel accepted the king's invitation to form a government to 8 April when he tendered his resignation was exactly 120 days.

In the last few weeks the only real issue had been not whether but when to go out; and in the end the timing of Peel's resignation had been almost faultless. Earlier it would not have been understood by all his followers; later it would have come in for justifiable criticism. As it was, the cabinet and the great majority of the party were satisfied that all had been done which was humanly possible. There were still a few Tory malcontents who would have preferred the last desperate plunge of another general election under the banner of the Duke of Wellington and *No Popery*. As against these

[1] Ellenborough, 8 Apr. 1835.

political primitives, however, it was known that Stanley and Graham were beginning to be impatient at the delay. Stanley, in fact, with the levity which amused one set of his acquaintances and shocked others, had been comparing Peel to a hunted fox who skulked along the hedgerows and at last turned up his legs in a ditch, instead of dying gallantly under the hounds in the open field.

Now the end had come, after a pitched battle and over a great issue. All that remained was a few days of routine administration. There had already been a discreet and parsimonious distribution of honours and patronage and Peel was not disposed to do much more in his last days of office. Five barons had been created, including Fitzgerald, Scarlett, and Manners Sutton; and the only peerage made on retirement was for Alexander Baring, whose health had not stood up to the strain of being minister in the Commons. For the rest, Peel's main interest in the field of awards and honours had been, as he expressed it to Ellenborough in February, 'the means by which we can stand well with the literary world'.[1] Croker had been urging a somewhat indiscriminate list of recipients for literary honours, not all of whom could be regarded as friendly to the government. 'I must be very cautious not to *confine* pensions to Whig or Liberal professors of literature', replied the prime minister mildly in January; and his awards were tempered with a judicious admixture of Tory figures. A baronetcy was conferred on John Barrow, the geographer; the poet Southey was offered another and when this was refused, he was given a pension. Other civil list pensions went to Mrs. Somerville, the scientific bluestocking whose book on *The Connection of the Physical Sciences* had appeared the previous year; to the wife of Professor Airey who held the eminent but unremunerative chair of astronomy at Cambridge; to the Sheffield poet and hymn writer, James Montgomery; and to Sharon Turner, the Anglo-Saxon historian. Wordsworth declined a proffered pension for his wife but encouraged by Peel and Lord Lonsdale he came to London in the spring to negotiate some official post for his son. This paternal pilgrimage was made fruitless by the termination of the ministry, but other awards from the royal bounty went to Mrs. Hemans the poetess, then in the last impoverished year of her short life, and to James Hogg, the Ettrick Shepherd, who

[1] *ibid.*, Corr. 6 Feb. 1835; *Croker*, II, 259.

replied disarmingly that though always poor and always happy, he had 'a particular facility in accepting of money'. To distribute largesse among literary and academic figures more eminent, as Peel put it, for their exertions than for their worldly wealth, was a welcome change from the usual run of political patronage. In doing so Peel was not only obeying the spirit of a recent House of Commons resolution on the future disposal of civil list pensions but demonstrating even in this field the readiness of his ministry to move with the times. It was a characteristic personal contribution to the growth of conservative enlightenment to argue, as he did to the king, the advantages of 'conciliating the confidence and goodwill of that most powerful class . . . immediately connected with the literature and science of the Country, and of encouraging the application of great talents and great acquirements to the support of the ancient institutions of the Country'.[1]

In the few remaining days before the official retirement of the ministry Peel was in noticeably good spirits. Once the decision had been made, his cares were over and he could look back on his Hundred Days without compunction and with some sense of achievement. The addresses of condolence, congratulation and support which were beginning to flow in offered gratifying evidence of the impression he had made on the country. From his own followers, headed by Lord Francis Egerton, came a hearty letter of confidence and thanks of a kind he was not accustomed to from that quarter. Another memorial expressing high approval of his conduct and with over a thousand signatures was formally presented to him by a deputation of metropolitan solicitors and attorneys. 'I had no idea there were so many,' wrote Peel light-heartedly to Croker, 'less that they were so nearly unanimous in their support of Conservative principles.'[2] But these were only two of countless similar testimonials that came pouring in from all parts of the kingdom: from Brighton, Norwich, Ipswich, Bristol, Leicester, Liverpool, Manchester, Rochdale, Leeds, Birmingham, and Huddersfield, from Yorkshire and Kent, from Edinburgh and Dublin, from the universities of Oxford and Cambridge, from magistrates, clergy, lawyers, freeholders, gentry, merchants and manufacturers, too numerous for the press to print in full more than

[1] 40302 f. 260.   [2] *Croker*, II, 273.

a selection, the mere enumeration of the continual additions to the list taking up several inches of news-column for several days on end. It was an exhilarating and almost unprecedented demonstration of public feeling.

IV

On 18 April the ministers delivered up their seals and Peel's first ministry came to its official end. Despite the unpropitious beginning its reputation had grown with its defeats and its credit was never higher than when it surrendered its power. This paradox was almost entirely the achievement of its leader. Not only had he taken on himself the main burden of the parliamentary conflict but he had done so in a manner which had raised immeasurably the public estimate of his talents and statesmanship. In the Commons his lucid and powerful speeches, his tenacious memory and mastery of the forms of the House, his courage and resource, had enabled him to dominate the benches even when he was beaten in the divisions. His first essay as prime minister had demonstrated a remarkable combination of firmness on essentials and patient persuasiveness in details which had first projected the cabinet along the path of active reform and then extracted it from an impossible parliamentary position without disunity or discontent. To a large number of his fellow countrymen he had presented a fresh and welcome political leadership, dissociated from the anti-reform image of old Toryism and yet different from the radical propensities of new Whiggery. *The Times*, which had given the government wholehearted support, recorded in monumental phrases the widespread and growing feeling. In a leading article published on the day of Peel's resignation, it spoke of the prospective loss

> of public services which ... no other Statesman in the British Empire could have rendered to his country with half the efficacy, or advantage, or honour, as the right hon. gentleman still at the head of His Majesty's councils, whose temper, capacity and powers have been daily developed by the arduous position in which he stood, until they reached a magnitude unlooked for by the most sanguine observers of his political course and absolutely unapproached by any Minister but one who has addressed Parliament since the opening of the present century.

Politics had changed when the voice of the Thunderer, however public and partisan, could compare Peel to the legendary Pitt the Younger. But the men who guided *The Times* were not usually far from the prevailing currents of public opinion. A few days earlier Greville had predicted that whatever the immediate outcome, nothing could prevent Peel's early return to office.

> He has raised his reputation to such a height . . . he has established such a conviction of his great capacity, and of his liberal, enlarged, and at the same time safe views and opinions . . . he stands so proudly eminent, and there is such a general lack of talent, that he must be recalled by the voice of the nation and by the universal admission that he is indispensable to the country.[1]

One thing at least was clear. Peel had emerged as a national leader, and as the *Annual Register* observed at the end of the year, 'not merely as the first but without a rival'. If the touchstone of politics is the ability to match need with performance, Peel had passed the test. Responsibility and crisis had evoked new energy and unsuspected talents. In the greatest office in the state he appeared a greater man than ever before.

Not the least part of Peel's success was that though he fought hard and skilfully, he had left no rancour. Unlike Stanley he had refrained from personalities and abuse and on one occasion indeed he had shown considerable restraint. Russell in the Speakership debate had admitted that the allegation against Manners Sutton of advising the dissolution was unfounded. Yet in private letters to supporters before the meeting of parliament he had lent himself to the allegation and one of these letters was handed to Peel on the first evening of the debate. When he specifically put the point to Russell and received his denial, however, he characteristically forebore to press the charge or produce the letter.[2] It was true that later in the session, when Hume observed in the House that his conduct over Irish tithes was inconsistent with that of a man of honour, Peel challenged the phrase with some heat and when he got no satisfaction wrote to Hume the same evening with a demand for retractation. Yet this with Peel was a question of pride rather than pique. The impartial Greville, while reflecting that it really was unnecessary to notice

[1] *Greville*, 3 Apr. 1835.   [2] *ibid*., 23 Feb.; *The Times*, 21 Feb. 1835.

anything Hume said, expressed patrician approval for Peel's rule
not to allow any impertinence to pass unchecked, particularly as
Peel's own language in debate was invariably free from dis-
courtesy.[1] Tact and restraint could not disarm his opponents but at
least made it easier for them to appreciate the ability with which he
had attempted the impossible. 'Nothing', said Lord Mulgrave
generously, 'in Peel's past political career led me to expect that he
would have done so admirably'.[2] Campbell, Melbourne's Solicitor-
General, admitted to his brother in March that 'Peel himself is a much
better man than any we can oppose to him. He really is exceedingly
dexterous and handy, as well as eloquent and powerful.'[3] Even
stern unbending radicals such as Hume could be heard to join in
what Greville called the general chorus of admiration.

It was not only his opponents and the public whom he had
impressed. Some of his own colleagues had been equally surprised,
though for different reasons. Those who had not known him
intimately and expected him on closer acquaintance to prove cold
and conceited, were struck by his warmth and friendliness. Wharncliffe told Greville that no man was easier to act with, more candid,
conciliatory and unassuming than Peel in the cabinet.[4] In his
handling of his subordinate colleagues, young men like Sidney
Herbert and Gladstone or older men like Bonham and Fremantle,
he had displayed a kindliness and informality which was completely
at variance with his public reputation. Gladstone, who was transferred to the under-secretaryship of the colonies in January, wrote
on that occasion to his father: 'I can only say that if I had always
heard of him that he was the warmest and freest person of all living
in the expression of his feelings, such description would have been
fully borne out by his demeanour to me.'[5] Power seemed to have
given Peel an assurance and ease of manner which in the past only
his intimates had habitually encountered. Graham, still loyal to
Stanley though not uncritical of his friend's defects as a political
leader, was particularly impressed by this unexpected side of Peel's
nature. He told Greville that the interview he had immediately after
Peel's return from Italy was 'cordial and obliging to the greatest

---

[1] *Greville*, 22 Mar. 1835. For Hume's grudging withdrawal see *Peel*, II, 291.
[2] *Greville*, 7 Apr. 1835.   [3] *Campbell*, II, 71.   [4] *Greville*, 9 Apr. 1835.
[5] *Gladstone*, I, 91.

degree, and without any appearance of that coldness and reserve of which he has been so often accused'. It was evident that he was looking forward to a union with Peel and the return of the Conservatives to office 'with as much zeal and fervor', noted Greville curiously, 'as if he had been a member of the Cabinet which has just fallen'. Obviously there had been times during the session when Peel had shown weariness and irritation; and one or two young men had been heard to grumble at his tendency to delegate too little to his subordinates. Government on a razor edge makes unusual demands on a leader and this was not always relished by his lieutenants. Francis Egerton complained that he got no encouragement when as a backbencher he had offered to speak in the disastrous Londonderry debate. Ashley, who had accepted somewhat grudgingly a junior lordship of the Admiralty, was annoyed on another occasion when Peel took out of his hands a reply to Hume on some question of naval estimates which he had taken some trouble to get up.[1] Yet there was not much of this, and more than a little justification for it in a hard-pressed minister. A front bench consisting of Goulburn, Hardinge, Baring, Knatchbull, Herries and Murray was not prodigally endowed with debating skill; nor was it unreasonable to exercise caution in letting young men loose in situations where a mistake could not be retrieved by the simple and overbearing logic of the big battalions. In the circumstances it was a small fault; if also a characteristic one. Conscious of his own powers and easily irked by the deficiencies of others, Peel was by nature always prone to take too much on himself.

Though the 1834–35 ministry had seemed at times a single virtuoso performance, however, there could be no doubt of its effect on Peel's position as acknowledged leader of the Conservative party. All minor and incidental criticism was forgotten in the general acclaim which greeted the close of his first ministry. When he stepped down from office in April 1835 it was to a more commanding position on his side of the House than he had ever had before. By a common process of political alchemy the actual parliamentary weakness of the government had served to strengthen its control over its followers. Only two difficult party issues had emerged—malt and resignation. The sense of the House had

[1] *Greville*, 17 Mar., 9 Apr. 1835.

supported Peel on the first; patience and persuasion had succeeded on the other. On the fundamental question of the government's general policy, however, there had been no real disagreement. The *Tamworth Manifesto* had been accepted, as much as anything of that kind could be, as the representation of the party's own views. Whatever the future might bring, the Peelite formula for Conservatism had now been endorsed not merely by his ministerial colleagues but by the rank and file of his followers. There could be no going back on that. For the rest, the future was now clearer and more hopeful than anyone could have expected six months earlier. The Hundred Days had given fresh heart to the scattered forces of Conservatism in the country at large. They had allowed a 'Conservative Party' in a real sense to be created. Previously it had neither numbers nor cohesion; now it had both. If William had done nothing else, he had put the leadership of the party firmly into Peel's hands and enabled him to revolutionise its parliamentary position. Its representation in the House of Commons was almost twice as large as in 1833; it had a majority in the House of Lords; it had the open support of the crown. With Stanley and Graham now operating on their flank, the Conservatives could muster an organised opposition more formidable than anything that had existed in the generation before 1834. For the first time since the Reform Act, moreover, they had taken the initiative in the constituencies and the wave of provincial Conservative and Constitutional Societies which had been formed under the stimulus of the general election and the new government provided a basis for continued electoral recovery. As Bonham wrote confidently to Peel later in the year, 'then we had to find candidates, organisers and friends in almost every place. *Now that work is done* and a tenth part of the exertions then applied would at least preserve if not increase our present strength.'[1] At the start of the crisis the king had likened his action to that of his father in dismissing the Fox–North coalition in 1783. The parallel was inexact; and the outcome different. Peel had failed to get the fair trial he asked for; he had been disappointed in his hope of attracting independent support. For this the primary reason had been the hardening of party divisions which the crisis and the dissolution had produced. Yet this emergence of a tighter

[1] 40420 f. 126.

and more organised party system, though it denied Peel at the time any repetition of the Pittite victory in 1784, in the long run worked to his advantage. It was clear now what post-reform politics were about and where post-reform party lines could be drawn. The Conservatives had everything to gain from such a clarification. For all its apparent futility and personal humiliation, the king's sole act had influenced the course of British politics more positively than anything the Crown had done since 1807. The beneficiary, however, was not the old, unhappy and frustrated William, but Peel and the Conservative party.

All these were substantial compensations to set off against the return of the Whigs to office, dissension and difficulty. Peel's own confidence in the future came out unmistakably in a brief, affectionate speech he made to some of his outgoing colleagues in April. Replying at a dinner in his own house to a toast proposed by Lord Lincoln, he said that he would not call them merely gentlemen, but rather warm and attached friends in whom he had complete trust and with whom it had given him great satisfaction to be associated. In undertaking the government he had never expected to succeed; but it was his conviction that good might be done, and he trusted that good had been done. If a Conservative government had not been strong enough to carry on the affairs of the country, at least they were strong enough to prevent any other government from doing serious mischief to its institutions.[1] He abstained from any further political speculation but it did not require much optimism among those listening to him that evening in the long dining-room at Whitehall Gardens to look forward to a time when the party would be back in power and Peel in office under conditions vastly different from those of November 1834.

[1] *Gladstone*, I, 94–5.

4

PEERS AND COMMONERS

The determination shown by the Whig–Liberal party in evicting the ministry was not accompanied by an equal alacrity among their elder statesmen in accepting office. On 9 April the king consulted Lord Grey who advised him to send for Lansdowne and Melbourne. When they appeared the king once more brought up his proposal for a coalition. Both men declared this impossible and the following day, 11 April, Melbourne was at last commissioned to form a ministry. His first and typical reaction was to try to persuade Grey to resume the premiership, or at least to take the Foreign Office. Grey, tired and resentful, refused all overtures; other difficulties were started by Melbourne's more aspiring colleagues; and the king, whose apprehensions mounted as the prospect of a right-wing Whig ministry waned, began to talk in disquieting terms of his scruples over the Irish Church and his coronation oath. The House of Commons which had been adjourned until 13 April met on that day only to hear Peel, as caretaker prime minister, propose a further adjournment to the 16th. On the 16th there was another adjournment until the 18th.

Meanwhile the king, who had tried without success to have his personal difficulties over the Irish Church referred to a committee of judges, obtained Melbourne's passive consent to write to Lord Lyndhurst (still acting Lord Chancellor) for advice. Melbourne had made it clear that the new government was committed to a settlement of the Irish tithe on the basis of the recent resolution of the House of Commons in favour of the appropriation of surplus revenues. William's enquiry whether he could consent to this without violating his coronation oath raised the possibility not only of a refusal to sanction the introduction of such a measure but in effect a refusal to sanction Melbourne's ministry at all. To require a member of the outgoing ministry to pronounce judicially on such an issue was, as even William realised, a somewhat unorthodox procedure. Lyndhurst's immediate reaction was to show the letter to his own leader who drafted a reply which the Lord Chancellor copied and sent to the king the same day. Peel, who had a low view of the obligation of the coronation oath and a high one of ministerial responsibility, phrased the letter in unambiguous terms. The ministers who proposed the tithes measure, ran the salient passage, 'must be responsible for the Advice which they might tender to your Majesty'.[1] But while uncompromising in his view of ministerial rights and royal duties, he was not without sympathy for the elderly monarch ensnared once more in the toils of parliamentary government. In the ensuing months he endeavoured in a confidential exchange of letters with Sir Herbert Taylor to exercise a moderating influence on the king's prejudices and temperament, neutralise the excitable advice of the Duke of Cumberland, and press home the simple but unwelcome lesson that nothing could be done to supplant the Whigs as long as they retained the support of the House of Commons. The day had passed when the Crown and the House of Lords between them could sustain a government. A 'cautious and judicious course', however unheroic, was, he told Taylor, the only path which the king could safely follow.[2]

Melbourne's second administration was finally announced to the world on 18 April. It contained few surprises. Brougham was excluded and the Great Seal put in commission; Wellesley did not return to Ireland; O'Connell was not given office. These omissions promised a quieter life for the prime minister. Indeed, with the loss of Althorp, Abercromby, and Ellice, the government was if anything less rather than more liberal than in 1834. On 20 April both houses adjourned for three weeks to allow the ministerial re-elections to take place. They did not provide the new cabinet with much ground for satisfaction. Russell was defeated in Devonshire and had to find a seat in Stroud. In Staffordshire and Inverness-shire by-elections created by the elevation to the peerage of Littleton and Charles Grant also resulted in Conservative victories. It was in a cheerful

---

[1] 40316 fos. 192–3. See also *English Politics*, pp. 16–17.
[2] 40303 fos. 235, 239.

mood that the leaders of the opposition gathered once more in London and the day before parliament reassembled was marked by a demonstration of Conservative strength and principles in the metropolis itself. On 11 May the merchants, bankers and traders of the City gave a dinner to Peel to which a number of his colleagues and friends were invited. It was an eminently political occasion and the speech which he delivered, though short in comparison with his usual parliamentary efforts, was the most significant public pronouncement outside the walls of Westminster which he had so far made.

It showed Peel to his audience in three important roles. As a politician he exhibited an authority and confidence never seen in him before; as a statesman he expounded his conception of Conservative principles in the settled and mature form from which he never subsequently departed; and as a party leader he pointed out to his supporters in the country the road to success and power. He disclaimed being a candidate for office; he paid his invariable tribute to the Duke of Wellington, which the duke reciprocated later in the evening; and he acknowledged the strength he had derived from public applause and confidence. Nevertheless, he reminded his audience a little unkindly, for all their demonstration of feeling that night, not one of the eighteen metropolitan M.P.s shared their political views. But the body of the speech was devoted to more fundamental matters. He warned his hearers that the dangers which threatened their constitution and forms of government could not be answered by simple reliance on the influence of the crown and the authority of the House of Lords. These were no longer impassable bulwarks 'which can be committed without apprehension to the storm and struggle of events'. The government of the country must mainly depend on the constitution of the House of Commons. The aim of Conservatives must be therefore to win an effectual influence in that branch of the legislature by all open and constitutional means. In this great task there must be no laziness, no apathy, no despondency; above all no attempt, not even the appearance of an attempt, to deny just political power to those who had been the beneficiaries of the Reform Act. Indeed, he added presciently, any change in the reform settlement would come from their opponents when they discovered that the act was incapable of excluding the influence of Conservative principles. There were, or should be, he continued, no barriers between the Conservative party and the new electorate.

> We deny that we are separated by any line of interest, or any other line of demarcation, from the middling classes. . . . What was the grand charge against myself—that the King had sent for the son of a cotton-spinner to Rome, in order to make him Prime Minister of England. Did I feel that by any means a reflection on me? . . . No; but does it not make me, and ought it not to make you, gentlemen, do all you can to reserve to other sons of other cotton-spinners the same opportunities, by the same system of laws under which this country has so long flourished, of arriving by the same honourable means at the like destination?

After this frank reference to his own social origins, Peel once more recited the basic tenets of the *Tamworth Manifesto*: the correction of proved abuses, the application of safe remedies, the abolition of patronage and sinecures; at the same time the preservation of limited constitutional monarchy and the rights of each branch of the legislature, the maintenance of the establishment, property and just privileges of the United Church of England and Ireland; and finally, a steady refusal to allow their mixed and balanced constitution to be transformed by a further succession of specious reforms into a democratic republic. Public order and commercial prosperity depended on this; this was the true interest of the middle classes and the electorate. 'That is what I apprehend by the Conservative principle and such is the ground on which we make our appeal to the country at large.' He ended by urging them to forget past differences, and join heartily with any past opponent who agreed with them that 'the Reform Bill is not to be made a platform from which a new battery is to be directed against the institutions of the country'.

Reported prominently in the columns of *The Times* next morning the speech made a sensation, more perhaps for its vigour and uncompromising style than for any explicit novelty. It was clear that the guiding lines of Peelite Conservatism had been laid down permanently by the *Tamworth Manifesto*, and that it was to an extension of the party's social basis and the organisation of the party's strength in the constituencies that Peel was now looking for the future of Conservatism. The ultra-Tories might have misgivings but the party as a whole praised the speech to the skies, as Greville said, and distributed copies of it all over the country.[1] It was an exhilarating overture for the opposition and when parliament once more addressed itself to its interrupted labours, the ministers were in a chastened frame of mind. Uncertainty about their new radical and Irish allies offered a private, the truncated session a public, reason for slowing down the pace of reform.

When the cabinet's programme was unfolded at the end of the month, it was seen that ministers were disposed neither to terminate nor essentially to modify the work of Peel's ecclesiastical commission, nor to bring forward another set of remedies for dissenting grievances. The only two major bills they did announce, however, were calculated to provide enough excitement to last for the rest of the session. One was a bill to reconstruct English municipal government; the other the Irish tithe bill which had so alarmed the king. The first, founded on a report of a commission appointed in 1833, was in a larger sense a consequence of the Reform Act. To enfranchise some of the new industrial towns without ensuring that they were adequately provided with municipal institutions, or to give the parliamentary vote to £10 householders without breaking down the close oligarchies of the older boroughs, was both administratively untidy and politically inexpedient. The Irish tithe bill, armed now with an appropriation clause, was another matter. It had been virtually forced on the old Whig cabinet by their own left wing; it was now to be forced on the country by the new Whig cabinet as a result of the circumstances in which they had returned to office. By his selection of this particular issue on which to defeat Peel, Russell had hung a Hibernian albatross round his own neck.

For the opposition, therefore, the two measures fell into different categories and demanded different tactics. For the municipal corporations reform, in fact, there was already in principle a wide body of support. The commission of enquiry had not yet presented its report when Peel left office, but it had featured in the attacks on his own legislative programme. Stanley had made it a criticism in his speech on the address that no pledge on that issue had been given by the Conservative ministry. Peel himself thought the case for municipal reform irresistible. His chief concern, however, was not

[1] *The Times*, 12 May; *Greville*, 24 May 1835; *Raikes*, II, 111.

immediately to join forces with Stanley but to secure a wide measure of agreement within his own party. It was still impossible to guess what Stanley's ultimate political ambitions really were; and the open contrast between his cordiality towards Peel and hostility towards the Duke of Wellington only created embarrassment. Indeed, it was largely for this reason that Peel had told Taylor in February to stop sending him any further reports from his niece on the inner councils of the Stanleyite party.[1] Even so, an overture from that quarter to make common policy on the municipal bill had already come in April. Sir James Graham spoke to Hardinge on the subject, evincing both Conservative sympathies and a desire to have some understanding with Peel. But he said he did not know Stanley's views though he expected that Russell would trim his sails to them, whatever they were, if they differed materially from Peel's. This sounded a more devious proposition than Graham probably intended, and Peel preferred to confer with Wellington rather than negotiate some temporary debating pact with the elusive Stanley. There was little point in discussing details until the government's plan was known but he urged the duke to read the commissioners' report so that they could discuss the problem at their next meeting. Flattered by Peel's co-operative attitude the duke replied promptly. He shared Peel's view that there had been abuse and corruption; he was anxious for an efficient magistracy and some security against grasping £10 householders. But he agreed that it should not be made a party question and declared his willingness to sacrifice personal views in order to keep a party together which would be strong enough to govern if called upon.[2] Peel himself was all for remedying practical abuses but, as he told Hardinge, they must take care that in doing so 'we do not infuse so much democracy into the constitution of this country as to make the working of a limited monarchy impracticable'.[3] His particular apprehension was that the government would place municipal government in the hands of an oligarchy of £10 householders with annual election of officers: a combination which he was disposed to think would lead to as much waste and jobbery as before.

In fact, however, the bill outlined by Russell in the Commons on

---

[1] 40303 f. 33.
[2] Wellington (24 Apr. 1835), ptly. pr. *Peel*, II, 313–14; 40310 f. 101.   [3] 40314 f. 89.

5 June provided for a municipal electorate of all permanent rate-payers, choosing their representatives for a three-year term of office. This, from a Conservative point of view, was a vastly superior arrangement; and Peel's speech which followed was one of general approval. He had studied the commissioners' report and was able to make a number of dexterous points based on their evidence against Russell's somewhat partisan presentation of the case against the old corporations. But in the main he contented himself with a promise to assist in providing the best possible system of municipal government and a plea to the government to provide ample time for consideration of details. Following the publication of the government's plan, and probably before the second reading on 15 June, Peel called a meeting of the members of his late ministry to discuss the bill.[1] The prevailing opinion among them was that the proposed franchise, fortified by the additional qualification of three years' residence and payment of rates, was preferable to the parliamentary £10 household franchise which was generally regarded as the worst for Conservative purposes. The way was open therefore for a consistent and constructive opposition in the lower house: and on this basis contact was renewed with the Stanleyites.

It was noticeable that in his speech on the second reading of the bill, giving personal approval to the main principles but reserving criticism of details, Peel referred more than once to his agreement with points previously raised by Stanley. By the time the bill entered on its committee stage (22 June–17 July) he had established in effect a working alliance with Stanley and Graham by which the two sides communicated to each other in advance their proposed amendments and gave mutual support in debate. Two of these amendments were of special importance. The first was to defeat the clause in the bill bringing to an end the institution of municipal freemen. Peel believed that this clause was primarily intended as an indirect way of destroying the parliamentary vote of a class popularly held to favour the Tories, though it had been left intact by the Reform Act. The other, moved by Peel himself, was to lay down property qualifications for borough councillors, varying accord-ing to the size of the borough. Both these and other amendments

[1] This seems implied by Peel's letter to Ellenborough of 28 July (Ellenborough Corr.) and his speech of 15 June.

133

were successfully opposed by the government and on 20 July the
bill received its third reading without further opposition. So far
all had gone well from Peel's point of view. The bill was better
than had been feared. The opposition had shown itself moderate,
statesmanlike and united. When the bill reached the upper House,
however, these agreeable reflections were rudely cut short. On
27 July the Conservative peers meeting at Apsley House agreed to
give it an unopposed second reading but to hear counsel at the bar
before going into committee. The general tone of the speakers,
even of Cumberland, was restrained. But it was evident that beneath
the surface there was considerable hostility to the measure and
more drastic amendments could be expected in the Lords than had
been put forward in the Commons. Indeed there was a feeling that it
might even be an issue on which the government could be evicted.

Peel, when sounded by Ellenborough for his views on this last
possibility, was blunt and uncompromising. Any notion of another
attempt to form a Conservative ministry he dismissed out of hand;
and he said it would be very difficult for him personally to suggest
or be party to any amendments he had not supported in the lower
House. 'The real truth', he ended pessimistically, 'is that it is impossible to prevail on the House of Lords and the House of Commons to
take the same views of many important public measures.'[1] If this
seemed a prematurely hopeless attitude to adopt, the fact was that
Peel was already angered and disheartened to see the agreement he
had established with his colleagues in the Lords collapsing like a
house of cards before the first breath of discontent from their followers. His forebodings were justified. The hearing of counsel (one
of whom was the ultra-Tory Sir Charles Wetherell) on behalf of
several threatened corporations, took the form of a general opposition to the bill, largely founded on criticism of the work of the royal
commission. Logically this pointed to a rejection of the bill; in any
case to a prolonged conflict between the two Houses. All Wellington's fine words about concessions of personal views to preserve
party unity seemed to have gone by the board; and Peel's leadership was once more in question.

The breach between Conservative policies in the two chambers
was soon a gaping void. On 31 July and 1 August Peel had meetings

[1] Ellenborough Corr. 28 July 1835; Kitson Clark, *Peel and Con. Party*, p. 269.

at his house of those peers who had served in his ministry and warned them that he could not take responsibilty for the action of the majority in the Lords. At a private dinner following the second of these he ran into Cumberland and Wetherell, hot from the House of Lords. The conversation soon swung to the great topic of the day. Cumberland spoke of honour and conscience, which was always a storm signal. Wetherell repeated his forensic arguments, to which Peel replied point by point. But all this was waste of effort. It was clear that Wellington had lost control and that the Tory peers were beginning to run riot. Peel's reply was to demonstrate his complete disassociation from them. The method he adopted was a dramatic one. On 3 August there were separate meetings of the two wings of the party. At Apsley House the peers decided to hear evidence against the actual principle of the corporation bill. A mile and a half away in Whitehall Gardens Peel announced his intention shortly to leave town and encouraged his House of Commons followers to follow his example provided they were ready to return when the bill came down from the upper House. 'I will not,' he wrote emphatically to his wife, 'be made responsible for the acts of the Lords.'[1]

For most of August, while the Tory peers under Lyndhurst's flamboyant leadership tore the government's bill to ribbons, Peel stayed at Drayton. He was not uninformed of what was passing on and behind the scene at Westminster. Fitzgerald sent long illegible and undated screeds describing in detail the proceedings of the Lords. Goulburn from time to time sent moderate and conciliatory letters, asking for advice on tactics and offering to communicate Peel's views to the party in the upper House. But Peel remained obdurate, reticent and unyielding. He flatly refused to open discussions with the Lords or even to allow Goulburn to pass his views on to them. It was trying conduct in a party leader; it was also a trying party to lead. Peel had moreover excuses of his own to offer. The session had been a long and difficult one and in the first half of it he had been under unusual mental and physical strain. Since receiving his summons from Rome the previous November he had scarcely had any appreciable respite, and his doctor, Sir Henry Halford, had repeatedly advised him to leave London and rest.

[1] Peel, *Letters*, pp. 133–4; *Greville*, 4 Aug. 1835.

Fundamentally, however, he was employing the only sanction left to him against the aristocratic mutineers of the party. Even to have appeared to condone their actions would have made nonsense of the new Conservatism he was preaching. It would also have destroyed his alliance with Stanley and Graham at a peculiarly critical moment. Already in the course of the debate on the municipal bill the hostile attitude of the Whig back-benchers had forced them to abandon their old seats on the ministerial side of the House and move across to the benches below Peel. To break the union now would be to leave Stanley betrayed and deserted, supported only by the half-dozen followers who had crossed the floor of the House with him.[1]

There was a consideration of another kind. If, as many thought and was perhaps true, the Tory peers were pursuing the dangerous ulterior objective of pulling down the government, this provided a still more compelling reason for holding aloof. Drawing-room intrigues by foolish peers, encouraged by the Duke of Cumberland's reactionary language and the petulant behaviour of the king towards his ministers, offered no foundation for policy as Peel understood it. It was true that among the peers' amendments there were some that he had supported himself; but there were others, such as the perpetuation of property rights in existing holders and a provision that a quarter of the new corporations should be composed of former aldermen sitting for life, to which he could not possibly consent. Beyond all technical details, moreover, was the fact that the attitude of the Tory peers, including their chief spokesman Lyndhurst, had been one of opposition to the whole principle of municipal reform. What was taking place was not the amendment of a bill; it was a direct challenge to the government and would be taken as such in the country at large. It was clearly the duty of the Whigs to stay in office. But they were being presented with a gratuitous justification for resigning; and Peel was not sure they would resist the temptation.

Meanwhile, slowly moving up in the rear like a second great thundercloud ready to add its lightnings to the overcharged atmosphere, was the Irish Church temporalities bill. On this there was no divergence of policy between the Conservatives in the upper and

[1] 40333 fos. 334–42; Goulburn, II/18 (Peel to Goulburn), ptly pr. *Peel*, II, 314; *Greville*, 3 July 1835; *Croker*, II, 282.

lower Houses. Yet that only made the defeat of the government more certain; and certain defeat on one major measure might well provoke the cabinet to defiance on the other. As introduced at the end of June the bill comprised a tithe settlement not radically different from that brought forward by Peel's ministry but with the addition of a set of provisions for the appropriation of a specific part of the revenues of the Irish Church. When the bill went into committee on 21 July Peel moved an instruction of which he had previously given notice, dividing the bill into two so that the section dealing with the extinction of some 860 parishes and the appropriation of their revenues could be considered as a separate measure. In a lucid and masterful speech, showing that command of detailed and complicated facts which the House of Commons found so impressive, and which impressed even his opponents, he demonstrated from the evidence of the government's own commission of enquiry that there was no surplus revenue and that the pretence of one would only arouse expectations doomed to disappointment. There were, he concluded, only two decided and intelligible courses for the government: either to reorganise the Irish Church revenues and satisfy its legitimate claims before otherwise disposing of its property, or to establish Roman Catholicism as the religion of the majority of the Irish people and leave Protestantism to its fate. What the Whigs were proposing to do, he observed, was to uphold the establishment of the Church of Ireland in theory while making its position untenable in practice. It was a great debating speech which won the wholehearted support of Stanley and Graham, and the votes of the majority of the English M.P.s of all parties in the House. With the aid of the Scotch and Irish votes the government defeated the motion by 319 to 282, but the narrow majority for the bill ensured its ultimate defeat. Passing through committee with little delay, since the opposition refused to offer amendments to the appropriation clauses, it went up to the Lords in August. In committee on 24 August the peers accepted substantially the first section of the bill but struck out the appropriation clauses by large majorities. The cabinet then abandoned the bill and acknowledged defeat by introducing a bill to waive repayment of loans already made to the Irish clergy to maintain them while the tithe question remained unsettled.

Four days later, on 28 August, the amended corporation bill came back to the Commons and with it the final crisis of the session. The political world buzzed with speculation. Would the government accept a second major defeat? Would they resign? Would either House accept a compromise? And, finally, what part would be played by Peel and the Conservative party in the Commons? Attendance on the opposition benches had thinned during August and on the 22nd Goulburn wrote to Peel to ask whether they should leave matters to be settled entirely by the government and the radicals. In his view the real issue was not the detail of particular amendments but the independence of the Lords as a branch of the legislature. This was impeccable constitutional doctrine but one which had practical political dangers. Peel in reply expressed his opinion that the ministers would never accept the peers' amendments or be allowed by their supporters to do so; and he doubted the policy of a small opposition party going into the lobbies to support the Lords. The technical right of the upper House to amend was uncontestable. What Peel feared was that the House of Commons would put forward some 'antagonist right' of its own. He still showed no shift from his earlier attitude of disapproving neutrality, however, and went off soon after to shoot with the Duke of Rutland at his lodge near Bakewell in Derbyshire. But the time for action was almost at hand. Fitzgerald warned Peel that it was not impossible that the government might try to persuade the Commons to accept the Lords' amendments and on 26 August Peel wrote an urgent note to Goulburn telling him to collect all the latest information he could and reply not later than Saturday 29th. Goulburn reported that Russell was holding a party meeting on the following Monday to consider the municipal corporations bill; that about a hundred Conservative M.P.s would be in London on that date; and that there was a general hope that Peel would be present.[1] Monday, 31 August, was the day of decision. Peel signalised his return to the political arena by appearing in town. Russell held a meeting at midday of his followers and supported by O'Connell advised them to accept a conciliatory policy.

In the afternoon the two leaders faced each other across the narrow gangway of the House. Russell made a temperate speech,

[1] 40333 fos. 336–42; Goulburn, II/18 (Peel to Goulburn, 26 Aug. [1835]); *Peel*, II, 315–17.

rejecting some of the Lords' amendments, accepting some, and offering concessions on others. It was not surrender, but it left the door of compromise as wide open as his party would tolerate. In the gap thus created Peel interposed the full weight of his authority. Not all that he had to say was easily stomached either by the men behind him or by the group of Conservative peers listening from under the gallery: and the cheers that encouraged him came principally from the other side of the House. But if, as many said, he 'threw over the Lords', it was in substance rather in form. He was at pains to answer Russell's strictures on the conduct of the peers; he defended their right to independent action; and he supported their proposals to have town clerks appointed for life, magistrates nominated by the crown, and Dissenters excluded from Church patronage. Nevertheless he kept his tone conciliatory. He said it was the duty of both sides to make sacrifices; and he welcomed the compromises which Russell proposed over the aldermen, the divisions of boroughs into wards, and the property qualifications of councillors. His speech was decisive; and with the two party chiefs bent on a settlement, the remaining differences between them were easily composed. Everything now depended on the pliability of the Lords, and by the beginning of September the solid front of the Tory peers was beginning to crack. Even the ultras realised that in the face of Peel's attitude there was no hope of forcing a change of government. Moderates like Ellenborough, Aberdeen, de Grey, Harrowby and Wellington—the exministerialist group—began to exert increasing influence; and Lyndhurst, who had led the party more as a brilliant advocate speaking to a brief than as a committed statesman, showed a graceful and professional readiness to change his course. At a meeting at Apsley House on 3 September, decisive not only for the fate of the bill but for the future of the party, the policy of conciliation triumphed. Lyndhurst, by undertaking to sponsor the Lords' amendments, preserved the upper House from humiliation and the party from open schism.[1]

The collision course which the peers had been steering throughout August had been altered at the last moment; but it had been a narrow escape and the crisis left its mark. Whether Peel could have exercised

[1] For a detailed account of the party meeting and the various manœuvres during the crisis see Kitson Clark, *Peel and Con. Party*, pp. 268–99.

any more control over the party in the Lords by remaining in London is doubtful. Yet to have attempted it would at least have been the proper and rational course. His temperament, however, had been too strong for his reason. He felt resentful against Wellington and Lyndhurst for having broken the agreement reached earlier in the session and his pride inhibited him from making any further appeals to them. He had done all that he could to influence the moderate peers of his party. When that failed, he chose to retire rather than hold empty authority as a nominal leader. His behaviour had not rendered him more popular: but the fact remained that the parade of ostentatious neutrality followed by the dramatic intervention of 31 August had been successful. Municipal reform had passed; the party had not broken up. Though there was discontent among the Conservatives, it was nothing to the discontent among the radicals who were outraged by the actions of the peers and dissatisfied at the concessions made to them by the government. The theme of House of Lords reform was a passionate topic of discussion among Liberals, Dissenters and radicals in the autumn of that year and at the end of the session O'Connell toured Scotland and the north of England in an oratorical campaign to secure an elective upper House. It was exactly this reaction which Peel had feared; and despite the temporary success of his policy in September, he still feared. Writing to Aberdeen on 19 September from Drayton he showed himself not unsympathetic to the apprehensions of the Lords and to the inconveniences of even occasionally alienating the ultra-Tory peers. But he insisted that it was right for the honour and character of the upper House that the corporation question had been settled; and he dwelt on the continuing threat to the independence of the House and the danger of a curtailment of its powers or a remodelling of its constitution under radical pressure from without.[1] The danger seemed real enough to him and to many other people. Already, at a grand dinner in his honour at Tamworth given by the local gentry and clergy together with townsfolk from Lichfield, Burton and Birmingham, he had devoted a large share of his speech to a denunciation of the radical attacks on the Lords and the drift towards 'an uncontrolled popular assembly'.[2] And the crisis was not yet over.

[1] 43061 f. 177.   [2] *The Times*, 5 Sept. 1835.

II

If Peel's behaviour during August had renewed the usual criticisms of his coldness and uncommunicativeness, there had also been an uncomfortable feeling that on this occasion he had been given some provocation. During the recess there was a move from several quarters to repair the damaged fabric of party unity. Even Wellington was conscious perhaps that over the corporations bill he had allowed himself to be carried along by his followers against his better judgement. In November he took advantage of a casual vacancy among the Irish representative peers to consult Peel as he had often done in the past. He received a prompt reply not only agreeing with what Wellington proposed but containing a friendly enquiry about his health and ending, 'ever, my dear duke, most truly yours, Robert Peel'. The older man was pleased at the success of his little olive-branch and told Arbuthnot that there would now be no embarrassment between Peel and himself whenever it became necessary for them to confer again.[1] As Christmas drew nearer Peel began to turn over in his mind the recurrent tactical problem of amendments to the address and sent Goulburn a memorandum on the subject. In January he received various communications on the need for concerted action at the start of the session. Hardinge sent on a letter from Arbuthnot which emphasised the readiness of the duke to discuss party tactics and the need to avoid even the appearance of a rift between the two leaders. Goulburn forwarded a letter he had received from Granville Somerset on the state of the party in the Commons. Two matters, according to that expert, needed particular attention. One was the growth of politically-minded agricultural associations and their effect, not so much on Lord Chandos, as on the more irresponsible 'fanatick Agriculturalists' in the party. The other was the Church question on which the rank and file would only be curbed by previous consent. Last session the party had been tolerably obedient to Peel's wishes and they would be again, wrote Granville Somerset, provided he let them know his views in advance and made it plain that he meant 'to continue actively at their Head and recognise them as his party on all main points'. He suggested therefore a preliminary meeting early in

[1] Wellington, 13 Nov. 1835; 40310 f. 117; Peel, II, 319.

February to which a full muster of the party would be summoned. Goulburn himself was eager for action. The liberal and radical successes in the first municipal elections under the new act had acted as a sting; a recent Conservative by-election victory in Northamptonshire as a tonic. An amendment to the address, even if defeated, would hearten the party provided it was supported by their whole strength, together with the Stanleyites, and was accompanied by a parallel move in the House of Lords.

In the centre of this bustle of party speculation Peel remained cool and cautious. He was unimpressed by the aimless energy of what Granville Somerset called 'agricultural radicalism'; he thought a mere Protestant demonstration equally indefinite. Nor was he enamoured of the fox-hunting approach to party tactics which many of his correspondents employed, as though his followers were a pack of hounds who could not be brought to cover without the certainty of a run, and an amendment was (as he expressed it to Croker) a kind of bag-fox brought along to guard against disappointment. If there was to be an amendment, his own preference was for one in defence of the constitution of the House of Lords. He was still uncertain whether Stanley was to be regarded as an occasional ally or a future adherent; and was inclined to think that the enigmatic third party was best left to decide its own political future. He was not sure whether defeat on an amendment, even by a mere thirty votes, might not injure rather than strengthen the institution they hoped to defend. While characteristically weighing up these pros and cons, however, he agreed that consultation was necessary and told Goulburn he would come up to town some days before the opening of parliament.[1] Early in January the party officials were instructed to proceed with the arrangements for an eve of session meeting and in the meantime he organised a kind of inner council at Drayton. Lord Harrowby and the young Gladstone were already his guests and as Wellington by a fortunate chance was staying at Lord Chesterfield's neighbouring seat at Bretby in Derbyshire, Peel rode over to persuade him to come to Drayton for a few days. The duke arrived on 20 January by which time the rest of the company was assembled, including Goulburn, Herries,

[1] 40333 fos. 346, 352, 356; Goulburn, II/18 (Peel to Goulburn, 3 Jan. 1836), ptly. pr. *Peel*, II, 318; *Croker*, II, 303.

Granville Somerset and Hardinge. In the discussion that took place Peel's reluctance to embark on a deliberate trial of strength and his continuing distrust of Stanley were both apparent. Of the two possible issues, an amendment on the Irish Church might not get the support of the majority of the Stanley party; one on the House of Lords, if defeated, might leave the upper House in a delicate position. It was agreed, therefore, not to put down an amendment in advance, even though one might be forced upon them by the terms of the king's speech, and to explain to a full party meeting (much, observed Peel, as he disapproved of them) the reasons for this abstention. If a somewhat negative decision, it left the politicians at Drayton with a happy sense of unity and sociability. The duke enjoyed himself, behaving towards his host and hostess with marked cordiality, relishing the deference with which he was treated, and hunting on one of his two days and shooting on the other before departing to Stratfield Saye. Peel's pleasure at receiving the great captain in his own home was equally evident. The last few days of holiday passed cheerfully. 'Our chief is in excellent health and spirits,' Lord Lincoln reported to Bonham on the 24th, 'and if he knocks over Whigs as cleverly and as surely as he does pheasants, woe be to them.'[1]

The Whigs, however, proved to be rather wilier birds. After all these preparations, the opposition began the session with a tactical defeat. The king's speech contained a reference to the need for a reform of the Irish municipal corporations on the same principles as in England and Wales. The Conservative peers took offence at this and the government accepted without a division an amendment to the address in the upper House, merely promising enquiry and redress. Peel, having told his party at a meeting in the morning that there would be no formal amendment, felt obliged subsequently to move a similar form of words in the Commons to avoid any appearance of divergence. The Whigs with cheerful inconsistency opposed this and carried their point with a handsome majority of forty-one, larger than they had enjoyed on any major issue in the previous session. Whether co-ordination of tactics between the opposition parties in the two houses was worth such an initial

[1] Newcastle. For the meeting at Drayton see 44777 fos. 23–8; 43061 fos. 181, 188; 40314 fos. 117, 135.

reverse was doubtful. Peel felt that among them all they bungl
the business, and his dislike of amendments and perhaps of gene
meetings also was only intensified. The one consolation was th
Stanley had delivered a strong speech against his old colleagues a
had been made angry by the sarcastic applause which he receiv
from the government benches. In fact, as the session got under wa
Stanley proved a more close and reliable ally than Peel in Janua
had been anticipating. Early on they took the same line in t
House over the minor question of the Orange Lodges, agreeing
principle to a dissolution of all political societies in Ireland thou
deprecating the particular condemnation of one. When the ma
legislative proposal of the session—Irish corporation reform—ca
before the House later in the month, the tacit alliance became
explicit one. The government bill was designed to sweep away t
seventy-one old Irish corporations, for the most part small corru
Protestant oligarchies, and replace them by a system similar to th
established in England of popularly elected corporations (based on
£10 franchise in the larger and a £5 franchise in the smaller tow
with property qualifications for councillors and aldermen. T
reform in the abstract was unexceptionable. The practical effe
however, would be to install Catholics in power in nearly eve
Irish borough. It raised therefore the constant dilemma whi
dogged all Irish politics: how to apply rational and acceptab
reforms to Irish institutions without destroying the Protesta
ascendancy.

Peel's particular fear was that a remodelled Dublin corporati
in the hands of O'Connell would at once become a platform f
Irish nationalist agitation and assume the appearance and somethi
of the character of an Irish parliament in constant session in t
Irish capital. The problem was to find a counter-remedy. On
January at his own request Graham came to see Peel and speaki
apparently both for himself and Stanley expressed a strong wish
act with him on the matter. The following day Peel held a meeti
of his Irish experts—Shaw, Fitzgerald, Goulburn, Jackson, Lefr
and Emerson Tennent. Their general conclusion was that the on
course satisfactory to the Irish Protestants would be the comple
abolition of Irish corporations and their replacement by the ordina
machinery of local government, with all general matters of admi

istration and justice in the hands of magistrates and other officials appointed by the crown. A memorandum embodying these tentative conclusions was sent by Peel to Stanley who approved the plan in principle but expressed a wish to talk over the details. At their interview the two men soon reached agreement. Though possibly taken aback by the novelty of extinguishing rather than reforming the Irish corporations, Stanley was ready to proceed on the basis of the new plan provided Wellington and Lyndhurst also consented to it. So the decision was taken, and probably the wrong one.

Peel could always be a persuasive advocate for any line of policy he chose to adopt, and his point about O'Connell and the Dublin corporation was a particularly telling one with his visitor. Both he and Stanley had a profound dislike of the great Irish agitator and of all men in politics they were the two whom O'Connell regarded as his bitterest enemies. It was unlikely therefore that they were able to view the problem with complete objectivity. It was true that O'Connell at the start of the session had proclaimed that the reformed English corporations would be 'normal schools for teaching the science of agitation' and what was rhetoric in England might become fact in Ireland. Nevertheless, to found a policy on O'Connell's oratorical excesses was in itself giving way to exaggerated fears; and the acceptance of the Irish committee's proposal was a tactical mistake from which it took several years to recover. Whatever the abstract justification, to deny to Ireland the kind of reformed municipal institutions granted to England was a national insult with which the Conservative opposition as a whole was never entirely happy and Peel in the long run found it impossible to persist. Wellington himself, though he concurred generally in the new policy, added realistically that it was improbable that the House of Commons would do so.[1]

It was unlikely that Peel disagreed with this forecast. His main object was to offer a constructive counterproposal rather than a blank negative to any proposed reform of the indefensible Irish corporations, and beyond that to chalk out a general line of policy which would keep himself, Stanley and the duke in agreement.

[1] 40310 f. 125, ptly pr. *Peel*, II, 323; Wellington (Peel to Wellington, 10, 12 Feb. 1836); 40318 f. 54 (year wrongly given as 1835).

Graham made it clear that he and Stanley regarded the Duke of Cumberland and the Orange peers as the chief obstacles to an alliance, and that for the present another dissolution or attempted change of government was out of the question. On all these matters there was complete harmony among all four men. Indeed the duke declared to Peel in a sudden outburst of epistolary exasperation that no one felt the inconveniences of Cumberland more than himself. When the Irish bill was read a second time on 29 February Peel indicated the course he proposed to follow and on the motion to go into committee the Conservatives moved an instruction to abolish Irish corporations and make such consequential arrangements as were necessary for justice and local administration. Despite the support of Stanley the amendment was heavily defeated by 307 votes to 243. This victory, when according to Hardinge in January the government only possessed a majority of twenty-five, was a cause of jubilation among the Whigs.

Some observers, Greville for example, thought that the opposition had made a mistake in erecting O'Connell and Catholicism as their constant scarecrows, and that the Conservative members themselves had been apathetic. That was not Peel's view. He told Wellington that the division had been a fair trial of strength. One or two Conservatives had scruples about extinguishing the Irish corporations; a few were absent through illness; otherwise all the party had done their duty. But the government had been able to bring up more than half the total membership of the House, mustering in all (counting the pairs) 332 votes. He was concerned less with the few Tory backsliders than with Stanley, who now feared that the large government majority would weaken the position of the Lords, and wondered whether it would not be wise for the opposition to offer a few compromises in committee. Peel, peculiarly sensitive to the dangers of departing from an agreed party line, persuaded him to abstain for the moment from any separate action and called a meeting of official peers to discuss whether anything could be done in the Commons to facilitate Conservative action in the Lords. There was also the allied question of whether to force a division on the third reading. But, as he wrote to Wellington, they were already having trouble in keeping their men together and it was essential to avoid a second and even greater defeat. On

12 March the joint meeting (seven peers[1] together with Peel, Goulburn, Hardinge, Shaw, Herries and Lefroy) decided that any change in tactics, even if suitable amendments could be devised, would only smack of panic and weaken party unity. The bill therefore was allowed to pass through committee without much opposition or alteration. On 28 March it received its third reading, against which the Conservatives in fact divided with marginally better figures than before. Even so a minority of sixty-one left little ground for satisfaction. Behind them, however, was the solid phalanx of the House of Lords. There, at the end of April, when the bill was about to go into committee, Fitzgerald carried by a large majority an instruction similar to that put forward by Peel in the lower House. The rest of the story was predictable. In June the Commons restored the original character of the bill; a conference failed to reach agreement; and the government finally abandoned the bill.

Equally predictable was the fate of the government's other main measure, another Irish Church revenue bill still embodying the crucial principle of appropriation. Employing the same tactics, and fighting on more favourable grounds, the opposition on this issue perceptibly improved their position in the lower House. Partly because the drafting of the bill made it difficult to separate the appropriation from the other sections, partly because Stanley and Graham were anxious to put forward some constructive solution of the tithe problem, the response of the joint opposition was a counter-motion by Stanley for leave to bring in a bill of his own. Though notice of the government measure came in April, the cabinet delayed the second reading until 1 June. Stanley's motion on behalf of his own bill, opposed by ministers as being in effect a hostile amendment, gave rise to a three-day debate which called up the principal speakers on both sides. Peel, speaking on the last day in answer to O'Connell, concentrated with considerable effect on the inconsistencies among government supporters. There were those, as he pointed out ironically, who said they wished to maintain a Protestant establishment while dwelling almost exclusively on Catholic grievances; those who favoured state expenditure on

[1] Lyndhurst, Aberdeen, Haddington, Fitzgerald, Ashburton, Wharncliffe, de Grey. Wellington, absent at Stratfield Saye, subsequently endorsed the decision. Wellington (Peel to Wellington, 11, 12 March 1836).

religion but only on the religion of the majority; those who supported the bill though they admitted it would not settle the tithe problem and preferred a voluntary system; those who thought that impoverishing the Irish Church would conciliate the Roman Catholics; and those who planned the disposal of a surplus without being able to demonstrate its existence. The real evil of the bill, he concluded, was not any reduction in the Church's revenues. 'The great evil of the bill is to be found in the provisions which divest the Church of its property, which change its character and destroy its independence.' It was a good attacking speech. He could afford to be destructive since the constructive contribution from the opposition had been left to Stanley; and the mixture of motives on the ministerial side of the House provided him with rich material for the close critical argument in which he excelled. The government won the division but only by thirty-nine votes; and when the battle over appropriation was renewed in committee their majority fell to twenty-six.

In July the bill went up for ritual sacrifice in the Lords. Given an unopposed second reading on the 22nd, it was then stripped of its appropriation clauses in committee and returned to the Commons at the end of the month. From something let fall by Melbourne the opposition leaders suspected that the government, on the ground that changes had been made in the financial clauses, might raise the question of privilege. Peel proposed in that case to move for leave to bring in a bill identical with that sent down from the Lords and arranged a conference with Stanley and Graham on 2 August to settle details and tactics once the government's intentions were known. The party calculations were that the minister would not have a majority of more than about two dozen, and Stanley made the long journey from Knowsley to be present.[1] In the event no exceptional measures were necessary. The Speaker ruled against Russell's contention of privilege but the government's motion to reject the amended bill was carried by twenty-nine votes. Three weeks later parliament was prorogued, Lyndhurst ending the session with a brilliant philippic against Melbourne in which he catalogued with cruel grace the government's long list of failures, frustrations, and unfulfilled pledges. It had in fact been a hard and

[1] Graham (Graham to Stanley, 26, 28, 30 July 1836).

disappointing session for the Whigs. The main legislation which they had succeeded in putting on the statute book related to the grievances of Dissenters: commutation of English tithe, registration of births, deaths and marriages, and the abolition of the compulsory Anglican marriage ceremony. To none of these had Peel raised much objection in principle, nor to the various Church bills (the first-fruits of the Ecclesiastical Commission) introduced by the government. Indeed the opposition to the latter came principally from the government's radical and dissenting supporters who saw with dismay this exhibition of practical co-operation between bishops and a reform ministry. But despite the agitation against both the Church and the House of Lords which continued to engage the energies of left-wing politicians, the government was in no mood for heroics. Neither disestablishment nor reform of the upper House were political possibilities without a greatly increased majority in the Commons; and dissolution on either issue would have been an incalculable risk.

For Peel, despite the blundering start, it had been a satisfactory session. There had been no rift between the commoners and the peers of the party; relations between himself and the duke were closer than they had been for several years; and the Stanleyites were being drawn slowly but surely into the orbit of the Conservative opposition. Despite Granville Somerset's forebodings, the agriculturalists had been kept within bounds; and on the Church question the party had enjoyed its best division of the session. The two major objectionable measures of the Whig ministers had been blocked but no real danger of their resignation had arisen to alarm the opposition leaders. Though the public scene was noisy and confused, for the moment all was tranquillity among the Conservatives. Most of August and the first part of September Peel spent at Cowes on the Isle of Wight where he had rented Norris Castle: a pleasant maritime retreat from parliamentary labours which he only left for a brief visit to shoot grouse with the Duke of Rutland on the Derbyshire moors. The excursion involved six days' travelling for the sake of five days' shooting; but he did not grudge the time, he wrote afterwards to Goulburn, 'for I know few things more agreeable than the rapid change of scene in such a country as England'. When he tired of looking out of his carriage windows he read Bailly's memoirs, one of a series of sources for the French Revolution published in eighty volumes which he had lately acquired. The descriptions of those crowded and tumultuous episodes nearly half-a-century earlier—the recall of Necker, the demand for popular assemblies, the abolition of tithe, the sentimental apotheosis of liberty, the attack on the aristocracy, the demagogues of yesterday denounced as the reactionaries of today, the complaints by ministers of the ingratitude of the public—'all these things following in rapid succession made me doubt for a moment', he told his old friend, 'whether I was not reading the *Annual Register* of 1836 instead of the "Mémoires de Bailly"'.

No revolutionary cries disturbed the calm of his room at Norris Castle where he sat writing to Goulburn that August day, nor the peaceful panorama of the Solent from the Needles to Spithead with the trees spreading their foliage over the water's edge and the racing yachts gliding past beneath his windows. Yet to Peel that autumn seemed full of reminders of France's revolutionary past. In late September he crossed the Channel with Julia. They visited Jersey, St. Malo and Nantes and then went up the Loire to pay the call on Talleyrand at Valençay which Hudson's summons from Rome had obliged them to forgo in 1834. Early in October they were in Paris, dutifully making the round of the fashionable salons. 'Sir Robert is playful and prudent,' observed one flippant English-woman, 'seems perfectly happy doing lion and lark, and only prims when Lieven calls him to the Bar.' He had two long conversations with Louis Philippe, another veteran of the Revolution, who showed him marked civility; and the Peels dined with the royal couple at Neuilly. Peel, whose knowledge of French was literary rather than colloquial, could speak English with the king. At dinner, however, he sat next to the queen, who tried to overcome the linguistic barrier by shouting in French, enunciating each word slowly and clearly as though he were deaf. 'J'es-père que vous—vous plais—ez—à—Pa—ris'—a mode of communication which drew the amused attention of the other diners and made Peel fidget.[1]

By November they were back at Drayton with the harvest over, the partridges in the stubble, the autumn house-parties beginning

---

[1] *Letters of Countess Granville*, ed. F. Leveson Gower (1894), II, 216; *Raikes*, III, 35–41; 43061 f. 195.

to assemble, and the shadow of the coming session falling across his correspondence. The experience of the previous year was a warning against premature political decisions. Yet it was important to maintain the mood of party unity and Peel started to collect a few political guests for early December. The duke was invited but though he promised to come later his health was indifferent and he said he was unlikely to walk or even ride that winter. Aberdeen was another to whom an invitation was sent, together with Goulburn, Ellenborough, and Ripon. The last was a significant inclusion. Of the four leading members of the third party, Ripon was closest to the Conservatives, followed by Graham, with Stanley in the centre and Richmond still on close terms with the Whigs. But not all those invited were able to come and there were others like Lord and Lady Jersey whose presence was merely social. The indeterminate character of the eventual gathering was reflected in the indeterminate nature of the discussions.

> Peel is as you know a *most cautious* man [Ripon reported to Graham afterwards] and never likes to commit himself to a course any [illeg.] length of time before he has to decide. But he seems to think that if Government determines to let certain vital questions be *open* questions as regarded themselves and their friends (that however I cannot bring myself to think possible) an appeal might be made to all moderate men of all parties. . . . I suspect that Peel's great difficulty is the State of Ireland, which certainly is terrific and apparently incapable of a peaceful settlement in *any* hand.[1]

Yet if Ireland was insoluble, something could perhaps be done in the larger island. The previous month Peel had unexpectedly been offered a novel platform from which to expound his political views. In mid-November he received the simultaneous news of his nomination and election as Lord Rector by the students of Glasgow University. To be invited to fill an office held by Adam Smith, Sir James Mackintosh, Brougham and Stanley was personally flattering. To have won the honour in whiggish Scotland against a Whig competitor, Sir John Campbell, was politically important. Even though acceptance meant a journey of four hundred miles in the depths of winter and on the eve of a parliamentary session, Peel did not hesitate.

[1] Graham, 26 Dec. 1836; 43061 fos. 197, 199.

I feel that I had no alternative [he wrote to Graham], that it would be inconsistent with the advice I have given to others and my own feelings as to the state of public affairs, and the necessity of unremitting exertions on this behalf of all who wish to preserve a National Church, and the Constitution of their Country, if I were to damp the ardour of the academic youth of Scotland by a cold refusal of this distinction.[1]

The inauguration took place in January and in the meantime he borrowed a copy of Stanley's rectorial speech from Graham, accepted an invitation to call at Netherby on his way north and received advice from the Tory historian Sir Archibald Alison and from Graham himself on the complexities of local politics in Glasgow and Edinburgh. His visit could hardly fail to be a political occasion; and he was invited to make public appearances at both places. But while a dinner at Edinburgh would have taken on the form of a High-Tory demonstration, in mercantile Glasgow moderate middle-class opinion was ripe for the preaching of Peelite Conservatism among former Whigs. Graham, though he felt it prudent not to attend the rectorial himself, primed Peel with information and counsel on these Scottish subtleties. 'Tho' this performance in Glasgow will be of the tight-rope description,' he reported irreverently to Stanley, 'yet our Bob may keep his legs there; in Edinburgh he must either break with the High Tories or neutralise any good effect which the amalgamation of Parties might produce at Glasgow.'[2] Of the two main functions in Glasgow for which Peel had to prepare himself, it was (so it struck Graham who saw him on his way north) the academic one which caused him most nervousness. The *genus* undergraduate was something with which he had had little contact since he had left Oxford over a quarter of a century earlier, and the red-gowned Scottish species was totally unknown to him. His rectorial address could only add one more to a series of conventional academic exercises in which to be memorable was an achievement and to be original impossible. The political banquet at Glasgow, though he did not care in general for such public festivities, was a more familiar setting; and for Scotland he had an affection ever since his first visit there in 1809. His other speech would

---

[1] Graham, 29 Nov. 1836.   [2] 12 Dec. 1836.

be about matters that had the immediate colour and impact of contemporary issues; and it was this which he determined to make his main effort.

On 11 January, in the spartan simplicity of the common hall of Glasgow University, from a long narrow platform in the centre of the room where a double line of professors precariously sat above the sea of student faces, Peel delivered his rectorial speech. Speaking for over an hour he expounded the theme of the career open in British society to talents, ambition, and effort. He instanced himself and his rival for the rectorship—one an Englishman, son of a man who was the founder of his own fortune, the recipient of honours from a Scottish university; the other a Scot, a traditional son of the manse, who had attained the highest eminence at the English Bar. But, he warned them, hardship was a condition of success. He quoted Burke: 'our antagonist is our helper'. He preached the gospel of self-control, economy, sound habits, and classical education. He pointed to the wider horizons opened by the new mechanical age. 'The steam-engine and the railroad are not merely facilitating the transport of merchandise, they are not merely shortening the duration of journeys, or administering to the supply of physical wants. They are speeding the intercourse between mind and mind, and they are creating new demands for knowledge.' He bade them finally to look back to the example of great men in the past and forward to the commands and consolation of religion. It was, as he admitted, no novel doctrine; but it was earnest, important, much of it true and all of it in character. Two crowded days followed. He dined with the Principal and the professors in Faculty Hall; he presided at a meeting of the University senate; he visited the Royal Exchange and made an impromptu speech standing on a chair. He went to Lanark, a notorious centre of radicalism and received the freedom of the burgh with not a sign of the formidable Lanark mob against which he had been warned. He received addresses from the merchants and tradesmen, the presbytery, the police board, the educational society and the Church Extension Society of Glasgow; from Edinburgh, Aberdeen, Perth, Paisley and Dunfermline, from Clackmannan and Stirlingshire, Cupar and St. Andrews, Annandale and Jedburgh. The freedom of the city of Glasgow, which the whiggish majority on the town council refused to bestow on him, was purchased in the form of a merchant burgess ticket by the subscriptions of over 2,000 working men in the city and presented to him in a silver box with an address from the 'Conservative Operatives of Glasgow'.

Meanwhile the last-minute preparations were being made for the great banquet on Friday, 13 January. As no public edifice in Glasgow could accommodate the enormous number of persons who subscribed at 25 shillings a head to be present, a temporary hall of timber and tarpaulin was built in the garden of a private house in Buchanan Street. Over forty yards square, it had twenty-four columns to support the roof and with a sublime disregard for fire hazards two enormous gasoliers were installed to give illumination. In twenty-six short winter days, despite snow, rain, frost and picketing by trades unions who objected to the use of non-union labour, the whole structure was erected and decorated in time to house and dine over 3,400 guests. There was turtle soup and venison on the platform; cold meat, chicken and lobster in the body of the hall; sandwiches and biscuits in the gallery; and port and sherry in unlimited quantities for all. For Glasgow it was an unprecedented political and social occasion; and as Peel viewed the vast assembly from his place at the centre of the circular platform, beneath a great set piece of solid rock symbolising the 'British Constitution' and surmounted by the words 'King', 'Lords', and 'Commons', it might well have seemed to him that here was the real foundation for the Conservative electorate of the future.

When the dinner, the loyal toasts, and the band-playing were over, he launched into his speech. For nearly two hours, encouraged by constant applause and cheers, he held the enthusiastic attention of his great audience. He began by mentioning the many personal ties that bound him to Scotland. Then he turned to politics. He appealed to all those who had supported the Reform Act. If they still held to the principles of that great settlement, this was the place where they ought to be. 'I see the necessity', he told them, 'of widening the foundations on which the defence of the British Constitution and religious establishments must rest. . . . With me you ought now to combine for the defence of the existing institutions of the country.' Like them he was an enemy of corruption and abuses; like them he did not want the great machine of

government to stand still. He wished to see that machine function-
ing as it should, 'animating industry, encouraging production,
rewarding toil, correcting what is irregular, purifying what is
stagnant or corrupt'. But it could only operate well if its foundations were secure and its motions free from perpetual meddling
and disturbance. Abandoning metaphor for more specific issues,
he said he was resolved to maintain the national establishments
which connected Protestantism to the state in the three kingdoms;
he meant to support the authority of the House of Lords, as an
essential element in the country's mixed form of government. He
then spent considerable time in denouncing as illusory the various
plans for a reform of the upper House which were being advocated
and in defending the peers against the charge of obstructionism.
He invited his hearers to consider the case of America, to consider
even more closely the case of revolutionary France, before casting
aside the blessings of their own constitution. He urged them to use
their electoral influence as well as express their political sentiments;
and he ended in a flourish of optimism and oratory. The twin
themes of Church Establishment (with particular emphasis on the
Church of Scotland) and House of Lords were taken up by speaker
after speaker, by peers, gentry, clergy, professors, lawyers and
politicians ranging from the Marquess of Tweeddale and the
Moderator of the General Assembly to the Principal of Glasgow
University and Mr. W. E. Gladstone, M.P., during the remainder of
the long excited evening. The dinner which started at five o'clock
ended reluctantly at half-past one in the morning by which time
only the nineteenth toast had been reached of the thirty-seven
heroically listed in the programme.[1]

All that Peel said, he had said before. He was not a philosopher
expounding novel truths but a politician propagating a cause. He
said what they expected or what they wanted to hear. Yet it was
not only what he said but how he said it which made the effect.
Gladstone thought Peel's speech 'explicit and bold; it was a very
great effort'. Some of the more ordinary and more representative
members of the audience thought so too. One of them, Thomas

[1] For a full account of the Glasgow visit see *Description of the Banquet in Honour of
Sir Robert Peel etc.* by James Cleland (Glasgow n.d.). See also Graham, 29 Nov.
1836–15 Jan. 1837; *Peel*, II, 327–35; *Graham*, I, 245–52.

M'Cosh, a precise Scots lawyer from Ayr, wrote his impressions of the evening to his brother four days later.

> Sir Robert fully came up to the high opinion I had formed of him. His appearance certainly was not very marked or uncommon, and until he commenced to speak I could not have said that there was anything extraordinary about him. He is certainly handsome and good-looking and he has an open honest countenance but we often see all this in ordinary characters. But when he commenced to speak and to explain himself he was overpowering. I never heard a more impressive person, nor one who seemed himself to be more convinced of the truth and honesty of what he was delivering. No one who heard him, if his mind was allowed to have fair play, could fail to say he was an honest man—and his arguments were equally conclusive that he was a sound politician. What a sad contrast betwixt his oration and those that we hear of being delivered at similar meetings of the other party. They delight to vilify and blacken their opponents applying to them all the low and dirty epithets they can think of whilst Sir Robert treated his opponents all as gentlemen.[1]

The spread of Conservative feeling owed not a little to this persuasion that its chief spokesman was above all an honest man.

Peel himself was in no doubt of the enormous success of the meeting and indeed of his whole trip, even though (as he admitted afterwards to Graham) some allowance had to be made for his own plebeian and industrial origin and his explicit abandonment of High Toryism. Leaving Glasgow at night immediately after the banquet he arrived at Netherby still flushed with pleasure and excitement—'more elated and communicative', Graham told Stanley, 'than I have ever seen him'. What Graham further noted was Peel's hopefulness about the future and his evident desire to win the alliance of the Stanleyites. He asked about Stanley's movements and pressed Graham to call at Drayton on his way to London for the start of the session. Though he did not mention office, he was optimistic about the outcome of a general election while doubting whether Melbourne had the power to dissolve. Graham cautiously declined the invitation to Drayton but he agreed to be in London on the 28th for the opening of what promised to be an even more

---

[1] I owe permission to quote from this unpublished letter to the kindness of Miss Mary Mauchline of Burnside, Glasgow.

critical session than the previous one.[1] After a night's rest Peel resumed his journey south to receive the plaudits of his friends and prepare tactics against his opponents.

III

The new session began quietly. There was a party meeting on 30 January at Peel's house but the mild speech from the throne provoked no amendment to the official address and the opposition was content to let the government take the initiative. With three Irish measures—corporations, tithe and poor law—on the legislative programme the session would clearly not lack activity or acrimony. On two out of the three bills all argument had long been worn to shreds and Peel's prime interest was to keep together his unicorn team of peers, commoners and Stanleyites. The auguries were favourable. He was in close touch with Wellington and the start of the session was marked by a private dinner at Whitehall Gardens at which for the first time Stanley met the duke.[2] When the new Irish corporations bill, showing little change on that of the previous year, was introduced later in February the opposition played the same opening gambit as before. Lord Francis Egerton moved an instruction to committee for the total abolition of the corporations which was defeated after three days of debate by eighty votes. For the opposition this was a worse result than in 1836 and Peel was both angry and depressed. Part of the disaster was due to the idleness and apathy of his own supporters, some being absent without excuse and others leaving London without making a pair. Yet the division emphasised the lesson of the previous session. The Irish corporations bill was not good ground on which to fight and the opposition was unlikely ever to turn out in full strength against it. Some of Peel's followers urged him to take up instead the question of the Irish Church; but this seemed to him a shortsighted policy. A constructive proposal from the Conservative benches meant concessions. Concessions could be exploited by the government without necessarily leading to a settlement. In any case the Whigs were in control of the parliamentary programme. The wiser course was a change of tactics.

[1] Graham (Graham to Stanley, 15 Jan. 1837).
[2] *Gladstone*, I, 102; *Croker*, II, 313.

Stanley and Graham were reluctant to hold up much longer a reform of the indefensible Irish corporations; they did not wish to drive the cabinet to resignation; and they were anxious to avoid another direct collision between the two Houses when the bill went up to the Lords. Peel's thoughts were travelling along the same road. He was impressed by the feeling in Ireland, which affected even the Irish Conservative M.P.s, that it was invidious to deny to one part of the United Kingdom what had been granted to the other two; and he did not want to tie his hands on a question which if he took office might demand immediate solution. The complications lay with the peers. Lyndhurst was absent in Paris and the Duke of Wellington was suffering from rheumatism which sent him off periodically to Bath. Correspondence in such circumstances was no substitute for consultation.

Meanwhile, early in March the government had introduced a bill to settle the problem of church rates in England. Its basis was an ingenious plan whereby the revenues from episcopal and cathedral property under new administration were to yield a surplus which would replace the old church rate. Once again the Whigs were putting forward a financial solution based on future expectation; and Peel made play both with this and with the counter-argument that any increase in church revenues would be better devoted to the improvement of small livings. The Anglican Whigs were not happy at the measure and in mid-March the government resolutions were only carried by twenty-three votes. For the opposition the un-popularity of the church rates bill, the opposition of the bishops, and the Anglican agitation in the country, all strengthened the case for dropping the Irish corporations bill and concentrating on the more favourable Church issue. Nevertheless Wellington was anxious that the peers should be supported on the corporations question by preliminary opposition in the House of Commons. Peel himself felt that consistency and policy required them to divide on the third reading of the bill. Stanley was not averse to this provided the opposition conducted the debate in such a way as to leave the door open to compromise in the upper House. The line he favoured was one of postponing the Irish municipal bill until more was known of the government's other two Irish measures. There was much in this suggestion which Peel found attractive. The corporations bill could be turned into a lever for extracting concessions on the tithe and poor law. In turn a tithe bill without the appropriation clause and a poor law establishing a reliable system of rating for franchise purposes would go far towards making a reform of the Irish municipal corporations—the grant, as Peel put it, of political privilege capable of bad use—more acceptable because more safe. In any case postponement rather than rejection would outmanœuvre the ministry and deprive them of an excuse to retire if defeated. If in the end the government used the pretext of the corporation bill to resign, it was all the more necessary in Peel's view to make known in advance any concessions which a Conservative government would be ready to make when in office.

Intellectually, therefore, he was willing to accept Stanley's suggestion. Politically he was placed in a dilemma. If he did not accept Stanley's proposal, he and Graham would probably break away on a line of their own. If he did accept it, he would have to persuade his colleagues, especially those in the Lords, to accept it also. The duke, anxious to do his duty, was not sure where his duty lay. Ill and out of humour he did not take kindly to what he thought were mere political manœuvres. He did not like the corporations bill as it stood; he could not see his way clear in the upper House; and there was the question of his absent and volatile lieutenant. Early in April he received a letter from Lyndhurst which not only argued for a rejection of the bill on the second reading but took for granted that this was the understanding reached with the House of Commons party earlier in the session. Peel, however, patiently maintained his ground. At a meeting at Lord Aberdeen's of all the available members of his 1834–35 cabinet, held the day before the third reading in the House of Commons, agreement was finally reached on the change of tactics. Lyndhurst was still not back from Paris but Wellington, though failing through deafness to appreciate the extent to which he was committing himself, agreed to dissuade his colleagues from any precipitate action in the Lords. When the debate came on in the House of Commons on 10/11 April Peel was able therefore to support Stanley's plea for delay until the government's intentions on the Irish Church were known. In the face of this clear indication of willingness to compromise the government's majority dropped to fifty-five. In the next two weeks the reluctant and distrustful duke was slowly brought into the line of battle. Lyndhurst arrived back from Paris on 20 April and three days later the inner group of Conservative peers met Peel and agreed on the new party line. This was explained to a larger meeting of peers at Apsley House on 24 April; and on 5 May Wellington secured the postponement of the committee stage of the bill for a month until more was known of the government's bills for tithe and poor law.[1]

Only one incident disturbed the new harmony. This was later in May when Richmond wrote to Stanley, and Melbourne spoke to Wharncliffe, in terms which suggested that the cabinet might abandon the appropriation clause in return for concessions on the corporations bill and would be prepared to negotiate with Stanley to that end. This, to a cynical mind, suggested an attempt not only to achieve a compromise but also to divide the opposition. Whether intended or not it might have had this practical result. But Stanley made it clear that he would do nothing without Peel and Wellington, and sent copies of his correspondence to Peel. There was a feeling among them all that no confidential negotiations should be undertaken with the government on such an issue; and the attempt to detach the Stanleyites—if it was an attempt—failed. For a moment, however, Peel had been placed in an embarrassing position. Stanley had sent him Richmond's correspondence with a request to keep it confidential. Before he could obtain permission to show it to Wellington, he received a curt note from the duke who had heard the news from another source, protesting against any private communications with the government.

This, however, was merely a ripple on the surface and in the event the tactics of conditional postponement proved more effective than any obstructionism could have done. The Irish tithe bill, with a 10 per cent tax on ecclesiastical revenues substituted for an educational appropriation, only received its second reading in the Commons on 9 June. The Irish poor law bill, supported by Peel and Stanley but increasingly attacked by O'Connell and the Irish brigade, floundered hopelessly in committee. In the Lords therefore

---

[1] The voluminous correspondence on the Irish Corporations can be traced in 40316 fos. 201, 206 (Lyndhurst); 40310 fos. 162–211 (Wellington); 40318 fos. 56–89 (Graham); Wellington (Peel–Wellington, May–June 1837); Ellenborough (Apr.–June 1837); Graham (Mar.–May 1837); *Peel*, II, 335–47.

Lyndhurst on 9 June successfully moved a further month's post-ponement of the corporations bill. By this time the whole legislative programme of the government was beginning to disintegrate. No major bill had passed or seemed likely to pass; the Irish nationalists were critical; some of the English radicals led by Roebuck were in open revolt against the cabinet's passivity; rumours of resignation or dissolution abounded. With parliamentary politics in this state of deadlock the cabinet was rescued from its hopeless situation by the death of an old man at Windsor. On 21 May Wellington had warned Peel that William IV was seriously ill and at the end of the month Sir Henry Halford, the royal physician, told him that the king's constitution was finally breaking up. On 9 June came the first bulletin and though William lived to see the sun set on one more anniversary of Waterloo, the end came early on the morning of 20 June. Two days later a message from his young successor announced that all controversial legislation would be abandoned and parliament dissolved as soon as was practicable. Less than a month later the last session of William IV's last parliament came to an end.

What the character of the new political era would be, with another parliament and another sovereign, could only be a matter of speculation. In retrospect the session of 1837 had brought Peel marginal and hard-fought gains. Almost from the start he had acted incessantly as mediator and arbiter of the opposition, especially in the question of the Irish corporations. He had put Wellington's views to Stanley and Graham; Stanley's views to Wellington and Lyndhurst; the commoners' views to the peers and the peers' views to the commoners. His chief concern had been to prevent separate action by Stanley in the lower House and separate action by Wellington in the upper. In this he had succeeded; and in the process had further eroded the position of the Whigs. Yet though unity of action had been maintained, it had only been by constant strain and effort. There was no reason to suppose that the future would be any less difficult. Between Stanley and Wellington there was still a sediment of the old hostility. The wayward Lyndhurst, even while the king lay dying, had annoyed his leaders and offended the moderates by delivering a violent speech on the second postpone-ment of the Irish corporations bill which went far beyond what had been agreed at a meeting at Peel's house only two days earlier. The independence of the Lords which Peel defended in public, and the co-operation between the Conservative parties in each House which he laboured to achieve in private, were not easily reconcilable. Nevertheless the double objective had been realised and the opposition in both Houses had been outwardly more united and more organised than ever before. Though the peers were restive, at least they had been kept in leash; and the last delicate stage had been reached in Peel's long courtship of the Stanley group. The 1837 session had seen in fact a silent transformation in their relationship with the Conservative Party. From political allies they became political associates; and personal conference had increasingly replaced formal correspondence. On 26 April, for example, Stanley and Graham had both been present with Peel at a meeting of leading Conservative peers at Lyndhurst's house to discuss the Irish corporations. They were present at a similar meeting at Peel's house four days later and again at Aberdeen's house on 2 May. In June they had been members of an unofficial opposition committee to prepare amendments to the bill in the House of Lords.[1] The Derby Dilly, with little more now than its 'six insides', had found stabling at last. These achievements, however, had only been made possible by the exercise of all the patience and persuasion which Peel possessed. When he went over his session's accumulation of correspondence, what impressed him most was not the success that had been secured but the difficulties that had been surmounted. 'Few people', he wrote in July in a memorandum put in with his Irish municipal papers, 'can judge of the difficulty there has frequently been of maintaining harmony between the various branches of the Conservative party—the great majority in the House of Lords and the minority in the House of Commons consisting of very different elements that had been in open conflict within a recent period.'[2]

[1] Ellenborough (under dates cited).   [2] *Peel*, II, 338.

5

SQUIRE OF DRAYTON

Although the Peel family was never again to exhibit the vast concentration of wealth present between 1815 and 1830, Peel himself
had been left a rich man. His father's fortune had continued to
increase even after he retired from active commercial life. By the
time of his death his personal and real estate, despite the large sums
already settled on his children, amounted to nearly £1½ million.
Even in the post-war agricultural depression the Tamworth estate
was probably worth nearly £500,000, and he possessed over
£890,000 in funds. Of this great inheritance about £450,000 was
bequeathed to his five younger sons and three daughters, leaving his
eldest son with the settled Tamworth estate and four-ninths of the
residuary estate, amounting to about £154,000 net, the remaining
five-ninths going to the other sons. Peel already had the income
from the trust fund of £100,000 set up at the time of his marriage,
together with £230,000 in 3½ per cent annuities settled on him for
life. Together these yielded an income of some £11,000 per
annum, to which the further inheritance of £154,000 might be
expected to add another £5,000, making a total income from
funded property of about £16,000. The settled estate comprised
Drayton Manor and the lordship of Drayton Basset and Fazeley,
land and houses in Tamworth, Drayton and neighbouring parishes,
and an outlying estate of about 1,000 acres at Oswaldtwistle in
Lancashire. The main estate covered about 9,000 acres, a third of it
in Warwickshire and the rest in Staffordshire. With an annual
rent-roll of some £25,000, Peel after 1830 was in possession of a
gross income from all sources of over £40,000 per annum.[1] This,

[1] The wills of the 1st (8 June 1830) and 2nd (17 Aug. 1850) baronets in Somerset
House, Principal Probate Registry, provide much information. Details of funded

though only half the amount which Lord Durham once memorably defined as the sort of income a man could jog along on, was by most contemporary standards undeniable affluence. In the previous decade the interest on trust and annuity stocks settled on him by his father, his salary of £6,000 per annum as secretary of state, and a small rental from his personal landed property, had amounted annually to about £20,000. But his marriage, his new house in Whitehall Gardens, and his buying of pictures had involved him in heavy outlays and he was overspending his income up to the time of his father's death. The inheritance which came to him in 1830 was therefore peculiarly welcome. It lifted him out of his indebtedness, absorbed the loss of his official salary, and provided him with a substantial surplus on which to live.

As squire of Drayton and leader of a party, he found his expenses inevitably rising with his enhanced status. At Whitehall Gardens alone his establishment in 1835 included, in addition to female staff, a male cook, a butler, four menservants, three stablemen and two other helpers.[1] Though some of these moved between London and Staffordshire, the house at Drayton needed many more. Eleven years later he was compounding for assessed taxes on fourteen male servants, two occasional servants, five four-wheeled and two two-wheeled carriages, twelve riding horses and eight dogs.[2] This was only part of a general establishment headed by the house-steward, Mr. Grundy, and the estate-steward, Thomas Hill. The latter had served his father and continued to serve him until he retired on a pension in 1845 when he was succeeded by John Matthews. Accustomed since boyhood to a luxurious standard of existence, Peel liked to live well and generously. He enjoyed good food, fashionable

property in 1830 and 1850, and the rentroll for 1850, are in Goulburn. Acreage of the settled estate in J. Bateman, *Great Landowners of Great Britain and Ireland* (1883). Peel made only a small addition (255 acres) to the entailed estate. The only significant change between 1850 and 1873 (the date of the parliamentary return on which Bateman's figures are based) was that the Oswaldtwistle estate which was about 1,000 acres at Peel's death, had diminished to 400 acres. Peel's rentroll in 1850 from Drayton, Tamworth, Fazeley, Bonehill and Oswaldtwistle was £25,762. His son (Sir R. Peel 3rd bt) had a rentroll in 1873 of £24,532. The decrease is easily accounted for by the reduction in the property at Oswaldtwistle. Greville in 1831, on the authority of Grant, said that the Peel rentroll was £22,000 (Greville, 7 March 1831).

[1] 40607 f. 223.   [2] 40609 f. 111.

clothes, expensive furnishings. His town house saw a constant succession of dinner parties throughout the parliamentary session, and Drayton was rarely without guests during the autumn and early winter whenever Peel was in residence. His entertaining was famous for its quality and style. At the formal dinners at Whitehall Gardens the arriving guest would encounter four or five powdered and liveried footmen in the hall who severally relieved him of his outer garments. He would then proceed upstairs with the flunkeys stationed on each landing calling out his name from one to the other until he arrived in the drawing-room to be greeted by his host. When they went in to dine, he would probably find himself eating off plate in company with thirty other guests attended by the same intimidating platoon of servants in their orange and purple livery.[1] The meal itself equalled the setting. 'I never saw a more splendid and sumptuous repast in my life,' wrote Lord Talbot after dining with Peel in June 1833. 'Beautiful and excellent in all its parts.'[2] Even the cynical and irreverent Disraeli was impressed by the food when he dined at Peel's house in February 1839. He arrived late to find 'some twenty-five gentlemen grubbing in solemn silence'. But, as he told his sister appreciatively, 'the dinner was curiously sumptuous—"every delicacy of the season"; and the second course of dried salmon, olives, caviare, woodcock-pie, foie gras, and every combination of cured herring, etc., was really remarkable'.[3]

If Peel entertained handsomely, he also gave freely. Most members of parliament were expected as part of their constituency duties to subscribe for local and charitable purposes. As a wealthy man with property in three counties, Peel was more than ordinarily exposed to appeals to his purse. Where his personal inclinations were revealed was perhaps in the frequency of his donations for religious and educational objects. From a surviving memorandum-book a few characteristic examples may be given: (1839) £10 for Drayton Sunday School, £500 for the Lichfield Diocesan Church Building Society, £50 and an annual subscription of five guineas for the Lichfield Diocesan Education Society, £500 to the Tamworth

---

[1] See, for example, the description by Edward Barton in 1846 (*New Letters of Edward Fitzgerald*, ed. F. R. Barton (1923), pp. 108–15.
[2] *Mr Gregory's Letter-Box*, ed. Lady Gregory (1898), p. 332.
[3] *Lord Beaconsfield's Correspondence with His Sister* (1886), p. 121.

Corporation for widening the Lady Bridge; (1840) £20 to the Tamworth soup fund, £31 to the Staffordshire Bible Society, £7 to the Lichfield Agricultural Society; (1841) £50 to maintain the service at the church at Oswaldtwistle, £5 to the Tamworth coal committee, £50 for a new church at Nuneaton, £100 for a new church and parsonage at Sutton Coldfield, £50 for the relief of the poor at Tamworth, Fazeley, and Bonehill; (1844) £140 for the repair of the Town Hall at Tamworth, half a crown for every man employed on his farms, gardens and drainage operations for a Christmas dinner; (1846) £52 to pay a debt of the Tamworth National School; (1847) £20 to Tamworth Bible Society; (1848) £50 to repair the church at Oswaldtwistle.[1]

Without being spendthrift, Peel clearly thought that wealth was to be used rather than hoarded. It would appear from his Bank of England account books between 1830 and 1836 that he was with-drawing on average over £30,000 a year; and as he also kept an account locally at Tamworth it is probable that his total annual expenditure was well in excess of this. During his decade in opposi-tion from 1831 to 1841 there was no sign that he was saving money. Though his buying of paintings fell off, he was steadily enlarging his landed property. Even before his father's death he had become a Staffordshire landowner by the purchase in 1827 of Lord George Cavendish's estate at Tamhorn. For this he paid £32,500—'as cheap a purchase as ever was made', wrote his neighbour General Dyott who had advised him to make it.[2] Apart from a farm on the Isle of Thanet bought early in his career, possibly as a parliamentary qualification, his acquisitions were almost entirely in Staffordshire, except for an estate of some 150 acres at Sutton Coldfield in War-wickshire. As early as 1837 he was able to declare from the election hustings at Tamworth that

all my own interests are identified with agricultural prosperity. It is true that I am under the deepest obligation to commerce and manufactures; and I am proud to acknowledge them; but all my present pecuniary and personal interests are centred in the prosperity of agriculture.[3]

[1] Memorandum Book in Goulburn.
[2] *Dyott*, II, 10.
[3] 'Speech from the Hustings, 24 July 1837' (Tamworth Pub. Lib.).

Five years later he extended these interests still further by paying nearly £5,000 for the manor of Hampton-in-Arden in Warwickshire, designed perhaps for his second son Frederick to whom he bequeathed it in his will drawn up the same year. After that his activities slackened. He told his brother William in 1845 that he had already bought more land than he proposed to leave to his eldest son and was not anxious to increase his estate except in special circumstances. Such a case did occur in 1845, however, when a farmhouse with some 250 acres of land within the manor of Drayton and almost surrounded by the Peel estate came on the market. He bought it for over £18,000 and to raise the money sold stock to the same amount which was not replaced until the following year. In his later years his investments, probably with a view to settlements on his other children, were mainly in securities. By 1850 he had £50,000 in 3½ per cent stock besides the trustee fund and annuity stock received from his father. At the end of his life his private fortune, apart from the entailed estate and the two large trust investments, totalled about £120,000, more than half of it in land, exclusive of such additional items as the house in Whitehall Gardens (valued at £20,000), his notable collection of paintings, his books, furniture and farm stock. He had spent or given away more than he had received and though still a wealthy man, was less wealthy in 1850 than he had been in 1830. On the other hand he had become a more considerable landowner than his father and it is clear that the decline in his funded property was at least partly accounted for by his real estate purchases. Though his political enemies sometimes alleged that he had increasingly disengaged himself from the landed interest, he had in fact committed himself more deeply to it. 'So far from my brother having increased his Property to the amount stated in the *Standard*,' wrote Colonel Jonathan Peel to Goulburn in October 1850, with reference to one of these journalistic insinuations, 'I should think he had decreased his personal property by at least the value of the Land he purchased.'[1] The available evidence more than confirms this.

One expensive personal luxury Peel did allow himself. This was the building of new Drayton Manor. Certainly his father's old house was too small and too plain to warrant retention or justify extension.

[1] Goulburn.

Yet the zeal and money which Peel devoted to his new house derived as much from his aesthetic interests as patron of the arts as from his social needs as landowner and politician. The combination of Peel money and taste, Robert Smirke the fashionable architect of the Tory aristocracy, and William Gilpin, the great landscape gardener then nearing the last decade of his long life, promised a spectacular achievement. Plans for the new house were drawn up as early as the summer of 1830 and all through 1831 there were regular conferences between Peel and his two experts. Progress in the troubled winter of 1831–32 was slow. It was not until the summer of 1832 that the body of the house was being roofed, though the new gardens had by that time already been laid out. Old Drayton Park had not been a naturally picturesque site but observers agreed that every art and artifice had been employed to embellish the surroundings. The old manor was left standing until the last; and from the windows of his cramped and condemned house Peel could watch in the intervals between parliamentary sittings the tardy progress of his great new building. At the beginning of 1835 Smirke announced that it would be ready in the autumn and in the spring estimates (one of £1,700 and another of £2,700) were being obtained for the furnishings of the principal apartments.[1] In February books, paintings and furniture were taken out of the old house which was then demolished.[2] With painting and papering going on inside and the outside stonework still to be pointed the new house was still uninhabitable and for a time the Peels were without a country residence. On his visit to Drayton that summer Peel occupied quarters in his steward's house. By December, however, even though the house was still unfinished and the heating apparatus not working properly, Peel was at last able to entertain guests under his own roof. On 3 December old General Dyott was present at the first formal dinner-party in the new house—'which certainly is a splendid mansion: perhaps not a more magnificent room in the kingdom than the library'. But. he confided to his diary, 'I cannot admire the *tout ensemble*: the two lengthened galleries on entrance are not in harmony with a country gentleman's country residence'.[3]

---

[1] 40607 fos. 187, 190, 210.
[2] Peel MSS. (G. Fawkes to Lady Peel, 14 Feb. 1835).
[3] *Dyott*, II, 217.

During the next twelve months the great work slowly came to a conclusion, six years after its commencement. In the autumn of 1836 Peel's collection of political portraits was being transferred from Whitehall Gardens to the gallery at Drayton and the whole house was repainted while the Peels took refuge in the Isle of Wight, the Channel Islands and France.

Peel Fold at Oswaldtwistle, the old house of the Peel family, was a simple yeoman's farmhouse; old Drayton Hall, built by his father, a plain unimaginative country mansion; new Drayton Hall, a great Victorian pile. Peel had set out to construct for himself a house which should combine the domesticated elegance of the late Elizabethan or Jacobean manor with the comfort, opulence and modernity of contemporary taste. With no restrictions of space and almost none of time or money, the result was by later aesthetic standards a florid and ambitious failure. Built in the reign of William IV, it was one of the first great examples of the disintegration of taste more commonly associated with the reign of his successor. It had everything except style; all the separate excellencies without unity of execution. Cupolas, balustrades, towers, gables, mullioned windows, an Italian campanile, marble and mahogany, stained glass and parquet floors, failed to conceal the essential ponderousness of the building while successfully obliterating all sense of architectural tradition.[1] General Dyott's verdict was the instinctive comment of a plain man but it went to the heart of the matter: the failure was in the whole, not the parts. It was a fault, however, not of a single patron or architect but of the age. Drayton Hall was conspicuous because it was one of the early examples of Victorian architectural eclecticism on a grand scale; but it was to be followed by countless others in the course of the century. What struck the first visitors to the house, however, was its opulence and above all its comfort. They were perhaps the criteria which gave the nineteenth century its characteristic art and architecture. Lord Talbot, who inspected the new hall when it was half-finished in October 1833, wrote enthusiastically to his old friend Gregory, 'upon my word, a very handsome house with every conveniency and even magnificence'. Haydon the painter, who stayed at Drayton in 1838, recorded in

[1] Cf. the comments of J. M. Crook in his art. 'Sir Robert Peel: Patron of the Arts' (*History Today*, XVI, no. 1, pp. 8–10).

his diary that 'the House is splendidly comfortable & a noble consequence of Integrity and Trade'. And Victoria, after her visit with
Albert in 1843, said to Aberdeen afterwards, 'Well, what you told
me is quite true. Drayton is certainly the most comfortable House
I ever saw.'[1] To a generation accustomed even among the rich to
draughts, discomforts, smells and general inconvenience in all its
old houses, the provision of efficient plumbing, mechanical heating,
and furniture designed for physical comfort, was something to be
given a higher valuation than that commonly allowed by a posterity
able to take such amenities for granted.

Whatever its qualities, it was Peel's second and favourite home for
the rest of his life; and despite its size and ornateness, it had something of the atmosphere of a squire's residence which even the
lengthened galleries could not destroy. With its dogs and horses, its
home farm, estate office, dairy and stables, Drayton Manor was
essentially a country mansion and the heart of a substantial landed
property; and both Peel and his wife had simple tastes which they
were still able to indulge in their great Staffordshire home. Charles
Adderley, who became Conservative M.P. for North Staffordshire
in 1841, used to relate how he was sitting with Peel after breakfast
at Drayton one beautiful summer morning when his host asked
whether he would like to see the partridges. Taking some corn from
a basket in the corner of the room, Peel went to the open french
windows, held out his hand and began to call. After a minute or
two a partridge appeared; then one or two more; and in a short
time a whole covey was feeding inside the room.[2] When he was
detained in London during the spring and summer months Drayton
was never far from Peel's mind. Julia would send him down violets,
strawberries and new potatoes and from the great library in Whitehall Gardens overlooking the busy Thames he could write, as he did
one day in September 1843, 'My heart is far away basking with you
in the bright sun on the terrace or dawdling about on your walk'.[3]
Of all the houses in which they had lived together, it was the one
Peel and his wife loved most.

[1] *Mr Gregory's Letter-Box*, p. 333; *Haydon*, IV, 462; Peel MSS. (Peel to Lady
Peel, n.d. [1843]).
[2] Mitchell Collection, IV, 93 (Tamworth Pub. Lib.).
[3] Peel, *Letters*, pp. 230, 249, 266.

Outside politics, paintings and books, in fact, Peel was by inclination more of a countryman than a townsman. Social visits, formal dinners, public occasions he learned to tolerate though never to enjoy. For club life he had little time and less interest though he made dutiful appearances from time to time in the Carlton. When his eldest daughter, in her mother's absence, had to be chaperoned during the London season, Peel undertook the duty of escort in the spirit of a necessary but penitential exercise. 'Julia has had very nice partners at her two balls,' he wrote to his wife in July 1839, 'and offers for every dance if I could have stayed, but I do get so tremendously bored after a certain time.'[1] Life in Staffordshire on the other hand was a pleasure beyond the mere relaxation in the country from political affairs. He had told his neighbours on his father's death how much he looked forward to settling down as a country gentleman and despite the demands and restraints of his political career, he took an unobtrusive part in the life of his county. The local gentry and their ladies were constantly invited to his house; he attended the Lichfield Races and acted on occasion as steward of the course; he applied his mind to the deliberations of turnpike trustees; he facilitated the introduction of the new poor law by giving a great dinner in January 1836 to neighbouring landowners and members of Tamworth Corporation at which one of the Commissioners explained the working of the act; he became president of the new farmers' club started at Tamworth in 1843; and he was vice-president of the Lichfield Agricultural Show in the same year. His national position made it necessary for him to move discreetly in local politics but from 1835 onwards he took an active share in promoting and supporting Conservative candidates in the county. At the 1837 election, for example, he breakfasted a hundred voters at Drayton before leading them off in a cavalcade to attend the nominations at Lichfield.[2]

With his parliamentary constituency of Tamworth he had through his family and property a special connection. The Drayton estate covered a large block of business and residential property in the borough, including ten inns and the Peel Arms Hotel, as well as

[1] ibid., p. 166.
[2] Dyott, II, has many references to Peel's activities, hospitality and small acts of personal kindness to friends and neighbours.

grazing and orchard land on the outskirts; and his father had taken both a paternal and proprietorial interest in the town. He had subscribed to the repair of municipal buildings, supported the local branch of the British and Foreign Bible Society founded in 1811, established a savings bank, and in 1820 founded a free school for poor boys who received annually a suit of clothes as well as their schooling. On his death he left the school an endowment of £6,000 and appointed his two elder sons and his son-in-law, the Rev. William Cockburn, as trustees. His heir carried on the tradition by erecting a new building for the school which he opened in person in January 1838. When this in turn proved inadequate, he had a larger school constructed in 1850. He also founded the first public library and reading-room in Tamworth and delivered the inaugural address there in 1841. He had succeeded his father as High Steward of Tamworth in 1830 and was the last person to hold this traditional dignity which became extinct with the passing of the Municipal Corporations Act in 1835. Three years later it was proposed to resurrect the office and Peel was invited to take it again. He declined on the grounds that the Act had placed the government of the borough in the hands of the mayor and corporation, and that it would not be proper to revive the High Stewardship without the formal consent of the crown customary before 1835. This in the existing circumstances of national politics it might not have been very prudent to request.[1] But with or without this ceremonial status, Peel remained the most powerful and influential figure in the borough. Though to the ordinary townspeople he seemed an aloof and awe-inspiring figure and his measured periods more suited to the House of Commons than to the tavern dinner or the market-place hustings, they were nevertheless proud of his national reputation. For Peel in turn the connection with the borough, like his experiences as landlord and Staffordshire magnate, was not without value for his work at Westminster. As squire of Drayton and member for Tamworth he had his own roots in English provincial life.

[1] For Peel's connection with Tamworth see esp. H. Wood, *Borough by Prescription: History of the Borough of Tamworth* (Tamworth, 1958), pp. 64–7; Mitchell Collection; *Staffordshire Advertiser*, 6 Jan. 1838.

II

By the autumn of 1837 Peel was into his fiftieth year. Sedentary employment and good living had left their mark and the long determined face painted by Lawrence in 1825 had grown noticeably broader and more fleshy. But his red hair, though duller, was still luxuriant. As he grew older he tended to wear it in long waves each side of his head and down to his neckcloth behind, a style which increased the florid appearance of his face when seen from the front. Only the profile still showed the lines of the curving nose and firm chin. His general health had remained excellent. He still suffered from an occasional suffusion of the eyes; and an ill-advised shooting experiment with a new type of cartridge in the 1820s had damaged his left ear and left a continual buzzing sound which tended to increase painfully whenever he was tired and overworked. Otherwise his constitution was unimpaired and despite his height and growing weight, his legs could still carry him through a day's shooting. Even military friends like Hardinge were full of admiration for a physique which after eight months confinement in London could enable him to tackle the roughest of moorland ground. His first serious indisposition, an attack of sciatica, came in 1837 towards the end of the parliamentary session. He had to remain in his room for several days, and though he attended the debate on the address to the queen at the death of William IV, he used a crutch to walk into the House. News of his illness got into the press and he was sent a number of remedies by sympathetic members of the public. To Aberdeen, who had forwarded one lady's agreeable prescription for a cure—a trip to the south of France—he wrote amusedly that 'my gratitude to those who are good enough to suggest remedies varies (not very rationally perhaps) with the Pleasantness of the Prescription'.[1] Even after he went down to Drayton, however, the pain and lameness continued. When rest and the more conventional treatment of Benjamin Brodie failed to bring relief, he tired of the role of invalid and went off to shoot with the Duke of Rutland at Longshawe.

Having tried what *materia medica* and what Repose would do for Sciatica, and without complete success [he reported to Aberdeen]

[1] 43061 f. 204.

I bethought me of a novel remedy—Grouse shooting upon Ground which for Rocks, pitfalls, Bogholes and quagmires Scotland has no parallel. I went on persevering (in Torture after a tumble) until I was well, at least able to walk 7 or 8 hours a day without pain for the first 4 or 5 and free from it the next morning. Pray note the prescription, should you ever be troubled with a similar disorder.[1]

Even this heroic treatment was not entirely efficacious. When Graham came to Drayton at the end of September Peel was still lame, though this did not prevent him from going out shooting with his guest three days running and walking stoutly though (Graham thought) still in some pain.[2]

While Peel was beginning to experience these first signs that even his superb constitution was not invulnerable, his wife's health perceptibly improved during the 1830s. With her last confinement in 1832 and her husband free for almost a decade from ministerial cares, it was perhaps the happiest period of her married life. She still retained much of her early beauty. On Gladstone, when he visited Drayton in 1836, she made the impression of a 'matronly lady who seems to combine the fondness and fragility of youth with a mother's practised character'.[3] But beneath the surface serenity there were depths not readily visible to a twenty-seven-year-old bachelor politician immersed in the affairs of Church and State. Always a temperamental woman, Julia Peel became more nervous and emotional with middle-age. Her passionate absorption in her husband, after the early jealousies, had settled into a close and happy companionship. She was concerned now not about him but for him, for his success, his good name, and his safety. He had been from the start of their marriage the centre of her existence and her emotional dependence on him increased with the passage of years. When they were apart they still corresponded constantly and affectionately; and Julia never tired of telling her growing sons about their father's doings and urging them to read his speeches. Apart from him her only interest was her home and children. As Peel rose in the public eye, she seemed to withdraw from it. She never became a great hostess; her intimates were few; her social life no more than dutiful. In her husband's essentially masculine

[1] 43061 f. 205.
[2] Graham (Graham to Stanley, 3 Oct. 1837).
[3] 44777 fos. 23–8.

world she was content to remain on the fringe; and it was only established friends like Goulburn, Croker, Hardinge and Bonham who came to know her well. She often did not accompany Peel on visits when her presence would have been natural. London she never seemed to care for. She escaped to Drayton as early in the summer as was possible even at the cost of separation from the husband of whom she saw so little during the parliamentary session. Her attitude to grand festivities was not unlike that of Peel's. 'I was civil to all,' she wrote to him unenthusiastically of a ball at Tamworth which she attended with her children in 1843, 'and spoke to all I knew.' Like him, she was happiest at Drayton among her children and flowers—'the place of all I love best'.[1]

With seven children, five of them boys, the years after 1832 were a procession of comings and goings at the start and end of term, letters home and long summer holidays at Drayton. The boys went to preparatory establishments either at Brighton under the Rev. Dr. Everard, or at Hatfield under the more famous Rev. F. J. Faithful. Both had a clientele among the sons of the gentry and aristocracy and the young Peels mixed at an early age with the scions of Russells, Aberdeens and Bentincks. Robert, the eldest, went to Harrow in 1835, followed by Frederick in 1836 and William in 1837. The two younger boys, John and Arthur, when the time came to launch into public school life, broke family tradition by going to Eton. Peel had not been satisfied with what he learned of Harrow during Frederick's career there and the change was perhaps a silent criticism of his old school. He made a similar deliberate alteration in the choice of universities. Robert went as a matter of course to his father's old college. But Christ Church in 1841 was no longer the place it had been under Jackson, Gaisford and Lloyd; and the second son went instead to Trinity College, Cambridge. 'With every prepossession in favour of Christ Church,' their father wrote to Gladstone in 1845, 'I sent my second son to Cambridge, after recent experience of the want of discipline, and neglect of the opportunities of application and of academic distinction, prevailing at that College.'[2] When Arthur, the only other son who attended a university, went up to Oxford in 1848, it was to a smaller college with a growing academic reputation, Balliol.

[1] Peel, *Letters*, pp. 219, 267.   [2] 44275 f. 254.

Robert, who sauntered away his Oxford days with a servant and an allowance of £500 a year, was a disappointment to his parents; but the fault was not altogether the expensive and frivolous atmosphere of his college. Small, dark, almost foreign-looking, and volatile, Peel's eldest son was a freakish contrast to the three generations of Robert Peels who had preceded him. Deriving his temperament and physical characteristics to all appearance entirely from his mother's Anglo-Indian family, he possessed good looks, vivacity and a quick intelligence with none of the traditional Peel qualities of soberness, integrity and purpose. He had not distinguished himself at school; he came down from Oxford without a degree; and when he chose the typically dilettante profession of diplomacy in 1844 he was already a cause of anxiety to his parents. Appointed to Madrid he threw up the post after a couple of years and when he returned to London in 1846 Peel asked Aberdeen, the Foreign Secretary, to speak forcibly to him about the favoured treatment he had already received and the need to disarm charges of nepotism by the efficiency with which he discharged his duties. But all exhortation and advice were wasted, then as throughout his eccentric career. Posted to Berne, he was soon writing to his father that he regretted leaving Spain, was bored with the 'dull monotony of Swiss seclusion' and would rather resign his position than remain there much longer.[1] It was fortunate for his parents, as they watched his capricious nature unfold, that the other sons in their different ways showed more reassuring Peel qualities. The ablest intellectually, and in character the most solid and dependable, was the second son, Frederick. At Harrow he became head of his house, was a strong competitor for various medals and scholarships, won the prize essay which his father had founded, was *proxime accessit* in verse and ended by winning the Lyon scholarship in 1841. At Cambridge he got a first-class degree, coming sixth in the classical tripos, and went on as his father had before him to read for the bar and enter parliament. Throughout his student years his father was always ready with advice, criticism, and encouragement, drawing on his own classical knowledge to provide hints on reading and reflection for his hard-working, dutiful son. Frederick's closest relationship, however, was with his mother. The qualities he inherited from his father were

[1] 43065 f. 175; 40609 f. 126.

those needed and appreciated by her own very different nature; and he was her favourite son to the end.[1] With a great sense of duty and responsibility, and more than ordinary talent, Frederick Peel lacked, however, the urge of ambition. He grew up a pleasant, able, serious man, resembling his more distinguished father in many but not all respects. To G. C. Lewis, who knew them both, the difference seemed mainly intellectual. Peel, he thought, would have made a fortune at the bar as an advocate; Frederick would prove a first-rate judge.[2] But there was a temperamental difference as well. The son was content in the end to be a minor politician and a respected country gentleman. What was missing was the driving force which would have enabled his intrinsic talents to leave their mark on the world.

Peel's own unacknowledged favourite among his sons was the active and spirited William. As a small boy he fixed his heart on the navy and Peel did everything to foster his ambition. When William was still a boy at Harrow, his father consulted Hardinge, the only service man among his close friends, and Graham, a former first lord of the Admiralty, about his career. With their advice and encouragement, after only two years at school William entered the navy as a midshipman in 1838 at the age of thirteen. His lively letters home left no doubt of the enthusiasm with which he was embracing his profession. Two years later on board H.M.S. *Princess Charlotte* he saw action off the coast of Syria and sent home accounts of the operation showing such maturity and intelligence that his proud father could not forbear to pass them round among his friends, including that supreme authority on service matters, the Duke of Wellington. The duke returned them with laconic advice to encourage William to write down his observations on any action in which he took part, revising the account afterwards and leaving on the paper both the errors and the correction. 'This habit will accustom him to an accurate observation and report of facts; which are most important, destined as he most likely is to direct and carry on great operations.' This comment on his son by the greatest

[1] Peel, *Letters, passim.* I am also much indebted to private information from Mrs. A. H. Soames (last surviving daughter of the 3rd Sir Robert Peel) and from Sir William Dugdale, Bt., of Merevale Hall, Warwickshire, who knew Frederick Peel in later life. See also G. W. E. Russell, *Collections and Recollections* (1904), pp. 131–2.

[2] Graham (Lewis to Graham, 5 Nov. 1849).

captain of the age moved Peel as no praise of himself could have done. 'He was so delighted with the Letter', wrote Wellington a trifle cynically to one of his female correspondents, 'as to have become quite gay and *déboutonné*. The Person who told me said that he had never observed such an effect produced by a Letter. The Man became one of a different Character.' The incident and the comment were both typical. Wellington respected Peel for his public qualities but was easily amused or irritated by the personal attributes of his complex and incomprehensible colleague. Peel's political dealings with the duke, on the other hand, were always apt to be cramped and self-conscious as a result of his civilian's veneration for Wellington's achievement as a soldier.

In this instance there were no politics to cloud Peel's gratification. All that he learned of his son's progress, directly through his letters home and indirectly through his naval acquaintances, strengthened Peel's fondest hopes.

> I can hardly justify on any reasonable grounds my early presentiment that my boy (if it please God to spare and protect him) will be a distinguished man [he wrote to his old friend Goulburn in December 1840]. But I must say that everything I have heard from him, or of him, since he entered his profession, has justified and confirmed it.[1]

In July 1841, after three years afloat, the young sailor son came back to England tall, bronzed, well-mannered, 'and with an intelligence and aplomb in his conversation' (reported Croker who saw him first), 'more like 26 than 16'.[2] William only stayed a short time in home waters, however, before going off to China in the *Cambrian* and on his return he immediately applied for a gunnery course on H.M.S. *Excellent*. His six years as midshipman ended in May 1844 and he was determined to qualify as soon as possible for promotion as lieutenant. In the event he obtained a first-class certificate after only five months of a course for which candidates were allowed fourteen months and no one had previously taken less than eight.[3] This single-minded energy was after Peel's own heart. The qualities

---

[1] Goulburn (6 Dec. 1840); 40310 f. 333, ptly pr. *Peel*, II, 451–2; *Wellington and His Friends*, p. 151.

[2] 40321 f. 458.

[3] 40460 fos. 201–3.

his father had shown in business and himself in politics were being exhibited by a Peel in yet another sphere. It was moreover one in which he had a particular interest. A man of action himself, Peel respected and admired the fighting services. He had grown up in the atmosphere of a great war; to him as to most Englishmen of his generation Trafalgar and Waterloo were names of undying association. In his letters to William at sea he urged him to read Southey's *Life of Nelson* and constantly held up the great admiral of his boyhood as a pattern for his son's career.[1] The qualities of ambition, patriotism, and dedication present in his own nature he recognised and encouraged in his third son. In William's active and warlike profession he found perhaps vicarious outlet for some unsatisfied dreams of his own.

William's early departure from the home circle made a gap in the row of growing children. Until 1840, while Robert and Frederick were still at Harrow, it was less noticeable. With Arthur at school in Brighton and John at Hatfield, the end of the summer term saw a bustle of boys arriving from different directions at Whitehall Gardens to stay a night or two and perhaps be taken to a theatre by their aunt Miranda before being despatched by their busy father to the peace and safety of Drayton. After that year the gap widened. Between Frederick and the fourth son John was a difference of four years and the one had scarcely started at Eton before the other went up to Cambridge. Increasingly the three younger children, John, Arthur and Eliza, tended to form a group of their own, fishing and boating together in the summer, playing with the new gilt india-rubber balls which their mother asked Peel to buy for them in August 1843, or riding their horses while Julia accompanied them across the park in her pony-carriage. By then their elder sister had already left her parents' roof. Julia, called Tooti by her family, was a general favourite. Educated at home, she had been more in the company of her father and mother than any of the rest of the children. She had been with them in Rome in 1834 and shared the excitement of the journey back to Dover. She was with them again in France in 1837; and she frequently stayed on at Whitehall Gardens after Lady Peel had left for the country. With her mother's charm and good looks, she remained candid and

[1] Lawrence Peel, *Life and Character of Sir R. Peel* (1860), p. 4.

unspoiled. Haydon, whose political sympathies were with the opposite camp, met her when he went to view Rubens's *Chapeau de Paille* in her father's gallery one April day in 1838.

> Miss Peel was with her French governess—a beautiful, domestic and interesting Girl is Miss Peel. She came out into the Gallery and received me most kindly. . . . Miss Peel had not a bit that air of coquetting fashion of the Whig Women. She looked like her Mother & her Father—good & domestic. She has beautiful eyes, and is very handsome.[1]

When in 1839, at the age of eighteen, she began to go out to London balls and receptions, she attracted great attention and it was not long before Lord Villiers, the son and heir of the Earl of Jersey, was showing a marked interest.

For a great-grand-daughter of old Parsley Peel of Fish Lane to become a future countess and for the yeoman stock of the Peels to ally with a family which had furnished a minister to one Stuart monarch and a mistress to another, was not without a certain piquancy. Until Villiers's parents showed their inclinations, Peel's own pride held him back. 'I think our object should be', he wrote to his wife after an encounter with the Jerseys at a ball given by the Duchess of Somerset in July 1839, 'to keep on good terms just as usual but to show, very decisively if it be necessary, that we think of no closer connection.' Fortunately there was no political enmity to vex the course of young love. As a former Whig who had come over to the Tories in 1830 Lord Jersey had been given a court appointment in Peel's ministry of 1834. Villiers himself, as Conservative M.P. for Weymouth, was one of Peel's party followers. In June 1841, when Julia was twenty, the engagement was announced. It was celebrated by the indefatigable pen of Croker with a set of verses and, if Lady Palmerston is to be believed, Lady Jersey went round triumphant at a match which offered both a great political alliance and a handsome dowry. On 14 July the marriage took place at St. George's, Hanover Square. The wedding, attended by Prince George of Cambridge and his sister Princess Augusta, was one of the great social events of the season and more than one observer was struck by the affection with which Peel replied to Prince George's

---

[1] *Haydon*, IV, 472.

toast of the newly married couple.[1] 'The conviction of your happiness', wrote Peel to his daughter a few days later, 'is the only thing that can reconcile me to the loss of your society. . . . I need not say how sincerely I pray to Almighty God that every blessing may attend you. If among the presents you received was a little purse, put the enclosed into it.' The young couple took up residence at Upton in Warwickshire, in an old country house which Julia's parents did not think entirely suitable. Next year Lady Peel assisted in finding them 'a nice, clean, pretty house' in Grosvenor Place and there on 10 May 1842 a third Julia was born. Peel and his wife were now grandparents.[2]

III

The Peels had brought up their children in a close family relationship governed by firmness and affection. When John was miserable and homesick in his first few days at Eton in 1840, his first unhappy letter home was forwarded to Drayton with a scribbled note from Peel, 'my dearest, you must write and comfort the little fellow'. But when there was trouble at Harrow he sent a stern warning to Frederick, telling him that for the sake of himself, his family, and above all his younger brothers, he must resist the temptation weakly to follow his companions. 'Do not listen to the silly advice that only turns industry and honourable exertion into ridicule. . . . Write to us immediately and comfort us. Tell us that you are fulfilling the promise you made to us, and that you are resolved not to swerve from the path which will lead you to honour.' This close superintendence continued even after school was behind them. 'My dearest Frederick,' his father wrote in December 1841, 'however occupied I am, you are never out of my thoughts. Let me know how you are going on at Trinity College, who are your friends and what you are reading.'[3] It was an age when moral exhortation and parental vigilance was a matter of course not only among the respectable middle classes but also increasingly among the aristocracy of English society. What would otherwise have been

[1] *Neumann*, II, 171; *Lieven-Palmerston Corr.*, ed. Lord Sudley, p. 214; Peel, *Letters*, p. 165. Croker's poem is in Peel MSS.

[2] Peel, *Letters*, pp. 179, 190, 197.

[3] *ibid.*, pp. 162, 170, 184.

commonplace was given a personal character in the case of Peel and his children by the deep affection he had for them and the religious conviction which underlay his code of behaviour.

Peel's Christianity was undemonstrative. He paraded his religion as little as his emotions but it would be equally absurd to doubt the genuineness of either. In the country he regularly attended church either at Drayton across the park from the manor-house, or at nearby Tamworth, where he frequently made the Sunday walk to service and back again, sparing both his servants and horses. In London he was an inconspicuous attender at various churches. Greville, for example, noticed him in the somewhat incongruous company of Lord Brougham at the Temple Church in May 1843. The same year he attended Whitehall Chapel on Good Friday and took Holy Communion there in company with his daughter on Easter Sunday. At Drayton he made it a rule to read prayers to the whole household, including the family, guests, and all the domestic staff; and, though few knew of this, he practised his own private devotions.[1] He rarely made any references to such matters, even in letters to his wife. Yet it was conviction rather than convention which made him end his rectorial speech at Glasgow with a plea to look to religion for support in tribulation, admonition in time of prosperity, and comfort in time of death.

His own sectarian beliefs were essentially moderate. He thought it proper for the State to support the Church but he had little love for dogmatic exclusiveness or priestly monopoly. He could not bear the clerical authoritarianism of the Roman Church. He disliked the doctrinal extremism of the Tractarian Anglicans. In his second Glasgow speech there was a revealing passage describing an occasion when he had attended service with a Highland shepherd and 'heard the sublime truths and pure doctrines of our common faith enjoined and enforced according to the rites of his church'. He continued in words that fell gratefully on the ears of his Presbyterian audience though they made less kindly reading for his former constituents of

[1] A copy of a prayer said to be constantly used by Peel and found after his death is printed in *Recollections of Lady Georgiana Peel*, ed. E. Peel (1920), p. 206. It also appeared in the newspaper press under the title of 'The Statesman's Prayer'. The version given by Georgiana Peel seems to be genuine. An MS. copy is in the Windsor Archives docketed 'copy of prayer found in Sir R.P.'s private box on his dressing-table 1850' (RA./A 83/52).

Oxford University. 'Think you that I have adverted to differences in ceremonies and forms? Think you I have troubled myself with questions of church discipline or church government?' Though Peel was a loyal Anglican throughout his life, his Anglicanism was not in the Laudian High Church tradition of his old tutor Bishop Lloyd, who had cause to lament before his death the low Protestant views of his most famous pupil. To Peel the Establishment was the seemly institutional embodiment of the purified religion adopted by the English people at the time of the Reformation. Arguing with Lloyd over the repeal of the Test and Corporations Acts in 1828, Peel characteristically observed that 'in these times it is not very prudent to lay down general doctrines with respect to the essential attributes of the Church, unless we are quite sure that they are safe doctrines for all parts of our empire'. His own definition of the Establishment was entirely secular. 'That is the Established Church of England to which the King must conform—whose chief ministers have a right to seats in the House of Lords—which has an unalienable claim to ecclesiastical property.'[1] A supporter of Protestantism from conviction of its rightness, a supporter of the Established Church from conviction of its utility, he was prepared to defend the Church of Ireland as the missionary church of the minority and the Church of England as the institutional church of the majority.

Tolerant and undogmatic as he was, there were limits to his tolerance. The liberty and protection which he conceded to all conscientious beliefs he did not think should be construed as liberty for public attacks on Christianity or protection for the propagation of atheism. There was an instance of this during his Home Secretaryship in 1828 when Robert Taylor, the anticlerical agitator, was imprisoned for blasphemy. Joseph Hume wrote to Peel on Taylor's behalf, asking him to peruse for his enlightenment a sermon by Tillotson on the subject of persecution. But Peel, who knew his English theological writing at least as well as Hume, retorted by recommending two other sermons by Tillotson, bearing more immediately on Taylor's case. One was on the dangerous folly of scoffing at religion; the other on the rights of the civil magistrate 'to establish the true worship of God in such manner as he thinks best, to permit none to affront it, or to seduce from it those that are under

[1] *Peel Memoirs*, I, 80.

his care'.[1] Fourteen years later almost to the day Peel was writing to another Home Secretary drawing his attention to 'the exhibition of revolting infidel publications and placards' in Holywell Street, off the Strand, London. He added, 'you may safely go to the extreme range of the law in suppressing these nuisances and it would be as well, I think, to direct the special attention of the Police Commissioners to the subject and desire them to *harass* the offenders'.[2]

For Peel religion was essentially something inward and personal. He disliked undue manifestations of piety in those not required by their calling to bear witness to their faith. When bigots and fanatics began to wrangle, it was his experience that Christian charity and humility flew out of the window. Reserved himself in his own religious professions, he did not relish religious exhibitionism, sectarian monomania, or collective sanctimoniousness either in private or public life; though he lived in an age when all three were conspicuous features of society. If it was the duty of the civil magistrate to defend religion, it was no business of the government in his view to appeal to the Deity as a political ally. When Lord Kenyon in 1845 suggested a special public acknowledgement of dependence on God's mercy at the time of the Irish famine, Peel dryly commented that it might seem somewhat inconsistent at the same time to leave in full operation human restrictions on the import of food. He made an even more cutting criticism of a suggestion emanating from the pious High Church member for Oxford, Sir Robert Inglis, that the parliamentary vote of thanks to the Army in India for the victories at Aliwal and Sobraon in 1846 should include a specific reference to divine providence. 'Considering the sanguinary nature of great battles,' he wrote, 'and that (however just the cause) many thousands forfeit their lives through no fault of their own, too direct a reference to the special intervention of Almighty God is not very seemly.' As it was, he had already toned down the religious fervour of the draft resolutions of the House. 'They almost made it appear,' he told the queen ironically, 'as they were originally drawn, that the fire of artillery on the confused mass of Sikhs, after they had been driven into the Sutlej, had been directed by Divine Providence, and was an agreeable sight to a merciful Creator.'[3]

[1] *Peel*, II, 44.   [2] 40448 f. 88.   [3] RA/A/18 (3 Apr. 1846); *Peel Memoirs*, II, 153–5.

Yet with all his distaste for cant and fanaticism, he could deal gently with enthusiasts, however misguided. There was an odd instance of this in 1836. In the early months of that year Spencer Perceval the Irvingite conceived himself directed by God to be the instrument of divine communication to leading members of the Privy Council on the state of the nation. The receptions he met from different politicians were curious and revealing. Lord Howick listened politely; Melbourne argued with him; Stanley turned him out; Lord John Russell excused himself; the Duke of Wellington evaded capture. Peel's turn came towards the end of January when Perceval and a fellow enthusiast descended on Drayton Manor—like beings from another world, recorded the young High Anglican Gladstone who was a guest there at the time. They announced to Peel, in the same cloudy and barely intelligible language that they used to other statesmen, that they were commissioned by God, through the ministry of a small but increasing sect, to draw attention to the state of national sin and apostasy, to the certainty of retribution, the speedy coming of judgement, and the awful responsibility resting on those who refused to listen to divine warning. Peel dealt patiently and seriously with the son of his old prime minister and his equally crack-brained companion. He impressed on them the duty and necessity of verifying those powers which they claimed to possess and proposed to them a test of their alleged inspiration. In each of their separate congregations at London and Manchester one person, among those claiming to be inspired, should be set to expound the same text and prophesy on the same subject. If they found that they agreed in their interpretations, it would constitute *prima facie* evidence in their favour. This attempt to meet religious fanaticism with commonsense and the rules of evidence was as characteristic as it was unsuccessful. Peel ruefully told his guests afterwards that it was impossible to tie them down in any way to the matter of proof. Nevertheless he said goodbye to Perceval with great warmth and kindness when the Irvingites departed in the evening.[1]

Peel's own religion was a simple, rational, pious Protestantism. The enthusiasm of the 'Saints', the high sacerdotal principles of Gladstone, were as foreign to him as the intellectual pessimism of

[1] 44777 fos. 25–8; *Greville*, 1 Feb. 1836.

Melbourne or the tortured self-examination of Lord Ashley. When in 1838 a copy of Gladstone's book *The State in its Relations with the Church* came down to Drayton, Peel glanced through the pages and then laid it aside with the dry remark that 'that young man will ruin a fine career if he writes such books as these'. For himself he felt that his business and his duty were with the affairs of the world and Christianity something to be expressed in practical conduct rather than in external observances or metaphysical speculation. He read theology regrettably more for the sake of the dialectics than the divinity; and his library was not conspicuous for a wealth of devotional literature. Yet it was perhaps not without significance that it contained copies of those classic seventeenth-century manuals on the practical duties and rules of conduct of a Christian, Jeremy Taylor's *Holy Living* and *Holy Dying*. Peel could only have approved what the Bishop of Down wrote: 'A king . . . a judge and an advocate, doing the works of their employment according to their proper rules, are doing the work of God, because they serve those necessities, which God hath made, and yet made no provisions for them, but by their ministry.'[1] There was a faint mundane echo of this in a correspondence in 1833 between Peel and Lord Mahon over the character of Walpole as depicted in Mahon's draft sketch for his *History of the Reign of George I*. Peel thought that Mahon underestimated Walpole's talents, courage and patriotism and had ascribed to the man the corruption more properly due to the age. As for Mahon's invidious comparison between the heroic figure of Strafford on the scaffold and Walpole dying unromantically in bed of the stone, Peel observed that one might as well contrast armour with a velvet waistcoat or a helmet with a wig. 'No doubt the cumbrous dress in which a corpulent Minister sweats at a Levee in the dog days is a much worse subject for a picture . . . than the flashing armour.' But all such comparisons must take note of contemporary conditions and different circumstances 'imposing different duties, and calling into action different qualities'.[2]

Because religion to him meant in effect duty and conduct, Peel also had faith in the progress of society and the spread of education and scientific knowledge. With so little dogmatic content to his

[1] *Holy Living*, ch. 1, sect. 1.
[2] Stanhope, *Miscellanies*, pp. 73–4.

own mind, he apprehended no danger to religion from the growth of secular knowledge. Indeed he welcomed it as a means of curing some of the evils and bridging some of the divisions of his troubled contemporary society. In his speech when opening the Tamworth Reading Room in 1841 he asserted that there was nothing in knowledge which should harm religious belief. Only unwise men and fools formed unworthy conclusions of Divine nature and the Divine universe; and he expressed his conviction of the harmony of the Christian dispensation with all that reason assisted by revelation told them of the course and constitution of Nature.[1] In religion as in politics Peel was essentially robust, optimistic, unmetaphysical and practical.

Yet there was one matter in which he refused to allow either the teaching of religion or consideration for his wife and family to affect his conduct. He had schooled his nature to patience and forbearance in ordinary personal and political dealings. What he could not tolerate was a reflection on his courage or integrity. On several occasions his sharp and sometimes unreasonable resentment at insult led him to the time-honoured demand for satisfaction or apology. This reaction, however, was entirely defensive. Few politicians more carefully avoided giving offence and provocation. In public he was scrupulously courteous to his opponents. In private life he neither spoke harshly of them nor allowed his less inhibited wife to do so. The nature of duelling makes the challenge the remedy of the injured party; and Peel never received a challenge in his life. Though Peel was easily provoked, however, what he was provoked to do was still an accepted social convention. Duelling did not vanish from English society until later in the century. When he began his career it was, for all but a few eccentric individuals, a contingent but unavoidable necessity of social life for all who called themselves gentlemen. It was not until 1844, for example, that the Articles of War were amended to allow army officers to tender or accept apologies in case of insult or injury without reflection on their honour; and the last actual encounter in England took place after Peel's death.

What complicated the issue for Peel was his prominent position

---

[1] *Sir Robert Peel's Address on the Establishment of a Library . . . at Tamworth on 19 Jan. 1841* (London 1841).

in public life and the fact that during his own lifetime the convention was dying out. The first imposed a particular obligation to follow the convention; the second made it a particular subject of remark. His plebeian origin would have come in for the inevitable sneer had he seemed to shirk this final test of good-breeding; his exposure to public attack made certain that there would be the opportunities. Peel's acceptance of the duelling code was not only normal but almost a necessity. Yet before the end of his career it was becoming an increasingly obsolete custom. Cardwell, born a quarter of a century after Peel, once put the matter in terms of simple chronology. Had he been personally insulted in his own bitter election contest of 1841, he said afterwards, he would have been thought a coward had he not fought. In 1847, in a similar situation, it would have been a doubtful point. 'In 1851 I should have been regarded as an idiot if I had thought of such a course.'[1] But these were the rapidly changing manners of society to which the older man scarcely had time to adapt himself. Even so, there was something excessive in Peel's sensitivity on points of honour. It could superficially be ascribed to the social uncertainties of a parvenu, concerned to prove himself a gentleman precisely because others did not take it for granted. Yet other politicians of no better social origin did not always show the same sensitivity. It might be explained, along with other traits such as his shyness, reserve with strangers, and unusually affectionate manner with intimates, as the mark of a childhood that had known too much discipline and too little love. What is beyond doubt is that underneath the intellectual caution and professional restraint of Peel's character was an emotional, impulsive and self-conscious nature. Anything which touched his proud and prickly temperament on the raw evoked a response which was too strong for reason or reflection. In those moments, rare but revealing, his pride and temper gained the upper hand.

IV

The general election of 1835, when Peel and his brother William were returned unopposed for Tamworth, was the first time for

[1] Cardwell (Cardwell to Goldwin Smith, 3 Nov. 1864).

many years that the constituency had not been divided, amicably or otherwise, between the Castle and the Manor interests. Lord Charles Townshend's retirement had been voluntary. Peel said publicly that he had not used his personal influence to exclude him and that, rather than expose the borough to family feuds, he would cheerfully abandon one seat. Contemporary electioneering habits made it inevitable, however, that he should be accused from time to time of coercing his tenants. At the hustings in 1837 he made a reference to these charges and, seeing one of his tenants beneath him in the crowd, unwisely asked him whether he had ever been coerced. The opposing party enjoyed the incident and turned it into verse.

> 'O where is the tenant will say I have threatened him?
> I've tenants enough in the crowd there below—
> Peter Bird, did I threaten you ever, my Peter?'
> 'Did you threaten me? Never—O no, my love, no.'[1]

This was good-humoured enough; but the result of the contest, in which Peel and a new Conservative candidate, Captain A'Court, beat a Castle candidate in the shape of Captain John Townshend, R.N., led to something less than good humour on both sides. Peel had already been charged with using his electoral interest in the borough to bring in A'Court when William Peel decided to retire. In his speech at the close of poll Townshend declared angrily that his defeat was a personal triumph in view of Peel's failure to live up to his explicit declarations that he would not interfere with the second seat. Peel denied that he had directly or indirectly made any attempt to decide the fate of his brother's former seat; and there is no evidence that he did so. After the election, however, Townshend was reported in the London *Globe* of 18 August as having said in a speech delivered a fortnight earlier that Peel had been guilty of a violation of honour, principle, and truth and that it would be impossible for his word to be trusted again. He followed this up with equally violent language at a Liberal election banquet at Tamworth on 20 August. 'Sir Robert Peel under the mask of secrecy had exerted his utmost influence to return Captain A'Court and prevent his (Townshend's) election; and he had done it in utter contempt of

---

[1] The author of the doggerel was the well-known journalist Cyrus Redding, then active in Staffordshire politics (see his *Fifty Years Recollections* (1858), III, 147).

reiterated declarations and promises solemnly and publicly made.

On 22 August, when the first report of these charges came to him, Peel wrote a stiff letter to Townshend. He sent it to Hardinge to deliver personally and asked his old friend to make the necessary arrangements when he received a reply. Hardinge was at Walmer with the duke and, after a hasty consultation with his host, came up to town. Using his discretion he withheld Peel's letter and to avoid publicity sent his servant to Townshend's house in the country with a private note covering the grounds of complaint but avoiding a peremptory demand for satisfaction. In the meantime Townshend had gone to Ireland in the company of Alston, the Liberal M.P. for Hertfordshire. The resultant delay, coupled with the speculation already roused by Townshend's speeches, made it difficult to preserve secrecy and Bonham, who had accidentally learned of the affair when visiting Hardinge, acted for a while as intermediary in the various exchanges of correspondence that ensued. When Townshend was eventually located, however, he showed no sign of retracting and merely named Alston as his second. On 31 August Peel went up to town in response to a summons from Hardinge and in the expectation that his antagonist would have arrived there from Ireland. Townshend failed to appear, however, and as public interest in the chances of a meeting was growing, Peel returned to Drayton and Hardinge to Walmer. By this time Lawrence Peel at Marble Hill, Twickenham, was growing anxious about his brother and Bonham went down to impress on him the need for caution. In the early days of September it seemed as if nothing could avert an encounter. The two seconds were discussing the rival merits of Hounslow and Birmingham as meeting-places; on 5 September Peel wrote to Bonham asking him to smuggle his case of pistols out of the library at Whitehall Gardens and bring them down to Drayton; and Hardinge arranged to join his principal under cover of a shooting party of the more conventional kind. In the end, however, the seconds settled the affair. Alston secured and Hardinge accepted a full apology from Captain Townshend, withdrawing the offensive words and admitting that they were based on an erroneous impression. The old duke pronounced that the apology was 'satisfactory and complete'. The retraction appeared in the press; and honour was satisfied. It would have been acutely embarrassing to the Whigs in fact had there been any other outcome. Alston told Hardinge privately that if their respective parties had gone out, he would not have allowed Townshend to fire. What particularly stung Peel, however, was that soon after the offending speech, Townshend had been appointed to the command of a ship. He asked indignantly what would have been thought if he had done the same for an obscure captain who had tried to insult Melbourne or Russell. But perhaps the posting was susceptible of a more charitable explanation.

Peel's friends at least were thankful at the happy issue. One of them, Archdeacon Singleton, who had been at Drayton during the days of waiting, wrote to congratulate Hardinge on his sense and firmness. Cleric though he was, he admitted that it was difficult to know how the affairs of the world could be ordered without such incidents occurring. But 'having had the happiness of seeing Sir Robert Peel in the singular felicity of his domestic life, after witnessing the regularity of his morals and his quiet piety, the mere possibility that he should have put all to hazard upon the garrulous malice of a madman or the foolish obstinacy of one whom the offender might have selected as a friend, is most *sad and appalling*'. Peel himself remained outwardly calm and even cheerful throughout. The only sign Singleton noticed was on one evening walk when Peel referred repeatedly to the stillness and beauty of the scene as though moved by some unusual emotion. Much had changed in Peel's life since as a young unmarried man he had chafed in desperation at his inability to bring O'Connell into the field. Yet age and responsibility had made no difference to his actions, only to the measure of what he was prepared to risk.[1]

One pleasure, however, he could feel in this period of anxiety—the support and loyalty of his friends. 'Never mention any personal inconvenience,' Hardinge wrote to him on 29 August. 'The occasion is to be lamented but any honest man owes you such a debt of gratitude, that exclusive of my personal attachment, I shall ever be

---

[1] For the Townshend affair see 40314 fos. 183–231; Cardwell (GD 48/53/103–10); *Peel*, II, 350–1. The last generous word was spoken by Townshend, writing to Lady Peel after Peel's death. 'I cannot resist telling you how thankful I felt that all differences between us had been buried in oblivion. Of this I am amply satisfied by the kind—the more than kind—manner in which both you and he received me. *There was much to be forgiven.*' (*Peel*, III, 558).

anxious to prove how sincerely and devotedly I am yours.'[1] It was characteristic of Peel that the reserve he exhibited to strangers was offset by the affection he showed in his own small circle. If his close friends were few, they were staunch; and as he grew older he never lost the capacity for making new ones. Hardinge, the firm, competent, professional soldier who had been with Moore at Corunna, Wellington at Vittoria and Blücher at Ligny, was over forty and Peel little short of that age before they came to know each other well. Since then their personal relationship had steadily deepened. Another man, only four years younger than Peel, was about to join this select company. The same general election which produced the Townshend affair saw Sir James Graham evicted from the seat in Cumberland which he had held since 1827. Inevitable as it was, this final severance from the Whigs brought Graham to the point at which, unconsciously perhaps, his personal as well as his political allegiance was transferred to Peel. Receiving a friendly letter of condolence from Drayton after his defeat, he replied with obvious emotion on 8 August:

> In my retirement I shall constantly remember the generous kindness which you have shown to me on every occasion, and, if you will allow me the expression, I trust we shall always continue friends. I do not believe there now exists between us one shade of difference of opinion on public matters, and my confidence in you is such, founded on personal regard and respect, that my inclination will be strong to prefer your judgement to my own.[2]

With that letter the decisive point in Graham's career was reached. It was symbolised by his acceptance at last of an invitation to stay at Drayton the following September. As he wrote, almost apologetically, to his late leader Stanley, had he once more refused, it would have shown an inclination to be on less friendly terms with Peel than his conduct towards Graham would justify.[3] It was the end of the Derby Dilly and the beginning of one of the closest friendships in the lives of both men.

---

[1] 40314 f. 201.
[2] 40318 f. 100 (pr. *Peel*, II, 349).
[3] Graham (1 Sept. 1837).

MONARCH AND MINISTERS

The accession of the Princess Victoria produced a brief lull in the parliamentary world. The first queen regnant since Anne, the youngest monarch since the sixteenth century, she brought to politics a breath of novelty which was both agreeable and disconcerting. Peel had been one of the great mob of nearly a hundred privy councillors in Kensington Palace on 20 June when dressed in mourning she took the oaths and received in silence the roomful of elderly politicians who came up one after the other to kiss her hand. Though short and without pretensions to good looks, she had pleasant blue eyes and a clear attractive voice; and they were all disarmed by her naïve mixture of calmness and inexperience. Peel was full of admiration for her bearing on this first public occasion and found the opportunity to express in the House a couple of days later what he had been privately and less formally saying to Greville and others in the interval. Part of the attraction, besides her youth and her sex, was the contrast with her immediate predecessors, William and George, her ageing uncles, Sussex and Cumberland, and even with her mother the Duchess of Kent, whose relations with Sir John Conroy were not above suspicion. The unpleasant Duke of Cumberland succeeded under salic law as King of Hanover but the loss of the German possessions of the crown after more than a century of personal union received hardly a comment from the insular British public. Indeed, there was little popular enthusiasm even for the queen. Her youth and secluded upbringing made her virtually unknown to most of her subjects; and they had little cause in recent years to venerate the monarchy.

Before William's death there had been talk of a regency. But as Victoria had reached her legal majority of eighteen in the previous month, it seemed (to Peel among others) better that she should enter on her reign with no formal tutelage of any kind. It was reasonable to assume that she would continue the ministry already in office; as a family adviser she had her uncle Leopold, King of the Belgians; and as a domestic companion her governess, the Baroness Lehzen. What became obvious in the next few months, however, was that Victoria and Melbourne, despite the forty years gap in their ages, were soon on close and even affectionate terms and that the prime minister was spending a disproportionate amount of his time at Court. Sir Herbert Taylor had been pensioned off and no successor was appointed; Melbourne himself took on the duties of secretary to the queen. The Whig government, after suffering the last cantankerous years of William IV, now enjoyed the personal as well as the public confidence of the monarch. What Melbourne would do with this court card remained to be seen. 'As yet,' Aberdeen wrote to Peel from Scotland on 11 August, 'he has not lost the sense of responsibility under which he acts; and I believe is reluctant to use the power which he possesses; but certainly I think that no minister has ever been in such a situation since the Protector Somerset.'[1]

Victoria's predilection for the Whigs was personal rather than political: little more indeed than an extension of her rapid adolescent attachment to the kind, cynical, charming Viscount Melbourne. In turn the prime minister, who had been fretted by William IV almost to the point of resignation, found a fresh source of pleasure as companion and mentor to a young and adoring queen. Yet personal relationships at that august level could hardly fail to exert some influence on the lower reaches of politics. Marginal as the influence of the crown now was in the parliamentary constitution, it was given continuing weight by the balanced state of parties left by the general election. The Whigs' hustings propaganda had extracted full advantage from the queen's name and this had already provoked a partisan reaction from their opponents. What profit they had realised from it was difficult to assess, though Aberdeen thought that in Scotland at any rate it had made a difference. Even so the election results narrowed still further the gap between the two great parties in the House of Commons. The crucial question had

[1] 40312 f. 290.

been whether the Conservatives could consolidate the advantages fortuitously presented to them two and a half years earlier or whether the Whigs in office could arrest or reverse the Liberal decline. The registrations of the previous autumn had given the Conservative party managers grounds for hope. Before the general election they were expecting to win an additional twenty-five seats in Scotland and England which, when offset by accepted losses in Ireland, would yield a net gain of fifteen seats in the House. With the Conservatives able to build on the foundations laid in 1835 and the Liberals reinvigorated by a new reign, both sides poured men and money into the field. As a result the 1837 election was the hardest fought and in some respects the most critical contest between the first and second Reform Acts. In the event the gains and losses on both sides in Scotland and the English boroughs neutralised each other; in Ireland there was the expected decline in the Conservative total; but twenty-three English county seats were captured by the opposition to which the only Liberal reply was Graham's defeat in Cumberland. With about a dozen members still loose in their allegiance, exact calculations of party strength were not easy. But by the fourth week of August, when the last of the contests were over, Bonham estimated that the Conservatives would muster 317 in the new House of Commons as against the ministerial 341. Ross's more stringent calculations, throwing out all the doubtful men, were slightly less favourable: 313 to 345. In the previous session the nominal party figures had been 295 and 353 respectively. This majority of 58 had now been reduced to no more than 32 and as Ross observed not all of those were likely to support the government on every issue.[1] With the advantage of office on their side, the Liberals had still not been able to stop the Conservative revival. They had lost their majority in England and Scotland, and only Ireland and O'Connell remained between them and a Conservative government. It now seemed simply a matter of time and one more trial of strength. Already on 7 August at his election dinner at Tamworth Peel pointed to the unbroken course of Conservative recovery and warned his hearers to be prepared at any time for another election. Some of their opponents, he observed, said

[1] 40424 f. 97; Graham (Hardinge to Graham, 13 Aug. 1837); Goulburn, II/18 (Peel to Goulburn, 21 Aug. 1837).

'agitate, agitate, agitate'. 'The advice which I give to the Conservatives is this—"register, register, register".'

A feature of the election had been the defeat of several well-known radicals—Roebuck, Hume, Ewart, Thompson and Hutt—and the reduction of Grote's majority in the City from 1,400 to 6. Nevertheless the Conservatives themselves had not come off unscathed. In particular the defeats of Sir George Clerk, Bonham and Ross had removed the entire opposition staff of chief and assistant whips and made it necessary, in Granville Somerset's cavalry phrase, to remount the establishment. A quick decision was necessary since Holmes, a former chief whip, was back in the Commons after an absence of some years. He was a vulgar, bustling, thick-skinned man, a protégé of the Lowthers, and it was certain that unless forestalled he would lay claim to his old office. It was equally certain, as Granville Somerset wrote to Peel on 9 August, that the bulk of the party would not tolerate him. Apart from his manners and his conversation, which were not to everyone's taste, his indiscretion, his inquisitiveness, and his excessive familiarity with the whips of the other party raised doubts of his trustworthiness. Peel, who had his own opinion of Holmes and knew moreover that it was shared by Wellington and Hardinge, needed no warning. The obvious successor was Sir Thomas Fremantle, who had been considered for the post in 1835 and was universally liked and trusted. As assistants, Granville Somerset recommended two new men, Henry Baring and Cecil Forester, the first of whom had already been active at headquarters in the recent electoral campaign. Within a week Granville Somerset wrote with Peel's authority to offer the post to Fremantle and received his acceptance.[1] Parliament was not due to assemble until November and for Peel there was little more to do in clearing up the aftermath of the election except write letters of condolence to the defeated, thanks to the active, and congratulation to the victorious. The business of arranging election petitions could safely be left to the party managers and once the Townshend affair was off his mind, Peel was able to enjoy a brief period of relaxation marred only by the persistence of his sciatica. He did not believe various post-election rumours that the ministers would fall back on a Conservative policy or would propose a coalition or would even

[1] 40424 fos. 47, 82, 95; 40333 fos. 372, 375; 40314 fos. 138, 185; 40341 f. 1.

seek the first opportunity of resigning in order to embarrass their opponents. Resignation without manifest necessity, he told Goulburn, was the most hazardous, unpopular and ridiculous of all political manœuvres.[1]

In the late autumn he took Julia and their eldest daughter for a short continental holiday. Travelling by way of Antwerp they visited Munich, where they met the King of Bavaria. At Stuttgart Peel was approached by the diplomatic representative of the new King of Hanover whose autocratic behaviour after his accession had done nothing to assist the Conservative cause in the British general election. What the king wanted was both to justify his policy and to persuade Peel to defend it in the House of Commons. Peel declined either to comment on the one or to undertake the other, though he did write to the king discreetly advocating a moderate and conciliatory course of action in his new domain. Their tour continued on a royal note with interviews in Paris with Louis Philippe and the Duke of Orleans, and calls on old acquaintances like the Princess Lieven who reported to her gossips that she never saw Peel looking better or more resolute.[2] By the middle of November they were back in London ready for the new session. Members of both houses were already assembling and the clubs and drawingrooms resounded to a hubbub of talk and speculation. On 14 November Peel spent much of his time at the Carlton, welcoming supporters and issuing invitations to small House of Commons club dinners where old and new M.P.s could get to know each other and their leader.

Six days later came the formal opening of parliament. It was preceded in the morning by a great meeting of some three hundred Conservative M.P.s at Peel's house. For the first time at one of these general gatherings Stanley was present, tacitly acknowledging his junction with the party. Peel addressed the throng full of spirit and apparently eager for action. He realised that his men were scenting blood and was ready himself for a demonstration of party strength, provided it could be made effective. The queen's speech,

[1] Goulburn, II/18 (21 Aug. 1837). An excerpt given in Peel, II, 479 is wrongly dated 1841.
[2] Wellington (Peel to Wellington, 14 Nov. 1837); Peel, II, 352–4; Corr. Princess Lieven and Earl Grey, ed. G. Le Strange (1890), III, 249.

delivered in person that afternoon, offered however no opening for the opposition. It did not mention church rates or church reform and contained only mild references to the unfinished topics of the previous session—Irish municipal reform, Irish tithe and Irish poor law. What criticism there was came from radicals like Wakley, Hume (who had been brought in for Kilkenny by O'Connell) and Grote, whose reaction to the reverses of the general election was to demand a further instalment of electoral reform. But Russell, to Peel's surprise, underlined the deliberate innocuousness of the queen's speech by emphatically repudiating on behalf of the government any patent radical nostrums such as the ballot, lower voting qualifications and shorter parliaments. Peel rubbed salt into the radical wounds by claiming that the reduction in the Liberal majority was due to a real change in public opinion; and a radical amendment in favour of parliamentary reform was crushed by the combined forces of government and official opposition. It was an odd start to the session. With the Conservatives spoiling for a fight, the ministry seemed equally anxious to avoid one. Nevertheless with 298 men packing their benches and a further sixteen or seventeen absentees to be reckoned on, the opposition were reconciled to the tameness of the proceedings by their own visible strength and the pleasing sight of discord among their opponents.[1]

For the moment all was harmony in the Conservative ranks and Stanley's open adhesion produced general satisfaction. On his arrival in London Peel had long and unreserved conversations with him on political affairs and at a second party meeting at Whitehall Gardens on 6 December Stanley himself made a short speech, saying that in spite of all past disagreements with Peel, there was now complete unity between them on every public issue. The formal enrolment of this distinguished recruit was celebrated with a select dinner party given by Peel three days later at which Stanley was the guest of honour. The host's pleasure was evident in the unusual animation with which he and Stanley talked to each other during the meal. Indeed, contrary to Peel's habits on such occasions, the conversation was dominated by the two great men at the head of the table who indulged in a long and lively discourse ranging from Talleyrand

[1] Graham (Peel to Graham, Stanley to Graham, 21 Nov. 1837); *Beaconsfield Letters*, pp. 117–19.

and George IV to the affairs of Prussia and Canada. Graham was still nursing his election wounds in Cumberland. But the party managers were trying to find another constituency for him and he was kept in touch by Peel and Stanley with all that was passing. The only business of importance before Christmas was the arrangement of the new civil list. Under radical pressure the Chancellor of the Exchequer, Spring Rice, had reluctantly agreed to appoint a committee to enquire into all existing pensions on the list, some of which dated as far back as 1769. Althorp in 1830 had refused to upset the rights of established pensioners and Spring Rice himself had rejected a similar enquiry in 1834 as painful and useless. With these helpful precedents Peel moved in a biting speech on 8 December a series of amendments designed to protect royal prerogative and uphold the previous practice of government. He was defeated by over sixty votes but it was a notoriously embarrassing issue for M.P.s blessed (or cursed) with large middle-class constituencies. Peel was far from being disappointed at the result of an exercise which he had undertaken on grounds of principle rather than of expediency. Indeed at the party meeting on 6 December, when he told his followers of his intention to divide the House on this issue, he said he did not expect everyone to follow him in such an unpopular course.[1] A fortnight later parliament adjourned for the recess. It had been originally intended to reassemble in February but the startling news that the political unrest in Canada had broken into open revolt made the cabinet decide at the last minute to bring forward the date to mid-January. With the radicals sulky, and arrears of legislation from the previous session still to be cleared off, the government now faced trouble from yet another quarter.

II

The Canadian crisis had been threatening ever since 1831. Essentially it was a fusion of two endemic problems: the inescapable friction between a crown executive and a colonial legislature, particularly over matters of finance and ministerial responsibility, and local nationalist and religious separatism in Quebec. Two simultaneous though dissimilar risings in upper and lower Canada transferred

[1] Graham (Stanley to Graham, 17 Dec. 1837); 44777 fos. 36, 40.

these issues from the departmental files of the Colonial Office to the floor of the House of Commons. The effect was curious and instructive. Both problems could be transposed without much difficulty into British political terms. All that was necessary was to substitute the grievances of the English radicals for those of the popular party in upper Canada, and the position of the Catholic Church in Ireland for that of French Catholics in lower Canada. In the movement for democratic control, the attacks on the upper chamber, and the demand for the application of church revenues to secular purposes, the parliamentary radicals in Britain could see in the colonial mirror their own image. Their dislike of the aristocratic structure of the state extended to the colonial establishment; they assumed and openly hoped that the colonies would soon drop away from the mother country; and their attitude towards the Canadian rebels was one of scarcely veiled encouragement. This, if unpatriotic, was at least logical. The effect on the other groupings in British politics was more complicated. The Whigs were torn between their instincts towards liberal concessions and their responsibilities as an imperial government; the Conservatives between their respect for executive authority, and their instinct to make the most of ministerial difficulties. It was not the first time that a colonial problem had disruptive consequences for domestic politics; and Canada presented a dilemma not only to the cabinet but to the leader of the opposition.

During the Christmas recess correspondence between Peel, Stanley and Wellington verified their common attitude to the fundamentals of the Canadian question. Though the government might require and deserve criticism on details, the Conservatives as a party must support them in all practical measures for suppressing the revolt. Until peace was restored, there was little value in discussing the future of Canada; though Peel privately thought that there would have to be a complete remodelling of the 1791 constitution. The summoning of parliament on 16 January came in his view either too late or too early: too late for an immediate demonstration of support for the crown, too early for any scheme of permanent settlement. However, when the House of Commons did reassemble, it was met by Russell with proposals for the suspension of the constitution of Lower Canada, a loyal address from the

House, and the despatch of Lord Durham armed with wide powers to put the government's policy into effect. Peel, while remarking on the absence of any message from the crown to underline the urgency of the crisis, pledged support for the address and next day the government laid before the House its detailed measures in the shape of a Canada bill. Its main provisions enabled the Governor-General to pass legislation in Council during the period of suspension and to convene a body formed from provincial representatives and members of the nominated Council to assist him in working out a settlement. Peel was not happy at statutory provisions for erecting a new 'representative' body at a time when the legal representative assembly of Lower Canada was suspended and that of Upper Canada still intact; and Russell had to explain that this was not an operative part of the bill but merely an authorisation to the Governor-General to call together such a body. In the Lords the Duke of Wellington showed himself more sympathetic to the ministers and more concerned with the prompt suppression of the revolt, expressing his conviction in a characteristic phrase that a great country could have no such thing as a little war. The difference of emphasis was not crucial but it was symptomatic. Many of the rank and file of the party in the Commons were dissatisfied at the apparently uncritical support for the government which Wellington was prepared to give; and Peel was not unaware of the undercurrent of feeling.

On 20 January there was a meeting of leading party men at Peel's house to discuss the whole issue—the duke, Aberdeen, Wharncliffe, Haddington, Fitzgerald, Ellenborough and Ripon from the Lords, Stanley, Francis Egerton, Granville Somerset, Hardinge, Fremantle, Pollock, Follett, Holmes, Eliot and others making up a fair cross-section of the party in the Commons. Peel restated his objections to an advisory 'convention' and suggested that the opportunity should be taken to change the constitution of Lower Canada. There was little or no dissent from this although Ellenborough and possibly Wellington secretly favoured an outright rejection of the bill. When on 22–23 January the debate in the Commons took place Peel made a powerful attack both on the details of the bill and on the government's laxity in previous years which had allowed Canadian affairs to reach such a state. Over the weekend the Conservative party whips had been quietly bringing up their men and with many Irish radicals still absent, and some English radicals hostile to the bill, there seemed a good chance that the government would be beaten.[1] But the experienced Whigs could see the danger. Ellice dexterously appealed to Russell to alter the bill in the light of Peel's criticism and so avoid a party collision over the amendments of which the opposition leader had given notice. Russell consulted his colleagues and next day agreed to make changes both in the preamble and the enacting clauses of the bill on the lines Peel had suggested. The opposition was triumphant and Peel accepted the surrender in a rather unpleasant and contemptuous speech. He turned down Russell's plea that the House should now acquiesce in the principle of the measure and reserved his right to criticise the outcome of the instructions to Durham which the cabinet had thought fit to draw up three months before the new Governor-General was due to sail and four months before he could possibly arrive. Further changes were subsequently made in response to points raised by the Conservative legal experts and the bill finally passed at the end of the month. The government had been given a mauling and their wounds were made to smart by the ridicule poured on them by the radical member Harvey who painted a lively picture of the cabinet as a set of inferior attorneys hastily throwing their crude notions together in an ill-digested draft which had to go for revision to a leader of the bar before it could be made acceptable. In the Lords the bill received the reluctant support of Wellington and Aberdeen and passed through all its remaining stages early the following month.

Having tasted blood, some of the opposition wanted to go on to the kill. Despite Russell's 'finality' language at the start of the session, faith in the ministry's ability to resist radical pressure was beginning to wear thin. To some politicians the debate on Grote's annual ballot motion in mid-February revealed the true writing on the wall. It was defeated by 198 to 315 votes but the majority was mainly composed of Conservatives. Only four cabinet ministers voted with Russell; a large number of Whig ministers together with their chief whip absented themselves; and three junior ministers

[1] Ellenborough, 20 Jan. 1838; *Greville*, 28 Jan. 1838; *Beaconsfield Letters*, pp. 129–30.

voted with Grote. Peel thought it a significant and unsatisfactory division: two hundred votes in the House of Commons for the ballot and only some sixty ministerialists voting against it. If this happened when the Whigs were in power, it was easy to imagine what they would do in opposition. It was the old dilemma in another form. Until the Conservatives could obtain a firm majority of their own, it was safer to leave the Whigs in the strait-jacket of office. How long it would be possible to keep them there was another matter. Molesworth had already given notice of a motion of censure on Lord Glenelg, the colonial secretary, and attempts had been made to enlist the support of the Conservatives. Peel discouraged Knatchbull when he raised the matter. Nevertheless feeling at the Carlton was running strongly in favour of joining Molesworth and evicting the government; and it began to look as if any other course might split the party. Peel, Wellington and Stanley were all disinclined on principle to any alliance with radicals, particularly on an issue which might bring about a change of ministry. But what was needed was not principle but action. Peel refused to commit himself and took soundings with his absent colleagues. To support Molesworth's motion he thought would be politically wrong; to vote with the government impossible; to abstain from voting shabby and irresponsible. This left by a process of elimination only one course: to move a separate amendment behind which the whole Conservative opposition could unite. Wellington unwillingly agreed that the party must vote one way or another in the debate but he wanted Peel to make it clear that the opposition did not wish to provoke a crisis and would not be answerable for its outcome. He thought the greatest evil that could befall the country would be to have a Conservative ministry forced on the queen at that particular time. In general he was full of gloom. Whether he looked at Canada, or the problems of Ireland, or the probable tactics of a Liberal opposition, he could only see lions in their path.

With this statement of their difficulties Peel could only agree. But the difficulties argued themselves; what he wanted was a formula for action. Granville Somerset assured him that the majority of the party would vote for Molesworth's motion unless something acceptable could be offered in its place. Since the debate was fixed for 6 March a decision could not be delayed much longer. As soon as Wellington, Stanley and Graham (who in February had been returned to the Commons as M.P. for Pembroke) were back in London, there was an inner council of the leading men of the party. This was followed by a general party summons to a meeting at Peel's house on 5 March. Some two hundred members attended and although the bustle of horses, cabs and carriages in the narrow street outside gave a clear indication of something unusual afoot,[1] the secret was well kept. No one outside the party knew what had been decided until Sandon rose the following evening halfway through the debate to move that an address be presented to the queen, expressing full support for the suppression of the Canadian rebellion and the establishment of a sound constitution in the colony, but declaring that the situation had arisen largely through the dilatory and irresolute conduct of her ministers. It was a neat two-headed formula guaranteed to unite the Conservatives and repel equally both radicals and Whigs. The debate, which had started tamely with a long speech by Molesworth and an unconvincing one by Palmerston, now came to life. Stanley got in some telling strokes against Palmerston and on the second night, to the cheers and laughter of his supporters, Peel made a lighthearted, ironic and devastating speech. He concluded with an invitation to the government, if they were dissatisfied with Sandon's amendment, to make the issue a straightforward one of explicit confidence in the diligence, forethought, judgement and firmness of the Secretary of State for Colonial Affairs. The opposition tactics succeeded perfectly. Ruffled by Peel's tone of condescending superiority, Russell made a short angry speech, inviting Molesworth to withdraw his motion so that there could be direct trial of strength between the parties. This with some reluctance Molesworth did, declaring at the same time his inability to vote either for or against the government; and the debate ended with a ministerial victory on conventional lines by twenty-nine votes. It was an interesting debate because it was the first time since the general election that the rival party strengths had been brought into direct collision; and when the Conservative whips analysed the division they had no reason to be displeased. They had 287 votes cast, 11 pairs, and 2 tellers; 14 were absent and there were 3 vacancies: a total party strength of 317, exactly the

[1] *Haydon*, IV, 463.

figure which Bonham had calculated after the election.[1] Added to this was the satisfaction that the radicals had been outmanœuvred, the opposition kept together, and Whigs given no chance to resign. It was a satisfaction particularly felt by Peel. Though forced almost against his will to a challenge on the Canadian issue, he had kept control of his followers and demonstrated to them that, strong as they were, they still could not provide a working majority. He had not expected to beat the government; he had not wished to. But the outcome had both confirmed his leadership and given a warning to the Whigs.[2]

From the position of power in which the Canada debate had left him, Peel was now able to adopt an attitude of measured conciliatoriness towards the government. On 27 March there was a significant exchange across the gangway between the two leaders. Russell asked whether the opposition intended to press for the total abolition of the Irish corporations. Peel in turn asked what were the intentions of the ministers on Irish tithe and the Irish Church generally. Russell replied that in view of all that had happened he did not wish to continue a contest over appropriation, and Peel promptly reciprocated by expressing his own wish for a settlement of the corporation and tithe questions provided security for the Irish Church was assured. There was in fact a general desire to bring these complex and interminable controversies to an end. The leaders of the opposition in both Houses felt that their previous resistance had narrowed the ground to the point where agreement was possible. The result of the 1837 election made doctrinaire attitudes by the Whigs untenable. It was a justification of all that Peel had been working for since 1832: the elastic defence of the great institutions of the state or the Fabian policy, as Graham called it, of wearing down the enemy without attempting major victories or risking major defeats.

It was this theme which Peel made the substance of a notable speech he delivered on 12 May at a great Conservative banquet organised in his honour. Three hundred and fifteen friends and supporters, all but two of them members of the House of Commons, dined him at the Merchant Taylors' Hall under the chairmanship of Lord Chandos. In the gallery seventy ladies headed by

<hr>

[1] Ellenborough, 7 Mar. 1838.   [2] *Greville*, 9 Mar. 1838.

Julia Peel looked down on the festive scene dappled with patches of colour where the setting sun shone through the painted windows of the old guild-hall. With Stanley and Graham seated with him at the upper table, Peel took this unprecedented opportunity of expounding directly to his own followers his conception of the nature and policy of Conservatism. He told them that his great object for some years past had been to lay the foundations of a great party which should diminish the risk and deaden the shock of a collision between the two deliberative branches of the legislature, check the precipitate zeal for alteration of the laws and constitution of the country, and say 'to the restless spirit of revolutionary change, "Here are the boundaries where all further aggression must stop"'. Its basis had been the unreserved acceptance of the Reform Act of 1832 combined with a firm resistance to any extension of the reform movement which might have the effect of destroying the mixed government left by that great constitutional enactment. They had enjoyed from the start the unrivalled moral authority of the Duke of Wellington; they had gained the adherence of some of the leading men of the reform ministry. Now they were a great and powerful party. But, he warned them, they must still bear in mind that they were a Conservative party and could not use the tactics which had sufficed the opposition in former times. 'This is a fact which I wish our impatient friends to remember.' Not only did they follow the principles on which all government ought to act but they had actually been performing many governmental functions. Their task had not been to resist but to preserve. On numerous occasions (he mentioned Canada, the move to exclude bishops from the House of Lords, the repeal of the Corn Laws, and the ballot) they had come to the rescue of the ministry against the ministers' own nominal supporters. They had rejected the temptation to unite for the sake of temporary party victories with those in fundamental disagreement with them. By doing their duty even in support of the government they had established new claims to the confidence of the electorate for becoming the government themselves. He repeated once more the basic constitutional and religious principles of the Conservative party—the defence of the settled institutions of Church and State, and the preservation of the customs and habits which had contributed to form the character and achievements of

Englishmen in war and peace, in industry and commerce, and in social improvement. What they sought, ran his peroration, was liberty without licence, and the preservation of that religion which was at once the consolation of the virtuous man and the guarantee of civil and religious liberty.

He sat down to loud and protracted cheering from the long tables in front of him. The remaining speeches were more partisan and less didactic. Stanley spoke as a former member of a great historic party, from whose traditions the Whigs of 1838 had lamentably departed, who now found his spiritual home among those who were united to defend the British constitution in church and state. Graham followed as a Liberal who regarded the Reform Act as the *ne plus ultra* of concession and saw in the present Liberal ministers if not the ability at least the will to accept further far-reaching changes of a democratic nature in Church and parliament. Lord Douro replied to the many compliments heaped on his absent father, the Duke of Wellington. Palmer, the senior M.P. for Berkshire, proposed as a back-bencher the health of Peel's cabinet of 1834. Goulburn toasted the Conservative electors of the United Kingdom; Egerton their noble chairman. With a final flurry of toasts and compliments the assembly finally dispersed at midnight full of wine, enthusiasm and cordiality. It had been a unique party occasion designed not only to honour their leader but also to celebrate their own achievements as the most powerful opposition ever known in British parliamentary history; and the party managers took care to secure adequate publicity for it. Within a few days a full account of the proceedings and speeches, prefixed by an encomiastic sketch of Peel's life and character, was printed by the *Conservative Journal* office and distributed all over the country.[1] Both Peel and the Conservative party had come a long way since the dark days of 1832 and in a sense the Merchant Taylors' Hall banquet marked the summit of his work as creator of the new Conservatism. Office still eluded him; and party unity and discipline was a tender growth that needed delicate handling. Yet for the future the main problem was how to use the power he had secured rather than how to secure that power.

Two days later, when Russell introduced his resolutions for

[1] *Authentic Report of the Conservative Festival etc.* (London 1838).

settling the Irish tithe question, the Conservatives staged a kind of epilogue of the Merchant Taylors' banquet on the floor of the House. The resolutions, though ambiguous, were generally accepted as meaning the abandonment of the appropriation principle on which the government had come to power three years earlier. To underline the moral victory Acland moved the formal rescinding of the two resolutions of 7 and 8 April 1835 on which Peel's ministry had been defeated and forced to resign. For the ministers, above all for Russell, it was a humiliating occasion. It was bad enough to wade through the mire of recantation without having their faces rubbed in the dirt; and by the same token it was a personal triumph for Peel. Acland's motion was defeated by nineteen votes: but the result was unimportant. It was the contrast with 1835 that mattered. To add to their exhibition of moral inferiority, when the ministers came in July to expound the detailed machinery of their tithe plan, they once more saw their proposals taken up and improved by the leader of the opposition. Some years previously parliament had voted a million pounds for the relief of Irish tithe-owners unable to secure payment. Not all this money had been expended but on the other hand fresh arrears of tithe had been accumulating. Peel proposed in committee a fresh mode of dealing with the problem. A commission should be appointed to ascertain the entire amount of tithe outstanding and the circumstances of each case. The round sum of £300,000 still left from the parliamentary grant should then be distributed *pro rata* among tithe-owners in purchase of their interest. Where the debtors were occupying tenants, the tithe-owners were to have the option of enforcing their claims or accepting the *pro rata* grant in settlement. The proposition was well received and subsequently, with reluctance and some changes of detail, it was accepted by Russell on behalf of the government. With that the tithe bill passed easily through both Houses and early in August the great appropriation issue was finally laid to rest.

The Irish poor law bill, on which there was little disagreement between the two major parties, had already gone through the Commons in April and received its third reading in the Lords early in July. The last of the trinity of Irish measures which had consumed such an inordinate amount of parliamentary time since 1836 did not have so happy an outcome. In May, following his favourite procedure, Peel held an inner meeting of some thirty members of the party on the Irish municipal corporations issue. A committee was appointed to draw up a series of resolutions on which it was hoped a compromise settlement could be reached with the government. These were explained to a full party meeting at the Carlton on 21 May and a week later, when Russell moved to go into committee on the bill, Peel outlined them to the House. He accepted first of all the principle of popular election for the eleven larger cities and towns in the first two schedules of the bill; he would agree to a £10 franchise provided it was on the *bona fide* rating valuation established by the new poor law and subject to residence and payment of rates. The other smaller towns he was prepared to leave with the option of applying for corporate rights but would not impose it on them. This handsome offer was favourably received by Russell; less so by his own restive followers. At a subsequent Liberal party meeting at the Foreign Office there was so much dissatisfaction that in the end the government insisted on fixing the franchise at £5. An attempt by Peel to restore the £10 rating failed by twenty votes and the bill went up to the Lords. In July Lyndhurst and the Conservative peers re-inserted the £10 qualification and in August the bill came back to the Commons. Russell in turn offered the compromise of a £10 compound rating of which a fifth could be made up by maintenance cost, repairs, and insurance: in effect therefore a net valuation of £8. This was rejected by the Lords and the bill was therefore abandoned. It was a narrow margin of difference in which to persist but Peel, who had only with great difficulty secured the support of his party for his original compromise proposals, felt that he had gone further in concessions than even his opponents had expected and that Russell's hostile attitude to the Lords precluded a settlement.[1] Even the Stanleyites, who had strongly supported Peel's conciliatory move, were not unduly concerned. Graham wrote to Stanley after the session that he did not think they had lost much by the rejection of the municipal bill compared with the immense advantages of the tithe and poor law settlement.[2]

On 16 August a long and laborious session came to an end. The House of Commons had sat for 173 days, the longest uninterrupted

[1] See his speech of 2 Aug. 1838.
[2] Graham (Graham to Stanley, 18, 20 May, 21 Aug. 1838).

period so far that century. Spanish affairs, the budget, the poor law, trade union activities, the protection of children in factories, had all at different times come up for discussion in the intervals between the major debates on Irish legislation. At the very end of the session the conduct of Durham in Canada and his arbitrary transportation of detained persons to Bermuda without trial had provoked strong parliamentary criticism. The government rounded off their unhappy record by disallowing his ordinances and rushing an indemnity bill through parliament on the day before prorogation. But this did end the tale of trouble. If the radical attacks on the Church and the House of Lords had noticeably slackened, the economic depression of 1837–38 had brought a harsher climate to the country as a whole and piecemeal remedies were beginning to be put forward from many different quarters. Ashley's attempt to stiffen the clauses of the 1833 Factory Act for the protection of children in factories had been turned down by the leading men of all parties—Russell, Poulett Thomson, Peel, O'Connell and Hume—as involving unprecedented, damaging and shortsighted restriction on the employment of labour in industry. But it secured a significant degree of support from back-benchers. Another piece of social legislation favoured by the experts was running into increased opposition as its operations spread to the distressed areas of the industrial north and midlands where the problem was not so much pauperism as unemployment. This was the new poor law of 1834 whose unpopularity had been exploited by some Conservative and radical candidates in the 1837 election.

The coronation in June attracted a throng of distinguished visitors to the capital and for some weeks London had worn a gala appearance with innumerable fêtes and banquets. But with the autumn, unemployment, poverty, and high prices in many parts of the kingdom soon obliterated the recollections of these summer festivities. The democratic reform programme of the doctrinaire radicals was taken up by working-class agitators; a new movement, 'Chartism', began to be mentioned in the newspapers; and before long the British public were becoming ominously familiar with such names as Stephens, Oastler, Vincent, and Feargus O'Connor. Dangerous as they seemed, these were social rather than political problems. They affected Melbourne's cabinet as an executive responsible for law and order, rather than parliament as a body responsible for policy and legislation. There was another movement born of the depression years of 1837-38, however, which though less dramatic, and initially less publicised than Chartism, was capable of becoming a more explosive issue in parliamentary politics. It concerned not so much the problems of the poor as the interests of the rich. For over twenty years the Corn Laws had been a political target for democratic radicals and a fiscal problem for successive administrations. Since 1837 Villiers had made it his particular crusade in parliament without achieving much beyond periodic publicity. But in September 1838 was founded the Manchester Anti-Corn Law Association and with it the nucleus of a campaign for the repeal of the Corn Laws drawing its support from wealthy manufacturers and merchants and impelled by class jealousy and hard material motives. The marked increase in petitions to parliament praying for repeal at the start of the following session was a clear sign that a new wind was filling the sails of the repeal movement. From being an item in the general radical programme it had taken the first step towards a separate nation-wide agitation.

All these social discontents and nascent organisations added to the difficulties of the Whigs. Yet in a sense they strengthened their position as the only possible administration and placed further restrictions on the conduct of the opposition. To the perils confronting a minority Conservative ministry catalogued with gloomy satisfaction by Wellington in the spring could now be added the Condition of England question. For Peel therefore the Fabian tactics were still the right ones to employ; from that point of view the session had been successful. It was true that at times a hard and contemptuous note had entered into his criticisms of the government when both policy and magnanimity might have dictated a more conciliatory approach. With a prime minister as often at court as in Downing Street, and an aristocratic cabinet whose instincts were less Liberal than his own, Russell had carried the burden of representing the government in the lower House almost single-handed with courage and fortitude if not always with great skill. The balance of debating power was now markedly with the opposition front bench; and they had little to gain from inflicting humiliation on him. Yet the problems of a party leader are more within his party than without; and Peel had his own followers to contend with. Throughout the session he had been under repeated pressure to adopt a more aggressive attitude towards the government. All his parliamentary skill had been necessary to devise opportunities for his impatient party to blow off its head of steam without wrecking the fragile machinery of equilibrium between ministry and opposition. His actions, however, if not always his words, had remained uniformly moderate and cautious; and despite the grumbling of his back-benchers at the eternal talk of compromise, he had never lost control of the party. It had not been easy; and at the end of his speech on the Lords' amendments to the Irish Corporations bill he had let fall some significant words on how he had laboured to bring about a compromise at the expense of great misconception, personal abuse and sacrifice of feeling. This was not exaggeration. Peel himself would have gone further in compromise on Irish corporations but he had been obliged to carry with him both his followers in the Commons, including an influential and stiffnecked Irish squad, and also the leading Conservative peers. The £10 franchise he had offered had been the limit of concession he had been able to obtain. Once the party line was settled, he felt unable to withdraw from it when the Lords' amendments came down at the end of the session. Even so, his insistence on compromise had left a residue of unconsumed resentment in the party. Graham during the autumn heard so much criticism of the alleged slackness of Conservative leaders during the past session and saw so many signs of rebelliousness, that he wrote to Bonham in October asking him to do what he could from his position of influence in the Carlton to soften internal animosities and keep the party together. 'My own apprehensions have always been', he added gloomily, 'that in this Parliament we shall never divide again so strong as we were on the day after the dinner to Peel.'[1]

III

Early in August Peel returned to Drayton where Julia and the children had preceded him a month earlier. In contrast to previous years the autumn was passed peacefully at home. After the boys had

[1] 40616 fos. 20–1; cf. *Greville*, 23 Aug. 1838.

gone back to school in September there was a constant succession of
mainly masculine parties marked laconically in Peel's engagement
book 'to shoot and dine'. In October he was the guest of Lord Lichfield and the officers of the Staffordshire yeomanry at Lichfield. In
December there was a grand and somewhat military gathering at
Drayton which included the Peninsular veterans Lord Hill, Fitzroy
Somerset, Hardinge and the Spanish General Alava, together with
the Duke of Rutland, Lord Ripon, Stanley, Arbuthnot and Sandon.[1]
What little political communication seemed necessary before the
meeting of parliament took place verbally with Stanley, Ellenborough and Aberdeen at Drayton and by correspondence with
Wellington and Graham. It was still Peel's view that unless something unforeseen happened, the government would stagger on
through their difficulties and the less said by the opposition the
better. He declined several invitations to speak at public meetings
and when Graham was elected rector of Glasgow University in
succession to himself at the end of the year, he sent a gentle warning
against making any specific declarations on behalf of the Conservative party. During the autumn Graham had received a number of
letters from Lord Tavistock which he thought were inspired by
Russell as a precaution in case the government were driven to the
last resort of coalition. Peel was not convinced by this interpretation.
He was more inclined to think that a few more lost by-elections
would convert Russell to the ballot.[2] In January, when it was
learned that Wood, the Chairman of the Manchester Chamber of
Commerce, would second the address at the start of the next session,
he concluded even more cynically that the cabinet was preparing in
the last eventuality to take up the repeal of the Corn Laws and
'retire from their dishonourable position, setting fire to all within
their reach'. This was the uninhibited expression of his vacation
thoughts; but behind it was a more settled and positive attitude.
Difficult as the task of succeeding to the Whigs would be, with a
hostile sovereign and an evenly balanced Commons, there was no
alternative for the opposition but to proceed steadily along their
chosen path, avoiding any alliance with the radicals but otherwise
not too minutely calculating the consequences.

[1] Goulburn, Peel's memorandum book.
[2] Graham (Graham to Stanley, 21 Sept., 9 Dec.; Peel to Graham, 5 Dec. 1838).

On the eve of the 1839 session it looked as though the government might well seek to escape from their mounting difficulties at home and abroad. Durham had thrown up his post in Canada and returned home in a pugnacious mood which he took care to make known to the public on both sides of the Atlantic. Brougham in the House of Lords was malevolently active against the Whig ministry which had excluded him in 1835. The political world was full of talk of a possible dissolution; and Peel was being pressed to give notice of some amendment to the address which would rally the opposition in full strength at the opening of parliament. For Wellington, it was true, the embarrassments of the ministers only increased his reluctance to take sides against them. He went so far as to opine to Arbuthnot that the Conservatives should not accept office even if they secured a majority. He disliked the radicals; he hated the idea of an alliance with Brougham; he thought popular feeling was against the Conservative party; and he had persuaded himself that the Reform Act had made government almost impossible. With many of these sentiments Peel agreed. Yet, as he said to Arbuthnot, even on public grounds it was essential to keep the party together as a brake on the radical excesses of the government. Abstention from opposition would simply mean that the opposition would soon cease to exist. On 26 January he wrote to Wellington, arguing that even without any gratuitous attacks on the government, Canada and the Corn Laws would almost certainly come under parliamentary discussion and that it was important therefore to consider what their attitude should be. On the first of these issues he thought it sensible to abstain from any expression of opinion until they heard what Durham and the cabinet each had to say. On the second, the indications were that the government would leave it an open question while instituting an enquiry into the operation of the law. If so, an amendment to the address might be unavoidable. Wellington, though he did not think Melbourne would make the Corn Laws a cabinet question, agreed with this attitude of cautious preparedness. Graham on the other hand held that the corn question would be raised by the cabinet in one form or another and that it would be impossible for the opposition not to defend the principle of protection if not all its details.[1]

[1] 40318 fos. 131–5; 40310 f. 252; Peel, II, 378–81.

In the event neither the best nor the worst of these anticipations were realised. Parliament reassembled on 5 February and though the queen's speech contained no reference to the Corn Laws, the question was raised in a significant manner by the movers of the address in both Houses. In the Commons Wood incongruously coupled a description of the prosperity in industry and commerce with a demand for the repeal of the Corn Laws to enable these interests to meet foreign competition. Peel pounced on this inconsistency in a long speech covering foreign affairs, Canada, the government's laxity in dealing with Chartist disorders, and the increasing vindication of his prophecies that the concessions made in 1832 would never satisfy the forces of popular radicalism. Russell combined a declaration on the finality of the Reform Act with a warning that the time had come to review the Corn Laws. But there was little excitement in the debate and a radical amendment in favour of a reform of the electoral system was easily beaten. The real discussion on the Corn Laws came later. In the middle of February the mass of petitions sent to both Houses in favour of repeal gave the opportunity to Brougham in the Lords and Villiers in the Commons to raise a debate on the issue. Peel was obliged by the form of the discussion on that occasion to confine his argument largely to a statistical demonstration that there had been no decline either in exports generally or in those particularly affected by wages and the cost of living. In March, however, there was a wider debate lasting five evenings on Villiers's motion for a committee of the whole House to enquire into the 1828 Corn Law. Peel took advantage of this to enter into a comprehensive review of the reasons adduced for a revision or repeal of the act.

His speech was destructive and critical; inevitably so since he was faced with conflicting and exaggerated arguments from his opponents and two suggested alternatives to the existing system—the complete free trade demanded by the abolitionists, and the fixed duty proposed by some members of the government. He showed a rational willingness to consider the varied contentions of free traders; he made skilful use of statistics; and he was sensibly sceptical of the theoretical arguments of individual political economists. He agreed that the argument that protection in corn injured the poor was an important one, and added (a significant proviso for Peel personally if not for the general debate) that if the Corn Laws could be shown to be inconsistent with an improvement in the condition of the labouring classes, then 'the Corn Law is practically at an end'. The evidence of savings banks at Liverpool, Manchester, Glasgow and Leicester, however, was one argument to the contrary. The Chartist denunciation of the repeal agitation as a middle-class attempt to lower wages was another. The entry into the country of large quantities of foreign corn even under existing law as a result of the bad harvests of 1838 was a third. In general, he argued, there was no evidence that the Corn Laws had held back the growth of industry; no evidence that free trade would throw open large markets to British manufacturers. In any case no British legislation could prevent the growth of industrialisation in Europe or America. If, on the other hand, for marginal or speculative advantages British agriculture with its burden of local and national taxation was exposed to free competition, the demand would inevitably and justly be made to deprive the other great economic interests of the country of the protection they enjoyed. He turned finally to the government. Unable to put forward an agreed policy and unwilling to offer a united opposition to the motion, they seemed ready (as he phrased it with mild humour) to enter into a fishing committee, baited with the delusion that they would catch a corn bill. Even if the opposition had favoured free trade in corn, this would make them pause. But when invited to follow distracted counsels, divided colleagues, contradictory evidence and inconclusive arguments, they must decline throwing the existing Corn Law into the lottery of legislation in the faint hope of securing a better system.

It was a good speech but a negative one. His positive advocacy of protection was more conventional and less prominent. It was not his business at that stage to offer constructive solutions: nor was it necessary. A majority of 147 against the motion adequately conveyed the weight of cross-party feeling against tampering with the sacred cause of agricultural protection. For the opposition it was an eminently satisfactory result. Despite support for Villiers's motion from Russell, Palmerston, Howick, and Spring Rice, some seventy ministerialists had voted with the Conservatives to make up the majority. Some agricultural hotheads, led by the inevitable Chandos (who in January succeeded his father as Duke of Buckingham) wanted to exploit the victory with a motion of censure on the government for their attitude towards the Corn Laws. A representative from the agriculturalists in the Carlton waited on Peel with this proposal the following morning. He successfully discouraged what he described to Wellington as this 'egregious folly'. Even so, he and the duke were placed in a position of some embarrassment only a few days later by the action of some of their followers on another issue.

In January 1839 had occurred an event noteworthy even in the endless catalogue of Irish crime: the assassination at Durrow Abbey, Kings County, in his own grounds and in broad daylight, of an elderly, inoffensive, unpolitical nobleman, Lord Norbury. The exacerbation of party feeling which resulted spread from Ireland to Westminster. A motion by Shaw early in March asking for a return of crime figures over the last four years led to a two-day debate in the Commons. Later the same month a move was made to secure a committee of enquiry in the House of Lords. Peel, having consulted Wellington, gave his opinion that there was little to be gained but that he would not object to a general enquiry if it was strongly desired by the Irish members of the party. The actual motion put forward by Lord Roden on 21 March was for an enquiry into Irish crime since 1835. His speech took the form of a direct attack on the administration of Lord Normanby who had recently retired from the Lord Lieutenancy to take over the Colonial Office relinquished by the unhappy Glenelg. Wellington supported the motion on the assumption that it had been agreed with Peel and the government not unnaturally took it as an indirect motion of censure. When it was carried in the upper House, Russell at once announced that he would seek a resolution of support from the House of Commons after the Easter recess.

In the interval O'Connell indulged in inflammatory speeches on behalf of his Precursor Society movement in Ireland, and the Conservative leaders took counsel together. Wellington was angry with the partisan extravagance of the Irish peers and also perhaps at the false position in which he had been put. Peel, more calmly, suggested that the best reply from the opposition would be simply that it was premature to ask for the approval of the House of Commons on the administration of Ireland before the results of the enquiry into Irish crime and agitation were available. He suspected that the ministers would not be unwilling to find a pretext for resignation and his suspicions were confirmed by two indications of the pessimistic feeling in the cabinet. One account, passed on by Greville through Graham, was to the effect that Russell anticipated an early end to the ministry and would be prepared to give Peel independent support if circumstances made it possible. The other, more factual, was a message from Melbourne to Wellington through the discreet if unconventional channel of the latter's niece Lady Burghersh, that in the event of resignation he would advise the queen to send for the duke. Wellington, less concerned with tactics than with consequences, concluded that the ministers were preparing to go out and told Arbuthnot that he in turn would advise the queen to send for Peel.[1] This information was duly reported to Peel but it is unlikely that either Greville's story or Melbourne's message made much difference to his tactics. He had already made up his mind that it was essential not to meet the government's motion of confidence in their Irish administration with a direct negative which might complicate future Conservative policy in Ireland and even, if supported by the radicals, lead to the immediate resignation of the ministry.

There was considerable speculation on how the opposition would meet the government's challenge, but Peel's parliamentary dexterity was not so easily caught out as this. The series of resolutions he brought forward followed the lines he had suggested to Wellington and received the general approval of the party. When the great debate came on he contented himself with a light satirical speech which raised a good deal of laughter in the House. The phrasing of Russell's motion which called for approval of the government of Ireland 'of late years', allowed him to enquire gently whether it covered the administration of Lord Wellesley in 1821–28, when he was himself Home Secretary, or merely the period since 1830 which however included his own ministry of 1834–35. He denied emphatically that the Roden committee was designed as a censure on the government and was careful himself to avoid any imputation of censure. In fact the more significant feature of the debate was a separate amendment by Duncombe in favour of electoral reform and a warning from Leader that if the motion had been one of general confidence in the Whig ministers, some ten or twelve

---

[1] *Greville*, 6, 10, 13 Apr. 1839; 40341 fos. 62–72; *Peel*, II, 387.

radicals would vote against it. The position of the ministry, observed the indignant member for Westminster, was that Mr. O'Connell governed Ireland, and Sir Robert Peel governed England. The leader of the Conservatives was satisfied with power without place or patronage; the Whigs with place and patronage without power. Let any honourable man, he concluded, say which was the more honourable position! The protracted debate spread over five evenings ended at last on 19 April with the defeat of Peel's amendment by 318 votes to 296. If Leader was right, twelve discontented radicals alone stood between the cabinet and defeat. It was an insubstantial barrier.

Meanwhile, in February that annual feature of the parliamentary scene, the Irish Corporations bill, had once more put in an appearance. Its terms were basically those proposed by Russell at the end of the previous session: a net annual rating of £8 as franchise qualification, together with a new proviso that all resident ratepayers should be enfranchised when the new poor law administration had been established for a period of three years. When it came up for second reading on 8 March Peel and Stanley supported the government against some of their own more uncompromising followers. With a new bill and a fresh session Peel felt free to reconsider his course. Since the poor law and tithe questions were now settled, he thought it a matter of obligation to promote the one remaining measure of the Irish trilogy and a matter of commonsense to make the marginal concessions which the political situation demanded. This tender handling of the government did not recommend itself to Tories like Sir Robert Inglis or Irish members like Shaw who brought forward various hostile amendments when the bill went into committee. But the disunity in the opposition was soon overshadowed by even greater discord among ministerial supporters. In April trouble struck the government from yet another quarter. The emancipation of the West Indian slaves in 1833 had provided for a period of Negro apprenticeship due to end in 1840. Abolitionist activity in 1838, however, had accelerated this timetable. The cabinet had felt obliged to pass an act for the better protection of the Negroes; in Jamaica under executive pressure the Assembly agreed to end apprenticeship in 1838. In the meantime a further stringent bill went through parliament dealing with the controversial question of prison and workhouse administration in Jamaica. When the news of this reached the colony, the strained relations between governor and Assembly finally snapped. The Assembly refused to carry on its functions until it received an assurance of its continued legislative independence; attempts at conciliation failed; and in April 1839 the cabinet introduced a bill to suspend the constitution and put the island under the rule of the governor and a reinforced council.

It was the Canadian solution applied to a smaller problem, with less provocation and greater haste. The measure was criticised by several leading Conservatives—Peel, Stanley, Goulburn, and Gladstone—and on 23 April Peel expressed the hope that the Jamaican Assembly would be given a further interval for reflection. On the motion to go into committee on 3 May he again showed his dislike of the bill. While not defending the action of the colonial planters, he thought that the tactless conduct of the government had precipitated the crisis. The decisive attitude was, however, that of the left-wing Liberals. The radical section of the party was divided between democrats and abolitionists; but several leading speakers like Hume and Grote attacked the severity and injustice of the bill and on a division at the end of the adjourned debate the government majority sank to only five. It was typical of the desultory and disordered session of 1839 that the final crisis came in this accidental fashion. Peel had argued in good faith for a policy of delay; the Jamaica dispute certainly offered no very attractive ground on which to take office. The government had expected before the debate to have their full majority and even as it was they had not actually been beaten.[1] But nine of their usual supporters voted against them and in the context of all that had passed that session it was enough. The following day, 7 May, Melbourne resigned office and advised the queen to send for Wellington. The situation which had been talked about for so long had suddenly arrived.

IV

On the morning of Wednesday, 8 May, Peel had a note from Wellington to say that he had been summoned to Buckingham

[1] *Greville*, 5, 10 May.

Palace. It had gone half-past one when there arrived at Whitehall Gardens a red-waxed envelope with the royal seal. It contained in big sprawling legible writing a single sentence. 'The Queen requests Sir Robert Peel to come to her as soon as he can, if possible by two o'clock.' Message and notice could hardly have been shorter and by the time Peel had got into court dress and driven to the Palace it was just after the desired time. He was under no illusions as to what awaited him. It was only because she had no choice that the queen was sending for him; and if he was not previously aware of his deficiencies in dealing with strange young women, he had just been told of them in a letter which an old friend, Lady de Grey, had sent him the day before warning him with more candour than tact that it would be difficult with his reserved and cautious manner to overcome the queen's prepossessions for Melbourne. Waiting for him in the Palace was a short, sulky young woman of twenty in a state of suppressed anger, misery and nervousness. With her heavy Hanoverian face, sharp nose and receding chin, it was an unmistakable granddaughter of George III who confronted Peel when he was ushered in.

The opening exchanges were stiff but civil. Victoria said that on the advice of the Duke of Wellington she had sent for him to form a ministry; that she had parted with her late government with regret; that she hoped he would not want to dissolve parliament as she had great objection to dissolutions; and that she wished the duke to be a member of the new administration. Peel replied that he would do all in his power to help; that he would not advise dissolution before giving the present parliament a trial but presumed the queen was not laying down an absolute condition; and that he would regard the duke's assistance as indispensable. There was some talk of particular offices and a mention of Goulburn's desire to stand for the Speakership and the test that this might provide of the government's ability to control the House. The queen spoke of her friendship with Melbourne and Peel agreed that she could not at the start give him the same confidence and that he did not expect her to give up seeing her late prime minister. But he emphasised the difficulties of his task, expressed his surprise at the resignation of the Whigs, and said that he would like the queen to demonstrate some confidence in her new ministers and that the Household would be a mark of this. He left with the understanding that he would submit names for all the principal offices on the following day. That evening he conferred with his chief colleagues: Wellington, Aberdeen, Lyndhurst, Ellenborough, Stanley, Graham, Goulburn and Hardinge. Among other matters the question of court appointments came up for discussion. It was an inescapable even if minor problem. In the first place, as a result of Melbourne's careless partisanship, an unusually large number of women holding Household posts were close relatives of the outgoing Whig ministers. They included the wife of Lord Normanby, two sisters of Lord Morpeth, a sister-in-law of Lord John Russell, a sister of Lord Howick, and a daughter of Spring Rice, in addition to several wives and relatives of Whig peers. Secondly, under the rule of the dominant Paget clan, the whole tone of court life was notoriously lax. Lord Conyngham, the Lord Chamberlain, and Lord Uxbridge had both installed their mistresses on the palace staff; and the recent scandal of Lady Flora Hastings had provoked savage comment in society and the press. Peel thought that those ladies immediately connected with the Whig party would and certainly should resign; and he had a talk with Lord Ashley on the kind of person who ought to compose the entourage of a young unmarried queen. That the queen attached importance to the question of household appointments was obvious, since she had mentioned it to both Wellington and Peel. Since Peel, however, had no intention of interfering with the subordinate posts of maids of honour or of removing all the ladies of the bedchamber it was not a problem which seemed to offer any peculiar difficulties.

This was a rational assumption. What the group of elderly politicians talking that evening failed to realise was that the strong emotional relationship between Victoria and Melbourne made them both a little less than rational during this crisis. In the case of the young inexperienced queen this was excusable; in her former prime minister less so. Immediately after her interview with Peel she had written a full account to Melbourne and in his reply the next morning he had advised her among other things to press the question of the Household strongly as a personal matter but not to let negotiations break down on it if Peel was unable to accede. The queen acknowledged this in an appealing little letter saying that she would do all he said and begging him to be what he had always been—a father to one who never wanted support more than she did at that moment. Back came an instant and sympathetic note to tell her that if Peel pressed for the removal of those of her Household who were not in parliament, he would be pressing her more hardly than any minister had ever pressed a monarch before. It was fortified with this encouragement that Victoria faced Peel when he returned soon after one o'clock on 9 May. The interview began quietly with a discussion of political offices. When they moved to court appointments the queen signified a wish to have Lord Liverpool, to which Peel readily agreed as she in turn did to his proposal of Lord Ashley. 'Now about the Ladies,' began Peel and was at once cut short. She could not give up any of her ladies, said Victoria firmly, and had never imagined such a thing. Peel asked if she meant to retain them all. 'All', came the stubborn reply. He tried to reason with the determined and excited young woman facing him across the yellow closet-room in which their interview took place. He begged her not to come to any precipitate decision. He pointed out that some of her ladies, for example Lady Normanby, were wives of her late ministers. That did not matter, replied the queen, for she never talked politics with them; and she counter-attacked by mentioning some of the Bedchamber women and maids of honour related to Tories. Peel said he did not mean the subordinate posts but the mistress of the robes and the Ladies of the Bedchamber. Those, replied Victoria promptly and with disconcerting lack of logic, were of more consequence than the others. She could not consent to part with them and it had never been asked before. Peel reminded her that she was queen regnant which made a difference: Victoria said it did not. He urged her on public grounds to make concessions; she refused to admit this as a consideration.

When all his arguments were exhausted Peel went off to get the duke who tried his own powers of persuasion alone but with equal unsuccess. Peel then saw Victoria once more and told her he would have to consult his colleagues and come back that evening. When the stillborn cabinet discussed the situation there was general agreement that difficulties over the Speakership and the certainty at the outset of being in a minority in the House of Commons made it indispensable to have some mark of public confidence from the queen. If she was determined to keep all her ladies of the Bed-chamber, they could not go on. Soon after five o'clock Peel returned to the Palace and informed Victoria of their decision. She said she would reflect but was certain that she would not change her mind. Even that minute concession was due to Melbourne who had been startled to receive a note from the queen telling him that Peel 'had behaved very ill and has insisted on my giving up my Ladies'. In his reply he admitted that he had never anticipated such a demand but urged Victoria to listen to what Peel and Wellington had to say and take time before coming to a peremptory decision. He came himself later that evening, heard Victoria's excited firsthand account of her interviews, and departed to consult in turn his own colleagues. At two o'clock in the morning the waiting queen received a note from Melbourne advising her to inform Peel that having considered his proposal to remove the Ladies of her Bedchamber she could not consent to a course contrary to usage and repugnant to her feelings. Copying the whole phrase word for word from Melbourne's letter the queen wrote another single-sentence communication for Peel and retired triumphantly to bed. The message went off at nine o'clock the next day. Peel sent his reply the same morning: a long careful document recapitulating the succession of events, stating the impression of both himself and the duke that the queen wished to reserve all the appointments of Ladies of the Bedchamber, and reiterating their agreed view that the difficult political circumstances facing the new ministry made it essential for Peel to have the public proof of the queen's support implicit in permission to make some changes in her Household. When Melbourne came that afternoon he read the letter and started visibly at the phrase 'some changes'. For the first time he realised that Peel had only made limited requests for changes. But some or all, said the exhilarated and happy young woman sitting with him, was the same. For practical purposes it had to be the same for the Whig cabinet who had gone too far in their support for the queen to withdraw now.

The news that the Whigs were in again spread like wildfire over the capital. Disappointed Tories spoke of planned intrigue; Whigs of Peel's dictatorial and unreasonable behaviour: and the rebellious radicals, to whom the events of the last few days had come as a douche of cold water, hastened to restore good relations with their party. The wildest accounts of the rupture were circulated but few knew the details. The public was still in some uncertainty even after the parliamentary accounts given by Peel and Russell on 13 May. Peel, while explaining and defending his own actions, said as little as possible about the queen's. Russell's speech left it unclear whether or not Victoria had really thought Peel was asking for the removal of all her ladies. A similar restraint was shown by Melbourne and Wellington in the Lords on the following night. In fact, however, as some neutral observers like Greville began to perceive, the Whigs had placed themselves and their youthful sovereign in an unfortunate and unconstitutional position. The root of the trouble was Melbourne's dual and contradictory role as prime minister and private secretary to the crown. He was the only person to whom Victoria could turn for guidance and this in turn created the remarkable situation in which the queen took the advice of one cabinet in dealing with another. It was true that the Whig leaders had been misled by Victoria over what precisely Peel had been asking her to do; but they had taken remarkably little trouble to find out. Melbourne had every disposition to be fair to his political successor but he had allowed himself to be carried along by Victoria's ardour and his own generous affection. Constitutionally the defence of the Whigs was that there was no recent nor any clear precedent governing the appointment of Ladies of the Bedchamber to a queen regnant. It was an accepted convention that in the case of a king's Household the high officers should either be neutral in politics or support the ministers of the day, and that those who held seats in either House of parliament should vote with the government. The question was how to apply a principle established in another context to the novel circumstances of a young unmarried queen. The Ladies of the Bedchamber did not sit in parliament; but it was a reasonable extension of the existing constitutional practice that they should not be selected from women having close ties with leading members of the opposition. Melbourne himself had occasionally intervened even in the appointment of ladies-in-waiting and had asked Victoria to support his government by accepting his recommendations.[1] Certainly there were good human reasons for dealing gently with the young and unhappy Victoria. On the other hand

[1] 40432 f. 77.

Peel was faced with a hostile parliamentary majority, and a sovereign clearly averse to granting a dissolution, determined to remain on terms of intimacy with his predecessor, and notoriously unfriendly to the Conservatives. To have taken office without the public mark of confidence implicit in the retirement of some of the leading Whig ladies and their replacement by Conservatives would have been almost advertising the stop-gap nature of his administration. The justice of his request seemed so obvious that he had never anticipated any difficulty on this score before the interviews with the queen took place.

The decisive role, however, was played by Victoria herself. It was evident from the start that she had made up her mind to yield as little as possible to Melbourne's successor. The question of the ladies became important because it was the first issue demanding immediate decision on which there was room for disagreement. But Victoria's hostility was because she was losing her minister, not her ladies. As she said significantly to Russell afterwards, 'I have stood by you, you must now stand by me'.[1] In the circumstances it would have needed unusual charm and flattery to have coaxed her out of her rebellious mood; and what Peel presented was only patient reasoned argument put forward by a large, shy, self-conscious man. She recorded afterwards that she could not make out what he meant; it is unlikely that she wanted to. She found him cold and odd but she was scarcely an impartial witness. There was clearly a temperamental antipathy; yet this was not the important factor. The old duke, more versed in the ways of women, she liked better; but his arguments still made no impression on her. As for the Whig allegations that Peel's manner had been harsh and peremptory, Wellington (who was no uncritical devotee of his colleague) told Greville that he had never seen Peel so gentle and conciliatory and that there was nothing at which Victoria could have taken offence.[2] Yet all this was useless against an emotional girl of twenty with strong will and strong temper. Exploiting the somewhat confused loyalties of the Whig ministers, Victoria had her way and the partisans of the two sides were left to circulate their own misleading versions of what happened. The Conservative party managers were left with the gloomy conviction that they now had to contend with an unnatural

[1] *Greville*, 10 May 1839.   [2] *ibid.*, 15 Aug. 1839.

alliance of the crown and the mob; and some Conservative M.P.s later in the year gave relief to their feelings by public and indecorous criticism of the queen. Peel kept his feelings to himself. To be denied office in the circumstances of 1839 was no great hardship. But he had gone to the palace ready to show respect and sympathy for the young queen and he would have been less than human had he not felt that part at least of the hostility he had encountered was personal to himself. To that extent the Bedchamber incident was a blow to his self-confidence. What rankled most keenly, however, was the charge that he had behaved in a mannerless and overbearing way towards the young girl who was his sovereign. Nevertheless he would not retract an inch from the constitutional position he had taken up. Replying in June to an address of approval from Shrewsbury he made a public and explicit statement that the sex of persons made no difference to the general principles governing appointments of state, however much the exercise of ministerial authority might be restrained by personal consideration for the monarch; and he added that any necessity for change was not of his making but that of the ministers who had in previous years given such a marked political character to the queen's Household.[1]

V

With a powerful opposition temporarily disabled from taking office and a weak ministry temporarily disabled from resigning the 1839 session took on an even more desultory character. The cabinet seemed to be floundering in a sea of executive problems. They could do little except with the tacit connivance of the Conservative leaders; and in the general paralysis of liberal policy the enthusiasm drained from their supporters both in the Commons and in the country at large. It was true that some belated marginal concessions were made to radical opinion. When Grote's annual ballot motion came up on 18 June it was made an open question and seventeen members of

[1] For the Bedchamber incident see *VL*, I, 154–75; *Girlhood of Queen Victoria*, ed. Viscount Esher (1912), II, 159–77; *Peel*, II, 388–407; *Hodder*, pp. 130–2. Victoria herself may be allowed the last word. Talking about it in 1897 to Sir Arthur Bigge, she said 'Yes! I was very hot about it and so were my Ladies as I had been so much brought up under Lord Melbourne; but I was *very* young, only 20 and never should have acted so again. Yes! it was a mistake.' (RA/L 17/56).

the administration including one cabinet minister voted for it. But as it was lost by almost exactly the same number of votes as in the preceding session, any progress made was not very perceptible. In the budget arrangements, which for the third year running showed a deficit, a new uniform penny postage was instituted despite the criticisms of Peel and Goulburn and the virtual certainty of a loss of unpredictable dimensions on the initial operation of the scheme. But these titbits were of little significance compared with what happened on the three important remaining issues of the session: education, Canada, and Jamaica.

The essence of the educational dispute of 1839 was that it was a religious dispute. The outcome was a measure of the Anglican and Conservative revival which had taken place since 1830. With the passing of relief measures for dissenters in 1836, and the firm programme of Church reform initiated by Peel's Ecclesiastical Commission of 1835 and continued by his Whig successors, the vulnerability of the established Church had largely disappeared and it was increasingly able (as the victory over Church rates in 1837 had demonstrated) to reassert its influence in English society. The conflict between Church and Dissent in the field of education was almost inevitable since it was a widening area in which the boundaries between the claimants were ill-defined. Most thinking people, except for advanced educational theorists like Wyse and Slaney in the Commons or Brougham in the House of Lords, held the view that education was the province of religion. The question was, which religion. It was true that without state aid the educational growth of the country would be stunted and inadequate. But the distribution of the annual parliamentary grant of £20,000 instituted in 1833 through the two great religious agencies, the Anglican National Society and the Dissenting British and Foreign Society, had carefully avoided the danger of either state direction or confessional monopoly. The Whig scheme of 1839, however, as outlined by Russell in February and expressed more specifically in a Privy Council minute of June, cut across both the existing pattern of state assistance and the deepest instincts of churchmen and Wesleyan Methodists. While increasing the annual grant to £30,000, it laid down that this sum would not as before go preponderantly to the National Society nor necessarily to any particular religious agency. Secondly, it involved a deliberate and increasing measure of state control through an educational committee of the Privy Council and a system of government inspectors for all schools in receipt of grants. Finally it took a step towards a more secular type of education by the institution of a non-confessional normal school for teacher-training. The general body of Non-conformists, with some misgivings over the extent of state direction, accepted the plan as redressing the balance between Church and Dissent. It came from a government which they still regarded as their political friend, and it owed much to the impetus of the radical Central Society for Education founded in 1836. To that extent therefore it could be regarded as a further liberal advance towards religious equality. For precisely the same reasons it was regarded by Anglicans as a direct attack on the position and authority of the Church.

The Conservative and Anglican forces in the country were not unprepared. As early as 1837 Peel had forecast that after the failure on appropriation and church rates, the next agitation would be on education. On that he had two things to say. First, a system of state education excluding or barely tolerating the intervention of the Church would mean an end to the Establishment and ultimately perhaps to all religious feeling at all. Second, there was no better ground on which the Church could fight since it had the means of defence in its own hands. He anticipated little difficulty in beating off the attack provided Church and laity worked together to provide the means of defence. The answer to the criticism of Church education was for the Church to make its education better and more widely available. 'It won't suffice,' he told Croker, 'to abuse the Government plan.'[1] In fact, in the intervening couple of years the young Anglicans of his party, notably Acland, Gladstone, Ashley, Sandon and Praed, successfully campaigned for the adoption of a new diocesan system of education; and an intensive Anglican agitation, culminating in a grand meeting of the National Society in May 1839, had already set the stage for resistance by the time Russell brought forward his specific resolutions in June.

In the Commons the full debating strength of the opposition was deployed: Peel, Stanley, Graham, Ashley, Gladstone, Inglis and

[1] *Croker*, II, 323.

229

Francis Egerton. Peel had various objections to the government plan, including the essentially political character of the educational committee of the Privy Council. But the crux of his argument on behalf of the Establishment was 'that no system of national education shall be founded which studiously excludes from the superintendence and control of education, given to the children of the establishment, the dignitaries of the Established Church'.[1] He had no wish to see the Church interfere with the education of Dissenters. His case was that no central board should be set up which did not include Church representatives, since that would be a denial either of the intrinsic connection between education and religion or of the national position of the Church. This was a much more careful and restrained claim than some of those put forward by High Anglicans, including such young war-hawks of his own party as Gladstone and Acland. The meeting of the National Society in May had passed a resolution not only asserting the necessity of religious instruction as part of any national system of education but claiming for the clergy of the national Church the right to superintend that instruction. Russell, speaking immediately before Peel, had in fact alleged that this attitude was at the root of the opposition to the government measure. But Peel was at pains to dissociate himself from this extreme and monopolistic position; and his arguments probably carried more weight with the House as a whole than did Russell's. The debate in which he spoke was on a motion to go into committee of supply. The government majority fell to five on that division and to only two on a subsequent motion to increase the grant to £30,000. In July the House of Lords led by the Archbishop of Canterbury carried by an overwhelming vote a motion for an address to the Crown protesting against the plan. The executive machinery of the Whig scheme, which needed only financial support from the Commons to be effective, made a formal victory for the opposition out of the question; but falling parliamentary majorities and rising public agitation were enough. The government fell back on a slow campaign of retreat and after negotiations with the Church leaders a settlement was finally reached the following summer. The unpopular normal school had already been sacrificed; and the cabinet agreed further to revert to the old system, which

[1] *Speeches*, III, 645 (20 June 1839).

favoured the Church, of allotting grants in proportion to private subscriptions and to submit the school inspectors to episcopal superintendence and appointment. It was an Anglican victory which not only endorsed the political recovery of Conservatism but convinced many Dissenters that the value of the Whig alliance was now exhausted.[1]

In the more secular sphere the fate of legislation on Canada and Jamaica once more illustrated the grip of the opposition on all effective government action. Earlier in the session there had been desultory discussions in the House of Lords on the various papers laid before parliament, including Lord Durham's report, and in May a royal message formally recommended the union of the two Canadas. In June Russell moved in the House of Commons the adoption of the recommendation in principle. But he proposed to defer any final legislation and continue the emergency powers of the governor and his special council in Lower Canada until 1842. Peel criticised the adoption in advance of an abstract resolution on union before the House had time or information to consider its permanent policy towards Canada; and Russell, who had also received strong protests from Upper Canada, agreed in the course of the debate to withdraw that part of the bill. There was opposition from colonial reformers like Molesworth, who were angered by the refusal of the cabinet to implement immediately the Durham report; but though Peel criticised the details of the temporary arrangements, he was clearly in favour of delay and did not press his arguments. In this he was supported by Wellington who was afraid that Durham and Brougham would together stage a demonstration in the House of Lords. As a result the bill passed the upper House at the end of session with surprisingly little difficulty. Much the same pattern marked the course of the government's Jamaica measure. Having resigned because of their failure to get adequate support for the suspension of the Jamaican constitution, the ministers could hardly persist in that policy. Swallowing their dignity—a disagreeable process in which they had some practice of recent years—they adopted the principle urged by Peel in April. A new bill was brought forward designed to give the Jamaican Assembly one more opportunity to rehabilitate itself by accepting the legislation proposed by

[1] For a more detailed account of this episode see my *English Politics*, pp. 76–9.

the executive government and reviving the annual acts which had expired in the interval. The opposition leaders agreed to give the bill an unopposed second reading and to amend in committee. This burden was mainly left to the party's legal expert, Sir Edward Sugden; but Peel made a strong speech on the third reading on 19 June renewing Sugden's criticisms of the clause empowering the governor to legislate over the heads of the Assembly if they did not pass the necessary bills within a period of six weeks. The government carried the clause by ten votes but it was later struck out in the House of Lords. When the bill returned to the Commons in July, Russell advised an acceptance of the Lords' amendments and it finally passed therefore in the shape which Peel had originally recommended. On 27 August parliament was prorogued and those assiduous politicians still in attendance were free to depart to the country or the continent as their fancy pleased.

Peel had already left for Drayton on 3 August. In the middle of the month he took his wife and elder daughter to Longshawe for a week's shooting and at the end of the month he entertained some of the celebrities who had gathered at Birmingham for the meeting of the British Association. First came the Marquess of Northampton, the president, and a bevy of professors—Whewell of Cambridge, Wheatstone of King's College, London, Forbes of Edinburgh, and Lloyd of Dublin, together with Lyell the geologist, and Fox Talbot the pioneer of British photography. Next came Buckland, another geologist, Hallam the historian, a Professor Shephard from the United States, and another professor from Basle. This intellectual galaxy was succeeded in September by more aristocratic and worldly figures: the Duke and Duchess of Cambridge, the aged Princess Augusta, Prince Esterhazy, the Earl and Countess of Aylesford, Lords Forester and Ward, the Earl and Countess of Bradford, Lord Talbot, the Earl and Countess of Warwick, the Duke and Duchess of Sutherland, the Marquess of Anglesey, and the Hardinges. Peel was clearly making full use of the luxurious accommodation available in his new house and later in the autumn came the most distinguished guest who had so far graced its walls. On 11 November the dowager Queen Adelaide arrived, escorted by the Tamworth troop of the Staffordshire Yeomanry and attended by a large retinue which included Lord Howe, the Earl and Countess of Denbigh, a chaplain and various maids of honour. On the 12th the royal party went in state to Tamworth, accompanied by a cavalcade of local gentry, to meet the mayor and council and attend a service in Tamworth Church. Next day there was a similar excursion to Lichfield and the visit ended on the 14th.[1]

As the first enthusiasm for Victoria had dimmed, Queen Adelaide's popularity had risen, especially in Tory circles. But there was little political significance in the visit. Certainly it could not be interpreted as a gesture of conciliation from Windsor even though the queen was on markedly better terms with her aunt than with her mother. There was no sign that Victoria had softened her feelings towards the opposition party; and the angry and senseless animus of many Tories against her continued to break through at various public dinners during the autumn. Even the rumours current from October onward and confirmed in November that the queen was to be married failed to soothe partisan hostility. Peel, who had been asking Arbuthnot for news of the marriage in mid-October, was assured by Lord Howe before the end of the month that it was certain to take place.[2] Little was known of the intended bridegroom, Prince Albert of Saxe-Coburg-Gotha, except that he was as young as the queen and reputed to be a Liberal. The most that could be said from the Conservative point of view was that marriage might weaken Victoria's dependence on the Whigs. As Graham put it in a letter to Peel in November: 'No change can well be for the worse; and in such circumstances almost any change becomes desirable.'[3]

---

[1] Goulburn, Peel's Memorandum Book.
[2] 40341 f. 112; Peel, II, 408.   [3] 40318 f. 155.

THE YEAR OF VICTORY

'No man, it is probable,' observed the *Annual Register* in 1839, 'ever deserved better of a party than Sir Robert Peel of his. . . . Unassisted by the powerful faculties, the temperate wisdom, and the parliamentary tactic and address of their leader in the House of Commons, they could scarcely, it may be thought, have recovered with such steady rapidity, and with so few reverses, from the prostration in which the revolutionary struggle of 1831 and 1832 had left them.'[1] Contemporaries of all shades of opinion were impressed by the rise of the Conservative party since 1834. From a broken and discredited minority it had become in half a dozen years a formidable and organised opposition knocking at the doors of power. Many forces had been at work to produce this result and most of them had little or nothing to do with Peel. The return of normal electoral influences after the excitement of the reform crisis, Anglican resentment at Dissenting attacks, Protestant dislike of Irish Catholicism, English dislike of O'Connell, the anxieties of moderate men over continued radical demands, the political ambiguity and administrative deficiencies of successive Whig cabinets—all these things would in any case have caused a reaction in the country. When in 1835 and 1837 it became a matter of translating these shifts of opinion into votes and seats, much was also due to the superiority of the party's electioneering organisation, to Granville Somerset and his energetic central committee, to Bonham with his endless correspondence and large strapped book of electoral secrets, and to the countless forgotten figures who ran the party associations and committees in the constituencies.

But these fears, interests and activities needed a focus if they were to be effective; and this Peel supplied. As the outstanding parlia-

[1] 1838, p. 115.

mentarian of the age, he offered unrivalled leadership at the centre of power. His Tamworth formula of moderate and judicious reform, promising both security and progress, had the attraction for his own generation of a political novelty. His restraint and realism in session after session had enlarged and consolidated the forces of Conservatism both in parliament and in the country at large. Since 1835 his technique of parliamentary leadership had developed in flexibility and persuasiveness. His characteristic procedures of consultation, by letter with a few close colleagues in the vacations, and during the session with the inner ring of official men, with *ad hoc* committees, and with groups of leading debaters, followed on special occasions by explanatory meetings of the full party, helped to give the Conservatives a cohesion and purpose which no party in opposition had ever had before. The importance of this was as much for the future as for the present; the organising of opposition had also been a preparation for government. At leisure Peel had been able to bring together the team of men who would form the next Conservative administration. He had been given five years to accomplish what in 1834 he had been asked to do in five weeks. From that point of view the recruitment of Stanley and Graham had a significance far greater than their votes in the lobby or their talent in debate. They had materially helped to liberalise Conservative policy in opposition and they guaranteed a more broadly-based administration than that of 1834 when next in office.

But this was only part of Peel's work as leader. In the larger society outside Westminster his influence, though more pervasive and intangible, had done much to widen the area from which the party drew its support. To the liberal but moderate men among the squirearchy and great landowners who increasingly felt that the Whigs were compromised by their radical and Irish allies, Peelite progressivism offered a safe and acceptable alternative. The adaptation of old institutions to new conditions provided an idealistic challenge to young and sympathetic minds and more than one observer noted how many of the rising aristocratic generation, including sons of traditionally Whig families, were enlisting under Peel's banner. He was also extending the party in another direction. Though Tamworth Conservatism and most of Peel's public speeches revolved round the central theme of the defence of the

Church and the constitution, he had repeatedly and deliberately addressed himself not only to the aristocracy but to the professional, mercantile and industrial middle classes. One of his great achievements had been to persuade large sections of those monied and respectable men that their true interest lay in maintaining the fundamental institutions of the aristocratic state and in the peaceful evolution of the mixed constitution left by the Reform Act. This was the more subtle and indirect aspect of Peel's work; in the long run perhaps the most significant. The importance he attached to it was evident less in the main themes of Conservative propaganda than in the language of his speeches, in the direction of his arguments, in his choice of place and audience, and in his personal interests and inclinations. It was evident, for example, in the *Tamworth Manifesto* itself, in the City speech of May 1835, and at the Glasgow banquet of January 1837. It was implied in his constant emphasis on the interdependence of industry, commerce, and agriculture, or in his other favourite theme that it was the continuity of British political life and institutions which had shaped the character of the British people. It was seen on a smaller scale in his Tamworth Reading Room speech of 1841, which brought down on him the attacks of Tories and High Anglicans for its secular and utilitarian outlook. It was seen again in his scientific and literary patronage when prime minister in 1835, or in his growing habit of inviting to his home distinguished professional and academic figures to diversify the usual run of political and social guests. Even his bourgeois family origins and the industrial source of his own wealth he had turned into electoral assets rather than aristocratic disadvantages.

Hybrid himself, he was making the Conservative party a hybrid organisation as well. Middle-class opinion, of whose power he had been aware ever since he returned as a young man from Ireland in 1818, was being increasingly tapped to supply wider support and a more liberalised tone to the parliamentary party. Most observers, indeed, recognised by the start of Victoria's reign that Conservatism was other and larger than landed Toryism. The latter supplied the necessary nucleus of strength, the irreducible minimum of a party of the right; but Conservatism provided the element of growth, the indispensable electoral condition for a party aiming at power.

Translated into parliamentary terms, Peelite Conservatives still formed a minority of the party, but they comprised nearly all the leading men, as well as the leader himself; and they represented an element in the electorate which was decisive for the difference between opposition and office. If Conservatism was to succeed, it had to become a national party; and a national party, even with the limited post-1832 electorate, had to be a composite party. The Whigs had been grappling, uncertainly and sometimes half-heartedly, with that necessity. But by 1840 they were being out-gunned and outmanœuvred by the leader of the opposition in the battle for the confidence of central moderate public opinion. For this task of harmonising middle and upper class interests all Peel's previous career seemed to have prepared him. His aristocratic education and sympathies, his middle-class origin and affinities, his administrative training, his non-partisan intellect, his passion for efficiency and good government, his immense parliamentary experience—all the varied qualities which were in conflict in the years 1831-32 had by 1840 fallen into a clear pattern. If there were discords and complexities both in his own position and in the nature of the party he led—and the internal history of the Conservative party since 1835 provided ample evidence of both—they were inseparable from the forces which had brought Peel and his followers to the brink of power. A more homogeneous party with a more unsophisticated leader would have offered less difficulty and suffered less strain. It would have laboured under only one disadvantage: that of never coming into office.

Office, however, was something for which Peel's party seemed to hanker even more than Peel himself. Success had given him three hundred impatient followers for whom the Conservative defence of the constitution in the thirties was not an end in itself but a prelude to Conservative rule in the forties. It was true that the opposition had achieved its main objects; that it had powerfully influenced Whig policy and legislation; that it had in fact, as Peel said in his Merchant Taylors' speech, been carrying out some of the functions of government. But these things were not enough. Peel might seem satisfied with power alone; his followers wanted the place and patronage that were its usual concomitants. By the end of 1839 office seemed only a handsbreadth away. The radicals were still restless; the country disordered; Howick and Charles Wood had resigned from the government in a huff. Since 1837 the Conservatives had gained seven additional seats through by-elections and had only lost one; and the autumn registrations showed continued Conservative advances. The fiasco of the Bedchamber incident had merely piled frustration on top of impatience. By the beginning of the new year Graham was urging Bonham not to let Peel remain in ignorance of the tone of desperation prevalent in the party.[1] Yet Peel was as aware as anyone that the point had been reached when he might soon have to face the practical consequence of power which was office; and office meant not merely loaves and fishes for his followers but personal responsibility for all the problems with which the Whigs were unsuccessfully struggling and others unknown which time would certainly uncover. To Goulburn, who in November was suggesting a motion of censure on the government's budgetary deficits, he rejoined that what they ought rather to be thinking about was how to remedy them. 'In other words, more startling to a House of Commons,' he added dryly, 'what new taxes could be imposed?'[2]

The immediate problem, however, was how to prepare an attack on the government which would not be just a bloodless exercise for his impetuous followers but a serious trial of strength. To use the Conservative resources merely to harass and obstruct was a negation of all he had been advocating. But in the existing temper of the party the only alternative was a deliberate attempt to overthrow the ministers. In the middle of December he wrote to the duke, Goulburn, Stanley and Graham. His starting point was the strong feeling among their followers in both Houses in favour of an attack on the government and a general impression that the Whigs no longer possessed a sure majority in the Commons. On that basis he placed four issues before his colleagues; the policy of an attack, the method, the timing, and the place, or more explicitly, whether it should be in the Commons or the Lords, or simultaneously in both. He made his own view clear that if an attack was desirable or inevitable, the best procedure would be a direct vote of no confidence brought forward as soon as possible. Amendments to the address were becoming outmoded and would be particularly incongruous on an

[1] 40616 f. 146.   [2] Goulburn (25 Nov.) ptly pr. *Peel*, II, 411.

occasion when parliament would be tendering its congratulations to the queen on her approaching marriage. Separate issues such as Jamaica or foreign policy might attract unwelcome radical allies in the lobby and prove an embarrassment when in office. On the other hand to prevent any premature action by their followers, it would be necessary to give notice of a motion at the very start of the session. His quartet of advisers showed various reactions. The duke, pessimistic as ever, thought it would be regrettable if Peel even had the option of taking office. Ranging a jaundiced eye over the political horizon, he pointed out that a Conservative government would have to do many things for which their supporters were ill-prepared and disunited. Stanley was inclined to agree with the duke. Graham for his part concentrated on tactics. He doubted whether a vote of no confidence would succeed without defections from the ministerialists but he thought the vote would be so close as to give no comfort to the cabinet; and if they dissolved he believed Peel would get a majority. Above all, he thought it impossible to keep the party together without launching a direct attack on the government; and a collapse in the numbers and morale of the opposition would be the greatest of all calamities. He favoured therefore a no confidence motion in the Commons, leaving the Lords in their proper role as a defensive rather than an offensive body. Goulburn agreed with Graham. He thought feeling in the party left no choice but to attack early and that a vote of no confidence, as Peel suggested, was the best mode of procedure.

Peel sent the various replies round his little circle of correspondents but in the succeeding weeks it was clear that he sided with Graham and Goulburn against his two more aristocratic and olympian colleagues. To Arbuthnot he wrote on 20 December that strong as the duke's arguments were, and notwithstanding the unresolved problem of the queen's household, the choice lay between displacing the government or dissolving the party. Meanwhile he discussed with Graham and Goulburn the difficulties which the parliamentary timetable might impose on an early dissolution and obtained from Fremantle and Bonham their most recent calculations of party strengths and the probable results of a dissolution. From these experts he received further confirmation of the temper of the party and practical justification for aggressive action. Bonham in particular was emphatic and optimistic. He thought the opposition would succeed on a vote of confidence and that a general election would produce a handsome Conservative majority. It was immaterial whether Melbourne or Peel dissolved parliament, he wrote, since the slight marginal advantage possessed by government (affecting about a dozen constituencies at most) would be offset by the anti-governmental temper of extreme radical constituencies. He enclosed an analysis of the House which indicated that the thick and thin ministerialists numbered one less than the opposition, the balance being held by eight doubtful members, eight independent radicals and eight vacancies. Enough votes would be forthcoming from these floating elements, he thought, to give the Conservatives victory. Sending this to Wellington on 5 January Peel argued that in these circumstances action of some sort was unavoidable and that the danger was not loss of office but the utter discouragement of the party. Even to appear to avoid a trial of strength, 'would, I apprehend, lead to that which I assume to be a great public evil, the breaking up of the powerful Conservative party. I write to you, what I do not write to any other person.'[1] The old duke, overborne though not convinced, gave way and Peel went up to London to meet his colleagues on the eve of what seemed likely to be a decisive session.[2]

In the first few weeks all went well. Much of the early parliamentary discussions revolved round the hapless and unknown Prince Albert and in the course of them the opposition was able to score handsomely off the government. There was criticism of the omission of any mention of his Protestantism in the official marriage announcement; Wellington successfully objected to the inclusion of precedency regulations in his naturalisation bill; and on 27 January his proposed £50,000 civil list allowance was reduced by the House of Commons to £30,000. The larger figure was on the basis of precedents laid down in more spacious ages, and was unpopular with both sides of the House. The cabinet had accepted it without any

[1] Wellington.

[2] For the exchange of letters between Peel and his colleagues, see 40310 fos. 308, 314, 323 (Wellington); 40341 f. 144 (Arbuthnot); 40333 fos. 392–402 (Goulburn); 40318 fos. 163–73 (Graham); Goulburn (Peel to Goulburn, 15, 26 Dec. 1839, 1 Jan. 1840); Wellington (Peel–Wellington, 15, 20, 25 Dec. 1839, 5 Jan. 1840); *Peel*, II, 415 seq.

consultation with the opposition; and in the division it was opposed not only by Conservatives but by Liberals and radicals who swelled the majority to over a hundred. Russell's angry accusations of disloyalty to the crown merely stiffened the temper of the opposition. A misleading report[1] had come to Peel that £30,000 was the figure originally proposed to the queen and rejected by her. But even before this he and Wellington were considering a motion for reduction and he took a human and somewhat malicious pleasure in reflecting that the queen had received a salutary warning that she could not rely indefinitely on the forbearance of the Conservatives or the parliamentary majority of the Whigs. When the great no confidence debate came on immediately afterwards, however, the false dawn of these early and trivial successes soon vanished. The motion had been entrusted to a solid country gentleman, Sir John Yarde Buller, M.P. for South Devon, who in his opening speech on 28 January made much of the government's failures in dealing with Chartist disturbances, especially the riots at Birmingham the previous July and the armed insurrection in Monmouthshire at the end of the year, led by a former magistrate, Frost, who had been appointed (and later dismissed) by Russell. For four nights the debate ranged backwards and forwards over the whole field of politics and administration, with all the leading speakers on each side called up, and charges and counter-charges of party disunity and incompetence hurled across the gangway. Macaulay, back from India and one of the three new Liberal ministers brought into the cabinet at the end of the previous session, warned Peel that if he came to power he would lose the confidence of his party without gaining that of Ireland. Peel speaking on the final evening accused Macaulay of preaching in his capacity as minister the sacred duty of agitation, and Russell of commanding an ill-found ship manned by a crew still squabbling over whether they should remain anchored to the monarchical constitution or run before the wind of radical change.

Metaphors apart, however, much of his speech was taken up with an indictment of the disunity, administrative weakness, and financial incompetence of the government; the remainder in answering the demands made during the debate that he should declare his own

---

[1] From Arbuthnot, see 40341 f. 159; cf. *Peel*, II, 432.

attitudes on the great questions of the day. It had been alleged that he did not dare to expose his views because he would simultaneously expose the divisions in his party. He retorted that he preferred to do that rather than purchase precarious support by concealing his intentions. He asked no men to change their conscientious beliefs. But, he continued, 'I will not be the instrument for giving effect to opinions in which I do not concur'. He then outlined the various topics on which he had been challenged to give his views. On the Hansard privilege case both parties were divided, so that his case was no worse than that of the ministers. He supported the new poor law and thought the agitation against it wicked and dangerous, though he would revise any of its enactments that were harsh. On education he would give means to the Church to extend its activities to all classes, but not the power to interfere with the education of Dissenters who ought to receive separate assistance. He would maintain all the provisions of the Reform Act. His views on the Corn Law were unchanged. He thought a liberal protection to agriculture indispensable in the general interest of the community and a graduated duty better than a fixed. Finally he embarked on a defence of his conduct over Catholic emancipation which in its length and indignation showed how vulnerable he still was to the taunts and accusations of his opponents on this eleven-year-old episode. But he declared his readiness to act on the basis of civil equality in Irish administration, provided this did not mean encouragement of agitation or injury to the Established Church; and he said again that he could not take part in any administration in which his principles could not be enforced. It was unlikely that he made any converts; but he had done two things which were of importance for the future. He had indicated, as clearly as circumstances and his own prudence allowed, the nature of his future administration; and he had given notice to his followers that if he was to govern, it would be on his terms and only his.

The long acrimonious debate finished on 31 January and when the division took place the opposition saw their motion lost by 308 votes to 287, a large and unexpected majority of 21 for the government. Two factors had combined to shatter the optimistic forecasts of the Conservative party managers. Of the doubtfuls and independent radicals ten came down on the side of the government; five were absent; only one voted with the opposition. Even Howick and Wood, the 'Grey Pouters' as Graham called them, whose neutrality had been hoped for, voted with their party. In the second place the Liberals had been strengthened by the return of six members in by-elections which had taken place since the start of the session and there were nine Conservative as against eight ministerialist absentees.[1] The direct threat to the continuation of Whig rule, and perhaps the violent atmosphere of the debate, had rallied the Liberal party. The opposition on the other hand not only failed to pick up floating support but had shown less zeal in attendance than their opponents. It was a humiliating failure and Peel felt, not altogether with complete justice, that he had been misled by his whips and hurried into a false position. The result safeguarded the Whig cabinet for the rest of the session and aggravated the tensions and divisions within the opposition. It was true that in April a party attack on the government's China policy led by Graham ran the ministers to a narrow margin of nine votes, and Stanley's Irish registration bill obtained a second reading in March before it was smothered in committee. But the rest of the session was marked by a kind of brooding restraint on the part of the opposition which was a sign of tension within. The remaining issues of the 1840 session in fact not only made another trial of party strength difficult but threw a material strain on the newly created unity of the Conservative party.

One of these issues had been referred to by Peel in the Yarde Buller debate. This was the Hansard libel case which from its small beginnings in 1836 had by 1840 brought the House of Commons into conflict with the law courts in defence of its own powers and pretensions. In 1837 a select committee which had Peel as one of its members decided in favour of upholding not only the privileged position of parliamentary publications but also the exclusive right of the Commons to decide its privileges. By January 1840 the Commons were faced with the necessity either of abandoning their defence of Messrs. Hansard or of punishing the sheriffs of Middlesex for obeying the instructions of the Court of the Queen's Bench. Throughout the long development of the conflict Peel had argued tenaciously and uncompromisingly for the sole jurisdiction of the

[1] See the analysis in *English Politics*, p. 206.

House of Commons. In this he took the same ground as Russell and the majority in the Commons. But opinion was not unanimous and many members of his own party, including his two chief legal experts, Sugden and eventually Follett, took the side of the law courts against the lower branch of the legislature. Outside the House it was clear that the legal profession in general and a majority of peers, including Wellington, were equally ranged against them. To some observers it seemed that Peel positively enjoyed speaking as a champion of the House of Commons rather than as a leader of a party. In fact, however, he was angered at the violent language used against him by the Tory press and by some of his own followers; and his private resentment probably stiffened his public attitude. It was probably also true that his example prevented the opposition from making party capital out of the issue. Greville indeed thought that only Peel's influence had stopped the mass of his followers from using the Hansard case to discredit both the Whig ministry and the reformed House of Commons.[1] But while it lasted, and it lasted a long time, the Hansard controversy imposed a considerable strain both on party unity and Peel's leadership. There was one particularly painful evening on 7 February when Russell proposed legislation to end the deadlock. Peel, smarting apparently under a taunt from Roebuck, spoke intemperately, restated all his strong opinions, took the lead out of Russell's hands to the annoyance of his own followers, and declared he would reject an enabling bill and only accept a declaratory one. 'It is curious', wrote Graham unhappily to Stanley the next day, 'that Peel who often is languid in his attack on his adversaries, puts forth superior energy and strength when he combats his followers.'[2] It was not curious that Peel, a parliamentarian who had sat for thirty years in the Commons, should defend the rights of his own House. But he displayed an obstinacy which he would probably not have shown had he been in Russell's place and which perhaps owed something to an irritable fear that Russell would in the end give way.

The notorious difference of view between Peel and Wellington over the Hansard case and the absence of any communication

---

[1] *Greville*, 22, 24, 31 Jan. 1840.
[2] Graham (8 Feb. 1840), cf. also Arbuthnot to Graham, 9 Feb. 1840. The speech (not in *Speeches*) is in *Hansard*, LII, 60-8.

between them on the subject made additionally sinister the disagreements between them on other current matters of legislation.
When the Parliamentary Papers bill which settled the privilege
question came up to the Lords, Wellington showed considerable
restraint in allowing the bill to go through unopposed. It was by
no means certain that he would show the same restraint over Irish
corporations and Canada. Yet in the event he did so and the record
of the session showed no overt breach between the two Conservative
leaders on either issue. The Irish bill came up for a second reading
in February and Peel, backed now by Shaw though not by Inglis,
supported the government on the grounds that there must be an
amicable and final settlement of this interminable problem. The
opposition were in fact virtually pledged to the bill. Even so Peel
took care to embody in his speech a long explanation of its history
and his own changes of policy, and to adopt a conciliatory and persuasive mode of argument designed perhaps as much for his own
party as any. The Commons shared his view and the bill passed by
handsome majorities in March. When it went up to the Lords
Wellington recommended his followers to vote for a second
reading. Though minor amendments were made at Lyndhurst's
instance in committee, these were eventually accepted by the government and the bill became law in August. A similar forbearance
marked the duke's handling of the Canada question. The bill for
the union of the two Canadas introduced by Russell in March was
handled as a non-party issue in the Commons. When the Lords
discussed it at the end of June Wellington made it clear that he was
against an immediate and final settlement and in the end recorded his
own personal protest against the bill. Nevertheless he supported the
second reading and the only major amendments put forward by the
opposition in committee—the postponement of the operation of
the act for fifteen months instead of six, and powers to suspend the
members of the council—were accepted by the government.

This harmony with the lower House no doubt owed something
to the increased habit of party discipline among the Tory peers, and
something to the duke's dread of displacing the Whigs. But behind
the scenes there had been considerable apprehension in the weeks
preceding the decisions on both bills in the House of Lords. Although
Peel felt that the party was bound by its own previous actions to

pass the corporation bill, at the beginning of June Wellington was considering postponing it until Stanley's registration bill was through. On Canada he was even more uncompromising. Believing that union between the two provinces would lead to the secession of both, he was prepared to do all he could to defeat the proposal. He had consulted with Peel on Canada earlier in the session but since Easter there had been no political discussions between the two men and some of their closest friends began to feel disquiet. The duke, isolated by age, deafness and prestige from the common feeling in the party, lived in a logical, despondent world of his own and was apt to forget, even if he had rightly heard, what had been agreed on earlier occasions. He was liable therefore to announce idiosyncratic opinions and intentions without realising the consternation they caused to those who saw in him not a tired and ageing soldier but leader of the Conservative party in the House of Lords. By the beginning of June Graham, alarmed at the reports he had heard, dragged Arbuthnot up from the country to talk over the situation and to get him in turn to talk to the duke; and both men tried without success to make Peel call on Wellington. The danger in fact was more apparent than real. When he comprehended the general party attitude over the Irish bill the duke abandoned within three or four days his idea of postponement. Canada took a little longer but two days before the bill went into committee, Peel was able to tell Graham that the duke had yielded. 'I never varied in my opinion', he added, 'that the Lords would not and could not reject the Canada bill when they looked into the real state of the case.'[1]

An open breach between the leaders had been avoided, but there had been real disagreements and unnecessary pride on both sides. The duke, looking morbidly into the future, did not like to give the seal of his approval to anything which he thought would endanger the stability of the empire. Peel, also looking into the future, did not wish to handicap a prospective Conservative ministry with a load of unsettled problems and impossible attitudes. Given differences of opinion, differences of temperament made personal explanations peculiarly difficult. In Peel's case that *mauvaise honte* as Hardinge once described it, which always afflicted his relations with the

---

[1] Graham (5 July 1840), wrongly transcribed in *Peel*, II, 444.

duke, made him refuse all the entreaties of Arbuthnot, Graham and Aberdeen to talk privately with Wellington about the Canada bill. On the other hand the duke, conscious of his infirmities, disliked and avoided formal party meetings. Though in his more pessimistic moods he fancied that Peel deliberately concealed his opinions, he himself somewhat illogically preferred not to state his own views unless specifically asked. Graham with his dark emotional streak and Arbuthnot with his protective feeling towards the duke were both inclined to exaggerate the situation. At the start of September Arbuthnot wrote that he despaired of ever seeing Peel and Wellington act cordially together again in cabinet. This was probably too much even for Graham who sent back a reply which Arbuthnot showed the duke. Wellington observed, however, with his accurate commonsense that there had been no ill-humour between himself and Peel. They had differed on two important points and each thought himself in the right; but on each occasion he had sacrificed his own opinion rather than injure the party. As for the future he knew that he was always in harness and would be ready to serve when necessary. Encouraged by this Arbuthnot opened up a correspondence with Peel on general political and diplomatic topics and received in reply a number of long friendly letters which were passed on to the duke. What with British hostilities against China, the intervention in the Near East to prevent an Egyptian conquest of Turkey which gave William Peel his first taste of gunpowder, and an Anglo-French crisis which threatened war and nearly split the Whig cabinet, there was no lack of incidents to discuss and mutually deplore.

In October Arbuthnot went to Drayton and from those palatial headquarters reported back to Wellington that Peel's views on public affairs were exactly the same as the duke's. This drew from Wellington his invariable comment that though he and Peel were kept apart by their different occupations and distant residences, he found that without any consultation they generally came to the same conclusions. Peel for his part told Arbuthnot that nothing in private life gave him more satisfaction than unreserved communication with the duke and that no occasional and honest difference of opinion on isolated topics could diminish their respect or decrease their co-operation. The old duke was pleased and Peel went out of his way to demonstrate his personal friendliness by sending Wellington only a few days later the letters from his son William describing the operations on the Syrian coast.[1] By the time the first frosts were on the stubble and the politicians' thoughts were turning with perennial zest towards the new session, the rift between the two men was closed. It had never been as great as their friends had feared and, what was perhaps more remarkable, it had been kept from the public eye and left no resentment behind. What would have caused an upheaval in the party six years earlier could now be absorbed with little shock. If the 1840 session had been disappointing, it had not been disastrous.

II

Apart from his usual shooting excursion to Longshawe and a visit to Sudbury Hall to see Queen Adelaide, Peel spent the autumn and early winter at Drayton, entertaining a succession of diplomatic, political, artistic and scientific guests, including a Swiss savant, Professor Agassiz, who was full of his discoveries of glacial remains in the Scottish Highlands and von Neumann, the Austrian diplomat, with whom Peel had long conversations about the crisis in the Near East. Getting to Drayton from London, with the extension of the new Birmingham railway line to Derby, was now easier than ever. The journey took only six hours and a guest could leave Euston at one o'clock and be sitting down to dinner at Drayton by half-past seven.[2] But no great advantage was taken of these modern transport facilities to muster a great eve-of-session gathering. If the experience of recent years was a guide, the greater the preparation, the more certain the disappointment. Peel told Graham in mid-December that all he had done so far was to discourage an attack on some small point such as the eastern question on which radicals and Conservatives could agree; and said he would decide nothing until he had seen the duke, Stanley, Graham and a few others.[3] Nevertheless he was in close touch with his officials at the centre and despite the

[1] For the Peel–Wellington relationship see 40318 fos. 196–210 (Graham); 40341 fos. 168–209 (Arbuthnot); Graham (Arbuthnot to Graham, 11 Aug., 4, 6, 7, 11, 22 Sept. 1840); *Peel*, II, 438, et seq.

[2] Goulburn (Peel to Goulburn, 21 Oct. 1840).

[3] Graham (15 Dec. 1840).

result of the Yarde Buller motion, they were full of optimism. Bonham in October was watching the municipal elections and telling Peel that in England at any rate the Municipal Reform Act had done hardly any damage to the Conservative cause. In December he prophesied that at the next general election the Conservatives would be returned with a greater majority than they had enjoyed since 1820. There was no lack of parliamentary candidates ready to take the field on behalf of the party. The whips and agents were now in the pleasing position of being able to pick and choose with an eye to the future. Bonham indeed noted with professional satisfaction the number of fathers who, to strengthen their claims on the next Conservative administration, were ready to bring their sons in at by-elections even with the prospect of a second expense at the general election. At the end of the year, at Peel's request, he furnished his leader with the most recent state of the party and repeated his assertion that from their point of view a dissolution could not come too early.[1]

The memorable year of 1841 began palely and uncertainly. Parliament opened on 26 January and Peel went up to London four days earlier to meet his colleagues. For the start of a new session the parliamentary world seemed strangely quiet. The great controversies had been laid to rest; Whig policy appeared exhausted. The government presented the spectacle of a great engine continuing to glide silently forward under its own momentum though the power had been shut off. It seemed the end not only of the decade of the reform bill but of a whole era in politics dominated by the hopes and fears which that great measure had inspired. If so, the problems of the forties would be those which neither of the two main parties had been trained to meet. Something of this stillness in the political atmosphere affected the opposition leaders. Though Graham had suggested the possibility of an attack on O'Connell's Repeal of the Union movement, it was decided in the end not to move an amendment to the address. The principal topic of interest was foreign affairs and though Peel and Wellington in the debate on the address pleaded for better relations with France, there was no party demonstration. Even when interest in domestic affairs revived with the bill to renew the Poor Law Commission introduced by Russell at the

[1] 40428 fos. 342, 462, 485; 40616 f. 191.

end of January, the divisions in the Commons were not on party lines. The bill was attacked by such diverse back-benchers as Wakley the radical medico and Disraeli, the literary and slightly exotic Conservative member for Maidstone. But it was strongly supported by official Whigs and Peel was disinclined to oppose in principle a system for which no alternative was proposed. He criticised, however, the severity of some of the commissioners' instructions and returned to this point when the bill went into committee. With the best of intentions, he suggested, the commissioners sometimes displayed a harshness in vindicating their principles which was unnecessary, unjust and unwise.[1] His proposal for a five- instead of a ten-year extension of the commission was accepted by the government and the bill struggled on in the teeth of criticism which never seemed likely, however, to bring it to a halt. For a time the public mind was full of the poor law and its iniquities. In April Walter of *The Times*, running as a Conservative in a by-election at Liberal Nottingham, gained an unexpected victory entirely, it was thought, because of his opposition to the bill. The party could 'abstractedly' have had a better candidate, confessed Bonham apologetically to his chief, but not a better one for that place; and success might do something to bring his newspaper more firmly over to the Conservative cause.[2]

It was not until February, when battle was joined over the respective Irish registration bills of Stanley and Lord Morpeth, that party passions grew warm. Stanley's bill in purifying, would also have restricted the exercise of, the franchise. The Whig measure contained provisions not only for adopting the new poor law valuation but for reducing the county qualification from a £10 to a £5 beneficial interest. This was an issue which could hardly fail to rally partisans. It plucked once more at the sore nerve of the Irish problem; it involved O'Connell and the repeal movement; it harked back to the Lichfield House Compact, the Reform Act and even Catholic emancipation. Most important of all, it implied a deliberate alteration in the existing electoral system despite Russell's repeated pledges of the finality of the 1832 settlement. In his speech on the second reading on 25 February Peel argued that the proposed qualification was tantamount to a restoration of the old 40s

---

[1] Not in *Speeches*. See *Hansard*, LVII, 442–5 (19 Mar. 1841).   [2] 40429 f. 199.

freehold abolished in 1829 as a condition of emancipation. It was therefore a breach of that measure as well as of the Reform Act of 1832.[1] When after four nights of debate the House divided, the government majority sank to five, the same ominous figure that had brought about their resignation in 1839. But the Whigs once more demonstrated that they were, in the catch-phrase of the time, 'squeezable material' and after postponing the committee stage until after Easter, offered a compromise £8 rating. This yielded them little profit and no honour. Howick, the former cabinet minister, now independently brought forward a stricter franchise definition which was carried against the government. The ministerialists were divided; the ministers uncertain; and when on 29 April after a protracted and confused debate the crucial division was taken on the franchise qualification, there was a majority against the government of eleven. With that the parliamentary voters (Ireland) bill disappeared into the limbo of Whig legislative discards.

Its fate, however, was overshadowed by increasing political excitement on another issue. If office did not give the Whigs power, at least it left them the initiative; and there were rumours during April that they were planning some bold stroke in the field of finance. In the middle of the month Bonham was urging Peel to strike at the government before they could bring in their budget 'which will, I fancy, be attractive but revolutionary, in proportion to the desperate position in which they are now placed'.[2] Certainly the Whigs were in need of something new in the way of budgetary devices. Since Althorp's ill-fated budget of 1831 they had followed a hand to mouth financial policy, responding to the general radical pressure for 'cheap government' with steady reductions of direct taxes, and drifting into a position in which they were increasingly dependent on indirect taxation and increasingly vulnerable therefore to trade cycles and depressions. After 1837, with an industrial slump and increased expenditure on colonies and the armed services, their fiscal nakedness was made plain. They had no surplus in 1837; a deficit in 1838; and an even larger one in 1839 as a result of the introduction of the penny post. In 1840, faced with yet another deficit of two million, their new Chancellor of the Exchequer, Baring, tried to stop the rot by increasing both assessed taxes and

---

[1] Hansard, LVI, 1096–116.   [2] 40429 fos. 199–201.

customs and excise. Even this sudden reversal of policy had failed however to extricate them from their annual insolvency. Some other device was needed; it was found in the recent report of Hume's committee on import duties. It had long been a stock free-trade argument that British agricultural protection helped to maintain tariff barriers against British manufactures abroad, just as it was a stock agriculturalist argument that it would be unreasonable to remove protection from articles of food as long as British domestic manufactures were also protected against foreign competition. Hume's 1840 committee, skilfully rigged by the free-trade radicals with the assistance of some of the officials of the Board of Trade, made the first important breach in this closed circle of argument. Its report was designed to demonstrate that a decrease in the rate of duties on sugar, coffee and timber would in fact result in a higher actual revenue because of the resultant higher volume of imports.

Faced in the spring of 1841 with the failure of his high taxation policy and unwilling to have recourse to an income tax, Baring took the Hume Committee report as the basis for his next budget. At this point Russell made his own decisive contribution by insisting that if the great monopolies of sugar and timber were to be attacked, it would be impossible to exclude corn. The curious dual origin of the Whig budget of 1841 was reflected in the way in which it was brought before the Commons. On Friday, 30 April, before Baring rose to make his budget statement, Russell gave notice that he would move at the end of May for a committee of the whole House to consider the Corn Laws. The Chancellor of the Exchequer then outlined his part of the plan. He announced a deficit on the previous year of £1·8 million which he proposed to pay off by loan. For the coming year he estimated a gross deficit of £2·4 million on a revenue of just over £48·3 million. Disregarding certain extraordinary items of expenditure, the net permanent deficit he took as £1·7 million. To meet this he proposed to reduce the duty on foreign timber, slightly raise the duty on colonial timber, and decrease the duty on foreign sugar. In this way he hoped to raise £1·3 million and, if Russell's arrangement for corn was accepted, he would secure £400,000 from that source to bring his additional revenue up to £1·7 million. What Russell's proposals would be was not yet known although there could be little doubt of their nature; and there was considerable alarm and irritation at the prospect of five weeks' delay before they would be laid before the House. On 7 May, therefore, when the Commons went into committee on Baring's resolutions, Russell announced that his intention was to propose a fixed duty of 8s a quarter on wheat and lesser amounts on other cereals.

It was an odd budget, the most curious and controversial since 1831; and a certain unreality attended it from the start. Financially it was a gamble since it depended for success on the untested prognostications of a doctrinaire committee. For that the cabinet was risking the alienation of powerful interests and the embarrassment of their agricultural supporters. But the attack on the three great monopolies had the effect of transforming a budgetary expedient into a political demonstration. Certainly there was respectable liberal lineage for the principle it embodied; but free trade had not in the past been a Whig monopoly nor noticeably a Whig enthusiasm. In any case it was, properly considered, an anti-monopoly rather than a free-trade budget since its essence was the manipulation of tariffs so as to produce a larger revenue. Nevertheless in the atmosphere of 1841, with the Whigs confronted by the Chartist movement and the Anti-Corn Law League, industrial depression and social disorder, a powerful opposition and a vanishing majority, the budget took on deeper colours. There was practical justification and there might be political profit in raising, even in this limited fashion, a great national debate. If to the more orthodox members of the cabinet it was a painless way of curing a deficit, to their more Liberal and radical supporters it could be made to signify free trade *versus* protection, freedom *versus* monopoly, a large loaf *versus* a small. It was these wider if vaguer implications which gave the budget of 1841 its electoral value. It was turning away from the mistakes, defects and exhausted controversies of the past to erect a new banner under which the party could fight. Yet despite the obvious hustings appeal of the new policy, it failed to arouse much enthusiasm or conviction in the country at large. The Whigs had left their initiative too late; their policy smacked of electoral opportunism; there was a touch of desperation which did not inspire confidence. The chief excitement was among the interests and organisations directly affected by their proposals. The planters, shippers, merchants and sugar-refiners, the East and West Indian lobbies, chambers of commerce, colonial societies, anti-slavery associations, agriculturalists, and the Anti-Corn Law League, all plunged into the fray, organising, agitating, memorialising and petitioning. Whatever else the budget was likely to accomplish, it was inevitable that the separate propositions would be regarded as a whole and that it would unite all the separate opposing interests. The political winds, so zephyr-like at the start of the session, were rapidly whipping up to a gale. This was not altogether undesired or unintended by the government. But it was still a nice question whether the gale would blow the Whigs off the rocks or on to them.[1]

Yet the opposition also had a difficult course to steer. If free, or free-er trade, was the national trend, protection was still the national system. No great party could have a simple approach to these problems. For the Conservatives, who could look back on such Liberal economists as Pitt, Liverpool and Huskisson, it would have been suicidal to allow a protectionist or monopolistic label to be tied on them by their opponents. If the Whig position was complex and ambiguous, so too was that of the opposition. The truth was that the Whigs had suddenly decided to make a party issue out of a question which so far had not been a party matter at all. Even corn had been left an open question, whatever the importance attached by individual ministers like Russell to the merits of a fixed duty over a sliding scale. Peel approached the task of countering the government's new policy therefore with considerable doubt and caution. A programme which promised to meet a deficiency by a reduction of taxation and promote cheaper living by a destruction of monopolies could not be answered by mere negatives. To make positive alternative proposals on the other hand, when out of office and denied access to official information, violated his administrative sense. Though he was not without private ideas on how to remedy the government's endemic deficits, this was hardly the time to 'startle the House of Commons' with proposals for new taxation. Whatever was to be done, however, had to be settled quickly. On the Saturday following the double statement of Russell and Baring he called together a small group of House of Commons experts—

[1] For further discussion of the 1841 budget, see *English Politics*, pp. 176–83.

Stanley, Graham, Goulburn, Egerton, Sandon, Fremantle, Clerk, Hardinge, and Gladstone—to discuss what line the opposition should take. Stanley argued in favour of a motion condemning the financial statement and expressing lack of confidence in the ministers. Peel also touched on the question of a direct vote of confidence. He was not sure that the sugar duties alone provided good grounds on which to fight since ultimately it might be wise for the West Indies to surrender their monopoly. He was anxious in any case to avoid the slavery issue. Four courses seemed open to them: a general debate on the state of the nation; a direct vote of no confidence; an attack on the financial policy of the ministers, coupled with a declaration that they lacked the confidence and support of the House of Commons; and last, a specific opposition to the sugar proposals, to be followed if successful by a general motion of no confidence. To all these there were disadvantages. The first was too wide; the last too narrow; the second a mere repetition of the previous session. On the whole Peel and Stanley leaned to the third; but no decision was taken and it was clear that there was a strong feeling, expressed most tenaciously by Sandon, M.P. for the great commercial constituency of Liverpool, that sugar was the really vulnerable point in the ministerial proposals.

Sandon in fact wrote a long letter to Peel the same evening, reiterating his view that their best line was to take up the sugar question on its own merits, distinct from any question of general confidence in the government. It was the simplest and most natural tactic; it would undoubtedly get support from some Liberals; and it would not tie Peel's hands on larger issues since the recent emancipation of the West Indian slaves made British colonial sugar temporarily a special case. By concentrating on Whig financial ignorance and ineptitude it would relieve Peel of the necessity of declaring his own financial policy; and by avoiding corn it would assist the Conservative borough members. Peel, still doubtful, had further talks with Wellington, Aberdeen, Lyndhurst, Ellenborough, and Ashburton, as well as Goulburn, Stanley and Graham. Reconsideration produced a reassessment. When the original House of Commons group, reinforced by Granville Somerset and Eliot, met again on Sunday, Peel announced that he had changed his views and that there was now unanimous agreement on making the sugar proposals their initial object of attack. He then read them a memorandum he had prepared on the various alternatives. The notion of a grand inquest on the state of the nation he rejected. It might be exploited by Liberals and radicals to force a general committee of enquiry into the condition of the working classes and the effects of the Corn Laws. The opposition would then be caught in their own trap. He was anxious also to avoid being caught in the government's trap of either having to declare in detail his own intentions or appearing to evade the issue. On finance particularly it was essential to keep silent. If they came into office, they could do nothing that year except tide over the deficit with a loan while they examined the problem. This was hardly an impressive financial policy to announce; yet any other course would plunge him into embarrassment. To hint at a general revision of tariffs would leave trade and industry in uncertainty for a twelvemonth. To hint at increased taxation would give their opponents a gratuitous electoral advantage. He came down therefore on the side of a resolution on sugar, for the reasons given by Sandon, to be followed if successful by a direct challenge on the grounds that the government had lost the support of the House. Two other considerations were important. Even if the Conservatives took office at that moment, the need to renew the old sugar duties expiring in July would prevent an immediate dissolution. On the other hand to postpone their attack until Russell's corn resolutions came on in June would merely present the government with a popular election cry in the event of their defeat.

The timing therefore of the final overthrow of the government was crucial. From that point of view a two-stage plan of attack offered considerable advantages. There was every prospect of beating the ministers over sugar, and though defeat would probably not force them to resign, the opposition would be left in a position of superiority which would aid them in seeking the decisive verdict in the House of Commons which Peel thought sooner or later would have to come. So the decision was taken and all that remained was to arrange the details. Fremantle wanted Peel personally to move the resolution on sugar. He refused on the grounds that this would detract from the strictly economic nature of the debate; it would be better for him to remain in reserve for any general motion later on.

Instead he asked Sandon, whose arguments had largely carried the day, to undertake the task.[1] The wording of the motion was settled at a subsequent meeting and on 5 May formal notice of it was given in the House.

Two days later, prefaced by Russell's statement on the new corn proposals, the great debate began on the notice to go into committee of ways and means. Continuing by successive adjournments from 7 to 18 May it occupied eight evenings and called up over eighty speakers on different sides of the House. Russell, by taking the lead out of Baring's hands, set the stage for the grand ministerial case that this was not a mere question of budgets and tariffs but a conflict of principle involving the welfare of the cotton-spinners of Bolton and Manchester and Britain's imperial role as leader in civilisation, Christianity, liberty and the peaceful commerce of the world: a theme renewed by Palmerston when winding up the debate. Stanley tried to bring the discussion down from this rarefied atmosphere by insisting that the argument was not over free trade but protection, the policy common to both parties, and that the only difference between them was one of degree and circumstance. He put the case for special aid for the recently emancipated West Indies, denounced the financial administration of the Whigs, and accused them of concocting a crude set of budget proposals, affecting extensive interests, for party political purposes. Other Conservatives spoke of the encouragement to slave-grown sugar and Whig speakers challenged the opposition to say how they would meet the deficit. More ominously for the government Lushington said that as an abolitionist he could not support his party on the sugar issue; and several Whig agricultural members declared that they could not vote for the ministers in view of the connection between the sugar, timber and corn proposals.

Peel spoke on the eighth and final night. He argued the need for a temporary continuation of protection for West India sugar, refused to make sweeping statements on either slavery or free trade, and referred to his past association with Huskisson to prove that he was favourable to progressive relaxation of all restrictions on commerce. It was hardly for the Whigs, he observed, after their 1840 budget

[1] 44777 f. 65; Wellington (Peel to Wellington, Sunday, n.d. and wrongly docketed 8 June); 40425 fos. 417-20 (Peel's memorandum); 40429 f. 214 (Sandon to Peel).

to declare a proprietorial interest in free-trade principles and threaten, if driven from office, to pack them up and carry them away. He repeated his known views on the Corn Laws; he refused without access to official information to commit himself on timber. As for the deficit, this was the responsibility of the party which had been in office for the past decade. It was no use for the Whigs to represent themselves as martyrs to free trade and then call on him to furnish them with a financial policy. 'Can there be a more lamentable picture than that of a Chancellor of the Exchequer, seated on an empty chest, by the pool of bottomless deficiency, fishing for a budget?' Then he added, to the laughter of his supporters, in which he joined himself: 'I won't bite; the rt. hon. gentleman shall return home with his pannier as empty as his chest.' He ended with a challenge which foreshadowed the next stage in the opposition tactics. The vote that night would effectually be one of confidence; and if unfavourable would imply distrust in the competence of the ministry to relieve the country of its present embarrassments. The real evil was in their attempt to rule without the confidence of the House of Commons. It was not in their interest, in that of the crown, of constitutional government, and of the public interest, that they should continue any longer. He spoke with the confidence of success and the division the same night bore out that confidence. Sandon's motion was carried by 317 votes to 281. Only one Conservative was absent without a pair; only one (W. S. Lascelles, a free-trader) voted with the government. But fifteen Liberals voted against the government and eighteen more absented themselves.[1] It was an emphatic victory and even if it owed everything to divisions among the ministerialists, Peel had come out of the debate without departing from his carefully defined and balanced position.

What nobody knew, listening to him on the night of 18 May, was that he had recently been given private and additional grounds for confidence. On 4 May Melbourne had gone down to Windsor to warn the queen of the probability of defeat on the sugar question and prepare her for a resignation of the government. While at the Castle he had a conversation with his former private secretary, George Anson, a pleasant scholarly young man of twenty-nine who

[1] For an analysis of the vote see *Hansard*, LVIII, 673; *English Politics*, Appx. B.

in 1840 had been appointed secretary and treasurer to Prince Albert.[1] Anson told him that Albert thought there should be prior negotiation with Peel on the subject of the Household and the prime minister agreed that this might be done through Anson though not through the prince himself. On 8 May Melbourne wrote to the queen that the majority of the cabinet were in favour of resignation in the event of defeat over sugar, and the same day Anson sent a note to Peel asking for a private interview.

The meeting took place on Sunday morning, 9 May, at Whitehall Gardens. Anson explained that he came at the request of Prince Albert with the object of smoothing away any difficulties which might arise if Peel came into office. His specific proposition was that if Peel did not insist on any formal procedures, it would be possible to arrange the resignation of the Duchess of Sutherland, Lady Normanby, the Duchess of Bedford and in fact any ladies to whose continuance at court Peel might object. He assured Peel that if he dealt fairly and kindly with the queen, he would be met in the same spirit; and the prince would give him all the support in his power. Having first ascertained that Melbourne knew of the overture, Peel agreed at once that there was no need to raise any constitutional principle. He suggested, however, that the best course would be for the queen simply to inform him that the ladies immediately connected with prominent members of the government had sent in their resignations. He denied any wish to score a party triumph over the queen and repudiated with warmth the notion that his followers might press for such a triumph. Had the queen told him in 1839 that the three ladies mentioned had resigned, he said, there would have been no difficulty. Anson spoke of Albert's concern for the personal character of those appointed to the Household and Peel asked significantly whether the queen shared that anxiety. To this Anson replied somewhat cautiously that he believed he might say she did.

When Anson returned the next day to report that Peel's formula was acceptable, Peel said he hoped the queen fully understood the feelings with which he had made his proposals. He had not in 1839 committed himself to the appointment of any specific ladies, nor should he on this occasion without knowing beforehand the queen's

[1] He was the son of the Dean of Chester and a cousin of the Earl of Lichfield, see his obit. in *Annual Register*, 1849.

preferences. And, he added, with an awkwardness which betrayed how much the ill-founded charges of 1839 had wounded him, it was essential that the queen should understand he had the feelings of a gentleman and, when duty did not forbid, could not act against her wishes. Anson again alluded to Albert's views on the character of those holding court appointments and Peel observed dryly that it was astonishing how few really suitable people could be found for court or diplomatic posts. He assured Anson that he fully understood Melbourne's motives in sanctioning the interview and added generously that if the prime minister found himself in the end forced to dissolution rather than resignation, it would make no difference to Peel's appreciation of his conduct. Finally he suggested that the prince should let him have a list of ladies agreeable to the queen from whom a selection could be made. He must be seen to make the appointments but he would be entirely guided by the queen's wishes.

When this last was reported back by Anson, the queen at once took fire. She was prepared to leave to her prime minister all appointments of those holding seats in parliament but she asserted uncompromisingly her right to appoint the ladies of the Bedchamber, when approved by him, and her absolute discretion with regard to the other women. The prince therefore sent Anson back once more on 11 May to settle this problem of protocol. Peel confirmed that his proposal was for the queen to select and himself to appoint. Anson observed that the queen would prefer the reverse. This was awkward and Peel asked for time to consult the Duke of Wellington. The prince, however, who had set his heart on the success of his first venture into the realm of high politics, was afraid that delay would only stiffen the queen. He at once brought forward a compromise formula whereby the prime minister would notify the ladies concerned of the queen's intention to appoint, and the queen would announce to them personally their actual appointment. Peel, who had meanwhile spoken with the duke, cheerfully accepted this revised procedure. When Anson returned for his fourth interview on 12 May they went over a list of eligible ladies which Albert had prepared and discussed other appointments. Anson confided that Melbourne was particularly anxious that everything should go smoothly as the queen was pregnant again. Peel, to whom this interesting fact had already been imparted by a lady of his acquaintance, said the queen could rest assured that what happened in 1839 had left no trace in his mind except to make him want to do all he could to be agreeable to her. One final discussion took place on 13 May when Anson called to explain the queen's wishes over the male Household appointments. But this was a touchy subject and Peel, visibly recoiling, said he would prefer to leave matters open until the occasion arose. Offices for peers would have to be discussed with the duke and on those combinable with seats in the Commons he must reserve his freedom of action. Concession had clearly gone as far as possible.[1]

In the end it was all premature. Immediately after the defeat of 18 May the cabinet, against the inclination of their chief, reversed their previous decision and decided to dissolve rather than resign. Their electoral expert Parkes had advised Russell on 7 May that resignation followed by a Peelite dissolution would smash the party, whereas their own dissolution might at least preserve their existing strength; and in the weeks that followed opinion in the cabinet hardened in favour of an appeal to the electorate. On the 19th the final decision was taken. Next day Baring announced in the House his intention to move the ordinary annual sugar duties the following week and Russell indicated that he would proceed with his corn proposals early in June. It was as though nothing had happened or would happen; and on Sunday, 23 May, Anson called on Peel in evident embarrassment at the situation in which he and his principals had been left. Peel, whose cautious handling of the discussions Anson admitted to have been entirely vindicated, soothed the young man's emotions. He was convinced, he said, of the good faith of all those who had authorised their conversations; his own feeling was one of gratitude. If the result had been simply to disprove to the queen and Prince Albert the allegations made against him by his political enemies, it had been more than enough. It was a sympathetic and at the same time a clearsighted attitude. Peel had every reason for satisfaction. Through Anson he had been able to explain his position not merely to Victoria but to Albert and Melbourne. A great obstacle had been removed from his path; and

[1] RA/Y 54/27–44 (Anson memoranda); 40303 fos. 257–85, ptly pr. *Peel*, II, 455–8; *VL*, I, 268–74.

he had the first sign that in the prince he possessed a friend at court. Meanwhile, he had plenty to occupy his mind. It was clear that the Whigs intended to dissolve after bringing forward their corn proposals, in the hope that a free-trade cry in the towns would offset their certain losses in the counties. It was equally clear that the task of the opposition was to deny them this advantage. The second part of the opposition plan now came into operation. As soon as the House reassembled Peel gave notice that he would move on 27 May a resolution of no confidence in the ministry. Meanwhile he neatly avoided a controversy on the old sugar duties by himself seconding Baring's motion for their continuance.

Whatever happened in the House, it was now generally assumed that a dissolution was inevitable. The great no-confidence debate of May–June 1841, therefore, was not so much the operative cause as the opening cannonade of the electoral battle. The sense of Peel's motion, that the government lacked the power to carry its measures through the House and its constitutional duty was therefore to resign, was designed to make the issue general and constitutional rather than particular and polemic. His opening speech was conspicuous for its calmness and restraint. He gave a long historical review of parallel situations, attributed the weakness of the government to its perpetual oscillations between conservative and radical attitudes under various political pressures, and instanced the budget as the last great product of this inherent parliamentary instability. As for himself, his views on the great topics of the day were well known and on finance he could not and would not offer any constructive proposals while out of office. His case was that the House of Commons had the right to expect ministers to possess their confidence and ministers had the duty of listening to the House of Commons even when it was unfavourable to their views and hostile to their continuation in office. The ensuing debate, which, with the interruption of the Whitsun holidays lasted until 4 June, alternated between partisan attacks on policies and personalities, and abstruse arguments on constitutional practices and obligations. Macaulay endeavoured to make a distinction between confidence in legislation and confidence in administration; Morpeth defended the right of the government to dissolve rather than resign in the face of their parliamentary difficulties; Russell dilated on the iniquities of pre-

1830 Tory rule; Graham and Stanley dwelt on the long list of Whig legislative abortions; O'Connell prophesied disaster to Ireland from a Conservative ministry; Handley, a Whig county M.P., taunted Peel on his vagueness over agricultural protection. Replying on the fifth and last day of the debate Peel had little difficulty in disposing of the contradictory constitutional arguments of his opponents, and made a cutting reference to their conduct in dropping the poor law bill as an electoral liability while persisting in the corn resolutions as a probable electoral asset. The intention of the Whigs to dissolve, which Russell had at last openly admitted, made the question of confidence an academic one. But since Peel had been challenged by several Liberal speakers to state his policy in more detail, he repeated at length his position on corn: his concern to maintain an adequate protection, his conviction of the interdependence of manufacturing and agricultural prosperity, his refusal to bind himself to the detail of the existing law. He ended with another attack on the government's budget proposals, their sudden conversion that spring to the conclusions of a committee which they had not appointed and on which no cabinet minister had served, and their final action in stirring up class hostility over the corn laws and going to the country on a cry of 'cheap bread'.

From the statements of various Liberals who had voted against their party over sugar, it was clear that the rebels of May were rallying to the government once more. No one could predict with certainty the outcome of the debate and when at 3 a.m. on the morning of 5 June the House finally divided, it was in an atmosphere of unbearable excitement. The whips on both sides had made prodigious efforts and the Whigs even wheeled in the unconscious figure of Lord Halyburton, the member for Forfar, to be counted amid the jeers of the opposition. When the tellers forced their way through the crowd on the floor of the House towards the Speaker's chair and the black hair and immense whiskers of Fremantle were seen to be on the righthand side, a great roar went up. The Conservatives shouted and stamped and clapped, and when the result was announced—for the resolution 312, against 311—they shouted and stamped again. Every single member of the opposition had either voted or paired, and eight absent ministerialists had decided the issue. The narrowness of the victory made it the more intoxicating;

but no one could deny that it was decisive. The following Monday Russell announced the government's intention to wind up the necessary business of the session and dissolve parliament as soon as possible. A couple of weeks later the session was concluded and writs issued for a new parliament returnable on 19 August.

The general election which followed vindicated the prophecies of the Conservative election experts. Beginning at the end of June and continuing into the second week of July, it exhibited the usual medley of special influences, local cross-currents and unexpected results, overlaid by violence, corruption, and compromise. But beneath the confusion two general drifts of opinion could be dimly discerned: disillusionment with the last procrastinating and inept years of Whig rule, and a readiness to confide in the opposition and above all in the dominating figure of their leader. Against this a Whig electioneering platform constructed of future promises rather than of past achievements had little effect. How far public opinion of this kind was capable of translation into electoral terms was unknowable; but the confidence of the Conservative party managers stemmed not from any sudden shifts of opinion but from the preparations of the last six years, the state of the registration, and the efficiency of their electoral machinery. Even before the no-confidence debate took place the party election committee were positive of a minimum net gain of 35 seats, equal to 70 votes in a division. In July, with nearly 500 Conservative candidates in the field, their hopes steadily rose. Peel, though suffering from a lame and painful right leg as a result of his old complaint, sciatica, set an example of activity. Finding on his arrival in Tamworth that Captain Townshend, against expectations, was persisting in a contest for the second seat, he at once began a three-day canvass of the borough. Finding, as he expressed it to Goulburn, fresh strength as he went on, he then extended his activities to the county elections for Staffordshire and Warwickshire. At Tamworth his speech on nomination day contained little that he had not said before, but he emphasised naturally enough in such surroundings the importance of agriculture and attributed the distress in the country not to the operations of the Corn Laws but to other more technical causes.[1]

Speeches at Tamworth were perhaps not very important; and

[1] *Tamworth Election: Sir Robert Peel's Speech on Nomination Day, 28 June 1841.*

he and A'Court were comfortably returned at the head of the poll. Elsewhere, despite local upsets especially in the boroughs, the tide was running strongly with the Conservatives and by the third week in July it was generally accepted that they would have a majority of 76, or as Fremantle preferred to consider it, a round figure of 80. The cheap bread cry had failed to have any obvious effect in the towns. Over the United Kingdom as a whole, in urban constituencies with populations of over 10,000, the Conservatives gained twenty-six and lost nineteen, a net gain of seven. In the English counties their triumphant progress continued with a net gain of 22. Even in the unpredictable English boroughs they had improved their position on aggregate by half a dozen seats, including three in the Liberal strongholds of the City and Westminster. Scotland, partly because of the domestic Intrusion Controversy (in which Peel himself had been embroiled as a result of an interview he had given to a Scottish delegation at the request of the Duke of Argyll), yielded only minimal gains. But Ireland added to the tale of success with a net gain of eight seats, including one captured from O'Connell in Dublin. The Conservatives were still primarily the party of England and above all of the English counties. Nevertheless, without the forty-four Conservative M.P.s returned for the larger boroughs of over 1,000 electors, there would have been no victory. The result was a total which, as Ripon observed cannily to Graham, was enough for a working majority but not so large as to encourage the extremists of the party to try any undue pressure on Peel.[1]

It was in its way the first modern general election that the country had experienced. For the first time in British history a party in office enjoying a majority in the Commons had been defeated by an opposition previously in a minority. The powerful party organisations built up since 1834, and the appeal of a great opposition leader, had imposed on the defective and old-fashioned electoral structure left by the Reform Act of 1832 something which Britain was not to see again until after the Reform Act of 1867. 'The elections are wonderful,' wrote Croker flatteringly on 20 July, 'and the curiosity is that all turns on the name of Sir Robert Peel.' This was an exaggeration; but for all that it was probably true that without Peel the great Conservative victory of 1841 could not have

[1] 40446 f. 5. For Conservative gains and losses see 40485 f. 323.

taken place. On 27 July, in the customary resounding prose of its leader-writers, *The Times* pronounced a benediction on the result.

> No other nation has ever witnessed the spectacle, now exhibited by Great Britain to the admiration of the world, of a triumphant reaction of sound public opinion against the progress of a partially-successful democratical movement. And until now the world has never known an instance of a party being installed in power expressly by the voice of a great people—not for any pledges or promises which they have given, not for the sake of any particular measure or series of measures which they have advocated, but solely because the nation places confidence in their capacity and disinterestedness, and recognises in them a tone of principle which it feels to be necessary for wise and good government.

In his language at the Tamworth election banquet the next day Peel was more cautious and more colloquial. He observed that he was constantly being asked what he would do when called to office. His advice was to get rid of the old physicians before bringing in the new. Instead of offering his own prescription he attacked the Whigs for using the queen's name as though she were a partisan instead of what she was, 'the beloved sovereign of a whole people', and declared that the election results were due to the country's lack of confidence in the ministers. He paid a tribute to the thousands of 'unobtrusive individuals' up and down the country who had worked harder for the Conservative cause at the election than candidates themselves once used to do; and he reminded his audience that the victory achieved in the registration courts must continue to be secured there.[1] His restraint in speaking of the future was reasonable. Some weeks had still to elapse before the fruits of victory could be gathered in. Precedent and custom, as well as inclination, ensured that the Whigs would wait for the verdict of the new parliament rather than yield at once to the presumed wishes of the electorate. In the meantime Peel resumed consideration of the composition of his ministry which had intermittently engaged his thoughts since May and smoothed over a little storm that had blown up over the question of the Speakership.

The election of a Speaker in the new parliament was of more than conventional interest since a contest would provide the first

[1] *Speech by the Rt. Hon. Sir Robert Peel etc., 28 July 1841.*

trial of strength between the parties after the election. There had been some discussion of the problem at a casual gathering at Peel's house at the close of the session. The general feeling then was against any opposition to Shaw Lefevre, an outstandingly able Speaker who had won the general liking and respect of the House. Goulburn himself, who had been the opposition candidate in 1839 when Shaw Lefevre had succeeded Abercromby, was disinclined to a second challenge. After the general election, however, there was a move by various members of the party—the Lowthers, the Duke of Buckingham, and a few English and Irish back-benchers— to get rid of Lefevre on the grounds that he had shown bias in the choice of election committees. The controversy was taken up in the press; the hotheads of the Carlton ran after this new scent; and among the lesser fry Vyvyan and Disraeli were reported by Bonham, Peel's faithful watchdog in London, to be indulging in a great deal of abuse of the party leadership on the issue. Disraeli, in fact, was alleged by such different men as Stanley, Arbuthnot and Bonham to be the author of a somewhat insolent letter of advice to Peel on the subject which appeared in *The Times*[1] over the pseudonym *Pittacus*. The prime movers in the anti-Lefevre cabal, however, were country members like Tyrell of Essex, W. S. Blackstone of Wallingford, and Neeld of Chippenham. For 'that blockhead Sir John Tyrell', as he described him to Graham and an even greater blockhead, Sir Eardley Wilmot, who talked of putting himself up for the chair, Peel had nothing but contempt. But he judged it prudent to go through the motions of party deliberation and wrote to some two dozen leading party men to elicit their opinions. All but Lowther, Burdett, Jackson and Sugden were in favour of Lefevre, and some very sharply so. Bonham's persuasiveness and perhaps the hope of office succeeded in neutralising the Duke of Buckingham and for the sake of party unity Peel sent a long soothing letter to Tyrell. By the middle of August the small stir had subsided.[2]

[1] 2 Aug. 1841.

[2] For the voluminous correspondence on the Speakership question see 40476 fos. 18, 20, 24, 29, 31, 41 (Fremantle); 40484 f. 20 (Arbuthnot); 40485 fos. 273, 288, 316, 322, 338; 40486 fos. 7, 101 (Bonham); Graham (Stanley to Graham, 25 July, 5 Aug., Peel to Graham, 30 July 1841); Stanhope (Peel to Mahon, 3 Aug. 1841); Goulburn (Peel to Goulburn, 28 July, 3 Aug. 1841); *Peel*, II, 476–9.

Meanwhile more important problems, two strategic and one tactical, were pressing for consideration. It was of obvious advantage to decide on the distribution of offices as early as possible; and the state of public business at the end of the session ensured that the first great task of the new government would be finance. Fremantle and Bonham, the latter armed with provisional lists of appointments, came down to Drayton early in August to assist their chief with the first; and on the weighty problem of financial policy Peel had already in July begun a cautious and confidential correspondence with Goulburn, Graham and Stanley. Nothing for the moment could be allowed to leak out on either of those two matters. The tactical question of dislodging the Whigs, however, had to be settled by the time parliament met. Since there was to be no opposition on the Speakership, an amendment to the Address was inevitable. Peel thought it should follow the same lines as the no confidence motion of May attacking men rather than measures, and perhaps accompanied by a parallel motion in the Lords. For himself, after snatching a few days' shooting in mid-August, he proposed to be in London by the morning of the 19th and asked his chief colleagues to meet him there. The final decision was taken at inner party conferences on 21–23 August, by which time they had before them advance copies of the queen's speech. Even at that stage there was a fear that the reference in the speech to the Corn Laws indicated a readiness on the part of the government to stay in office and agitate the question until a suitable moment could be found for a second dissolution.[1] On 24 August, therefore, when the speech was read in parliament, the opposition moved in for the *coup de grâce*. In the Lords Ripon carried by a majority of almost two to one an amendment expressing no confidence in the ministry. In the Commons the process was more protracted. The moving of the amendment was entrusted to J. S. Wortley, the hero of an election triumph in the West Riding where he and Edmund Denison had defeated Milton and Morpeth, the eldest sons of two great Whig magnates, Lords Fitzwilliam and Carlisle. The debate, which lasted over four nights, was conspicuous for quantity rather than quality. Certainty of the outcome robbed the occasion of any flavour or excitement. There was a good deal of petty bickering; party and

[1] Ellenborough (24 Aug. 1841); cf. Graham (Peel to Graham, 4 Aug. 1841).

personal records were dragged over once more; Peel was again taunted for his silence over his own policies; and it was sourly forecast that he would be forced either to give way to the extremists of his party or, as he had done before over Catholic emancipation, to yield to popular pressure and take up the measures of his opponents.

Speaking on the final night Peel exhibited (except for a few sharp words to O'Connell) the calmness and objectivity that befitted a man on the brink of office. He congratulated the government on the restoration of friendly relations with France and said some sensible things on the folly of competitive armaments among the states of Europe. On domestic matters he again declined to say how he would deal with finance. He drew a distinction between his opposition to the three principal budget proposals of the government and his general and long-standing advocacy of free trade. He said no more than he had said before on sugar and timber; though he argued more cogently the case against a fixed duty on corn. On social distress he reaffirmed in even more striking language that

> if I could be induced to believe that an alteration in the Corn Laws would be an effective remedy for those distresses, I would be the first to step forward and say, at once, to those who are most interested in upholding the present system, the agricultural interest,—'it is for your advantage rather to submit to an alteration of the present Corn Laws than by insisting on their continuance to be the occasion of suffering such as has been described.' If any sacrifice of theirs could prevent the continuance of that distress, could offer a guarantee against the recurrence of it, I would earnestly advise a relaxation, an alteration, nay, if necessary, a repeal of the Corn Laws.

But what remained longest in people's memories was the warning he threw out at the end of the speech. He had been told, he said, that in exercising power he would have to be the instrument of opinions and feelings he himself repudiated. With his ideas of office, he observed contemptuously, he was little disposed to add this degrading condition to the other sacrifices it entailed. And the last two sentences of his speech ran like this:

> If I exercise power, it shall be upon my conception—perhaps imperfect, perhaps mistaken,—but my sincere conception of public

duty. That power I will not hold, unless I can hold it consistently with the maintenance of my own opinions; and that power I will relinquish the moment I am satisfied I am not supported in the maintenance of them by the confidence of this House and of the people of this country.

When the cheering died down Russell replied, defensively but not without sense and dignity. Then the division took place: for the address 269, for the amendment 360, a majority against the government of 91. It was all over and when parliament reassembled on Monday, 30 August, the resignation of the government was announced in both Houses. Already on 28 August Melbourne had told Victoria that the ministry was at an end and advised her to make arrangements for a new government as rapidly as possible.

III

At half-past twelve on Monday, 30 August, an open travelling carriage turned out of Whitehall Gardens, passed through St. James's Park and up Constitution Hill, and turned left into the Hounslow Road. It contained the solitary figure of Sir Robert Peel on his way to Windsor in response to a frigid summons from Victoria which had arrived by special messenger late the evening before.[1] It was the end of a decade of opposition, the start of a new period in his own life and perhaps in that of the country as well. He was inured to office; and he knew what it was like to be a prime minister. Yet power of the kind which was about to be placed in his hands was something he had never had before. At the age of fifty-three with a wider experience of public affairs than any other man then in politics, he was to be as much his own master as any parliamentary statesman can ever be; and no one knew better than Peel how commonly the world overestimates the freedom of action of the person at the head of a nation's affairs. 'Men, and the conduct of men', he had written to Mahon in the course of their Walpolean debate eight years earlier, 'are much more the creatures of circumstance than they generally appear in history.' He was as uncommitted as anyone in his position could hope to be; to a degree, in

[1] *The Times*, 31 Aug. 1841.

fact, which had evoked the exasperated comments of his opponents. But the limitations were there, in the needs of administration, in foreign affairs, in the facts of national economy and the movements of public opinion, in population statistics and trade returns, in the views of his colleagues, in the pledges, hopes and interests of his supporters, and in his own past career. For himself he had no choice. If his work in opposition meant anything at all, it was designed to lead up to that very day. Defence of Church and State, of the mixed and balanced constitution, of the great aristocratic interests, was only possible through an organised party; and an organised party could only be kept in being if it aimed at office. 'What are we fighting for,' he had asked Goulburn in 1839, 'but the predominance of our principles? and if the acceptance of office will advance them, office ought to be accepted.' Certainly the principles that served in opposition would hardly furnish more than the bare bones of a policy in office; but with the right men in power, he believed that the details of policy would come right too.

Waiting for him in the great castle above the Thames was another captive of circumstances: a dissatisfied and unwilling young woman in an advanced state of pregnancy. It would not be an easy interview, but he knew what the complications were and a solution had already been devised for them. Moreover there would also be at Windsor Prince Albert and his secretary Anson, both young, but men whom he felt he might trust. 1841 would not be a repetition of 1839. The real difficulties were elsewhere: in the problems that stayed in office when politicians went out; and in the unpredictable events that make improvisation three-parts of a politician's trade. For some of the immediate issues confronting him he was already prepared. For the rest he had made it clear to supporters and critics alike that he would govern according to his own conception of national duty. Yet he would not have been Peel had he not viewed the future with satisfaction and confidence. After nearly ten years during which his administrative talents had been lying fallow, he could set to work once more. He had seen too much to have any delusions about what lay ahead, but he had supreme confidence in his own powers. The frustrated energy which at times had made him irritated or contemptuous at the blunderings of the Whigs could now be released in constructive policy. In the prime of life, while his experience was still matched by his stamina, he could face with professional realism and self-reliance the greatest challenge of his career. It was a cautious, experienced, but very masterful man who at three o'clock drove up the hill past the sentries at the Henry VIII gateway and into the castle courtyard.

THE NEW MINISTRY

The audience with the queen on Monday, 30 August, was brief but civil. Victoria, who had just taken leave of Lord Melbourne, was visibly subdued and Peel tactfully told her that he had not presumed to come with ministerial recommendations at their first interview. It was agreed that he would write to her the following day and come again on the Wednesday after she had time to consider his proposals. There was a circumspect conversation about Household appointments with each almost inviting the other to make suggestions; and after assuring the queen of his anxiety to do everything that was agreeable to her, the new prime minister withdrew. It was all over in twenty minutes. Though only a beginning, at least it was a satisfactory one; and during the next few days Peel took pains to ensure that no jarring note was struck in the first inevitably constrained exchange of views. In this other interested parties took a hand. The three principal Whig ladies at Court—the Duchess of Bedford, the Duchess of Sutherland and Lady Normanby—had already sent in their resignations, and Prince Albert followed this up by telling two of his own Whig Household officers to resign. On Tuesday Anson called on Peel to inform him of the prince's wish, if agreeable, to appoint Lord Exeter, one of the most loyal Conservative party peers, as head of his Household. Peel encouraged the young secretary to talk and the conversation developed into a general canvass of names for Household appointments both male and female. Anson was able to mention some of the royal dislikes and Peel then suggested that, since he wished to meet the queen's wishes whenever possible, it would be helpful if he could see Anson and ascertain her feelings from him. On his return Anson reported this to Albert and it was arranged that before Peel's interview with the queen the next day Anson should have a preliminary talk with him on Victoria's reactions to his initial proposals. In consequence the second audience on 1 September passed off even more gratifyingly than the first.

With the discreet Anson acting as a softening medium between his three principals, the long list of Household appointments was filled up during the early weeks of September to the general satisfaction of both sides, though as Peel wrote to his old confidant Hobhouse on 18 September 'you can readily believe that this double object could not be attained without the most sedulous care and caution in every step'. He studiously consulted the queen's wishes on any office that affected her, abandoning suggestions which she did not like, and accepting those for whom she indicated a preference. In at least one instance he gave up an appointment which though politically useful turned out to be questionable on personal grounds. Having proposed Lord Powerscourt as Lord in Waiting, he subsequently became aware of a scandal about him at Bath. He therefore asked Powerscourt to call, put it to him that if there was any truth in the story he should resign his claim, and secured his withdrawal.[1] It was clear also that the queen, guided by Albert and prompted offstage by Lord Melbourne, was prepared to play her part in this courteous game of mutual concessions. Though Victoria's own letters were sometimes stiff, there was an unmistakably cordial note in Anson's flow of correspondence conveying private advice and suggestions on the part of Prince Albert. Anson occupied a remarkable position in these first few weeks. He was in practice acting as the real channel of communication between the prime minister and the queen through the prince, his nominal employer. Peel, so far from resenting this anomalous situation, had the sense to encourage it. Drummond, Peel's private secretary, detained Anson in fact after one of his interviews to tell him that the prime minister had taken a great liking to him and felt he could place absolute trust in him.[2] The queen on her side could also feel satisfaction. The arrangement, while sparing her personal embarrassment, brought her more success than she could have anticipated. It was true that Peel's solid parliamentary majority made it not merely possible, but as he observed to Anson, desirable to pay additional

[1] RA/Y 54/68-73; RA/C 22/12.   [2] RA/Y 54/73.

deference to the queen's wishes. Yet it was characteristic that Peel, recognising the signs of trust and fair dealing at court, not only came halfway to meet the queen but advanced far beyond what could have been expected in the way of concession. The queen admitted to Ashley that Peel had behaved very handsomely to her[1] and when Lord Melbourne heard all the details from Anson he grumbled like any traditional Whig that 'Sir Robert had allowed the Queen *far too wide a discretion* in the formation of the Household'. As for Peel, he let it be known that the queen had behaved most kindly and generously. To Ellenborough (who had a lift back in the prime minister's carriage from Slough on 1 September) he confided that 'Prince Albert is altogether with us'. For these large advantages a handful of court appointments was a small price to pay.[2]

Meanwhile the main structure of his administration was rapidly erected. On most of the important offices his mind had already been made up. As far back as June he had started thinking about the problem and after the detailed consultations with Bonham and Fremantle in August he was able to go to work immediately he had received his commission from the queen. With several of his closest colleagues there had probably been for some time a verbal understanding about their destined offices. In general three considerations governed his choice. He felt he owed a duty to those who had supported him in the forlorn venture of 1834; key positions had to be found for Stanley and Graham, the great converts of the post-1835 period; and for the sake of party unity some gesture had to be made to the ultras and the agriculturalists. Of the old cabinet Rosslyn was dead; Alexander Baring, who had already received his reward in the Ashburton peerage, was omitted; Herries having lost his election at Ipswich was temporarily ineligible; the inarticulate Sir George Murray was also out of the House of Commons; and de Grey after some demur consented to go as Lord Lieutenant to Ireland, his former post as First Lord of the Admiralty being taken by Haddington, the Lord Lieutenant of 1834–5. This left four vacancies in the original list of fourteen, enough to accommodate Stanley, Graham and Ripon of the Whig seceders of 1834 with one to spare. Keeping his cabinet at its former figure, therefore, Peel had virtually

[1] N & Q, vol. 187, p. 207 n.
[2] Ellenborough, 1 Sept. 1841; 40432 fos. 3 et seq.; RA/Y 54/68–73; VL, I, 309–13.

a readymade set of senior colleagues. The main problem was the redeployment of offices. The duke, because of his age and deafness, being prone moreover, as Peel expressed it to the queen, to sleep coming over him during protracted discussions, was relieved of departmental duties, leaving the Foreign Office to Aberdeen. The Chancellorship of the Exchequer which Peel had held in 1834 was now delegated to Goulburn. Stanley had the Colonial Secretaryship which Canada and Jamaica had turned into one of the most responsible and difficult offices in the Whig administrations; and Graham took the more laborious Home Secretaryship. Ripon accepted the Presidency of the Board of Trade at the cost of some mortification in going back to a post he had held twenty years earlier before his brief, inglorious months as prime minister in 1827. Hardinge, whose Irish Secretaryship in 1834-5 had shown Peel his unsuitability for paper-work, was transferred to the less demanding administration of Secretary at War. Wharncliffe became the President of the Council. The rest—Lyndhurst as Lord Chancellor, Ellenborough as President of the Board of Control, and Knatchbull as Paymaster-General—returned to their old posts.

The one vacant seat in the cabinet was offered in a calculated gesture of expediency to the Duke of Buckingham. He was a man without talent or even businesslike habits; but he had electoral influence, he was the darling of the Buckinghamshire farmers, and in the decade which had elapsed since he won a spurious reputation as Lord Chandos of the Reform Bill, he had made himself the titular leader of the agriculturalists. The summit of his career was reached with the presidency of the Society for the Protection of Agriculture in 1840. Malt had been the stumbling-block in 1834 but in 1841 there was more attractive bait for the vanity and greed which predominated in his irresolute character. What he wanted was the Admiralty and the Garter, but Peel knew his man too well to pay this inflated price. The Garter was left dangling. What he was offered was a choice of the two non-departmental posts which carried cabinet status—Lord Privy Seal or President of the Council—and he chose the former. Stanley, quoting the Duke of Richmond, opined that if Buckingham entered the cabinet, he should retire from the presidency of the Agricultural Society, which was primarily a political organisation designed to combat the Anti-Corn Law

League. With this Peel and the rest of his colleagues agreed in principle though it was perhaps wisely never made a stipulation.[1] With both Buckingham and Knatchbull in the cabinet, however, the agricultural interest had been given a gratifying representation and at the same time the danger of dissidence from that always potentially dissident element in the party was substantially reduced. Two passengers in a cabinet of fourteen was not in political terms an excessive supercargo. For the rest it was a workmanlike combination of ability and prestige. It was all settled in a day and a half of personal discussions and interviews and on 31 August Peel sent off to the queen the full cabinet list together with names for some of the Irish and legal posts.

Bonham's draft list of ministerial appointments in August[2] had covered not only the cabinet but a whole range of junior posts down to under-secretaries and assistant whips. The work of filling up the bottom tiers of the administration went forward therefore with almost equal promptitude. It might not have done perhaps had all potential office-holders shown Gladstone's ability to see three sides to every question and insist on discussing all of them. Summoned to Peel on the morning of 31 August he was offered the vice-presidency of the Board of Trade as second-in-command to Ripon and spokesman of the department in the Commons. For a quarter of an hour the young author of the *State in its Relations with the Church* urged his unfitness for this mundane post while Peel patiently and good-humouredly assured him of the important part which matters of trade and finance would play in the new administration and 'the sense which others entertain of your suitableness for this office'. Next day Gladstone followed up the interview with an acceptance covering seven sides of writing to which the busy prime minister replied in one.[3] Others were more succinct and by 3 September Peel was able to submit to the queen the full list of the Admiralty Board and Treasury including the two important appointments of Clerk as financial and Fremantle as patronage secretary. The party's chief of staff, Granville Somerset, took the Duchy of Lancaster; and the indispensable Bonham, though not in parliament, returned to his old niche as Storekeeper to the Ordnance.

[1] Ellenborough, 31 Aug. 1841.
[2] 40489 f. 393. [3] *Gladstone*, I, 178; 40469 fos. 6, 10.

Of the remaining young men of the 1834 vintage, maturer now by seven years, Lincoln became Commissioner for Woods and Forests, Sidney Herbert Secretary to the Admiralty, Eliot went as Chief Secretary to Ireland, and Lord Canning came in as under-secretary at the Foreign Office. In the lower strata of offices a sprinkling of Suttons, Barings, Corrys and Gordons demonstrated a decent regard for the claims of old party connections; while the ablest of Peel's own brothers, Colonel Jonathan Peel, was given an official but not very onerous appointment as Surveyor-General to the Ordnance. Of others who might have had posts, Francis Egerton and Lord Mahon disowned ambitions for office, and Sandon refused an offer of Woods and Forests made before Lincoln's appointment. Lord Melbourne privately deplored this to Victoria on the grounds that Lincoln was ignorant of the work, unused to business and reputedly of quarrelsome temper. Acting on this unofficial if slightly unconstitutional hint, Anson raised the matter with Peel but the prime minister remained unmoved. Though the Woods and Forests Department, which carried with it the super-intendence of royal estates and buildings, inevitably involved much direct business with the crown, it was still a political office; and among his young followers Peel had a particular affection for Lincoln. He assured Anson that he was 'one of the best men we have' and the issue was allowed to drop.[1]

There was of course the usual crop of personal difficulties which any prime minister has to face. Granville Somerset was a case in point. He was a first-class administrator who deserved well of the party. But he suffered from two handicaps: a physical deformity of his figure and a brusque unconciliatory manner. The first disqualified him from the post he wanted of Chief Secretary for Ireland, since Peel felt it would expose him to cruel ridicule in the Irish press; the second from Woods and Forests where he would be in close contact with the court. He accepted the Duchy but it came without the seat in cabinet which his central role in the inner party consultations of the summer might have encouraged him to expect.[2] Another example was Sir Edward Sugden who raised the old social difficulties about his wife and tried to make it a condition of his acceptance of the Irish Lord Chancellorship that he should get

[1] RA/C 22/12, 21.   [2] Ellenborough, 31 Aug., 2 Sept. 1841; RA/Y 54/69.

a peerage. Peel stood firm against any promises and told him flatly that as he was enjoying a pension for his brief judicial tenure in 1834–35, the question of a peerage could be no possible justification for refusing appointment.[1] The future of Lord Londonderry revived another old sore. He had said he would only take the Embassy at Paris or the Lord Lieutenancy of Ireland. For an Orange peer who was a notorious Russophile both were out of the question. To send him to Vienna was equally inexpedient; and since Stanley had been one of those who had strongly criticised his posting to St. Petersburg in 1835, this too presented difficulties. Peel thought of putting him at the Ordnance but encountered resistance from Wellington who thought he would do more mischief there than as a malcontent peer in the Lords. In any case Londonderry indicated that he would not consider the Ordnance unless it carried cabinet status; and when nothing came of anything, he was not slow to express dissatisfaction.[2] The veteran Herries presented an equally insoluble problem. He was out of parliament and there was the old quarrel of 1827–28 between himself and Lord Ripon to complicate matters. In an interview on 10 September Peel made it clear that the latter would not have prevented him from inviting Herries into the cabinet but in the circumstances he could not now do so without exposing himself to claims from other men who had failed to get themselves elected. The conversation was friendly and later the same month Peel sent for him to suggest he should put up for the seat vacated by Sugden at Ripon which its proprietor Miss Lawrence had placed at Peel's disposal. But he made no accompanying promise of a ministerial appointment. Herries, sensitive and awkward, took the view that if he stood for what was virtually a government borough without holding a government office, he would be apparently abandoning all political ambitions. This to Peel was surprising and probably vexatious; but all his attempts at persuasion failed. In the end the seat at Ripon went to Sir George Cockburn, the new First Sea Lord. Herries, one of the party's acknowledged financial experts, remained out of parliament in self-imposed exile until 1847.[3]

Another even more prickly and tortured man was Lord Ashley. As early as 30 August Peel repeated the proposal made and accepted

[1] 40480 f. 9.   [2] Ellenborough, 31 Aug. 1841.   [3] *Herries*, II, 192–203.

in 1839 of an appointment in the Royal Household. Ashley adopted the attitude that he was so committed on the Factory question that he could not take office unless the government fully accepted his policy on that issue. Three days later, having seen the queen, Peel renewed his solicitations. He argued that Ashley could reserve his position on a question which in any case could not come up until the spring, and he emphasised the difference between a court and a political appointment. But though he brought in Goulburn to add his entreaties, Ashley remained adamant. A few days later Anson tried to find a way out of the deadlock by suggesting that Ashley should be invited to take a position in the Prince's Household; but two more interviews with Peel proved equally fruitless. The prime minister clearly could not at that stage commit himself to the details of Ashley's factory campaign, though he said enough to indicate that when the government had been given time to investigate the problem, they might be able to come to some agreement. For the moment he used all his resources of patience and persuasion to overcome the other man's scruples. But Ashley was in a highly emotional and irrational mood. He had already pledged himself in writing to the West Riding operatives to take no office which would inhibit his activities on their behalf. From the start he probably had no intention of accepting anything. Yet he was mortified at not being offered political office; and to himself at least he justified his attitude by pouring out in his diary cynical suspicions of Peel's motives.[1]

If there were some candidates who could not or would not take office, there were some offices for which it was difficult to find candidates. The most eminent of these was the Governor-Generalship of India on which Peel was sounding opinion even before he was summoned by the queen. Lord Auckland was due to retire, leaving two current sets of military operations against China and Afghanistan to underline the necessity for a good and quick choice of a successor. Lord Heytesbury declined on grounds of age and health; Haddington preferred the Admiralty. Other names were canvassed with Ellenborough and the duke but there seemed an objection to every one. Ellenborough was opposed to Wharncliffe and Fitzgerald, and hankered for either a young man or a soldier.

[1] *Hodder*, pp. 182, 188–95; 40432 f. 67.

Peel thought Dalhousie too young, Granville Somerset unsuitable, Graham indispensable, and Hardinge useless for civil administration. A month of intermittent discussion uncovered nobody acceptable to both Peel and Ellenborough. Finally, early in October, Peel cut through the dilemma by asking Ellenborough to go himself to India, leaving his place at the Board of Control to be filled by Fitzgerald. His only misgiving, which he expressed privately to Wellington, was Ellenborough's 'tendency to precipitation and over-activity', though he said hopefully that this might be offset by his having good and steady advisers when he arrived. The duke, while endorsing the decision, was sceptical of the restraining abilities of the Council in India but pinned his trust with no less optimism to Ellenborough's own discretion and commonsense. This, in a man who had already told Peel that what he had to do was to choose a successor not to Auckland but to Akbar, an emperor who was his own minister, was not the most convincing of guarantees. As it was, Peel had to discourage Ellenborough's immediate desire, contrary to all recent practice, for an additional commission as Captain-General and Commander-in-Chief. He would have been even more disquieted had he been present at Ellenborough's parting interview with Victoria at the end of October when he informed the queen that if all went well out East, 'her troops would keep her birthday in the Palace of the Emperor of China and the Golden Island'. However, the die was cast and Peel could do no more than ask Wellington to impress on the new Governor-General with all the weight of his Indian experience and military prestige, the policy of mature consideration and avoidance of precipitate courses.[1]

In the meantime, by dint of working sixteen to eighteen hours a day up to the middle of September, Peel completed his other arrangements. Inevitably, as the administration took shape, the cloud of disappointment thickened behind it. It was an age which still had much of the old eighteenth-century candour in pressing personal requests; and by letter and interview Peel was beset for weeks on end by applicants for offices, honours, and promotions. Among the peers Beaufort and Wilton were aggrieved at not being

---

[1] Ellenborough, 29 Aug.–4 Nov. 1841; Wellington (Peel to Wellington, 9 Oct. 1841); 40471 fos. 37–9; *Peel*, II, 575–8.

offered a place at court; Glengall and Charleville thought that the Orange Ireland—in their persons—had been deliberately excluded; Lord Maryborough at the age of nearly eighty still fancied his claims; and Chief Justice Bushe came over from Ireland to bargain for a peerage before retirement only to return empty-handed and aggrieved. Lefroy proffered unsolicited advice on judicial appointments; and 'Chin' Grant wanted to be Chairman of Ways and Means.[1] Everybody who had ever had anything in the way of office, Peel observed to Greville, conceived that they had some sort of reversionary right to it, forgetting that younger men must be brought forward. But a decade of opposition had accumulated claims which left Peel with very little freedom of choice. The pressure was greatest on the parliamentary posts. 'I really believe', Peel wrote to Ripon, 'that with the exception of two or three appointments there has been an absolute claim which could not be disregarded for every Parliamentary office.' Those whose claims were more illusory made up in importunity what they lacked in qualification. When Francis Egerton in declining office hazarded the opinion that Peel's difficulties would be in the abundance, not the scarcity, of candidates, the prime minister replied somewhat caustically that he had not had a single application for office from anybody who was fit for it.[2] In practice his patronage covered little more than the parliamentary offices and the Household appointments; but an exaggerated notion was current of the range of his beneficence. As late as the end of October Peel was still spending a couple of hours each day in answering applications from those who, as he expressed it to Arbuthnot, 'either have no profession, or seek civil office instead of professional employment'.[3] The pressure was equally great from those who sought merely social advancement. Austere by nature on the question of titles, Peel could not persuade himself that the recent history of the House of Lords warranted an immediate reinforcement of new Tory peers. This did not save him from a heavy correspondence with Wellington on honours, promotions, lord lieutenancies and bishoprics. With the approaching confinement of the queen, there was another surge of requests from aspirants who optimistically assumed that the birth of a Prince of

[1] Greville, 4, 17, 22 Sept. 1841.   [2] ibid., 1 Sept. 1841; 40464 f. 17.
[3] Arbuthnot, p. 234.

Wales would be celebrated by a large creation of peers and baronets.

It was an expectation which Peel had no intention of satisfying, but the enormous number of applications he received moved him to mild irony. 'The distinction of being without an honour is becoming a rare and valuable one,' he wrote to Graham in late October, 'and should not become extinct.'[1] The business of patronage, as always, brought out the more intolerant side of his nature. To Croker, who in September sent him the draft of a *Quarterly* article on the new administration, he replied forcefully that a paragraph should be added on the difference between a prime minister in their own day and the Pelhams and Newcastles of the previous century. The reward for a position of such toil and anxiety, he continued, was not the curse of patronage which as a rule only made *dix mécontents et un ingrat*, but the means it provided for serving the country and winning honourable fame. Such a minister would not demean himself by humiliating submissions for mere party purposes. He would use his position to carry out the great principles his party supported; and if obstructed would retire from office, though not from power, since the country would do justice to his motives.[2] No doubt this uncompromising rhetoric was designed to stiffen the general theme of Croker's article that Peel was taking office on his own terms. But clearly it represented a side of Peel's own nature which power was likely to strengthen rather than diminish. It was a side which observers often found repellent. Even if the sentiment was unexceptionable, there was something which jarred in the expression of it. On the morrow of a great electoral victory Peel could perhaps afford to be autocratic; but political honeymoons do not last for ever.

II

The formal installation of the new ministry took place on 3 September at a Privy Council held at Claremont, Leopold of Belgium's country house at Esher in Surrey which he had put at the disposal of his royal niece. The outgoing and incoming ministers (the latter punctiliously clad in court dress) were all on the road together, to the amusement of Lord Brougham who drove out towards Kingston

<hr/>

[1] 40446 f. 106.   [2] *Croker*, II, 409–10.

to watch the spectacle. At Claremont the queen was flushed and nervous; Peel pale and quiet. Only he and the duke had private audiences and Melbourne's absence spared her the most painful of the leavetakings with her ex-ministers. The rest of the proceedings were routine and civil, although the atmosphere was notably muted.[1] In the succeeding days the re-elections of the House of Commons ministers took place without opposition and on 16 September the House reassembled with the new ministers sitting on the Treasury bench. The only purpose of this late autumn meeting was to deal with urgent and indispensable business and as soon as possible the session was brought to a close. Little of note took place. There was some unimportant party bickering, and Peel took the opportunity to tell the new House of Commons what he had told the old and was to repeat to Croker a few days later—his view of the office of prime minister, his right to propose such measures as he thought in the national interest, and his disdain for considerations of 'mere political support' which would make him the instrument of carrying other men's opinions into effect. Early in October parliament was prorogued. By this time the cabinet had settled down to its routine meetings and the work of preparing measures for the new session was already begun.

In personnel alone the administration which Peel had assembled was one of the more impressive ministries of the century; three past and three future prime ministers, and three future governors of India served in its ranks. Nor despite the long years of opposition was it excessively weighted by age. Though the cabinet itself had an average age of fifty-seven, only four of the fourteen were over sixty; and since these included Lyndhurst, Wharncliffe, and Haddington, they scarcely counted as the more influential group of ministers. The men most likely to form an inner ring of confidential advisers round the prime minister—the three secretaries of state and the chancellor of the exchequer—had an average age of only fifty-one. Peel himself at fifty-three belonged to the younger half of the cabinet. Oldest of them all was the seventy-two-year-old Duke of Wellington. He still retained his thin, soldierly figure, incisive speech and imperative accents. But his deafness was gaining on him and the old head with its silver-white hair, round blue eyes,

[1] Ellenborough, 3 Sept.; *Greville*, 4 Sept. 1841.

beaky nose and small, firm mouth, was beginning to droop. Although he still had astonishing reserves of energy, the decision to make him minister without a department was clearly right. Even so, with a sympathy which perhaps would not have occurred to the duke had their positions been reversed, Peel felt at the first few cabinet meetings that Wellington was finding a painful contrast between his new position and the one he had previously held.[1] The duke's former critic, Stanley, was on the other hand the youngest man in the cabinet, though visitors to the House of Commons with mental visions of the handsome Rupert of debate a decade earlier found this hard to credit. Of average height and thickset physique, Stanley was already showing the outward signs of his own careless, self-assured nature. He was beginning to develop a paunch and there was a lounging untidiness in his dress and manner which was a reflection of his habitual indifference to conventional forms. At the age of forty-two his temper was more under control, but he had lost nothing of the sharp tongue, quick mind, independent judgement and forcefulness in debate which had once marked him out as the prospective leader of the Whigs. His well-known sporting and racing interests—he and Wharncliffe were the only members of the cabinet who were also members of the Jockey Club—gave a curious duality to his life. Yet it would have been premature to assume he had abandoned any of his early political ambitions. As the most youthful and at the same time one of the most outstanding members of the Conservative cabinet, he had time on his side.

Graham, the man whose name had been so closely connected with Stanley, was a very opposite character. Tall, dark, heavy-featured, dignified, Graham did not easily show his real nature to outsiders. His speeches were weighty and sensible, but his hard voice and an occasional unfortunate phrase gave an impression of venom which was far from just. Behind the formidable façade Graham was a curiously humble man who always yielded to the attractions of a more forceful personality. At the outset of his career it had been Althorp, then Stanley, and now it was Peel. Part of this dependence came from the uncertainties of his own complex and emotional nature, constantly veering between apocalyptic gloom and boyish enthusiasm. Greville once said of Graham that he was either in the

[1] Cf. 40467 f. 148 (Peel to Stanley, Dec. 1841).

garret or the cellar; and this temperamental polarity was sharpened by his logical mind and quick imagination. He had a dangerous gift of seeing large issues in absolute terms, and a prophetic eloquence in describing what he saw. Russell later wrote of him that his sense of danger was as acute as that of an animal, and like some creatures of the wild he was fascinated by the object of his fear.[1] Yet he was an able and upright administrator, a loyal colleague, a devout churchman, and a sympathetic friend. Peel could scarcely have found a more diligent and congenial collaborator. His defect was perhaps that in the end he unconsciously absorbed so much of Peel's thinking that he could not offer the stimulus of an independent judgement. This was not true of Goulburn, though in popular estimation he was often dismissed as no more than Peel's *alter ego*. Like Graham, though shorn of Graham's more spectacular qualities, he was a sound administrator and a staunch friend. His speeches were usually dull, his personality limited, and when it came to the point he was always ready to subordinate his opinions to the superior judgement of his lifelong friend and political leader. But he possessed an equability of temperament and solidity of mind which enabled him to disagree with Peel without pushing disagreement to uncomfortable extremes. One of the most self-effacing, he was far from being one of the least valuable of the cabinet. Nevertheless his position as Chancellor of the Exchequer in an administration in which the prime minister was the acknowledged expert in finance and fiscal policy meant that he was permanently overshadowed. Increasingly his role became more that of an industrious permanent civil servant of objective judgement than that of an independent and equal colleague.

The Foreign Office, that most aloof, specialised and professional of all the great departments of state, was once again in the hands of Aberdeen who had held that responsibility in 1828-30. Personally and politically he represented the purest strain of historic conservatism. Pitt and Dundas had been his guardians; he had been a contemporary of Peel's at Harrow; he had gone to Vienna as Castlereagh's ambassador in 1813. His tragic family history—the early death of his first wife, the successive deaths of all three daughters of that marriage, and finally the death of his second wife in 1833—he

---

[1] *Clarendon*, I, 326.

had borne with stoic fortitude. While remaining on close and even affectionate terms with both Peel and the duke, however, he had only reluctantly returned to office as Secretary for the Colonies in 1834. A few years later he was persuaded by Wellington to undertake the leadership of the Scottish Conservative peers. Though he accepted what was for him the one congenial post of Foreign Secretary in 1841, his zeal for office remained at a low temperature. This, in a diplomatist, was perhaps no great disadvantage; in a Foreign Secretary it was possibly more so. Grave, mild, and conscientious, Aberdeen credited other persons with intentions similar to his own and was unwilling to believe that any of the foreign ministers with whom he dealt would do anything he would not stoop to do himself. His strength was in patient negotiation and conciliatoriness of approach. What he lacked was an element of toughness and scepticism. Although he was only fifty-seven, he seemed prematurely aged; and ill-health, or the persuasion of it, provided him with an additional reason for viewing office as a temporary and undesired burden. Nevertheless, after the last bellicose years of Palmerston's tenure of the Foreign Office, Aberdeen's high reputation abroad, his position in the party, and his influence among the Scottish peers, made him irreplaceable.

So much could not be said for some of his colleagues. Ripon, though experienced and knowledgeable in finance and trade, was an amiable, philosophic, mildly sceptical man who brought caution in politics almost to the point of immobility. Intellectually, however, he was a convinced free-trader of the Liverpool–Huskisson school in which Peel himself had been reared; and his instincts were always towards administrative liberalism. He wrote to Graham in July 1841 that the success of Peel's government would depend on its measures and that those measures must be based on 'an enlarged view of what the actual condition of society demands'.[1] If not exactly a cherubim with flaming sword, Ripon would always be on the side of the angels as far as the social and economic policy of Peel's government was concerned. Wharncliffe, the great Yorkshire magnate, chairman of Quarter Sessions and Lord Lieutenant for the West Riding, was contemptuously dismissed by Ellenborough as a mere county politician with a weakness for local patronage who

[1] 40446 f. 5.

would be quite unfit for the Governor-Generalship of India. But Ellenborough's judgements were not always very sound, and Wharncliffe was rather better than this peremptory verdict suggested. A grandson of George III's Lord Bute, he was perhaps denied by heredity the possession of first-class ability. Yet at least he matched his large property with fair talents. He was active, honest, liberal, and firm; and as Lord President of the Council he developed a keen and useful interest in the educational department which formed the main administrative responsibility of his office. Knatchbull, another of the country gentleman breed, was of perceptibly lower quality. Fussy, alarmist, a poor judge of men and intellectually out of his depth in the cabinet, he showed sense only in his realisation that he had been promoted beyond his deserts and in his longing to be out of office. The most that could be said for him was that he was a barometer of the feelings and interests of his class and on such matters as cattle, corn, seeds, malt and apples he could always talk with some authority.[1] Lord Haddington at the Admiralty was perhaps another to whose political career fate had been unusually kind. Greville allowed himself some sardonic reflections at the spectacle of a man devoid of interest and influence, lacking both real and apparent merit, who had served as Lord Lieutenant of Ireland, refused the Governor-Generalship of India, and consented to become First Lord of the Admiralty.[2] But Haddington in the cabinet scale of values was nearer to Wharncliffe and Aberdeen than to Buckingham and Knatchbull. He was an elderly man, not enjoying good health, but he made a sensible and efficient minister; and he gave a voluntary assurance to Peel that he would not job the Navy. This, at a time when the hunger of Scots for government patronage was still a tradition in politics and dockyard administration the most notorious area of government electoral influence, could hardly fail to bring satisfaction to a prime minister jealous for both the economy and the purity of his administration.[3]

III

During the last months of 1841 while cabinet ministers and their juniors accustomed themselves to the routine of office, the rather

[1] *Knatchbull*, ch. ix–xiii.   [2] *Greville*, 22 Sept. 1841.   [3] 40458 f. 257.

brittle relations between the prime minister and the queen were settling down on a more durable basis. It took a little time for Peel's self-consciousness to wear off and his constant and unnecessary reiteration to all who mattered that his one desire was to consult the queen's comfort and happiness clearly sprang from a painful sense that there were still memories, prejudices and misunderstandings to overcome. The queen complained that he was so shy that it made her shy too. At the second Council on 17 September, though Victoria seemed more at ease with her new ministers, Greville mordantly noted that when she talked to Peel, he could not help putting himself 'into his accustomed attitude of a dancing master giving a lesson'. In fact only a week earlier he had received a barely concealed reprimand from Victoria for his failure to notify her officially of the adjournment of parliament, coupled with a superfluous reminder that in future she would like to receive short reports of debates in both Houses as she had been accustomed to from her late ministers. Since Peel was not actually a member of parliament at the time, having vacated his seat on appointment, and was working for days at a stretch in assembling his administration, the omission was understandable, even though he was technically at fault.[1] But these minor embarrassments were soon left behind. In the growing volume of correspondence on parliamentary affairs, foreign policy and patronage Peel was invariably polite and punctilious though he gave little away on any point of substance. A virtual veto conveyed by the queen on 9 September against the employment of Lord Londonderry in any position of importance fortunately raised no argument since Londonderry made himself unemployable.[2] But Jackson, the new Irish Solicitor General, was firmly defended against Victoria's criticism that he belonged to 'the very violent Orange party'; and her mistaken impression that a redeployment of the exiguous Mediterranean fleet implied an actual reduction in forces was set right in detail.[3]

Relations were also softened in small ways. The queen offered a post as groom-in-waiting for one of Peel's sons, though it was politely declined on the double ground that the only two eligible

[1] RA/Y 54/76; C 22 II/25; *VL*, I, 322.
[2] *VL*, I, 323. Londonderry's name is omitted from the printed text but see 40432 f. 110.
[3] RA/A 11/65–7; *VL*, I, 352.

were both about to begin their university careers and that the position was too high for men so young.[1] Peel was more successful with a counterproposal a couple of weeks later to place Prince Albert at the head of a Royal Commission on Fine Arts which he wished to set up.[2] Closer contact with Albert had already brought about a markedly friendly relationship. The German prince, young enough to be Peel's son, with few friends and prepared through Anson to meet the prime minister on terms of trust, was a willing disciple for the great English statesman. Peel, on the other hand, like many of his countrymen in those pre-Bismarckian days, was something of a Germanophile. Sociable intervals at court soon uncovered common interests. One discussion on German literature about the beginning of October encouraged Albert to present to the prime minister a new edition of the *Nibelungenlied* accompanied by a note in the prince's large, boyish handwriting.[3] By November he was already inscribing himself 'always, my dearest Sir Robert, yours very truly Albert'. Further correspondence followed on such congenial topics as Dutch paintings and the decoration of the new House of Commons; and the warmth of the prince's regard began insensibly to infect the queen. Certainly by October the letters which passed between Peel and Victoria were taking on a more cordial and informal note; and in November Peel was able to write contentedly to Stanley that 'we are going on exceedingly well in all our relations with the Palace'.[4] By the start of the new year relations had become close and informal enough for Peel to be given an impromptu invitation to join Albert in what had become almost his only private relaxation, an hour or two of shooting in the early part of the day before Victoria claimed his attention. With a borrowed gun and dressed in his usual town clothes—thin shoes, pepper and salt trousers, and blue frockcoat—the prime minister took part in a ninety minutes' foray against pheasants, hares and rabbits in the domesticated landscape of Windsor Great Park.

During the late autumn in fact the emphasis slowly shifted from the problem of the court to the problems at the court. Chief of these was the delicate relationship between Victoria and Melbourne. Peel had shown no resentment at the advice which Melbourne had sent to him through Greville about the right way to handle

[1] 40432 f. 131.   [2] *ibid.*, f. 204.   [3] *ibid.*, f. 218.   [4] 40467 f. 121.

the queen, her dislike of hearing official matters from third parties and her preference for short clear explanations and brief audiences; and he made it clear in return that he had no jealousy of Melbourne's continued friendship with the queen.[1] Yet though he could scarcely have known of the freedom with which Melbourne was commenting to Victoria on many of Peel's candidates for office, he might well have suspected that the queen's emphatic views on particular individuals owed something to the other man's prompting. If for the moment he kept his thoughts to himself, there was one man at least who felt it his duty to speak out. This was Baron Stockmar, the prince's old tutor and family friend. Stockmar confided his disquiet to Anson as early as 21 September and two events early in October—Melbourne's attack on the government in the House of Lords and the queen's invitation to him to visit Windsor—brought matters to a head. An enquiry from Melbourne to the prince about the propriety of such a visit provided an opening and Anson went to see Melbourne armed with a memorandum on behalf of Albert drafted by the baron. The main consideration which Anson urged on his old master was that as long as the queen felt she could turn to Melbourne for advice, she would never be disposed to put real confidence in Peel. In the memorandum Stockmar went so far as to write that he had good cause to doubt whether Peel was sure in himself of the queen's goodwill. This was almost certainly true and probably accounted for much of Peel's visible self-consciousness when meeting the queen. The very next day, in a routine interview with Lord Liverpool, the half-brother of his former chief who had been appointed Lord Steward of the Household, Peel enquired whether the queen and Prince Albert were as satisfied in their relations with him as he was with them. Liverpool took the opportunity to talk about Stockmar's position at Court and expressed the hope that Peel would find time to see him. The following day the prime minister mentioned Stockmar to Anson who assured him that he could speak to the baron with absolute confidence. Nothing happened immediately but a fortnight later Stockmar himself saw Melbourne and tried to extract an assurance from him that after the queen's confinement their correspondence would be allowed to die a natural death.

[1] *Greville*, 4 Sept. 1841.

Stockmar's attitude was heavy and pedantic; and his earnest approach seemed the more unimaginative in the face of Melbourne's vexed and human reaction. Yet it was significant that Stockmar's objections were also felt by Anson, a man of instinctive tact who had every reason to deal gently with Melbourne. What they were most concerned with was not Melbourne but Victoria. It was her long-standing and still not extinguished prejudice against Peel and the Conservative party which made her correspondence with Melbourne a potential constitutional danger. As long as his influence remained with the queen, it was a barrier behind which less benign growths could shelter. There was notably the Baroness Lehzen, the queen's governess and friend, an ally of the displaced Conynghams to whom she owed her position at court, a violent Whig partisan, and a scarcely veiled enemy of Prince Albert. On one occasion in November she harangued the Court ladies on the impossibility of the queen's ever forgiving the Tories for reducing the prince's allowance; and after the queen's confinement she proclaimed that she would speak to Victoria once she had recovered about Albert's habit of discussing political matters with Peel and taking decisions before the queen could mention them to Lord Melbourne. Anson raised the Lehzen issue with Peel as early as 8 October and the prime minister had enquired then whether any means could be found to get rid of her. That there could be any such sinister influence interposed between husband and wife shocked Peel's own sense of personal propriety.[1] Both in personnel and organisation there was in fact an obvious need for a reform of the whole structure of the royal household. It was a task which the prince was anxious to take on and in October he had already started corresponding with Peel on the subject. Meanwhile there was the matter of the queen's confinement. Towards the end of October the prince warned the prime minister to his mild amusement of the approach of 'a certain event' and the summons came from Buckingham Palace on the morning of 9 November. Peel arrived at nine o'clock and the other ministers and officers of state whose presence was by tradition thought necessary on such royal occasions were gradually rounded up in the next couple of hours. Shortly before eleven Victoria's second child was born—a well-formed boy with large nose and blue

[1] RA/Y 54/87, 89, 98.

eyes, the future Edward VII—and immediately displayed by the
nurse to the assembled dignitaries waiting outside the bedroom.
According to the precedent he had established at the birth of the
Princess Royal the previous year, Albert took over control of royal
business in the succeeding weeks and the flow of confidential boxes
to the court continued without a check. For the first time Peel and
the prince found themselves in direct communication on affairs of
state and it was not until the last day of November that Albert
wrote to inform the prime minister that he could recommence his
correspondence with the queen. 'She only begs that in matters
which require more explanation you would for the present still
write to me or see me.'[1]

It marked another stage in the growing authority of both Albert
and Peel; and perhaps in consequence the prime minister allowed
himself the first overt sign that there were limits to his tolerance of
Melbourne's continued influence with the queen. Acting on the
assurances he had received from Liverpool and Anson, Peel used
Stockmar as the medium through which a warning could be conveyed. Despite the baron's earlier intervention the correspondence
between Victoria and Melbourne still carried on unabated. Indeed
the situation had been made worse by Melbourne's indiscretion in
mentioning it to Mrs. Norton who went round telling people that
he wrote daily to the queen and that she in return confided to him
everything. It is hardly likely that Peel was ignorant of the gossip;
scandal and malice usually find willing retailers. The opportunity to
reveal his misgivings came when Stockmar finally had an interview
with him in November. When they came to home politics Stockmar
expressed a pointed hope that the queen would increasingly find her
real happiness in her domestic relations. Peel seized the opening at
once. He assured Stockmar of his wish to please the queen and
indulge all her personal wishes, and said he would ignore any reports
he heard of Victoria's private life and opinions. But, he said with
emphatic reiteration, the moment he knew for a fact that the queen
was taking advice on public affairs from another person, he would
resign office. The warning had its effect. More than ever determined
to rescue the queen from her ill-starred relationship, Stockmar
wrote to Melbourne on 23 November, mentioning both Mrs.

[1] 40433 f. 69.

Norton's indiscretions and his conversation with Peel, and begged him to bring his correspondence with Victoria to a close. He received no more than a cold acknowledgement but this third onslaught could hardly have failed to shake Melbourne. His letters to the queen did not stop, but they came less often and their contents were increasingly less political.

But there were other influences at work to weaken the relationship. A second child, growing domesticity, deeper emotional dependence on Albert, his widening familiarity with the business of the monarchy, the discreet influence of Anson who for a time served equally as secretary to the queen and to her husband, the mere physical replacement of Melbourne's companionship by that of others—all these new elements in Victoria's life were gradually weaning her away from the first adolescent stage of her reign. Anson noted at Christmas that she was becoming less interested in politics and less prejudiced against her ministers, even if she would not have been prepared herself to admit any change in her attitude. Problems there would undoubtedly be for the new Conservative government, but they were unlikely now to arise at Windsor or Buckingham Palace.[1]

[1] For Peel's relations with the Court and Stockmar's activities see generally RA/Y 54/87–100; *VL*, I, 330–1, 337–43, 352–4, 360–3.

THE GREAT BUDGET

Few governments in the nineteenth century took office in circumstances as discouraging as those which confronted Peel's cabinet in
the autumn of 1841. The war in China had reached a stage at which
further military success seemed meaningless and peace endlessly
elusive. In India involvement in the treacherous internal politics of
Afghanistan had led to the dispatch of an occupying force whose
dangerous position was exposed by the native uprising of November
and finally collapsed with the disastrous retreat from Kabul in
January 1842. With the United States there was a festering dispute
over the north-east boundary with Canada aggravated by local acts
of violence on both sides. In the Near East the Syrian crisis had
left strained relations with France, the greatest naval and military
power of mainland Europe. The solution of these external problems
had to be accommodated to the slow tempo of diplomatic negotiation and the logistics of an age of sail and horse. At home the
pressures were more urgent. The increased expenditure for these
overseas commitments had fallen on an over-burdened national
exchequer. Since 1837 the revenue had failed to meet costs. For the
year ending April 1842 there was an estimated deficit of over £2
million, raising the accumulated deficit to some £7½ million. These
bare statistics were merely an index of the state of the country as a
whole. Trade was depressed, industrial manufacture stagnant. There
was severe distress in the textile areas. In towns like Bolton and
Paisley thousands lived on private charity and public subscriptions.
There had been a run of bad harvests and the cost of living was
abnormally high. A population increasing remorselessly by 15 per
cent each decade seemed to be outrunning its ability to feed, clothe
and house itself. Industrialisation, which to some appeared the

promise of a golden age, to others seemed a cancer at the heart of society.

In the few short years since Victoria's accession, the old constitutional and religious conflicts of the reform era had been thrust into the background by what Thomas Carlyle, in his pamphlet on Chartism the previous year, had called the *Condition of England Question*. The problem was manifest; the proffered solutions varied and dubious. From the angry and inarticulate mass of English society many separate voices were upraised. There was Ashley's Ten Hours campaign, the anti-Poor Law protest, and the Complete Suffrage agitation. There was the passionate working-class movement known as Chartism which concealed a diversity of leaders, aims and methods beneath the simplified banner of the Six Points. There was the smaller but better organised Anti-Corn Law League, more astute and single-minded but as violent and emotional in its denunciation of landlords and aristocrats as the Chartists in their attacks on mill-owners and capitalists. The agriculturalists themselves, slowly reacting to the threat from the Free Traders and Manchester men, had already made in the Duke of Buckingham's Protection Society their first fitful show of combined resistance to the Corn Law repealers. As prophesied at the time of the Reform Act ten years earlier, the field of coal was beginning to be arrayed against the field of corn, except that by 1841 it seemed more a contest between the plough and the loom. Like Kilkenny cats, the classes of English society seemed bent on devouring each other: proletarians attacking industrialists, industrialists attacking the landed interest, and individual humanitarians and politicians, many of them Tory Anglicans, taking up the cause of factory reform or joining the opposition to the new poor law. If Peel needed any reminder of the intensity of feelings in the society over which his ministry now presided, he promptly received it from various delegations that came up to London to see him in the course of the autumn: one for example from the Anti-Corn Law League, another from Tory manufacturers pressing for factory legislation, a third and most impressive from the West Riding Short Time Committee in October urging a restriction of factory hours and a reform of the poor law administration.[1]

[1] See Kitson Clark, 'Hunger and politics in 1842' (*Journal of Modern History*, XXV, 355 et seq.).

In this turbulent and angry situation the mental habits of the age, the structure of society and the poverty of administrative machinery, all imposed their restrictions on the government. The political executive could only act in limited fields and in certain directions. The frontiers of governmental action were admittedly ill-defined and open to argument but no sudden and revolutionary expansion was possible. An age in which cheap government was both precept and practice, state intervention the exception rather than the rule, was not one which could see a rapid transformation of the role of the state in society. Government could assist, it could not become responsible for the condition of the working classes. Ashley's campaign for shorter hours for women and children in certain industries, and the opposition of particular politicians to the new poor law, did not constitute a national policy. As a gesture of social reconciliation they had a wider significance; as a solution to the Condition of England problem they were peripheral. Peel's instinct, not always to the good of his reputation, was always to the practical measure rather than to the political gesture. No responsible statesman, he thought, could afford to abandon or mutilate the Poor Law of 1834, one of the greatest if most rigid of the administrative reforms of Whig–Benthamite policy in the post-reform era. The country gentry would have been the first to complain had there been even a partial return to the disorganised and expensive situation before 1834. In renewing the expiring law for a further six months in the short autumn session of 1841 he refused to accept any amendment and reserved wider consideration of the subject for the following year. This did not mean that either he or Graham was blind to the harshness of the system. On two occasions in September Peel found time among all his preoccupations to write to the Home Secretary asking him to enquire as a matter of urgency into specific allegations of cruelty and abuse that had come to the prime minister's notice.[1] But in their view it was the administration of the law rather than the law itself which needed review. In fact the doctrine of the Poor Law Commissioners was always harsher than their practice; and the genuine public reaction against the inhumanity of certain aspects of the law was being exploited by a venomous and exaggerated campaign led by *The Times*. Peel, like Russell before

[1] 40446 f. 29; Graham (Peel to Graham, 5, 21 Sept. 1841).

him, had to take on the parliamentary defence of an unpopular bureaucratic authority which lacked a parliamentary departmental head and was singularly obtuse in its public relations.

The problem confronting the government, however, was neither the poor law nor factory reform but finance. What parliamentary reform had been to Grey in 1830, finance was to Peel's ministry in 1841. Whatever else they accomplished would hardly signify; if they failed in this, they would fail absolutely. It was the issue which, more than any other, had brought down the Whigs; the issue on which the new ministers would be expected to satisfy the country; the issue on which would depend the success of most of their subsequent measures. Money, the sinews of war, was the backbone of any policy that sought to bring peace to the distracted society of 1841. Abstractly the problem presented no great difficulty. Most financial experts would have agreed that an income tax alone offered a reasonable prospect of raising additional revenue in a form that was simultaneously effective in operation, predictable in its yield, and equitable in its incidence. It was a tax which involved no interference with the processes of trade and industry, and placed no fresh burden on the poor. The question was not what tax, but what government would be courageous enough to revive such a tax, psychologically identified as it was with the dictatorial powers of a state at war and unique in its inquisitorial basis of assessment. Ever since the House of Commons had forced Liverpool's ministry to abandon the tax in 1816, it had lain in the armoury of theoretical economic policies, unused, repugnant but not forgotten. Between 1828 and 1831 there had been serious talk in ministerial circles of reviving it and only perhaps the instability of parliamentary support had stood in the way. Even so there had been general agreement by Peel, Herries and Goulburn in Wellington's cabinet of 1830 that an income tax must come. The issue was not a party one; Althorp and Parnell had been its champions among the Whigs. But there was more support for it among the ministerial Conservatives of the pre-1830 vintage than among the post-1830 Whigs who had responded mechanically to popular pressure for less taxation without ever evolving a considered financial policy. When Peel in 1833 had supported Althorp's resolution that it would be necessary to resort to a tax on property if the malt tax were repealed, Ellenborough thought his tactics wrong.

It was important, he believed, that the opposition should not give any encouragement to the Whigs to take up the policy of an income tax. 'It was too good a thing to place in their hands, and must be our stock-in-trade if we took office.'[1]

But Peel's tactical support for Althorp on that occasion did not mean that he had altered his views. In a debate on the penny postage bill in 1839, for example, he had dropped a significant hint that, in view of the general financial situation and the heavy taxation on raw materials and articles of consumption, a property tax might be the wisest expedient to adopt.[2] In facing the financial difficulties of 1841, therefore, Peel had at hand a policy laid down twelve years earlier. The defence of Church and State in the post-reform era had provided him with a parliamentary majority; but in economic affairs the precedents and traditions to which he looked back were those of Liverpool, Huskisson, Herries and Robinson in the eighteen-twenties. Office in 1841 was an opportunity to pick up the threads snapped short in 1830.

It is probable that Peel had made up his mind from the start to reintroduce the income tax. But he knew it would need much persuasion before all the members of his cabinet could bring themselves to accept it. He set to work early therefore on a few chosen colleagues. As soon as the returns of the general election indicated that there would be a substantial Conservative majority, Peel broached the subject verbally with Goulburn. In a judicious letter from Betchworth on 22 July[3] the prospective Chancellor of the Exchequer cast up the balance sheet of advantages and disadvantages. For the tax was first the certain yield of a revenue that would be more than sufficient to supply the immediate deficit; second the fact that it would fall only on the rich. Against it were its inquisitorial nature, the difficulties of either including or excluding Ireland, the risks of evasion, and the hazards of steering such a complicated and unpopular measure through parliament. If the decision were to be taken, he suggested two further points for consideration. It would not be worth setting up the cumbrous machinery of an income tax for less than an annual revenue of £5 million. This would leave a substantial surplus over the estimated deficit of £2 million on the

[1] Aspinall, *Diaries*, p. 321.   [2] *Speeches*, III, 659.
[3] 40443 f. 1, ptly pr. *Peel*, II, 490.

current year. This surplus should be used to reduce duties on consumer goods and so make the tax more palatable to 'the working classes at least' if not to others. His own preference was for drastic cuts in the duties on colonial and foreign sugar, both to assist the British planters and to facilitate agreement with Brazil on such matters as slavery and coffee. Sugar was an article on which Goulburn, with family interests in the West Indies, was always somewhat less than impartial.

On 28 July, Peel, just back from a hasty trip to Portsmouth to see his sailor son, briefly replied:

> Your letter states very clearly the comparative advantages and disadvantages of an Income Tax. In point of reason and sound policy the former in my opinion predominate. We well know however that that consideration constitutes no conclusive argument for the adoption of a financial measure, We will of course say nothing whatever on the subject, though as my belief is, that 'to this complexion we must come at last', we may as well be turning the subject in our minds and laying the foundation for at least full consideration.[1]

The next person to be brought in was Graham, then holidaying on the Isle of Wight, who returned Goulburn's letter on 1 August with one of his own which bristled with distrust. He agreed with Goulburn that it would be politic to reduce taxes on consumer goods such as sugar and raw cotton, and threw in a suggestion of his own that there should be an examination of the eleven hundred articles of dutiable goods that only yielded a negligible revenue. But the burden of his argument was that before the fate of the new government should be rested on such a desperate financial decision, everything should be done to eliminate waste and corruption in government departments, abolish non-productive tariffs, and reduce wherever possible naval and military establishments. 'Before an Income Tax can be mooted, the Public will justly expect that this duty has been strictly and honestly performed.' It followed in his view that Peel would not be in a position to decide on an income tax till some months after he had taken office. Graham at this stage showed all the marks of his Whig financial upbringing; and Stanley when approached was little better. He was less sanguine than Graham of possible economies, agreed with Goulburn that, if

[1] Goulburn, ptly pr. *Peel*, II, 491.

introduced, the income tax should be fixed at a high enough rate to allow a general tariff reduction, but argued forcibly that Peel had every justification for delay before coming to such a crucial decision. A proved permanent deficit in the revenue might in the end justify an income tax but it was a device 'I earnestly hope you will not resort to, except upon the most evident necessity'. To his old crony Graham he expressed a private view that any discussion of the tax at that moment was premature.[1]

What perhaps this correspondence proved to Peel was that if the instinctive repugnance of his colleagues was to be overcome in time for the 1842 budget, the process of conversion could hardly begin too soon. A start had been made, however, and he allowed an interval for the novelty to sink in before renewing his persuasions. No one knew better than Peel how familiarity wears away the initial discomfort of a new idea. Once the administration had been formed in September, he revived the subject on a more formal basis. From some of his old colleagues of the Liverpool cabinet he found more ready support than the two ex-Whigs had displayed. Wellington, for example, forgetting his qualms as prime minister in 1830, had read an article in the *Spectator* at the end of July recommending a searching review of the tariff and then, if the revenue could not be augmented sufficiently in that way, the resort to a property tax. The duke, or so Arbuthnot confided to Graham in August, thought this the first thing for Peel's government to do.[2] Even more encouragingly Ripon, who as prime minister had agreed in principle with Herries and Huskisson on the reintroduction of the tax in 1828, hailed Peel's suggestion in October as a 'bold and most judicious plan of finance'. Gradually the area of consultation widened. On 18 October Peel broached the idea with Lord Ashburton who, with the caution natural in a senior member of the great banking house of Baring & Co., agreed that the best way out of their financial difficulties was an income tax, provided the necessity of that hazardous step was clearly proved. If imposed at all, however, it should be at 5 per cent to yield a big enough surplus for Peel to be able to hold out the hope that the tax would be only temporary.

[1] Graham (5 Aug. 1841); 40467 f. 42; 40446 f. 9. The last two letters are pr. with many omissions in *Peel*, II, 492–4.
[2] Graham, 4 Aug. 1841.

'It would be next to insupportable', he added with feeling, 'to live in a country where such a tax were permanent.'

Peel had still not yet raised the matter in the cabinet and he continued a little longer his selective sounding of opinion. A week later he submitted the correspondence with Ashburton to Gladstone with a request for his views. The reply he received was a formidable demonstration of his young colleague's intellectual powers, even though what it exhibited was more the clarity and force which Gladstone could bring to practical matters than any depth of economic experience and judgement. Rehearsing all the standard objections to the tax, Gladstone took leave to doubt whether a yield of £5 million was enough to justify ignoring them. With praiseworthy constructiveness he put forward as an alternative the renewal of the house tax that had been proposed by one of his officials at the Board of Trade, J. McGregor, in a recent work on commercial and financial legislation. This old tax, repealed by Althorp in 1834, had brought in about £1·2 million *per annum*. But unpopular by its nature and inequitable in its administration, some hardihood would have been required to revive it in 1841. Simultaneously to remove its anomalies and extract from it enough revenue for immediate needs would have necessitated a considerable increase on the old rate and the imposition of that higher rate on a smaller number of taxpayers. It was this which Goulburn made his chief criticism of Gladstone's paper. Graham and Stanley were equally against it; and Herries, another outside expert consulted by Peel, though gentle in his comments on the house tax proposal, reiterated that the only policy right in principle was the restoration of the income tax. Peel answered Gladstone courteously and took the trouble to give his junior the reasons for his reluctance to accept the suggestion. He also circulated the paper to other cabinet members. But his private opinion was that a heavy house tax would be even more odious than an income tax. 'It would really', he remarked lightly to Ashburton, 'invest a property tax with a dangerous degree of popularity.'[1]

What Gladstone had in fact done, and it was a considerable service, was to demonstrate the absence of any acceptable alternative. In the

[1] 40469 fos. 75, 96; *Peel*, II, 498–504; Hyde, *Gladstone*, pp. 8–16; *Herries*, II, 205 et seq.

following weeks his more senior colleagues gradually came round to an acceptance of the prime minister's proposal as the basis of the government's budgetary plans. The Graham policy of economical reform was met in part by the appointment of a commission (suitably unpaid) under Granville Somerset to scrutinise and reorganise the revenue departments. Peel did not hope for much from such an enquiry but at least it gave earnest of their desire for economy. To Stanley he recommended a similar enquiry into the colonial establishments.[1] He was not prepared, however, to allow the decision over the income tax to wait upon the results of these leisurely activities. Indeed Wharncliffe told Greville afterwards that the basic principle of their financial policy was settled within six weeks of taking office. As far as Peel was concerned this was perhaps correct; but formally it was not. The elaboration of the new tax took even longer. On 9 December the cabinet agreed to call parliament together for the new session on 3 February. Peel then proposed that on 14 December they should begin detailed consideration of their financial and commercial policy and continue meeting as long as necessary.[2] It was not until 24 January that the final plan of the income tax was approved.[3] In its matured form it showed several important differences from the wartime tax of Pitt and Addington. The income exemption limit was fixed at £150, as compared with the previous exemption of £60; and the profits of farming were to be assessed at one-half instead of three-quarters of the rental. These concessions materially modified Goulburn's summer calculations of a yield of £4–£5 million from a rate of sixpence in the pound. In order to obtain an effective yield at all it seemed necessary in fact to raise the rate to sevenpence in the pound and even this was calculated to yield only £3·7 million. To extinguish the deficit and secure a surplus for tariff reform, the income tax had to be supplemented by other sources of revenue. Ireland, which had been exempt from Pitt's operations and lacked even the machinery of assessed taxes, was still exempted; but in compensation it was decided to increase the Irish spirits and stamp duties. In addition the duty on coal shipped for export in foreign vessels, which was showing a rapidly declining yield because of the operation of

[1] 40443 f. 27; 40467 f. 98, ptly pr. *Peel*, II, 495–6.
[2] Wellington (Peel to Wellington, 10 Dec. 1841).   [3] *Knatchbull*, p. 239.

reciprocity treaties, was extended to all coal exports. These new items of revenue, together with the income tax, were calculated to produce over £4 million; and with £4 million much could be done.

From the start there was general agreement that the massive engine of the income tax would have to be used not merely to meet the deficit but create a surplus; and that this surplus would, from both a political and fiscal point of view, be best employed in reducing the duties on consumer goods. The income tax was not introduced in order to make possible a reform of the tariff; but its introduction made tariff reform both possible and expedient. In his long explanatory letter to Ashburton in October Peel argued that capitalists would be serving their own interests by submitting to the income tax for a given number of years in order to enable the government 'to make without risk a decisive experiment in the reduction of duty on some of the great articles of consumption'. He went on, 'I would combine with this measure a review of the existing Corn Law . . . relaxing the amount of protection where it might safely be relaxed; and attempting to reconcile all just protection for agriculture with greater steadiness in trade.' Tariff reform and a new corn law were therefore the two wings (to use the old Catholic emancipation vocabulary) of the income tax, disarming opposition to the central measure with their promise of greater social justice and sounder commercial policy. Hume's Select Committee on Import Duties appointed in 1840 had familiarised the educated public with the notion that a wholesale reduction of duties might actually strengthen the tariff system as an instrument of revenue as well as bringing relief to commerce and industry. The *Spectator*, the *Manchester Guardian*, and the *Morning Chronicle* in 1840 and 1841 had all given support and publicity to the tariff reform campaign. Peel could not have failed to be abreast of the contemporary controversy, particularly after the Whigs had accepted the free trade argument in their 1841 budget.[1] But the Tariff Report had been

---

[1] The date of his well-known letter to Goulburn saying that he had not read the Report on Import Duties, given in *Peel*, II, 509 as 1841 is clearly wrong. The year has been added later to the original letter which is obviously 18 Dec. 1840 in reply to one from Goulburn dated 16 Dec. 1840. In this Goulburn observes that 'I have not myself read the evidence of the Import duties Committee which was of Jos. Hume's appointment and nomination but shall do so on my return home' (40333 f. 425). From what Peel said in a speech of 4 June 1841 (*Speeches*, III, 783) it is evident that he was conversant with the report by that date.

based on singularly slender and biased evidence, and bore all the marks of a doctrinaire thesis. The new ministers did not have the same confidence as their predecessors in the radically-minded officials of the Board of Trade. Indeed they viewed the propaganda activities of such men as McGregor with considerable distaste. If in the end the Conservative proposals seemed in harmony with the Tariff Report, they had been arrived at by a different route. They were designed as conscious experiment rather than as dogmatic policy; their object was to relieve consumers and manufacturers rather than to stimulate the revenue; and the expected loss was underwritten by the introduction of the income tax.

It was this which made the difference between the Whig policy of 1841 and the Conservative policy of 1842. Once the principle of the income tax had been accepted, Goulburn's initial suggestions of July were widened in discussions between Peel and Ripon in October to cover reductions in the duties not only on sugar, coffee, and brandy, but also on a large number (running to over six hundred) of minor articles yielding a low revenue but including many raw materials of industry. In all Ripon budgeted for a loss of over £2 million in duties. After the existing deficit was met, this would still leave nearly £500,000 surplus. In future years, Ripon assured Peel, similar substantial relief could be afforded to all classes of society as long as successive tariff reductions were made dependent on the success of the earlier experiment.[1] Major changes in sugar and coffee duties, however, were conditional on negotiating a treaty with Brazil containing enough reassurances on slavery to make politically acceptable the admittance of their raw products on competitive terms. Without such competition any further reductions in the duties on British colonial sugar, for example, would merely present the West India planters with an unassailable monopoly. By the beginning of November, however, it was clear that no arrangement with Brazil could be made in time to affect the supply of sugar for the following year. Peel instituted an enquiry into possible sources of 'free' sugar elsewhere but came to the conclusion that the sugar question must be postponed. Any premature alteration in the duties would form a weak point in his budget; and the Whigs, sore from their defeat on sugar the previous session,

[1] 40464 f. 33, ptly pr. *Peel*, II, 496.

would do all they could to trip up a Conservative government on the same sweet but slippery commodity.[1] There was no lack of other articles on which the duty could be lowered without complications. Gladstone named some in his long memorandum of 4 November—timber, oils, exported woollens, tea, and insurance. A few weeks later Peel himself was pressing Ripon to consider in particular the advantage of an extensive reduction of duty on colonial and foreign timber.

No large reconstruction of the tariff could, however, avoid the question of the Corn Laws. Indeed, corn and finance were the two questions on which Russell in the short autumn session had pressed the government for an immediate statement. To have maintained the existing law for yet another session might have been possible; it would hardly have been advisable. The activities of the Anti-Corn Law League and Russell's plan of 1841 had brought the issue to the front and many politicians were prepared to admit that the law was either objectionable in principle or defective in operation. The high protection afforded by the act of 1828 seemed to have created a quasi-monopoly in an age when monopolies of all kinds were under attack. The system of operating the sliding scale on a basis of average local prices was open to fraud and manipulation.[2] The revised law of 1828 had failed in fact to bring stability to either farmers or consumers. Perhaps no law could have done so. Wide fluctuations in price were almost unavoidable in the absence of large overseas sources of corn and at a period when even advanced farming techniques could not protect crops and harvests against the vicissitudes of the British climate. It is probable indeed that protectionist legislation was less decisive in influencing the price of corn than most people thought. Nevertheless, it would have been difficult in 1841 to have found a receptive audience for the argument that the corn laws were of little significance either way. Doctrinaire free-traders thought them obnoxious if not actually immoral; convinced protectionists considered them vital, even if defective. Between these

---

[1] 44275 f. 41; 40464 f. 75.

[2] The country was divided into twelve districts and the average price of corn sold in the towns of those districts over the six weeks preceding four specified dates in the year decided the port duties for the next quarter. It was alleged that prices were artificially forced up (e.g. by fictitious sales between corn dealers) to allow in bonded corn on suitable occasions.

two extremes a wide range of intermediate opinion was prepared for a change. Peel had studiously refrained from committing himself to the defence of the 1828 Act, as distinct from the general principle of protection; and it was largely accepted that some modification would be undertaken by the new government. To have left it alone would have been taken as mere truckling to the agriculturalist section of the party.

What Peel was doing in the autumn and winter of 1841 was making up his own mind on the right course to adopt in the welter of conflicting advice which surrounded him. How intrinsically liberal that mind was, however, he revealed early in October when Ripon presented his first long memorandum on a change in the corn laws. The revised scale of duties he proposed was based on two assumptions. First, that foreign corn could not be brought to Britain at a lower price than 35s a quarter, exclusive of duty; second, that the British grower would be reasonably compensated by a market price between 56s and 60s a quarter. Hence a sliding scale which provided a duty of 20s when wheat was 56s a quarter would suffice. Ripon's scale was considerably lower than that under the existing Act. Even so, it did not go far enough for Peel. 'I think the degree of protection your memorandum proposes is too great— greater than is required for any well-understood agricultural interest,' he replied on 17 October. He followed up this opening shot by suggesting the possibility of a scale which, to check specula- tion, would impose a short 'rest' by means of a fixed duty at the critical range from 56s to 64s and vary inversely with prices outside those points. He also urged Ripon to consider the possibility of lowering tariffs on other articles of food. 'We must substitute pro- tection for prohibition and must set about considering what will constitute fair protection. Live animals, or fresh meat, can surely require no great amount.' As if conscious of the startling nature of these comments, he added cautiously, 'I write to you of course in strict and peculiar confidence.'[1]

It was evident that Peel was sceptical of some of Ripon's basic assumptions. He doubted whether foreign corn could profitably be put on the British market at 35s and he distrusted the soundness of Ripon's statistics. Before coming to any conclusion he wanted more

[1] 40464 fos. 27, 37, ptly pr. but misdated in *Peel*, II, 496–7.

facts. In the following month he set up a committee to go into the question of the averages and pressed Ripon to get more details about the prime cost of wheat at the principal European and American ports, together with freight and insurance charges. It had already been decided to send a government official to Europe to enquire into the effects of British protective food tariffs and early in November he instructed Gladstone to add foreign corn exports to the subjects for investigation. He was also more conscious than some of his colleagues of the tactical considerations which would affect policy decisions. To Ripon's early proposal to admit Canadian corn free or at a minimal duty, for example, he observed that it should be linked with a proposal to reduce the duty on foreign as well as colonial timber and drew attention to the fears of British agriculturalists that free trade in Canadian corn would become a cover for the illicit import of American corn. In November he was asking the President of the Board of Trade whether it would be possible to associate changes in the Corn Laws with commercial agreements with foreign countries such as Russia to admit British industrial goods on more favourable terms.[1] Under this brisk and wide-ranging fire Ripon's department returned to the task of gathering information before formulating plans, while the cabinet committee of Ripon, Graham and Knatchbull addressed itself to the complicated problem of the averages. At Knatchbull's suggestion the Duke of Buckingham was added to this committee. Ripon made no demur since he assumed that it would not be necessary for Buckingham to be informed of the discussions going on about the Corn Laws themselves. Peel, however, thought this dangerously disingenuous and told Ripon to say categorically that the graduated duty itself was under review; that Peel had been collecting much information on the subject; and that both Peel and Ripon felt that other parts of the law needed serious attention.[2]

Advice on the Corn Laws was now coming in from other quarters. Gladstone, in his first cautious memorandum of November, aimed at better protection for the farmer and was impressed by the effect of speculators in driving up prices. Ashburton, while laying down the formidable axiom that 'our Conservative party is a party pledged

[1] 40464 fos. 48, 64, 69; 40469 f. 67; 44275 f. 67, ptly pr. *Peel*, II, 497.
[2] 40464 fos. 102, 111, ptly pr. *Peel*, II, 505.

to the support of the land . . . and that, that principle abandoned, the party is dissolved', nevertheless admitted that the protection given by the law was too high and its machinery defective. Graham doubted whether the increase in population was in fact outstripping improvements in agriculture and wanted a sliding scale that would provide between 50s and 60s a quarter for the home grower.[1] Peel also corresponded with R. A. Christopher, the influential M.P. for North Lincolnshire, who had been sounding opinion in his constituency on the need for a change in the Corn Laws. Encouraged by Peel's interest Christopher summarised what he believed to be the views of practical agriculturalists. The real desire of the farmers, he argued, was for a steady rather than a high price. Provided that the averages system could be remodelled to prevent speculation, he thought that on mixed or light soils a maximum duty of 20s when the price of corn was 50s would be adequate, though on cold clay lands the wheat farmer would want the last figure raised to 55s. In general he agreed that the farmer would obtain fair remuneration if he could sell at about 56s.[2] Meanwhile the Board of Trade continued to modify their original proposals. Further research brought Ripon round to Peel's view of the inability of foreign growers to put quantities of cheap corn on the British market. In December he concluded that foreign wheat could not profitably be sold in Britain at less than 50s to 52s a quarter, excluding duty. He therefore prepared a new scale of duties, incorporating Peel's suggestion of a fixed duty of 10s in the 55s–65s range, with a sliding scale above and below effectively protecting the home grower against excessive foreign competition.[3] While the President of the Board of Trade had thus cut his tariff by half, Gladstone under the educative influence of his labours at the Board, was also drastically reducing his estimate of the amount of protection needed for the British farmer. His third paper in January 1842 proposed a duty varying from 20s to 6s with a short sharp uniform descent aimed at providing no real inducement to imports of foreign wheat under 54s and no real protection for the domestic grower above 61s. This, however, was going faster and further than Peel thought the agriculturalists would tolerate. It would not do, he told his zealous young

[1] 40446 f. 181; Hyde, *Gladstone*, pp. 35–9.   [2] 40469 f. 88; 40493 fos. 341, 343.
[3] 40464 fos. 117, 124.

subordinate, to propose to them a mere 6s protective duty when the market price in Britain was 61s.[1]

By this time Peel felt the ground had been sufficiently prepared for a discussion in cabinet. In his first memorandum in December his object was simply to secure assent for the principle of revising the 1828 Corn Law. He went over the objections to the existing law—rapid price fluctuations, fraud and speculation. He argued for the removal of any superfluous duty—'uncompensated loss to incur the odium of unnecessary protection' as he neatly expressed it. He adduced impressive statistics to show the steady increase in population and the even greater increase in the consumption of foreign and colonial wheat. In addition he drew attention both to the lack of correlation between the periodic depressions in British agriculture and the import of foreign grain, and to the relief given to farmers by tithe commutation and the new poor law. His conclusion was that the government should propose to parliament at its next meeting a revision of the Corn Laws. It was a long paper, covering some fifteen sides of paper in print, and stripped of detail it was a plea for the adjustment of the law to the changed condition of society while preserving the principle of protection. As such it won without difficulty the assent of the cabinet.

The next and more difficult step was to obtain agreement on a new measure. On 22 January he read a second memorandum to the cabinet. The proposals he put forward were based on three criteria: the need to take into consideration the investment of capital in land and agricultural improvements, in effect the high level of rent as an element in the cost of production; the need for encouragement to domestic agriculture in general and to wheat growing in particular to ensure that the bulk of the supply was produced at home; and the need to eliminate fraud, speculation, price instability and excessive fluctuations in the import of foreign grain. He took as his starting point the figure of 56s a quarter as the price at which the British grower would obtain fair remuneration and foreign wheat could be admitted to qualified competition. This figure compared with an average of 52s 6d between 1831 and 1837, and 67s 2d for

[1] 40469 fos. 108, 125. Hyde, *Gladstone*, pp. 41–3, where the proposal for 'rests' is attributed to Gladstone in apparent unawareness of Peel's letter to Ripon of 17 Oct. 1841.

the three bad years of 1838–40. He also pointed out that if in fact there had been appreciable fraudulent speculation, those statistics exaggerated the actual market price obtained by the home grower. As far as European wheat was concerned, he estimated the general average price free on board at 37s 2d per quarter which freight charges would raise to 42s on arrival in Britain. For wheat from Hamburg and the Baltic ports, from which the main exports to Britain might be expected, the cost was slightly higher. Allowing for a profit, therefore, he took 45s as the minimum price at which any appreciable amount of foreign wheat could be sold on the British market. In time of glut, prices would be lower; but even in the cheapest year of the previous decade a duty of 12s would have been enough to give ample protection to the British farmer. He concluded therefore that a scale of protection providing a 20s duty when the home price was 50s, would offer complete security for the domestic grower. In detail, the scale he suggested imposed a duty of 20s at 50s a quarter dropping to a minimum of 1s at 73s. Within this framework he proposed a 'rest' in the duty between 52s and 54s and between 66s and 68s in order to diminish the temptation to hold back corn at each end of the scale; and he added that he would not be averse to increasing the extent of the rest period.[1]

In effect what Peel offered to his cabinet was a scale halfway between Ripon's first and second schemes, with two short rest periods instead of the single long one he had suggested in October, which perhaps came too close to a Whig 'fixed duty' to be comfortable. His detailed recommendations in fact were less drastic than his general arguments. In leaning to the side of a conservative rather than a liberal policy, however, his tactics were dictated by an unwillingness to startle those of his colleagues who had not shared in the preliminary discussions and an appreciation of the alarm which any lowering of the tariff would cause among the agriculturalists. What is beyond doubt is that the corn bill was drawn to Peel's own design and that he was determined to dispose of the issue at the earliest possible moment.[2] If the party had to swallow unpalatable

[1] The two memoranda are in Peel, *Memoirs*, II, Pt III Appx.

[2] The statement in Hyde, *Gladstone*, pp. 42, 47, which has unfortunately been followed by Halévy, *Age of Peel and Cobden* (1947), pp. 13–14, that Peel wished to postpone the issue until the end of the session or to the next, is based on a misreading of a letter from Ripon to Gladstone. Though dated by Ripon 2 Jan 1842 it belongs

medicine, it was best administered at the very start of the session. It was nevertheless true that his final proposals, as far as the few advanced free-traders in the administration were concerned, were open to the criticism that they provided the 'superfluous protection' which Peel himself had condemned. With wheat at 56s, for example, when by his own demonstration the home grower only needed an 11s duty to compete on level terms with foreign imports, he was given in fact 16s. The preferential margin of 5s seemed large; but what Peel was taking into account were the intangible factors—the relations between landlord and tenant, the need for stable prices and the avoidance of any sudden shock to a great national interest— rather than simply the economic concept of a 'remunerative rent' which was virtually impossible to translate into an actual figure.

In the end his scheme came remarkably close to that outlined by Christopher in November. Admittedly the latter, who had problems in his own constituency, later moved to a more protectionist position; but essentially it was the views of moderate, intelligent and sympathetic agriculturalists that Peel had to consider more than the ardent convictions of such recent converts to economic liberalism as Gladstone. Immoderate agriculturalists he could not hope to satisfy; but he did not wish to multiply unnecessarily their support. As it was the Duke of Buckingham, days before he knew the content of the second memorandum, was patently restive. Even Knatchbull, who thought his ducal colleague's views on protection absurdly exaggerated, was unhappy when Peel's detailed proposals came before the cabinet. His unhappiness redoubled when the decision was finally reached on the income tax. 'This Tax and the Corn Laws', he gloomily confided to his diary, 'will overset the Govern-

in fact to the following year (Jan. 1843) as both the contents of the letter and a docket on the back make abundantly clear. Peel's reluctance to which Ripon refers was to the projected Canadian corn bill of 1843. Even so, there is no reason to think that it denoted any more than a natural regret at having to stir up the corn question again. The key passage in Ripon's letter runs as follows: 'I quite concur with him [sc. Peel] in the reluctance which he has expressed to me to stir the question of the corn laws at all this session; a proceeding which might be followed by very serious and embarrassing consequences. At the same time I do not see how we can avoid giving effect to the expectations which Stanley's despatch and the discussion in Parliament naturally created in Canada; and we must therefore consider how the implied pledge can best be fulfilled.' The letter then goes on to discuss the details of the new tariff on Canadian wheat and flour (44285 fos. 276–81).

ment.' When on 27 January the cabinet came to discuss the Corn Law memorandum Buckingham strongly opposed it; and since he was alone in his opposition, there was every expectation that he would resign.[1] Between fanatic agriculturalists and fanatic Leaguers, the contents of his post-bag and the expectations of the public, Peel's search for an acceptable solution was strewn with difficulties. Nevertheless the rest of the cabinet were behind his plan and in favour of immediate action. Even Knatchbull's disquiet was more on account of the opposition he expected from the agriculturalists than any objections of his own to the scheme. In the cabinet in fact he expressed a decided opinion in favour of Peel's proposals. In the subsequent discussion the only change made was slight. The scale was raised by virtually one point so that the first reduction operated between 51s and 52s instead of between 50s and 51s. Otherwise the scheme put forward to the Commons in February was exactly the same as that propounded by Peel in Cabinet in January.

To have brought his colleagues to an agreed decision on politically the most difficult issue of all was a decided success for the prime minister. The success had been largely due to two things: the careful preparation and discussion that had gone on since October, and Peel's refusal to drive his colleagues into either a quick or drastic solution. The final plan fell short of his own economic convictions but his abstract views were tempered by his judgement of what was politically feasible. His recommendations to the cabinet were thus able to appear less extreme than those of the Board of Trade. When Gladstone learned the cabinet's decision he murmured mutinously of resignation. But Peel was able to inject something of his thirty years' political experience into his impulsive junior. Most of their colleagues, he wrote to Gladstone early in February, had their doubts on some point or other of the bill; but equally they disliked the existing law, thought the new one an improvement, and 'they look to that point, which must always be looked at by the members of a government, the prospect of carrying the measure they propose'.[2] Had he been able only to consider abstract considerations, he later told Gladstone, he would have proposed a lower rate of protection; but 'it would have done no good to drive Knatchbull out of the

[1] *Knatchbull*, pp. 237–40.   [2] 44275 f. 106; Hyde, *Gladstone*, pp. 45–6.

cabinet after the Duke of Buckingham, nor could I hope to pass a measure with greater reductions through the House of Lords'. In the event the only casualty was Buckingham. He resigned before the meeting of parliament, protesting friendship and assuring Peel that he would support the government on everything but corn. 'I doubt however,' wrote Peel dryly to de Grey, 'whether he will long remain proof against the influences by which he is surrounded.'[1] He was not proof either against an offer of the Garter and his acceptance of that delayed honour gave a certain air of absurdity to his gesture of resignation. The loss, such as it was, was repaired by appointing the Duke of Buccleuch to succeed him as Lord Privy Seal and getting the consent of another agriculturalist peer, the Duke of Richmond, for his son and heir, Lord March, to move the address at the opening of the session.[2]

II

Parliament was opened by the queen on 3 February with the customary ceremonial made even more splendid on this occasion by the presence of the King of Prussia who had come over for the christening of the infant Prince of Wales. Finance, corn and tariffs were given prominence in her speech and in the general atmosphere of interest and speculation the address was agreed to without a division. The only important event was Peel's announcement that he would make his first policy statement on the subject of the Corn Laws and follow it as soon as possible with his main financial and commercial proposals. On 9 February the public galleries of the House of Commons were filled as soon as the doors opened. Outside the excitement was made more boisterous by a massive demonstration of Anti-Corn Law League delegates who, frustrated in their attempts to enter the lobby, stood outside the House and shouted to M.P.s as they entered.

Soon after five Peel rose in a crowded House to announce the details of the corn bill. His opening remarks, sober, cautious and

---

[1] 40477 f. 160; *Gladstone*, I, 188.

[2] For a discussion of the brief participation of Buckingham in Peel's ministry see David Spring, 'Lord Chandos and the farmers, 1818–1846' (*Huntingdon Library Quarterly*, XXXIII, 274–7).

sceptical, set the tone of the whole speech. He did not think the distress in the country was due to the Corn Laws; he could not promise immediate alleviation of it by any legislative action; though he refused to believe that the springs of British industrial wealth had suddenly dried up. Abolition of the Corn Laws would not help industrial distress; it would merely add poverty in the countryside to the poverty of the towns. The crucial consideration for the working classes was not the abstract price of food, but their command through wages and employment of the means of subsistence. He went over all the arguments beaten out with his colleagues in the preceding months, but he did so with significant modifications, deliberately shortening the range of his speculation and concentrating on short-term considerations. He spoke of population increase but pointed out that in years of good harvests the country could still feed itself; the legislature must take into account good years as well as bad. He singled out the inevitability of price fluctuations as the prime objection to a fixed duty. He spoke of the need to enlarge the basis for taking the averages, while wondering whether the effect of fraudulent manipulation had not been exaggerated. When he had gone through all the details of the government scheme he made an appeal to the extremists on both sides. To protectionists he stressed the benefits they would receive from any measure that promoted greater price stability and prevented in particular the artificial lowering of prices at harvest time. He told them frankly that they could afford to part with some protection and it was only just that they should. To free-traders he pointed out that the new scale would in fact make a material reduction of duties (between 59s and 60s, for example, the existing duty of 27s 8d would be cut by more than half to 13s) and emphasised that the protection he wished to retain was not for the special interest of any particular class. 'Protection cannot be vindicated on that principle.' It was the welfare of all classes he had in mind. Yet agriculture had its special burdens and he could not subscribe to any policy which would make the country permanently dependent on foreign countries for a substantial proportion of its food.

It was a dry, balanced speech, weighted down by a mass of statistical information, and of necessity somewhat defensive in character. Middle of the road policies may sometimes command intellectual approval; they rarely excite enthusiasm. This was no exception. Yet though there was nothing in it to please extreme protectionists or doctrinaire free-traders, it offered something with which moderate men, uneasily aware of the pressures from all sides, could thankfully concur. Given Peel's premises—and they were probably those of the majority of the House—his technical solution seemed workman-like and adequate. Where the effect of regulation was so diversely calculated and expectation so often deceived, a cautious, experi-mental attitude had much to recommend it to those who conceded the need for some change while fearing the result of too much. Those were the men whom Peel's speech, sober, factual, undog-matic, looking to present difficulties and avoiding too long a view, was designed to convince. The greatest criticism was that he offered no final, absolute solution; the greatest merit that he offered an immediate, practical one. In that was the strength and weakness of his position. Greville thought the speech itself so elaborate that it bored his audience. If it reduced the political temperature in a House of Commons ringed by police and angry Leaguers, this was no great disadvantage. With greater shrewdness Greville also observed that it was the speech of an advocate rather than that of a statesman, and that it perhaps concealed rather than revealed Peel's true convic-tions. Wharncliffe agreed with him that the actual plan was some-thing of an anticlimax after the speculation caused by Buckingham's resignation, but insisted that it would have been impossible for Peel to do any more. Time had to be given to the agricultural interest before it would consent to any further modification.[1] The truth was perhaps that public and political opinion was so fragmented on the issue that no one solution would have commanded wide support. Peel's plan was acceptable, even if it did not evoke enthusiasm, as being the mean average of conflicting interests.

Subsequent debate in the Commons confirmed this. All three alternative propositions put before the House were decisively rejected. Russell's resolution in favour of a fixed duty was defeated by 123 votes, a larger margin than Peel expected; Villiers's motion for total repeal by a crushing majority of 303 votes which included the official Whigs; and Christopher's amendment for a slightly higher protective scale of duties by over 200. The debates contained

[1] *Greville*, 11 Feb. 1842.

little that was either new or noteworthy. Despite his earlier qualms Gladstone proved an acute and able defender of ministerial policy in the House. Cobden spoke vehemently in the Villiers debate and was answered even more vehemently by Ferrand in a popular and savage attack on mill-owners and manufacturers. In the Russell debate Peel answered an appeal by Roebuck to overcome his prejudices and show himself a great statesman with words which were an unconscious reply to Greville's strictures:

> I will tell the hon. and learned gentleman what I think belongs more to the true character of the minister of such a country as this. I think it more in keeping with that true character for me to aspire to none of those magnificent characteristics which he has described, and that the wisest and safest course for me to adopt is to effect as much practical good as I can, and not, by pronouncing panegyrics upon general principles which might obtain temporary popularity and praise, delay even a partial remedy for evils the existence of which all acknowledge.[1]

Partial remedy or not, it suited the temper of the House, as the comparative mildness of debate and large majorities demonstrated. A meeting of the party on 14 February, the opening day of the general debate on the bill, made it plain that though many Conservative M.P.s would have preferred a higher degree of protection, the great body were prepared to support the measure. In the event Christopher's academic protectionist exercise fell flat and even stout agriculturalists like Tyrell and Bankes stood firm with the government. The excitement was outside the House, in the violent proceedings of the Anti-Corn Law League conference in London, and in the industrial towns of Yorkshire, Lancashire and the Midlands where Leaguers, Chartists and Complete Suffragists met in innumerable angry meetings and effigies of the prime minister were publicly burnt. The agricultural districts were quiet and after an initial hesitation the farming community in general seemed disposed to follow the advice of their representatives in parliament. In Buckinghamshire the sedulous influence of its ducal patron so far prevailed as to produce a mild resolution against the bill from the local Agricultural Association; but this was predictable and unimportant. Inside parliament proceedings moved swiftly once the wearisome debates

[1] *Speeches*, III, 841.

in committee were over. In March, after a brief, firm and incisive speech by Peel, the second reading was carried by over a hundred votes and the bill finally passed on 5 April. The Lords offered even less obstruction and before the spring was out, the first of the three great government measures was safely on the statute book.

Meanwhile the second instalment of the budget had been unfolded. On 11 March Peel informed the House of the government's financial proposals. If corn had been the great social issue, this was the great technical issue. The secrecy surrounding the cabinet's decision had been complete and the interested speculation, though not of the same nature as that attending the corn bill, was considerable. The professional politicians on the opposition benches in particular felt that here was the weakest flank of the new ministry as it had been of the old. They did not think that Peel would dare to reintroduce the income tax in time of peace; and they had agreed to oppose any increased taxation designed to balance the budget since they themselves had offered to balance it by reductions. The importance of the occasion was made obvious by that fact that Peel himself made the opening announcement of policy although, as a government financial statement in a Committee of Ways and Means, it would have fallen more naturally to the Chancellor of the Exchequer. His speech, lasting over 3½ hours, was a model of lucidity and mastery of detail which had all the greater effect because of the shock of the principal proposal contained in it. 'The success was complete,' wrote Greville, 'he took the House by storm; and his opponents, though of course differing and objecting on particular points, did him ample justice.'[1] He began, in a quiet and serious vein, by exposing the actual financial situation. With no change in the revenue, there would be a deficit of £2½ million in 1843—an accumulated deficit therefore of £5 million in two years. This was not casual but part of an aggregate deficit amounting to over £10 million in six years or about one fifth of the annual revenue of the country. What was to be done? He would not, he said firmly, lay more taxes on the poorer classes. Despite all the taunts he had been subjected to over the corn bill, no man could be more convinced than he was that 'whatever be your financial difficulties and necessities, you must so adapt and adjust your measures as not to bear on

[1] *Greville*, 13 Mar. 1842.

the comforts of the labouring classes of society'. Further taxation of articles of consumption would be fiscally disappointing and socially undesirable. He glanced lightly at other possible expedients—a tax on gas, a tax on railway travel—only to reject them. He agreed that in the long term buoyancy of consumption would result in increased revenue from decreased duties. But long term was not short term; and it was the present situation with which they had to deal. So far, he pointed out, with the exception of coffee and rum, there had not been a single article on which the yield had recovered within five or six years after a considerable reduction of duty.

It had been after five o'clock when he began his speech and already an hour had gone by. But then, in a couple of sentences came the bombshell:

> Instead of looking to taxation on consumption—instead of reviving the taxes on salt or on sugar—it is my duty to make an earnest appeal to the possessors of property, for the purpose of repairing this mighty evil. I propose, for a time at least, (and I never had occasion to make a proposition with a more thorough conviction of its being one which the public interest of the country required)—I propose that, for a time to be limited, the income of this country should be called on to contribute a certain sum, for the purpose of remedying this mighty and growing evil.

He had already started to give the first details of the tax before the House recovered its breath and interruptions broke out. But order was soon restored and he continued with the statement of the machinery of the tax and the probable yield. With the figure of £4·3 million firmly before the House as the estimated revenue from the income tax, the new Irish duties, and the coal export levy, he turned to what the government proposed to do with it. Adding further sums for China and India to the existing deficit, he arrived at a figure of £1·8 million as the net surplus to be expected. This would be applied to a vast remodelling and rationalisation of the tariff system on the general principle of removing all prohibitory duties, reducing all import duties on raw materials to 5 per cent or less, and those on foreign manufactured goods to 20 per cent or less. Out of the 1,200 dutiable articles that made up the cumbrous book of tariffs, 750 would have their duties reduced with a loss to the exchequer of about £270,000. Though there would be no reduction of the duty on sugar while the present colonial monopoly continued, there would be decreases in the duties on foreign and colonial coffee resulting in a loss of £171,000. The duty on foreign timber would also be lowered, while Canadian timber would be admitted at only a minimal charge, bringing a further loss to the revenue of £600,000. Finally the export duties on domestic manufactures would be lowered with another loss of £103,000. As a result of these great and a few other minor changes, the government would be left with an estimated surplus of half a million. His clear but elaborate financial analysis over, he pitched his argument to a more rhetorical note and in his peroration compared the difficulties of the twenty-five years of peace since Waterloo with those of the twenty-five years of war that had preceded them. He adjured his audience to rise to the needs of the time as their fathers had risen to the challenge of revolutionary France. 'If you do permit this evil to continue,' he said grandly, 'you must expect the severe but just judgement of a reflecting and retrospective posterity.'

It was nearly nine on the Friday evening when he sat down at last to tremendous cheering from his party. The main debate did not begin until the Monday and over the weekend two things became clear. He had thrown the opposition into some confusion and he had put himself in a position which in a sense transcended party. Having come prepared to attack a mere multiplication of conventional taxes, the Whigs now had to decide their attitude on a point of principle. Peel on the other hand had laid down as his fundamental axiom that the rich should take on their shoulders the cost of rescuing the country from its financial ills. This was not a class but a national policy. Over corn the ministers had been criticised for timidity, compromise and social bias; over finance they startled parliament and country by the boldness of their proposals. At last they had vindicated the result of the general election and demonstrated their capacity to master a problem with which their opponents had signally failed. If he had done nothing else, Peel had made the country feel that it was being governed by a man who knew what was wanted and was ready to do it. Some of his parliamentary opponents were as sensible of this as his friends. One Whig M.P. came into the Travellers' Club on the Friday night and gave an account of his speech. 'One felt,' he said honestly, 'all the time he was speaking, "Thank God Peel is Minister".[1] This of course did not mean that there would be no opposition. Some manufacturers thought that they had been made the scapegoats of an aristocratic oligarchy. Some landowners thought it would ruin the landed interest. Cobden and Bright on behalf of the League were violently hostile. The former indeed rashly opined that 'the income tax will do more than the Corn Law to destroy the Tories'.[2] On the other hand the Chartists welcomed the tax as a measure of social equity and old Lord Melbourne observed with cynical commonsense that any middle-class protest meeting would risk being swamped by a lower-class vote in its favour. *The Times* somewhat illogically opposed the tax while supporting the tariff; but there was no general press campaign against it. People, especially politicians, had spoken of the impossible odium of such a measure for so long that its impossibility had become an article of faith. Now that an income tax was actually brought forward by the government there turned out to be a surprising amount of acquiescence among the rich; while those with less than £150 *per annum* were its natural and enthusiastic champions.

By the time the debate was resumed in the Commons the Whigs had rallied from their initial embarrassment and decided on a formal opposition. This was no great deterrent to Peel as was evident from a brisk masterful speech on 18 March, in which he said he had felt sure that the chief opponents of the tax would be precisely those who had run the country into its financial difficulties. But it meant that there would be hard fighting before the measure could be sent up to the Lords. In committee the cream of the opposition speakers—Russell, Francis Baring, Charles Wood, Howick, Sir George Grey, Hawes and Buller—rose one after another to denounce the tax. It was wrong in principle, not warranted by any real emergency, excessive in amount, unjust in its failure to distinguish between settled and precarious incomes, a blind to protect the corn and sugar monopolists, and unnecessary since there were other ways of meeting the deficit. Every advantage afforded by the rules of the House was exploited to obstruct the progress of the bill. Cobden took a prominent part in these delaying tactics, which depended for their success not on victory in the lobbies, which the solid government

---

[1] *Greville*, 13 Mar. 1842.   [2] *Cobden*, p. 241.

majority made impossible, but on the sheer consumption of time in debating motions for adjourning the debate until adjournment was forced on the government by the lateness of the hour.

These tactics were effective in postponing a decision until after the Easter recess, but they brought no long-term advantage to the opposition. Several leading Whigs, in fact, including Howick, protested in the end against this abuse of the rules of the House; and the respite provided no great evidence of public support for the opposition campaign. Peel's own impression was that there was less feeling against the income tax in the country at large than in the House of Commons and a wider endorsement than might have been expected for his argument that 'it is for the interest of property that property should bear the burden'.[1] He instanced with satisfaction to Prince Albert in mid-April a unanimous vote of approval for his financial and commercial policy from the Glasgow Chamber of Commerce.[2] Once the House was brought to a decision after Easter the Conservative voting strength began to tell. Indeed, the notable defections were on the other side. Roebuck the radical, Edward Ellice, and a back-bench Whig Raikes Currie, the member for Northampton, all declared their intention of supporting the ministry. Currie declared stoutly in words which perhaps found an uncomfortable echo in others of his party, that 'I think it an honest measure, because, while we impose no direct burden on the working classes, on the great body of the people, we severely tax ourselves.' He added, to ministerial cheers and laughter, that on his side they were only 'a *soi-disant* Liberal opposition . . . a popular opposition without a solitary puff of popular sympathy'. On 14 April the main counter-resolution, sponsored by Russell, was defeated after four nights of debate by 106 votes. The first reading was carried a few days later by 97 votes; and before the end of the month the second reading by 79 votes in a thin House and after a languid debate. In its final stages in committee the bill went rapidly forward and passed by 130 votes with less than 270 members present, every substantial opposition amendment having been rejected.

Three weeks earlier, on 10 May, Peel had introduced the third branch of his fiscal policy—the Customs Duty bill embodying the alterations in the tariff he had previously announced to the House.

[1] *Speeches*, IV, 27.   [2] 40434 f. 23.

This, in its detail and complexity, was not only a laborious legislative operation but ran a risk not previously encountered during the session: the risk of serious dissension in his own party. As far as parliament and public opinion were concerned, he had little to fear. Tariff reform was a consequential step once the principle of the income tax was accepted. It was in accord with the authoritative economic doctrines of the day; it had a national end in view; and the Whigs could not oppose it as a policy, as distinct from objecting to specific items, without repudiating their own budget of 1841. In his opening speech Peel could touch on precedents that began with the younger Pitt, took in Huskisson's policy of the eighteen-twenties, and finished with the Committee on Tariffs of 1840. He could quote with approval 'the general rule that we should purchase in the cheapest market and sell in the dearest', though this was not the happiest of quotations since it brought a cheer from the opposition benches in ironical reference to his own corn bill.[1] With greater effect he drove home the point that the whole object of his tariff reform was to reduce the cost of living for the country as a whole. Whatever the individual merits and drawbacks of any particular change, the total effect of what was proposed was 'to make a considerable saving in the expenses of every family in the kingdom'.[2]

Against this the official opposition was reduced to piecemeal criticism. They could deplore the absence of sugar and hark back to the compromise on corn. They could object to the new duty on exported coal and press for the abolition of colonial preference. But when Labouchere, in the first authoritative speech from the opposing front bench, said that he had heard with pleasure the main principles which the prime minister had laid down—when Hume, the high priest of radical orthodoxy, hailed with joy the conversion of the cabinet to free trade—it was clear that the main difficulties would not come from the other side of the House. The sour imputation of a late conversion was easily countered. Disraeli rose from behind his leader to deliver a grand historical disquisition on the identification of the Tory Party with the principles of free trade and the exact consistency of Sir Robert Peel's policy with that of Mr. Pitt. Gladstone with a shade more authority pointed out that since 1815

[1] *Speeches*, IV, 76 (10 May).   [2] *ibid.*, p. 62.

no equivalent period had seen so little done for free trade as in the seven years preceding 1841. Even on the question of reducing the duties on imported manufactured goods Peel was able to argue convincingly that 'high duties are a mere delusion'. They did not constitute a protection to the British manufacturer because of the prevalence of smuggling; and he enlivened what was by its nature a prosaic economic survey by producing a small bundle of unplaited straw, admitted at the minimal duty of 1d a cwt, which artlessly concealed within its recesses (as he proceeded to demonstrate to the House) a parcel of plaited straw subject to a duty of 17s 6d a cwt.

During the preceding weeks, however, when he and Ripon were interviewing innumerable delegations pressing for modifications of one kind or another in the long list of tariff changes, it had become obvious that the most serious objections would come from the agriculturalists. At the end of March Christopher told Fremantle, in a note which the chief whip passed on to his leader, that the farmers in his constituency were in a ferment over the new tariff and that he and his Lincolnshire colleagues were obliged to desert their parliamentary duties in order to be present at a county meeting of their indignant electors. 'They do not care for the income-tax nor are they very rebellious about wheat but on barley, oats and cattle they are, I think, with reason, dissatisfied.'[1] Similar pressure was being exerted on the ministers themselves. But Peel's attitude was inflexible. Only a couple of days after Christopher's complaint, the prime minister was arguing with Ripon against making any last-minute changes in response to what he dismissed as mere clamour. If they yielded to the agriculturalists, they would simply multiply their differences with the manufacturers. 'Concessions to any demand which we do not feel to be *bona fide* a good one will involve us in greater difficulties than direct opposition publicly offered.'[2] When on 10 May he came to make his preliminary speech on the tariff proposals, he spent much of it in explaining and justifying the reductions made in the duties on a whole range of imported farm produce from live cattle down to onions and potatoes. He was emphatic that the price of meat and cattle had been unduly high— 'extravagantly high'—and that despite increased supplies from Ireland and Scotland, prices were still rising. Did not this, he asked,

[1] 40476 f. 116.   [2] 40464 f. 196.

show clearly that population was growing faster than the available means of supply? What the new tariff was designed to do was merely to prevent exorbitant price rises in time of scarcity. It still offered a reasonable degree of protection to the British grazier. Indeed, he went on to say, he did not despair of seeing the country yet again exporting fat cattle. 'I believe that improvements in science and the application of chemical processes to agriculture may produce such results.' But as far as the agriculturalist wing of his party was concerned, his arguments fell on deaf or discontented ears. Not only were they—or their constituents—genuinely alarmed at the immediate reductions in duties on foreign agricultural produce, representing a more effective application of free trade doctrine over a wider front than the new Corn Law, but they were uncomfortable at the whole liberal tendency of the government's policy. To witness unsolicited compliments to their party leader from Whigs like Labouchere or radicals like Hume filled them with distrust. As George Palmer, the Conservative M.P. for South Essex, bluntly put it: if the government adopted free trade as a principle, who could tell where they would stop? If the tariff was passed, the next step would be a repeal of the Corn Laws. Protectionists by instinct, and representing protectionist constituencies, they could only reconcile themselves to the new tariff as a prudent concessionary adjustment of a basic protectionist system. If, as some were beginning to fear, the measure was no more than a halting-place in the march towards complete free trade, they were ready to sound the alarm.

Over foreign meat and cattle they were ready, in fact, to oppose. By existing law both were prohibited from entering the country. Live cattle, the simplest and most effective method of importing meat in an age before refrigeration, and one which might also encourage a remunerative home industry in fattening stock, the government now proposed to admit at a flat duty of £1 a head; dead carcasses at 8s a hundredweight. A deputation of county and agriculturalist M.P.s which waited on Peel failed to extract any concession. He told them that the duty envisaged was an adequate protection for them; and that the alternative method of fixing the duty on live cattle by weight, even if theoretically imposing no greater duty in aggregate, would involve delay and expense at the docks practically equivalent to an additional tariff. When after

Whitsun the House settled down to the detailed consideration of the bill, the discontent of the agriculturalists was expressed in a formal amendment by W. Miles, Conservative M.P. for East Somerset, that all livestock from foreign countries should be taxed by weight. This amendment, debated on 23 May, was defeated by 267 votes. But among the 113 who voted in the minority were 85 of Peel's usual supporters, and the large majority in favour of the government's proposal included 172 of his usual opponents. The extreme agriculturalist wing of the Conservative party, which had stood firm over Corn Law and income tax, had defected at last over meat.[1] The result of the division, however, was decisive. Though there was much subsequent debate about foodstuffs, all amendments whether from free-traders or from protectionists were easily repelled. By mid-June the customs bill had emerged from committee and it passed its third reading at the end of the month with a few valedictory words from Peel to the effect that great changes had been made for the general good—as great as possible without disturbing violently the important interests in the country—and he sincerely hoped that the result would be to promote commerce and give new openings to domestic industry.

In private he sent his congratulations to Ripon and the Board of Trade on their handling of the many deputations appearing before them and the skill with which they had presented their case in the House of Commons.[2] It had been a long parliamentary battle in which, besides Peel, other prominent members of the front bench like Goulburn, Graham and Stanley had taken a part. The man who had done most to enhance his reputation, however, was Gladstone. He had sat at Peel's side handing up the relevant papers during his major speeches. Among other tasks he had been put up to answer Russell on corn and Miles on cattle and done it on each occasion with knowledge and authority. Throughout he had conducted himself, Peel told Ripon on 16 June, with signal ability. The same day he wrote to Gladstone's father to tell him in flattering terms of the distinction his son had gained. 'At no time in the annals of

---

[1] The voting figures quoted are those supplied to Peel by his whips (40434 f. 91). Professor Aydelotte's analysis (incl. tellers) is: for the amendment Conservatives 86, Liberals 29: against the amendment Conservatives 213, Liberals 169 (*English Politics*, Appx. C).

[2] 40464 f. 219.

parliament has there been exhibited a more admirable combination of ability, extensive knowledge, temper and discretion.'[1] For a young politician who at the start of his office had protested his unsuitability and halfway through had threatened to resign, the end of the session brought nothing but success. It was something in which Peel could feel a double satisfaction. His judgement had been vindicated and he now possessed a promising reserve for any cabinet vacancy.

Behind him on the back benches, however, the atmosphere was ominously quiet. In April the pessimistic Knatchbull felt that the government had already lost the good opinion of the greater part of the agriculturalists. J. G. Lockhart, the editor of the *Quarterly Review*, wrote to Croker in June that there were clear signs of 'sulky disaffection' among the Conservative rank and file. The prime minister was not disposed to sit still under charges either of deferring to agitation or betraying the interests of farmers and landowners. To Croker, who was collecting material for the defence of the government's policy which appeared in the September *Quarterly*, he wrote sharply that the difficulty would be to prove that they had gone far enough in relaxing the tariff. Something had to be done to revive industry and commerce; something had to be done for the starving thousands in towns like Paisley. One might ideally prefer cornfields to cotton mills, agricultural labourers to factory workers; but nothing now could divert British society from the road of industrial expansion. 'Our lot is cast, we cannot change it and we cannot recede.' There had been no concessions to the Anti-Corn Law League in what the government had done over tariffs and corn. 'There is nothing I have proposed which is not in conformity with my own convictions. I should rather say, I have not gone, in any one case, beyond my own convictions *on the side of relaxation*.'[2] Those policies were still on trial but unless some improvements showed soon, they would be on the verge of a social crisis.

What coloured Peel's mind by the summer of 1842, and with it the whole statement of the case for his policy, was the social condition of Britain. It was not that the elements of that policy had changed, but that the balance had altered. Starting with an enquiry into the best means of balancing the budget, he ended with the broad

[1] *Gladstone*, I, 190. [2] *Croker*, II, 382–4; *N&Q*, vol. 187, 208–9.

concept of attacking poverty and restoring social stability. The only way open to the government to do this was to reduce unemployment and lower the cost of living, or in the more abstract language of the textbooks, to reprime the economy with increased consumption and demand. However dictated by the limitations of early nineteenth-century government, it was in fact a curiously modern economic formula; and he had arrived at it by a process of practical commonsense rather than by any doctrine. It would of course be absurd to accept the conventional debating point of the Whigs that Peel in 1842 was a convert to free trade. His membership of Liverpool's cabinet twenty years earlier was a sufficient attestation of his credentials as a liberal economist. The intellectual tradition of the ministerialist Pittite–Liverpool party was in fact more continuous and impressive than that of the Whigs. If there were any recent converts to free trade they were sitting in 1842 on the opposition front bench rather than alongside Peel. The Whigs had been when in office a party of tax reduction but not of tax reform, nor until 1841 of any coherent tariff policy. Yet some development in Conservative thought had certainly occurred. The work of Liverpool, Robinson and Huskisson in the twenties, whether in the famous series of reciprocity treaties or in the rationalisation of the tariff, had pursued strictly limited objectives. It would be an historical distortion to see in it a consciously designed stage towards a free-trade system in the absolute sense. Throughout the thirties Peel's views had shown no obvious advance on the position he had reached when he left office in 1830. The major issues of politics in that crucial decade were in any case not economic. Protectionism was still the national system; and when a defence of the Corn Laws became a tactical necessity after 1837, it was difficult for the Conservative opposition to lay any emphasis on other aspects of tariff reform. For Peel, as for most leading politicians, the broadening of his economic ideas was accelerated by the industrial depression of·1838, the report of the Committee on Tariffs in 1840, and the controversial proposals of 1841. During the Conservative party consultations over the Whig budget he clearly had at the back of his mind the possibility of new taxes and the general revision of tariffs which would then become possible. Between the summer of 1841 and the summer of 1842, however, the emphasis in his thinking steadily shifted from the financial and fiscal problems of government to the wider impact of governmental policy on the nation at large—to economic policy as a piece of social engineering.

In the end, as his autumn correspondence showed, his preoccupation was with the means whereby government could meet the dangers of a spawning, impoverished, and disorderly industrial society. What had caused this shift of emphasis was obvious. It was the rapid deterioration in the state of the country during the actual year in which he put his first great legislative programme through parliament. The harrowing experience of governing England in 1842, the worst year perhaps which the British people endured in the whole of the nineteenth century, acted as a forcing-ground in which his ideas developed almost from month to month. Revolutionary as the great budget of 1842 had been, by the end of that terrible year of starvation and violence Peel had convinced himself that he had done too little rather than too much. The Condition of England question was a more savagely educative process than any economic textbook.

CHAPTER

10

DISTRESS AND DISORDER

When Peel's government took office in the autumn of 1841 it was obvious that the combination of Chartism, Anti-Corn Law League propaganda and widespread unemployment threatened serious trouble in the industrial districts during the coming months. Graham, the minister most nearly concerned, was prophesying in October a winter of unrest. Even apart from possible outbreaks of disorder, the demands of the organised operatives of the north were passionate and far-reaching. The Short Time Committee from the West Riding which interviewed Peel wanted not only a ten hours act for children but the exclusion of women from the factories, reform of the poor law, and a general enquiry into the use of machinery and the causes of manufacturing distress.[1] Peel gave no pledges and was sceptical of some of their arguments. But he listened sympathetically and, as Ashley told him afterwards, the deputations from the factory districts were '*much* pleased by their conferences with *you*', though less so by those with Graham.[2]

In the next few months this first favourable impression rapidly faded. At the end of December Ashley learned from Graham that factory reform had not yet been discussed in the cabinet and he had not consulted any of his colleagues on the question. Two weeks before the start of the session Ashley's not over-large stock of patience ran out. Convinced that the government intended to oppose the ten hours demand, and determined to push the question irrespective of party, he asked Bonham whether he should in those circumstances resign from the Carlton. If he meant this as a warning

[1] Kitson Clark, 'Hunger and politics in 1842' (*Journal of Modern History*, XXV, 361).
[2] 40483 f. 36.

to the government, he succeeded at least to the extent that Bonham asked his permission to lay the letter before Graham. The Home Secretary sent it back on 21 January with a regretful note of his own, saying that he hoped to meet Ashley halfway in a more friendly spirit than that which had inspired the latter's correspondence with Bonham.[1] But halfway-houses were not habitations in which Ashley could comfortably dwell. The same day he was already writing a somewhat peremptory note to Peel, pointing out that five months had elapsed since he had brought the factory question to his notice, and asking the prime minister to say whether he had made up his mind to resist or concede the principle of the ten hours restriction for persons between thirteen and twenty-one. As might have been expected, Peel replied that he was not prepared to pledge himself or the government to a ten hours bill. He added, however, that the Home Secretary had under consideration a measure for regulating hours of labour and the education of children in factories which he would willingly discuss. Ashley then asked whether the government would resist a bill brought forward independently. Peel answered somewhat frigidly that he had given all the information he could require and Ashley was free to take any line he wished in parliament. Sending the correspondence to Graham the same day the prime minister added caustically that 'there are limits to coaxing a Gentleman, who is angry with everybody because he has embarrassed himself'. Ashley, reinforced in his conviction that the cabinet had decided to oppose his campaign, then announced publicly, in a letter to the Short Time Committees in Cheshire, Yorkshire and Lancashire which appeared in *The Times* on 2 February, that Peel's government would resist the ten hours bill. This was not strictly true since Peel had merely said that he could not support it. But the distinction was not one which Ashley in his emotional frame of mind was ready to appreciate.[2] An article in the *Morning Post* a few days later, criticising him fairly enough for misrepresenting the government's attitude but using unfair and offensive language about Ashley's personal character, completed the breach. Coming when it did, and in a well-known Conservative

[1] See my note on 'Ashley and the Conservative Party in 1842' (*E.H.R.*, LIII, 679); f. also 40616 f. 237.

[2] 40483 fos. 36, 44–50; Graham (Graham to Ashley, 30 Dec. 1841, Peel to Graham, 6 Jan. 1842); *Hodder*, pp. 215–16.

journal, Ashley felt that the article must have been officially inspired.

The real damage to the government, however, was not the alienation of Lord Ashley. Torn between his neurotic tendency to regard all who were not with him as against him, and his Christian principles which enjoined charity even towards his enemies, Ashley would always remain an exasperating and unpredictable individualist. The effect on the operatives of the north was more simple and direct. The Short Time delegates had reported back in the autumn that at least Sir Robert Peel had a heart. Now they were told by the politician they had most reason to trust that the prime minister had ranged himself among their opponents. The compromise of the corn bill in February did nothing to remove that impression; nor did the renewal of the Poor Law Commission for a further period of five years later in the session. Such amendments as were made by the government were largely technical. Though under some pressure in the House to make statutory relaxations, in particular to authorise poor law guardians to give outdoor relief, Graham refused to budge on the main principles of the act. He argued from official statistics that in fact the workhouse system was not being rigidly enforced; that 86 per cent of those in receipt of relief in 1841 obtained it outside the workhouse; and that £892,000 was spent that year in workhouse relief compared with nearly £3 million on outdoor relief. These figures were not challenged but they did little to efface the image of the brutal bashaws of the new poor law. The realities of the situation justified Peel and Graham in their resolution to make no change in the actual law; but its sinister reputation remained. There was probably much truth in what Ashley wrote at the end of the session: that at the dissolution the previous year the mass of the working classes had placed some hope in Peel but that this hope was dissipated in 1842.[1]

Contrary, however, to Ashley's prophecy to Bonham in January, they were not driven from despair of any help from the government to an alliance with the Anti-Corn Law League. The League in fact, by its failure to make any impact on parliament, was being driven further towards the Chartists. Cobden at meetings of the League delegates in the spring used violent language about the need for physical force to overawe the ministers and did what he could to

[1] Hodder, p. 233.

vilify and discredit aristocratic government. But it was to Chartism rather than to the Manchester mill-owners that the industrial proletariat turned for leadership during the months when Peel was working his corn, tax and tariff bills through parliament. The League's London Conference was matched by the Chartist Convention in April. On 2 May came the presentation of the great Chartist petition to parliament. Six miles in length, purporting to have over three million signatures, and carried on a great framework by thirty bearers, the petition was accompanied by a huge procession which wound through nearly two miles of London streets. But the breaking up of the petition into fragments, which was physically necessary before it could be taken into the House, was symbolic of its reception by the legislature. When Duncombe, presenting the petition, moved that the petitioners be heard at the bar, he was opposed by the Home Secretary on the simple grounds that though nobody disputed the fact of widespread distress in the country, the political remedy prescribed by the Charter could not possibly be accepted. Peel restated this argument later in the debate with greater force. The Charter and the petition which accompanied it made demands which condemned not only the constitution but the whole structure of society. There could be no practical use therefore in listening to speeches at the bar in their favour. He sympathised with those who suffered from the existing distress, admired their fortitude, and respected their patience. But he saw no reason to think that the real end of government—the happiness of the people—would be better served by another form of constitution than that which they enjoyed.[1] It was of course inconceivable that the Charter could have been accepted by the House of Commons. But on the actual proposal to hear the petitioners perhaps the greatest damage was inflicted not by Peel, nor by Russell who spoke in much the same vein, but by two lesser politicians. One was Macaulay who delivered one of his grand constitutional lectures on the sanctity of property and the inadmissibility of universal suffrage. The other was Roebuck who, while defending the Chartists, denounced O'Connor, the presumed author of the petition, as a malignant and cowardly demagogue. The motion to hear the petitioners received less than fifty votes.

[1] *Speeches*, IV, 57–60 (3 May 1842).

'Moral force' Chartism had demonstrably failed and Peel's measures on corn, tariffs and income tax had simultaneously blunted the effect of the League's perfervid oratory. The liberal middle classes of the towns generally welcomed his proposals and showed no enthusiasm for the return of the Whigs. Even in Manchester, the *Guardian* praised the reintroduction of the income tax and with the passing of the new corn bill called for a halt in the activities of the League. As the House toiled away in committee on schedules and duties, Ashley watched the progress of Peel's policies with uncomprehending dissatisfaction. 'His success puzzles me', he wrote in March; but the explanation was simple enough. A combination of firm government and liberal legislation offered to propertied classes security for the present and promise for the future. In the racked and distressed society of 1842 these were no mean achievements. To Ashley imports and exports, tariffs and taxes, were mundane trivialities compared with the crusade to which he had dedicated himself. Every cheer in the House for Peel seemed only another obstacle to the ten hours movement. The Home Office had not yet disgorged its own factory proposals and the session seemed running to waste. At the end of March, however, he had a reconciliation with the prime minister. They shook hands, avoided old controversies, and Peel at least seemed pleased at the gesture.

In May came an opportunity for Ashley to advance his humanitarian work in another field. Two years earlier he had secured the appointment of a commission to enquire into the employment of children in mines and manufactures. In May 1842 the first report was issued to become the most famous Blue Book of the century. Ashley's sensational speech of 7 June on his motion to bring in a bill to regulate the employment of women and children in the mines, largely drew for its effect on the evidence of brutality, misery and sexual degradation contained in the report. The reaction from both parliament and the press was instantaneous and overwhelming. From Peel and Graham, to both of whom he sent copies of his speech, Ashley received generous recognition for his exposure of what Peel bluntly called the 'mining abominations'. 'I have read as much of the evidence as is possible for me to read amid the incessant demands upon my time,' wrote the prime minister. 'I admire equally the good feeling and the ability, the qualities of head and heart, with which you have forced this matter upon public notice.'[1] In the House Graham promised the assistance of the government and the bill went rapidly through its stages despite Ashley's grudging feeling that ministers might have been more active in its support. In the Lords matters did not go so smoothly. Buccleuch, who had at first agreed to take charge in the upper House, told Ashley that his colleagues felt that it should not be made a government measure. When the bill came up for discussion, Wharncliffe, possibly meaning to do no more than make this plain, announced in rather unfortunate wording that the government had determined to remain entirely passive. Nevertheless, with certain previously agreed amendments designed to neutralise specific criticism, the bill under Lord Devon's guidance and with the help of Wellington and Wharncliffe passed successfully through the House of Lords against the opposition of such *laisser-faire* champions as Londonderry and Brougham.

When it came back to the Commons Ashley was afraid that the bill as finally drafted would not expressly forbid the physical presence of women in the mines as distinct from working in them, and that this would be a loophole for evasion. Peel, to whom he confided his fears, had interviews with various other persons on the significance of the Lords' amendments. Like Ashley he preferred the principle of total exclusion for all purposes but as he explained in a letter of 4 August, the real difficulty lay in the undue severity of the original wording of the bill. The Attorney General, whom he had consulted, thought that the first draft would have had the effect of prohibiting, with risk of severe penalties to innocent third persons, the presence of a wife in the case of an accident to her husband or a daughter bringing a meal to her father.[2] These technicalities, together with the lateness of the session, led in the end to the acceptance of the Lord's amendments. Despite the taunts of the opposition and Ashley's temperamental misgivings, Graham was not unrealistic in claiming that the essential principles of Ashley's original proposals had been achieved: the prohibition of female labour underground, together with that of boys under ten, and the limitation of apprenticeship. Ashley's real dissatisfaction was with the continual postponement of Graham's factory bill, on which he

[1] 40483 fos. 68–70; *Peel*, II, 534.   [2] 40483 fos. 78–80; *Hodder*, pp. 229–31.

expressed his deep disappointment to Peel in July. The prime minister sent back a placatory note, welcoming a frank expression of his feelings even when critical of the government, and pointing out that no one could have anticipated the extent to which the session had been taken up by other matters. He himself had been obliged to neglect many things which only absolute necessity would have made him neglect. 'When there is a constant unvarying demand upon sixteen or seventeen hours of the twenty-four for months together, delays ... become unavoidable.' Ashley, though still sore at Graham's dilatoriness, was sufficiently mollified to promise not to raise the matter himself in the Commons.[1]

Two great measures of industrial regulation were perhaps more than could be expected in one parliamentary session. Nevertheless the wider subject of industrial distress and agitation was one which haunted the parliamentary discussions on commercial policy, taxation and corn laws. At the beginning of July the opposition forced a general debate on the issue. The actual motion put forward by Wallace, the Liberal M.P. for Greenock, was a specious one to the effect that the queen should not prorogue parliament until an enquiry had been instituted into the causes of the distress. But it provided an opportunity for speaker after speaker from the opposition benches to describe the distress in the localities known to them and to proceed according to their fancy either to place the responsibility on the ministers or to demand a change of policy. The motion was easily defeated but the insistence of the House on prolonging the debate owed something perhaps to genuine concern as well as to party tactics. A few days later, in committee of supply, the opposition again raised a debate on the general issues of the Corn Laws, the state of the nation, and the causes of manufacturing distress. Peel argued, as he had done so often before, that the Corn Laws in themselves had not caused the distress. But he said that if after fair trial the new Corn Law did not work, he would be the first to agree to its revision. He pointed to the over-capitalisation and unduly rapid expansion of the cotton industry as a partial reason for its difficulties; and he uttered some sharp words on the inflammatory propaganda of the League.[2] Though much heat, little light was generated by these debates. All acknowledged the distress; the

[1] 40483 fos. 72-6; *Peel*, II, 534. [2] *Speeches*, IV, 104-10, 114-21 (1, 11 July 1842).

confusion was over causes and remedies. The opposition itself was openly divided on views and tactics. The time-wasting and obstruction in the Commons were more the index of the indisciplined state of the Liberal Party than of any sustained attacking leadership. After his unsuccessful criticisms of the budget Russell made only fitful appearances in the House and opposition had degenerated into guerrilla warfare to which only Palmerston among the official Whigs lent some sort of front-bench benediction.

It was this circumstance which enabled Peel to end the session on an unexpected note of personal triumph. Early in August Palmerston staged one final attack on the government in the style of Lyndhurst's annual philippics against Melbourne a few years earlier. Under the pretext of moving for a return of bills presented during the session, he delivered an elaborate and sarcastic speech mainly directed at Peel personally. He reviewed the course of politics since Catholic emancipation, criticised the records of the new ministry both at home and abroad, and accused the prime minister of coming into power on a protectionist programme and carrying out a free trade one. It was a long, clever and not ineffective speech of the gladiatorial type, of no practical use except to please supporters and raise party morale. The disjointed and demoralised Liberal opposition were in need of some tonic before they broke up for the summer. But Palmerston, disgruntled by loss of office, contemptuous of Aberdeen, and irritated by the failure of many Whigs and most radicals to support his attacks on the government's foreign policy, had his own scores to settle. Few politicians could excel Palmerston in the great parliamentary set-piece, but on this occasion at least he met his match. Sermons from Palmerston on political consistency provided scope for sharp counterthrusts when Peel rose immediately after his opponent to second his motion. Equally effective were his barbed comments on the tardy conversion of the Whigs to the free trade policy of 1841, their painful wavering between dissolution and resignation, and the conspicuous absence that evening of Palmerston's colleagues on the opposition front bench. It was an entertaining and lively counter-attack, unusual among Peel's speeches in that much of it was personal. Its incisive tone probably owed something to its impromptu quality and even more to his resentment at the deliberate nature of Palmerston's attack on himself. His supporters showed their relish by laughter and cheers. Though Cobden acidly reminded them that there were more urgent matters before the country than the staged quarrels of Tory and Whig, Peel himself was exhilarated by his generally acknowledged victory in this parliamentary duel. He showed it a trifle unpleasantly in a letter to Julia next day.

Whitehall   11 August 1842

My dearest Love,

How I long to see you again. I am just come from the Council. I am fagged to death. The night before last, having drunk some strong green tea, I never closed my eyes and had a tremendous day to go through yesterday, preparing the [sc. queen's] speech, and seeing ministers and a Cabinet and then a speech of 2 hours in the House of Commons in the course of which I inflicted as sound a chastisement on Lord Palmerston as he could desire to receive. He meant to have it all his own way, and brought down Lady Palmerston, and a party who were to dine with him afterwards, to witness his triumph. You never saw a man look as foolish as he did under the flagellation which I gave him.

Parliament will be prorogued tomorrow. We have very unpleasant accounts from Manchester and that neighbourhood. Great rioting and confusion. The Anti-Corn Law League have excited the passions of the people and are among the first victims of their own folly. Read the account of last night's debate in the *Standard*.

Ever my own dearest love,
Most affectionately yours,
Robert Peel.[1]

He would probably never have written in such terms to anyone but his wife and it was a mark of the tiredness and strain of the session that he could write like that at all. In the heat of political strife few men are exempt from an occasional spasm of vanity and resentment; but a more impartial reader than Julia might have wondered whether power was not already beginning to affect her husband.

The strain on the ministers was not over yet. Though the trials of the legislative session were behind them, the burdens of executive responsibility grew heavier as the summer wore on. Nothing that parliament had done so far made any tangible effect on the distress

[1] Peel MSS.

in the country; and the frustrations of the Chartists and the Leaguers were driving both into violent and desperate courses. The government did not need parliamentary debates to remind them of the grim state of some of the industrial areas. From the time they took office petitions, deputations and the correspondence of the Home Office had kept them in daily awareness that the country was passing through one of its worst periods in living memory. The distress was extremely severe in the textile areas, particularly in Scotland where the unreformed poor law, excluding all able-bodied from relief and requiring a three-year residential qualification for others, was totally ineffective in dealing with large-scale industrial unemployment. A memorial from Paisley in February, for example, had drawn a grisly picture of long-standing and increasing destitution. In that one town there were 17,000 persons enduring slow starvation and the local relief committee with failing funds was being compelled to reduce steadily its already inadequate assistance. But some towns in England were in almost as desperate a plight. From Leeds the mayor and council reported in July that never within the recollection of its oldest inhabitants was the distress so universal, prolonged and exhausting. A charitable subscription of over £6,000 had been expended the previous winter in relieving the poor within the town. Nevertheless, the number of families assisted by the workhouse board had doubled since 1838. In the first quarter of 1842 some 4,000 families, estimated at 16,000 persons out of a total population of 80,000, were on the workhouse books. In outdoor relief the expenditure had gone up 23 per cent, from £3,900 during April–June 1841 to £5,200 in the same three months of 1842; and unemployment was still rising.[1]

Paisley and Leeds, however, were but items in a general catalogue of misery which included areas as different and far apart as Manchester, Marylebone, Clydeside, and the Potteries. Almost everywhere the story was the same. Poor law relief and local charity were both breaking down under the strain of the unprecedented calls made upon them. Early in May Peel was arranging with the Archbishop of Canterbury, the Bishop of London and the Home Secretary for the issue of a Queen's Letter inviting contributions in churches and chapels throughout the country for relief of distress in

[1] 40612 fos. 105, 114.

Lancashire and Scotland. Later in the month the cabinet decided to open a public subscription headed by £500 from the Royal Bounty, and to advance money from the Treasury for immediate distribution under a revived City of London Committee.[1] Even this could only be a partial alleviation; and though the weather was good and the harvest promised well, ripening corn in the fields was no remedy for starvation in the streets. Everything pointed to the situation growing worse before it grew better and towards the end of July Graham was growing anxious for the return of the Brigade of Guards from Canada before the onset of winter. He had reason for alarm. Chartism and the League, linked by Sturge's Complete Suffrage movement, already showed some signs of coalescing. In the spring of 1842, for the first time since 1831, there seemed the possibility of an alliance between middle- and lower-class agitators for a combined attack on aristocratic government. The League leaders, with falling funds and baffled minds, were talking in private of a campaign to withhold taxes and, more dangerous still, of closing down factories to produce unemployment on such a scale that the government would be forced into submission. Though their correspondence on these subversive themes remained, fortunately for the League, unknown to the Home Office, there were enough open threats by lesser men in the movement to be relayed to the government or reported in the national press. In July there were public memorials from Manchester and Salford urging their local M.P.s to stop supplies to the government. The same month a meeting of Chartists in Manchester sent a warning to Peel that the League members were preparing to excite the people to a breach of the peace by withholding taxes and closing down their mills. Even if nothing can.e of these threats, there was the contingent and scarcely less serious danger that urban authorities in the disturbed areas would refuse to act in a crisis. Already men of the class on whom the government were primarily dependent for preserving civil order in the provinces were uttering the language of disaffection. The mayors of Bolton and Stockport said they would not be responsible for keeping order until ministers made concessions to popular demands. The Provost of Paisley said he would not sanction the use of military to repress industrial disorder. The

[1] 40434 fos. 65, 81.

Borough Reeve of Manchester said that magistrates would resign rather than be the tools of aristocratic government. All these men were members of the League, as were the great majority of the J.P.s in Manchester, Stockport and Bolton.[1] To these ominous texts the itinerant lecturers of the League were supplying inflammatory chapter and verse.

The conventional language of the opposition politicians and newspapers in London, fixing responsibility for the state of the country on the prime minister and the government, took on a deeper significance when transferred to the provinces. Placards charging the government with direct responsibility for the sufferings of the people had already appeared in the industrial areas. One, headed 'MURDER', was printed at the expense of members of the League and issued for sale at a shop in Manchester kept by a printer under contract to the League. Cobden denied that the League was responsible for the placard; but this, like many of his other statements at this time, was more than disingenuous. In May 1841 a violent article had appeared in the *Anti-Bread Tax Circular* under the heading 'Murder'. Supported by a quotation from *Lamentations* iv, 9 ('they that be slain by the sword are better than they that be slain with hunger') it had argued that those who upheld the Corn Laws 'are virtually the murderers of their fellow creatures'.[2] It was a generation given to wild, emotional language, of which the Old Testament offered a rich and authoritative store; and no doubt most of it expressed feelings rather than intentions. Nevertheless, for the first time for many years, words like murder and assassination were beginning to be tossed up in the sea of angry recrimination that marked the summer of 1842. At a meeting of free-traders in London during July one speaker mentioned a conveniently nameless acquaintance who had asserted his readiness to assassinate Peel. While the speaker piously added that such extreme measures could not be approved, he opined that few tears would be shed on the day of Peel's funeral.[3]

Violence was in the air that sultry summer. On May 30 Peel

[1] N. McCord, *The Anti-Corn Law League* (1958), p. 127.
[2] A. G. Rose, 'The Plug Riots of 1842 in Lancashire and Cheshire' (*Trans. Lancashire & Cheshire Antiquarian Soc.*, LXVII, 81).
[3] Halévy, *Age of Peel and Cobden*, pp. 24–5.

was called out of the House by Graham to be told that an attempt had been made on the life of the queen as she was returning in her carriage to Buckingham Palace. In a state of visible emotion the prime minister went back to his place and moved the adjournment of the debate (the third reading of the income tax bill). He then left immediately to attend a meeting of the Privy Council hastily convened to examine the prisoner, a young carpenter called Francis. Another, less serious, attempt followed early in July. What Graham described as 'an hump-backed Boy of an idiotic appearance'[1] named Bean presented a rusty flintlock pistol of decidedly non-lethal capabilities at the queen as she was going along the Mall to the Chapel Royal. Neither of the two culprits had any political affiliations or motives; but assassination is an infectious activity and not all pistols could be guaranteed to be as innocuous as Bean's.

In August all the sweltering discontents of that hot summer came to a head. In many industrial areas long-continued unemployment had driven many of the men to leave their homes and go round the countryside in large bands, ostensibly begging for charity but over-awing the neighbourhoods through which they passed by their mere appearance and numbers. Where the operatives were not actually out of work, they were often on short time and reduced wages. Between April and June there were sporadic strikes and disputes between masters and men. In July an attempted reduction of wages at a colliery near Longton in Staffordshire precipitated a general turnout of colliers throughout the Potteries. The men on strike went round the pits extinguishing the steam engines and pulling the plugs from the boilers so that they could not be restarted. Crowds of them, many thousands strong, moved into the adjoining counties of Shropshire and Cheshire in an attempt to enlarge the area of stoppage. Simultaneously cotton-mill owners in the Ashton and Stalybridge districts of north-east Cheshire began a series of wage reductions. The operatives reacted with meetings to consider strike action at which local Chartists harangued the workers. By the beginning of August the two streams of industrial unrest merged into a violent movement to withhold all labour until the Charter was the law of the land. Colliers and mill-hands armed with bludgeons, pitch-forks, flails and pikes went round in their thousands,

[1] 40447 f. 31.

closing down pits and mills, breaking into buildings locked against them, and requisitioning money and food by scarcely less forcible methods. In some places the houses of magistrates and clergy, public buildings, police-stations, and workhouses were looted and set on fire. Two policemen were killed in Manchester and attacks made on the railroads. The original disturbances were in Staffordshire, Cheshire and Lancashire; but the example of disorder was soon followed in Yorkshire, Warwickshire, Tyneside, and parts of Wales and Scotland. By this time the Chartist leaders were being carried along, exhilarated or frightened according to their temperament, by the violence raging around them. The Chartist Convention Council meeting fixed for mid-August in Manchester showed the familiar divisions between personalities and policies. But before the Convention broke up, McDouall secured the issue of a fierce manifesto to the working classes, appealing to the God of battles and urging a universal strike.

Meanwhile the authorities in London had already begun their counter measures. On 13 August the alarming reports from Manchester were confirmed by the arrival of various magistrates from the disturbed areas. The 16th was the anniversary of Peterloo and it was feared that there would be a particular outbreak of demonstrations on that red-letter day in the working-class calendar. Peel promptly called the cabinet together and it was agreed to despatch a battalion of Guards north by rail the same evening. Dispensing with the usual formalities a Privy Council was summoned to meet at Windsor later that day for the issue of a royal proclamation warning all subjects against attending tumultuous meetings or committing any acts calculated to disturb the public peace.[1] Under this energetic leadership the local authorities, many of whom had seemed paralysed during the first week of rioting, began to recover their nerve and the overstrained military forces in the industrial districts reasserted their power. Where strong forces of troops and police were mobilised, the rioters usually dispersed to reassemble elsewhere. But in several places the troops had to open fire and there were a number of casualties, including a few killed (notably at Preston and Burslem) before order was restored. The speed with which troop reinforcements came up by rail from London and the south of England had,

[1] VL, I, 422.

however, a disconcerting effect on the rioters. By the end of August the worst was over and Graham could tell Peel that every day that passed was strengthening the hands of the authorities and weakening the instigators of disorder.[1]

The work of co-ordinating the efforts of police, magistrates and military, arresting ringleaders and preventing further outbreaks, was one that fell on Graham's department. But throughout the days of crisis the prime minister remained in close touch with the Home Office. One personal anxiety he was burdened with was the exposed position of his wife and children in the very heart of the disturbed area. Discreet arrangements were made to station a small detachment of cavalry where they could intercept any threatened march on Drayton or reinforce its defences if attacked. But in the confusion and ignorance of the early days this was a precaution rather than an absolute safeguard. On 15 August Peel snatched a couple of days to see his wife at Upton, the Warwickshire residence of their elder daughter whose first child had been born three months earlier. He arrived to find that Julia, anxious for the safety of their younger children, had already returned home. He followed her to Drayton and while there heard a report that the queen had been assassinated. Though the next down-train brought a contradiction of this alarmist rumour, he urged Graham to take special measures at Windsor for her protection. On the evening of the 17th he was back in London and next day went through all the provincial correspondence with Graham at the Home Office. London itself was under threat of disturbance, though the existence of the Metropolitan Police made it unlikely that the violence of the north would be repeated in the capital. A meeting at Lincoln's Inn Fields on 18 August was promptly countered by Graham with an order to disperse the crowd and arrest the ringleaders. Chartist meetings at Kennington Common and Paddington were met with a similar brisk demonstration of executive authority, backed by a strategic disposition of men and guns. Some twenty Chartists were arrested and the peace of the metropolis preserved by vigorous co-operation between the Home Office and the magistrates. Friday, 19 August, was a particularly arduous day. Peel and Graham, dining late at Whitehall Gardens on the Thursday, had their meal interrupted by

[1] 40447 f. 92.

a report from Mayne, the police commissioner, of a great gathering at Lincoln's Inn Fields. They promptly adjourned to the Home Office and Peel was there until the small hours of the morning, supervising police and troop dispositions to prevent the demonstrators from moving out of the City into Westminster. Next day he was back with Graham, interviewing the provincial stipendiary magistrates who had been summoned to London for consultation and conferring with the Lord Mayor, Sheriffs and the Attorney-General.

In the midst of all the hubbub he found a few minutes during the afternoon to write to Julia, reassuring her of his own safety and pressing her to return to London if there was any danger. News had come through that morning of fresh disturbances in the Potteries. It was reported that Beaudesert, Lord Anglesey's country house in Staffordshire, was threatened and that the men would then march on to Drayton. The afternoon train brought no confirmation of this. Nevertheless:

> I cannot tell you [he wrote] how uneasy I was made by the report brought from Birmingham by the first train. Remember to come up to me *at once* without the children tomorrow or Sunday if there be the slightest cause for it. Do not run the slightest risk, for your presence could not add to the security of the House.[1]

An alarm there had been at Drayton but Julia, a soldier's daughter, was not to be frightened away from her home by mere alarms. A brief note on Friday which arrived in London the same evening told her husband all was well and that he was not to come down himself. It was followed by a longer one on the Sunday:

> My own dearest love,
> During the whole of this late tumultuous scene and expected attack I felt anxious only to save *you* from an alarm for us, lest you might think things exaggerated. You will know that I was never guilty of a sentimental or ignoble fear. Our arrangements were quickly and vigorously made and should have been equal to an attack from two or three hundred till assistance had come. But then we expected three or four thousand. I am confident, however, that no men actually attacking doors and windows here would have left this place alive.
> I sent for Mr. Grundy and desired him to see to the preparation of

[1] Peel MSS.; 40447 fos. 50–94.

the supply of water. You see we were armed at all points! I have felt *furious* with the vile mob who contemplated an attack. I received a note last night from Mr. Bonham who sent us some carbines and ammunition by a most trustworthy person. When you come from the station do so as quietly as possible. I shall take care not to say when I expect you.

> Believe me,
> Ever most affectionately,
> JULIA PEEL.[1]

Like her husband, Julia's spirits always rose in an emergency. All her anxiety was for her husband.

Peel himself was clearly in need of rest after the strains of the parliamentary session. He had been considerably affected by the attempt on the queen's life at the end of May, more so indeed than the queen herself. Tiredness probably added to his nervousness about Julia. When he returned to London on 17 August he had seen his doctor, Seymour, about pains in his head from which he had been suffering and on his advice had been immediately cupped, with beneficial results. But there was little respite in his activities. At the end of August came the royal visit to Scotland on which his presence was required. With distress as severe and disorders almost as widespread as in England, it was hardly an auspicious moment to visit the northern kingdom. But the tour had been long planned; its postponement would be psychologically damaging; and, as Peel observed to Graham on 25 August, there was no more danger to the queen in Scotland than in England. All they could do was to take precautions, avoid the troubled districts, and hope for the best. The court party went north in the traditional nautical manner on board the old royal yacht. Peel employed a more utilitarian means of transport. Sending his carriage ahead of him with his private secretary Drummond, he and Aberdeen left Drayton on 29 August, travelled by rail as far as Darlington, and then by post to Edinburgh where they arrived the following day. Hazy weather delayed the *Royal George* and it was not until 1 September that she was towed by two steam tugs to Granton pier, where Peel and Aberdeen, clearly distrustful of sailing-ship schedules, had been waiting since four o'clock in the morning.

---

[1] Peel, *Letters*, p. 204.

From the start a certain air of improvisation and confusion surrounded the tour. Defective signals and Victoria's own restless nature resulted in inadequate notice being given for the queen's reception in Edinburgh. There was an initial difficulty in clearing the traffic for the royal procession in which Peel's hackney carriage formed an inconspicuous item. The provost and magistrates were not present to offer the keys of the city; and the bodyguard of Royal Archers hastily marching to meet the queen ran into the escort of dragoons and were thrown back in some disarray. The Town Council, abandoning their formal preparations on the news of the queen's imminent arrival, scrambled into their own carriages to catch a glimpse of her as she passed along the Portobello road to Dalkeith Palace where the Duke of Buccleuch was her host. An improvised second royal procession later the same day and a special visit to the Castle two days later soothed wounded Edinburgh susceptibilities; but the general impression of mismanagement persisted throughout the visit. A last-minute scare of scarlet fever in Holyrood made it necessary to transfer the official court reception to Dalkeith and there were two postponements while the harassed Buccleuch made preparations for receiving in his own residence the hundreds of loyal subjects from all over Scotland who were anxious to see the young queen. When the royal party began its round of the great aristocratic houses it was evident that the Scottish peers who entertained the queen had put themselves to great trouble and expense to meet their long-disused social obligations. Peel estimated that Lord Breadalbane had spent not less than £10,000 on his preparations and he quoted with relish when writing to Graham the remark of the schoolmaster at Aberfeldy. 'It's a vary proper thing for Breadalbane to give his countenance to the Queen, but he's spending a muckle deal o'siller.' Fashionable caterers and smart waiters had been brought up from London to rub shoulders with Scottish ballad-singers and Highland pipers. In the evening bonfires, illuminations, and fireworks (when rain permitted) lit up the summer landscape. Yet nearly every house where they stayed—Dalkeith, Scone, Taymouth Castle and Drummond Castle—gave Peel the impression of derelict mansions hastily put in readiness with rooms inadequately furnished and unwilling fires smoking in cold hearths.

In the intervals between public duties Peel climbed Arthur's Seat in company with Prince Albert and Buccleuch, accompanied the queen in pouring rain to Dalmeny, the seat of Lord Rosebery, and with Aberdeen and Anson attended Sunday service in the parish church at Dalkeith. It had been thought inadvisable on security grounds for Victoria to go herself and it was hoped, as Peel expressed it, that 'the presence of the Queen's ministers at the Kirk might do something to repair the absence of the Queen'.[1] On Tuesday, 6 September, the royal party left Queensferry by steamer to cross to the north shore of the Forth. Confusion and crowding still prevailed in the official arrangements and for a while Peel was left standing in the bows of the ferry-boat containing the carriages until beckoned on board the royal steamer. The tour then proceeded through Perth and Dunkeld to Taymouth Castle, the home of Lord Breadalbane, where a display of fireworks and Highland dancing, accompanied by a liberal distribution of whisky, took place against the familiar background of pouring rain. On Peel's advice the project of extending the trip as far as Dunrobin in distant Sutherlandshire was abandoned and on 15 September the queen re-embarked at Granton for the return voyage, accomplished speedily if unromantically in a commercial steamer. Peel left with Aberdeen the same day to travel back by the route they had come.

Despite the unreliability of weather and sail the visit from a political point of view had been a decided success. The enthusiasm and loyalty had been tremendous, even among the unemployed Scottish colliers. Nevertheless it had been a nervous operation. The lack of organisation and the defective security arrangements had been a constant source of anxiety to the prime minister. The excitement, the boisterous curiosity of the public, the physical pressure of the crowds which gathered round the queen's open carriage made him fear, as he reported to Graham, 'not one but a hundred accidents'. In Edinburgh, where the civic authorities had been particularly inefficient, a mob of about fifty or sixty 'Chartists and low blackguards', as Peel described them, had been allowed to run alongside the royal carriage all the way during the official procession on 3 September. Two lessons at least seemed clear to Peel. '*Private* tours in Scotland by the Sovereign', he wrote to the Home Secretary

[1] 40447 f. 126.

on 14 September, 'are not very practicable.' And as soon as he was back at Drayton he wrote to Haddington at the Admiralty on the need to procure an official steam yacht for the queen's use.[1]

For himself it had been far from a holiday. Apart from his anxieties for the queen's safety, the round of official functions and the constant arrival of red boxes from London had left him little time for relaxation. 'I have no great anxiety for the repetition of a similar visit,' he wrote dryly to Graham on hearing of the queen's safe arrival at Woolwich, 'happy as have been all the circumstances attending this.'[2] But at least it had reassured him that loyalty to the monarch was a deep-seated feeling among the great mass of the people. He himself had not been without some marks of public esteem. Passers-by had saluted him at Dalkeith; at Perth, where the party stopped for an address by the Lord Provost, he had been singled out by the spectators for a special cheer in which there were only a few discordant notes. Along with the prince, Buccleuch, and Aberdeen, he had received the freedom of the city of Edinburgh and had made a speech recalling his visit with George IV twenty years earlier. After going through Stirling and Linlithgow his hands were bruised and swollen from the constant handshaking with the crowd which pressed on both sides of his carriage. It was an experience he endured with some distaste. 'It is better, however,' he wrote to his wife, 'than having stones thrown.'[3]

II

By 22 September Peel was back in Whitehall Gardens to deal with the aftermath of the August disorders. Special Commissions had been appointed to deal with the rioters captured in Staffordshire, Cheshire and Lancashire, and a number of leading Chartists had also been subsequently arrested. Against the latter the law officers advised simple charges of conspiracy since treason would be difficult to sustain by any direct proof. A state trial of the Chartist delegates

---

[1] RA/A 13/12; Peel, II, 545.
[2] 40447 f. 168.
[3] For the Scottish tour generally see 40447 fos. 118–68; Graham (Sept. 1842); Peel MSS. (Peel to Lady Peel, 11, 12 Sept. 1842); Edinburgh Courant, 27 Aug.–24 Sept. 1842; Peel, II, 542–3; Peel, Letters, pp. 205–11; Vera Watson, The Queen at Home (1952), pp. 71–6.

was avoided and they were left to make their appearance in court along with the ordinary rioters. In the event they received considerably lighter sentences than the most of their convicted fellow-prisoners. O'Connor himself escaped entirely on a technicality. It was in fact difficult to establish any real connection between the Chartist Convention at Manchester and the violence in the country at large. In general the mass of evidence before the Home Office pointed to economic rather than political causes for the disturbances in the industrial areas. Shaw, the chief commissioner of police at Manchester, was emphatic that the whole affair had been primarily one of wages and that the political element was not dangerous. On this score the sympathies of the government were entirely with the workmen. At the start of the trouble in Staffordshire Graham reported to Peel that the masters were more to blame than the men. He was particularly anxious not to play the game of the Anti-Corn Law League, as he put it, by offering military protection to employers who reduced wages and increased profits at the expense of their workpeople. On 25 August he instructed General Arbuthnot, the new military commander of the Northern and Midland Districts, that while defending property against looters and men at work against intimidation by strikers, he should do everything he could to remove the suspicion that the government and the military were prepared to use force to make the workmen resume employment at what they considered inadequate wages. He added, moreover, that wherever the men had reason for complaint, Arbuthnot and his officers should urge employers to meet their grievances. Writing from Drayton next day Peel completely endorsed his distinction between the preservation of public order and the protection of masters against 'just and peaceable demands for a rise of wages'.

Up in Scotland the problems of employers and men had continued to exercise Peel's mind. 'I wish,' he wrote to Graham from Dalkeith on 2 September,

> we could with perfect safety and without adding to the excitement which prevails, appoint a Commission for the purpose of ascertaining the real truth as to the state of the relations between the employers and employed in the Collieries. I think it would be found that there are practical grievances—possibly not to be redressed by law—of

which the employed have just reason to complain. What law cannot effect, exposure might. I strongly suspect the profits in many of these collieries would enable the receivers of them to deal with much more liberality towards their workmen than they do. . . . Without appointing a Commission, could we get such a man as Horner, or one of the best of your Poor Law Commissioners, to make a tour through Staffordshire and Shropshire, and get at some part of the truth at least, without ostentatious enquiry.[1]

Graham acted immediately on the suggestion. A week later he sent Peel a confidential memorandum on the grievances of the colliers and promised a commission of enquiry as soon as the men returned to work. He added for good measure that he proposed in the next poor law bill to deal with the problem of apprenticeship which in the coalpits was 'slavery disguised'.[2] The condition of the coal mines in Staffordshire, Yorkshire, and Lancashire, often run on insufficient capital with the owners contracting for the work with gang-leaders or 'butties', was in fact among the worst in the kingdom. In November, when there was a renewed threat of industrial strife in Staffordshire, Peel wrote roundly to Graham that 'some of our Coal owners seem most hard-hearted and infatuated'.[3]

From the government's point of view the most disturbing aspect of the August rioting was the equivocal behaviour of some of the local magistrates and the fomenting of disorder by the Anti-Corn Law League. As early as 20 August Graham was contemplating a strict investigation into the conduct of those radical borough magistrates who had notoriously fallen short of their duty. During the next fortnight the Home Office accumulated a whole file of complaints against individual J.P.s and in the first week of September Graham instituted a formal enquiry into the allegations. But though there were ample grounds for suspicion, it was not easy to obtain proof of criminal negligence as distinct from timidity or supineness. A uniformly high level of efficiency could not be expected from an amateur magistracy and one of the lessons of 1842 was that it might be better to provide more professional jurisdiction in the provinces than to provoke a political wrangle by dismissing

---

[1] 40447 fos. 56, 94, 120; Graham (Shaw to Graham, 23 Aug., Graham to Gen. Arbuthnot, 25 Aug., Peel to Graham, 26 Aug. 1842).
[2] 40447 f. 134.   [3] Graham (20 Nov. 1842).

unsatisfactory J.P.s. A county court bill was already under consideration by the government and Peel was ready to discuss, as he wrote in October, 'how long the administration of justice can be committed to unpaid, and therefore to a considerable degree, irresponsible dispensers of it'.[1] Graham possibly still hankered after some exemplary dismissals. But at the start of December Peel gave a firm ruling that no magistrate should be removed except on specific evidence and even then (unless proved in a court of law) not unless he had been given an opportunity to defend himself. This effectively put disciplinary action out of the question. In the end the Home Secretary left the borough magistrates alone and contented himself with a circular letter to Lords Lieutenant on the conduct of the county magistrates during the disturbances.

The other proposal which he favoured was the appointment of assistant barristers to reinforce the unpaid magistrates at Quarter Sessions. This met with a cautious reserve on the part of the prime minister which was soon justified by the unconcealed opposition to it from cabinet colleagues like Goulburn and Wellington. It was not easy in fact for a Conservative administration to sponsor a proposal which would diminish the status and discourage the services of the country gentry.[2] The defects of local authorities revealed by the disturbances were only partial. After their initial hesitation the magistracy in general had responded well to the exhortations of the Home Office and the prompt military reinforcement of the threatened areas. At Bolton, Wigan, and Preston, for example, the civic authorities had on their own initiative prevented the entry of mobs of strikers trying to effect a general turnout; and Graham had been impressed by the assistance given by the mayors of Manchester and Birmingham despite the fact that they were both politically opposed to the government.[3]

The Home Secretary himself by his energy and commonsense had done much to ensure that the administrative defects for which he was seeking a remedy had resulted in no great national disaster. Given the fragmentary means at its disposal—the untrained JPs, a handful of stipendiary magistrates, a limited number of full-time

[1] Graham (12 Oct. 1842).   [2] Cf. *Graham*, I. 333–6.
[3] 40447 f. 86. See also generally F. C. Mather, *Public Order in the Age of the Chartists* (1959), pp. 64–5, 228–31.

police, and as a last resource the yeomanry and the professional troops—the executive had met and mastered the crisis with reasonable firmness and efficiency. Though Graham under the stress of the August events occasionally spoke in rhetorical terms of 'a servile insurrection' and convinced himself at one point that there was an organised movement throughout the country directed by delegates and long prepared,[1] he had at no time lost his nerve or his judgement. Never absent from his post in London for a single day during the whole of August, he set an example which invigorated the whole unwieldy structure of command stretching from the Home Office and the Horse Guards to the back-streets of Manchester and Wigan. On the eve of his departure for Scotland Peel sent a message of sympathy to his colleague for the labour and strain which he had undergone in the preceding weeks. 'I know no one', added the prime minister, 'who could have gone through them with so much temper, firmness and resolution combined, as you have manifested. Everyone interested in the peace and well-being of this country ought to feel, as I feel, very grateful to you.'[2]

There remained, however, one covert aspect of the 1842 disorder against which the firmness and activity of the Home Office seemed an inadequate shield. At the start of the trouble there was a widespread impression that the Anti-Corn Law League by reducing wages and closing mills had deliberately invoked disorder in order to bring pressure on the government. In Chartist mythology the Plug Plot, as the riots were known in Lancashire, was long attributed to a conspiracy of League mill-owners. At the time this belief was shared by many Conservatives and was given pointed expression in the Tory press. The language of League spokesmen in the preceding months and the fact that many League manufacturers were implicated in the wage reductions and lock-outs made this a natural conclusion. 'I consider the conduct of the Masters', John Gladstone had written to the Home Secretary on 19 August, 'particularly the radical portion of them, as the originating causes [sc. of the disorders] and I hope that they will take warning from what is passing sufficient to induce them to adopt a different line of conduct.'[3] Even if the League as an organisation could be acquitted

---

[1] See his letters to Wellington, Buccleuch and Egerton in Graham (20 Aug. 1842).
[2] ibid. (28 Aug. 1842).   [3] ibid.

of guilt, it could not be absolved from blame. The Chartists had certainly tried to turn the industrial troubles to their own purposes; but the Chartists themselves were caught up in an angry and emotional atmosphere to which the League had powerfully contributed. Not only economic distress but political agitation was prevalent all over the midland and northern industrial areas; and as an organ of agitation the League was second to none. Cobden, Bright, Sturge, George Thompson, Moore, Acland and many lesser orators of the League had helped to produce among the working classes not only a sense of unendurable evils wilfully inflicted but an apocalyptic expectation of some sudden dramatic change. Even in July Graham felt that the League had held out 'wicked temptations to open violence',[1] and the events of the following months seemed a complete vindication of his language. It was an opinion shared by authorities in the affected areas. 'I almost fear', wrote Sir Charles Shaw, the police commissioner at Manchester, at the height of the disturbances, 'that the anti-Corn Law League are still blind to the fact that their paid lecturers worked the people up to frenzy, making them ready to imbibe any folly, even that of "Chartism". It would be of great benefit to the District if they would suspend their meetings for a month or six weeks.'[2] The doubt in the minds of the ministers was whether the League had acted not blindly but with deliberate intent to exploit human misery as a weapon against the government. To Peel there seemed grounds at least for enquiring more closely into the connection between the League and the riots.

On 26 August, a few days before he left for Scotland, he asked Graham to collect from the reports of the League Conference earlier in the year those passages which bore on the present disturbances. He continued:

> It would not be impossible for a skilful person devoting his attention to it, and with a certain command of money, to discover much important matter with regard to the proceedings of the League. First, who were the agents employed by them? What was their character, and what their language and aim? For them the League is morally at least responsible. The course taken by such a fellow as Acland should be scrutinised. It would be feasible to trace the payments made to him. I have little doubt his expenses at *Tamworth* were paid by the

[1] Graham (letter to J. Sandars, 30 July 1842).   [2] *ibid.* (23 Aug. 1842).

League. There is a paper called the Anti-Bread Tax Circular. This should be carefully examined, its connection with the League if possible ascertained, and then selections from its language made. . . . If the nature of your secret service account precludes the application of it to this object, that need not be an impediment to the incurring of any necessary expense. . . . If we can bring no legal offence home to the League, it would have an excellent effect, having collected our evidence and arranged our proofs, to arraign the League in a careful publication, so careful as to admit of no reply, at the bar of public opinion—to bring forward the presumptive evidence that the League was at the bottom of these disorders.

Of course the names of all the members of the League should be ascertained, the acts of the members in respect of the stoppages of mills and the time and circumstance of stoppage carefully scrutinised. . . . A comparison of the exciting language used by the same men, as members of the League, with the language of the Proclamations issued by them and the acts done by them as Magistrates, would be a proper lesson to some of them. There is a prating self-sufficient fellow of the name of John Brooke at Manchester who ought never to hold up his head again. I see the mob at Manchester justly observed 'the same men that incited us to outrage yesterday are committing us to prison today'. I cannot tell you how strongly I feel the advantages of a *thorough* exposure, *founded on proof*, of the Anti-Corn Law League.[1]

Graham went to work at once on this suggestion. On the advice of Follett, the Solicitor General, he obtained the services of a rising young barrister (and later judge) Montague Smith who, wrote the Home Secretary with pleasurable anticipation, 'will track the Anti-Corn Law Leaguers in all their turns, and prepare evidence to convict them, if not legally yet morally, and beyond a doubt, of concert and full participation in the Councils which led to this dangerous outbreak'.

The material for investigation was certainly bulky enough. It was not until November that the dossier against the League was in Graham's hands. Four copies were privately printed, one of which was sent to Peel in the middle of the month. The question was what to do with the document now that it was ready. Graham's idea was to turn it into a pamphlet under some attractive title. But this involved awkward problems of editing, publication and government

[1] *ibid.*

sponsorship. Peel showed the paper to Croker who was staying with him at Drayton at the time. Croker had previously made an offer to work the material up for an article in the *Quarterly* but on reading the paper he thought it should appear as a pamphlet which he could then review. He was emphatic, however, that the evidence collected did not prove the complicity of the League in the actual riots, only their responsibility in bringing about a situation in which rioting was inevitable. This was probably no more than Peel and Graham had expected. In his own advice to Graham the prime minister showed more than a little dexterity as a publicist. The paper should be cut down to a more readable length; there should be no hint of official inspiration; and there should be no gratuitous advertisement for the arguments of the League against the Corn Laws. Everything should be concentrated on demonstrating the moral responsibility of the League for the August outbreaks. An appeal should be made to the working classes by pointing to the contrast between the language of the League magistrates before and after the riots and between the loss of wages suffered by the men and the savings made by the masters. The propertied classes on the other hand should be reminded of their fears at the time of the riots and the folly of supporting an organisation whose activities were liable to produce a repetition of such scenes in future.

> I would try to show that the loss of wages, the disturbance of the public peace, the cost of suppressing it, are all attributable to the League. The strong point, that which will tell among the people, among the working classes, is that they influenced and excited, that they made appeals to physical force, and when the People listened to the appeal and obeyed it, that then in the actual moment, the members of the League thought only of themselves. . . . In short my opinion is that detailed proof of systematic agitation on the part of the League is superfluous and that it will be advisable to confine the charge and the proof as much as possible to the one main prominent accusation against the League—that they are morally responsible for the outbreaks in August and for all the Mischief that flowed from it.[1]

Thus adjured Graham and Croker between them produced the famous article on 'Anti-Corn Law agitation' which, with some

[1] Graham (20 Nov. 1842); *Croker*, II, 389-90; 40448 f. 171. See also for this episode Graham (Peel to Graham, 26 Aug., Graham to Peel, 2 Sept. 1842); 40447 fos. 104, 344.

final revision by Peel, appeared in the *Quarterly* in December 1842. Portions of the article were also reprinted, on Graham's instructions, for distribution in cheap popular form.

In denouncing it as a dangerous, immoral and quasi-unconstitutional body, the government went as far as it could in striking back at the League. But their suspicions had gone beyond the actual facts. It had been the 'butties' of Mr. Sparrow, a Tory mine-owner, who had started the trouble among the colliers at Longton in June; and it was notice of wage-reductions by the Lees, Tory cotton manufacturers at Stalybridge, which was the first incident in the great turnout in the textile area in July.[1] Their example had been followed by Liberal and League mill-owners but there was no proof of any conspiracy among them. What had happened in reality was a series of industrial disputes, contagious but unorganised and unpolitical which the Chartists rather than the League endeavoured to exploit for political ends. Yet what had caused the rapid spread of violence and disorder was the preceding incitement and agitation. To this the League had contributed as much as any. The League leaders had talked both openly and privately of creating exactly the kind of situation that occurred in August. Individuals among them had played dubious roles in the actual disturbances. Bright, for example, closed down his mills at Rochdale when the turnout mobs entered the town. The League leadership itself had been torn between moderates and extremists. In fact the League had stopped short on the brink of illegality and their loud and disingenuous protestations of innocence—sometimes amounting as in Cobden's case to deliberate lying—concealed a lively fear that they had put themselves in danger of prosecution for the activities of their agents and their own provocative propaganda.[2] As it was, the violence of the 1842 disorders and the sharp counter-attacks of the Conservative press, followed by Croker's carefully documented indictment in the *Quarterly*, enabled the moderates of the League to win the victory over policy and direct its activities into more legal and constitutional channels. But it was many months before the fears, nervousness and strained tempers on both sides died down.

The riots and the prosecutions which followed crippled Chartism and frightened the League. They did little, however, to remove the

[1] Rose, 'Plug Riots of 1842', pp. 84–7.   [2] McCord, *op. cit.*, pp. 126–31.

economic causes of the disturbances. When the men returned to work, they did so mainly at the old wages, some at reduced rates; only a few obtained increases. Distress and widespread unemployment continued; and in some places the problem seemed endemic and insoluble. From Paisley, a town that haunted Peel all through 1842, came a memorial in December from the local clergy saying that despite the large grant made by the national Relief Committee, relief funds were almost exhausted together with all local sources of charity. There would soon be 10,000 persons without means of subsistence in the town for whom the choice would simply be one of starvation or crime.[1] If agitation was temporarily stilled, distress and disorder remained; and throughout the rest of the year the state of the industrial districts continued to gnaw at the minds of Peel and Graham. But all the proffered remedies seemed piecemeal; all attended by difficulties. Education and church extension were doubtless desirable, but there was little hope of persuading parliament to agree to financial support for the Anglican Establishment or even to a plan of national education. Graham even deprecated launching an enquiry into the lack of moral and religious instruction in the disturbed areas since it would only reveal 'brutal ignorance and heathenish irreligion' without being able to suggest a cure.

On a more mundane level, the August riots had drawn attention to the unpoliced condition of many industrial districts. Yet boroughs already had powers to create local police forces and other towns had the right to petition for borough status. A Rural Police Act of 1839 had even made it possible for county police forces to be set up. But the parsimony of local ratepayers and the anti-authoritarian prejudices of the general public made the evolution of a national police network a slow and painful process. The first wave of Chartist disorders had induced the Whig government in 1839 to bring in police bills for Birmingham, Bolton and Manchester. These at Peel's suggestion had resulted in the creation of police forces each under a Commissioner of Police directly supervised by the Home Office and working on the old preventive methods of the Metropolitan Police. In Manchester and Birmingham at least, as the Plug Riots proved, the experiment had been a success. But the Acts under which these forces operated expired in

[1] 40613 f. 53.

1842 when the local Watch Committees took over.[1] Peel had no doubt of the need for a professional police force in the provinces. But while the British public was grudgingly accommodating itself to this new feature of local administration, some stopgap measures were advisable. What was wanted in the industrial districts, he wrote in September, was some civil force capable of being called out quickly in an emergency but without the expense and unpopularity of the regular police. Graham, Wellington and Hardinge had already been at work on a scheme for organising army pensioners as an auxiliary military force in certain large towns like Manchester, Birmingham and Glasgow; and an Enrolled Pensioners Act the following session put on a statutory basis this useful local addition to the means of preserving order in the industrial areas.[2]

There were other ways of approaching the problem of industrial unrest which were less to the liking of the government. While Peel and Graham had a lively sympathy with the workmen on such matters as wages and truck, they recoiled instinctively from any notion of general legislative interference with industry. When a correspondent in September urged on Graham the statutory limitation of labour as a device for curing industrial depression, Peel expressed his conviction that nothing should be done to shorten hours of work for the sole purpose of preventing excessive production. It was difficult enough, he added, to impose such restrictions on moral grounds; on economic grounds it was next to impossible.[3] Similarly, though he recognised that the introduction of new machinery frequently led to a temporary decrease in the demand for human labour, all his instincts were against any attempt to limit artificially the development of industrial techniques. In his view the prosperity of the working classes was in the end inseparable from the prosperity of the manufacturers. The task of government was not to impede industrialisation but to soften its impact. For that he looked to his 1842 legislation, the revenue yield, the customs returns, and the prices of the main articles of consumption. In October he was studying Board of Trade figures for the price of

[1] Mather, op. cit., pp. 115–27.
[2] Graham (Peel to Graham, 18 Sept.; Graham to Wellington, 20 Aug.; Hardinge to Graham, 2 Sept. 1842); 40447 f. 130; Mather, op. cit., pp. 32, 89, 151.
[3] Graham (Peel to Graham, 18 Sept. 1842).

wheat and bread and urging an enquiry into the price of flour.

It had been one of the warmest summers in living memory and each time he travelled on the railroad between London and Tamworth he noted with a grateful eye the evidence of a bountiful harvest. Nature, if not man, had been kind to the government that year. The wheat crop proved to be 25 per cent heavier than in the two preceding years, and when this was known, bonded wheat kept in reserve was at once put on the market. As a result the price of British corn dropped steadily until by the end of the year the average price was only 40s a quarter compared with 62s 9d in January and 64s 5d in July.[1] When the agriculturalists began to complain of low prices, Peel reacted sharply. 'The danger is not low price from the tariff,' he wrote to Croker at the end of October, 'but low price from inability to consume, from the poor man giving up his pint of beer, and the man in the middling station giving up his joint of meat.' To Arbuthnot, who warned him that many ultra-Tories were still dissatisfied with the legislation of the previous session, he retorted that such men should look beyond their narrow interests and consider something more important to them and their property than the price of pigs or wheat. He quoted the case of Paisley, from the authorities of which he had just received a letter describing the distress, and to the relief of which he himself, with no connection with the town, had twice subscribed. There the poor were not even fit to emigrate. No rents were paid; no rates could be raised. There had been 150 bankruptcies among the local manufacturers; private charity was exhausted. That was the worst but not the only case.

> My firm belief is that you could not have during the coming winter the high prices of the last four years and at the same time tranquillity and security for property. . . . The true friend to the 'astounded' and complaining Ultra is the man who would avert the consequences which would inevitably follow if some of them could have their way.

When Sir Charles Burrell, Conservative M.P. for Shoreham in Sussex, grumbled to Fremantle the chief whip about the effect of

---

[1] *Annual Register*, 1842, p. 377; D. G. Barnes, *Hist. of the English Corn Laws* (1930), p. 253.

the tariff in lowering agricultural prices and criticised the official thanksgiving for the harvest ordered by the Queen's Council for 2 October, Peel commented tartly that

> this is the first intimation I have had that the thanksgiving for a good harvest was deemed 'inappropriate'. . . . If Sir Charles had such cases before him as I have before me of thousands and tens of thousands in want of food and employment, at Greenock, Paisley, Edinburgh, and a dozen large towns in the manufacturing districts, he would not expect me to rend my garments in despair if 'some excellent jerked beef from South America' should get into the English market, and bring down meat from 7½d. or 8d. a pound.[1]

At the heart of Peel's policy was now the conviction that the only way to overcome both the human misery and the social threat was to increase the purchasing power of the masses. Poor law, charity, schemes for encouraging emigration, were only palliatives. Steady employment and cheap food were the only permanent remedies. They were remedies moreover which would benefit all classes. As he had told Croker in August, 'We must make this country a cheap country for living, and thus induce parties to remain and settle here, enable them to consume more, by having more to spend'. In this he was, ironically enough, on common ground with some of the more intelligent Chartists. At the start of the year the Scottish *Chartist Circular* had argued in a leading article that:

> It is not of over-production that we have to complain; it is of our utter inability in consequence of the oppression we endure to obtain the means requisite for a sufficient consumption of the fruits of our national industry. An enlightened and popular Legislation would by securing to us the blessings of good and cheap government, and by encouraging trade at home, have placed within our reach, the abundant means of supplying all our reasonable wants, which would have rendered the power of production by automaton agency, a blessing instead of a curse; but the heathen 'Exclusives' who superintend the destinies of this injured nation instead of giving every possible facility to industry, have by enormous taxes which they have imposed on every necessary of life, rendered the working millions unable to purchase the products of their mutual labour.[2]

[1] 40476 f. 205; *Peel*, II, 530–3.   [2] 29 Jan. 1842.

There was little in this with which Peel would basically have disagreed. Certainly it would not have occurred to many to think that the government had pursued a Chartist policy or that the Chartists were, in fiscal matters at least, good Peelites. But there were more ways of helping the poor than Ashley or Oastler were prepared to consider. Peel's apparent obsession with tariffs and finance had its human and social side. Indeed, among all the remedies for the condition of England problem, the broad economic road along which he was leading the country offered perhaps the most immediate, practical and comprehensive way out from the country's miseries which any government in 1842 could have devised.

At least the experience of that tumultuous year convinced Peel that he must press on with the relaxation of the tariff. Butter and cheese must follow meat and cereals; even sugar must be looked at once more. It was reserved for Graham, however, the man who more than any other had come to share Peel's inner thoughts and feelings, to make the most startling observation of that long year of distress and disorder. The occasion was a discussion of the relatively minor question of colonial preference. Stanley in March had virtually promised the Canadians free entry into Britain for their corn if they would provide a safeguard against abuse of that concession by imposing a duty on American corn coming into Canada.[1] Though the Canadian legislature in October had done this, Graham was afraid of renewed discontent among the British agriculturalists and was inclined towards a postponement of any change in the existing Canadian corn duties. In a letter to Peel in December he emphasised the inexpediency of tampering so soon with the new corn law in the 1843 session. Nevertheless, he used one argument that was a revelation of the extent to which the whole principle of protection had been undermined in the thoughts of some of the cabinet. 'It is a question of time', he wrote. 'The next change in the Corn Laws must be to an open trade. . . . But the next change must be the last; it is not prudent to hurry it; next Session is too soon; and as you cannot make a decisive alteration, it is far wiser to make none.'[2]

[1] For the text of this letter see *Annual Register*, 1842, pp. [335-7.
[2] *Peel*, II, 551.

The end of 1842 came with no sign that the new year would offer any better dispensation than the old. The prime minister still stood, as HB the great cartoonist of the day portrayed him in November,[1] between the snapping crocodile of the League and the couched lion of the agricultural interest, brandishing his Corn Law in one hand and his tariff in the other. Whether either beast could be tamed, and how long they could be kept apart, were questions on which much future British political development depended. The industrial depression continued with its gaunt companions, unemployment and starvation; and it had been joined, if farmers and landlords were to be believed, by agricultural distress. The success of Peel's tariff experiment still hung in the balance and even the revenue had not recovered. An impoverished population and a contracting economy had inevitable effects on public finance. In the last quarter of the year excise, customs, stamps, and assessed taxes were all down by an amount which, if continued throughout the whole financial year, would more than absorb the whole yield of the new income tax. Though ministers had reason to congratulate themselves on their refusal to embark on the tariff experiment without the reinsurance of the new tax, the revenue from that source was coming in with painful slowness. The reduction in import duties under the 1842 budget legislation had taken effect at once, but it was six or more months before the machinery for the income tax assessments could be set up and the actual collection of money commence. As a result the second of the half-yearly instalments was not collected until after the financial year had ended. A serious financial miscalculation had in fact been made and for a time the revenue was

[1] In a sketch entitled 'A Pleasant Situation'.

running far below expenditure. Like its Whig predecessors Peel's ministry was heading inevitably for yet another deficit.

When the cabinet met at the end of October for the first round of pre-sessional discussions, it was in a chastened frame of mind. It was clear that there could be no more experiments while the 1842 budget was itself on trial, and the cabinet talks tended to range over peripheral topics like Canada, Ellenborough's regrettable conduct in India, the state of the industrial districts, education in Ireland, and Church extension in England. On 2 November the whole cabinet went down by special train on the Great Western railroad to attend a Council at Windsor, a novelty which moved Greville to reflect whimsically on the ability of a single Whig locomotive engineer to produce an instantaneous change of government. Nothing so dramatic happened, however, and out of all their discussions there emerged only two firm decisions. One, negative, was not to take up for the moment the explosive topic of Maynooth and Irish Catholic education. The other, more positive, was to institute the private enquiry into the condition of the working classes in the mining areas which Peel and Graham desired. Late November and December saw Peel at Drayton for the usual house-parties and in the second week of January he returned to Whitehall Gardens for the start of the session. There the violence that had hung in the air all through 1842 struck his own household.

On the afternoon of 20 January, at the Charing Cross end of Whitehall, Peel's private secretary Drummond was shot in the back at a few yards range by a man called Daniel MacNaghten. The bullet passed almost completely through his body and although superficially the injury did not seem mortal, he died five days later. His assailant turned out to be a mechanic from Glasgow, of illegitimate birth and erratic habits, who had thrown up his business about two years earlier under delusions of persecution by Jesuits, police, and the local Tory party. From his conversation after arrest it transpired that he had intended to shoot the prime minister and was under the impression that he had done so. More determined than Francis, better armed than Bean, he had only been prevented from firing a second pistol at his victim by a passing policeman, the weapon discharging harmlessly into the ground during the scuffle of arrest. In the previous fortnight he had been seen hanging round the public offices in Whitehall and on one occasion he had been questioned by a door-keeper outside the Privy Council Office from which Drummond had emerged shortly before the attack. Peel thought that he himself must have passed within a few yards of MacNaghten only half an hour previously. But it had not been a matter of thirty minutes but a grotesque error which had saved him. During the summer of 1842 MacNaghten, who had substantial sums of money at his disposal, had gone back to his native country. He had bought the two pistols at Paisley in July and was still in Scotland at the time of the queen's visit. It was possible but never proved that he had seen Drummond occupying Peel's carriage during the royal tour. The prime minister himself frequently travelled with the queen or Aberdeen, leaving his secretary to make use of the conspicuous Peel carriage with its coat of arms and liveried servant in which he had come up to Scotland. Drummond himself had joked about the mistake which many people must have made in thinking that he was the great man in person. He was almost the same age as Peel and though he did not otherwise resemble him, the error would have been natural in an age when there was no pictorial press to familiarise the provincial public with the physical appearance of public figures. MacNaghten must in any case have frequently seen Drummond moving between the Treasury and Whitehall Gardens. Though he had his own private house in Grosvenor Square, he was virtually a part of the Peel domestic household and had been with the younger children only a short time before he was shot down. Of all the idle servants and street-loungers about Whitehall who could have pointed out to MacNaghten a score of notabilities, it had never occurred to the morose and unsociable Scot to ask even one to confirm for him the identity of his intended victim. Only this frail accident of misunderstanding in a crazed and obsessed mind had prevented, thirty-one years after Perceval's death, the assassination of a second British prime minister.[1]

The attack, followed by the news that it had been meant for himself, and then by Drummond's death a few days later, was an

[1] RA/A 82, Peel to Prince Albert, 20 Jan.; /A 13 Peel to the queen, 25, 26, 31 Jan. 1843; VL, I, 455-8; Peel, II, 552-5; Greville, 26, 29 Jan. 1843; Annual Register, 1843; R. M. Bousfield and R. Merrett, Report of the Trial of Daniel M'Naughton (1843). There were several variants to MacNaghten's name; I have followed Peel's spelling.

emotional shock to Peel and still more to Lady Peel. It was soon evident that MacNaghten was mentally unbalanced and had no political motives. But the police had information that he had been in contact with other men, and as the prime minister wrote to the queen, 'It must be borne in mind that he was exactly the instrument which others would employ. Sir Robert Peel has no reason for surmising this to be the case, but the possibility of it ought not and shall not be overlooked.' Even without complicity there had been too much talk of murder, assassination and personal guilt in the previous twelve months. With Croker's *Quarterly* article fresh in people's minds, it was not easy to regard MacNaghten's act as entirely dissociated from the continued current of public agitation. Julia Peel's anxieties about her husband's safety in the summer seemed to have received a cruel vindication and she herself for a time was completely prostrated. Peel absented himself from the cabinet dinner on the day of Drummond's death and excused himself and his wife from a forthcoming visit to Windsor. As late as 30 January Julia was still so weak from grief and strain that she was confined to bed. Concern could not cease with MacNaghten's arrest. The queen's injunction to Peel to be careful and not expose himself to danger was entirely reasonable. Drummond's death was followed by a number of threatening letters to the prime minister; and another crazed person called Dillon, who had been pestering the Treasury for years, began to send menacing notes to Goulburn and haunt the neighbourhood of Downing Street and the House of Commons. He was put under police surveillance for a month and Peel later persuaded his colleague to apply to the courts for protection.[1]

All this gave a sharp edge to a passage between Peel and Cobden in the House a couple of weeks after the opening of parliament on 2 February. The occasion was Howick's motion for a committee of the whole House to investigate the distress in the country. Cobden, speaking on the 17th, the last of the five evenings of debate, savagely accused the prime minister of personal responsibility for the state of the nation.

---

[1] RA/A 14/2; Graham (Peel to Graham, 16 Feb. 1843); Knatchbull (Knatchbull to his wife, 26 Jan. 1843). Goulburn took Peel's advice and in March obtained a warrant for the arrest of Dillon, a former naval and coastguard officer with an ancient grievance against the government (see *Annual Register*, 1843, Chron., p. 23).

You took the Corn Laws into your own hands. . . . You acted on your own judgement. . . . You are responsible for the consequences of your own act. . . . You passed the law, you refused to listen to the manufacturers, and I throw on you all the responsibility of your own measure. . . . I must tell the right hon. Baronet that it is the duty of every honest and independent member to hold him individually responsible for the present condition of the country. . . . I tell him that the whole responsibility of the lamentable and dangerous state of the country rests with him.

Cobden had used such language before at League meetings. But repeated in this direct and passionate manner across the floor of the House only three weeks after Drummond's funeral, it had a visible effect on the prime minister. Rising immediately after Cobden, and speaking with unusual intensity in a House already keyed up by the personal nature of Cobden's attack, he began an immediate retort.

The hon. gentleman has stated here very emphatically, what he has more than once stated at the conferences of the Anti-Corn Law League, that he holds me individually—

Here the repressed excitement of the House broke out, but Peel continued—

individually responsible for the distress and suffering of the country; that he holds me personally responsible; but be the consequences of these insinuations what they may, never will I be influenced by menaces either in this House or out of this House, to adopt a course which I consider—

The sentence was never finished. By this time loud shouts were coming from different parts of the chamber. Cobden rose to explain that he had not said that Peel was personally responsible but that he was responsible by virtue of his office. There were cries of dissent; and Peel contradicted him pointblank. In the general hubbub of shouting, calls to order, and appeals to the Chair, Cobden was unable to make himself heard and had to sit down. Peel resumed more calmly, corrected his phraseology to say that Cobden had twice declared he was individually responsible, and then dropped the issue. After the speech Cobden apologised with ill grace. He said he had merely intended—and believed that everyone in the

House except Peel had understood what he meant (shouts of No! No!)—to throw responsibility on him as head of the government. In using the word individually, he said sneeringly, he had used it as Peel used the first pronoun singular. He treated him as the government, as he was in the habit of treating himself. Peel contented himself with replying that Cobden had used the word individually in such a marked way as to make Peel and others put on it a different construction; but he was bound to accept the construction Cobden now put on the language he had employed.

It was an unpleasant episode and attracted for a time much public comment. The enemies of the League tried to make out that Cobden had ruined himself, its supporters that a perverted and atrocious meaning had been put on Cobden's words in order to destroy his reputation. If Cobden had any misgivings, they were drowned in his own resentment. There was, he wrote to his brother soon after, in a letter that was a remarkable expression of the political passions of the time,

> a pretty general notion that Peel has made a great fool of himself, if not something worse. He is obliged *now* to assume that he was in earnest, for no man likes to confess himself a hypocrite, and to put up with the ridicule of his own party as a coward. Lord —— was joking with Ricardo in the House the other night about him; pointing towards Peel as he was leaning forward, he whispered, 'There, the fellow is afraid someone is taking aim at him from the gallery.' . . . He [Peel] is looking twenty percent worse since I came into the House, and if I had only Bright with me, we could worry him out of office before the close of session.

It was clear from the remainder of the letter that Cobden had previously decided to concentrate his attacks on the prime minister and his speech in the debate had been deliberately framed. That it could be construed as an incitement to violence against Peel bitterly incensed him. But Cobden in these years constantly let his vocabulary outrun his judgement and he himself was largely to blame if other people took his words at their face value. The charge of either cowardice or feigned indignation showed a certain ignorance of Peel's character. A month later, when the queen suggested that during her renewed pregnancy[1] Albert should deputise for her at

[1] Princess Alice was born on 25 April 1843.

long and fatiguing *levées*, she showed some concern that she would be exposing him to the kind of physical attack she had experienced the previous year. Peel, in reassuring her of the unlikelihood of such an occurrence, added lightly that

> it may tend to remove or diminish your Majesty's anxiety to know that Sir Robert Peel has *walked* home every night from the House of Commons, and notwithstanding frequent menaces and intimations of danger, he has not met with any obstruction.[1]

So far as Peel was concerned, the episode was soon dismissed from his mind. It was another three years before he realised how much it had continued to rankle with Cobden.

II

The Howick debate on 13–17 February was a foretaste of the whole session. In the queen's speech the ministers had avoided controversies and gave no promises of any major legislation. Though peace had been made with China and a treaty signed with the U.S.A., these successes in foreign policy had been offset by Ellenborough's grandiose and embarrassing activities in India. In domestic affairs, in view of the state of the revenue and continued distress in the country, the government contented itself with consolidating rather than extending the work of the previous session. The parliamentary gap created by the absence of any large programme of government legislation was promptly filled by the opposition. Motions of various kinds were brought forward which, if useless for any practical purpose, enabled them to monopolise parliamentary time and score debating points against the ministry. If these tactics were less effective than they might have been, it was because the opposition themselves were deeply divided on the right solutions for the problems which they insisted on discussing. Howick's motion was a typical example. His speech was able and temperate but suffered from the disadvantage of serving no particular object except as a fingerpost pointing towards free trade. It was not clear whether he intended an indirect approach to the repeal of the Corn Laws or a general vote of no confidence in the government. As a

[1] *VL*, I, 473; *Cobden*, pp. 263–4.

result succeeding speakers rode various hobby-horses off in different directions and though the debate was protracted, it was also shapeless.

The main excitement in the earlier part of the proceedings was caused by Gladstone when answering Howick on the first evening. Trying to balance one conflicting consideration against another, he lost the thread of his argument and allowed his recently acquired economic convictions to come to the surface. In consequence he spoke so often of temporary factors and the mutability of Corn Laws as to create joy for the opposition and alarm among the Tory agriculturalists. Peel by gestures tried to indicate to his younger colleague that he was getting on dangerous ground; but the damage was done.[1] On the last evening the Tory Blackstone of Wallingford announced his complete lack of confidence in the ministers, described Gladstone's speech as neither distinct nor satisfactory, and gave a warning that the farmers though slow to move were alive to their own interests. If nothing was done to reassure them, he said darkly, they would soon be found in opposition to the government. Peel in his closing speech was careful and soothing. He repeated the statement he had made at the start of the session that he was not contemplating another change in the Corn Laws; he argued the case for moving slowly in anything affecting the great economic interests of the country; pointed to the first faint signs of recovery; and diverted attention in his peroration to the hopeful prospects following the settlement with China and the U.S.A. and the establishment of more friendly relations with France. A majority of 115 on the division demonstrated not only the solidity of the government majority but also perhaps a lack of conviction by the opposition that Howick's motion was likely to produce anything of value.

Nevertheless this was only the first of a number of time-wasting general debates on the state of the country. Ward, the Liberal M.P. for Sheffield, moved in March for an enquiry into the peculiar burdens on the land in a speech which was an attack on the privileged position of the landowners. George Bankes retorted with a counter-motion deprecating the continued existence and activities of the Anti-Corn Law League. Peel pointedly dissociated himself and the government from this quarrel between bellicose back-benchers.

[1] *Gladstone*, I, 194, but wrongly dated.

In May, after the Easter recess, came Villiers's annual motion for a committee of the whole House to consider the Corn Laws. Continuing over five nights the debate attracted the usual cast of speakers, repeated the usual repertory of arguments, and revealed the endemic divisions among the opposition between outright repealers and supporters of a fixed duty. Gladstone, taught by his February blunder, took a more purist protectionist line and quoted figures to show that the prices of barley, oats, beans, peas, beef, mutton and wool were lower than in 1835, the previously cheapest year of that generation. Blackstone, noting but scarcely mollified by this change of language, argued in somewhat oblique fashion that if the tenant farmers were moving towards free trade in corn it was because they distrusted the government and preferred to meet their fate at once rather than die by inches. To this he added some caustic observations on the unwillingness of the gentry and magistrates to stand behind the farming community. Peel, while repeating that he would be ready to change the existing Corn Law if it proved a failure, declined to accept its failure as proved. Having extracted from Villiers a confirmation that he wished to abolish at once all protective duties and all monopolies and preferences, regardless of the effect on the revenue, he left it to the House to accept or reject this simple proposition. The House by a massive majority of 256 emphatically rejected it. Even so the division showed, as Peel noted when reporting to the queen, that the numbers in favour of repeal had increased since the previous session.[1] Finally in June Russell himself brought forward another motion for a committee on the Corn Laws in a fishing speech tentatively arguing for a fixed duty but indicating a readiness to accept any compromise. The exhausted House gave only one evening to this belated and threadbare proposal. With the opposition hopelessly split, Peel bringing up the rear of the debate had little difficulty in disposing of the issue. Seizing on the admission that a fixed duty would have to be suspended in time of scarcity, he was neatly sarcastic at the vagueness of the motion before the House. Russell had admitted that his proposition would not bear rain, he observed; he would find if he got into committee that it would not bear criticism. A diminished and uninterested House by a majority of 99 ensured that it ran the risk of neither.

[1] RA/A 14/56.

In the intervals between these parliamentary set pieces, the government carried on with its own modest set of legislative proposals. At the beginning of May Goulburn introduced the budget in a speech which was largely a tale of deceived expectations and unexpected losses. Customs and excise were down mainly as a result of the unsettling effect on the wine trade of the prolonged negotiations with Portugal; though it was also true that timber and coffee had shared in the general depression. The tax on exported coal and the Irish spirit duties introduced the previous session had proved failures. When to these was added the loss by miscalculation on the income tax, the result was a gross deficit on the year of £3¼ million. On the other hand there had been some uncovenanted benefits. Government expenditure had been down on the estimates and China had paid over a sum of £750,000. With various other items to swell the credit column, the chancellor was able to reduce the deficit to a net figure of a little over £2 million as compared with the estimated surplus of £500,000. It was not a picture that at first blush conveyed an impression of government foresight or financial dexterity. Yet Goulburn, in presenting his balance-sheet, was able to strike a note of firm and cheerful optimism. In the first place the revenue in the previous year had clearly reflected the abnormal depression of the period. In the second, there were already signs of national recovery. The returns for the last quarter of the financial year showed distinct improvement; trade and industry were beginning to revive; there was less unemployment. Already in the Howick debate of February Graham had been able to report that even in Paisley, that grim barometer of the country's economic health, there was rising employment and a falling demand for relief. From the financial point of view the most encouraging fact was that the income tax, calculated modestly to yield less than £4 million, in a full year was obviously going to produce over £5 million. In consequence Goulburn proposed no special measures to meet what could now be regarded as a temporary deficit. The extraordinary charges of compensation to opium holders and payment to the East India Company arising out of the China War he debited to future indemnity remittances from the Chinese government. For the ordinary revenue and expenditure of the country he estimated that the current year with no changes in taxation would show a surplus of £750,000.

It was a paradoxical situation. The government had perpetuated the dismal run of large deficits. Almost all its calculations had been falsified by events. On a dozen technical points its financial policy was open to criticism. Even if the whole of the unexpectedly large revenue from the income tax had been collected in the first year, it would still not have produced a surplus. Yet the discussion in the House was brief and temperate. Indeed a more ostentatious attack was subsequently launched by Lord Monteagle (Melbourne's late Chancellor of the Exchequer, Spring Rice) in the House of Lords at the end of the session. In his own contribution to the budget debate Peel showed no disposition to stand in a white sheet. He pointed to the extraordinary severity and unexpected duration of the industrial depression. He observed that if all the income tax instalments had been recovered during the year in which they fell due, there would have been only a slight deficit. He easily disposed of Hume's argument that the income tax had contributed to the loss of revenue by showing that the principal deficiencies had occurred not in assessed taxes but in customs duties. As for the future, he reaffirmed his faith in the rightness of the government's policy and declared that they would continue with their tariff reductions as soon as the state of the revenue permitted.[1]

It was clear that on the major proposition he carried the bulk of the House with him; and it was this that made the individual items of miscalculation relatively insignificant. If there was one lesson that stood out, it was that the crucial innovation of the income tax had stood between the country and financial disaster. As Peel asked the Commons, 'Where should we have been now if the income tax had not been imposed?' When to this was added the growing feeling that the country had at last turned the corner of the great depression, it was not easy for fair-minded men to escape the conviction that the fundamental policy of the government was sound or deny them the credit for introducing and maintaining courageous measures. Reproaches for its mishandling of the financial situation were among the least of the burdens which the ministry had to bear during the 1843 session; and Peel's reputation as a financier was in no way impaired by the uncertainties that surrounded the first year's working of his new

[1] *Speeches*, IV, 245 (8 May 1843).

policy.[1] It was obvious now that it would need two years rather than one for the full effects of his 1842 budget to be realised; but the principle behind that budget was not discredited.

In the circumstances the only important economic measure introduced by the government in the session was Stanley's Canada corn bill and this in a sense was an appendix to the 1842 legislation rather than a new departure. The cabinet had decided in January that it was committed to take action[2] and this had been announced by Stanley early in the session. As Graham had anticipated the agriculturalists at once scented danger. By the time Stanley brought forward his resolutions on 19 May it was already being muttered that the government was plotting to overthrow the protective principle of the 1842 Act by introducing foreign corn through the backdoor of Canadian preference. Stanley himself, appearing in a rare role as chief government spokesman, admitted that had it not been for his promise the previous year he would not have introduced a measure likely to disturb the agricultural interest. But, he argued, he was bringing forward his bill not as a free-trade measure but as a boon to Canada on the principle of imperial reciprocity laid down as far back as the 1828 corn bill. In detail he proposed to admit Canadian corn at a nominal duty of 1s a quarter with equivalent duties for Canadian wheat-flour.

From the official opposition no great danger threatened. Peel already knew from Anson, who had his information from Melbourne, that the Whigs were split on the issue. Many of them, led by Palmerston and Labouchere, wanted to oppose—some on the contrived grounds that as free traders they must object to the corn tariff established by the Canadian assembly against the U.S.A. But Russell, Macaulay, and Ellice, together with Lords Melbourne, Morpeth and Spencer, were equally determined to support the principle of the bill.[3] The real threat to the ministers came from the benches behind them. Graham was under the impression as late as 17 May that many Conservative M.P.s intended to vote against the bill. If they did, he confided gloomily to de Grey, 'our overthrow is inevitable'.[4] In the event Stanley's resolutions were formally opposed by Labouchere and Howick with an amendment

[1] Cf. Stafford Northcote, *Twenty Years of Financial Policy* (1862), pp. 41–50.
[2] *Knatchbull*, p. 247.   [3] 40436 fos. 290–4.   [4] Graham, 17 May 1843.

asking the crown to withhold its assent from the bill of the Canadian legislature. The debate showed the familiar divisions among the opposition and mixed but moderate feelings among the Tory agriculturalists. Peel himself, with his usual tactical skill, narrowed the technical issue to two points. The first was the constitutional impropriety of Labouchere's amendment and the embarrassment which would be caused to the Crown by a request to veto one of the first measures of the new independent and united legislature of Canada. The second was the impossibility of granting imperial preference (which nobody seriously opposed) without previously ensuring that it would not be used as a cover for cheap importations of foreign wheat. On general grounds, he went on to argue, it was of the highest importance to assist the fragile unity of the recently disturbed and rebellious Canadian colonies by giving practical encouragement to their only two important exports, timber and corn. Unless they secured the friendship and co-operation of the Canadian assembly, Canada would remain the weakest part of the whole empire.

Peel spoke on Monday, 22 May, at the close of the debate on the second evening. By that time the ministers were confident of success. The previous Friday, the morning of Stanley's introductory speech, the government supporters had been summoned to Downing Street. There they were addressed by Peel and Stanley who described the nature of the measure, the circumstances under which it was introduced, and the consequences of rejection. The ministerial explanations were well received and it was clear at the close of the meeting that no great number would persist in opposing the bill. When the division took place on Monday Labouchere's amendment was heavily defeated by 344 votes to 156. It was almost an embarrassing majority since the ministers now faced the probability that the agricultural M.P.s would feel free to conciliate their constituents by an occasional adverse vote in the later stages of the bill. It was true in fact that the government majority dropped during the subsequent proceedings but at no point did it fall below eighty. In the Lords the bill went through without amendment, though with some harsh words from protectionist peers, and with that the government were safely over their one difficult party issue.[1]

[1] 40436 fos. 304, 322; RA/A 14/61-5.

The other major piece of legislation introduced by the government in the 1843 session ended disastrously. At the end of February Ashley had carried an address to the Crown on the subject of education for the working classes. In the debate Graham took the opportunity to outline the scheme for pauper and factory children on which he had been working ever since he took office. The events of 1842 had merely strengthened the conviction of leading members of the cabinet that a greater effort at education must be made in the industrial districts. As Graham hopefully put it, now that the police and soldiers had done their work, parliament should approach the problem of national education in a non-partisan spirit. The House, apart from a few apprehensive expressions from individual spokesmen for the Anglican, Dissenting and Roman Catholic interests, was clearly sympathetic. It was noticeable, however, that Peel, more cautious than his colleague, confessed that he had more faith in the effect of Ashley's speech in encouraging individual efforts than in the result of direct intervention by the legislature. His caution was justified when in March Graham introduced his bill to regulate the employment of children and young persons in factories. He had hoped to postpone the discussion of the education clauses of the bill until after Easter. But under pressure from various opposition members expressing anxiety on behalf of Dissenters and Catholics, he was forced to agree to a general debate on the educational aspect when the bill was read for a second time at the end of the month. Much of Graham's preparations in 1842 had been devoted to discussions with Church leaders with the object of avoiding a renewal of the Anglican opposition to a system of state-directed national education which had wrecked the Whig plan in 1839. The concessions he had made, however, seemed to have the effect of placing the new schools under the practical control of the Established Church.

The House of Commons, predominantly Anglican and genuinely concerned for the state of the working classes, gave a second reading to the bill but the publicity provided by the debate stirred Dissenting opinion in the country into devastating activity. Petitions began to pour in and the progress of the bill was halted by the government until after the Easter recess in the hope that the tide of dissenting resentment would recede Even so Peel was not sanguine. 'The High Church party is not satisfied with the bill,' he told the queen on 25 March, 'but their opposition will be less formidable than that of the Dissenters.'[1] His fears were more than realised. The interval merely allowed dissenting agitation to become organised. Public meetings were held all over the country; an unprecedented mass of petitions flooded into the Commons; Roman Catholics and Wesleyans threw their weight behind the mass of Protestant dissenters. Hasty modifications announced by Graham after Easter failed to allay the sectarian storm. On 15 June the government acknowledged defeat and Graham withdrew the educational clauses. It was clear by this time that to use the parliamentary majority to put through the bill would inflame religious hostility to a point at which the practical operation of the educational scheme would become impossible.

Ashley himself, in admitting this to Peel, released the ministers from any moral obligation they might have felt to him, though he pressed hard for the factory regulation clauses to go through. With this Peel was in complete agreement. He told Ashley on 17 June that the cabinet had resolved that the rest of the bill, including a modified clause relating to the inspection of schools, should be neither abandoned nor postponed.[2] But already much time had been lost; and more had to be spent in disentangling the educational clauses. A month later Ashley himself was obliged to admit that the lateness of the session, the pressure of other business, and the departure of many M.P.s favourable to factory reform, made it advisable to postpone the bill until the next year. In making this formal announcement to the House Peel took care to say that Ashley approved the postponement. But perennially suspicious of the government and morbidly hostile to Graham, Ashley felt that the ministers had not expressed enough disappointment at the abandonment of the bill and made a point of extracting from the prime minister a promise that the subject would be resumed the following session.[3] Alternating between high moral exhortation and angry distrust, Ashley's correspondence with Peel and Graham was a curious psychological study. It said much, both for their good nature and the respect they had for his integrity, that Ashley was treated so gently by the Conservative ministers. Peel himself was

[1] 40436 f. 138.   [2] 40483 f. 112. Cf. *Peel*, II, 560–1.   [3] *ibid.*, fos. 122, 124.

always friendly and courteous, ready to return amicable acknowledgements even to the most bitter letters from Ashley. The only
time he had been noticeably dry and official had been at the start
of 1842 when Ashley had tried to pin him down to a commitment
on the factory issue. Yet the upshot of the session's work was that a
sectarian opposition had claimed what Peel called a 'sorry and
lamentable triumph'; factory regulation was put off for yet another
year; and Ashley's relations with the government retained their
uneasy blend of intimacy and distrust.

As the 1843 session demonstrated, economic depression had not
weakened the power of religion to stir up historic discords in
British society. In Scotland the internal conflict over the right of lay
patrons had steadily widened since the 'Veto Act' of the General
Assembly in 1834. In subsequent judicial cases the Scottish law
courts and the House of Lords had ruled against its validity. When
the Non-Intrusionist leaders canvassed the leading Conservatives in
1840, they realised that there was little to expect from the opposition
when they came to power. Peel refused to pledge himself to the
Duke of Argyll's bill which sought to legalise the Veto. He deprecated the theocratic claims of the Evangelical party and studiously
ignored the veiled threat of secession which was made during his
interview with their delegates. Chalmers, who led the deputation,
found the opposition leader bland, cool and cautious and preferred
the other Conservative politicians whom he saw. But neither
Aberdeen nor Graham could be shifted from their adherence to
Peel's position. Graham in fact, with Peel's hearty approval, took
the unusual step as Lord Rector of going to Glasgow the same year
to vote against Chalmers's candidacy for the Chair of Divinity.[1]
The issue came to a head in 1842 with the 'Claim, Declaration and
Protest' of the General Assembly against lay patronage and state
intervention, and the assertion that acts of parliament affecting the
Church without its consent were null and void. The attitude of the
government was primarily and perhaps inevitably legalistic. They
were concerned to uphold the law courts and ultimately the
sovereignty of parliament against the illegal acts of individual
Presbyteries and the General Assembly. They felt a duty to protect
individual sufferers such as the seven ministers of Strathbogie sus-

[1] 40318 f. 226.

pended by the Assembly for obeying the orders of the Court of Session. Yet they were also embroiled in a more personal sense in this passionate Scottish controversy, partly because of its disruptive political effects, and partly because the Crown itself owned patronage rights in about a third of the Scottish parishes.

Within the cabinet the ministers primarily implicated in the dispute were Graham as Home Secretary and Aberdeen as the leading Scottish peer. But Peel himself could hardly avoid being involved, however distastefully, in a conflict where all his training and prejudices ranged him on the side of the civil authorities against ecclesiastical pretensions. He gave in fact much time and attention to the matter. With Aberdeen he was prepared to go halfway to meet the demands of the Church by giving sanction to the use of a veto by the presbyteries provided that they did not act as irresponsible instruments of the popular wishes of the congregation. But even before he came to power, the prospects of compromise were rapidly vanishing. 'There seems to me', he noted dryly in 1840, 'a great deal of ill temper on both sides.' Once in office Peel tried to formalise negotiations through his Scottish Solicitor General. As long as the dominant party in the Church refused to accept any degree of judicial review or deal sympathetically with the ejected ministers, it did not seem to Peel that any early legislation could be successful. But with Non-Intrusionists making preparations for secession and the deadlock between the General Assembly and the State beginning to set hard, it was clear that the government could not stand aloof much longer.

Peel thought it pointless for cabinet ministers to indulge in barren assertions that they intended to uphold the law; and undignified for them to enter into an epistolary wrangle with the General Assembly on points of civil and ecclesiastical jurisdiction.[1] If the government were to intervene at all, it should be to make a clear factual statement of the existing law of patronage. On the prime minister's advice this was eventually done by Graham in his letter to the Moderator of the General Assembly in January 1843. Fundamentally the ministers' attitude was that patronage should be exercised within the framework of the law but with full regard to the judicial rights of the Presbytery. They particularly

[1] 43062 f. 219.

objected to the refusal to accept a patron's nominee even for the intermediate stages of trial and presentation. What the 'Veto Act' of 1834 had done was to substitute, on doubtful legal authority, the popular veto of the congregation for the acknowledged legal right of the presbytery to reject on specific grounds. If that were accepted all right of patronage disappeared; and it was this which the government, as Graham's letter ended by saying, firmly condemned.[1]

When in March Fox Maule moved unsuccessfully for a committee of the whole House to consider the claims of the Non-Intrusionists, Peel made it clear that he would not vote for any committee merely intended to recognise the claims put forward by the dominant party in the Assembly. The Church of Scotland was a Church established by law and subject therefore to regulation by the civil power. 'If a church chooses to have the advantage of an establishment, and to hold those privileges which the law confers— that church, whether it be the Church of Rome, or the Church of England, or the Presbyterian Church of Scotland, must conform to the law.'[2] If a declaratory act was needed, however, it might properly be passed by parliament to maintain the rights and discipline of the Church. The government was prepared to legislate, on the lines indicated by Graham's letter of January, if the opportunity arose. In fact Graham promised in May to take steps to establish the rights of presbyteries to object and the powers of church courts to adjudicate on such objections. But it was already too late. The same month Chalmers led over four hundred ministers out of the Kirk and into the secessionist Free Church of Scotland. However embarrassing and incomprehensible to the government, the Disruption was a fact.

Nevertheless the Old Kirk remained with its old problems, or at least a measure of uncertainty on particular aspects. The General Assembly proceeded in consequence to repeal the Veto Act and in June Aberdeen introduced a bill to regulate on orthodox lines the admission of ministers to Scottish benefices. It met with much criticism both from those who disliked the virtual abolition of the Veto Act of 1834 and those, like Brougham, who thought it went too far in giving an equivalent veto to the Church Courts.

[1] For Graham's letter see *Annual Register*, 1843, pp. 463–70.
[2] *Speeches*, IV, 200 (8 Mar. 1843).

One lively issue was whether the bill, as the government was advised by its Scottish judicial experts, was simply declaratory of the law of Scotland or enacted new law. The Whig law lords took the latter view and the cabinet itself was uncomfortably divided when it discussed the matter in the second week of July.[1] In fact that issue was never clearly settled. When the bill came to the Commons Follett, the Solicitor General, cheerfully said that it could be described as either an enacting or a declaratory bill, though it did not expressly call itself either. Peel stuck to his own views and asserted that the bill defined the rights of patrons, congregations and the Church in strict conformity with past practice. In the end therefore the policy of the government was vindicated in the limited sense that it was enshrined in statute. But the Disruption was an open and permanent proof of its failure to solve the actual problem.

Peel's deliberate delay during 1842 had bought him no advantage; though it is probable that no advantage could have been bought in 1842 at a price the government would have been willing to pay. Failure perhaps was unavoidable. A civil government faced by rebellious churchmen, acting however intemperately on grounds of spiritual conscience, is at a disadvantage in any liberal-minded society. The situation was worsened in that it was also a conflict between passionate Scots Presbyterians reared on a separate tradition of Church–State relationships, and a parliament, largely Anglican and Erastian, to whom the whole problem was alien and irritating. Disruption was probably inevitable even before the Conservatives gained power in 1841. The policy of restrained but legalistic firmness followed by Peel's ministry was a doomed casualty of the engrained differences between English and Scottish historical traditions which the Union of 1707 had concealed rather than obliterated.[2]

The secession in Scotland, occurring simultaneously with the Dissenting attack on Graham's bill and O'Connell's repeal agitation in Ireland, was at least confirmation of Peel's view that any request by the government for public money to assist the Anglican Church would merely raise a sectarian storm. Church Extension had been

[1] 44777 f. 91.
[2] See also Peel, II, 468–74, III, ch. iv; Graham, I, ch. XVII; J. T. Ward, Sir James Graham (1967), pp. 197–202; A. B. Erickson, Sir James Graham (1952), pp. 197–210.

under intermittent discussion ever since the ministry took office. Even before the summer of 1842 there was general agreement that something must be done in the industrial areas to create new parishes, build additional churches and schools, and raise fresh endowments. The difficulty was finance. Inglis's proposal for a parliamentary grant of two or three million pounds merely showed his political naïvety. Goulburn's suggestion for creating a fund by the sale of crown livings or a special tax on clerical livings was a more realistic policy though not a promising one. Peel thought that the main need was for church building, since the Ecclesiastical Commissioners had already been authorised to provide endowments out of surplus cathedral funds. To start a new fund for churches, moreover, might encourage private subscriptions.[1] After the violence and disorder of 1842 the prime minister's mood became noticeably sharper. He told Henry Hobhouse in January 1843 that it was impossible to defer any longer the consideration of a remedy for social evils of such pressing danger; to postpone it indefinitely would be criminal. What he wanted was not public funds, which he thought would only lead to public enquiry and controversy, but a better use of church property and a wider appeal for private assistance. Goulburn still favoured a small parliamentary grant but to this the prime minister would lend no backing. The extreme Anglican argument of a state church, therefore state support, irritated him. Logic of this kind simply could not be applied to politics.

> We cannot go further, I think, in that direction [he wrote to Graham in December 1842], than loan without interest. Can we go so far? . . . It is very well for clergymen and for Sir Robert Inglis to argue that it is the duty of the State to provide religious edifices wherever they are wanted, and that Dissenters are bound to build and repair and endow their own churches, and those of the Establishment also—and this by new Taxation whenever requisite—but you and I know that the Church and religion would suffer, and peace and charity would be sacrificed.[2]

After intensive discussion with Graham, Hobhouse, Gladstone and others, Peel and Goulburn met the Archbishop of Canterbury and the Bishop of London early in January and impressed on them

---

[1] 40443 fos. 100–2 (Jan. 1842).   [2] Graham, 22 Dec. 1842, pr. *Peel*, II, 550.

the need for a special effort at church extension in the northern industrial areas.[1] The two ecclesiastics promised to look into the available church resources and further meetings took place in the early spring. Peel's object was clearly to stimulate the Church into a policy of self-help. He continued to resist even the efforts of that great and moderate church politician, Bishop Blomfield of London, to secure some state aid for the purchase of building sites. But in the course of the session he put through an unobtrusive and uncontroversial piece of legislation which materially facilitated the Church's voluntary effort. This was the Populous Parishes Act which enabled the Ecclesiastical Commissioners to create parishes in districts of over 2,000 population and provide a stipend even before a new church was built. For this purpose the Commissioners were empowered to anticipate further funds falling to their use (mainly from expiring leases) by an advance from the Queen Anne's Bounty of up to £600,000. In introducing the bill he appealed to wealthy persons, particularly those connected with the manufacturing districts, to assist in endowing the new parishes. Privately he turned precept into practice by subscribing £4,000 to the Commissioners for use in London and the industrial parts of Staffordshire, Warwickshire and Lancashire. Equally characteristically he forbade any publicity for this handsome donation even for the laudable purpose of inspiring other benefactions.

This was not the only personal contribution he made to the voluntary efforts of the Church. Following the collapse of Graham's bill in June, the Anglican National Society started a special fund for establishing schools in manufacturing and mining districts. Peel headed the list of original donors, followed by the two Archbishops, Bishop Blomfield, Lord Harrowby, Sidney Herbert, and Abel Smith. When the list was sent to the queen by the Archbishop of Canterbury, the royal couple on Anson's advice made an equally generous contribution. By the end of July, only three weeks after the fund had been instituted, a total of over £32,000 had been raised to which the queen, the Dukes of Portland and Northumberland, and the prime minister had each contributed £1,000.[2] Parsimonious

---

[1] 40435 f. 240.

[2] RA/F 37/59–72; *Christian Observer*, 1843, pp. 573–4. Peel's donation is wrongly given as £5,000 in *Peel*, II, 562.

with the public purse, Peel was generous with his own. His only anxiety was that there should be no quarrelling within the Church on the purpose of the fund. If agreement could be reached, he had told Graham, 'I mean to subscribe liberally less as a minister than from connection with the manufacturing districts'.[1]

III

The closing stages of the 1843 session were marked by bitter and prolonged debates on Ireland. The disturbances in that country which accompanied O'Connell's repeal campaign induced the government in May to introduce an arms bill to control the possession of dangerous weapons. Though of the conventional nature on which past ministries, whether Tory or Whig, had been accustomed to rely in time of unrest, it was sharply contested in the House of Commons. The second reading gave rise to three nights of violent debate on familiar party lines. When the bill went into committee it was resisted clause by clause with repeated amendments and divisions. During its slow and acrimonious progress fresh debates on Ireland were started in both Houses. The most important of these was on Smith O'Brien's motion for a committee of the whole house on the state of Ireland. Though formally defeated, it had the practical effect aimed at since it led to a general debate on Irish affairs extending over five evenings. In the third week of July the cabinet was forced consequently to lighten their programme of government business by jettisoning the factories, ecclesiastical courts, and county courts bills. Even so it was not until 9 August that the Irish arms bill reached its final stage in the House of Commons. A fresh source of obstruction was then found in the enrolled pensioners bill which the Rebecca riots in South Wales during the summer had done nothing to render less urgent. With the House sitting some fourteen hours a day to get through its remaining business, Cobden, Bright, Duncombe and Hume delayed the passage of the bill by all the devices which the rules of the House allowed. To defeat these filibustering tactics the government had to organise a body of some forty supporters ready to sit up all night if necessary to resist repeated motions for adjournment. Thus forti-

[1] Graham, 10 July 1843.

fied the ministers refused either to give way to the obstructionist minority of a mere dozen or to accept the compromise proposals put forward by other opposition members. In the end they finally carried the bill through without alteration.[1]

The long, harassing and largely unproductive session came to its belated close on 24 August and with it the ministry had virtually completed its second year of office. There had been few changes in its composition since the end of 1841. Peel tended to keep his colleagues as long as possible in the offices to which he had appointed them; and the one minor reshuffle of 1843 was an enforced one. Fitzgerald had died in May and Ripon at once asked to succeed him, or at least to transfer to any cabinet seat vacated by Fitzgerald's successor. His ill-health had for some time left Gladstone in virtual charge of the Board of Trade and Ripon wanted to relinquish entirely the responsibility for that over-worked department.[2] Peel had already anticipated this in his proposals to the queen and without delay offered Gladstone the vacant presidency with a seat in the cabinet. Lord Dalhousie, a young Scottish peer whom Wellington was anxious to bring into office, was promoted to Gladstone's old post, a move which held two further advantages. It gave assistance to the duke in the House of Lords where Ellenborough's departure for India and Fitzgerald's death had depleted the front bench; and it dispensed with a by-election.[3]

For a government in mid-passage trials of electoral popularity were best avoided. There was proof of this in July when Bright at a second attempt won the seat at Durham vacated by Fitzroy's appointment as Governor of New Zealand. Another free-trade success followed in the City of London by-election in October when Pattison, an unsuccessful Liberal candidate in 1841, but now backed by the intensive efforts of the League, narrowly beat his Conservative opponent Thomas Baring despite the confident hopes entertained by Bonham and Fremantle. It was true that this was a failure to capture a seat and not an actual loss but a League triumph in the metropolis itself was ominous. Graham, conveying the news to Peel, opined that the result would go far to seal the fate of the

[1] 40437 fos. 151, 157; RA/A 15/48–51.
[2] 40464 fos. 360, 366, 435.
[3] Wellington (Peel to Wellington, 13 May, 22 May 1843); 40460 fos. 52, 76.

Corn Laws and would encourage agitation and resistance to the government.[1] Peel himself had attached enough importance to the result to make one of his rare overtures to Wellington to use his influence with the Rothschilds to gain the Jewish vote. But the duke, aware of the ultimate object of the Rothschilds to secure the admission of Jews to parliament, was not sanguine of success.[2]

There was little doubt in fact that support for the new Conservative ministry had waned perceptibly since 1841. Greville, returning in July after a month abroad, was struck by the critical attitude towards the government both in society and in the press. There was a mood of anticlimax, of expectations aroused and unrealised, of personal disappointments and disillusionment. Part of it was due to the fact that the great problems confronting the ministry in 1841 had still not been solved; part to the middle course Peel had followed on many aspects of his policy; part to Peel's own inability to compensate for the inevitable frictions of political life with the small change of flattery and attention. The interminable Irish debates and the defensive attitude of government spokesmen had left an impression of compromise and irresolution. Too balanced to please extremists, too cautious to offer instant remedies, Peel had concealed rather than revealed his fundamental thoughts on the Irish problem. As a result he had pleased nobody. Knatchbull, the outsider in the cabinet already tired of office and longing for the peace of private life, was writing bitterly in his diary in August of Peel's cold and discourteous manner even to his colleagues in office. 'It will be found when he dies, that no minister ever possessed fewer friends or would be personally less lamented—in his policy he is deficient in purpose and in courage.'[3]

Within the party the frustrations and suspicions of the agriculturalists were still fermenting. In the London clubs the current political joke in the spring was that the Tories were like old walnuts: they were hard to peel. Later in the session a more exotic note was given to the party's discontents by the emergence of the independent and critical group of idealists known as Young England whose ideas were an attractive and youthful compound of romantic High Churchmanship, feudal sympathy for the industrial poor, and

[1] 40449 f. 117.   [2] 40460 fos. 127–9, ptly pr. *Peel*, II, 570–1.
[3] *Knatchbull*, p. 252.

veneration for an imaginary past. In the Irish debates in July Peel reported to the queen that four members of the party had voted against the government: Baillie Cochrane, Smythe, Manners and Ferrand. Over the Irish arms bill in August he mentioned that in the course of the debate D'Israeli (as the prime minister still spelled it), and Smythe had made speeches which seemed to indicate that they would in future oppose the government.[1] In voting power the Young Englanders were negligible. But they had connections with other Conservative politicians like Henry Baillie, Peter Borthwick, Henry Hope, Stafford O'Brien, Monckton Milnes, and even Ashley; they had the benevolent support of *The Times*; and the circumstances of the 1843 session gave them an admirable opportunity to bring themselves before the public eye. Greville noted their activities in his diary for the first time on 11 August, when contrasting the civility of Peel's regular adversaries in the Irish debate with the bitterness and insolence of his *soi-disant* supporters. 'Disraeli and Smythe, who are the principal characters, together with John Manners, of the little squad called "Young England", were abusive and impertinent.' If they were, the prime minister took it calmly. In referring to Disraeli's speech on the third reading of the arms bill on 9 August, for example, he good-humouredly bantered him on his belated misgivings over the party's Irish policy and on his failure to signalise his new-born zeal for the subject by anything more decisive than an abstention from the division.[2] Nevertheless their existence was a cause of minor concern to the party whips if not the party chief. Fremantle in September warned Peel that if Borthwick was disappointed in his hope of a diplomatic appointment he might join 'the party of malcontents, G. Smythe, D'Israeli & Co.'[3]

But Young England was only a symptom and as it turned out a transient one of the general period of political depression through which the government was passing. Even the royal couple at Windsor were uneasily aware of their ministers' loss of popularity. In a conversation with Aberdeen in November the queen surprised him by suddenly asking whether he thought the government was stronger or weaker than it had been. The Foreign Secretary replied

[1] RA/A 15/20, 43; 40437 fos. 35, 125.   [2] *Hansard*, LXXI, 460–1.
[3] 40476 fos. 266–7.

diplomatically that certainly it was less popular but that had little to do with strength or weakness. The grumblings of disappointed politicians and the discontent of sections of the public were of little consequence as long as its majority held firm in the House of Commons.[1] This was also the view of Greville who having enquired more searchingly into the political situation, concluded in August that no serious injury had been done to the government, whatever the loss to their credit. No other party or set of individuals had enhanced their position; and there was in fact no real rival to Peel. The Whig talk of his imminent downfall was moonshine. Once trade revived and Irish agitation died down, it would be seen that there was no basis in fact for the passing clamour against the government.[2]

Certainly there was not the slightest wish at Windsor for a change of ministry. In her November conversation with Aberdeen, the queen had said with engaging candour that 'she knew that the Whigs talked confidently of coming into office soon; but that she hoped there was no danger of it, and that it would be a very long time before they did'.[3] All that had happened between the royal couple and Peel since 1842 had only strengthened the prime minister's standing at court. On several delicate matters he was already acting as a trusted family adviser. In the winter of 1842-3, for example, there had been an unpleasant scandal about the relations between Prince George, son of the Duke of Cambridge and a cousin of the Queen, and Lady Augusta Somerset, daughter of the Duke of Beaufort. Peel was instrumental in obtaining a satisfactory denial of the rumour from Prince George and was thanked somewhat prematurely by Albert in November for bringing 'this disagreeable affair to an end'. Unfortunately the queen, untaught by the Lady Flora Hastings episode, persisted in believing the scandal and allowed her views to become known. The Dukes of Cambridge and Beaufort angrily protested and, failing to get satisfaction from Albert, appealed to the prime minister. Further negotiations followed and in the end Peel was able to assure the outraged ducal parents that the queen was entirely satisfied and begged that the matter might be dropped.[4] The affair ended without any

---

[1] 40454 f. 6, ptly pr. *Peel*, II, 571.   [2] *Greville*, 6 Aug. 1843.   [3] 40454 f. 6.
[4] 40435 fos. 134-57; *Greville*, 7 Nov. 1842, 7 Feb. 1843.

open reflection on the queen. But it left strained relations with the Cambridge family; and there was much correspondence between Peel and the queen in 1843 over the duke's persistent refusal to attend royal *levées*. This was not the only royal quarrel to involve the prime minister. In 1842 and 1843 he was also in correspondence with Victoria and Albert over the claim of the King of Hanover to some of the crown jewels. This was a complicated and acrimonious issue which Peel was successful in removing to the calmer and more leisurely atmosphere of a special legal commission.[1] In a happier context, when the royal couple were looking for some rural retreat of their own, the prime minister was able to bring to their notice Lady Isabella Blachford's estate at Osborne on the Isle of Wight. It was a spot well known to him from his stay at Norris Castle in 1836, combining privacy, fine views over the Solent, safe sea-bathing, and scope for planning and improvement. To avoid publicity and an inflated price Peel himself set on foot the third-party negotiations which led in the end to a lease of Osborne for one year with an option to purchase.[2]

Even the personal relationship between Peel and Victoria was growing warmer. On meeting the queen for the first time after Bean's attack Peel was moved to tears. Victoria on the other hand showed unusual sympathy over Drummond's assassination and was filled with true Hanoverian indignation when MacNaghten was acquitted on grounds of insanity.[3] On his visits to Windsor Peel was relaxed and unselfconscious enough to drop into his mild joking vein at mealtimes[4] and he was evolving his own ways of handling the royal pair. Their constant interest in state affairs was sometimes encouraging, as in their lively support for strong measures to repress the disorder of 1842 and 1843, and equally forcible condemnation of the obstruction of the Leaguers in the House of Commons; sometimes embarrassing, as when Albert, in response to the views of the Portuguese court, tried to persuade Peel to modify the British attitude to the commercial treaty with Portugal in the summer of 1843. But none of this caused real concern to the

[1] RA/C 58/28; *VL*, I, 439, 487. The final adjudication, favourable to Hanover, was not made until 1857.
[2] RA/F 21/1 (Oct. 1843).
[3] *VL*, I, 469; Martin, *Prince Consort*, Pt. I, 24.
[4] Cf. Lady Bloomfield, *Reminiscences* (1883 new edn), p. 33.

prime minister. When misgivings were expressed in the cabinet in July over the projected visit of Victoria and Albert to Ostend to see King Leopold, following their official visit to the French Court, Peel assured his colleagues that 'they will be as reasonable as possible—but it does not do to thwart them. I know how to manage them—the way is to receive the proposals without objection and show a willingness to meet their desires—then as difficulties appear, they will grow cool.'[1]

The final open mark of favour came in November when, to the chagrin of some of the Whigs, Victoria and Albert visited the prime minister at Drayton. It was a quiet domestic occasion, in keeping with the comfort and orderliness rather than grandeur and formality which the visitors discovered in Peel's country home. Before dinner on the first day Julia and all the ladies waited on the queen and presented her with a bouquet. Matilda Paget, one of the Maids of Honour, reported that Lady Peel was 'truly kind . . . the Queen has looked pleased and happy, and it has not been the least formal'. The dinner, as might be expected of Peel's cook, was excellent and the prime minister had the pleasure of toasting his sovereign under his own roof. Next day, when the prince departed for Birmingham, Victoria went round the dairy and kitchen garden, and after lunch the ladies sauntered about the hall and looked at illustrated books while waiting for the arrival of the old dowager queen Adelaide who was coming over from Witley to see her niece.[2]

Albert's wish to visit the great industrial and radical town of Birmingham had necessitated certain precautions and Graham had troops and police available in case of disturbance. Peel made the local arrangements in Staffordshire and at Birmingham but he had no real apprehension except from the immense crowds expected to appear. The mayor and many of the council were Chartists but, the prime minister assured Graham, fully as loyal as their neighbours.[3] The event justified the prediction. As he wrote afterwards to Stanley

Everything that has passed here and in the neighbourhood has left a strong impression on the minds of the Queen and the Prince that loyalty and devotion to the Monarchy are deeply grafted in the minds

[1] 44777 f. 86.   [2] Bloomfield, *op. cit.*, pp. 53–4.   [3] 40449 fos. 231–2.

of the English people. They say, and *they* include Colonel Thorn the Military Officer in Command—that there were 250,000 people congregated in Birmingham. *More meo* I strike off 100,000 from the estimate. Still, universal concord and universal satisfaction among such a multitude as will remain after my abatement of numbers, are very striking amid all the discontent, disunion, and disloyalty.[1]

It was something that little more than a year after the scenes of August 1842 the representatives of the monarchy could tour the factories of Birmingham capitalists and be entertained by a Chartist mayor without a single unpleasant incident. In his own more rural and deferential neighbourhood Peel commemorated the royal visit by giving a shilling to each of the school children of Tamworth, Drayton and Fazeley who lined the royal route and a hundred guineas to the mayor of Tamworth to be applied to 'some sort of carousing for the poorest of the town and of the hamlets', not forgetting those in the workhouse.

It was a satisfying end to a not very satisfactory year; and made all the more so by the growing signs of national recovery. In September Peel had been on one of his regular visits to shoot with the Duke of Rutland at Longshawe where he unexpectedly encountered a somewhat embarrassed Lord John Manners, the leader of the Young Englanders.[2] From there he wrote to Victoria of the unusually fine weather, the prospects of a good harvest, and the strong likelihood that the price of provisions would keep reasonably low in 1844. Besides which, he added, almost all branches of industry were showing improvement.[3] To Ellenborough, in distant India, he described at the start of November in more measured but still optimistic terms the 'chequered state of our affairs here'.

> The balance of good preponderates. We have friendly feelings established with France and the United States. Apparent harmony and prosperity in Canada—a moderate price of provisions. The Income Tax producing more than we calculated and causing little grievance and even little complaint—a surplus of revenue instead of a great deficit. The cotton manufacture flourishing—trade generally reviving. On the other hand we have (I hope I may say) have had,

---

[1] 40468 f. 85.   [2] C. Whibley, *Lord John Manners* (1925), I, 170.
[3] RA/A 15/60–3.

a troublesome social distemper in South Wales. We have that great standing evil, which counterbalances all good, the State of Ireland.[1]

Few governments are long without problems; no nineteenth-century British government was without the problem of Ireland. But domestically at least it looked as if the ship of state, so long wallowing in the uneasy trough of 1843, was beginning to feel a new wind stirring its sails.

[1] Ellenborough Corr. (1 Nov. 1843); 40472 fos. 102-4.

12

THE SERBONIAN BOG

The cabinet of 1841, with four ex-Chief Secretaries among its members, was as knowledgeable on Ireland as any of the century. But it was a mark of the Irish problem that knowledge often only brought pessimism. In private conversation at Drayton some five years earlier Peel had made the depressing comment that though the political troubles of England could probably be cured, the state of Ireland was to all appearances hopeless. The fundamental weakness was the inability to secure the ordinary administration of justice, since its basic institution—the jury system—rested on a presumption of identity between the jurymen and the state which in Ireland simply did not exist. Two years later, in December 1837, during a discussion of religious affairs on the continent, he let fall the significant remark that what the English had conspicuously failed to do in either Ireland or Canada was to establish a working relationship with the Catholic Church.[1] Diagnosis, however, is a logical preliminary to prescription. Pessimistic as these observations were, they contained the germ of most of Peel's later Irish policy.

When he came to power in 1841 English affairs inevitably took first place in his mind. The preceding decade had seen a substantial number of Irish reforms—tithe, Church of Ireland, municipalities, and poor law. Of the remaining problems susceptible to immediate legislative remedy there was nothing that called urgently for attention. In the circumstances of both islands a period of quiet and sensible administration in Ireland had much to commend it. During the years of O'Connell's collaboration with the Whigs much of the fire had gone from the Irish nationalist party. In anticipation of a Conservative victory the Irish leader had started a new agitation for

[1] 44777 fos. 23, 40.

the repeal of the Union, but that issue in itself isolated him from his political allies in England. The general election of 1841 had reduced his parliamentary following to the coachload of passengers with which he had derisively compared Stanley's party in 1835; and the first two years of the Repeal Association saw only a slow and hesitant advance. In the autumn and winter of 1841 Ireland seemed moderately quiet and Peel was content to leave it in that rare and happy state. In September he was urging the new Lord Lieutenant to exercise patronage on merit rather than party expediency and in January he observed dryly that the proceedings of the Repeal Association suggested a desire for martyrdom which the executive should carefully abstain from gratifying.[1] To Graham he remarked that 'when a country is tolerably quiet, it is better for a Government to be *hard of hearing* in respect to seditious language than to be very agile in prosecuting'.[2]

What was more disturbing in the first eighteen months of office was the personal friction in the new team of Irish officials. Earl de Grey, who had gone to Ireland as Lord Lieutenant with the lament that it was perfect banishment, was a handsome, good-humoured man of the world with a pretty, talkative wife, a sister of the prominent Orange peer, Lord Enniskillen. Underneath his easy manner, however, there was a vein of intractability. He soon revealed a combination of ultra-Protestant predilections, mediocre political sagacity, and jaunty confidence in his own capabilities, which indicated that he would not be the easiest of viceroys to control. The Chief Secretary, Lord Eliot, son and heir of the Earl of St. Germans, was his opposite in every respect except their common aristocratic background. Liberal, high-minded, sensitive and emotional, Eliot had strong views but lacked strong personality. A man of great kindness and integrity, he responded readily to sympathetic treatment but was prickly when ignored or opposed. He was unable to sustain his point of view with the tact, patience and persistence which a Chief Secretary needed when dealing with his technical superiors. The impulsive gestures with which he was liable to assert himself alienated his colleagues and shook their confidence in his judgement. The third member of the trio, Lucas, the under-secretary, was an Irish Protestant landowner and a former M.P. for co.

[1] 40477 fos. 17, 138.   [2] 40446 f. 231 (Dec. 1841).

Monaghan. Peel regarded him and John Young of Cavan as the ablest of the Conservative Irish members. But he was antipathetic to Eliot and conscious of his own importance as deputy to the Chief Secretary and immediate adviser to the Lord Lieutenant during the six months of the parliamentary session. It was a familiar situation in the history of Irish administration since the Union but familiarity did nothing to reduce its awkwardness. The oddity was that Peel, with more experience of the realities of Irish government than any other nineteenth-century prime minister, should have perpetuated by his choice of men the endemic weakness of the system. The explanation must be sought partly in the limited field on which he could draw for Irish appointments, partly in the besetting need to preserve a political balance in the composition of the Irish executive. But a balance of political views needed the oil of confidence if it was not to lead to constant friction over policy. Any personal clash between Lord Lieutenant and Chief Secretary at once brought into the open the inherent anomalies of their constitutional relationship.[1] The other members of the Castle junto were of little help in this situation. Sugden, the Lord Chancellor, was a good academic lawyer with little practical sense. The Attorney-General Blackburne was in disagreement with many of Eliot's views. Both were apt themselves to take decisions without much consultation.

While conscious of Eliot's occasional tactlessness and forced by political expediency to make greater allowance for Irish Conservative opinion than his impetuous subordinate, Peel was generally on the side of the Secretary in his unequal struggle with unsympathetic colleagues in Dublin Castle. He deprecated the series of prosecutions and dismissals from the magistracy which the Lord Chancellor and the Attorney-General began on their own initiative in the autumn of 1841; he upheld Eliot's protest against the proposed appointment of the uncompromising Protestant Dr. Elrington to the bishopric of Meath in the summer of 1842; and he persuaded a reluctant Lord Lieutenant to promote Howley, a Roman Catholic barrister, to the rank of Third Sergeant in the following year. On the wider problem of the relationship between Lord Lieutenant and Chief Secretary his attitude, based on his own unrivalled experience, was even more sharply defined. Aware as early as December 1841 of

[1] For a fuller discussion of these problems, see *Mr. Secretary Peel*, chs. 4, 11, and 15.

Eliot's resentment at lack of consultation, he advised Graham to make his communications to the Irish government as far as possible through the Secretary.[1] He thought de Grey too apt to keep his subordinate in the background and to overlook the fact that Eliot's unique parliamentary responsibilities entitled him to 'great deference and authority'. Continually to hold the balance between the jarring elements at Dublin Castle threw much needless work on the senior ministers in London. The growing discordancies among the Irish officials during 1842 which broke out even on the floor of the House of Commons made the prime minister comment sharply to Graham in October that it was impossible for them to go on as they had been doing, collecting different opinions from each member of the Irish government. Those officials must either decide collectively or simply put the facts before the cabinet for a ruling. 'We are invited, not only to govern Ireland in details, but to solve the difficulties arising from the discrepancies of opinion of those on the spot.' Eliot's solution was to abolish his own office. In a letter written the following December he observed bitterly that 'an efficient Lord Lieutenant necessarily renders the office of Secretary a sinecure, and it seems to me that the presence of one in Ireland, except as a preparation for his parliamentary business, might be dispensed with'.

A crisis of this nature was something the prime minister was not prepared to tolerate. If it did happen, it would be taken as proof of the inadequacy of the existing constitutional methods of governing Ireland and would compel the ministry to recast the system entirely. In that case his remedy was the reverse of Eliot's. 'The basis of a new arrangement would be the abolition of the office of Lord Lieutenant —in my opinion a great evil, but a lesser evil than discord between the Lord Lieutenant and his representative in the House of Commons.' But he exerted his authority to ensure that it did not happen. To de Grey he sent an urgent plea to avoid disagreement with Eliot and enclosed the Secretary's letter as proof of the seriousness of the situation. To Eliot he wrote a long and sympathetic reply covering twelve sides of paper, in which he analysed from his own experience under three viceroys the complex position of a Chief Secretary,

---

[1] The misprint in *Peel*, III, 36 (Peel to Graham, 6 Dec. 1841) of 'do not like' for the correct MS. version 'do not dislike', blunts the force of this particular expression of views.

assured him of the importance attached by the cabinet to his views and of Peel's own complete confidence, but reminded him that on the Secretary rested the main responsibility for overcoming the intrinsic difficulties of the situation. 'The contest with them makes his office a most valuable preparatory course for higher duties; the complete mastery of them proves his qualification for those higher duties.'[1] Touched by this kindness and mollified by a conciliatory letter from de Grey in response to Peel's promptings, Eliot agreed to carry on. Even so Graham, who was conspicuously less sympathetic than Peel in his attitude to the Chief Secretary, observed hopefully to the prime minister at the end of the year that the Earl of St. Germans could not be immortal and there were some great advantages in an hereditary peerage.

The difficulties were only papered over, however, and each minor crisis caused new cracks to appear. In June 1843 Lucas tended his resignation partly on grounds of disagreement on policy, partly on internal administrative grievances. The Lord Lieutenant, loth to let him go, seized the opportunity to point out the deficiencies of his other subordinates. He was, he assured Peel, without a single man on whom he could rely. Even when Eliot was present his advice and judgement were nil. Sugden, like Eliot and himself, was a stranger to Ireland and had no knowledge of mankind. The Attorney-General was away; the Solicitor-General was absolutely useless.[2] Peel thought Lucas's behaviour shabby and said so. But though de Grey succeeded in retaining him, the Lord Lieutenant himself was not viewed with much favour by Peel and Graham. In July the Home Secretary suggested that as soon as de Grey left Ireland they should consider abolishing his office and governing Ireland through a Secretary of State for Ireland assisted by one under-secretary in London and another in Dublin.[3] Their basic dissatisfaction with de Grey was over his persistent refusal to carry out the government's stated policy of admitting Roman Catholics to a reasonable share in official patronage. On this question Catholic emancipation in 1829 had worked a great change in Peel's mind compared with his youthful attitudes when he first went to Ireland in 1812. To govern

---

[1] 40448 f. 124, pr. *Peel*, III, 41; 40480 f. 200.
[2] 40478 f. 67, ptly pr. *Peel*, III, 53.
[3] 40448 fos. 356, 358.

on the old Ascendancy assumption that there were only two classes in Ireland, friends and enemies, would inevitably lead to the monopoly of power by a few families. Even the 'specious priniciple', as he described it, that when Protestant candidates were better qualified than Catholics they must be appointed, should not in his view be too literally adopted. 'We must *look out* for respectable Roman Catholics for office.' To that extent political expediency had to take precedence over alleged administrative efficiency. The government must do in Ireland what they were trying to do in Scotland over the Kirk dispute. Though they could not hope to conciliate inveterate enemies, they should endeavour to 'give satisfaction to a great body of moderate men and withdraw them from the ranks of our opponents'.

To expect de Grey, however, of his own accord to look out for respectable Roman Catholics was evidently useless. Indeed, he told Peel flatly in August that 'conciliation is a chimera'. Faced with this direct repudiation of the government's policy, Peel once more intervened with the full moral and intellectual weight of his office. In a long thirteen-page letter to the viceroy on 22 August he expounded in clear terms the principles on which he required the Irish executive to act. Policy and justice, he wrote, demanded not only a liberal but an indulgent estimate of the claims of Catholic candidates for office. Emancipation in law was useless if it was not followed by equality in practice. Long years of legal privilege had given the Irish Protestants habits, connections, training and expectations which perpetuated their hold on official posts. If this historic monopoly continued, the active and talented Roman Catholics would use the political opportunities now open to them to work systematically against the whole system of Irish government. 'Every avenue to popular favour is opened, and if every avenue to Royal favour be closed, we have done nothing by the removal of disabilities but organise a band of mischievous demagogues.' If, as de Grey asserted, no favours could conciliate the mass of Roman Catholics, it was hard to see how the government of Ireland could be carried on or the Union long maintained. Even though two-thirds of the Irish members were political opponents of the Conservative government, their attitude was still materially affected by the policy of that government. In turn their attitude would affect the whole body of Roman Catholics in Ireland. Even apart from that influence there were many in that body on whom a liberal policy would have a conciliatory effect. The maintenance of the Church of Ireland and the existing distribution of property placed severe limitations on the distribution of local patronage to Catholics. It was all the more necessary therefore to favour them in those areas of patronage, particularly civil office and the Bar, where these limitations did not apply.[1]

To this communication, in itself a minor state paper which received the unqualified endorsement of Graham, Stanley and Sugden, the Lord Lieutenant made a token surrender by the promotion of Howley. In the latter part of August when de Grey came to England to take a cure at Buxton, Peel and Graham had a long discussion with him on the patronage question. Even after this they were still far from satisfied. The prime minister thought that de Grey still misunderstood the relative positions of Lord Lieutenant and Chief Secretary. He told Graham privately that he would not have stayed in the Secretaryship an hour if he had been excluded from consultation on patronage as Eliot had been; and he was displeased at the series of exclusive Protestant appointments in the senior ranks of the Irish constabulary which Eliot had reported.[2] Short of making drastic changes in the Irish government, however, all he and Graham could do was to continue their exhortations and take on a larger burden of Irish decisions than they had a right to expect.

One of the early disagreements within the Irish government was over education. In 1831 Stanley as Whig Chief Secretary had put through a plan for national schools administered by a mixed Board of Commissioners which included Murray, the Catholic Archbishop of Dublin. Despite the hostility of most Anglican and some Roman bishops, the scheme had worked well in so far as it provided a network of Irish elementary schools. As a means of promoting mixed as distinct from national education it had largely failed. The majority of schools were either Anglican or Roman or Presbyterian with each Church extracting what sectarian advantage it could from the system. With the arrival of a Conservative ministry in 1841 the Archbishop of Armagh, the Anglican primate, supported by the Lord Lieutenant, urged a return to the practice of making a separate

---

[1] 40478 fos. 160–6, ptly pr. *Peel*, III, 56–60.
[2] 40449 f. 7, ptly pr. *Peel*, III, 60.

state grant to the Anglican Church Education Society. Even Stanley, the author of the mixed schools policy, was inclined to favour the suggestion on the analogy of the English system. Eliot, on the other hand, was adamantly opposed to any breach in the national scheme. It would probably result, he warned Peel, in the resignation from the Board of both Murray and the Anglican Archbishop of Dublin, Whately; and would be felt by moderates on both sides as a blow at the whole concept of national education. A separate Anglican grant would inevitably be followed by a demand by the Presbyterians for a similar concession. The National scheme would then become an exclusively Catholic organisation, setting up at the taxpayers' expense 'a little Maynooth' in every parish.[1] Peel refused to be rushed into a decision and forbade the Lord Lieutenant in November 1841 to carry on any discussion with the Irish primate on the subject. But in the course of 1842 continued Anglican pressure, debates in the House of Commons, an open clash of views between Eliot and Jackson, the Irish Solicitor-General, and the proposed election of Elrington, a known opponent of the National system, to the diocese of Meath, made it imperative for the cabinet to decide formally whether to continue the existing system or not. The situation was complicated by a renewed move by the Catholic hierarchy to obtain an increased grant for Maynooth.[2] Eliot, convinced of the inadequacies of the college and sympathetic to the creation of a 'well educated clergy' in Ireland, was already advising a committee of enquiry.

It needed no special perspicacity on Peel's part to foresee the sectarian controversies which would ensue. But he promised to bring both issues before the cabinet in the autumn and had further discussions on the subject during the summer with Graham and the Lord Lieutenant.[3] On 7 November the cabinet deliberated on the two knotty problems of Irish education and Maynooth. The upshot was a decision neither to institute an enquiry into Maynooth nor to make a separate grant for Anglican education in Ireland. It was the line of least trouble, and no doubt recommended itself as such.

[1] 40480 fos. 76, 104.
[2] For the earlier history of the seminary at Maynooth, see *Mr. Secretary Peel*, pp. 149–51.
[3] 40480 fos. 118, 120, 132.

Yet even if there had been any disposition on the part of his colleagues to take up these dangerous issues, Peel was disinclined to make any move. The discussions of the previous months had convinced him of the importance of maintaining the only system which offered some faint prospect of bringing children of different creeds side by side and giving them a simple undenominational education. With Eliot he felt that any special concession to the Anglican Church would lead to a progressive disintegration of the whole organisation. Politically it would cast doubt on the liberalism of the government and destroy confidence in their proclaimed intention of governing Ireland not for the sake of one class or sect but for the good of the entire nation. To a letter of protest from the Irish primate he returned a reasoned but decisive answer. The Archbishop Lord George Beresford, one of the most aristocratic figures on the Irish bench, was he thought 'an honourable and upright man' but he was determined to leave him in no doubt as to the strength of the government's resolution. He was rewarded by a public declaration from the primate and his bishops accepting the government's decision and pledging themselves to abstain from further agitation on the question of the National schools.[1] 'Peel has been stout on the education question', Graham wrote approvingly to Stanley, 'and he would have had no peace if he had faltered.'[2] As for Maynooth, the prime minister judged it impossible at that stage either to appoint a commission which would have the confidence of both parties or to frame any acceptable terms of reference for its enquiries. Eliot, gratified by the successful issue of the education controversy, was prepared to accept this ruling; though he still felt that great benefits would be obtained by putting the college on a sound financial footing. He had recently been approached by Matthew Flanagan, the secretary to the Maynooth trustees, and took care to forward to Peel the statement which the latter had drawn up of the case for an additional grant. At the same time he was able to report that the Trustees appreciated the government's difficulties and were ready to wait for a more propitious moment.[3] For the time being therefore that infinitely more controversial issue was laid on one side.

[1] 40480 fos. 145, 195; Graham (Peel to Graham, 20 Nov. 1842).
[2] *Graham*, I, 358.
[3] 40480 fos. 149, 153.

II

In the first six months of 1843 the repeal movement came suddenly and explosively to life. The first sign was the popular support evidenced at various county meetings at the start of the year. This was followed at the end of February by a successful motion for repeal petitions at a meeting of the Dublin Corporation when O'Connell went far to conciliate moderates by declaring his readiness to accept an Irish parliament with limited powers. After Easter the movement gathered momentum with a series of monster meetings all over Catholic Ireland. The flow of subscriptions rose sharply. Clergy and educated laity as well as peasantry began to enrol. A number of Catholic bishops became members, including the redoubtable MacHale of Tuam who like some medieval prince-bishop joined at the head of a hundred of his priests. The radical nationalists of the Young Ireland group, with their newspaper, *The Nation*, threw their weight into the campaign. Financial support and the cheaper currency of anti-English threats came from America and Canada. Offers of aid in the forthcoming struggle were made in the bellicose French liberal press. In Ireland a nation-wide organisation collected funds and a central council began to ape some of the activities of an Irish Legislature. Flushed with success O'Connell increased his pressure. He now proclaimed as his objective a membership of three million, repeal wardens in every parish and the summoning of what would be in effect a national convention in Dublin to prepare for the repeal of the Union. The year 1843, he announced, was to be the Repeal Year. What made the situation all the more dangerous was that O'Connell, a past-master in the gentle art of legal disruption, took care to keep within the forms of the constitution while making psychological use of the threat of popular disorder.[1] The Irish government which had previously underrated the danger reacted violently when it realised the extent of the crisis. On 6 May the Lord Lieutenant sent off a despatch to London in which a highly coloured assessment of the situation was coupled with the lame excuse that until the last few weeks the movement had been

[1] For the rise of the Repeal Movement see C. G. Duffy, *Young Ireland* (1880); K. B. Nowlan, *Politics of Repeal* (1965), ch. II; R. B. McDowell, *Public Opinion and Government Policy in Ireland* (1952), chs. 8, 9.

utterly undeserving of notice. De Grey in fact had been caught off guard and showed it by the panic of his language.

> Let whatever you do be strong enough. Temporary if you please, to make it palatable, but durable enough to give it fair play. Let no morbid sensibility, or mawkish apprehension of invading the Constitution which might influence some minds and perhaps secure some trifling support, be allowed to weigh.[1]

The central government had been more observant. In the middle of April Peel had written to Graham on the unpleasant state of Ireland and the need for local police and military reinforcements. Even before de Grey wrote, two regiments of cavalry had arrived in Dublin from England and two infantry regiments were on their way out.[2] Having taken these precautions the prime minister and the Home Secretary were inclined to view matters more coolly, particularly since Eliot in London advised against any precipitate action. Nevertheless the Irish Conservatives in both houses were restive and had communicated their fears to the Duke of Wellington. In any case it was impossible to ignore the Lord Lieutenant's letter, even if Peel had no intention of being swayed by it. A cabinet on 8 May, attended by Eliot and the Attorney General, formally endorsed the official view that no extraordinary counter-measures should be undertaken until actual treasonable offences were committed. Stanley, laid up by gout, sent Peel a letter which he read out to the cabinet, deprecating any legislation aimed at the repeal movement. To the ministers in London the situation appeared considerably more complex than it did to the Lord Lieutenant in Dublin Castle. The Irish officials themselves were not unanimous; Eliot would clearly have no relish for piloting a coercive measure through the Commons; and with the Anti-Corn Law League imitating O'Connell's tactics and language in England, it would seem invidious to attack only one movement and foolhardy to attack both.[3] Peel wrote back to de Grey, asking him to confer with the Chancellor on the possibility of new security legislation but to bear in mind also the perennial difficulty of all Irish penal enactments—the unwillingness of Irish juries to convict. He agreed however that newspapers guilty of

---

[1] 40478 fos. 39–44, ptly pr. *Peel*, III, 46–7.   [2] 40448 fos. 273, 289.
[3] 40468 f. 14; 40448 f. 297, ptly pr. *Peel*, III, 47.

seditious language should be prosecuted since in the present circumstances failure to secure conviction was a lesser evil than complete passivity.[1]

In the meantime, to placate the Orange faction and reassure the moderates, an official declaration upholding the Union was made in both Houses the day after the cabinet meeting. To underline the seriousness of the statement Peel was present in the House of Lords when Wellington made his reply to a prearranged question from Lord Roden, the Grand Master of the Orange Order. The prime minister himself made the parallel statement in the House of Commons. The duke, more extreme in his private utterances, was circumspect in his official one. Peel by contrast thought it politic to accompany the cabinet's moderation behind the scenes with an uncompromising severity of speech in public. The government, he said, would do all in their power to maintain the Union. They would use all the apparatus of prerogative and law to that end. They would not hesitate to ask parliament for fresh powers if necessary. Finally, with a deliberate repetition of the words used by Lord Althorp on a similar occasion in 1834, he warned the Repealers that though he deprecated war, and above all civil war, there was no alternative which he did not think preferable to a dismemberment of the empire.

Defiance was thus answered by warning but for the time being the cabinet was not prepared to go further. On 15 May they decided that there were no good grounds for banning a great repeal meeting to be held in Tipperary and left it to the Lord Lieutenant to gather more reliable information before recommending action. Though the duke announced ominously that they would soon have to consider the means of carrying on *la grande guerre* in Ireland and later advocated calling out the yeomanry, his more pacific colleagues contented themselves with a resumption of military recruiting and unobtrusive measures to expedite the return of garrison troops from Canada.[2] In Dublin the executive was more active and more intemperate. The Lord Lieutenant told Peel on 11 May that he proposed to issue circulars requesting the county lieutenants to caution magistrates under pain of dismissal against attending meet-

[1] 40478 f. 47.
[2] Graham (Graham to de Grey, 15, 17, 21 May; memorandum by Wellington (18 May 1843).

ings or abetting measures likely to cause mischief. Sugden then proceeded on his own authority to dismiss Lord Ffrench, a Galway magistrate, for declaring his intention of attending a repeal meeting and followed that up by removing another twenty-four J.P.s for actual or in one case merely presumed support of the Repeal movement. Action against magistrates had earlier been discussed between Graham and the Lord Lieutenant but this precipitate step, which the Home Secretary attributed to Sugden's 'vanity and self-sufficiency', gravely embarrassed the ministers. They could not disavow what had been done but on 1 June Peel sent Sugden a scarcely veiled rebuke, reminding him that the dangerous situation made it all the more necessary to consider 'what particular thing should be done, at what time it should be done, and in what mode'.[1] As long as the repeal meetings were conducted legally, it could scarcely be an offence to be present at them; and Sugden had omitted even the elementary precaution of warning the magistrates concerned not to attend them. Their dismissal in fact was a false step. The effect was to drive even more Liberal and Whig Irish gentry into the repeal movement.

The general support in England for the government declaration of 9 May disintegrated still further when the Irish arms bill was introduced by Eliot at the end of the month. In itself it was a normal security measure of a kind previously passed by the Whigs in 1838, dealing with the registration of firearms, the prohibition of lethal weapons such as pikes and daggers, and the sale of gunpowder. But it was fiercely opposed by the Irish and English radicals, and severely criticised by the official Whigs as a confession of bankruptcy in the Irish policy of the government. With passion and obstruction attending the progress of the arms bill through parliament, other difficulties gathered thick and fast round the government. Clanricarde in the House of Lords censured the dismissal of Lord Ffrench. O'Connell at a repeal meeting at Mallow declared that the time was approaching when they would have to live as slaves or die as freemen. Graham, stung by reproaches in the Commons against the barrenness of the government's Irish policy, retorted that unless the House was prepared to grant fixity of tenure or abolish the Church of Ireland, it was difficult to see what further measures of conciliation

[1] 40448 f. 303; Peel, III, 51–2.

could be proposed. It was the type of unnecessary outburst into which Graham's temperament was apt to betray him in moments of strain. He realised the mistake at once and apologised for it in a characteristically modest and conscience-stricken letter to Peel on 18 June.[1] In a subsequent debate in July, on Smith O'Brien's motion for a committee of enquiry into Irish grievances, he did what he could to tone down his previous words. But the damage had been done and a general impression created that in fact the government possessed no positive policy on Ireland at all. It was not entirely true; but what was true was that the government had nothing they were ready to bring forward that session. Irish woes and Irish politics did not lend themselves to easy improvisation.

For the moment, between the pressure of their opponents and the pressure of their own supporters, they were pinned into an uncomfortably tight corner. The Lord Lieutenant was pleading for sharper measures against the agitation in Ireland and on 8 and 11 June the cabinet deliberated at length whether it would be feasible either to prohibit organised assemblies for the repeal of the union or to suppress the whole repeal organisation. To accomplish the latter would mean, in effect, giving the Lord Lieutenant powers to stop any meeting of any kind for any purpose. Without much disagreement but with many fluctuations of views in the course of the discussion, the cabinet finally decided that the first course would be impolitic and the second impracticable. Even for the more limited purpose the passage of a bill through parliament would be difficult; its operation ineffective; its failure disastrous. The more drastic alternative offered even greater hazards. Even if such extraordinary powers could be obtained from parliament, it was difficult to see how the Lord Lieutenant could use them. Reliance on juries was hopeless; even magistrates would be impotent to deal with meetings held in chapel or after mass, or by corporations and other closed bodies. More important still, harsh legislation might simply give fresh stimulus to agitation; and the agitation would not be confined to Ireland. As Peel wrote to de Grey on 12 June:

> I firmly believe, in the present state of things, from the party opposed to us, there would be banded against the measure, that is against a measure of simple unqualified coercion, the Whig party, the Radical

party, the Chartist party, the Anti-Corn Law League party—all those parties, by whatever name they may be called, who are in favour of democracy or of mischief and confusion.[1]

A general constitutional opposition of this kind would do more to encourage the repeal movement in Ireland than simple agitation and disorder. In face of the total political situation confronting them in 1843, therefore, the cabinet decided not to seek any fresh coercive powers. A policy of prudent forbearance by the executive and the chance of some tactical mistake by the agitators seemed to offer the only hope of coming through the crisis.

It was a policy of sense, but it was not heroic. When accurate if not actually inspired reports in the press of the cabinet decisions made it obvious that no positive action was intended, feeling in Irish Protestant circles against the government mounted steadily. There were criticisms of Peel, attacks on Eliot, and demands for the prosecution of O'Connell. The Lord Lieutenant continued to press for firmer measures, though he was told bluntly by Peel in July that the Irish arms bill had involved them in enough difficulty and they wanted proof that fresh legislation was necessary.[2] In private Peel was thoroughly dissatisfied with the state of Irish affairs and beginning to feel that Ireland represented the most vulnerable aspect of his parliamentary position. He told the cabinet in a fit of ill-humour, that though they could not now abandon the arms bill, they would not carry it. It had been badly drafted, nobody seemed to understand it, and the new Attorney General, T. B. C. Smith, had proved a disappointment. In the Commons, he added, Russell had not only lost control of his party but probably had a secret understanding with O'Connell. The great object of the whole agitation was to drive out the government.[3] In those circumstances it was not surprising that Peel was more intent for the time being on getting the ill-assorted Irish team to work together and instilling some rudimentary political sense into the Lord Lieutenant's patronage policy than embarking on more ostentatious activities.

Meanwhile in Ireland O'Connell was multiplying his monster meetings and using ever more threatening language. At Tara in Meath, the site of the palace of the old Irish kings, a meeting took place in August which outdid all its predecessors. It passed into

[1] 40478 fos. 79–84.   [2] ibid. f. 103.   [3] 44777 f. 91.

legend as the meeting of the million and even more sober contemporary accounts placed the number of those who attended at 500,000. Whatever the size of the assembly, it was the most formidable, Peel told the queen, in point of preparations and numbers that had yet been held. To flavour the government's disquiet there was a report that some twenty Frenchmen were present and in communication with O'Connell.[1] The undercurrent of tithe and tenant-right agitation which accompanied the repeal movement strengthened Wellington's conviction that the whole social order in Ireland was in danger of collapsing. It became unpleasantly apparent to Peel and Graham in September that the duke was aching to go himself to Ireland to take charge of the situation. This was unthinkable but even Graham was so far infected by the growing unease as to complain bitterly of the inactivity of the Irish law officers in enforcing elementary law and order. 'I begin to despair of the Irish Executive,' he wrote to the prime minister in September, 'it does not only sleep, it is dead.'[2] Peel remained cooler and more detached. When secret papers compromising the repeal movement fell into government hands, he warned Graham not to attach too much importance to them as O'Connell had probably nothing to do with their production. 'Among all conspirators in Ireland', he observed cynically, 'there is a love of mystery and of secret association which tempts them in contravention of the wishes and orders of the Leaders, to prepare and carry about with them Papers like that referred to.'[3]

There were in fact some signs that if the worst was not yet over, at least O'Connell himself was in a dilemma. By the very success of his campaign, he had excited Irish expectations to the point where it would be dangerous for him to go further and humiliating to retreat. The real question for the government was a tactical one. What they had to decide was the exact point at which it would be possible to intervene in such a way as to silence O'Connell and bring the repeal movement to a halt. Materials for legal action against the agitator were beginning to accumulate. He had attacked the queen's speech at the end of the session and issued a counter-manifesto which implied that there was no hope of obtaining redress for Irish

[1] RA/A 15/52.   [2] 40449 f. 23, ptly pr. *Peel*, III, 62-3.
[3] Graham, 18 Sept. 1843.

408

grievances by legal or constitutional means. His announcement of a final monster meeting to be held at Clontarf on 8 October was couched in more martial terms than usual; and the issue was decided by the appearance of placards summoning the attendance of 'Repeal Cavalry' at the meeting. O'Connell had alluded at earlier meetings to the existence of 'cavalry' among his mass supporters; and this fondness for military metaphors combined with customary Hibernian exuberance probably led to the phraseology of the notorious Clontarf placards.[1] There is no evidence that O'Connell himself was responsible. They were in fact withdrawn and the more innocuous title of 'Repealers on Horseback' substituted. But by then it was too late to retrieve the blunder.

At this point de Grey was still in England on his Buxton cure. On 3 and 4 October there were long meetings between himself, Peel, Graham and the available English and Irish law officers. Even apart from the cavalry placards, the legal experts were of the opinion that there was sufficient evidence in the speeches and writings of O'Connell and other repeal agitators to sustain a charge of treasonable conspiracy and as Peel prudently qualified it, 'on which an honest jury ought to convict'. They also ruled that the forthcoming meeting at Clontarf, independent of proof of alarm to the queen's subjects, was illegal and ought not to be tolerated.[2] After two days' discussion, therefore, it was decided that de Grey and Sugden should return to Ireland with full authority to apprehend O'Connell and leading members of the Association, to ban the Clontarf meeting, and if necessary to disperse it by force. Peel, who had come up from Drayton for the consultations, remained in London to await the outcome of events. Graham simultaneously made military and naval arrangements to reinforce the authorities in Ireland should the need arise. Now that the crisis had arrived, Peel and Graham were determined to see the matter through and the duke was positively 'enchanted' that decisive action was to be taken at last. Even when it was learned in London that O'Connell had repudiated the cavalry placards, the Home Secretary after consulting Peel instructed the Lord Lieutenant to proceed at his discretion as planned.[3] Legalistic

[1] Duffy, *op. cit.*, p. 360 n.   [2] 43063 f. 11.
[3] Graham (Graham to Irish Attorney-General, 3 Oct.; to Stanley, 4 Oct.; to Wellington, 5 Oct. 1843).

doubts among other members of the Irish executive delayed the announcement of the Lord Lieutenant's proclamation until 7 October. As soon as it appeared, however, O'Connell abandoned the meeting and called on his followers not to put themselves in conflict with the law.

It was a startling surrender; but in retrospect not surprising. At the age of sixty-eight, with declining physical powers, O'Connell was temperamentally incapable of departing from the line of legal agitation he had consistently pursued throughout his career. In that lay the fundamental flaw in his strategy. If the great parade of force staged by the Repeal Association was never intended to be more than a psychological weapon against the government, then it was essentially a battle of nerve and judgement: a battle which the ministers won. O'Connell had never devised any policy on what was to be done if popular pressure was answered by legal action; and his passive surrender forfeited the confidence if not immediately the support of his younger nationalist allies. Nevertheless it was not clear then either to friends or enemies that he had reached the final turning-point of his long tempestuous life; nor that the repeal movement had received a decisive check. In the situation at the time there seemed no reason for the government to refrain from following up their first successful blow at the Association. To have done so indeed might have weakened its effect. A week later O'Connell and half a dozen leading Repealers, including the editors of the two most important nationalist newspapers, were arrested on charges of conspiracy. Bail was given and in the interval before the trial (which in the event did not begin until the following year) O'Connell instructed his followers, to Peel's satiric amusement, to refrain from acts of disturbance and agitation, and to act 'patiently, quietly, legally'. To the ministers O'Connell in the law courts was like an old fox in his home coverts. Though the government had driven him to earth, there was no sentimental disposition on Peel's part to underrate the wiliness of his adversary.[1] For that reason O'Connell's continued retraction of some of his former language, including a statement of his willingness to reduce his demands for 'repeal' to one for a federal and subordinate Irish legislature, aroused the curiosity of the prime minister. 'What has chiefly surprised me in the

[1] Graham (Peel to Graham, 15, 21 Oct. 1843).

recent events in Dublin', he wrote to Stanley on 21 October, 'is that O'Connell does not see the impolicy of the submissive tone which he now takes. What must his former partisans think of him when he abandons, in face of the threatened prosecution, Repeal of the Union for a Federal Parliament?'[1] It was a long time before Peel and Graham realised that in bringing O'Connell to trial they had not only halted the Repeal movement but broken the morale of the old Irish leader.

III

To Peel, as to any politician not blinded by interest or prejudice, the repeal movement was only one and not the most important element in the Irish problem. It was symptomatic, in that it represented the kind of agitation which could always be thrown up by the existing social conditions of Ireland; but it was negative, offering no possibility of solution or compromise; and it was an irritant in so far as it obstructed the application of more fundamental remedies. The sudden check administered by the executive in the autumn of 1843 was the beginning and not the end of the government's Irish policy. In a letter to Graham a few days after O'Connell's arrest, the prime minister laid down as an axiom that 'mere force, however necessary the application of it, will do nothing as a permanent remedy for the social evils of that country'. It was the duty of government to look beyond the present. The time might come when to a Britain at war stability in Ireland might be a matter of national importance. 'Let you and I ponder on these things and say nothing to others until we have talked them over.'[2]

One step however had already been taken. Ever since the middle thirties the subject of Irish agrarian reform had been under intermittent public discussion. Revolving round such proposals as the extension of Ulster tenant-right to the other Irish provinces, legal fixity of tenure, and compulsory compensation for improvements to outgoing tenants, it had formed part of O'Connell's repeal campaign, it had been urged by Irish members like Sharman Crawford, and taken up by liberal Whigs like Lord Howick. In the general

---

[1] 40468 f. 72.   [2] 40449 f. 105.

debate on the state of Ireland in July 1843 the relations of landlord and tenant had figured prominently in both opposition and government speeches. Peel, in his own contribution to the debate, while warning the House (perhaps unnecessarily) of the danger of any measure which seriously affected the rights of property, freely admitted the unsatisfactory condition of the Irish peasantry, hinted at legislative protection for tenants wantonly evicted without compensation for improvements, and pledged the government to take into consideration the whole question of landlord and tenant relationships.[1] Discussions between Peel and Graham during the summer led to a decision to appoint a small commission to enquire into the law and practice of land occupation in Ireland. While they were still corresponding on the subject Lord Devon, a liberal and occasionally resident Irish as well as English landowner, wrote to Peel urging him not to entrust the enquiry to a committee of the House of Commons in which he feared a demagogic spirit might be present. Peel, quick to seize the opportunity, asked him in return whether he would serve as chairman if a small commission were appointed instead. Devon's prudence, reliability and legal knowledge of landlord and tenant relations in both England and Ireland marked him out as an admirable head for such an enquiry and his acceptance was felt by Peel, Graham, and Wellington to be an initial success in what would clearly be a difficult undertaking.[2] To find three or four other knowledgeable, intelligent and unbiased men did not prove easy. Having secured the services of G. A. Hamilton, the Conservative M.P. for Dublin University, and John Wynne, another Irish Conservative, Peel in the end left it to de Grey and Eliot to choose two more from the other side of politics, merely stipulating that one should be a Catholic.[3] Sir R. A. Ferguson, Liberal M.P. for Londonderry, and T. N. Redington, Catholic Liberal M.P. for Dundalk and a future Whig under-secretary for Ireland, were in this way added to the list. The commission was deliberately given wide terms of reference; and Peel and Graham scrupulously avoided giving any private directives to its Conservative members. By the

[1] 11 July 1843 (*Speeches*, IV, 268 et seq.).
[2] Graham (Peel to Graham, 23 Sept.); Wellington (Peel to Wellington, 30 Sept. 1843).
[3] Graham (Graham to Stanley, 7 Oct.; Peel to Graham, 28 Oct. 1843).

start of 1844 the Devon Commission, despite its mixed politics, was already harmoniously at work.[1]

In a political world dominated by landowners and an age which attached some sanctity to the rights of property, Lord Devon and his colleagues were clearly treading on dangerous ground. But Peel was preparing to venture even more deeply into the Serbonian bog of Irish affairs where not only whole armies but policies and administrations had so often sunk without a trace. Dealing with a nation three-parts Catholic it seemed logical in principle to come to terms with the Roman Catholic Church; and it made sense tactically to isolate O'Connell and the repeal movement by driving a wedge between them and the Catholic hierarchy. Nevertheless, the task of securing an understanding between the British government and the Roman Church was herculean even in contemplation. There were several ways of approach which Peel had been turning over in his mind during the summer of 1843. At the start of his ministry he had confessed to Stanley that though he recognised all the difficulties of their relationship with the Catholic Church, he doubted whether in existing circumstances parliament and public opinion would be ready for a dispassionate review of that relationship.[2] Two years later it was a different matter. If O'Connell had done nothing else, he had reinserted the Irish problem into the centre of British politics. What Chartism had done for the condition of England, the repeal movement had done for the condition of Ireland. With his economic schemes launched and the crisis of 1842 behind him, Peel now had both opportunity and incentive to lay the foundations for a constructive Irish policy. Among the 'more comprehensive measures' about which he wrote to Graham in October, he had raised the question of state salaries for the Irish clergy. He had already discussed this delicate matter with Victoria and Albert. They were clearly taken with the notion of conciliating the Irish priesthood in this way, though Peel had warned them of the political difficulties of doing so out of public funds to which among others the unendowed Protestant dissenters would have contributed. Graham faithfully echoed his doubts and endeavoured to preserve the silence enjoined on him. But even within official circles he was being pressed by Eliot and Sugden who both favoured such a policy; and Eliot at

[1] Graham (Graham to Lord Devon, 13 Jan. 1844).   [2] 40467 f. 144 (26 Dec. 1841).

least he encouraged to think further on the question of clerical salaries and Maynooth.

The caution which Peel impressed upon Graham and Graham in turn on Eliot was understandable. To follow firmness by conciliation was a sound enough policy in the abstract; but there was no certainty that the effect produced by the firm action of October would last even until the next session. Given the indifferent quality of the Irish law officers and the grotesqueness of Irish judicial machinery, there was every ground for assuming that the trial of O'Connell would end in failure, the agitation be renewed, and all Ireland be in a turmoil again by next spring.[1] A similar gap between desirability and practicability existed over the Maynooth question. Eliot was once more urging the claims of the college and a generous settlement of that issue might smooth the way for a formal concordat with the Pope. Yet there was no guarantee that British public opinion would tolerate an increased grant to Maynooth. The general anti-Catholic feeling in England had increased rather than decreased since Catholic emancipation; partly because of disillusionment at the failure of that measure to halt Catholic-nationalist agitation in Ireland, partly because of the growing uneasiness in dissenting and moderate Anglican circles at the spread of the apparently Roman-inspired Tractarian movement in the Church of England. A significant remark was let fall by Stanley when arguing in favour of allowing Eliot to proceed with an enquiry into the state of Maynooth. If it did nothing else, he observed, it would elicit factual information which might 'render familiar ideas which at present would not even be permitted to be discussed'.[2]

It was not only Peel and his inner ring of ministers who were beginning to consider in private what would have been political suicide to advocate in public. Even the Lord Lieutenant, taught by office and yielding to the logic of the situation, proposed in October that an approach be made to the Pope in the hope of curbing his Irish bishops. Informal relations between the British government and the Curia already existed. Thomas Aubin, an attaché to the Legation at Florence resident at Rome, had acted as a channel of communication since 1832; and Metternich, scenting in Ireland the distant smell

[1] See Graham's letter of 25 Oct. 1843 (40449 f. 136, ptly pr. *Peel*, III, 67).

[2] To Peel, 21 Oct. 1842 (the date given in *Peel*, III, 67 is 1843 but see D. A. Kerr, *Peel, Priests and Politics*, p. 258, n. 130).

of revolutionary liberalism, had in 1843 put the good offices of the Austrian diplomats at Rome at British disposal.[1] Graham, at Peel's request, passed de Grey's suggestion to Aberdeen. When a few weeks later Metternich asked for the assistance of the British government in suppressing seditious literature emanating from Malta and affecting the Papal States in Italy, the British ambassador in Vienna hinted in return that the Pope might well be asked to do something similar in Ireland. Peel, while careful to avoid any bargain whereby British censorship in Malta would be offered in exchange for Papal restraint on clerical demagogues in Ireland, was not averse to extracting some profit from the situation. He instructed Graham to prepare 'a nosegay of the acts and speeches and writings of priests' in Ireland and pass it to Aberdeen. 'If we cannot regale his Holiness with the bouquet, let Metternich have it.'[2] This was rough wooing; but Peel was too English and Protestant to entertain much veneration for the Bishop of Rome. In more serious vein he suggested that the Pope and Metternich should be asked whether they thought the actions of some of the Catholic clergy in Ireland were not disgraceful to religion and dangerous to thrones in other places besides Britain.

Though desirable, an understanding with the Pope was too fugitive a prospect to be allowed to hold up the development of Peel's plans for Ireland. When the customary presessional cabinets started in November it soon became clear to the other members that the informal discussions between Peel and his immediate advisers had reached a point when major decisions on the Irish problem would soon have to be faced. The prime minister did not attempt to hurry his colleagues. There was enough on the government's immediate programme to take up the attention of the cabinet until after Christmas. The initial Irish discussions centred on such surface topics as O'Connell's trial, agrarian disorders and the progress of Repeal. It was only towards the end of January that Peel, supported by Graham and Wharncliffe, suggested the possibility of doing something for Maynooth. Parliament opened on 1 February and the only references to Ireland in the queen's speech concerned the Devon Commission and a projected reform of the county franchise. Irish affairs however

[1] J. F. Broderick, *The Holy See and the Irish Movement for the Repeal of the Union* (Rome 1951), pp. 163 et seq.
[2] *Graham*, I, 402 (27 Nov. 1843).

at once came before parliament in the form of opposition motions put forward by Normanby in the Lords and Russell in the Commons. It was obvious that a grand assault was intended by the Whigs; equally obvious that if the government was to present a firm front, more general discussion and agreement on future Irish policy was required than had so far taken place. The debates were to begin in both Houses on 13 February. Two days earlier Peel circulated a memorandum to the cabinet emphasising the need for an immediate decision on the general line to be followed by ministerial spokesmen. He took as his two assumptions that their opponents would call for an explanation not only of the government's past actions but of its future intentions; and that a particular attack would be made on the position of the Irish Church. Since it was equally axiomatic that the government had to defend its administrative record and could make no concessions on the vital issues of church property and establishment, it followed that the only course open to the cabinet was to consider more constructive ways of conciliating Irish Catholics. There were two special topics to which he called his colleagues' attention. The first was the state of Maynooth College and the expediency of appointing a commission to investigate and improve its standard of education, with the inevitable corollary of an increase in its parliamentary grant. The second was a subject frequently touched on in the Commons: the connection between the financial dependence of the Irish Catholic clergy on their parishioners and their participation in political agitation. What Peel suggested was not a state endowment to remove them from this dependence but the more innocuous step of altering the law so as to allow landed proprietors in Ireland to make endowments for Catholic parish priests. While admitting the difficulties of the question he also stressed the policy, 'now that we have resisted agitation and steadily enforced the law', of detaching from the ranks of their irreconcilable opponents in Ireland those who were not yet committed to violent attitudes and still believed in the union of the two countries.[1]

This formal document had a mixed reception in the cabinet. Gladstone and Goulburn argued against an increased grant for Maynooth, mainly on the grounds that it would do little good in Ireland and much harm in England. Aberdeen, Hardinge and Knatch-

[1] 40540 fos. 19–25 (memorandum of 11 Feb. 1844), ptly pr. *Peel*, III, 101–3.

bull maintained a judicious silence. The rest clearly favoured the proposals. Stanley observed that the principle of support for Maynooth was as much embodied in the existing grant as in any extension and the duke probably expressed the feelings of the majority when he bluntly said that since it was impossible to withdraw the grant from the college, they might as well try to make it efficient. When Gladstone argued that it would strengthen the demand for payment of state salaries to the Irish clergy, Peel answered decisively that the opportunity for making such a provision from state funds had long passed. If it ever came, it would be at the expense of the revenues of the Church of Ireland. A narrower division existed over the tactics. Peel and Wharncliffe thought that it was unnecessary to make an announcement of their intentions in the forthcoming debate; Stanley and Graham thought otherwise. That minor point was involuntarily settled by Gladstone. On the 13th, the opening day of the Russell debate, the cabinet met again to discuss the relative merits of a royal commission or a parliamentary committee for the enquiry into Maynooth. Gladstone, following some interior logic of his own, said that he supported an immediate statement of their Maynooth policy in parliament but that his objections to the policy itself remained unchanged. Graham and Wharncliffe at once interjected that in that case they advised no statement; and Peel settled the issue by observing that it would be fatal at that moment to have a division among themselves. It was a small episode but a disquieting one. For the first time since the new Corn Law of 1842 the faint shadow of a resignation on a question of principle had been cast across the cabinet.[1]

In the circumstances it was unavoidable that the great Irish debate, launched by Russell with a formal motion for a committee of the whole House to examine the state of Ireland, was little more on the government's side than a holding operation. Graham and Stanley, speaking early in the debate, made the most of the positive steps on which the cabinet was agreed—the increased education grant, the enlargement of the county electorate, and legal facilities for Catholic parochial endowment—but the general character of the ministerial speeches was inevitably defensive. Peel himself was not satisfied with the situation even though he had nothing but praise for the way in which his colleagues, particularly Stanley, had carried out their

---

[1] 44777 fos. 115, 119 et seq.

difficult roles. On the chance that opinions might have matured during the progress of the long and continually adjourned discussions in parliament, he sent round a second memorandum on Saturday, 17 February, suggesting another cabinet before the end of the debate. With the general principles already laid down he had no quarrel. What he wanted was the chance to reinforce the principles with further concrete proposals. He emphasised that the points he mentioned were for consideration only and that he would abandon any views of his own on minor matters rather than cause disunity. Nevertheless, he added sombrely, 'I view our future position in respect to Ireland and the administration of affairs in Ireland with great anxiety'. Once more he impressed on the cabinet the need to make reforms while it was safe to do so. He drew on historical parallels, not omitting the crisis of 1828–29, to show that reform refused merely led to enforced concessions. He reiterated that law and order in Ireland depended on the co-operation of the respectable and influential Catholics; and he laid down the naked principle that every concession short of abandoning the Church of Ireland and the Union must be made sooner or later if those two basic features of the Anglo-Irish relationship were to be preserved. The additional matters he raised were of a miscellaneous kind. One was the question of the so-called Ministers' Money, a tax levied on houses in Irish corporate towns for the benefit of the Church of Ireland. This, he suggested, might be abolished if suitable compensation could be found. Remaining Irish clerical sinecures could be dealt with on the same lines as those followed by the Ecclesiastical Commissioners in England. On higher education for Irish Catholics he wondered whether Trinity College could be extended or new provincial academies set up. Could they not establish institutions which like Oxford and Cambridge would offer a general academic education to Roman Catholics intending to enter the Church as well as to ordinary undergraduates? Had they anything to lose by widening the municipal franchise, seeing that repealers were getting majorities in most of the leading towns in southern Ireland?

This was radical reform with a vengeance, and a somewhat shaken cabinet recoiled instinctively from any immediate decisions on this unexpected supplementary list of reforms when it came to discuss the memorandum the following Monday. Nevertheless, Peel left his colleagues in no doubt that he attached central importance to Catholic education, both lay and clerical, as a means of improving and conciliating the Irish professional middle classes; and that he saw little hope for official Irish Protestantism unless this kind of social stability could be secured. As he left the cabinet room at the end of the inconclusive meeting on 19 February his last words were 'Depend upon it, the attack upon the Church of Ireland can only be staved off by liberal concessions'.[1] When four days later he wound up for the government on the ninth and last evening of the debate, he stressed that the most important aspect of the whole question was future British policy towards Ireland. What he had to say on that score was said generously and at length. Yet there was little in fact that he could add to what had already been said on behalf of the government by previous speakers.

From Peel's point of view therefore the great parliamentary debate, and the cabinet discussions that provided the invisible counterpoint to it, was only the first stage of a new Irish policy. At the end of the month he pressed home the lesson in a third memorandum to his cabinet.[2] He listed the principles which they had publicly acknowledged: maintenance of the Union and of the Church of Ireland, equality of Protestant and Catholic in the service of the state, substantial uniformity of parliamentary franchise between the two countries, private endowment of Catholic clergy, an appreciably larger grant for National schools, a readiness to take up the problem of Irish academical education. The task now was to decide what could be done immediately to put these principles into practice. Such an opportunity, he reminded his colleagues, might not come again. The temper and result of the Irish debate had been highly favourable to the government. Executive action in Ireland had crippled O'Connell's authority and brought about a temporary lull in agitation. Now if ever was the time to detach moderate Irish Catholics by concessions that could be made without loss of prestige on the part of the government or inconsistency with their stated policy. The practical matters he suggested for early legislation were

[1] ibid., f. 127; 40540 fos. 230 et seq. (memorandum of 17 Feb.), ptly pr. Peel, III, 105-7.
[2] 40540 fos. 26-39 (draft), 40-55 (fair copy), endorsed 'Irish policy, circulated Feb. 1844.' Date probably 27 Feb. since it was read by Gladstone, 28 Feb. (44777 f. 129).

municipal and parliamentary franchise, education, and Roman Catholic endowments. He devoted much space to an argument for the reform of Maynooth; and on this his language was particularly strong.

> I am oppressed by the strong feeling that we incur a great responsibility, not parliamentary but moral, by leaving the vote as it is—by sending out annually fifty spiritual firebrands, prepared for mischief by ourselves, to convulse the country. The Lord Lieutenant tells us that the real enemies of the Government and the really powerful incendiaries are the young priests. . . . The College of Maynooth as at present governed and scantily provided for, is a public nuisance. If principle is violated by educating Roman Catholic priests, the present vote violates it, and in the worst manner, for we have no compensation for our violation of principle. We educate Priests, more than half the number required for the yearly supply of all Ireland, and the wit of man could not devise a more effectual method for converting them into sour, malignant demagogues, hostile to the law, from all the sympathies of low birth and kindred, living by agitation, inclined to it and fitted for it by our eleemosynary but penurious system of education.

This broadside delivered, he returned at the end of the paper to his old theme of the endemic danger of the Irish situation, and the need to snatch the fleeting opportunity that presented itself to bestow reforms on Ireland rather than have them extorted later by force.

In this trilogy of Irish papers in February 1844 Peel had in fact exposed both the essence and detail of his whole future policy. Though their form and timing had been dictated by the current parliamentary situation, the implicit argument was an exercise in rigorous logic. As long as Ireland remained disaffected, the United Kingdom was embarrassed in its foreign relations and vulnerable in time of war. Ireland would remain a source of danger until it was efficiently governed. It could not be efficiently governed as long as Irish courts and juries were useless to provide the foundation of law and order. They would continue to be useless until the professional middle classes in Ireland identified themselves with the state. They would not so identify themselves until they and their Church were given political and cultural as well as legal equality. This full equality could only come if professionally, educationally, and socially they were given the same opportunities as Protestants. To achieve this, after centuries of inferiority, parliament and the taxpayer must come to the assistance of the Irish Catholics both lay and clerical. To his colleagues in the cabinet this devastating dialectic was almost unanswerable. Even Buccleuch, who started out with a strong Protestant bias, confessed that he had been completely converted. Only Gladstone, on grounds of past pledges and present principles, remained unhappy and unconvinced. But under the private persuasions of the prime minister, who offered a massive array of considerations for his junior to digest, and warned by his other colleagues of the dangers to which he would be exposing the government, even Gladstone was prepared for the moment to let matters take their course. The real difficulty before the cabinet was not to decide on their ultimate objectives. It was, as the old duke had said about Maynooth, the mode of arriving at them which was not easy to decide.

The reform of the Irish franchise, which on the face of it was one of the least exceptional of the government's promised measures, was an early casualty. Introduced by Eliot in April, it had two objects: to remedy the defects of the legal machinery and, by enfranchising the £5 freeholder, to bring about a closer approximation to the English county electorate. It was opposed however by the Irish Liberals and threatened to become a protracted party issue. Rather than risk delay to more important business the government first postponed and then finally abandoned the measure. A better fate attended the charitable trusts bill which after a tranquil passage through the Lords came down to the Commons at the end of July. The essential object of the bill was to encourage private endowment of Catholic clergy. To achieve this, it was necessary to offer stronger guarantees for the impartiality of the statutory body administering such endowments. The existing Board for charitable trusts had since its inception early in the century been composed exclusively of Protestants although three-quarters of the trusts were Catholic. The new measure introduced by Graham provided for a mixed commission of three *ex officio* members (two of whom could be Catholic) together with five Protestants and five Catholics, the removal of legal obstacles to the private endowment of Catholic chapels and benefices, and the reference to the Catholic members of the board of any question affecting the doctrine, discipline and law of their Church. The bill passed with minor opposition from some of the Irish members, and Peel was sceptical of the motives of those who did oppose. He told the queen that many of them admitted privately that they only did so on orders from Ireland. 'There are many parties in Ireland', he added for Victoria's enlightenment, 'who desire to have a grievance and prefer the grievance to the remedy.'[1] The success of the Charitable Trusts Act however largely depended on the co-operation of the Catholic hierarchy. As O'Connell and MacHale, the bishop of Tuam, both realised, the new measure, by reconciling some Catholics, would divide all. There was a vociferous press campaign in Ireland against the bill and MacHale made private representations at Rome for a ban on the acceptance of seats on the board by Irish bishops except with the consent of the Pope and the rest of their Irish colleagues. Nevertheless, despite pressure from below and lack of support from most of the Irish hierarchy, Archbishop Murray of Dublin when approached by the Lord Lieutenant agreed in principle that three of the five Catholic commissioners should be prelates, including himself and the primate. He also suggested candidates for the other two places.[2] Even so, the battle to secure the co-operation of the Irish bishops proved long and arduous.

One obvious tactical move for the government was to bring counter-pressure to bear at Rome. Aubin had died in May but, despite the growing need for close relationships with the Curia, Peel preferred to continue with the traditional method of indirect diplomatic representation. In July Gladstone, with one of those sublime illogicalities which periodically staggered his colleagues, offered himself for the post: an offer which Peel met with forbearing silence. To some extent the previous *démarches* of 1843, with the customary tardiness of Roman diplomacy, were beginning to bear some fruit. In October Cardinal Franzoni, the Prefect of Propaganda, wrote to the Irish primate, making no mention of the repeal movement, but enjoining abstention from political activities on both bishops and clergy. Yet something more than this was needed to counteract MacHale's activities. Murray and Anthony Blake, the most influential Catholic lay member of the Board, apparently favoured an official approach to Rome by the government, as the best method

[1] RA/A 16/112 (30 July 1844); 40438 f. 376.   [2] 40439 f. 65.

of strengthening their own position.[1] Peel promptly instructed the Foreign Office to represent privately to the authorities at Rome that they should not decide on their attitude to the Charitable Trusts Act until they had heard both sides of the argument. Early in October a new diplomatic representative, William Petre, who although not a conspicuously devout Catholic was acceptable to Rome, was despatched to press the government's case. By December encouraging reports were coming back from Petre of the disposition of the Papal Court to recommend peace and civil obedience in Ireland. Peel impressed on Aberdeen and Graham the need on the one hand to keep Petre instantly informed of Irish developments and on the other to repay the confidence of Archbishop Murray by communicating to him the progress of Petre's negotiations at Rome.[2] The wary diplomats of the Papal Curia, far removed from the noisy scene in Ireland, in the end refrained either from condemning the repeal movement or openly supporting the Charitable Trusts Board. Nevertheless neutrality in itself was a defeat for the O'Connell and MacHale party, as O'Connell's frantic attacks on the Franzoni letter gave ample evidence.

By this time the battle for the Board was won. A meeting of the hierarchy in November agreed that individual bishops should act on their conscience with regard to the Board. Crolly of Armagh, the Catholic primate, had at first refused to serve. When approached again, however, he admitted the fairness of the government's intentions and, resenting rather than intimidated by the popular pressure, finally agreed after the November meeting to become a member of the Board. Bishop Kennedy of Killaloe first accepted and then at the last moment withdrew, despite Peel's injunctions to his officials in Ireland to use every means that tact and diplomacy suggested to prevent the Irish bishops from being 'bullied out of their engagements to the government'.[3] His place was taken on the recommendation of the other commissioners by Bishop Denvir of Down.[4] Even

---

[1] This seems to be the reasonable interpretation of Peel's letter to Graham (Graham, 30 Sept. 1844).

[2] *ibid*. Peel to Graham, 30 Sept, 22 Dec.; Graham to Heytesbury, 23 Dec. 1844; 40479 fos. 75, 84. The Lord Lieutenant was instructed in Dec. to show Petre's letters at his discretion to Archbishop Murray. See also Broderick, *op. cit.*, pp. 184–202.

[3] Graham (Peel to Graham, 5 Dec. 1844).

[4] McDowell, *op. cit.*, pp. 214–16; *Peel*, III, 126–33.

Murray at one point hesitated; but in December it was possible to announce the membership of the new Board. It was a triumph for the government and, wrote the Lord Lieutenant cheerfully, an embarrassing rebuff for O'Connell.

IV

If the Devon Commission and the Charitable Trusts Board were only the first planks in the government's new Irish policy, at least the situation at the end of 1844 was appreciably more hopeful than it had been during the first half of the year. The trial of O'Connell in the spring had presented the usual mixture of inefficiency and absurdity that Peel and Graham had come to expect from Irish judicial proceedings. Either by design or negligence the jury list was so imperfect that it resulted in an exclusively Protestant and Conservative jury. In the course of the proceedings the chief justice in an engaging slip referred to the defence as 'the other side'. At one point the Attorney-General challenged one of the defending counsel to a duel. 'How strange it is,' observed Graham icily, 'that nothing can be done in Ireland without a blunder, when Irishmen alone are employed!'[1] In February the defendants were found guilty but to Peel's regret sentence was postponed until the following term, a delay which enabled O'Connell to resume his place in the Commons. His return to Westminster was attended by the same comic spirit that had presided over his trial. On 15 February, when he was hourly expected to arrive, a crowd of his admirers gathered in Parliament Street 'through which I passed with considerable applause', Peel reported to Victoria, 'in consequence of having been mistaken by the great majority for Mr. O'Connell'.[2] In May sentences of fine and imprisonment were passed by the court but on appeal to the House of Lords in September the verdicts were quashed. Since the law officers had been of the opinion that the appeal would not succeed, O'Connell had already started his term of imprisonment. He was thus given the political advantage of a triumphal release from his otherwise comfortable prison quarters in Richmond gaol. Though the English judges advised that the verdict was good, the decision lay with the law lords in the upper House. They divided three to

[1] *Graham*, I, 403.   [2] 40438 f. 82.

two in favour of the appeal: Lyndhurst and Brougham being over-ruled by the three Whigs, Cottenham, Campbell and Denman. If it was not a political verdict, it seemed so; and when it was clear that the appeal was going to succeed, some of the lay peers foolishly tried to assert their long-disused right of voting.

To Peel almost every stage of the proceedings had been unsatis-factory. He regretted the delay in passing sentence and had been opposed to allowing O'Connell to start his sentence before the result of the appeal was known. On the question of the procedure in the House of Lords, however, he made it clear from the start that politi-cal bias among the law lords could never justify the intervention of the government or of its supporters. 'The permanent evil of over-ruling the majority of the Law Lords by the vote of the unprofessional Peers', he wrote to the indignant Brougham, 'would have been, I think, greater than the reversal of the sentence. I think it is very important in a case of this kind that the Government should be clearly in the right.'[1] In the larger game he was playing with the Irish ecclesiastics, the fiasco of the Lords' verdict was a sacrifice he could afford.

Among all the popular rejoicings at O'Connell's release there remained a dilemma for the great agitator which Peel at least was able to recognise. O'Connell's first instinct, he thought, would be to exploit his momentary triumph to unseat the government. For that purpose he would try to renew his old alliance with the Whigs. But O'Connell's younger followers would be unlikely to acquiesce in a tame return to these tactics of the thirties. They would press him to carry on with the repeal agitation accompanied by as much popular disturbance in Ireland as was consistent with their own safety.[2] It was a diagnosis that came very close to the truth. The momentum of the repeal campaign had been arrested and for the next two years the nationalist movement in Ireland was torn by internal disputes over personalities and tactics which the ageing O'Connell was unable to suppress. But not everything was left to the fratricidal tendencies of Irish politics. In the autumn of 1844 the prime minister was urging the Lord Lieutenant to meet O'Connell's federalist propaganda by some counter-effort in the Irish press, duly 'seasoned for the Irish palate'. Acting on the hint Eliot in October was able to arrange

[1] Peel, III, 125-6.   [2] Graham (Peel to Graham, 14 Sept. 1844).

with the rising young Irish barrister Isaac Butt to write a series of articles in the *Morning Herald* attacking O'Connell's views. That a Conservative government in 1844 had engaged the services of the future founder of the Irish Home Rule party was an irony which it was reserved for posterity to appreciate.

If the political situation in Ireland was improving, the administration too was by this time on a sounder footing. Early in 1844 de Grey had expressed a desire on grounds of health to retire by the early summer. Although the protracted O'Connell trial provided an argument for delay, by May he was growing impatient for release. Peel could hardly have been sorry to see him go, but the problem of a successor offered all the customary difficulties. As early as March Graham had gone through the peerage and extracted a list of some two dozen names to all of which there seemed some, in a few cases an insuperable, objection.[1] By midsummer a decision could no longer be avoided. Buccleuch was asked, hesitated and declined after consultation with his former guardian Lord Montagu who grandly opined that the post was incompatible with Buccleuch's 'commanding position in Scotland'. Graham proposed Richmond but Peel, unwilling to risk another refusal, was reluctant to approach him unless sure of an acceptance. The only other candidate Graham could suggest was Lord Canning; but Wellington, when consulted by the prime minister, demurred at the instantaneous promotion of an under-secretary to a Lord Lieutenancy. In the end Peel brought up the name of Lord Heytesbury[2] who had not been on Graham's original list, though he possessed considerable experience of public life and had been nominated by Peel for the governor-generalship of India in the abortive ministry of 1835. This time all went smoothly and before the end of July the new Lord Lieutenant was installed in Dublin Castle.[3] The contrast between the new and the outgoing viceroy was not unlike that between Whitworth and Richmond during Peel's own Chief Secretaryship thirty years earlier. A self-made man and a career diplomat, Heytesbury had served his country abroad during the first thirty years of the century and had been

---

[1] 40449 f. 358.

[2] William A'Court, 1st Baron Heytesbury (1779-1870).

[3] For the search for a new viceroy see 40450 fos. 40, 54; 40460 fos. 214, 216; Wellington (Peel to Wellington, 18 June 1844); 40478 fos. 261-305.

rewarded with a peerage in 1828. With no controversial record in domestic politics to prejudice him, at the age of sixty-five he faced his task in Ireland with calm, objectivity and a practised talent for administration. It was fortunate for the government that it was he and not de Grey who had to handle the delicate negotiations with the Roman Catholic bishops over the membership of the Charitable Trusts Board in the months immediately following his arrival on the other side of the water. Minutely instructed by Peel on all the essential features of the ministerial policy towards Ireland, Heytesbury at once showed himself a sensible and sympathetic coadjutor. His first two patronage appointments went to Catholics; he was diligent in searching out for promotion those rare animals in the Church of Ireland, Conservative clerics who supported National education; and he struck up a good relationship from the first with Eliot.

But in Ireland the only certainty was misfortune. The new partnership so promisingly begun lasted only six months. In May, when it looked as though de Grey would be retiring almost at once, Eliot had declined an offer of the Secretaryship at War on the grounds that he would be of more use to the government in Ireland. Within a few months of securing a sympathetic chief, however, the event to which Graham had once looked forward to with relief occurred when it was least opportune. In January 1845 Lord St. Germans died and Eliot's career in the House of Commons came to an abrupt end. It was a loss for the Irish government and an embarrassment for the cabinet even though Peel extracted what profit he could from the situation by making it the occasion for a general reshuffle of offices. The three possible men for the vacant Chief Secretaryship were Lord Lincoln, Sidney Herbert, and Fremantle, who had been promoted Secretary-at-War when Eliot refused it. Lincoln was ruled out by the misfortune of possessing a notoriously Protestant and Tory father. Herbert, whom Peel thought the best candidate of the three, was offered the post but refused for family reasons to leave England for more than a year. The prime minister then used his authority with Fremantle to press him into an acceptance. Of his temper, loyalty and official experience there was no question. As chief whip he had been universally popular in the House; as a magistrate he had served as chairman of Quarter Sessions. His mother and sisters were Catholic; he was related by marriage to an old English Catholic family; and his views on Ireland were impeccably liberal. These assorted qualifications were probably the deciding factor in Peel's mind. The one drawback was his inexperience in debate and this in fact turned out to be a greater handicap than was foreseen at the start of 1845.[1] His talents would have been more suited to the chairmanship of the Board of Customs for which Graham would have preferred to reserve him. But time was pressing; there was no other obvious candidate; and a harassed prime minister could not afford to meet parliament without an Irish Secretary in a session in which Irish affairs were going to loom large.

[1] For the choice of a successor to Eliot see 40479 f. 275; 40451 fos. 21, 23; Graham (Graham to Heytesbury, 28 Jan. 1845).

DIFFICULTIES AND DISSENSIONS

The year 1844, which saw the end of the O'Connell case and the beginning of Peel's new deal for Ireland, was a year of mixed fortunes for the government. Ministers carried all their important measures but only at the cost of an intolerable strain on the loyalty of their supporters. At the start of the session the cabinet was in a mood of cautious optimism. Trade and industry had continued to improve; the financial situation had righted itself at last; parliamentary opposition was fragmented; Chartism had declined; and the League had fallen back on more constitutional methods of propaganda. The Corn Law of 1842 had shown itself the best technical instrument so far devised for reconciling the demands of consumer and producer. Since September the official average price for wheat had only varied between 50s and 52s a quarter, a lower level than had been recorded in all but seven of the previous fifty years. The instinct of the ministers was to leave well alone. In January there had been some discussions in the cabinet whether corn should be mentioned in the queen's speech. The unanimous feeling was that it should not, though Wharncliffe got into deeper waters by saying that if they were asked about the Corn Law, they should speak up stoutly on its behalf. Peel retorted that it would be impossible for the government to commit itself on that, as on any other question, irrespective of circumstances. The law had fulfilled expectations and there was no intention of changing it. The choice, he ended significantly, lay between the 1842 Act and repeal; at least there was no other step they themselves could take. Wharncliffe insisted that the important thing was to express a conviction of the continued need for protection; but to this, as Gladstone noted, Peel avoided any direct answer.[1]

[1] 44777 f. 115.

The prime minister's inclination was clearly towards silence rather than stoutness on corn. Nevertheless, in the debate on the address, he did something to reassure the agriculturalists by saying that the government had never contemplated, and did not contemplate, any change in the existing law. This, if not the positive affirmation of faith for which Wharncliffe had asked, was at least a subscription to orthodoxy; and it did much to put the corn issue at rest for the 1844 session. Neither Cobden's attempt in March to appoint a committee of enquiry into the effects of protection on tenants and farmers, nor Villiers's annual motion against the Corn Laws in June attracted much interest or support.

The general recovery of industrial production and commercial confidence encouraged the cabinet in fact to carry out a classic financial operation. With capital seeking investment, interest rates low, large gold reserves in the Bank of England, and government stock at a premium, Goulburn early in March obtained the ready sanction of parliament for an unprecedently large refunding scheme. Some £250 million of 3½ per cent consols, which at the start of the year stood at 102½, were converted to 3¼ per cent stock with a further reduction to 3 per cent envisaged after a ten-year period. The immediate gain to the revenue was £625,000 per annum; the ultimate saving £1¼ million. All the financial pundits approved; the City was prepared; and the operation went through with a minimum of difficulty.[1] This was a happy augury for the budget and when Goulburn presented his accounts and estimates at the end of April, he had a cheerful story to unfold. Duties for the year 1843–44 were up on the estimates, as was the yield of the income tax. Expenditure had been slightly less than forecast. As a result there was an overall surplus of £4·1 million or, deducting the deficit of £2·7 million inherited from the previous year, a net surplus of £1·4 million. His estimates for the current year at £48·6 million expenditure and £51·7 million revenue were equally encouraging. Nevertheless, in view of the expiry of the income tax in 1845, the government did not propose any sweeping reductions in taxation. Little more than a third of a million was set aside for remission of duties on a selection of items: glass, vinegar, currants, coffee, marine insurance, and wool. Replying to miscellaneous criticisms of the income tax, particular

[1] Cf. Peel to Victoria (RA/A 16/30, 31), 6, 7 March 1844.

duties, and the establishment estimates, Peel made it clear that the budget was to be regarded as a holding operation. The estimates had been pruned as severely as the government thought safe. It was too early to decide whether the income tax was to be renewed; and no further manipulation of the tariff was possible until that decision. To make large prospective cuts in the tariff revenue would in effect be to settle in advance the crucial question. With this the House was not particularly inclined to disagree and the budget legislation went through with exemplary despatch.

The more important financial innovation, what Peel later described as 'the most important Bill of the Session', was the Bank Charter Act.[1] In 1833 the charter of the Bank of England had been renewed for twenty-one years with a proviso that the government could terminate it ten years before its expiry on giving a year's notice. That notice had to be given within a six-months' period starting on 1 August 1844 and ending on 31 January 1845 and it had to be in the form of a resolution of the House of Commons. Parliament rarely met before 1 February but could easily and often did remain in session after 1 August. It was obvious therefore that if the government was to exercise its option, it would have to do so in the 1844 session. With Peel's interest in finance, it was unlikely that he would have missed this statutory opportunity of revising the Bank's charter. There might even have been some attraction in the notion of placing upon the foundation of 'Peel's Act' of 1819 a Peelite Bank Charter Act in 1844. But the case for revision rested on stronger ground than this. Though the subject was both abstruse and acrimonious, there was at least a general feeling that changes should be made. The Act of 1819 had put the currency back on the gold standard but that in itself had not ensured that there would always be enough bullion to cover the note issue. The Bank of England had come to accept its role as guardian of the currency, custodian of the gold reserve, and ultimate source of loans to the economy. But these different functions were not always easy to

---

[1] For much of what follows see J. H. Clapham, *Bank of England* (Cambridge 1944), II, ch. III, and *Early Railway Age*, ch. xiii (Cambridge 1926); A. Feavearyear, *The Pound Sterling* (Oxford 1963), pp. 226–77; R. G. Hawtrey, *Century of Bank Rate* (1962), pp. 18–20; Peel's speech of 6 May 1844 (*Speeches*, IV, 349 seq.). For a professional banker's favourable views, see G. G. Riley, 'Peel and the Bank Act, 1844' (*Institute of Bankers Journal*, Feb. 1963).

reconcile. There was no legal restriction on its issue of paper and the situation was further complicated by the existence of over four hundred private or joint-stock banks entitled to issue their own notes. Four times in recent memory, in 1825, 1832, 1835-36, and 1838-39, there had been financial crises exhibiting the same distressing symptoms: speculation, high prices, a flight of gold abroad, and undiminished issues of notes by the country banks. In the last of these the bank rate had risen to the abnormal level of 6 per cent, its bullion reserves had fallen to a point at which the convertibility of its notes had been endangered, and recourse had to be made to the humiliating expedient of raising loans in France and Germany to tide over the emergency. In the wake of these crises had come the familiar trail of bankruptcies among the provincial banks. In 1840 twenty-four had failed, of which seventeen had paid no dividend. Over the five-year period no less than eighty-two had collapsed, more than half totally insolvent.

The controversies aroused by these events centred on the Bank of England. The key to the problem seemed to lie in the relationship between note issue, bullion reserves, and holdings of deposits and securities. But there was no agreement among the experts on which way the key ought to be turned. The banking school led by Thomas Tooke and James Wilson argued that once the metallic value of notes was fixed, the volume of currency should be left to the discretion of bankers. Circulation should depend not on a fixed quantity of money but on prices and wages, and through them on the current level of economic activity. It was a highly modern and sophisticated theory which took into account the growing role of other forms of credit besides notes, such as cheques and bills of exchange. But its weakness was that it offered no machinery for checking speculation, inflation and excessive credit, though Wilson advocated the active use of the bank rate to stimulate or damp down the money market according to the needs of the moment. The orthodox currency school, which found its natural stronghold in the Bank of England, argued for a strict relationship between paper issue and gold reserve. The logic of this pointed to more regulation and more centralisation than the British banking system had yet achieved. When an important select committee of the House of Commons enquired into banks of issue in 1840-41, Samuel Jones Loyd, the future Lord Overstone and main champion of the currency school, spoke in favour of a fixed ratio between notes and bullion and G. W. Norman, a director of the Bank of England, expressed the need for a single national bank of issue and an end to the circulation of country banknotes.

From the start therefore the question of rewriting the Bank's terms of reference revolved exclusively round the currency question. The real nature of the Act of 1844 was conveyed not by its popular name of the Bank Charter Act but by the first part of its formal title, 'an act to regulate the issue of bank notes'. The Act itself was largely the Bank's own solution to its own problem. Nevertheless, in approaching the issue in 1844, Peel could draw on his own long experience of currency investigations commencing with the committee of 1819, and continuing with another in 1832, which like its successor of 1840–41 heard much and said little, and a third more recent one on joint-stock banks in 1836–38. By the time he came to serve, as one of its leading members, on the 1840–41 committee, his mind was probably made up. It was significant that while he took a lively interest in the evidence of Jones Loyd, Palmer and Norman, he did not even trouble to attend when Tooke appeared. One result at least of all these enquiries was that there was no need to hold another. As early as October 1843 Peel reminded Goulburn of the need to review the Bank charter question in all its aspects. The Chancellor of the Exchequer assured him that every spare moment he was immersed in a sea of blue books and before the start of the session produced a memorandum on the subject. In this, in his usual civil service fashion, Goulburn analysed the problem and argued the advantages and drawbacks of various courses of action without coming to definite conclusions or making specific recommendations.[1]

On 13 January he and Peel met Cotton, the Governor of the Bank, and his deputy, Heath. Two important things they discussed were the question of a single issuing authority and the division of the Bank into separate issue and banking departments. The Bank favoured a single bank of issue but to this Peel and Goulburn clearly felt there were insuperable objections. To place a monopoly of issue

[1] 40539 fos. 183–91 (undated but written just before the 1844 session); 40444 fos. 136–8.

in the hands of a government agency, as Ricardo had long ago advocated, would be to expose the system to political pressure from the House of Commons at every time of financial stringency. It was difficult enough for the Bank to stand up against public opinion. There was even less hope of finding financial wisdom and firmness among parliamentary politicians. On the other hand, if note issue was entrusted solely to the Bank of England, there would be difficulties of another kind. Without control of the banks in Scotland and Ireland, its power of regulation would certainly be incomplete and probably ineffective. Even more daunting was the existence of the other banks of issue in England who would undoubtedly offer a formidable opposition to any legislation which extinguished their rights merely to create a monopoly for the Bank of England. So radical a solution seemed to Peel both financially undesirable and politically dangerous. There were many country bankers and they had many friends and clients in the House of Commons. 'Between the Bankers and their customers', Goulburn had opined pessimistically in his memorandum, 'there will probably be a cordial co-operation in resisting the change.' In the circumstances Peel looked characteristically for a middle way between existing practice and ultimate objective. What he wanted was some process whereby gradually, painlessly, almost voluntarily, the rights of issue of the country banks could be brought to a close and the Bank of England become in practice the sole issuing authority.[1] In the fourth week of January he brought the question before the cabinet.[2] In his customary way he presented three courses to his colleagues, though his argument pointed inexorably to one of them. They were the maintenance of the existing system, the prohibition of all issues of paper money except by a public board responsible to parliament, and a third course—'an intermediate one between complete acquiescence in

[1] 44777 f. 111.

[2] ibid., f. 117. Clapham (Bank of England, II, 179) is probably wrong in suggesting that Peel's well-known memorandum was written during the Easter vacation. The two drafts of the memorandum (one rough holograph by Peel and the other a fair copy with emendations by Peel) are undated. But they are put with Goulburn's memorandum in the Peel correspondence of Jan. 1844 (40539 fos. 193, 209). Gladstone's memoranda (44777 f. 117) make it clear that Peel opened the discussion on the Bank Charter on Tuesday, 23 Jan., and there was a general discussion on 25 Jan. It was probably on the first of these occasions that Peel read out his memorandum, extracts from which are printed in Peel, III, 134-9.

the present system and radical subversion of it'. He admitted that if he had the task of establishing the currency for a new society, he would find it difficult to resist the argument for a public board of issue. But, came the familiar practical observation, they were dealing with three kingdoms and a great inherited weight of separate habits, institutions and interests. In such circumstances the chance of success with a new theoretical system would necessarily be uncertain, the consequence of failure plainly disastrous. His advice therefore was for the middle way which 'violates no existing right . . . takes precautions against future abuses . . . ensures by gradual means the establishment of a safe system of currency'.

In defining more clearly the issuing responsibility of the Bank a start could be made by creating a separate department for that purpose, a device which banking experts inside and outside the Bank had been considering for half a dozen years. Following the cabinet discussions Cotton at Peel's request sent in a memorandum on the division of the Bank and early in February came a second paper embodying the general views of the Bank authorities. Working with these and other papers at Drayton during the Easter vacation Peel put into shape the details of the measure. On 6 May in a long, lucid and able speech he introduced his plan in the House of Commons. On the theoretical side he approached the problem as a convinced adherent of the currency school; and he laid excessive emphasis on the danger of an over-issue of notes unsupported by reserves. His proposals were that the Bank should be separated into departments of issue and banking; that the issue of notes should be related to specific amounts of bullion and securities; that there should be a fixed fiduciary issue of £14 million, with the remainder based on bullion; and that a fiduciary issue above £14 million should be permitted only in an emergency and with the consent of three ministers of the Crown. Private banks of issue were to be restricted; no new banks of issue were to be created; a weekly statement to be published of all bank issues. The bill was to apply only to England; legislation for Scotland and Ireland would be introduced next session. The whole purpose, as he summarized it at the end of his speech, was an act which 'shall inspire just confidence in the medium of exchange' and 'put a check on improvident speculation'. Before and during these parliamentary proceedings there was a formal exchange of letters between Goulburn and the Bank; but this was little more than ceremonial. The gist of Peel's proposals to parliament had already been contained in the Bank's memorandum of February. Little opposition or informed criticism came from the House. Though Peel's theoretical exposition contained nothing that was new to the experts, he had at least made M.P.s understand the rudiments of a complicated question and by sheer clarity of explanation had given a certain attractiveness to what the *Annual Register* called, and no doubt many back-benchers found, a 'barren and repulsive subject'.

Between 6 and 20 May, when the House went into committee on his resolutions, Peel changed his mind on one important point. He withdrew the proposal for sanction by ministers of emergency issues (a suggestion which had originated with the Bank) on the grounds that it was advisable to preclude any kind of statutory government interference. In return he proposed to give to the Bank a limited power of increasing its note circulation in cases where country banks terminated their own issue rights. In this shape, and with the support of the Whigs' chief financial expert, Charles Wood, the bill passed into law against negligible opposition. While it was still in parliament a number of bankers individually and collectively pressed him to relax the stringency of the issue regulations. To many experts the bill seemed too rigid and because of its rigidity likely to cause a crisis from the sheer knowledge that the Bank would not be able to exercise its discretion, as it had done in the past, in issuing and lending during time of bullion shortage. To Peel however the essence of the bill was to restore and retain confidence in the currency by the guarantee of convertibility into gold at all times. If it did not do this, he told the Governor of the Bank of England, 'the whole measure is a delusive one'. He had removed the emergency clause precisely to stiffen the credibility of the currency and all appeals for relaxation left him unmoved. That monetary crises might recur he did not deny. He never claimed for the Act that it would prevent undue speculation or ensure a constant volume of paper currency. But if the legislature could establish some sort of safeguard, however limited, he thought it right to do so.[1] If despite that an emergency came and with it the need to take emergency

---

[1] See the closing passages of the speech of 13 June (*Speeches*, IV, 391).

measures, 'I dare say men will be found willing to assume such a responsibility'. He preferred to let the crisis find the men, rather than the men bring on the crisis.

In retrospect it is clear that Peel over-simplified the relationship of note issue to financial stability and price levels. Like many of his contemporaries he exaggerated the inflationary effects of the country banknotes. But he erred in good company. Peel was not a professional economist, merely a politician of considerable experience trying to apply what he believed to be sound economic principles to an admittedly defective financial system. The currency school to which he belonged thought perhaps in unduly mechanical terms. There was more to be said not only for Thomas Tooke but for the other Thomas—Attwood of Birmingham, the great advocate of paper currency—than Peel would ever allow. Attwood and his followers, whose views were dismissed somewhat contemptuously by Peel in the Bank Charter debate, were the precocious theorists of a managed currency and price stabilisation. But this in the eighteen-forties was not a practical alternative. The Bank certainly wanted no truck with such novel and risky doctrines and there was probably more danger at the time from an unregulated system than from an over-regulated one. Attwood for all his originality was remarkably blind to the effects of prices on exports and the balance of payments.[1] The prime minister's practical sense, as well as his economic prejudices, inevitably made him lean towards the simplicities of a fixed currency and a legal framework, furnished with its own automatic control, free from political manipulation. For all its rigidity the Act of 1844 served as the basis of the country's currency policy for the next eighty years. Only three times in that period did it prove necessary to take emergency powers to extend the fiduciary issue. Only once was the statutory limit of £14 million actually exceeded. No doubt the growing skill of the Bank in evolving its own methods of controlling money and credit helped to make the 1844 Act succeed in ways which owed little to its actual clauses.[2] But for the public at large the currency question was finally settled by the Act of 1844 and the professional critics were left to argue with each other over

[1] Cf. S. G. Checkland, *Rise of Industrial Society in England* (1964), pp. 196–201, 422–3.
[2] *ibid.*, p. 201.

the abstruse technicalities of a subject from which popular interest
had largely receded. The stately progress of the measure through
parliament was a political tribute to the prime minister even if all
the economists did not join in the applause.

II

In November 1843 the cabinet had formally decided to bring back
Graham's factory bill shorn of its educational clauses but retaining
the restriction of a 6½-hour working day for children which would
at least offer the opportunity for part-time education.[1] As introduced
by Graham in February the revised bill raised the age limit for children from eight to nine, maintained the normal maximum of
twelve hours for young persons and women, and added various
provisions to strengthen the powers of factory inspectors and protect
operatives against dangerous machinery. When the bill went into
committee in mid-March Ashley moved an amendment to reduce
the legal maximum for women and young persons to ten hours.
The ensuing debate showed complete lack of party unanimity on
either side of the House. Supporting Graham were Milner Gibson,
the Liberal member for Manchester, radicals like Bright and War-
burton, and the Whig economists Labouchere and Baring. Against
him were ranged other official Whigs including Sir George Grey,
Russell, and Lord Howick, and influential back-bench Conservatives
such as Lord Francis Egerton and Sir Robert Inglis. What was also
clear was that there was a powerful cross-section of Conservative
members, including many younger men like Acland and Lord John
Manners, who were completely indifferent to economic arguments
in their support for Ashley's humanitarian campaign. In embodying
the twelve hours maximum in the bill, however, the government
was merely maintaining a norm laid down as far back as 1802 and
upheld by successive ministries in a long line of factory acts. In
1833 the Whigs themselves had resisted an Ashley amendment to
bring in a ten-hour day and continued to resist similar amendments
six years later. Russell's change of attitude in 1844, in Greville's
opinion, did his reputation little good.

What was never contradicted, what in fact was tacitly accepted

[1] 44777 f. 103.

by both sides in 1844, was that whatever regulation was made for women and young persons would decide the effective working day for men also. In effect if not form the House of Commons knew that it was legislating for the entire textile factory population. It was this knowledge which was the basis of the argument, much used by Graham, that to shorten the working day would mean a severe loss in productivity, in profits, and ultimately therefore in wages. The supporters of the ten-hour clause argued that the reduction in wages would not be as great as the 25 per cent which Graham quoted; but they did not deny for the most part that there would be some reduction. The most that Ashley ever claimed—and that on a subsequent occasion—was that a fall in wages would not necessarily take place. A more characteristic attitude was that of C. Buller, a supporter of Ashley, who said that the fall would only be 9 per cent. The general acceptance by the speakers on both sides that production and wages would inevitably be affected added further point to Graham's statement that the manufacturers in general had only agreed to the restrictive clauses of the bill on the express understanding that the government would continue the normal twelve-hour working day.

It followed from this common assumption that the issue was not a simple one between humanitarians and economists, or between *laisser-faire* and state intervention. The admissibility of government interference was acknowledged by all but a few die-hard radicals. The real dilemma was what kind of intervention was justified in this particular case and what the consequences would be. Was it in the long run more humane to limit hours still further if the result was not only a loss to manufacturers but a decrease in the standard of living of the textile workers themselves? That many of the assumptions in the debate were proved in the end to be wrong or exaggerated did not make the contemporary problem less genuine or less painful. There were in addition more political considerations which the cabinet had to bear in mind. Much of the readiness of the country gentry to vote for Ashley could be attributed to their resentment against the Anti-Corn Law League and its provocative activities in the rural areas. 'A great body of the agricultural members,' Peel wrote to the queen, 'partly out of hostility to the Anti-Corn Law League, partly from the influence of humane feelings, not foreseeing the certain consequences as to the Corn Laws of new restrictions upon labour, voted against the Government.'[1] The not unreasonable fear of the ministers was that further restraints on the manufacturers at the hands of a land-owning legislature would increase the class-feeling behind the anti-corn law movement. Any buffet from the agricultural lion would be answered by a snap from the crocodile of the League. On 16 March, when it was uncomfortably clear that Ashley might carry his amendment, the cabinet discussed their tactics. The notion that either the government collectively or Graham individually should resign was for the moment put aside. Nevertheless Graham made it clear that he could not accept the ten-hour clause even if it passed. In this he was supported by Peel, though Aberdeen, Wharncliffe and Goulburn appeared ready to compromise. What chiefly haunted the cabinet discussions, however, was the probable stimulus to the anti-corn law movement which was visibly growing in strength even in the House of Commons. Graham with his usual harshness of expression opined that the Corn Laws would not survive twelve months if the amendment were adopted.[2]

The conflict of feeling evident in the cabinet came out clearly in Peel's own intervention two days later. In the morning he had arranged with Graham to see two experienced factory inspectors, Horner and Saunders, on the crucial question of the effect of a ten-hour restriction on wages and profits. It is clear that nothing transpired at that meeting which made him change his views. Indeed it was Horner's estimate that a reduction of the working day to ten hours would produce a 25 per cent reduction in wages which Graham quoted to the Commons the same evening.[3] When Peel came to make his own speech his basic argument was the inevitable decrease in productivity already emphasised by Graham. Because of the important sector of the national economy affected by the bill, he pointed out, this would have more than local repercussions. The textile industry accounted for £35 million out of a total national export of £44 million. The proposed restriction would reduce its working week by ten hours, a total of seven weeks in the entire year. The crippling effect of this on British textiles in the foreign

[1] RA/A 16/39; 40438 f. 156 (19 March 1844).　　[2] 44777 f. 149.
[3] 40449 f. 351; Graham (Peel to Graham, 17 March).

market would soon produce a reduction in wages; and this in turn would lead either to decreased home consumption or prolonged industrial strife. Given this premiss, it was inevitable that Peel should fight against a proposal which seemed to threaten all that he had been working for since the 1842 budget. The fact that some at least of the support for Ashley was dictated by political motives merely made him more determined not to give way; and on the purely humanitarian issue he resented bitterly the imputation that the advocates of the ten-hour clause had a monopoly of Christian benevolence. 'I am told', he said referring to a phrase of Fielden's, 'that it is a question between mammon and mercy.' If this were the real alternative, he would unhesitatingly choose the comfort and welfare of the labouring classes rather than the financial gain to the country. But the antithesis, he argued, was unreal. The prosperity of the industrial workers and that of industry were inseparable. Stagnation in commerce meant hardship for the poor; and a prolonged industrial depression was something he did not wish to witness again. 'I shall never forget as long as I live the situation of Paisley in 1841 and 1842.'

He did not ignore the effect of long hours. 'If my wishes could prevail I would have women employed in labour only eight hours a day.' It was a question, however, not of private wishes but of what was desirable to achieve by legislative action. If humanitarianism was to be their only guide, he would prohibit a great deal of the agricultural work carried out by women in the depths of winter with no protection against the weather. But nobody proposed, and it would be impractical for parliament to attempt, to protect all labour—industrial, agricultural and domestic—on purely humanitarian grounds. Why then, he asked, should parliament single out a few particular kinds of labour 'which are at your mercy, because they are congregated in large factories and brought under your eye'. He quoted instance after instance of far worse conditions in other branches of industry. Was the House prepared to legislate for these too, he enquired. There were cheers all round him and shouts of 'yes'. Astonished but undeterred the prime minister persisted in his argument. What they were asking for was so comprehensive as to be impossible. The government had attempted as much legislative interference as was wise and safe; and, he added defiantly, he could not and would not acquiesce in Ashley's amendment. But neither his language nor his arguments were enough. The same night the House divided against the government 179 to 170, to the cheers and hat-waving of many Conservative members.

It was a blow to the government but not necessarily a fatal one to the bill. To carry his point Ashley would have to move for the insertion of ten hours instead of twelve when clause 8 of the bill was reached; and in a larger House it was not impossible that the decision would be reversed. On 22 March, however, the House plunged itself into hopeless confusion by voting by a majority of three against twelve hours and by a majority of seven against ten hours. Next day an unhappy cabinet discussed the situation. With probably a hundred of their own party ready to vote against them and Graham as rigid as ever, the issue of resignation now seemed alarmingly real. If they did not resign, the question was whether they should abandon the bill, persist with it, or accept a compromise. Some of the leading Ashleyite Conservatives—Mahon, Egerton, Sandon and Beckett—had signified a readiness to accept eleven hours. But in the cabinet Peel, Graham and Stanley opposed any compromise and it was obvious that they felt strongly about the treatment of the government by its nominal supporters. Graham in particular was in a hard mood, ready to abandon both bill and office. During an interval between discussions Peel saw the queen who viewed the possible resignation of the cabinet with horror and begged him to consider her own position. In the end therefore they postponed a decision until the 25th when Graham had to announce the government's intentions to the Commons.

On the morning of that day the ministers gathered at Peel's house to decide their fate. All were present except Knatchbull. Peel opened the discussion by saying he strongly objected to a compromise. It would only buy a temporary peace; it would not end the ten hours agitation; and the surrender would weaken the authority of the government. He was supported by Stanley. The only two members who argued for a compromise were Gladstone and Wharncliffe; though some of the others did not exclude the possibility of yielding at a later stage. Peel however said flatly that he regarded any interference with the bill as wrong in itself and would not be willing to add anything to what was already in it. A somewhat silent cabinet agreed therefore to abandon the bill and bring in a new one simply amending the law with regard to young children and leaving intact the existing hours for adults.[1]

After Easter the parliamentary tussle was renewed with tempers that had hardly cooled in the interval. The new bill was largely a repetition of the old except that it avoided the question of hours for women and merely brought them into the same category as young persons who were already limited to twelve hours by the 1833 Act. Ashley in consequence could only bring forward his expected motion on the third reading. In these circumstances the bill passed quietly through its intervening stages until 10 May. When the crucial debate came on Ashley's amendment Peel made it clear that the government were staking their existence on the outcome of the division. He took time to argue that the additional vigour and freshness of factory workers resulting from a shorter day would not compensate for the loss of two hours' production since the decisive factor was not human muscle but machinery. He showed his sensitiveness to the humanitarian plea by a long philosophical digression on the limits of legislative action and the impossibility of drawing moral distinctions between working days of twelve, ten, or as Fielden had proposed, eight hours. And he ended with an emphatic statement of his intention to resign if the bill was not carried.[2] It was an uncompromising speech delivered with greater energy and force than some of his audience had ever heard from him and it made a profound though not necessarily sympathetic impression on the House. Faced with the ultimate sanction and exhorted by the whips, the government supporters mustered in strength and Ashley's amendment was defeated by 297 votes to 159, a large and surprising majority of 138. This was a hundred more than the whips had calculated and more than the House itself had expected; so much so that the figures were hardly credited when they were read out.[3] The hard line had proved successful; and the bill quietly passed into law in June.

For the ministers, especially for Peel and Graham, the justification for their stand was twofold. They regarded Ashley's amendment not as a simple issue of a couple of hours more or less, but as a threat to

---

[1] For the discussions in cabinet see 44777 fos. 151, 155; 40438 fos. 164, 168; RA/A 16/42, 43.
[2] *Speeches*, IV, 366 et seq. (13 May 1844).   [3] RA/A 16/69.

the economic recovery of the country with a further probability that the working classes themselves would be the first to suffer. In this they may have been—probably were—mistaken; but the mistake was genuine. 'I admit,' said Peel in his final speech, 'that I am afraid of foreign competition.' He spent much time on expounding the need for Britain to export if she was to live and added tartly that 'as if we were not satisfied with the experience of the last four years, when manufacturing prosperity is returning, we don't permit six months to elapse before we try to reduce our amount of labour from sixty-nine hours per week to fifty-eight'.[1] But behind this conviction was a further resentment that the party had deserted him and allowed a motley majority with wildly assorted motives to override the deliberate policy decision of the ministers. Stripped of its detail, his closing words on 13 May constituted a request, almost a demand, that his supporters, if they supported him as head of a government, should accept the cabinet's decision on what was the right thing to do. To Gladstone, disapproving of the prime minister's action and already half-severed from him over Maynooth, it seemed odd that ministers who preached concession to Irish Catholics should stand stubbornly on what they called their principles over the factory question. But he misunderstood their attitude. The issue was not whether policy should be based on expediency but whether, when the cabinet had deliberately come to a major decision on policy, they should continue in office when they could not enforce it. Against Russell's acid observation in the Commons that ministers were taking all legislation out of the hands of parliament, could be set Graham's sombre remark in the cabinet that if parliamentary government meant that government could be overborne by its own supporters, the famous query of the Duke of Wellington at the time of the Reform Act—how could the queen's government be carried on?—had gained redoubled force.[2] It was this which made Peel and Graham talk so much, as their younger colleague noted unsympathetically, of honour and principle. Paradoxically the more the party rank and file demanded the liberty of acting on their own views, the more the leaders could claim a similar freedom for themselves. When those leaders became ministers of the Crown, their sense of individual responsibility was immeasurably increased. By

[1] *Speeches*, IV, 372.   [2] 44777 f. 151.

training and temperament Peel took a high, almost a high-handed, view of the position of the executive. This was the issue which fundamentally was at stake in the division which took place in the early hours of 14 May.

Yet within a month he was facing an exactly similar crisis. This time it was over the old question of the sugar duties. A prudent inactivity had been exhibited by the government on this issue ever since the great controversy of 1841. But by 1844 the time had come when they could avoid legislation no longer. Their earlier reluctance had been understandable. The whole question was an inextricable and explosive compound of commercial, financial, political and humanitarian elements. The supply of sugar to the United Kingdom was a virtual monopoly of the British West Indies on whose product there was a duty of 25s 3d a cwt. compared with the virtually prohibitive rate of 63s on foreign sugar. The domestic consumption of sugar was growing but the ability of the West Indian planters to keep pace with it had not only been halted by the emancipation of their slave workers but actually diminished. Prices therefore were rising and a combination of monopoly and high prices was not one which public opinion would accept indefinitely. Simply to reduce the duty on West Indian sugar, however, would be of little use. As long as the monopoly continued a reduction of duty would enrich the West Indian planters rather than bring down prices for the British consumers. It would also have a considerable effect on the revenue. Sugar was the most valuable single item of dutiable British imports, accounting for about a third of the total return from the customs. It would be quixotic to throw away such a large revenue with no corresponding benefit to the British public. The alternative was to look for other sources of supply. Slave-grown sugar was inadmissible. The Conservatives had used the anti-slavery argument when in opposition in 1841 and could not go back on their previous attitude. The West Indian planters, to whose difficulties Peel was not indifferent, would have had every right to complain if after they had been forced to emancipate their own slaves they were exposed to the competition of other slave states. And if they complained, they had a powerful lobby in parliament to see that their complaints would be heard. The history of negotiations with Brazil had demonstrated the hopelessness of persuading slave states by mere commercial inducements to abandon their peculiar institution. The only other source of free sugar, and that a limited one, was the East Indies, in the slowly developing plantations of Java and the Philippines. Under the existing most-favoured nations treaty with Brazil, however, no terms could be offered to the East Indies which would not also admit on equal footing the slave-grown Brazilian sugar.

So far it was deadlock. But after 1844 the deadlock would be broken since in November of that year the Brazilian treaty expired. The ministers were already under pressure from the opposition to announce their future sugar policy and in the voluminous discussions that went on in ministerial circles during 1843 it was generally accepted that free trade in sugar was bound to come sooner or later. But first it was essential that the East Indies should be encouraged to greater production by being given a practical pledge of the British government's intentions. A large, immediate reduction in the duty on foreign sugar, however, could hardly be given without making a proportionate reduction of duty on imperial sugar. This would merely give a season's bonus to the West Indies while the East Indies extended their plantations to meet the British demand. The ministerial plan was therefore divided into two stages in order to overcome the short-term difficulties of increased demand and limited supply. The first stage would take effect in 1844, the second in 1845. For 1844 it was proposed that the duties on free sugar would be reduced so as to leave a preferential margin of 10s for the imperial product. This was announced by Goulburn when introducing his budget in March, though the details were left until later in the session. Even in April the Chancellor of the Exchequer was still uncertain of the best course of action. But at the beginning of June, with the factory bill through and the Bank Charter bill favourably launched, he brought his sugar bill before the House. His immediate proposal was after November to admit 'free' foreign sugar at a duty of 34s plus the usual 5 per cent. In the subsequent debate both Goulburn and Gladstone made it clear that the permanent settlement would be effected in 1845 when it was known whether the income tax was to be retained and to what extent therefore further tariff reductions could be made. Goulburn's proposition, however, ran into cross-fire from free traders who wished to reduce the duty on all foreign sugar regardless of origin and from protectionists who objected to a decrease in imperial preference. A resolution by Russell to abolish the distinction between free and slave sugar was comfortably defeated, but on 14 June came an artful motion by P. Miles, M.P. for Bristol and a leading West Indian spokesman, to reduce the imperial duty to 20s and retain 34s for foreign refined sugar (the main East Indian export). It attracted support from both free traders and protectionists and was carried against the government by twenty votes.

As early as 11 June Peel had been apprehensive of an alliance between the opposition and some of his own supporters. Taught by the factory bill experience he convened a party gathering at his own house on 13 June but said grimly afterwards that it was 'the most unsatisfactory meeting he had ever known'.[1] Strong language was used by some of the West Indian representatives and it was obvious that there was no prospect of retaining their support.[2] The split in the party over sugar was not unexpected, therefore, but its extent was shattering. With a hundred more members voting than had taken part in the disastrous ten-hour divisions, the government had suffered an even greater defeat. Had it not been for over half a dozen members of the opposition who had voted for the ministry, it would have been even worse; and to rub salt into the wound both mover and seconder of the victorious motion were Conservatives.

When next day the cabinet discussed the situation Peel was in a mood of profound pessimism. In 1841, he pointed out, they had argued that if the Whigs could not carry their measures in the Commons, they should resign. Now they were themselves in exactly the same position and for the moment he could not, or in his anger would not, see a way out. He thought that it would be too dangerous to attempt a reversal of the vote. Even if it were possible, it would damage the reputation of the House, especially after the factory bill episode less than four weeks earlier. On the other hand he could not accept Miles's motion, nor was he prepared to fall back on the expedient followed by Baring in 1841, a tame renewal of the old duties. He could think of no means of extricating the government from their predicament and on the whole seemed inclined towards resignation. Stanley and Graham, who had seen him privately beforehand, agreed with this fatalistic conclusion. Not all their colleagues, however, were prepared to throw in their hands so soon.

[1] 44777 f. 188.   [2] *Greville*, 21 June 1844.

Aberdeen thought they should decide nothing in anger and at least sleep on any decision. Goulburn with his homespun commonsense saw grave disadvantages in resigning on an issue which would not be understood in the country as one of principle. Gladstone thought the same; and the deaf old duke burst out, 'God, I am against quitting! I have seen the consequences of quitting before, and I say, continue if you can.' In the absence of Buccleuch and Lyndhurst it was decided after three hours' discussion to postpone a final decision.

The following day, Sunday, 16 June, they met again at Aberdeen's house. Peel had in the interval seen the queen, who was friendly and sympathetic, roundly condemned both opposition and renegade Conservatives, hoped no resignations would be necessary, and laughingly said that she could hardly send for Mr. Miles to form a government. This was a point; and though Peel was still feeling hard, he was a shade less intransigent than on the previous day. Nevertheless, he told the cabinet that it was incompatible with his personal honour either to adopt Miles's motion or renew the old duties; and both he and Stanley talked of the incapacity of disgraced men to serve their country. It was known that many of their followers were anxious that the government should not resign and it was anticipated that some formal demonstration of confidence would be made before the House met the following day. On this, however, Peel merely made the icy comment that if the party wanted to demonstrate its confidence, the way to do so was by voting for the government's proposal. Granville Somerset, a newcomer to the cabinet and professionally alive to the problems of party management, asked what arrangement could be made to allow those who had given their vote to Miles to support a new proposal without reversing their previous stand. Peel said pessimistically that if anything like that was attempted, Russell would merely carry a motion to postpone the whole issue until the following session. Others disagreed with this, and also with Graham's gloomy observation that the mass of the party was not only unruly but actually hostile.[1]

Next day Peel saw Miles and Sandon in Gladstone's presence and stated clearly and quietly the view of the government. He then went over with Gladstone the commercial aspect of the issue in

[1] For discussions in cabinet see 44777 f. 188; RA/A 16/81-3; Graham (Graham to de Grey and Lyndhurst, 15 June 1844).

preparation for his speech of explanation the same evening. Sandon had already impressed on Gladstone that apart from a few discontented or hostile individuals, the mass of the party was still solidly behind the government and anxious to avoid its resignation. On the other hand they were unwilling to rescind their vote of Friday for the sake of their own reputation and that of the House of Commons. To satisfy the honour of both ministers and back-benchers was a task of some nicety; but Sandon's diagnosis of party feeling was clearly more realistic than Graham's. An independent meeting of some two hundred Conservative M.P.s was held at the Carlton the same day under the chairmanship of Sir John Yarde Buller, the respected member for South Devonshire. With only five or six dissentients, including Disraeli and Ferrand, they passed a resolution:

> That this meeting has heard with deep regret the rumour of an intended resignation on the part of her Majesty's Ministers, a step which in their opinion would be fraught with the most disastrous consequences to the best interests of the country, and while they reserve to themselves the full exercise of an independent judgement upon all measures submitted to the consideration of Parliament, they take this opportunity of expressing a grateful sense of the services which have been rendered to the Empire by Her Majesty's ministers, an anxious desire for their continued maintenance in Power, and a firm determination to afford them a general and cordial support.[1]

This at least was an olive branch, though it still did not settle the question of tactics. All the information reaching Peel suggested that a direct reversal of Miles's motion was out of the question; and half the cabinet did not even wish to attempt it. At their final meeting on the Monday, however, they agreed on the compromise which had been virtually implicit in Peel's remarks the previous day. It was decided to make a marginal concession, as Granville Somerset had suggested, to enable their errant followers to change their attitude without actually eating their words.

That evening in the House of Commons Peel moved for the imposition of a 24s duty on British colonial sugar, thus restoring the preferential margin of 10s which the government had originally proposed. It meant that half of Miles's composite motion was retained, though the lesser half; and it left all those who had voted for

[1] RA/A 16/85.

449

it, unless specifically committed to the 20s duty, technically free to
vote again. The ground for manœuvre had been minimal; and the
device was paper thin. Not surprisingly the opposition took the line
that what the House was asked to do was in fact to reverse its previous decision; and not only the official opposition. Disraeli made a
clever mocking speech which aroused considerable applause,
attacking the prime minister for 'menacing his friends and cringing
to his opponents'. But the atmosphere, taut enough in any event,
was made worse by Peel himself at the start of the debate. He first
explained in considerable and perhaps unnecessary detail the background to the sugar proposals, emphasising its part in the general
financial programme of the government and the importance of its
timing. Then, towards the end of his speech, he spoke with undis-
guised resentment of the means whereby the Miles motion had been
carried. He talked of a combination between the opposition and
some of the government's usual supporters; and he said this obliged
the government not only to resist it but to bear in mind also that
acquiescence would encourage similar combinations in future. He
referred to previous difficulties thrown in the way of government
legislation; regretted the loss of confidence on the part of their
former friends; but asserted grimly that the ministers would continue
to put forward the proposals they thought right, even though they
did not get the support they ought to receive, and needed to receive,
if they were to carry their proposals into legislation. His manner was
sharp and offensive, and he spoke as though completely detached
from the benches behind him.

Gladstone at his side had cold shivers run up his spine as he listened
and felt at the close he had been hearing the government's death
warrant. Peel himself thought it was the end. Indeed perhaps it was
this conviction which made his speech so hard and unforgiving.
In a brief note to the queen, scribbled from the front bench after he
had sat down, he warned her that the House was likely to reject
his motion by a considerable majority and that this second rejection
would have inevitable consequences for the stability of the government.[1] If any one person saved the day it was Stanley. In a deft
speech at a critical point in the debate he gave a sharp riposte to
some supercilious remarks by Lord Howick about the agriculturalists

[1] RA/A 16/85 f. 86.

and made a soothing appeal to the government's old supporters for fair and generous treatment. When the division was taken there was a formal majority for the motion of 255 votes to 233; but what the figures could not reveal was the internal feelings of those who made that majority of twenty-two possible. Talking with Conservative members afterwards Gladstone was convinced that a deep wound had been inflicted on the party's morale. 'A great man', he recorded sorrowfully, 'had commited a great error.'[1]

Peel himself, once his victory was won, realised how far he had put himself in the wrong. A few days later when Duncombe facetiously moved to omit the customary words 'freely and voluntarily' from the preamble to the sugar duties bill on the grounds that it had notoriously been done under coercion, the prime minister seized the opportunity to make a brief conciliatory speech. He disclaimed any such 'arrogant a sentiment' as that his party should vote for every measure introduced by the government or that all their measures should be completely adopted; and he acknowledged the 'generous support' which his followers had frequently given him. With that the open quarrel was patched up. What could not be restored so easily was the shattered confidence on both sides. That there had been much misunderstanding was clear enough. To Peel and Graham the sugar question was a cardinal aspect of the government's economic policy and its defeat a wanton dereliction of duty on the part of their followers. To the rank and file of the party the sugar duties seemed a minor issue and rumours of resignation that had swept through London over the weekend had taken them by surprise. Lord Sandon, who was bold enough on the Saturday evening to write a letter to Peel remonstrating against any thought of resignation, argued that the defeat on Miles's motion had been merely one of detail, involving a loss of only £400,000 in the current year. A government with a majority of a hundred on any matter of principle had no right to regard such a defeat as a fatal affront. Sandon's attitude was simple, probably not unrepresentative, and certainly revealing. Plainly the party did not realise how seriously the government would view the matter; nor did the cabinet—or some of them—realise how unimportant the issue seemed to the party.

[1] 44777 f. 194.

451

But behind this mutual lack of comprehension was a larger issue. The ministers claimed freedom in the national interest to propose such measures as they thought right, even though they conflicted (or could be deemed to conflict) with the social and economic interest of their supporters. The individual M.P. on the other hand tended to interpret his party allegiance as only committing him to support his leaders on matters of general principle or when their position as ministers was at stake. 'You cannot expect', wrote Sandon in his letter of 15 June, 'that upon all points, whether of individual interest or class interest, the whole of your supporters should sacrifice everything to this general but honest allegiance.' There was a perceptible gap in fact between the concept of party loyalty held by the ministers and that held by the ordinary party member. Perhaps this looseness provided a necessary margin of tolerance in the new party machines built up so rapidly after the Reform Act. Men conditioned by the style of politics that obtained before 1832 could not rid themselves immediately of their traditional notions of political independence, whether applying to ministers or to back-benchers. A more rigid party structure would probably have broken under the strain. As long as individual M.P.s disdained to vote invariably as members of a disciplined and obedient party phalanx and ministers refused to allow the views and interests of their followers to dictate policy, a certain looseness was inevitable if the system was to function at all. But for a masterful prime minister and a government working at high pressure in an antiquated parliamentary framework, the weakness of the system was hard to bear. 'Declarations of general confidence', Peel had replied laconically to Sandon on 17 June, 'will not, I fear, compensate for that loss of authority and efficiency which is sustained by a Government not enabled to carry into effect the practical measures of legislation which it feels it to be its duty to submit to Parliament.'[1]

A great deal in these circumstances depended on management. But in June 1844 neither the prime minister not his recalcitrant followers were in a very manageable mood. It seemed to Gladstone that Peel, and those members of the cabinet like Graham who shared his attitude, were allowing themselves to be influenced not only by the particular difficulties thrown in their way over sugar

[1] *Peel*, III, 150-2.

but by their weariness with the unending drudgery of office and by a resentful feeling that the party only exerted itself in order to criticise and oppose its leaders. There was a similar sense of disillusionment in the party; particularly among those who, protectionist by interest or conviction, saw the government following a general policy of free trade, who heard Peel and Gladstone talk the language even if they did not adopt the full prescription of radical economists, and who hungered in vain for some words of sympathy from their leader for the threatened cause of agriculture. Sore feelings led to inflexible attitudes and out of these came the situation in which Peel felt forced for the second time to reassert his authority, only in turn to be accused of coercing the House of Commons and behaving despotically towards his own followers. Though the strained feelings inevitably died down with the passage of time, the future could never be the same. It was not so much that a permanent scar had been inflicted on the relationship between Peel and the Conservative Party as that a silent change had come over the relationship itself. Many Conservatives probably thought what Lord Ashley actually said in a letter sent to Peel on 19 June; that this second reversed vote at the bidding of the prime minister was 'tending to a dictatorship under the form of free Government'. He looked back on it, added Ashley painfully, in astonishment and grief, convinced that the mischief done was irreparable.[1] This was the real sting. Opinions on the constitutional propriety, as on the political justification, of Peel's action might differ. What was undeniable was that he had handled the whole episode as badly as any in his long parliamentary career.

III

Stanley's speech in the sugar debate, perhaps his greatest single service to the government in the House of Commons, was ironically also his last. Early in August parliament adjourned for a month to allow time for the Lords to deliver their verdict in the O'Connell case. With the work of the session substantially completed, Stanley at his own request was moved to the upper House. It was an action,

[1] 40483 f. 134. For the subsequent exchange of letters between Peel and Ashley see ibid., fos. 136–40, ptly pr. Peel, III, 153–4.

to borrow the jargon of his own favourite pursuit, bred by pride out of disappointment. The Colonial Office had declined in interest and importance since Whig days. Heavy as it was, the work of government had fallen mainly on a few departments—the Home Office, Treasury and Board of Trade—and there was little scope for general debaters in the Commons. Finance and commerce, subjects that seemed to absorb an increasing amount of parliamentary attention, had little intrinsic interest for Stanley;[1] and he felt his time and talents wasted as night after night he sat silent on the ministerial bench. In the House of Lords on the other hand he would be spokesman for the government over the whole field of policy, a valuable reinforcement to the ageing Wellington, and automatic successor when the duke, thirty years his senior, finally left the stage. Wellington raised no opposition and Peel could not do so, though he felt an understandable pang at losing without warning so formidable a debater from the Commons. The matter was settled in a few days by an exchange of letters between the three men which said much for their sense and mutual trust.[2] With one outstanding colleague gone, another in his own self-doubting fashion was on the way out. In July, during a temperate non-party debate started by Wyse on Irish education, Peel had pledged the government during the recess to review the question of Irish academic reform, including Maynooth, and to announce their intentions at the start of the next session. For this he had obtained the consent of the cabinet and had an additional assurance from Gladstone that he would do as little as possible to embarrass his colleagues and would leave the timing of his resignation in Peel's hands.[3] The government was now committed to action and after all the discussions in cabinet it was predictable what that action would be.

To ministers now entering on their fourth year of office the interval between winding up the business of one session and starting on that of the next seemed to grow shorter each year. The autumn recess in 1844 was even less of a respite than usual for Peel because of a period of acute anxiety over his youngest child, the twelve-year-old Eliza. Early in September the report of her illness, at first diagnosed as scarlet fever but from the symptoms possibly diphtheria, brought Peel and Julia hurrying down from London by the first

[1] Cf. *Gladstone*, I, 194.   [2] *Peel*, III, 154-9.   [3] 44777 f. 198.

454

train. For nearly a week Eliza lay on the edge of death while her stricken parents, forbidden to live at the Manor, lodged with her two brothers in the nearby steward's house. Peel's visit to Scotland with the queen was cancelled; Aberdeen took his place; and Graham was put in charge of affairs in London while the prime minister remained in virtual quarantine. Fresh cases of the illness appeared among the maidservants and after the crisis was over Peel sent Julia and the boys to Brighton where Eliza joined them in October. Peel himself returned to London on 18 September. Most of what was left of the autumn he spent between Whitehall, Brighton and Windsor. Not until the last part of October did the Peels return for a week to Drayton and after that brief visit began the work of preparing for the first of the November cabinets. It was a peaceful time for the partridges and pheasants in the stubble-fields round Drayton that season. But though most of Peel's observation of the countryside had to be made from the windows of his railway compartment between London and Birmingham, at least it had been a good season. Earlier in the summer there had been fears of a drought but by the end of June the queen was able to send Peel a well-formed ear of wheat which, replied the prime minister diplomatically, was calculated together with 'the beautiful rain of the last twelve hours' to allay all his apprehensions.[1] By September the price of wheat was down to 47s 7d a quarter and remained under 50s until Christmas. This, flanked by the mounting evidence of the success of the government's tariff policy, surpassing Peel's most sanguine expectations, ensured that financially and commercially at least there would be few problems during the following session. The real difficulties would come over politics and religion.

During the late autumn Graham and the Lord Lieutenant had been working out the details of the various Irish educational schemes. The close contact established through the Charitable Trusts Board enabled them to tap expert and influential Catholic opinion; and this in turn helped to shape official policy. Blake, for example, produced a memorandum arguing powerfully for the specialised training of priests which was eventually accepted despite Peel's earlier speculations on the desirability of joint education. The direct access to informed Catholic circles also made it unnecessary, in the

[1] 40438 f. 234.

view of the ministers, to appoint any preliminary commission of enquiry. They had enough detailed recommendations without that. The first fruits of the new alliance began to appear even before the Trusts Board was gazetted in December. By mid-November Graham was able to embody his work in two Home Office memoranda privately printed for cabinet circulation. That on Maynooth included appendices written by Lord Heytesbury and Anthony Blake.[1] Apart from the factual descriptions of the impoverished condition of the college and the familiar political arguments for its improvement, the paper contained a number of specific proposals: the incorporation of the trustees to enable them to hold property and grant degrees, an increase in the salaries of the principal and professors, an extension of the training period, the doubling of the value of scholarships, and the appointment of a body of Visitors to exercise general supervision on behalf of the government. The adoption of all these reforms would involve raising the total parliamentary grant from £9,000 to £25,000. The other paper,[2] on Irish collegiate education, outlined no less than four schemes for cabinet consideration by various authors including Blake and Wyse, the Irish Liberal M.P. for Waterford. All envisaged the establishment of provincial colleges under one eventual academic organisation though there were divergent recommendations for the future of Trinity College and Maynooth. Graham, however, wished to keep the Maynooth question separate from the colleges despite the Lord Lieutenant's inclination to include it in whatever new university scheme was eventually set up.

The first meeting of the cabinet on 19 November merely reviewed the course of events in Ireland since their last meeting. Three days later they discussed the collegiate scheme with what to Peel were highly satisfactory results. In principle they agreed to leave Trinity College alone, found provincial colleges probably at Cork and Belfast with professors nominated by the crown, and group these into a new university with powers to grant degrees in arts and law. Peel was prepared to leave the delicate matter of chairs of theology to private endowment, though some members of the cabinet showed sensitivity over the loss of central control which this would entail

[1] Graham (H.O. memorandum of 16 Nov. 1844).
[2] RA/D 14/7, dated 15 Nov. 1844.

Finally on 25 November they gingerly turned to the subject of Maynooth. There was general acceptance that something must be done for the college; and though Peel emphasised the political importance of establishing effective visitorial powers, he did not wish even this to stand in the way of a general reform. With the prime minister pressing his colleagues for a clear decision in principle, Gladstone now made his formal though hardly unexpected statement that he could not support such a plan as a member of the government. In answer to a blunt query from Stanley he said somewhat mystifyingly that he would not necessarily oppose the plan as a private member. If he resigned, he tried to explain to his colleagues, it would be on grounds of consistency with past opinions, not because he thought their present policy either unnecessary or objectionable. This did not seem a very convincing reason and even now Peel tried to avoid a public breach. At their last meeting on 6 December he recommended that Graham should leave the details of the Maynooth bill until after the new colleges were dealt with. On that procrastinatory note the autumn cabinets came to a close and ministers went off for their last few weeks of comparative leisure before the session began: Peel to entertain a galaxy of scientists at Drayton and Gladstone to brood self-consciously over his position in the seclusion of Hawarden.[1]

From there he wrote to Peel on 2 January a long and involved letter marked secret but inadvertently sent open through the post. But there was little danger that an inquisitive postmaster would have gleaned many cabinet secrets from it. 'I really have great difficulty sometimes in exactly comprehending what Gladstone means,' the prime minister commented dryly when forwarding the letter to Graham, '. . . I take for granted, however, that the letter means to announce his continued intention to retire, and I deeply regret it.'[2] When he saw Gladstone in town a week later he met him with his usual friendliness, talked frankly of the danger that the government might be shipwrecked on the issue, spoke of the growing public resistance to Maynooth, and asked Gladstone to stay in office until the last possible moment. Peel was clearly using every argument that might have weight with his younger colleague. Nevertheless to say

[1] For the autumn cabinets see 40439 fos. 155–7; 44777 fos. 206, 212.
[2] Graham (n.d. but early Jan. 1845).

of Maynooth as he did that 'I think it will very probably be f.
to the government'[1] argued a surprisingly fatalistic attitude. In 1
during December and January it had become increasingly clear t
in a Church of England torn by the Tractarian and ritualistic c
troversies, among English Dissenters increasingly opposed to s
establishment in any form, and in Scotland still shaken by
Disruption, the Maynooth proposals, combining the twin princi
of state support and encouragement to Romanism, would prov
a storm of reaction. The solid, sensible Goulburn, who had b
listening to opinion at Cambridge, wrote Peel a long letter on
subject early in January which concluded pessimistically tha
should not be surprised if the flame of real religious apprehension
the consequences of the measure was to burn as fiercely as eve

In the second week of January the ministers reassembled in Lon
for a last round of discussions before the session began. Peel was
prepared to delay over Maynooth and as late as 20 January s
Gladstone a friendly letter, begging him to consider how benefi
a change had already taken place in British relations with Irel
and the Papacy. But rather than risk misunderstanding the youn
man reaffirmed his position in writing and this time Peel bowed
the inevitable. With Eliot and Gladstone quitting their posts
both Lonsdale and Knatchbull hinting at retirement, a major
shuffle of offices was now forced upon him. He had already in
begun to discuss them with Wellington before the final break. C
of his main concerns was to reinforce his depleted speaking ta
in the Commons. To avoid any jealousy at the promotion o
junior, however, he first offered a seat in the cabinet to Lons
who since succeeding to his father's title and estates the previ
year was anxious to be relieved of his duties at the Post Office.
offer was refused but the compliment was disarming and the P
master General agreed to stay on for the time being. Next San
was invited to succeed Gladstone at the Board of Trade. On learn
of Gladstone's reason for retiring he hesitated and finally decli
because of the difficulties likely to be created by his ultra-Protest
constituents in Liverpool. Peel then made the best of an unsatisfact
situation by promoting Dalhousie to the presidency of the Board

[1] 44777 f. 212.
[2] 40445 f. 5 (6 Jan. 1845). For a fuller extract see *English Politics*, p. 95 n. 2.

Trade, but without cabinet rank. Sir George Clerk was made vice-president though Peel would have preferred Cardwell for this post. But crude by-election considerations once more intervened. Cardwell's constituency of Clitheroe was peculiarly vulnerable to the Anti-Corn Law League and he had to be content with Clerk's old post of financial secretary to the Treasury.[1]

He was able to do something, however, for his other young men. Sidney Herbert succeeded Fremantle as Secretary at War; and together with Lincoln was promoted to the cabinet. When Knatchbull made his unnoticed departure from the ministry in February, W. B. Baring, Lord Ashburton's son, took over the Paymastership and Jocelyn, the son and heir of Lord Roden, succeeded to Baring's post as secretary to the Board of Control. Limited as his range of choice had been, Peel had once more shown his preference for the younger men and in Edward Cardwell he had enlisted another outstanding personal recruit. Only thirty-two, son of a wealthy Liverpool merchant, a Balliol man and a double first, Cardwell had made his mark as a defender of government policy in 1844. Lacking Gladstone's brilliance but possessing greater calmness and caution, and endowed with a pleasant if somewhat ponderous temperament, he was soon on intimate terms with the prime minister. When Hardinge went to India in 1844 Cardwell took over his house next to Peel's in Whitehall. Peel had been accustomed to walk back home with Hardinge late at night after the House had risen. It was not long before he fell into the same habit with Cardwell.

IV

Parliament was opened by the queen on 4 February and Gladstone's explanation of his resignation, couched in highly personal terms, made little impact. The immediate attention of the House was concentrated not on Maynooth but on the financial and commercial matters which occupied most of the first eight weeks of the session. In bringing forward the budget only ten days after they assembled Peel justified the exceptionally early period on the grounds that the queen's speech had contained a clear hint that the government intended to renew the income tax. It is not improbable also that he

[1] RA/A 17/8-17.

wanted to launch a scheme which included both that and a final settlement of the sugar question well before the House became involved in the acrimonies of Irish legislation. What he had to propose, however, was a series of exceptionally well-matured measures. Planning for the 1845 budget had in fact started a year earlier. During the Easter recess of 1844 Goulburn had submitted to Peel a long-range forecast of government finances for the next two years, together with his preliminary thoughts on the policy they should adopt. At that stage he was looking forward to a surplus of £3 million in April 1845. If he could retain that for a year, he said with a wistfulness peculiar to chancellors of the exchequer, he could put everything on a sound basis; but to expect such a financial paradise was hopeless. In the following year the revenue situation would worsen; partly because the accidental relief from one quarter's debt interest on the new $3\frac{1}{4}$ per cent stock in 1844-45 would not recur; more drastically, because the income tax expired in 1845. The further outlook was even less promising. If the income tax was not continued, there would be a small surplus of about £250,000 in April 1846 and a gross deficit of £2·3 million in April 1847. Even if the estimates could be pruned by a million, the net deficit forecast for 1847 would still be £1·3 million. The first question to be decided therefore was the renewal of the income tax; or rather, since he virtually took renewal for granted, for how long it should be renewed. If for two years, it would expire in 1847; and that year would almost certainly see a general election. With an orthodox Treasury horror of submitting such a question to the hazards of the hustings, he recommended that the tax should be renewed for three years. To put their planning on a firm basis, it should be done by an act introduced in the 1844 session.

This point established, he turned to the question of tariff reductions. Clearly another administration of income tax medicine should be accompanied by the sweetening of tax reductions elsewhere. Here again Goulburn's characteristic financial caution asserted itself. The income tax after all, he reasoned, was a temporary tax, peculiarly unpopular, liable therefore to be suddenly terminated. It had been abolished in 1816 against the will of Lord Liverpool's ministry. In a reformed parliament the chances were even greater of some sudden parliamentary revolt against it. Any further reduction of taxes on this insubstantial basis must be undertaken warily. A complete repeal of tariffs meant an absolute loss. If the loss ever had to be made up by means other than the income tax, it would involve them in the unpopularity of restoring old or imposing new duties. His advice therefore was for a reduction rather than a repeal of tariffs, in the hope that at best larger consumption would eventually mean a restoration of revenue, or at worst that it would be politically easier to increase existing tariffs if ever they faced a deficit. These considerations, he admitted, would not apply to a repeal of the duty on wool and vinegar because the loss of revenue was relatively trifling, only £125,000 in all. They would, however, apply to glass (£750,000) and raw cotton (£760,000) and other articles where the relief to trade and industry would be larger than mere revenue statistics would suggest. In any case, he wished to retain a surplus as a guard against unforeseen contingencies and he suggested a figure of between £126,000 and £210,000 as the maximum amount of tariff reductions that should be contemplated. These figures he arrived at by the cautious method of reckoning the available sum for tariff experiment as the equivalent of the interest over three or four years on his nest-egg of £1·4 million, the unexpected surplus over the estimated income tax yield.

Peel's reaction to this sketch of future financial policy was illuminating. Writing from Drayton in the peace of Easter Monday, he laid down as his first axiom that there would be great difficulty in renewing the income tax unless they proposed reductions in taxation which not only benefited the mass of the population but were clearly seen to do so. Sugar, therefore, on which Goulburn confessed himself at a loss to know how to proceed, Peel thought would have to be included in any tariff revision despite all the known difficulties. He agreed about wool and vinegar. On raw cotton he made the revealing comment that there might be political complications because of the factory question. 'It would be thought that we unduly favoured the Manufacturer if *we at the same time* protected him from the reduction of the hours of labour, and relieved him altogether from the duty on the raw Material.' On income tax he argued that renewal for three years would be in a different category to a renewal for two. Firstly, they had never concealed their view that a total period of five years was desirable to allow time for the full advantages of tariff reductions to be realised. Secondly, renewal for yet another term of three years would look remarkably like a permanent arrangement. The political argument of the general election in 1847 was not one which could publicly be brought forward. In any case he did not think that the tax would be endangered by a general election provided it offered a substitute for taxes pressing heavily on trade and industry. 'I would rather incline', he concluded, 'to renewal for two years for the purpose of trying the experiment of beneficial and popular reductions within certain limits of amount.'

This correspondence[1] was of course only a preliminary exchange of views and information, intended as a basis for further discussion when Peel returned to London; and neither man was expressing any decided conclusion. Nevertheless the difference of approach was characteristic. Goulburn was clearly looking at the problem from an orthodox financial point of view. He was concerned primarily to keep the national balance-sheet straight; he wished to retain as large a surplus as possible as an insurance against the future; and he was not prepared to trust too much to the cover provided by the income tax in view of its politically vulnerable nature. His advocacy of a three-year renewal was prompted by distrust, not by a zeal for experiment. Peel on the other hand was more fluid in his thinking, more drawn to the possibility of another large tariff experiment, but at the same time more alive to all the political factors involved in their budgetary decisions. His leaning towards a two-year renewal of the income tax was prompted by a desire to remove political obstacles to another great fiscal operation, not by any financial objection. It was probably this consideration which ensured that Goulburn's desire for an income tax renewal bill in the 1844 session was not gratified.

In the largely verbal and unrecorded discussions which took place during the rest of the year there was clearly an important assimilation of viewpoint. The growing evidence of an increasing surplus for 1844 strengthened the case for a massive tariff reform in 1845. But since that in turn would inevitably entail a large and immediate loss of revenue, it also strengthened the case for another long-term renewal of the income tax. Up to the last, therefore, the Chancellor of the Exchequer fought a determined rearguard action for financial

[1] 40444 fos. 185–90.

caution. By December 1844, as a result of the non-expenditure of certain sums and the continued improvement in the revenue, it was estimated that the surplus in April would be over £4 million. Yet what seemed significant to Goulburn was that without the income tax and the adventitious current savings, there would have been a deficit of over £1·6 million. Similarly, looking forward to April 1846, he could certainly calculate on a surplus, even without the income tax, of over a million. But this was so dependent on non-recurrent items that it would be foolhardy on the strength of it to repeal any taxes. The case for a renewal of the income tax was therefore impregnable. Even with the income tax he wished to retain £1½ million as a safeguard, leaving a maximum of £2½ million for tariff reductions. If the income tax was to be renewed for only two years, he thought it over-sanguine to expect the revenue to cover both the deficit and the tax losses from tariff reductions within such a short period. In that case they could only reduce tariffs and not repeal them. The nature of the tariff experiment would depend therefore on the term for which the income tax was renewed.[1] The problem for the ministers was paradoxically that there would be an excess of money in 1845 and the reasonable certainty of a shortage in the two following years. By February the estimated surplus had risen to over £5 million and though a large payment for exchequer bills on account of the opium compensation reduced this to a book balance of just over £3 million, Peel did not feel that the Treasury could take refuge behind this insubstantial screen.[2] He accepted Goulburn's calculations; he agreed on the importance of safeguarding the revenue not so much in 1845 as in 1846 and 1847; but within this general financial framework he was prepared to discard Goulburn's cautious reservations about the amount of tariff reforms that they could undertake and the size of the surplus revenue they should hold in reserve. To Goulburn's solidity in finance Peel added ruthlessness and imagination. In its perfected form the budget of 1845 was that phenomenon more often seen in war than finance, a bold stroke of policy secured by a thorough organisation of resources. As a piece of administrative planning it was one of Peel's masterpieces.

[1] ibid. fos. 349–58 (memorandum on budget of 1845).
[2] Goulburn (Peel to Goulburn, 13 Feb. 1845).

As in 1842 the prime minister himself introduced the budget. In his speech on 14 February 1845 he made it clear to the House that the expected real surplus in April was in excess of £5 million, even though £½ million was composed of non-recurrent items. If the income tax was allowed to lapse but no other changes were made, there would still be an excess of £2·5 million for the year 1845–46. Nevertheless, he went on to demonstrate in his usual lucid fashion, the financial situation would begin to deteriorate in the course of the year and grow rapidly worse after 1846. In the first place the government proposed to increase services expenditure by £1 million, mainly on the Navy. This would reduce the real surplus to £1½ million. In addition, the estimated revenue for 1845–46 included a sum of over £½ million from the China indemnity, which would not be repeated in later years, and a half-yearly instalment of £2·6 million income tax collected in arrears which would fall due after April 1845 even though the tax was allowed to expire. This joint non-recurrent sum of £3·2 million more than accounted for the surplus to be expected in 1845–46. In other words, for 1846–47 and possibly for future years, there would again be deficits on the normal revenue and expenditure of the country. The question was whether to wait until 1846 to devise ways of meeting these prospective difficulties. The answer given by Peel on behalf of the government could scarcely have surprised his audience. It was to make provision at once for a deficit that was still two years ahead, or more bluntly, to renew the income tax. If they did this, they would have a nominal surplus of £5 million. Deducting from this the increased naval estimates and the adventitious China indemnity, they would be left with a working surplus of £3·4 million. 'I now, Sir,' observed the prime minister, 'approach that most important part of my statement I have this night to make, namely, what is the mode in which that surplus, or any part of that surplus, shall be applied for the relief of taxation.' He did not keep the House long in suspense. If the renewal of the income tax turned government solvency into positive affluence, at any rate for 1845–46, the government for its part proposed to return almost all the available surplus back to the public in the form of remissions of those taxes 'which in our opinion press more onerously on the community than the income tax'. He outlined them one by one. A complicated reorganisation of the sugar duties which basically brought the duty on colonial products down to 14s and on foreign free sugar to 23s 4d. The abolition of all export duties on British goods, including the ill-fated coal tax of 1842; the complete abolition of import duties on 430 of the remaining 813 articles in the Book of Tariffs, mainly those on raw materials for industry; the abolition of the duty on raw cotton; and the abolition of the excise duty on glass and auctions. The total loss to the revenue he estimated at £3·3 million of which more than a third was incurred over sugar. In return he asked for the renewal of the income tax for a further period of three years.

In this massive exercise in tariff reduction, far exceeding the initial experiment of 1842, the position of sugar had been predetermined. Cotton, the raw material of the country's largest single export industry, was another obvious item which had figured in the Chancellor's early budget planning. Goulburn had also wished to remove the excise duty on glass, again to improve its competitive position in the foreign market. Where Peel's hand was detectable was in the lengths to which he carried the suggestions more cautiously advanced by the Chancellor of the Exchequer and the extent to which he was ready to exhaust their surplus in so doing. In this there was a perceptible change in his attitude since 1842. Partly it was the difference between budgeting for a surplus and budgeting for a deficit. In 1842 he had asked for an income tax as a desperate expedient to meet a crisis. His budget then had been a courageous but limited experiment. In 1845 it was a grander but infinitely safer operation. What was new was the conviction born of the experience gathered over the intervening three years.

From one point of view the experiment of 1842 had been vindicated and he could have rested on his financial laurels.[1] Under the shelter of the temporary income tax the initial loss from the tariff reductions was gradually being made good by an expanding economy and a buoyant revenue. Even without the income tax the ordinary revenue was now almost equal to the ordinary expenditure. Had the income tax been granted for five years, as he would have preferred, the end of that period would probably have seen a complete recovery of the ordinary revenue. But what might have been an argument for abandoning the income tax, Peel turned into an

[1] Cf. Stafford Northcote, *Twenty Years of Financial Policy*, pp. 61-2.

argument for further experiment. Indeed, it was not now so much an experiment as another instalment of a tried and successful policy. Two things had been the subject of practical verification between 1842 and 1845. One was the effect of the income tax on other sources of public revenue, and the other the effect of reduced tariffs on industry and commerce. No counterbalancing decrease in the yield from other taxes had been detectable as a result of imposing the income tax. As for the second, everything seemed to show that the free trade theory of lower tariffs yielding higher revenue was in the long run correct. What Peel invited the Commons to do in 1845 was to accept a further and in a sense unnecessary period of income tax in order to make possible a further and even more comprehensive demonstration of that theory. For the full results of this to show, three years was a short enough period. As he told the House in committee a few days later, he would again have preferred a term of five years. Nevertheless, 'I do think there are good grounds for hoping that at the end of three years we may be at liberty to discontinue it.' He was not so egotistic as to assign all the credit to the government's tariff policy. 'I see many causes combining to increase the prosperity of the country'—the expansion of industry, the accumulation of capital, the spread of railways, the growth of population. But all these were working to the same end and justified his optimism.

With the official Whigs denouncing his income tax as an inquisitorial and probably permanent infliction but nevertheless signifying their intention of voting for it, Peel had no fear of the outcome of the debate. 'It is evident', wrote Albert cheerfully, 'that everybody wants you to bear the abuse of it and still have the 5 million in case of getting into office.'[1] This was the view of others, including HB the political cartoonist, who published a lively sketch of Peel reclining luxuriously on a couch labelled Income Tax, enviously watched by Russell and Baring.[2] In such circumstances isolated

---

[1] 40439 fos. 294, 296.

[2] HB Political Sketches, No. 830, 'Small Insinuations', 5 Apr. 1845. It may be mentioned here that Mr. Hyde is quite wrong in his suggestion (Hyde, Gladstone, pp. 16, 25) that in 1845 Peel had a passing inclination to replace the income tax by a house tax. In the letters he refers to as his authority he has misread 'window tax' as 'income tax'. What Peel raised with Goulburn in March and October 1845 was the possibility of substituting a house tax for the socially undesirable window tax. The Chancellor

efforts by Roebuck, Buller and others to secure changes in the method of raising the tax were easily defeated. By Easter the income tax bill, the sugar bill and the tariff had all gone through the Commons; and Easter was early that year. The success strengthened his confidence and confirmed his judgement on tactics. 'I would not admit any alteration . . .', he wrote somewhat jauntily to Hardinge during the recess. 'This was thought very obstinate and very presumptuous; but the fact is, people like a certain degree of obstinacy and presumption in a minister. They abuse him for dictation and arrogance, but they like being governed.'[1] The only part of the budget which provoked much acrimony was sugar, that historic if slightly inconsequential tilting ground between the two parties. 'Sugar is a rock,' wrote Graham to his old companion Stanley, 'but we have steam enough to *bump* over it; and the Rads and the Doctrinaires will protect us from the Whigs, if the country gentlemen do not bodily desert in sullen sadness.'[2] This was the rub. Nothing had been done for agriculture; it had not even been mentioned in Peel's opening budget speech. All that the silent country squires behind him had heard was one more panegyric on free trade. All that they were invited to undertake was one more long stride towards economic liberalism. The agricultural question had been discussed between Goulburn and Peel in December but only to dismiss any possibility of reducing the malt tax. Picking their way delicately past the embattled fronts of the landed and manufacturing interests, the ministers felt safe in making no concessions to the agriculturalists provided they imposed no further sacrifices on them. But the omission did not go unquestioned. George Bankes, William Miles, Robert Palmer and Tyrell all voiced their resentment that agriculture, alone among the great national interests, was to receive no compensation for the continued burden of the income tax. It was unlikely that Peel's subsequent argument of the benefits to be derived by farm labourers from cheap cotton or by farmers from a repeal of the auction duty did much to diminish their dissatisfaction.

was against this on grounds of technical difficulties and the unpopularity of the house tax. Peel's final comment was that if the difficulties were too great, it would be better to abolish the window tax altogether (40445 fos. 36, 38, 217).

[1] *Peel*, III, 270.
[2] Graham (14 Feb. 1845).

V

It was not only the budget that gave the sulky agriculturalists an opportunity to vent their feelings. The session was not many weeks old before they found one man on their side of the House who was prepared to announce audibly what many of them were beginning to feel. The first occasion came almost accidentally in the Post Office debate of February. The previous session Duncombe had started a campaign against Graham on the question of opening letters in the Post Office under Home Office warrant. The government had met the attack by appointing a select committee to enquire into the general law and practice of opening letters. Its report completely exonerated Graham but the subject was dragged up again in February 1845. It had already been given exaggerated and slightly hysterical publicity in the press and some official Whigs joined in the renewed offensive even though they could not pretend that their own practice when in office had been any different. It was in fact largely a personal attack on the unpopular figure of the Home Secretary who was cut to the quick by the shabby behaviour of his old Whig friends and colleagues. Other interested parties lent their hand to this exercise in baiting the minister. Half a dozen dissident Conservatives voted against the government; and Disraeli was particularly prominent in stirring up trouble.

On one occasion, in the course of what Peel described to the queen as a flippant and hostile speech, he made an absurd and erroneous charge against Bonham, whom he rightly described as one of the prime minister's 'intimate friends'. This was that he had been implicated in treasonable conspiracy some forty years earlier.[1] It was crushingly refuted by Peel and an apology extracted. In the course of his speech he referred to Disraeli's accusation against himself of simulated warmth, and dryly remarked that he on the other hand was perfectly prepared to believe that Disraeli's bitterness was entirely sincere. He only begged him not to support a hostile notion in an allegedly friendly spirit; and he quoted Canning's well-known line 'save, oh save me, from the candid friend'. A week later, when seconding a motion of Duncombe's to bring Post Office officials before

[1] For details see my article on F. R. Bonham in E.H.R., LXIII, 506–7.

the bar of the House, Disraeli returned to the attack in a studied and effective oration. He enlarged on the tyranny of Peel's leadership, delivered his famous phrase that Peel had caught the Whigs bathing and walked away with their clothes, and alluding to Peel's quotation, made a delicately sarcastic reference to Peel's desertion of Canning in 1827. 'The theme, the poet, the speaker—what a felicitous combination!' It was a new style of oratory, cool, mocking, oblique, by a politician who was rapidly showing himself one of the greatest masters of satiric invective that the Commons had ever heard. It would have taken a Canning or a Brougham to have replied in kind; and Peel made no attempt to alter his own very different parliamentary style or even to reply to Disraeli at length. Instead, towards the end of his own speech in the same debate, he merely expressed the hope that Disraeli would feel more at ease now that he had discharged himself of the accumulated venom of the previous week. The hon. gentleman, he observed, had the advantage of leisure in which to prepare his attacks. He had encountered them before and never thought it necessary to reply. Nor would have done so the other night had not Disraeli said he had seconded the motion against the government in an entirely friendly spirit. He had no desire to fetter the gentleman's independence, but if he thought he was entitled to withdraw his confidence because of what had happened twenty years ago, he need not have waited for an accidental quotation to open his eyes.

It was beyond all doubt by this time that even if Young England was becoming little more than a memory, Disraeli had embarked on a personal vendetta against the prime minister. After his behaviour in the 1843 session it had been taken for granted by the ministers that he was no longer to be regarded as a supporter. Graham had been astonished at receiving a request in the December of that year for a piece of patronage for Disraeli's brother. Disraeli had made the same request a few months earlier and the renewed application was couched in a sarcastic and contemptuous tone as though he almost expected a second refusal. 'It is a good thing when such a man puts his shabbiness on record', Peel wrote back when informed of the incident by the indignant Home Secretary. 'He asked me for office for himself and I was not surprised that being refused he became independent and a patriot. But to seek favours after his conduct last session is too bad. However, it is a bridle in his mouth.'[1] When at the start of the 1844 session Fremantle had felt obliged to enquire whether he should send the usual letter from the prime minister requesting attendance to Manners, Smythe, Disraeli and Cochrane, Peel had instructed him not to write to either Disraeli or Smythe. He then received a letter of protest from Disraeli to which he replied politely, expressing his satisfaction that his scruples were unnecessary and that he could still regard Disraeli as a supporter of the government.[2] The reconciliation was as thin as the paper on which it was written and in the course of 1844 Disraeli began to address himself to a wider and more appreciative audience for his sallies against the prime minister than Young England had ever provided. But it was in 1845 that he became, in Roebuck's biting phrase, 'a sort of Paganini playing upon one string'. He had found the role in the House that exactly suited his superb if specialised talents and a situation that might have been created to display them. And what to other men might have been a bridle, to him was only a goad. The Post Office affair had been a mere episode. There were other more permanent issues on which the temper of the Conservative party could be tried.

Throughout the early part of the session the old question of free trade and agricultural protection continually emerged to rasp the nerves of the country party. In March Cobden moved for a select committee on the alleged agricultural distress and the effect of protection on the rural classes. In one of the most skilful, because most temperate, of his free trade speeches he analysed the condition of the agricultural industry and asked for proof that protection either before or after 1842 had done anything to satisfy the farmer's grievances. In his customary note to the queen on the debate Peel reported that Mr. Cobden had made an 'able speech' and had been answered for the government by Mr. Sidney Herbert.[3]

It is possible that the prime minister found it not only able but virtually unanswerable. The story has often been told how, as Cobden went on speaking, Peel began to make notes, his face growing more and more solemn as the speech continued. Finally, it is said,

[1] Graham (22 Dec. 1843), ptly pr. *Peel*, III, 425.
[2] See my article 'Peel and the party system', in *Trans. R. Hist. Soc.*, 5th ser., I, 61.
[3] RA/A 17/50.

he crumpled up his paper and whispered to Sidney Herbert, sitting beside him, 'you must answer this, for I cannot'. It is not unlikely that the incident, or something like it, actually occurred. Certainly Peel remained silent on this occasion and Herbert replied for the government with a speech which, perhaps because it was extempore, was not of the happiest. In announcing the intention of the government to move a direct negative, he referred to the sensitivity of the agriculturalists and the misinterpretation that might be put on the appointment of yet another committee; and he added that it was distasteful to him, as an agricultural representative, to be always coming to parliament whining for protection. The agriculturalists had some protection and he thought they should be content with what they had. It was a speech that was remembered, and not kindly, by the Tory back-benchers. A few nights later W. Miles moved that in applying the surplus revenue, consideration should be given to the relief of agriculture. It was in substance a planned attack on the government's free trade policy and the Central Agricultural Protection Society circularised the local societies, urging them to bring pressure to bear on their parliamentary representatives to support it. The ensuing debate revealed all the underlying tensions on the government side of the House. Newdegate declared that Cobden was the high priest of free trade and the treasury bench his fellow worshippers who chanted the appropriate responses. Escot, the Conservative member for Winchester, defended his leaders and asserted that the motion was only intended to put the agriculturalist members right with their discontented constituents. Disraeli, in an ironic speech, dwelt on the inconsistencies of the prime minister and the contrast between his attitudes to the country gentry when leader of the opposition and when minister of the crown. Once he had been the fond wooer of the agricultural interest. Now he 'sends down his valet who says in the genteelest manner, "We can have no whining here"'. If they were to have free trade, he said acidly, he would rather have it from Cobden than from a leader who had betrayed the confidence of his party. And he ended with his memorable line that a Conservative government was an organised hypocrisy.

It was a brilliant speech which evoked applause and laughter from the House. They did not like or trust Disraeli, but they enjoyed listening to him; and what he said was balm to many of the inarticulate men around him even if they did not join in the joyful cheers that rang out from the opposition benches. When Peel came to defend the government's economic policy later in the debate, he briefly referred to Disraeli's charge. In 1842, he reminded the House, the same member had defended him against the kind of attack he was now himself making. He attached the same value, he added contemptuously, to the panegyric and the attack. He was merely surprised that both came from the same source. As Peel must have realised, Disraeli in himself constituted no great threat. The danger was in the situation which he was trying to exploit. Miles's motion attracted in fact less than eighty votes. Yet there was no mistaking the general atmosphere of disaffection among the protectionist back-benchers. Graham at least was in a distinctly pessimistic mood the following day. 'There is a bad spirit and an angry feeling in our Ranks,' he reported in his gloomy dramatic vein to the Lord Lieutenant. 'The House is surcharged with Electric Fluid and an explosion after Easter is quite possible.'[1] Graham was prone to exaggerate his fears and probably a number of motives were present among the supporters of Miles's motion: a genuine protectionist spirit in some, a desire to placate constituents in others, and in a few personal disappointments and ambitions. Nevertheless, it was an uncomfortable overture to the great parliamentary debate over Maynooth.

In February Graham had gone through the cabinet draft of the Maynooth bill with Blake. By March it was in its final shape: acceptable, as the Home Secretary put it, to the Catholics and unexceptionable to the ministry.[2] John Young, chief whip in succession to Fremantle, had gone through the lists and reported that there was no danger of defeat. The House of Commons, more exempt than the general public from the prevalent anti-Romanism, was clearly favourable to a generous settlement. Liberal and Irish votes would more than make up for Conservative defections. The real resistance would come from outside the House; from the revived *No Popery* passions of England and Scotland. It was this which would make Maynooth the crucial issue of the session. Already petitions, mainly hostile, were pouring in; public protest meetings were being held

[1] Graham (18 March 1845).
[2] *ibid.* (Graham to Heytesbury, 9 Feb., 18 March 1845).

up and down the country; and even by-elections were beginning to be affected. At Exeter Hall, the unofficial headquarters of English evangelical Protestantism, an anti-Maynooth Conference set up a committee to fight against the bill by every legitimate method of pressure and publicity. Even the staid Deputies of the Three Denominations, who had supported Catholic emancipation in 1829, sent in a forcible memorial to Peel against a measure which brought the state into formal connection with the Romish religion and subsidised it from public funds.[1] On 3 April the prime minister expounded the details of his long-awaited measure to the House of Commons. In its final form the bill fixed the annual grant at £26,000, made a special non-recurrent advance of £30,000 for new buildings, put the cost of repairs and maintenance on the Board of Works, and established an effective system of annual visitation. Peel spoke at moderate length, calmly and discreetly, though the cheers and counter-cheers which followed his successive observations were evidence of the strong feelings among his audience. A steadfast loyalty to their own creed, he argued placatingly at the end of his speech, was perfectly compatible with an attempt to improve the training and character of those who—whatever the House decided—would continue to be the spiritual guides of millions of their fellow-countrymen.

Despite the energetic opposition of Inglis and other Conservative Protestants, he was given leave to bring in his bill by a majority of over a hundred. Even so it was an ominous feature of the division that so many of the minority came from the government benches and so many of the majority from the other side. Tactically the one danger to the government lay in the possibility that High Protestants moved by anti-Catholic feeling and radicals opposed to any state endowment for religion might combine to defeat the bill on some technical point. Ward had already given notice that on the second reading he would move an amendment that the money for Maynooth should be taken from the revenues of the Church of Ireland. A motion such as this, reviving the old appropriation quarrel of the thirties, would certainly attract much liberal support. In conjunction with some of the ultra-Protestant Conservatives it might put the government in a minority. The debate on the second reading began on Friday, 11 April, and for some days before there was considerable

[1] 40612 f. 168.

uneasiness among members of the government. But Peel did not waver. In the last resort he was ready to stake the existence of his ministry on passing the bill. Nevertheless, their best chance of success, he told Stanley, was to go on with the bill in the ordinary way. If defeated by a combination of interested parties on the amendment he would still move the second reading on the following Monday against which the same incongruous alliance could not again be assembled. There was a general belief that if beaten on Ward's motion the government would resign, and he was careful to do nothing to weaken that salutary impression. 'I have great confidence', he told Stanley, 'in the effect of a steady declared intention of a Government to carry a particular measure, or to throw on others the responsibility of defeating it.'[1] These tactics proved remarkably effective and at the last minute Ward withdrew his amendment. According to Peel's information it was because he had heard of the determination of some members to use his motion, though not in sympathy with it, to destroy the bill. Lord Sandon told the queen that Russell had been instrumental in persuading Ward to withdraw.[2] But whatever the cause, the safety of the bill was now assured, even though there was to be much talking before it passed into law.

The six-day debate on the second reading uncovered all the cross-currents in the House. Liberal Conservatives joined forces with the Whigs and Irish against the ultra-Protestants and doctrinaire radicals. The representatives of the two English universities were evenly divided, Goulburn for Cambridge and Estcourt for Oxford supporting the bill against the opposition of their colleagues Law and Inglis. The Young Englanders split, Disraeli attacking Peel as the great parliamentary middleman while Smythe and Manners supported the bill if not the author. The Leaguers too were separated, Cobden being in favour while Bright opposed. Despite the repeated taunts of inconsistency even from those who, like Macaulay, declared their readiness to vote for the measure, Peel made a gentle and conciliatory reply. The debate, he said, had been honourable to both supporters and opponents of the bill. If there were to be reproaches, they should fall on the authors of the bill, not on the bill

---

[1] 40468 fos. 311, 313; 40440 f. 15; RA/A 17/68 and D 14/101.
[2] 40440 f. 21; RA/A 17/71.

itself. He earned his reward in the general cheering which greeted his speech and in the division which followed. The bill passed by a majority of 147, larger than Peel or anyone else had expected. When in the committee stage Ward revived his motion in a more innocuous form he was comfortably defeated by an even larger majority than that which had been secured on the second reading. The renewed debate was mainly conspicuous for a demand by Macaulay that Peel should answer the brilliant and merciless piece of oratory in which he had assailed the inconsistencies in the political career of the prime minister during the debate on the second reading. Peel had largely ignored it at the time and even on this occasion showed remarkable restraint. It was as though he had consciously subordinated all his energies and feelings to the one purpose of piloting the bill safely through. Having made a temperate answer to Macaulay he continued:

> While I give the hon. gentlemen opposite entire credit for the motives which induce them to support this motion, and while I am quite willing to transfer to them, on account of their uniform advocacy of Roman Catholic claims, all the merit which is due to our proposal, and all the gratitude of the Roman Catholics from it, still my anxiety remains unabated, that in the present state of public feeling in Ireland, the measure may receive the sanction of the House.[1]

Yet the longer the debate over Maynooth dragged on, the deeper became the issues thrown up by it.

Already much of the argument had turned not on the abstract merits of the bill but on the record of the men who brought it forward. As the inquest continued, the more sharply Peel began to define his own position in the storm of criticism which swept around him. In one of his last contributions to the debate, he harked back—as so many of his critics had done—to the crisis of Catholic emancipation in 1829. His conduct on that occasion had been contrasted unfavourably by his enemies with that of Gladstone in 1845. He too had wished and had intended, he told the House, to retire from office in 1829. He had been dissuaded from doing so for reasons which, looking back across the gap of sixteen years, he still felt justified.

[1] *Speeches*, IV, 503 (23 Apr. 1845).

I do think [he said in an illuminating sentence] I acted a more honourable part in consenting to retain office and proposing that measure;—that I took a part more for the character of a public man—than if I had said to my sovereign and my colleagues, 'You shall be exposed to the obloquy of proposing this measure while you still retain office; I will advise the Crown to give its assent to the measure, but I will shrink from the responsibility of bringing it forward.'

For exactly the same reason, despite all the taunts and sarcasms to which he had been subjected, he had thought it his duty to bring forward the Maynooth bill. 'So much, Sir, for the principles on which I think public men ought to act in retaining office.' On the third reading of the bill he returned once more to the same basic issue: the duty of ministers as against the claims of party interest and personal consistency. He regretted, he said, the severance of ties with political friends who honestly disapproved of what the ministers had done. But, notwithstanding, he must claim for the government, for any government,

> the absolute right, without reference to the past and without too much regard for what party considerations must claim from them, to risk even the loss of confidence of their friends, rather than abstain from doing that which conviction tells them the present circumstances require. . . . It seems to me that a misapprehension is entertained in some quarters with respect to the position of a minister of the Crown. I am as proud of the confidence as any man can be, which a great party has placed in me; still I never can admit that he owes any personal obligation to those members who have placed him in a certain position.

He would gladly retire to the obscurity of being a private member rather than hold office

> by the servile tenure of the advice I gave to my sovereign upon every subject, being exactly in conformity with every opinion which every member of that party might hold. . . . I claim for myself the right to give to my sovereign, at any time, that advice which I believe the interests of the country require.[1]

Maynooth went through, with larger majorities and less technical damage to the government than could have been expected. Apart

[1] *Speeches*, IV, p. 506 (28 Apr.), 520 (21 May 1845).

from Gladstone, only Pringle, a junior lord of the Treasury, and Lord Redesdale, the Conservative chief whip in the House of Lords, resigned on the issue. But the damage to the party had been incalculable. Of all Peel's measures, the Maynooth bill had come nearest to a repudiation of the classic constitutional doctrines, the defence of Church and State, on which the Conservative party had been built up in the thirties; and it had been carried only by the aid of the official opposition in the Commons. On the second reading the Conservative party had divided 159 to 147 in favour of the bill; on the third reading 148 to 149 against. It was the solid mass of over four-fifths of the Liberal votes which had supplied the comfortable majorities in the House.[1] Following the session of 1844 in which Peel had strained discipline to the limit over factory hours and the sugar resolutions this fresh division was shattering. He had won his bill, but in the process had finally destroyed the morale of the Conservative party. Despite his studied conciliatoriness in the House, the prime minister in private had shown the grim and at times almost reckless determination which had marked the crises of the previous session. He told Croker on 22 April that he looked with indifference at the storm of opposition to the bill, 'being resolved on carrying the bill, and being very careless as to the consequences which may follow on its passing, so far as they concern me'.[2]

What those consequences might be was only too clear. As Aberdeen expressed it privately to the Princess Lieven the same month, just as emancipation in 1829 had left a root of bitterness which led to the overthrow of 1830, so this in turn might have a similar outcome.[3] The faithful Graham reflected the mood of his chief in more dramatic language. 'The country gentlemen cannot be more ready to give us the death-blow than we are prepared to receive it,' he had written to Croker in March in the aftermath of the budget discontents; and while the long debates were taking place on the second reading of Maynooth, he unburdened himself in black prophetic strain to his distant colleagues in Ireland and India:

The bill will pass but our party is destroyed. The result may probably resemble the consequences which ensued on the carrying of the

---

[1] For the full voting figures see *English Politics*, p. 151 n.
[2] *Peel*, III, 176.   [3] *Aberdeen*, II, 140.

Relief Act.[1] . . . A large Body of our supporters is mortally offended, and in their anger they are ready to do anything either to defeat the Bill or to revenge themselves upon us. . . . We have lost the slight hold which we ever possessed over the hearts and kind feelings of our followers. . . . In a party sense it has been fatal, and the old High Tories will not see that they can only govern on Peel principles in a Reformed Parliament, and if they reject the only man who has the wisdom and capacity to lead them thro' the difficulties of the Age in which we live, they must be content to see power transferred to their political opponents.[2]

This was the heart of the matter. The Maynooth contest had been over something larger than Maynooth itself. The split in the party was a symptom as well as an effect.

Raikes, who knew his club world though he was no very active politician himself, believed that the real reason for the revolt of the Tories was their underlying grievances about protection and free trade, and their feeling that Peel would sooner or later repeal the Corn Laws themselves. Otherwise, he concluded, Maynooth would have passed with a clear Conservative majority in its favour.[3] This was probably at least a half-truth. Peel himself was not unaware of the diverse nature of the motives among the opponents of the bill. 'Tariffs, drought, 46/- a quarter for wheat, quicken the religious apprehensions of some,' he had written scornfully to Croker, 'disappointed ambition, and the rejection of applications for office, of others.' What angered him above all was that his four years' achievement apparently counted for nothing as far as his party was concerned. Trade and industry were flourishing, the working classes better off, Chartism extinguished, the Church stronger than ever, demands for radical reform no longer heard, the financial system on a firm footing, the revenue buoyant. 'But,' he wrote ironically to Hardinge at the end of the Maynooth struggle, 'we have reduced protection to agriculture, and tried to lay the foundation of peace in Ireland; and these are offences for which nothing can atone.'[4]

---

[1] The reference is to Catholic emancipation.

[2] Graham, 22 March (to Croker); 12, 18 Apr. (to Heytesbury); 23 Apr. 1845 (to Hardinge).

[3] *Raikes*, IV, 422–5.

[4] 40474 f. 314, ptly pr. *Peel*, III, 273 (27 May 1845).

The vital question concerned the future. If Maynooth was merely an excuse to express the latent discontents with Peel's leadership, those discontents would not cease with the passage of the bill. It might be true, as Raikes thought, that the malcontents were only waiting for their chance and the next opportunity might prove decidedly more fatal. Yet as tempers cooled, intentions might flag. Even if the essential unity of the party had disappeared, it was still doubtful whether the bulk of the Conservatives would be ready to overthrow a minister for whom they had no substitute, and whose standing in parliament, in the country at large, and with the crown was never higher. Maynooth had scraped bare the bedrock of the relationship between Peel and his party. But in itself it had decided nothing; and the rest of the session was equally indecisive.

The Irish Colleges Bill, introduced by Graham in May, had in fact a more friendly reception than had been anticipated. It was known from Blake that the Catholics would not insist on the incorporation of Trinity College so long as they eventually had a second university in Dublin. The cabinet decided therefore to propose simply the establishment of three colleges, one at Cork, another at Galway, and the third probably at Belfast, leaving open the question whether they should be grouped in one central university or given independent powers to grant degrees. Inevitably opposition came from Inglis, who denounced the absence of theological faculties as creating a gigantic scheme of godless education. In this he was given incongruous support in the later stages of the bill by O'Connell. But it was not easy to inject religious rancour into the debate and with both Whigs and most of the Liberal Irish M.P.s favourable to the bill, its passage through parliament was singularly uneventful. The firmness of the prime minister ensured that as little *odium theologicum* as possible attended its proceedings. A belated demand from the Irish Catholic hierarchy that only Romans should be appointed to certain chairs was flatly turned down, as was a formal request from the Irish primate for a grant from public funds for Anglican Church schools. Peel was the last person to yield to these opportunist tactics and the Church of Ireland was in his view the last institution in Ireland to put forward fresh pretensions. In later discussions with Graham in the summer, he made it clear that the northern college must on no account be located at Armagh, the spiritual capital of Irish Anglicanism. 'It must be *Presbyterian*', he added, 'or it will be worse than useless.'[1] The retention by the ministry of these and other administrative details considerably facilitated the parliamentary proceedings over the bill and once it was through the main work of the session was over. The last few months were in fact curiously lacking in spirit, as though Maynooth had exhausted passions on both sides. A highly complicated set of resolutions on the state of the labouring classes introduced by Russell at the end of May fell flat, as did Ward's motion in June for a committee on the peculiar burdens and exemptions of the landed interest. Another hardy annual, Villiers's motion for the abolition of the Corn Laws, was chiefly remarkable for the further evidence it provided of Lord John Russell's crablike progress towards a completely free trade position and for the singularly unimpassioned explanations of the continuing need for the corn laws offered by Graham and Peel. Had Villiers's resolution been for gradual abolition, Lord Howick observed acidly at the end of the debate, the speeches of both ministers would have been taken as in favour of the motion.

But party spirit seemed to have disappeared along with party unity. The news which reached the country during the session of the Maori risings in New Zealand provoked a good deal of debate on colonial administration in June and July among those interested in such matters. But though the House of Commons ministers had to bestir themselves in defence of Lord Stanley's colonial policy and the whips scurried round to secure suitable majorities in a thin and largely indifferent House, it was not an issue calculated to raise partisan passions or topple ministries. At the end of the session the administration looked, if not as strong, at least as immovable as it had ever been and Peel both indispensable and irreplaceable. Greville, who in April had observed that 'everybody knows that the Tory party has ceased to exist as a party', in August was remarking on the flat state of politics. All loyalty and enthusiasm had gone, yet nobody anticipated and few even hoped for a change. The mirage of office which had floated before the Whigs at the time of Maynooth had vanished, leaving an arid prospect of endless opposition. The Tories, for all their dislike of their leader, could see no alternative to him. Despite his unpopularity the prime minister like an inscrutable

---

[1] Graham (Peel to Graham, 27 May, 17 Aug.; Graham to Heytesbury, 9 Feb., 10 May, 4 June 1845).

colossus still bestrode the political world. 'Everybody expects that he means to go on, and in the end to knock the Corn Laws on the head, and endow the Roman Catholic Church,' the diarist ended his ruminations, 'but nobody knows how or when he will do these things.'[1]

[1] 21 Aug. 1845.

CHAPTER

14

THE RESPONSIBILITIES
OF EMPIRE

'It is very curious', wrote Wellington to one of his women friends a few weeks before the Conservatives took office in 1841, 'that Sir Robert Peel should have the reputation of being entirely ignorant on foreign Affairs. They say that Palmerston has very little consideration for him, and that the foreign Ministers have no confidence in him.'[1] It was natural not only in 1841 but when judgement came to be passed on his career as a whole that Peel's achievement in domestic policy blotted out other activities. Most people had forgotten his early support for Canning in the eighteen-twenties. His utterances on foreign affairs as leader of the House of Commons under Wellington, or later still as head of the opposition, had never been taken as indicating any particular interest. But ignorant or not, as prime minister Peel was ultimately responsible for the foreign policy of a country which still retained the prestige of victor in the Napoleonic Wars, which wielded the greatest sea power in the world, and which had imperial responsibilities in every quarter of the globe. His detailed administration ensured that the affairs of four continents came to his desk; and in Europe, India and America issues arose between 1841 and 1845 which demanded more than merely departmental attention.

The first came quickly in India. The Afghan crisis, born largely of Palmerston's anti-Russian policy, was an inescapable legacy from the last government. In the spring of 1842 Peel could only wait for the outcome of what he described as 'the most absurd and insane project that was ever undertaken in the wantonness of power'. Ellenborough, the new Governor-General, arrived at Madras in February to be

[1] *Wellington and His Friends*, p. 166.

greeted by the news of MacNaghten's murder and the destruction of the Kabul garrison. His first reaction was that the evacuation of Afghanistan must be deferred until the prestige of British rule had been restored; and the letters from Peel and Wellington that were sent off at the end of March and the beginning of April agreed that decisive measures should be taken, as Peel put it, for 'retrieving our military credit'.[1] The government, before the arrival of Ellenborough's first despatch, had already anticipated his wishes for reinforcements of men and material. Though Peel enjoined caution and deliberation, Ellenborough once in the seat of power acted promptly. His promptness however took the unexpected form of an order for the remaining troops in Afghanistan to withdraw without even making an attempt to recover the prisoners and hostages in Afghan hands. When the news reached London the prime minister reluctantly accepted the decision, already many weeks old, of the man on the spot; but all his instincts were against it. 'I think it questionable, however,' he confided to Fitzgerald in July, 'whether orders should have been given for the immediate withdrawal of our troops.' To Ellenborough he suggested at least some negotiations before evacuating Kandahar if only to give an appearance of deliberate action to the withdrawal.[2] By May the military situation had improved with the defeat of the besieging Afghan army by the garrison of Jellalabad and Pollock's forcing of the Khyber. Lord Ellenborough, already showing signs of the delusions of grandeur which was India's subtle gift to successive viceroys, complacently took credit for the victories while casting doubts on the military talents of the men who had won them.

Nevertheless, he still ordered evacuation and it was not until July that he gave Nott permission on his own responsibility to retire in a circuitous route north-east through Kabul and the Khyber rather than by the direct road southwards through Quetta. Peel, up in Scotland with the queen, thought that this was placing an unfair burden on General Nott. At the same time he was emphatic that nothing but 'very severe and overpowering necessity' should induce them to evacuate Afghanistan without at least one deliberate effort to rescue the women, children and officers, over a hundred in

[1] Ellenborough Corr. (6 Apr. 1842); 40471 fos. 159, 177, ptly pr. Peel, II, 582–3.
[2] 40471 f. 193.

all, held captive in Kabul. When he returned south he wrote from Windsor on 24 September to express pointed approval of Nott's courage and discretion and a strong hope that he would decide to march on Kabul. In the event the Nelsonian initiative of the commanders in the field effected what the prime minister fervently desired. Nott took the more hazardous course, captured Ghazni, entered Kabul and linked up with Pollock coming up from Jellalabad. The prisoners were released and the two armies returned to India, bringing with them from Ghazni on Ellenborough's somewhat theatrical orders the gates of the Hindu temple of Somnauth captured eight centuries earlier. It was an irony concealed from the Governor-General that the gates were in fact not the originals but replicas of much later date. As it was he celebrated the triumph with two bombastic proclamations from Simla which, whatever their effect on the natives, were calculated to make the worst possible impression at home. The first, addressed to the princes and peoples of India, deeply offended the Christian susceptibilities of the British public by its oriental and pagan phraseology. The other, by its slighting reflections on Ellenborough's predecessor, aroused sharp resentment among the Whigs.

In all these military operations of 1842 the home government was inevitably in a disadvantageous position. They only learned decisions long after they had been taken and they knew that any instructions they sent out might be overtaken by events long before they arrived. To a great extent therefore they were confined to the role of spectators. But Peel, from his wider experience, was more conscious than Fitzgerald of the need for withholding criticism when it would be too late to alter action, for stating the government's views only in the most general terms, and for restraint in approving particular policies when the next mail might show them to have already been discarded by the volatile Governor-General. Nevertheless, the first six months' experience of Ellenborough's rule in India filled Peel with concern. He thought the new Governor-General had misjudged the position in Afghanistan and by the inconsistency of his orders had created a dangerous situation on the frontier from which he had only been rescued by the initiative and steadiness of the soldiers. His disquiet was increased by an interview he had with Lord Auckland on his return to England in which the outgoing Governor-

General made strong representations about Ellenborough's tactless behaviour towards the civil servants in India. Fitzgerald was plainly unhappy not only with Ellenborough's policy but with the fact that he was writing in a highly irregular fashion direct to the queen and that Wellington in his own correspondence on military matters with the Governor-General did not always keep in line with official cabinet policy.

Much of the prime minister's activity in Indian affairs had to be directed towards supporting the President of the Board of Control and advising him on the best way of handling the erratic Governor-General who complacently assumed complete approval by the cabinet for all his actions. 'Lord Ellenborough should not', wrote Peel dryly in October, 'construe the unwillingness to disturb decisions, or apparent decisions, by the expressions of regret and dissent, into approbation.' Nevertheless it was undeniable that the Afghan expedition had ended in brilliant success and in December Peel sent a letter of congratulation to the Governor-General. Inserted, however, among the general expressions of appreciation were a number of specific warnings. Peel cast doubt on the policy and legality of bringing Akbar Khan, the Afghan chief responsible for the murder of MacNaghten, to trial; he dropped a significant hint about the parliamentary and public reactions in Britain to the Simla proclamations; and as a marked tribute to the two generals, Nott and Pollock, he announced his intention against precedent of giving both the G.C.B. although neither had the intermediate honour of the K.C.B.[1]

As anticipated there was sharp comment in the press on Ellenborough's behaviour. As soon as parliament reassembled in February 1843 the opposition mounted a brisk attack. W. B. Baring, the secretary to the Board of Control, who had little experience of public speaking, gave a floundering performance which left the case of the government worse than he found it. The situation was restored however by what Henry Baring described as 'the best speech Peel ever made with the worst cause'.[2] All the prime minister did was to emphasise the military victories in Afghanistan and ask

---

[1] 40471 f. 259; Ellenborough Corr., 3 Dec. 1842, ptly pr. *Peel*, II, 600. For Indian affairs generally see *Peel*, II, ch. XX; III, ch. I.

[2] *Greville*, 12 Feb. 1843.

in effect whether Ellenborough was to be disgraced for one act of indiscretion; but he did it with remarkable skill.[1] When the Whigs unwisely returned to the attack in March the temporary public excitement had subsided. Wellington in the upper House, Peel and Stanley in the lower, stoutly defended Ellenborough's general policy and the hostile resolution was easily defeated. It was difficult in fact for the opposition speakers to disentangle their particular criticisms of Ellenborough from the general patriotic pride in the success of British arms in Afghanistan to which Peel had so dexterously appealed in his February speech. Managing Whig and radical critics of Indian policy was simple compared with the task of managing an ebullient Governor-General located ten thousand miles away from his nominal superiors with an interval of three to four months between the despatch of his letters home and the receipt of further instructions. There were times when the problem of India seemed little more than the problem of Lord Ellenborough.

Hard on the Afghan crisis came the affair of Scinde. The original invasion of Afghanistan through Quetta and the Bolan Pass had involved a passage through the territory of the Ameers of Scinde and the enforcement on them in 1839 of a new treaty. Suspicion of the loyalty of the Ameers during the Afghan War provided Ellenborough with a factitious justification for imposing on them at the conclusion of hostilities a further treaty involving the cession of territory. An expected and not unwelcome clash of arms resulted in the defeat of the Ameers by the bellicose Charles Napier in the spring of 1843, followed by the annexation of the whole province. In a despatch of the previous November Ellenborough had given a clear warning of what he was about and hinted at resignation if he was not supported at home. This was little more than a species of political blackmail. Relations between the Governor-General and the Court of Directors in London were already strained and on receipt of this last message from Ellenborough the unhappy Fitzgerald, standing uncomfortably between the Company and its autocratic servant in India, was half inclined to resign himself. Peel energetically refused to listen to such a counsel of despair.

Instead of thinking of retiring, maintain your own ground [he wrote in January]. Inform Lord Ellenborough that he has had every support

[1] *Speeches*, IV, 144 (9 Feb. 1843).

which it was possible for him to receive but that you will insist upon your right, and your duty, freely to express your opinion upon every act and every matter of public concern connected with the administration of affairs in India.[1]

But Fitzgerald was not the only sufferer. Peel had to undergo considerable trials of his own patience. When Ellenborough took leave of the queen before going out to India, he asked whether he could write to her directly, and Victoria had incautiously agreed. Though ministers gradually became aware of this palace correspondence, they made no remonstrance until April 1843 when Victoria showed Peel a letter she had received from Ellenborough suggesting that many difficulties of local government might be removed if the queen became empress of India with the princes as her feudatories. In the face of this imaginative but improper suggestion Peel sent to the Governor-General on 6 April a measured rebuke. In the first place, he wrote, 'direct communications between the Governor General of India and the Sovereign of this country, without the knowledge or intervention of the Sovereign's responsible advisers . . . are open to considerable objection in point of constitutional principle', however innocent the contents of such communications.' The objection was even weightier if 'they tender opinions or advice to the Sovereign on political questions or convey suggestions calculated to make an impression on the mind of the Sovereign in reference to the treatment of such questions'. On the specific title of empress the prime minister coolly excluded any proposal to the queen except through her responsible ministers. It was obvious that he disapproved of it but his main concern was to instil into his distant subordinate the rudiments of constitutional propriety. Ellenborough dutifully accepted the rebuke and promised to send any future material for the queen through the prime minister and to confine himself even then to matters of fact.[2] He was always more ready to accept plain speaking from Peel than from his immediate departmental chief or the Court of Directors; and when Fitzgerald removed himself from any further Indian complications by dying in May 1843, his replacement by the easy-going Ripon meant that the prime minister became even more involved in the continuous

[1] *Peel*, III, 4.
[2] Ellenborough, 29 Oct. 1841; Corr. 6 Apr. 1843; 40471 fos. 290, 304.

narrative of strained relations between the Governor-General and the authorities at home.

Peel warned Ellenborough in June of the effect which improved communications with India was having on the amount of attention given by parliament and the press to Indian affairs and himself expressed serious doubts about the justice of the actions taken against the Ameers.[1] As more information on this episode became available, others beside the prime minister became alarmed at the soaring flights of Ellenborough's Indian policy. Lord Ashley, the self-appointed keeper of the government's conscience, was moved to warn Peel on 10 June that if it came to a formal vote in parliament he would have to record his condemnation of the actions in Scinde. The Court of Directors themselves were patently uneasy and their continual criticisms were already embarrassing the complicated system of authority in India. Ripon at the start of August asked in cabinet whether he could inform the Directors that the government shared their disapproval of the treatment of the Ameers. In view of the obscurities of the situation in Scinde and the fact that no specific instructions had yet been sent to Ellenborough, the prime minister preferred to retain a neutral position and the cabinet accepted his sketch of a reply to the Directors in place of the draft which Ripon had placed before them.[2] Failing to obtain government support, the Directors turned sulky. A fortnight later Peel was showing considerable asperity towards both parties in the dispute:

> The treatment of the Ameers [he wrote to Ripon] is really disgraceful to the character of this country. In my opinion direction ought to be given without loss of time to treat the Ameers with every degree of consideration. We have taken their territories, and despoiled them of their private property. Surely we need not inflict further punishment and privations.

As for the Court of Directors:

> Tell the Chairs that it would be infinitely more creditable to the Court to recall Lord Ellenborough, and manfully to take upon themselves the responsibility of a change in the Indian government, than to paralyse that Government both at home and abroad by acts

[1] Ellenborough Corr. (6 June 1843); 40471 f. 318; *Peel*, III, 6–7.
[2] 44777 f. 95.

demonstrating distrust and dissensions among the chief authorities who have to conduct the administration.[1]

Ripon acted on this directive but the immediate reaction of the Court was disappointing. Willing to wound but as yet afraid to strike, the Directors at the end of the month placed on secret record their strong condemnation of the treatment of the Ameers in a form which made it incumbent on Ripon to transmit it to the Governor-General.

It was clear, however, that an explosion would soon come either in India when Ellenborough received Ripon's despatch or in the Court of Directors, some of whom wished to put the secret resolution of August in their public minutes. In warning Ripon of this probable development the chairman of the Directors expressed a meaning hope that they would hear by the next Indian mail of the Governor-General's resignation. What he wanted was obviously that the government itself should recall Ellenborough. This Peel was not prepared to do nor to commit himself on the general question of Scinde until he had fuller information. He instructed Ripon to reply as coldly as possible to the chairman, making it plain that the responsibility for removing the Governor-General must rest with the Court. Though he was already turning over in his mind possible successors for Ellenborough, he would not budge from his position until the cabinet was able to come to a considered judgement on the Scinde affair. While he was in London in October waiting for the news of O'Connell's arrest, a fresh batch of Indian mail arrived which made it probable in his opinion that the government would have to confirm what Ellenborough was doing in Scinde. This in turn made precipitate action by the Directors doubly objectionable. He countermanded a temporising despatch by Ripon and on Wellington's advice a decision was left over to the following month. At the end of October fuller information arrived from India, including an able vindication by the Governor-General of his general policy which was patently designed for ultimate publication. With some reluctance but bowing to the compulsion of logistics— 'time, distance, the course of events', as Peel expressed it succinctly to Ripon—the cabinet finally decided to accept the annexation of Scinde.

[1] 40464 f. 447, ptly pr. Peel, III, 9 (17 Aug. 1843).

Peel's doubts had not been removed. He continued to press for better treatment of the captive Ameers; he was still concerned, as he had told Ellenborough in July, about the expense and security of the newly-acquired territories; and he took pains to ensure that Ripon's despatch conveying the cabinet's decision was couched in terms which justified the government's earlier hesitations.[1] When complaints came from Ellenborough of the delay in receiving the cabinet's support, he reacted sharply:

> I cannot see any proof, in the facts that have reached us in regard to Scinde [he wrote to Ellenborough at the beginning of 1844], that the difficulties in respect to that country and its future administration have been aggravated by the course taken by the cabinet. . . . Considering the consequences involved in a decision and the nature of the information transmitted to us in the first instance, the immediate unhesitating approval and confirmation of everything that was done could hardly have been expected.[2]

The position of the government was now clarified in relation both to Scinde and to the Court of Directors. The news of the incorporation of Gwalior as a protected state proved, however, that there was no predictable end to Ellenborough's expansionist policy. When it became obvious in April 1844 that the Court had at last decided to recall him, Peel instructed Ripon to make no admission that could justify their criticisms, to disassociate the government entirely from their action, and to refuse to discuss the question of a successor. The expected dismissal came at the end of the month, and with Ripon out of action through illness most of the correspondence dealing with the appointment of a new Governor-General was handled by the prime minister. Though protesting against the decision of the Directors, the government could not with decency refuse to assist them in finding a suitable candidate. But with the full backing of the cabinet Peel told them that he would leave them with their full legal responsibility unless he received an assurance that they would give their support and confidence to his own nominee. The Directors, already shaken by Wellington's public condemnation of their action as the most indiscreet exercise of power he had ever known, promptly gave the prime minister the guarantee he sought.

[1] 44777 f. 107.   [2] *Peel*, III, 19.

Peel handled them peremptorily, but what was paramount in his mind was the need to restore to the office of Governor-General the status and independence without which no public man worth his salt would ever accept it. Hardinge, in fact, to whom Peel offered the post on 2 May, refused at first to take it after the way in which Ellenborough had been treated. The available candidates were few enough. Ripon suggested Graham, but the prime minister, with the dictum that 'the Home Office is more important than India', was inclined to send out a military man, either Hardinge or Murray. Hardinge had turned down a proposal in 1842 that he should go out as Commander in Chief mainly on account of his wife's health. This time, after Peel had urged the difficulties of the government and assured him of the warm support of the queen and the Duke of Wellington, he finally accepted the Governor-Generalship. He stipulated however that there should be a clear understanding with the Court of Directors that he would go out not merely as a colleague of Ellenborough's but as a kinsman and friend who would make it his object to carry on Ellenborough's policy.[1]

Once Hardinge had signified his willingness, the prime minister acted swiftly to bring an unpleasant situation to a conciliatory conclusion. On Saturday, 4 May, he saw the Chairs and said he would assist them on one condition. They must give him an assurance that if he proposed a man of whom they approved, they would give him their entire support. He then named Hardinge as the candidate whom he thought fitter than anyone else. There was a meeting of the Court the same day and Peel told them to go back, report what had occurred, and send him the required assurance in writing. Within two hours he had his guarantee and in another he had seen Hardinge again, and got his final acceptance. The crisis was over and he drafted the same day a brief paragraph for Aberdeen to give to *The Times* announcing the new appointment and emphasising the friendly relations between the government and the Court in arriving at the decision.[2] To fill the vacancy at home left by Hardinge's departure Granville Somerset was at last promoted to the cabinet, though he declined the offer of the Secretaryship at War. That office was taken by Fremantle. It meant the loss of an efficient and popular Chief

[1] Ellenborough Corr. (Hardinge to Ellenborough, 6 May 1844).
[2] 43063 fos. 260–2.

Whip; but men of ministerial quality were scarce and his value in one office could hardly be made a justification for denying him advancement to another. An equal if personal sacrifice was made by Peel. In sending Hardinge to India he was sending away one of his closest and most loyal friends.

There remained the problem of the dismissed Governor-General. In a long, tactful letter Peel informed him of the final developments, assured him of the undiminished confidence of the queen and the cabinet, and told him that he was being recommended for an earldom and the G.C.B.[1] What Peel also had to consider was the need to maintain good relations with the Company and avoid public controversy when Ellenborough returned home. For that reason most of the cabinet were against an immediate announcement of his earldom since it might be taken as a snub to the Directors.[2] There had already been several awkward debates in the Commons on Indian affairs during the session. Lord Ashley in February had moved for an address to the crown on behalf of the Ameers of Scinde; and the recall of Ellenborough at the end of April provoked further acrimony. On 7 May, the day after Peel's despatch to Ellenborough, Hume moved for copies of the correspondence between the Governor-General and the Court of Directors. But with the official Company spokesmen in the House, as well as the official Whigs, counselling a suspension of judgement, the Commons agreed with Peel that it would be improper to send out a new Governor-General carrying documentary evidence of past differences of opinion among the authorities at home. The reluctance of the government to add fresh material to the controversy was soon vindicated. A letter arrived for his successor couched in what Graham called Ellenborough's Asiatic style outlining plans for an invasion of the Punjab with an army 'with which I could march to the Dardanelles', renewing the suggestion of enthroning the queen as Empress of a consolidated India, and looking forward to the day when Egypt would ultimately fall to British arms. In circulating the despatch Peel added the restrained comment that if its contents became known to the Court of Directors, 'it would not dissatisfy them with their recent letter of recall'. A second letter to himself on the same subject

[1] Ellenborough Corr. (6 May 1844); 40472 f. 171, ptly pr. *Peel*, III, 26.
[2] 40472 f. 178.

but written in more temperate prose was answered by Peel in June with the sober remark that 'I for one shall very sincerely deprecate the necessity for intervention by force of arms . . . [and] sincerely hope the necessity for any such proceedings may be averted, and that we may be left at liberty, without incurring any risk from our forbearance, to consolidate and improve our present Empire'.[1]

Ellenborough's eastern *avatar* was now almost at an end. One of his last acts was to send Ripon a long despatch, clearly framed for future use, containing some vituperative charges against the Directors of jobbery and intrigue. Hardinge reached India at the end of July. Though military seniority prevented Peel from giving him the additional appointment of Commander in Chief in India, his commission was drawn up so as to allow wide authority over the army; and he departed with the fresh honour of the G.C.B. to mark the prime minister's opinion of his proper ranking among military men. By the autumn Ellenborough was back in England, meditating revenge on the Court of Directors and pressing for the publication of papers to vindicate his policy. Death and time had invested Fitzgerald with rarer qualities as President of the Board of Control than Ellenborough had been prepared to recognise at the time. His resentment now was concentrated against the unfortunate and still living Ripon. But while Peel was ready to defend publicly the actions of the late Governor-General, he would not tolerate internecine warfare within the government. The Ellenborough episode had demonstrated all the weaknesses of what Peel had described to Ripon a year earlier as 'the anomalous and absurd principle on which the government of India is conducted'.[2] Yet as long as ministers had to work with the East India Company within the antiquated system of dual control, it was essential to preserve the recently restored harmony.

As soon as Ellenborough was back, Peel offered him Lonsdale's office of Postmaster-General and a seat in the cabinet, with the alternative of succeeding Buccleuch as Lord Privy Seal. He made it clear, however, that though his colleagues would stand by his past policy in India, they would not sanction any future attack on the Court of Directors.[3] Ellenborough refused both offers, intimating

---

[1] *ibid.* f. 205; *Peel*, III, 29–31.   [2] 40465 f. 124.
[3] Ellenborough Corr. (16 Oct. 1844); 40472 f. 245.

(as Peel wrote to Hardinge with some amusement) that 'his head had been so full of grand conceptions and schemes with great results, that Post Offices and Privy Seals were beneath his notice'.[1] The prime minister was prepared to wait until the customary neglect of the British public for retired Indian viceroys had exercised its deflating influence. But when Ellenborough, to Ripon's discomfiture, began a paper war with the Board of Control, Peel intervened at the start of the new year with a long, cool letter refuting his charges. The ex-Governor-General had many gifts, not least imagination and a kind of intuitive prescience, but he lacked a sense of measure. In his thirst for ends he overlooked the problem of means; and he was impulsive and tactless in human relationships. With all his extraordinary powers, Peel observed once in the cabinet, Ellenborough had not the faculty of managing men.[2] The history of his governorgeneralship was an admirable illustration of Peel's own approach to the same problem in circumstances which could scarcely have been more difficult. The defence, against criticisms which he often felt to be justified, of a wayward subordinate too far away to be controlled but for whom the executive government was ultimately responsible, was an exercise in balanced judgement which made it one of the most illuminating episodes in Peel's record as prime minister.

It was the more noteworthy since Peel was in fundamental disagreement with Ellenborough's ideas. The prime minister disliked the high-handed treatment of the native princes, was opposed to unnecessary expansion of British rule, and had complete disbelief in the theory that the position of Russia had any real relevance to British policy in India. When the Tsar Nicholas came over on a brief visit in 1844 Peel had a conversation with him on Indian affairs which convinced him that the rumours of Russian intrigues on the Indian frontier were largely the invention of the French press, even though it was clear that Nicholas was equally sensitive to any talk of British advance into the Punjab. The Russian government had its own public to consider. While there was Russophobia in England, there was also Anglophobia in Russia. The essential need, in Peel's view, was to establish confidence and understanding between the two governments. He did not despair that statesmen, whatever national pride and prejudice might demand, could be brought to

[1] *Peel*, III, 264.   [2] 44777 f. 172.

494

act sensibly. When Count Nesselrode, the Russian minister, paid him a parting visit in October 1844, they had a frank discussion on the Francophile party in Russia who were indoctrinating the Russian public with the idea that there were no assignable limits to British expansion in India and that a clash between Russia and Britain in the foreseeable future was on that account inevitable. In response to Nesselrode's insistence on the desire of the Russian government to preserve friendly relations, Peel explained the peculiar and dangerous situation arising from the anarchic conditions in the Punjab and read him an extract from Hardinge's latest despatch in which he reported the assurances he had given to the native states of the north-west and his hopes that intervention in the Punjab would prove unnecessary. 'I . . . convinced him', the prime minister wrote to Hardinge, 'that the consolidation and improvement of the vast domains we possess in India were objects much nearer your heart than the extension of our empire, or the gratification of the cravings of our army for more conquests and more glory.'[1] He attributed the sentiments to Hardinge; they were also his own. The road of imperial expansion had few attractions for Peel.

II

Peel's dealings with Aberdeen offered an instructive contrast to those with Ellenborough. Where in his correspondence with the Governor-General he seemed invariably liberal and pacific, with his Foreign Secretary he often appeared hard and sometimes aggressive. Part of the contrast was due to his habit, when discussing matters with his colleagues, of putting strongly all the counter-arguments; not so much because he believed in them but in order to test the strength of the case presented to him. Since policy was at least partly influenced by the temperament of the man framing it, he tried to counteract any eccentric tendency by applying an opposite bias of his own. Dealing with such opposed personalities as the dashing opinionated Governor-General and the gentle tolerant Foreign Secretary, there was all the greater need for him to complement their temperamental deficiencies. To be an Ellenborough to Aberdeen, an Aberdeen to Ellenborough, was part of his prime minister's duty. Even when

[1] 40474 f. 168; *Peel*, III, 258–62.

this large allowance is made, however, it is also true that there were sensible differences between Peel and his Foreign Secretary. They were differences of temperament rather than of policy. Peel was less trusting, less optimistic, more inclined to deploy all the means of influence open to him to arrive at a given end. Aberdeen was more sanguine, more conciliatory, more ready to announce openly his intentions and rely on the goodwill of the other side. When on one occasion Peel remarked somewhat tartly that one needed 'that charity which believeth all things' to trust the French government, his Foreign Secretary retorted that 'charity should not only *believe all things* but should *never fail*'.[1] This to Peel was merely unrealistic.

Both men were agreed that the maxim for British foreign relations must be to walk softly but Peel was considerably more inclined to carry a big stick. Ends and means however cannot satisfactorily be separated in the conduct of foreign policy; and since the prime minister exercised as close a supervision over the affairs of Aberdeen's department as he did of the other great offices of state, the Foreign Secretary had to argue his case more often than he would have preferred. Peel on the other hand had to impart some of his own energy to the curiously devitalised figure of the Foreign Secretary. A reluctant candidate in 1841, Aberdeen continued in office with an absence of zeal and ambition which in a less conscientious man might have had more serious consequences. As it was, any passing physical depression was enough to turn his thoughts to retirement. As early as September 1842, after only a year in his department, he was describing to Peel his distressing medical symptoms, like 'a gentleman walking about with his head under water', and hinting at resignation. Peel replied forcefully that his departure would be the greatest misfortune for the government and to himself an irreparable loss. Aberdeen did not press the issue but begged Peel to release him at some convenient moment. He had long since lost any real wish for office, he added, and it was only his relations with Peel that gave him any satisfaction in his work. His picturesque symptoms remained and a month later he told Peel dolefully that he had to postpone working on several matters since 'my head is completely *submerged*'. Whatever the trouble was, and it was probably no more than mental fatigue, it seemed a recurrent phenomenon.

[1] 43064 f. 176; 40454 f. 411 (11 Feb. 1845).

In October 1843 he was complaining to Peel of again experiencing the 'noise, confusion and distressing sensations in the head' from which he had suffered the previous year.[1] It would only have been human on Peel's part to conclude that Aberdeen needed the spur as much as Ellenborough the bridle.

Certainly there was no question of allowing the Foreign Secretary the same undisturbed and almost private conduct of foreign affairs that Palmerston appeared to enjoy under the placid rule of Lord Melbourne. Between Peel and Aberdeen there was an incessant correspondence. The prime minister not only discussed general matters of policy but scrutinised all levels of diplomatic activity. He read, criticised, and amended draft despatches and instructions, suggested new points for consideration, and proffered his views on diplomatic appointments. He even showed a Palmerstonian tendency to criticise the style of diplomatic despatches. 'I wish', he wrote to Aberdeen in November 1842, 'you would require your foreign ministers and Ambassadors to write *English*. I read some despatches yesterday from Lord Stuart and I think Mr. Mandeville or Mr. Hamilton or I believe both, which are too slovenly for endurance.' Or again, 'surely it would be better to pay Mr. Goldsmith his accustomed salary and tell him to do nothing—at any rate, not to write such abominable stuff as the enclosed'.[2] If he rarely sought to override the Foreign Secretary, he frequently sought to influence him; and he was capable of taking a firm line when the occasion seemed to justify it. The degree of attention he gave to foreign policy was almost excessive. When, for example, Aberdeen wrote to him in November 1843 on the problem of the defence of Monte-Video, apologising at the same time for interrupting Peel in his preparations for the royal visit to Drayton, the prime minister took the trouble to write back a letter of over seven sides of quarto.[3] On the other hand, when even the ever-vigilant prime minister occasionally nodded, Aberdeen was ready with a vigorous rejoinder. Receiving a letter of protest from Peel in the winter of 1843–44 against concession to France in the matter of right of search, he wrote back: 'My dear Peel, I am afraid that you have read Guizot's letter without much attention, and mine with still less, for there is no

[1] 43062 fos. 89, 91; 43063 f. 50; 40453 fos. 171, 176.
[2] 43062 f. 186; 43064 f. 36.   [3] 40454 fos. 18-20.

question whatever about any *concession* on the subject of our Treaties.'[1] Yet with all their differences of style and temperament, and occasional disagreements over policy, nothing ever happened to shake the essential personal confidence between the two men.

When the Conservative ministry took office in 1841 one of the immediate and dangerous foreign problems was the strained situation with the United States. Bad blood had existed at least since 1831 when the arbitration settlement by the King of the Netherlands on the Maine–New Brunswick frontier line had been rejected by the American Senate. Since then the dispute had grown worse with the *Caroline* incident of 1837 when an American steamer carrying arms to the Canadian rebels had been captured and destroyed by loyalists in the St. Lawrence. Early in 1841 a British subject named McLeod had been arrested in New York for being concerned in the attack and a party to the death of one of the Americans on board. Palmerston's unconciliatory diplomacy had widened the breach and to the frontier issue was added the wider question of the right of inspection at sea. The British government maintained a squadron off the African coast to suppress the slave trade and for this purpose had treaty agreements with certain other European powers permitting a limited right of mutual search at sea. The American government had refused to participate in the treaty. Nevertheless British ships claimed the right to stop suspicious ships flying the American flag to ensure that it was not a fictitious colour run up by slavers to conceal their identity. Feeling in the United States was increasingly roused and a hostile report by the Committee on Foreign Affairs demanding preparations for national defence was accepted by Congress in the spring of 1841. Among all his other preoccupations in October 1841 Peel found time to circulate a cabinet memorandum arguing that the possibility that 'some immediate and decisive demonstration on our part may be necessary' made some precautions advisable in case war was forced upon them. A meeting of Aberdeen, Stanley, Graham, Haddington and the prime minister, agreed on 18 October to strengthen the naval forces at Gibraltar and Halifax and to hold reinforcements ready to go to Bermuda if requested.[2]

[1] 40454 fos. 50–2.
[2] Wellington (Peel to Wellington, 18 Oct. 1841); *Peel*, III, 387.

At the same time Peel could see that the right of stopping ships on the high seas, though necessary for effective control of the slave trade, was not covered by any known international law, was open to abuse by individual ship's commanders, and might easily lead to a maritime war. His instinct therefore was for negotiation and agreement; and he was further encouraged by a pacific article in the *New York Herald* which suggested that advantage be taken of a new government in Britain to settle all outstanding issues between the two countries. He sent the article to Aberdeen on 31 October and followed it next day with a hint to write officially to the Admiralty requesting precise information on the instructions given to H.M. ships on their exercise of the right of search. 'We ought in my opinion to check as far as possible wanton visits, from the sheer love and hope of gain.' From officious captains of the Africa squadron his thoughts turned a fortnight later to the quality of British diplomatic representation at Washington. H. S. Fox, one of Palmerston's appointments who had been minister there since 1836, was not in high repute as a diplomat. His critics alleged that he did not mix in society, knew little of American opinion, and 'spent the greater part of the day in bed'.[1] What was equally damaging in Peel's eyes was that he was strongly anti-American and little hope could be placed in any negotiation conducted through him. Peel and Aberdeen gave their attention therefore to finding a more suitable agent for effecting, as the prime minister broadly defined it, a conciliatory adjustment of all outstanding difficulties with the U.S.A.

Out of this came the appointment of Lord Ashburton as special envoy with plenipotentiary powers. It was a happy choice. As a former cabinet minister and member of a great banking firm, Ashburton brought both political authority and practical business sense to his mission. Through his American wife he was already known to Webster, the new Secretary of State, who himself had banking interests. The two men approached their task with a determination to come to an agreement and in less than six months settled the immediate issues between the two countries.

Ashburton accepted his commission just before Christmas, was formally accredited in January, arrived in Washington in April and

[1] See General Greene's account to Goulburn in Aug. 1843 (40444 f. 81); 43061 fos. 308, 343; *Peel*, III, 388.

signed the Anglo-American convention in August. Throughout the period of negotiation Peel showed himself eager to reach a settlement. An agreement on the maritime problem was not enough. 'I think we *must* come to an agreement on the boundary,' he wrote to Aberdeen in May. For Canadian susceptibilities, particularly in view of the anti-British sentiments still smouldering among Canadian politicians, he had little sympathy. If the colonists expected to receive imperial protection while refusing to accept imperial policy, it would be better in his view to separate peacefully rather than continue with political friction inside and strained relations outside the Canadian frontier. 'Seeing that the Boundary question invades no principle, I would go as far as we could safely go, in the present state of the Canadas, in accommodating matters in so far as that Question is concerned.'[1] The new north-east frontier settled between Ashburton and Webster, though embodying substantial concessions to the Americans, satisfied both the prime minister and his Foreign Secretary. Indeed Aberdeen thought it in one material respect superior to the old arbitration line of 1831, since it pushed the border back from twenty-five to fifty miles south of the St. Lawrence and Quebec.[2] The question of right of inspection at sea was quietly abandoned. Instead there was an agreement between the two countries that each would maintain anti-slavery squadrons off the African coast with provision for joint action. Though savagely attacked by Palmerston in the *Morning Chronicle*, the Washington treaty was approved by both orthodox Whigs and their more radical supporters. The country as a whole, more interested in good commercial relations with its best customer, shared Peel's fundamental attitude that minor arguments over the strategic value of barren lands in the North American continent were unimportant compared with the possibility of war with the United States.

For the government it was an early and welcome diplomatic success, marred only by a certain coolness when Ashburton returned home in the autumn. His grateful ex-colleagues offered him a viscountcy and the red ribbon of the Bath. He considered his services entitled him to an earldom. Peel, backed by Wellington, thought this excessive in principle, awkward as a precedent, and

[1] 43062 f. 48 (16 May 1842), ptly pr. *Peel*, III, 388.
[2] 40453 f. 161; 43062 f. 80.

objectionable in its implications. Such an effusive reward might be taken as a sign that the government had been seriously afraid of war with the U.S.A. A slightly unpleasant exchange of letters between Peel and the mortified diplomat took place in October and in the end the prime minister was obliged to ask Aberdeen to let Ashburton know that he did not wish to continue the correspondence.[1]

Personal ambition apart, the one outstanding issue left untouched by the Webster–Ashburton treaty of 1842 was the Oregon question. The Louisiana purchase, which opened up to the United States the remainder of the continent from the Mississippi to the Pacific, made it inevitable that there would be eventual friction over the northwest boundary with Canada. The popular American doctrine in the eighteen-forties of Manifest Destiny at least made manifest that there was a strong desire among the American peoples to extend their Pacific territory north-west to meet the Russians in Alaska. The Anglo-American agreement in 1818 had fixed the 49th parallel as the frontier as far as the Rocky Mountains but left the ultimate fate of the Oregon territory beyond the mountains unsettled. As a temporary measure both powers had assumed common ownership of that undefined and largely uncolonised coastal area. To this extent therefore Ashburton had fallen short of Peel's hope of settling all outstanding issues.

Immediately after Ashburton's return Aberdeen suggested that Fox should be instructed to open the Oregon question with Webster and ask that Everett, the new American minister in London, should be given powers to conclude a treaty.[2] With this Peel warmly agreed; but pacific as Webster's diplomacy was, the political situation in America made it difficult for Washington to move as fast as London would have liked. It had been judged impossible to include the Oregon question in the negotiations with Ashburton and in the following two years the latent hostility of the American public and President Tyler's difficulties with Congress prevented any progress in what was an increasingly dangerous situation. Time moreover was on the American side, since once the tide of emigration to the

[1] 40453 fos. 169, 206; Graham (Peel to Graham, 19 Oct.); Wellington (Peel to Wellington, 16 Oct. 1842).
[2] 43062 fos. 121, 123.

Pacific coast began to flow, the American settlers would soon out-number the British. The official American claim was to all the territory up to the parallel 54° 40′ and on the most optimistic forecast in London would hardly be reduced to less than a continuation of the 49th parallel across the mountains to the water's edge. This line, if extended to Vancouver Island, would exclude from British control the entrance to Puget Sound and the harbour which constituted the most valuable part of the territory. Aberdeen's proposal was to negotiate for an extension of the 49th parallel to the Pacific only, leaving Vancouver Island in British hands and the entrance to the Columbia river free to both countries. This would clearly be an advantageous settlement, the most the British government could hope for, and more perhaps than they would get by arbitration. Peel endorsed this line of policy in language stronger than Aberdeen was in the habit of using. He suggested that they should obtain the views of the British settlers in Oregon and resort to arbitration rather than make any concession that fell short of Aberdeen's proposal. 'I should not be afraid of a good deal of preliminary bluster on the part of the Americans,' he wrote to the Foreign Secretary. 'The best answer would be to direct the *Collingwood* to make a friendly visit when she has leisure, to the mouth of the Columbia.'[1]

The indolent Fox had been replaced by Pakenham, but his negotiations in 1844 with the new Secretary of State, Calhoun, made little headway. Even so Peel remained unconvinced of the need to surrender any material British interest. In October Pakenham put forward a new plan which Aberdeen thought worth adopting. It was that each side should take the extreme claims of the other as its formal frontier, leaving the intermediate zone as common territory. This suggestion Peel styled dryly as 'a very novel one at least' with little advantage for the present and much likelihood of future trouble.[2] Aberdeen then fell back on the alternative of arbitration, only for this in turn to be rejected by the American government.

President Tyler's closing message to Congress at the end of the year indicated perhaps a more conciliatory approach to the problem than he had previously shown. But the future lay with the new President, Polk, elected on an enthusiastic expansionist Democratic ticket. His inaugural address in March 1845, asserting the American

---

[1] 43064 fos. 32, 34; 40454 f. 268 (Sept. 1844).   [2] 40454 fos. 278–84.

'clear and unquestionable' claim to Oregon, came close to Peel's definition of preliminary bluster and was taken up by Russell in the Commons. Peel, while deprecating the attempts of both Russell and Polk to bring a matter under confidential diplomatic discussion before the bar of public opinion, nevertheless used the opportunity to declare that the British right to Oregon was equally clear and unquestionable. The issue, he hoped, would be settled amicably. But if not, and their rights were infringed, they were 'resolved and prepared to maintain them'. This was something more than a little counter-bluster of his own. Behind the scenes the prime minister was showing himself ready to support his words with action. At the end of February he had questioned Aberdeen's optimistic assumption that the balance of local power on the banks of the Columbia was or would necessarily remain in Britain's favour and suggested that a frigate with marines and artillery should be sent under sealed orders to the mouth of the Oregon.[1]

The negotiations resumed with the new Secretary of State, Buchanan, in 1845 still failed to reach agreement, and at the end of the year the American government recommended to Congress the termination of the 1827 convention providing for joint occupation of the Oregon territory. The refusal of the British government to concede anything on the vital issue of Puget Sound and Vancouver Island, and the strong language used by Peel in the spring, inevitably produced angry words from the American politicians. Nevertheless, once matters were brought to a head, it was clear that Congress had no real will for a rupture with Britain at a time when American relations with Mexico were rapidly moving towards war. In accepting in April the President's recommendation, Congress added a clear directive to the U.S. government to renew its efforts for an amicable settlement. On the British side, outside the strict limits of the question at issue, Peel took care to do nothing that might ruffle American susceptibilities. In September 1845 he had advised strongly against any response to overtures from Mexico for the assertion of British interests in California,[2] and was equally positive five months later in forbidding any unusual naval activities on the Great Lakes that might flutter the war hawks in the United States.[3] Aberdeen

[1] 43064 f. 178; 40454 f. 413 (23 Feb. 1845).   [2] ibid. f. 357.
[3] Ellenborough Corr. (8 Feb. 1846).

was hopeful at the end of 1845 that the new year would see a final solution to the Oregon question and a conciliatory passage was inserted in the queen's speech at the opening of parliament in January which was patently designed to appeal to the peace party in Congress. By the early summer of 1846 it was clear that Peel's waiting game had succeeded and that the opportunity for making a satisfactory settlement had come at last.

III

India and Canada were problems of the imperial frontier. To Peel's ministry, as to most nineteenth-century British governments, foreign policy was basically European policy. In that field the dominant feature was the relationship with France.[1] It was a complex and uneasy association. Though geography and national interests threw up specific issues from time to time, the fundamental problem was formed by past conflicts, by mutual distrust, and by fears for the future. Alone among the great states of Europe France still appeared a revolutionary and unstable society. Alone in Europe it offered a challenge to British sea power. On the surface there seemed in 1841 the prospect of a new era in Anglo-French relations. The Near Eastern crisis, and the isolation of France marked by the Quadrilateral Treaty of 1840, had brought about the fall of Thiers and the installation of the more pacific Soult-Guizot ministry. The following year had seen the return of France to the concert of Europe in the Straits Convention and the replacement of Palmerston by the conciliatory Aberdeen. But strained feelings remained; and while in France national pride was still ruffled, the new British prime minister represented a tougher strand of continuity in foreign policy than was realised at the time. Though the diplomatic world was frequently reminded that Palmerston was the exponent not so much of a Whig as of a Canningite foreign policy, it was too often forgotten that in this at least Peel had been a supporter of Canning when Palmerston was still in the obscurity of the secretaryship at war. In the early days of the ministry it was the superficial contrast with his Whig predecessors which attracted attention. Peel impressed the public on both sides of the Channel by the soothing words he

[1] For the background of what follows see esp. J. Hall, *England and the Orléans Monarchy* (1912), ch. IX.

uttered about France in August 1842 when answering Palmerston's attacks on the government's foreign policy. Despite their domestic and personal antipathies, however, Peel was in some respects closer to Palmerston in his attitude to foreign affairs than he was to Aberdeen.

Even before he took office in 1841 Peel had expressed the discouraging view that Guizot's policy of armed peace was more dangerous than the crackbrained projects of Thiers.[1] Towards the end of 1842 he showed considerable anxiety over the scheme for a customs union between France and Belgium. Though he rejected a Prussian proposal for a great powers conference as an unnecessary humiliation for France, he was not prepared to assume as lightly as Aberdeen that the plan of union had been permanently abandoned.[2] He showed an equally lively apprehension of French readiness to extend their influence over their southern neighbour. The tortuous and sordid history of the Spanish marriages which dragged on throughout his ministry provided ample reason for British distrust of French aims and methods. In 1840, in the course of the endemic Spanish civil conflicts of the period, Christina the queen-mother had been forced to leave Spain. She took up her residence in Paris and Espartero became regent on behalf of the young Queen Isabella. Although she was only twelve years old the question of her marriage soon developed into an international issue and remained one for the next six years. The restoration of French influence in Spain became a primary aim of Guizot and Louis Philippe; and there was a well-founded suspicion that they were assisting Christina and the anti-Espartero faction in return for the promise of a marriage between Isabella and one of Louis Philippe's sons. The official French attitude was that she ought to marry one of the Spanish or Neapolitan Bourbons, even though on physical, mental and political grounds a certain unattractiveness adhered to these notoriously degenerate descendants of Philip V.

Peel placed no trust in Guizot's assurances of disinterested neutrality towards Spain. On the other hand there was some disadvantage for Britain in appearing to support Espartero and a reactionary military junto. In October 1841, Peel was half-inclined to sound opinion in Austria and among the northern powers. The primary object of British diplomacy was after all to resist a revival of

---

[1] *Neumann*, II, 161.   [2] 43062 f. 186; 40453 f. 253.

Louis XIV's Spanish policy and other powers besides Britain had an interest in this.[1] Next month he was suggesting to Aberdeen the advisability of a formal communication to Spain, supporting the right of the Spanish government to be the sole arbiter of the marriage of Isabella and assuring them that Britain would not be party to any conference or secret treaty to settle the matter over the heads of the Spanish people. At the same time he was anxious that the Spanish government, while protecting their northern frontier, should offer no provocation to France that might serve as a pretext for armed intervention.[2]

When early in 1842 the French government officially proposed that Isabella should marry one of the Bourbon princes, Aberdeen reiterated the British view that the decision was one solely for the Spanish government. But he made the all-important reservation that a marriage with a son of Louis Philippe would necessarily be open to the objection that it would upset the balance of power in Europe. Since Metternich in Vienna took the same line, a temporary deadlock ensued. Difficulties continued to mount in Spain for Espartero, and there was a strong suspicion in both Madrid and London that France was at the bottom of the trouble. When in June 1843 a military *coup d'état* forced the Regent into exile, Aberdeen began to waver. What he feared was that the victorious party in Spain would marry Isabella to a French prince in return for a French alliance. To circumvent this he proposed joint intervention by France and Britain to restore peace in Spain. What this also implied however was an abandonment of the British principle that Spain alone must decide on the royal marriage. To that extent it was a significant concession to French diplomacy and both Guizot and Louis Philippe hastened to welcome the overture.

In September came the visit of Victoria and Albert to the Chateau d'Eu near Le Tréport. The occasion allowed the French king and his foreign minister to cement the new diplomatic alliance by showering Aberdeen with protestations of the unselfish nature of their intentions. Reacting rather differently Peel regarded the meeting as an opportunity to give a warning to the French government. 'I hope you will let Louis Philippe understand', he wrote to Aberdeen

[1] 43061 f. 289; 40453 f. 30; ptly pr. *Peel*, III, 390.
[2] *ibid.* fos. 327, 337, ptly pr. *Peel*, III, 390–1.

on the eve of his departure, 'that we cannot conceive it possible—which of course means that we shrewdly suspect—that he may contemplate, by various cunning devices, under the pretence of friendly concert with us, rendering the marriage of the Queen of Spain with the duc d'Aumale inevitable.'[1] The king however assured Aberdeen that he had no intention of a marriage with the Spanish royal house for one of his sons and wished to act in agreement with Britain in all matters affecting Spain.[2] Aberdeen for his part consented to recommend to the Spanish government the choice of a Bourbon descendant of Philip V and on this happy conjunction of views the *Entente Cordiale* was announced to the world. The phrase, coined by Aberdeen, was taken up with alacrity by Louis Philippe and his minister and constantly employed by them to advertise the allegedly close relationship between the two great western powers. Peel, if not Aberdeen, was less convinced that there was much reality behind the phrase. But he was sufficiently politic to insert a sentence in the queen's speech at the start of the 1844 session referring to the 'good understanding happily established' with the French government.

The year 1844 demonstrated how fragile in fact the *entente* was and how deepseated were Peel's suspicions. The occasion of difference was provided by the overlapping spheres of influence of the two countries on the other side of the world. In 1840 the British annexation of New Zealand had neatly forestalled a projected French colonising expedition. In part compensation a French squadron under Admiral Dupetit-Thouars had taken possession of the Marquesas Islands and later, without authorisation, declared a protectorate over Tahiti. Though British missionaries had long been active in the island, and Queen Pomare had twice offered to put her territory under British protection, the British government had no legal standing in Tahiti and no grounds for protest at the French action. Nevertheless, the local situation was riddled with religious, commercial and personal rivalries; the behaviour of the French admiral had been high-handed; and the hostile attitude of the British consul Pritchard, who encouraged Pomare to appeal for British assistance, led at the end of 1843 to the deposition of the queen and the annexation of the island by the French commander. Both governments

---

[1] 40453 f. 434; *Peel*, III, 453.   [2] 40453 f. 446.

were embarrassed and each tried to conciliate the other: Guizot by repudiating the annexation and reinstating Pomare, Aberdeen by ordering the troublemaking Pritchard to be transferred elsewhere. In July 1844, however, the news reached London that Pritchard had been arrested, thrown into jail and ultimately deported from Tahiti. In fact he had acted in a highly offensive way to the French authorities and was at least partly responsible for the native unrest which followed the annexation. At the relevant time moreover he seems to have ceased to have occupied the post of consul. But these finer details were at first unknown in England and if they had been, would probably have had little effect on the public outcry which greeted the news. Roused simultaneously by the reports of the French expedition to Morocco and the bombardment of Tangiers, bellicose national feeling ran high on both sides of the Channel. While Guizot was under attack in the French assembly for his alleged abandonment of Admiral Dupetit-Thouars, Peel had to face the most dangerous force in contemporary British politics, the outraged susceptibilities of Evangelical Protestantism.

Pritchard had originally been a member of the Methodist missionary organisation in the Pacific and his appearance in August at a great meeting at Exeter Hall was the signal for most unsaintly speeches by leading representatives of the Saints. 'Grief and indignation cannot go beyond what I feel against the French aggressions in Tahiti,' recorded Ashley emotionally in his diary. 'A peaceable and helpless people, a State presenting, as such, the only Christian model in the world, are subjugated by savages and powerful Europeans, and inundated with bloodshed, devastation, profligacy and crime.'[1] On the first report of Pritchard's arrest questions were immediately put to the prime minister in the House. Peel, having consulted Aberdeen, made it clear that the action against Pritchard had been taken without the authority of the French government and he hoped they would make instant reparation. But he also stated roundly that, presuming the truth of the reports, 'I do not hesitate to say that a gross outrage accompanied with gross indignity has been committed upon this country in the person of its officer'. Or so at least he was reported in *The Times* next day, though *Hansard* does not record the last nine words. When Jarnac, the French *chargé d'affaires*, saw

[1] *Hodder*, p. 289.

Aberdeen the same day in some consternation, the Foreign Secretary tried to explain away Peel's words by attributing them to faulty reporting. But the prime minister was not disposed to take shelter behind so obvious a subterfuge. He believed the version in *The Times* to be incorrect but stood by the remainder of the sentence which had appeared in all the papers and caused in fact the main sensation. In a note to Aberdeen of 24 August which was passed on to Jarnac, he said he would be extremely sorry if Guizot were to rely on the presumed inaccuracy of the report of his words in parliament when in fact those reports were not only substantially correct but constituted an expression of opinion which he was not prepared to retract or deny.[1]

This was disconcerting; but Guizot, who had his problems at home, was disposed to temporise until tempers had time to cool in both countries. In this, despite the urgent warnings of Jarnac, he clearly underestimated feeling in Britain. The Tahiti and Moroccan events together had undoubtedly incensed Peel. He thought they demonstrated at best Guizot's loss of control of French policy and at worst complete lack of good faith; and he was not prepared to wait. Following a cabinet meeting on 13 August Aberdeen warned Guizot that unless satisfaction was soon offered, he would have to send a formal request for redress to the French government. To drive the point home he read Jarnac a confidential letter from Peel which must have confirmed the Frenchman's conviction that the British prime minister was no diplomat. In the letter Peel pinned the blame for everything on Guizot:

> If he chooses to send out expeditions to occupy every place where they can find the pretence for occupation and if the commanders of those expeditions occupy other places not contemplated by their Government, and if M. Guizot has not the power or courage to disavow them, *he* is responsible for whatever may occur in consequence of such proceedings.

If the French consul in Tahiti got up a plot with the French admiral 'to swindle Queen Pomare out of her sovereignty', he should not be surprised that local residents protested and made 'an unjust

[1] For this incident see the art. by Jarnac in *Revue des Deux Mondes* (3 Période, Tome IV), on 'Sir Robert Peel'; *Hansard*, LXXVI, 1575 (31 July 1844); *The Times*, 1 Aug. 1844; Hall, *op. cit.*, 360 et seq.

usurpation uncomfortable for usurpers'. As in Tahiti, so in Africa. The original annexation of Algiers was a violation of French engagements to Europe, and had led to the present trouble. Unless Britain held strong language to France about Tunis and Morocco, it seemed likely that they too would meet with the fate of Algiers. 'I do not', he finished crushingly, 'attach the slightest weight to the disclaimers of M. Guizot and the King.' At half a dozen French ports along the Channel, he pointed out, naval preparations were going on and the only conclusion could be that France was preparing for a naval war with Britain. In sending a fleet to Morocco the French government was presuming on British naval weakness in the Mediterranean.[1]

A different kind of importance would have to be attached to this outburst had it not been written expressly for Aberdeen to read to Jarnac. But it was clear all the same that Peel was genuinely indignant. If Knatchbull is to be believed,[2] he was using much the same language in the cabinet. The end of a session which had seen the clashes with his own party over the factory and sugar bills had left him in a perceptibly sharp temper, and the Pritchard affair was only the last of a series of unsatisfactory episodes in the chequered history of Anglo-French relations since he took office in 1841. In itself it was, as he later admitted to Hardinge, a trumpery cause of quarrel. But he had to take into consideration the angry feelings of the public and the pressure of the opposition. In the circumstances he thought it both a point of honour and a political necessity to extract an immediate promise of financial compensation from the French government. If it took strong language to startle Guizot out of his passivity, he was ready to supply it.[3] But the Moroccan expedition was probably at least as much an irritant as the Tahiti affair.

Writing to Wellington a few days afterwards, the prime minister expressed the hope that his letter to Aberdeen would have a salutary effect on the French government. He had done all he could, he added, to smooth the way for the French king and would deplore the end of peace. 'But we must not allow Louis Philippe to establish a character at our expense. The only way to prevent this is to convince

---

[1] 43063 f. 303 (12 Aug. 1844); 40454 f. 206, ptly pr. *Peel*, III, 394.
[2] Writing long after the event and after he had parted with Peel (*Knatchbull*, p. 253).
[3] Cf. 40474 f. 168 (4 Oct. 1844]; *Peel*, p. 263.

him that we are in earnest and that we are prepared for a Naval War.'[1] Such language was meat and drink for the duke. It was hardly, however, the preferred diet of the Foreign Secretary. Aberdeen's advice was to make no hostile demonstration against France, avoid any public reference to the state of Anglo-French relations, recognise the internal difficulties confronting Guizot, and accept in due course any suitable form of reparation the French government might think it politic to offer. There was, he argued, no rational ground for a quarrel between the two countries. Though the fact of French naval preparations was indisputable, they had after all been going on for some time. He admitted that no trust could be placed in French assurances, as witness the attack on Tangiers; but British rearmament would only make war more probable.

Few of his arguments elicited much sympathy from Peel. If Guizot could not control French policy, he replied, he should not be surprised if the British government consulted its own interests and security rather than 'the delicacies and difficulties of his position as minister'. The question of compensation to Pritchard was of minor importance compared with the accumulated proofs of hostile naval preparations by France. The real question was whether they could place any trust in French policy. Failing that, it was common prudence to ensure that if war broke out, the French would not have a decided superiority at sea at the start of hostilities.

I do most earnestly advise that we should without delay consider the state of our naval preparation as compared with that of France. Matters are in that state that the interval of twenty-four hours— some act of violence for which the French ministry is not strong enough to make reparation or disavowal—may not only dissipate the shadow of the *Entente Cordiale* but change our relations from Peace to War. Let us be prepared for War. Some may think the preparations for it will diminish the chance of peace, that the fact of our strengthening ourselves may give alarm or umbrage to the French. I think it is very doubtful whether it would have any such effect. My belief is, from all I have seen of the French people and their Government, that they are much more likely to presume upon our weakness than to take offence at our strength[2]

[1] 40460 fos. 254, 256.
[2] 43063 f. 324 (21 Aug. 1844). For the rest of the correspondence see *ibid.*, fos. 333–54; 40454 fos. 225–9.

The Tahiti affair in August 1844 was little more than a nine days' wonder. While it lasted there was an undoubted war scare on both sides of the Channel. Guizot, however, in characteristically oblique fashion, while defending the right of the local French authorities to expel Pritchard, made an offer of financial compensation which was frigidly accepted by the British government. Early in September, when parliament was finally prorogued, the speech from the throne announced a satisfactory conclusion to the dispute. The return visit of Louis Philippe to England in October symbolised the resumption of the sorely tried *Entente*.

Nevertheless the old distrusts and fears had been revived; and there was always new material on which they could feed. In December Peel was highly critical of a proposal by Guizot, approved by Aberdeen, to appoint a mixed Anglo-French commission to consider the existing treaty right of search at sea and explore other ways of suppressing the slave trade. When however the Foreign Secretary pressed for an acceptance in order to strengthen Guizot's position at the next meeting of the French Chamber, the prime minister—feeling perhaps that he had tried his colleague far enough—gracefully yielded. 'You have a fair right to ask for confidence in your judgement,' he wrote on 4 January, 'in a matter of such great and in point of time, urgent importance, and I waive all objection to the Commission.'[1] But as fast as one matter was cleared up, another took its place. The Spanish marriage question still occupied the dynastic thoughts of the French king and the return of Christina to Spain in the spring of 1844 enabled the Neapolitan Bourbon prince, Count Trapani, to be put forward as their joint candidate for Isabella's hand. Though the queen-mother secretly assured the British government that she still favoured a Coburg suitor and had no intention of allowing Louis Philippe to dictate to her, by the end of the year there were well-founded rumours that the French government was pressing for a marriage between Isabella's younger sister and one of the king's sons. Since the queen was still physically immature, and her marriage for the time being out of the question even in the brutal dynastic politics of Spain, this new development was regarded by Peel as yet another example of French perfidy.

[1] 43064 f. 158 (see also fos. 101, 103); 40454 fos. 382-4.

If the King of the French is, as I dare say he is [he wrote to Aberdeen on 20 December], meditating an alliance between the Duc de Montpensier and the sister of the Queen of Spain, the proceeding is underhand and dishonest. It is not an actual breach of honourable engagement to this country, but considering the state of health of the queen of Spain, the effect will not probably be very different from an alliance with the Queen herself—and there is but little prospect of a *bona fide entente cordiale* between England and France if we are constantly on the look out for being cleverly overreached. *Entente Cordiale* implies at least frank and honest declarations of intentions.[1]

In fact it was not until seven months later, when the diplomatic world of Europe was alive with rumours of the projected marriage, that Guizot, honestly or otherwise, announced the French intention to Aberdeen. He added the soothing assurance that it was not an immediate event and in any case would not take place before the queen herself had married. This belated disclosure met with an understandably cool reception in London. When in September 1845 Victoria and Albert paid a second visit to the Château d'Eu, Guizot and the French king did all they could to quieten British suspicions. They said positively and explicitly that until Isabella married and had borne children, they would regard any marriage between her sister and a French prince as out of the question. The Foreign Secretary thought this was ample assurance and he was willing to leave any consideration of a French marriage until the occasion arose. With this the prime minister, more guardedly, was prepared to agree. The French government, he wrote to Aberdeen in October, could not expect any statement of the British attitude until the precise circumstances in which the marriage would take place were known.

Though Aberdeen was content with French promises, however, he was deeply distressed at the policy of his own government. At the end of 1844 he had criticised a programme for new coastal defences approved by the Duke of Wellington as 'a system which would virtually stultify our whole policy for the last three years'. This from Aberdeen was strong language. It was all the greater proof therefore of his conviction that any naval and military

[1] 43064 f. 124.

rearmament by Britain would have a politically disastrous effect on the Anglo-French *entente*. Disagreement on this fundamental issue complicated relations between Peel and Aberdeen throughout 1845. Publicly Peel continued to take any reasonable occasion to promote good feeling between England and France. At the start of the 1845 session, when the announcement of increases in the navy estimates and the parliamentary inquest on the Pritchard case exposed him to attacks from Russell and Palmerston, the prime minister spoke of the state of Anglo-French relations in unexceptionable terms and emphasised the British wish to maintain an amicable understanding with her neighbour. But behind the scenes his distrust of the French government's will or ability to maintain that friendship remained; and he would not accept Aberdeen's argument that the new British naval and coastal defence programme was either militarily unnecessary or politically inexpedient. French activity at Dunkirk, Calais and Boulogne justified in his view defensive precautions on their own side of the Channel. If they were not carried out in peacetime they could not be completed until six months or a year after the start of hostilities. Knowledge of such defensive readiness, he argued, would in fact be an additional guarantee of peace. Aberdeen in turn remained unconvinced. At the Château d'Eu Guizot had laughed at British anxieties and the Foreign Secretary returned home full of gloom at what he thought was the mistaken policy of his own country. On the night of his arrival he had a discussion with Peel on the naval programme. Neither this nor a subsequent conversation with Graham did anything to remove his apprehensions. A week later he sent Peel what was in effect a conditional resignation. He recorded his deliberate conviction that there was less reason to distrust the French government or fear the end of peace than there had been in the four previous years. But he qualified this absolute declaration of faith by admitting that in spite of everything 'it is possible that war may suddenly, and when least expected, take place. It is also certain that sooner or later this calamity must fall upon us.' But, he added, at the moment both countries were acting under the influence of panic and ignorance and he was conscious of such a change in the attitudes of leading members of the cabinet that he felt completely isolated. He suggested therefore that he should be allowed to retire quietly as though by prearrangement before any open difference of opinion on policy occurred or could be suspected.[1]

Peel refused to connive at such an arrangement. It would be improper and useless, he wrote back on 20 September, to attempt to conceal the true reason for Aberdeen's retirement. Quite apart from public considerations, he added, the loss to himself would be irreparable. He showed the correspondence only to Graham and the duke, but to Wellington he made it clear that they must try to achieve a compromise between taking reasonable military precautions and maintaining their declared policy of close and friendly relations with France. His own personal opinion, he confided to the duke, was that Louis Philippe and Guizot, in so far as it rested with them, were bent on preserving peace. He was equally convinced that the security of the country should not depend on the personal attitudes of individual rulers of France. Precautions they must take, though they should be gradual and unostentatious. With all this the duke heartily agreed, pointing out from his own long experience that a similar combination of opposed principles had governed the attitude of the victorious powers towards France in 1815.[2]

In this way the personal crisis was averted and the correspondence between the prime minister and Foreign Secretary fell back into the more familiar channels of argument over policy. The only difference was that Peel perhaps now put a conscious check on the more extreme expressions of his views in order to avoid any unnecessary ruffling of his colleague's feelings. In October Aberdeen sent for his edification a long letter from Guizot on a text which was Aberdeen's own that the old maxim 'if you want peace, prepare for war' had become obsolete in the advanced state of society and the more sophisticated relations between the Great Powers. Peel returned it without comment, but on being pressed by the Foreign Secretary for his observations, he offered some mild general reservations. He agreed, he wrote, that Guizot's policy 'as a Minister and especially as a minister of Louis Philippe is a pacific policy'. But as for the text of the sermon, 'I think it very difficult without reference to circumstances to maintain or deny the soundness of the axiom'. As far as

---

[1] 40455 f. 159; 43064 f. 337; ptly pr. *Peel*, III, 401.

[2] 43064 f. 349 (to Aberdeen, 20 Sept.), draft in 40455 f. 167; 40461 f. 235 (to Wellington), 21 Sept. and his reply (f. 237) of 22 Sept., ptly pr. *Peel*, III, 401–7.

Britain was concerned, he took leave to doubt whether the reverse of the proposition was true. There was no guarantee of peace in being defenceless. 'We ought in my opinion even in the midst of peace, to be at ease upon *vital* points.' As for France, neither Louis Philippe nor Guizot were immortal; and no reliance could be placed on their successors. 'When I reflect on the Revolutions in government that have taken place in France, on the military genius and recklessness and want of principle in the people of that country . . . I cannot feel confidence in the maintenance of peace.'[1] In this letter, more perhaps than anywhere else, Peel was expressing his fundamental views on the French problem. They were perfectly compatible, however, with a genuine desire to keep on friendly terms with France. Only a week later, when discussing the difficulties being encountered by the French in Algiers, Peel observed that the duty or at least the inclination of the British government must be to help in extricating them from their troubles. 'I think there is a *gentlemanlike* policy,' he added, 'which nations as well as individuals would do well to adopt.'[2] Not least perhaps, though he refrained from saying so, across the Channel.

To the end, therefore, the differences between Peel and Aberdeen on foreign policy remained differences of emphasis rather than of objective; and they were never allowed to grow to intolerable lengths. The one serious personal crisis of September 1845 was resolved without either man sacrificing his basic opinion; and at no time was there any withholding of views or information from each other. Though at times Peel's insistence on the full exchange of confidential papers led to slight friction between Aberdeen and Wellington in the overlapping spheres of foreign policy and defence, it was a small price to pay for the greater coherence which resulted. Peel's object was peace, but peace without abandoning British interests or foregoing the advantages of power and influence. His pacifism was tempered by a concern for national security and an ingrained scepticism for the professions of other interested parties. The *entente cordiale* with France was for him not so much a necessity of international life as a marriage of convenience from which much of temporary utility could be extracted. He was frequently irritated by the delinquencies and minor infidelities of the other partner and

---

[1] 43065 f. 43, ptly pr. *Peel*, III, 410.   [2] *ibid.* f. 73 (23 Oct. 1845).

was not prepared to suffer in silence. He believed in plain dealing, plain speaking and occasionally firm action. More important still, he looked both to the past and to the future; and in the long run would not trust Britain's safety to anything but her own resources. Less diplomatic than his Foreign Secretary, he had perhaps a more realistic concept of national interest. The end of his ministry not only left the country on more peaceful terms with its two great maritime rivals, France and the U.S.A., but saw it better prepared for war.

IV

The question of national defence which strained Aberdeen's relations with his colleagues in 1845 was one which the government was bound to face sooner or later if it remained in office. Expenditure on the armed forces during the thirties had fallen to a dangerously low level and though in the last three years of Whig administration an additional £2 million was being spent annually on the army, navy and ordnance, this had only partially repaired the neglect of previous years. The new Conservative ministry, preoccupied with domestic and financial problems, showed no great zeal in its first two years to continue even this belated and limited rearmament. In the nature of services administration any changes of policy took one or two years to be reflected in actual economies; but the total services expenditure steadily dropped after 1842 until in 1844 it was the lowest for six years. Long before this the service chiefs had been uttering warnings about the state of national defence. Hardinge, for example, in June 1843 was expressing his concern about the depleted stocks of arms and accoutrements in the country; and Haddington in the following January spoke in the cabinet of the serious under-manning of the navy.[1] While the economic situation remained uncertain, these isolated voices had little hope of receiving much attention from the prime minister. By the spring of 1844, however, Peel was sufficiently impressed with the argument for establishing defensible maritime bases along the Channel, or 'harbours of refuge' as they were called in the current vocabulary, to be ready to take the first economical step of appointing a commission of enquiry. The case for precautions of this kind rested primarily on the sudden

[1] 40474 f. 80; 44777 f. 117.

acceleration of French naval preparations and the largely unpredictable effects of steam navigation on naval strategy in home waters. It was these long-term considerations which prompted the first hesitant movement towards a Conservative armament programme rather than the war-scare with France that blew up suddenly later that year.[1]

Nevertheless, the Anglo-French crisis of that year provided a more realistic background for the arguments of the service chiefs. Haddington in July drew Peel's attention to the shortage of capital ships in commission and asked for a modest addition of 3,000 seamen at a cost of £150,000 to raise the effective total of line of battle ships from eight to twelve. It was not, as he restrainedly added, an excessive figure for the first maritime power in the world. Peel was prepared to consider the point to the extent of sending the letter to Aberdeen and authorising Haddington to raise the matter in cabinet. He warned the First Lord, however, that they would have to consider very carefully the political repercussions in France and told him to talk privately with Aberdeen beforehand. The door for discussion was now open and the next two months saw a brisk circulation of papers on the state of the navy. Peel, with the aid of that ex-Whig First Lord of the Admiralty Sir James Graham, subjected Haddington's department to a succession of critical broadsides in a manner that would have been painfully reminiscent to the staff of Dublin Castle thirty years earlier. Why, with more money and more men, were there fewer ships of the line in commission? Could they not man more ships with smaller crews? Could he please be supplied with details of ships' complements at different dates and in different categories on the enclosed form of return? How many men were carried by line of battle ships and frigates at Trafalgar, in 1813, in 1830, 1834, 1839, and 1844? What were the comparative naval strengths of France, Russia, and the U.S.A.? Above all, why with £6 million annually voted for the navy, was it only possible to send to sea seven battleships? Haddington argued back convincingly that the discrepancy between higher expenditure and fewer ships in commission was due to the development of more costly steam-vessels and the prolonged effect of the 1836–38 economies which the Whig government had concealed by reducing ships' crews even lower than

[1] 40460 fos. 161–73 (Peel to Wellington).

the official low-manning scale which they themselves had introduced. The situation reported by the Admiralty was in fact pathetic in its revelation of naval weakness. In the summer of 1844 there were only nine capital ships in commission: three as guard-ships in home waters, one in Ireland, one in the Mediterranean, one in the Pacific, one in Indian waters, and two returning home to be paid off.[1]

On the technical strength of the Admiralty's case Peel was in the end satisfied. There remained however the diplomatic opposition of the Foreign Office. Peel was prepared to sanction the immediate commissioning of one additional battleship in place of the two asked for by Haddington. But discussions with Aberdeen made it plain that the Foreign Secretary was against even this small increase. Indeed he brought forward the awkward personal argument that it would be inconsistent with the general assurances he had been giving the French government, particularly in his talks with Jarnac over the Tahiti incident. His main criticism was directed at the timing of the decision and he made a suggestion which Peel duly passed on to Haddington that large frigates should be used in distant waters like the Pacific so that all the available battleships could be concentrated at home. A further expedient which Peel was ready to approve was that the two ships about to be paid off or two others should be recommissioned, leaving the nominal total unchanged and avoiding an actual decrease.[2] Though the sailors were prevented by considerations of high policy from increasing their official front-line strength, there was much that could be done in other ways to improve the situation. At the end of 1844 the Admiralty was preparing plans for floating defences and naval impressment, and the Ordnance produced its long awaited report on harbour defences. To a prime minister deep in preparations for the next budget, the result made anything but cheerful reading. 'There are *awful* reports from a Commission on the state of defences of all the great Naval Arsenals and Dock Yards,' he wrote ironically to the Chancellor of the Exchequer on 7 December. 'One would suppose that each was at the mercy of a handful of men, and that it will require an enormous expenditure to give to each—not complete—but the most ordinary means of Defence.'[3]

---

[1] See the correspondence in 40457 fos. 170–261.   [2] *ibid.*, f. 263.
[3] 40444 f. 323.

The Admiralty plans he remitted to a technical commission, along with a recommendation from the Duke of Wellington for an enquiry into the use of armed merchant steamers in case of war. But Stanley at the same time was raising the question of the defences of Canada, and while reminding him of the need to cast a cynical eye on all professional representations from below, Peel could see that there was little hope of compensating for naval increases by reductions in the military establishments. As far as the Navy was concerned, he accepted that a great effort would have to be made in 1845. Herbert was estimating that an expenditure of £750,000 would be needed for the fleet alone, excluding the cost of the harbours of refuge and the defence works for dockyards and arsenals. To Wellington, the omnicompetent authority to whom all matters of defence and strategy were ultimately referred, the prime minister unburdened himself at Christmas on the dilemma confronting him. There were two considerations, he wrote, which must govern their actions: the state of national finances and the effect of rearmament on other powers. It was good economy as well as good policy to make timely provision for the protection of vital interests. But even if the country was richer than it was, there would have to be a selection among all the claims crowding in on them. Financially the plain fact was that after thirty years of peace the national revenue—excluding the income tax—was still insufficient for normal expenditure. Diplomatically they must neither appear to threaten other powers by hostile preparations nor appear so weak as to invite their aggression.[1]

Within these limitations there were two compelling reasons which led the government to embark on rearmament in 1845. One was the thirty years of parsimony and neglect since Waterloo which had resulted in the virtual absence of any new defences, the deterioration of what already existed, and the manifest inability of the army and navy to carry out efficiently their normal peacetime duties. The other was one which weighed particularly heavily on the duke's mind: the effect of steam power on the security of the British Isles. The latter was inevitably the more intangible problem and the naval experts themselves offered conflicting advice to the prime minister. In June 1845 Sir George Cockburn, the First Sea Lord, produced a memorandum on steam navigation and invasion which appeared

[1] Wellington (26 Dec. 1844); 40460 f. 322; ptly pr. *Peel*, III, 197.

to demonstrate that whether in number of steam ships completed or under construction, in size of ships or in engine power, the British Navy was actually superior to the French. His conclusions were promptly contradicted by Haddington on the ground, which turned out to be true, that the French Navy list which Cockburn had used in his calculations was out of date. While Haddington admitted that in steam ships Britain had an advantage which would probably continue until 1847 his point was that the French had and would continue to have superiority in home waters. The essence of the threat posed by French steam power was its ability to strike a sudden blow across the Channel. The British advantage rested in the reserves of trained men in the mercantile marine and the existence of a large steam merchant fleet which the Admiralty was already making plans to convert into an auxiliary force in time of war. But in their nature these assets would take time to realise in action. They provided no defence against a sudden *coup de main* by a reckless French government.[1] While making full use of Cockburn's figures, therefore, Peel was not disposed to pass over lightly the wider considerations pressed by Haddington. The summer of 1845 saw the prime minister involved in a mass of correspondence on naval defence, recruitment, reserves, and harbours of refuge. He not only closely supervised the progress of defence works sanctioned by parliament but raised fresh queries of his own, the defence of London, for example, against surprise attack.

He did not lack warnings from elsewhere about the responsibilities resting on the government. The million pound naval programme announced early in 1845 inevitably drew public attention to the question of national defence. At the end of the session the redoubtable Palmerston entered the controversy with a speech in the House of Commons drawing attention to the inadequate state of coastal fortifications and the danger to British security from the new element of steam navigation. Faced in public with the dilemma which he had discussed in private with the Duke of Wellington seven months earlier, Peel made a cautious and non-committal reply. He repudiated Palmerston's more pessimistic statements while refusing for obvious reasons to give details of the defences of the country. He made friendly and hopeful reference to France and deprecated any arms

[1] 40458 fos. 57–76.

race between the great powers. He agreed with the general principle advanced by Palmerston of the need to have sufficient strength to deter an aggressor but enquired ironically what had prevented the Whigs during their period in office from taking the measures which the Conservative government was now pursuing. As for the future, he said firmly, his hope was, 'that this country will never depart from that policy which has secured its safety, namely, that of being strong as a naval power, and at the same time not attempting to enter into competition with the great military powers of Europe'.[1] The Duke of Wellington, indifferent to the conflicting considerations which hampered Peel, thought his remarks were dangerously optimistic if not actually misleading. All his professional hackles raised, he determined to put on record his opinion that if war broke out, the country was incapable of defending itself. As the faithful Arbuthnot warned Peel, 'he says that steam makes a bridge for the French and not for us, they having an army of near 400,000 men and we not having one thousand for any sudden emergency'.[2] The duke's first impulse was to submit his protest to Stanley, who was Secretary for War, as well as Colonies, but in the end he transmitted it to the prime minister with the oblique remark that he should dispose of it as he thought proper. The long and detailed memorandum which he enclosed drew a forceful picture of the dangers of invasion and made the caustic observation that if only party and political prejudice would permit, the true national policy would be to raise an army of 100,000 men for the defence of the British Isles. Though he recognised that this was out of the question, he begged Peel at least to consider increasing the regimental depots to battalion strength, reorganising the militia of the three kingdoms, and enrolling a further 10,000 army pensioners.

Stung by the oddity of an official protest sent in so private a manner, and still more perhaps by the implicit criticism of his speech in the Commons, Peel returned the document at once with the advice to send it to Stanley. Next day he sent another letter on his own account to place on record the practical justification of what he had said in parliament. 'Whatever be the real state of our defences,' he began dryly, 'I presume even the strictest regard for truth does not compel

---

[1] *Speeches*, IV, 566 (30 July 1845).
[2] 40484 f. 185, ptly pr. *Peel*, III, 200.

a Minister of the Crown publicly to proclaim that the country is in a defenceless state.' In the succeeding pages of his own even longer memorandum he went closely into the details of the available information on naval and military strengths and coastal fortifications which had served as a basis for his reply to Palmerston. His account demonstrated that though there were many deficiencies, the general situation was not as bad as the alarmists had painted it, and that much was being done at that moment to improve it. The estimates for the Navy and Ordnance had been increased by £1,100,000 and Peel had authorised the Admiralty to spend another £100,000 on converting ships of the line to screw propellers and improving their armament. After years of discussion harbours of refuge had been sanctioned at Portland, Dover and Harwich. The Ordnance had been permitted to exceed the estimates if necessary to improve the defences of Portsmouth, Sheerness, Pembroke and the Thames estuary. The effective strength of the army in the United Kingdom had been increased by about 10,000, or almost a quarter, since 1841; and though this was still far below what the duke had propounded as necessary for security, there were cogent political and financial reasons which made it difficult either to enlarge further its front-line strength or to reintroduce compulsory militia service. He ended, however, by welcoming Wellington's co-operation and promised to keep him informed of all measures of military and naval defence under consideration by the various departments, and to bring his views before the queen. 'I fully admit that precautionary measures for our security ought to be taken,' ran one characteristic passage. 'The question is as to their extent, their urgency in point of time, the best mode of adopting them with reference to that which I cannot but deem a very important consideration, the great increase of our *relative* strength, and the avoiding provocation or temptation to hostility *before* we are prepared.'[1]

Wellington, who had been piqued by the return of his own document, responded more cordially to this long exposition of policy and Stanley, to whom Peel sent all the correspondence, sided firmly with the prime minister. The duke, as he admitted in his reply, had made his military calculation on the assumption of a war on home

[1] 40461 f. 168, ptly pr. *Peel*, III, 207–16. For remaining correspondence between Peel and Wellington see 40461 fos. 154–82.

soil. For the politicians, however, the overriding priority was naval security; coastal defences and the home garrison were merely adjuncts. Military needs were therefore subordinate to the prime task of keeping control of the narrow seas. As for the colonies, it was accepted by Peel and Stanley that in the event of war they would be virtually indefensible. The enormous cost of putting Britain's far-flung empire in a state of security at all points would never be tolerated by either parliament or the public. With the possible exception of Canada, however, naval supremacy would ensure the ultimate safety of all the overseas possessions. Picking a middle path between the military alarms of the duke and the diplomatic alarms of Aberdeen, the government went forward therefore with its selective and unostentatious rearmament. Before Peel left for Drayton in August he authorised Haddington to equip two more ships of the line with heavier guns and screw propellers, making six in all of this class not provided for in the naval estimates. From Staffordshire he continued to press the military authorities on the question of reservists and stocks of percussion guns and accoutrements.

During the autumn the activity of the departments responsible for defence showed no sign of slackening. Early in September Graham, Herbert and Haddington were down at Drayton discussing various matters connected with military defence both at home and in the colonies. The heightening of tension over the Oregon dispute made the protection of Canada an urgent question even though the multiplication of defence projects, as Peel wrote half-humorously to Stanley, 'will make peace so expensive that many will think actual war a more tolerable evil than such a state of burdensome and anxious suspense'.[1] It was not surprising that the Foreign Secretary after his return from the Château d'Eu in September was alarmed at the bustle in the service departments and the apparent preoccupation of most of his leading colleagues with defence questions. Oregon was only one example of the extended commitments of British power all over the world which collectively made its European position so vulnerable. The real potential enemy against which these general security preparations were being made, as was freely admitted in all the discussions, was of course France. Indeed, when a son of

[1] 40468 f. 359 (5 Sept. 1845).

Louis Philippe could publish[1] a pamphlet discussing the possibility of war with Britain, and the British ambassador in Paris could warn his government that plans for a sudden invasion of England were under serious consideration in France,[2] it was inevitable that this should be so. While Peel battled with Aberdeen's threatened resignation, the Duke of Wellington for all his seventy-six years was making a personal tour of the coastal defences in the straits of Dover. In October he sent to Peel a copy of the twenty-page report on the results of his inspection which he submitted to Murray.[3] But by then a more pressing danger had emerged to distract the prime minister's attention.

[1] *Note sur l'état des forces navales de la France* (1844), see Hall, *op. cit.*, p. 356.
[2] Graham (Graham to Stanley, 6 Sept. 1845).
[3] 40461 fos. 257–79.

THE AUTUMN OF CRISIS

Wellington's stiffness over defence policy in August 1845 had been caused to some extent by his feeling of isolation. In warning the prime minister Arbuthnot had dropped a hint that it would be an advantage if Peel could see the duke more often. In his reply a fortnight later Peel acknowledged the justice of the criticism but asked how he could be expected to find time for this during the parliamentary session. He continued rather wearily:

> The fact is that the state of public business while Parliament sits is becoming in many ways a matter of most serious concern. I defy the Minister of this country to perform properly the duties of his office —to read all he ought to read, including the whole of the foreign correspondence; to keep up the constant communication with the Queen *and the Prince*; to see all whom he ought to see; to superintend the grant of honours and the disposal of civil and ecclesiastical patronage; to write with his own hand to every person of note who chooses to write to him; to be prepared for every debate, including the most trumpery concerns; to do all these indispensable things, and also sit in the House of Commons eight hours a day for 118 days. It is impossible for me not to feel that the duties are incompatible, and above all human strength—at least above mine.[1]

For a man normally so reticent this was a significant outburst.

By the summer of 1845 Peel in fact was clearly feeling the accumulated strains of office. The letter to Arbuthnot was neither a mere excuse nor a passing spasm of distaste. In July he had told the queen that the habit of debating everything in the House of Commons and the rapid increase of business in all departments of state made it very difficult for a minister 'to perform in a satisfactory manner his

[1] 40484 f. 197 (14 Aug. 1845) ptly pr. *Peel*, III, 218.

duty towards Your Majesty and the Country'.[1] A couple of days later Gladstone, invited to dinner with his former chief, congratulated him on not only the state of public business but the fact that he seemed to be bearing up under his labours at least as well as in previous sessions. Peel made a gesture of dissent, complained of a feeling of tiredness in his head, and spoke of the intolerable strain of attendance in the House of Commons on ministers already overburdened by the enormous growth of detailed administration in their departments. He even admitted that it had occurred to him whether it might not be best for a prime minister to be in the House of Lords. This clearly would involve placing much trust and much responsibility on the Leader of the Commons. It was a system, he observed, which had worked in 1828 because the duke had been ready to accept the judgement of his subordinates in all civil matters. But the unspoken implication was that it would not in other circumstances and with other men; and he refrained from saying, what he might have said, that even under the duke it had not worked well in 1830.[2]

There were many reasons for Peel's weariness. The Maynooth session of 1845 that was just ending had seen the passage of legislation as important and controversial as any brought forward by his ministry, harried by criticism and opposition from every part of the House. If Ireland for a change was quiet, France, the U.S.A. and defence problems had more than filled the gap. Admittedly all this was no more than the familiar grind of politics of which no professional politician had a right to complain. But it took a greater toll because of Peel's prodigious outlay of energy in the previous four years. Incessant activity in a period of prolonged crisis at home and recurrent difficulty abroad had left the prime minister by 1845 a tired man. To some extent he had himself to blame. It was from choice as well as necessity that he took so much on himself. Certainly the structure of administration in itself made great demands upon him. With the promotion of Stanley, the transfer of Hardinge and Fremantle, and the resignation of Gladstone, the ministerial bench in the lower House had become uncommonly threadbare. Since the heads of the Admiralty, Foreign Office, Colonial Office, Board of Control and Board of Trade were all in the Lords, Peel had to answer in the Commons for five major departments in addition to his normal

[1] RA/A 17/134 (10 July 1845).   [2] 44777 f. 229.

duties as Leader of the House. Though the cabinet itself remained of manageable size, the distribution of offices even by mid-nineteenth-century standards had become decidedly unbalanced. Underlying this slight but perceptible deterioration since 1842 in the machinery of the administration was Peel's own besetting tendency to take too much into his own hands. Though the Chancellor of the Exchequer and the Chief Secretary were both in the House, it had been the prime minister who had introduced the 1845 budget and brought in the bill for Maynooth. Defensible as both actions might be, they were nevertheless a manifestation of something which ran all through his ministry. Behind the parliamentary scene was his constant minute supervision of the work of every department. This close scrutiny was both a strength and a weakness. It immeasurably improved and tightened the administration as a whole. But it imposed a degree of labour on the prime minister himself which, as he was beginning to perceive, was scarcely sustainable even for the lifetime of one parliament. The passion for efficiency which drove him on year after year was beginning by 1845 to defeat its own purpose.

To give a small illustration from one, and that not the most important nor the most complicated department, his correspondence with the Admiralty even in the critical winter of 1845–46 was dealing with such minor concerns as a pension for Lady Sale, the exploration of a new line of communications through Trieste, the claims of a certain Captain Warner to have invented a new long-range explosive, the disposal of trophies from the Sikh Wars, and medals for the China campaign. The fact that the prime minister had to speak for the Admiralty in the House of Commons was only a partial justification for this constant immersion in petty detail. The effect, when multiplied by every department in the government, had two damaging consequences. It helped to produce a continuous mental and physical pressure on his working life; and it reinforced his temperamental disinclination to spend much time on cultivating the goodwill of his followers. During the parliamentary session he even found it difficult to carry on regular meetings of the cabinet. Once policy had been laid down in the autumn, the cabinet met during the session mainly to deal with particular contingencies. The flow of government business was maintained by direct communication between the prime minister and the department involved. Gladstone on a subsequent occasion went so far as to say to Peel that his government had been carried on not by a cabinet but by the heads of departments in communication with him. This, if an exaggeration, had a large element of truth. It did not strike Peel however as anything but the proper way to get the business of government done. Departmentalism, an actively supervising prime minister as the main unifying force, the implicit confidence of the separate ministers in each other, was his own recipe for good administration. He compared it favourably with Melbourne's system of government by departments without any centre of unity.[1]

The cost, however, was excessive. Only a minister with Peel's physical stamina and capacity for mental concentration could have stood the strain so long; and by 1845 he was beginning to realise that he had overtaxed his resources. Yet he was temperamentally incapable of altering his own style and standards. Though he saw the advantages as well as the disadvantages of a prime minister in the House of Lords, it was not a device to which he was prepared to resort himself. There was no immediate prospect of an escape from his own political position; nor did he consciously think of an escape. But the problem remained and would have to be solved sooner or later. 'The failure of the mind', he added grimly in his letter to Arbuthnot, 'is the usual way as we know from sad experience.' From a man who remembered the suicide of Castlereagh and Romilly, Liverpool's stroke, and Dudley's lunacy, this was not an extravagant remark. In his more tired and depressed moments it was not easy to prevent such thoughts from entering his mind. There was a curious passage in a speech he had made in 1837 which had momentarily illuminated this dark side to his temperament. He had been reminding the House of Commons in a debate on the civil list pensions of 'those ministers who, fretted to premature decay by the restless agitation of political life are now in their graves'. He continued in the same sombre vein.

Consider the life of intolerable labor and care—the briefness of the career—the causes of the death of many of those who have reached the summit of precarious power in this country. Look back upon the history of this country from 1804 to 1830, a period of twenty-six years, and you will find that death has swept away nearly all the ministers, with two exceptions, who had successively presided over

[1] See the conversation with Gladstone in July 1846 (44777 f. 261).

the destinies of this country during that eventful period, and that the combined tenure of office by those two embrace. only three out of twenty-six years. Call to mind the fate of Castlereagh, of Canning, of Liverpool, whose deaths were hastened by their devotedness to the services of their country.

And he quoted a remark made to him by Lord Liverpool shortly before his stroke that no one knew what it was like to be prime minister for seventeen years and never open his post without a feeling of apprehension.[1]

Even without the larger cares of state, there was enough in the life Peel led to produce an accumulated intellectual fatigue: the mass of correspondence on every conceivable subject that piled up on his desk, the constant visitors and delegations in the morning, the long hours in the crowded stuffy House listening to speech after tedious speech until the small hours of the next day. It was an additional affliction in those circumstances that his one permanent physical disability affected his head. Since he took office his old trouble from the shooting accident in the eighteen-twenties had recurred with increasing intensity. The symptoms, as he described them once to Bunsen,[2] resembled the noise of boiling water in his ear. He was rarely free from some inconvenience and under the stress of prolonged work he suffered actual pain. His doctor, Brodie, with the bland assurance of Victorian physicians, told him that just as some overworked one part of their body, and some another, so he overworked his brain. This diagnosis offered neither comfort nor cure; and it would have taken a less imaginative man than Peel to ignore the possibility that abnormal symptoms in his head might be a forewarning of mental collapse. The trouble was probably never more than the effects of purely physical damage to one ear. But it had never been adequately diagnosed or cured. Not until he went to an ear specialist, W. Wright, in March 1846 did he receive some practical treatment which after four or five months materially relieved the symptoms and improved his hearing.[3] From the summer of 1845 to the spring of 1846 the condition was probably at its worst. Even at the end of June 1846, when discussing his position with Aberdeen

---

[1] *Speeches*, III, 456 (8 Dec. 1837).   [2] *Bunsen*, II, 40.
[3] W. Wright, *Deafness and Disease of the Ear* (1860), pp. 111–13.

and Graham, he suddenly said, putting his hand up to the side of his head, 'Ah, you do not know what I suffer here'.[1] The unexpected crisis of the Irish potato disease had to be met by a prime minister whom tiredness, anxiety and pain had made more than usually inflexible.

II

The potato blight which struck central and western Europe in 1845 first became noticeable in the late summer of that cold, cheerless year. The preliminary sign was a dark blotching of the leaves. This would gradually spread until the whole plant became limp and dead, emitting a faint odour of decomposition. When dug up the stalks below ground were often rotten and the tubers spotted with centres of decay which spread inward to infect the whole flesh. Potatoes which seemed sound on digging ended up as a stinking mass. Neither soil nor type of potato seemed to make any difference. Whole areas either escaped entirely or were completely ravaged. The disease was caused by a minute fungus of the genus *botrytis*—*phytophthora infestans*—not previously known to scientists. It took the form of a mould with fine branching filaments bearing spores which broke away when ripe and drifted in the air like wind-borne seeds to settle on other plants. The filaments had rootlike strands which grew in the cell-tissues of potato leaves and killed their growth. Once established in a plant the fungus would not only multiply but spread downward to the roots and tubers. It was for this reason that apparently healthy potatoes would subsequently rot in store or carry the disease into the next season. The species of fungus concerned was described by various European scientists, notably Dr. Montagne in Paris, as early as August 1845 and by his British friend and collaborator, the eminent mycologist the Rev. M. J. Berkeley of Northamptonshire, in the *Journal of the Horticultural Society* in January 1846. But there was wide disagreement among the experts as to the exact cause of the disease. For another generation scientists worked on the problem without coming to an accepted conclusion as to the life cycle of the fungus and therefore as to the proper prevention and cure of the potato blight itself. Not until fifty years later were there successful

[1] 44777 f. 245.

experiments with copper sulphate sprays, and it was another thirty before the meteorological conditions necessary for the spread of the disease were precisely formulated.

At the time Berkeley's fungus hypothesis was not generally accepted in England. More authoritative figures than the clerical botanist, such as Professor Lindley of London University, thought that the fungus only attacked plants already weakened and diseased by climatic conditions. The fungus was taken to be a symptom and not, as Berkeley argued, a cause. Lindley in consequence had a fatalistic attitude towards the disease even though he was one of the first to sound the alarm in the *Gardeners' Chronicle and Agricultural Gazette* of which he was the editor. The Lindley school of botanists were right, however, in the sense that the disease could only reach epidemic proportions in certain atmospheric conditions: heavy dews, moderate night temperatures, and cool days with considerable cloud and rain.[1] The late summer of 1845 was a textbook example of these conditions. It was in fact the abnormal weather accompanying the potato blight which made the atmospheric theory seem the more reasonable hypothesis. After a hard foggy winter the spring was cold and wet. Not until June did the warm weather arrive and with it the promise of good growth after the unusual moisture of the preceding months. Planting and weeding went forward rapidly and in the south the early hay crop was gathered in ideal conditions. About the middle of July, however, the rains came once more. For over a month the sky was overcast with repeated rainfalls, high winds, and low day temperatures.[2] The weather, which for some years had been the ally of the government, had turned traitor at last; and the correspondence of the leading ministers became increasingly spotted with allusions to the prospects of harvest.

Immersed though he was in problems of defence, foreign policy and Irish education, Peel by early August was already beginning to be apprehensive. From Drayton he wrote to Prince Albert on the 11th, mentioning the wretched weather of the preceding day and his fears that there would be a sharp increase in the price of wheat. For the rest of the month the frequent references in his letters to the

[1] See E. C. Large, *The Advance of the Fungi* (1940), ch. 1; P. M. Austin Bourke, 'Emergence of potato blight, 1843–46' (*Nature*, vol. 203, Aug. 1964).

[2] See the monthly weather accounts in *The Farmer's Magazine*, 1845.

weather reflected with alternate hope and pessimism the changing appearance of the sky. On 14 August he reported seeing from the railway the flattened cornfields between Watford and Coventry. Though no rain had fallen for twenty-four hours, he told Graham, the sun was still very coy and round Drayton they were cutting oats and bringing in hay simultaneously. On the 16th he added at the end of a letter to Goulburn that 'we are all looking here with surprize and pleasure at the novelty of the Sun—its first appearance on the stage this summer'.[1] It did not perform for very long. On the 19th there were ten hours of incessant rain, the worst (he told Graham) so far. Meanwhile his colleagues in other parts of the kingdom were sending in their own bulletins. From Betchworth in Surrey Goulburn wrote hopefully on 21 August that after a deluge of rain the weather at last seemed more settled and the corn crop in his neighbourhood was not yet badly damaged. Graham, still at his desk in Whitehall, reported on the 16th a dark cold day with a northerly wind though no rain, more like November than summer. Towards the end of the month there was some improvement. On 28 August Peel was able to tell the queen that the last few days, though not warm, had at least been dry. Harvest was going on rapidly round Drayton and he had hopes that there would be a sufficiently good crop to ensure that food prices would not rise too steeply during the winter. Nevertheless, though he was feeling decidedly more cheerful at the end of August than at the beginning, it was not very comfortable to have to rely on the British climate for political optimism. As so often happened it was Graham who brought into the open the underlying issue.

> I know not that the state of affairs is really sound [he wrote to Peel on 15 August] when Ministers are driven to study the Barometer with so much anxiety, but under no Law will it be found easy to feed twenty-five millions crowded together in a narrow space, when Heaven denies the blessings of abundance. The Question always returns, what is the Legislation which must aggravate or mitigate this dispensation of Providence.[2]

The return of more normal weather about a week after Graham put his gloomy question relieved the general apprehension of the

---

[1] 40445 f. 136.   [2] Graham.

ministers over the wheat harvest. But by then the damage to the potato crop had already been done. The first report of the disease in England came from the Isle of Wight. Then on 11 August Graham was warned by a wholesale potato-merchant named Parker of the extent of the disease in Kent and Essex. 'I am given to understand it is so in Holland and Belgium,' added his correspondent, 'and should it be general in this country, it will be a shocking calamity for the poor.' Graham forwarded the letter to Peel and before going off to Netherby in the middle of the month ordered further enquiries to be made. His anxieties were increased by finding the disease general in Cumberland. But the question uppermost in his mind and in Peel's was the extent to which it had affected Ireland. In England a failure of the potato crop might be a calamity; in Ireland it would be a disaster. First reports were reassuring but by the third week in September they knew that the disease had made its appearance in the sister island. Everything now depended on how far it had spread and whether the sound part of the crop would last the winter. 'I deeply regret', wrote Peel on 19 September, 'the forebodings as to the Potato Crop in Ireland. There are bad accounts of the state of it from Belgium, Holland and the adjoining districts.'[1] At the end of the month Peel warned Graham that the wheat harvest in Poland was poor and there would be none to spare for export. Already he had been asked by an Anti-Corn Law League candidate in South Lancashire to repeal the duty on maize; and an even better-known League member, the Quaker philanthropist Joseph Sturge, had pressed him for the admittance of foreign wheat duty-free by Order in Council.[2]

But the focus of attention was Ireland. By 8 October it was clear that a crisis was looming in that afflicted country. Reports from a number of branch offices of the Bank of Ireland forwarded by Goulburn indicated that while the oats and barley crops were fair, the wheat harvest would be down by a third, and that in many districts the potato harvest was threatened with complete failure.[3] Other reports from Ireland varied according to the locality and temperament of the writers. But by the middle of October even the professional reluctance of the Home Office and Dublin Castle to assume the worst was giving way. By 13 October Peel had virtually made

---

[1] Graham. [2] ibid., 28, 29 Sept. 1845. [3] 40445 f. 219.

up his mind that Ireland was facing a major disaster. While ready to concede the notorious uncertainty of all Irish reports, he foresaw already that the government would have to consider what executive and legislative measures would be necessary to relieve the now almost certain famine. Long experience of Irish conditions enabled him to dismiss at once such misguided palliatives as stoppage of distilleries and prohibition of grain exports. 'The removal of impediments to imports', he wrote to Graham, 'is the only effectual remedy.'[1] His letter crossed one from Graham written the same day which could only have confirmed his views. Taking for granted that the ports would have to be opened, the Home Secretary with his usual terrifying logic put three fundamental questions to his chief. 'Could we with propriety remit duties in November by Order in Council when Parliament might so easily be called together? Can these duties, once remitted by Act of Parliament, be ever again re-imposed? Ought they to be maintained with their present stringency, if the people of Ireland be reduced to the last extremity for want of food?' In three sentences Graham had summed up the whole crisis.[2] Two days later when sending Graham's letter to the duke, Peel warned him that they would have to give the subject their early and serious attention.[3]

On 17 October the Lord Lieutenant confirmed that the Irish potato crop had failed almost everywhere. What sound tubers remained were being hastily put on the market before they became infected. There were no stocks left from the previous year; and the price of cereals was already beginning to rise.[4] In the nature of Irish economy the real pressure on food supplies would not come until the spring. But this interval only offered time for investigation and precautionary measures; it could not be made an excuse for delay. If the seed potatoes were taken for food or carried the disease into the following year, the effects of the blight would be felt throughout 1846 and perhaps longer. If all this was true it was clear to Peel that the government would have to be prepared for immediate decisions. The first need was for authoritative confirmation of the extent of the potato failure. Next came the subordinate problem of preserving

---

[1] Graham, 13 Oct. 1845.
[2] ibid.; 40451 fos. 376–80; Peel, *Memoirs*, II, 113–16.
[3] Wellington; 40461 f. 295.   [4] 40479 f. 507.

either by chemical means or by processing into flour the surviving sound potatoes. For this scientific advice was essential. In the third week of October Lyon Playfair, the distinguished chemist, came down to Drayton at the prime minister's invitation. Buckland the geologist and Josiah Parkes the agricultural drainage expert were already there and all three men seemed to think that something could be done to prevent the worst effects of the blight by the treatment of sound or slightly affected tubers. Nevertheless, from an examination which the party made of diseased potatoes at Drayton, it was obvious that prompt action was necessary if any remedies were to be in time. At Peel's request Playfair returned to London on 19 October to carry out further experiments with Lindley the botanist and then go with him to Ireland to advise the Lord Lieutenant.[1] Meanwhile the Irish government were instructed to ask Professor Kane of Queen's College, Cork, to prepare specimens of affected potatoes in various stages of decomposition. Kane, who was the author of a recent work on the *Industrial Resources of Ireland*, had in fact already begun an investigation on behalf of the Irish Agricultural Society. By the time he was joined by the two scientists from England, it was known beyond all doubt that the blight had affected the potato crop to a greater or less extent in every part of Ireland. With any further proof of the extent of the disease rapidly becoming irrelevant, the Lord Lieutenant chiefly wanted scientific advice on how to preserve potatoes dug up in apparently healthy condition, how to prevent a perpetuation of the disease, and how to secure sound seed for the following year. Heytesbury, who was in no sense an alarmist, was by this time deeply apprehensive. The most reliable reports already suggested a deficiency of 50 per cent in the potato crop; but the continual rotting in the pits made even this estimate optimistic. Food prices were going up sharply and there was growing panic among the Irish population.

The observations of the scientists merely confirmed the pessimism of the authorities. Playfair's preliminary report suggested that the situation was even worse than the public realised and he placed so little confidence in palliative measures that his first recommendation was to explore the possibility of securing potatoes from Spain and the Mediterranean. All that Peel could oppose to this was the grim

[1] *Playfair*, pp. 98-9.

remark that 'the knowledge of the whole truth is one element of security'.[1] The final report of the two scientists on 15 November formally advised the prime minister that at the lowest estimate half the Irish potato crop was useless and that if seed potatoes were deducted, only three-eighths could be assumed at that date to be available for food. Lindley, who saw Peel and Graham on 10 November immediately after his return from Ireland, told them bluntly that not only half the crop had already gone but unless the Irish peasant took precautions (which he thought they would not do) the rest might follow. Moreover, he added with a percipience which suggested that he did not entirely reject the fungus theory, he was afraid that the taint of the disease was still in the soil and would infect even the clean seed planted the following year.[2] With reports from England and Scotland indicating a failure of the potato crop only marginally less severe than in Ireland, it was now beyond any doubt that the government faced a great crisis. Already pressure was mounting in Ireland for official action to allay panic and in the larger island the Anti-Corn Law League was demanding that the ports should be opened for the free entry of corn. The growing public apprehension of industrial distress in England and agrarian famine in Ireland during the approaching winter made further delay in executive action a serious political matter.

What seemed overwhelmingly evident to Peel and Graham as early as the beginning of October was that any effective governmental intervention to prevent famine and disease in Ireland would have catastrophic consequences for the position of the Corn Laws in England. The prime necessity was to secure a large supply of foodstuffs at a time when Europe generally was anticipating an acute shortage. Merely to admit an exotic cereal such as American maize would be not only to rely on a little-known and unpalatable food but to invite instant attack on the retention of duties on wheat and oats. To suspend temporarily the duties on all foreign cereals would be to confirm the argument of the League that the Corn Laws aggravated scarcity and their abolition would secure plenty. A suspension of the Corn Laws would be unpredictable in its duration; their ultimate reimposition only conceivable at the cost of violent public

[1] ibid., pp. 99–100; Peel, Memoirs, II, 138–40.
[2] Graham (Graham to Stanley, 11 Nov. 1845).

controversy. Already in their minds the 1842 Corn Law had been undermined to the point of being simply a political and economic expedient. If that expediency was now swallowed up by the Irish famine, the last argument for protection had been destroyed. In a remarkably outspoken letter to the Lord Lieutenant on 15 October Peel gave it as his opinion that the only real and practicable remedy for the Irish famine would be 'the removal of all impediments to the import of all kinds of human food—that is, the total and absolute repeal for ever of all duties on all articles of subsistence'.[1] It is not surprising that he wanted complete confirmation of the certainty of famine before taking action. Yet the significant fact was that he was already prepared to think in these absolute and uncompromising terms. Even before Playfair and Lindley had left for Ireland he assumed, or at any rate felt bound to act on the assumption, that the government would have to intervene. This in turn meant that parliament would have to be called together in November either to ratify emergency action by the executive or to proceed to immediate legislation.[2] Peel had been invited to Windsor Castle for a three-day visit on 27–30 October and before he left Drayton he took his first decisive step. In a circular dated 21 October he summoned a meeting of the cabinet for the 31st to consider the reports of the potato disease in the United Kingdom.[3]

On that day the ministers gathered at Whitehall Gardens where Peel was confined to his room by a sharp attack of gout. The first meeting was devoted to a presentation of all the information on the situation in Ireland that had come either to Peel or to the Home Office. Next day, Saturday, 1 November, they reassembled at the same place to hear the prime minister read a long memorandum. He took as his starting point the clear evidence of a grave deficiency of food, not only in Ireland but in parts of England and Scotland, which might prove worse than anticipated and would in any case begin to take effect at the very start of the new year. He then discussed what the government ought to do. His first proposal was the appointment of a Commission under the Lord Lieutenant to provide employment by means of public works and loans and in the last resort to give direct relief where other measures were inapplicable

[1] Peel, Memoirs, II, 121.   [2] Cf. his letter to Goulburn of 18 Oct. (40445 f. 228).
[3] Copy in Wellington.

or impossible to organise in time. But, he went on, the provision of substantial public funds for such a purpose would entail a meeting of parliament and if this took place, the wider question would at once be raised.

> Can we vote public money for the sustenance of any considerable portion of the people on account of actual or apprehended scarcity, and maintain in full operation the existing restrictions on the free import of grain? I am bound to say my impression is that we cannot.

Past precedents in similar circumstances, the present example of Russia, Holland and Belgium, all pointed to the suspension of the Corn Laws as an inevitable consequence. The mere summoning of parliament would reveal the extent of the crisis. He could not disguise from himself that 'it will be dangerous for the Government, having assembled Parliament, to resist with all its energies any material modification of the Corn Law'. If the Corn Laws were to be suspended, was it to be done by Order in Council or by legislation? Executive action had the advantage of speed but required instant decision by the cabinet and proof that delay would have been dangerous. To submit the issue to parliament would be more constitutional and allow further time for reflection. He suggested therefore that they should meet again in a week's time on the general assumption that parliament would be summoned not later than 27 November, the date to which it had been formally prorogued. But, he warned his colleagues, it would be necessary for them to decide, before calling parliament, on their final policy. 'We must make our choice between determined maintenance, modification, and suspension of the existing Corn Law.'[1]

What Peel wanted to do was clear enough; but it was not the general wish of the cabinet. In the discussion which followed there was no agreement either on the course to be followed or even on whether it was necessary to undertake any extraordinary measures. All they could decide was to authorise the Lord Lieutenant to make preliminary arrangements on the lines of Peel's proposals and to meet again on 6 November. To some at least it seemed as though Peel had embarked on a course that was both disastrous and unjustifiable. Not only did they feel that it was not for a Conservative

---

[1] Peel, *Memoirs*, II, 141 et seq.

ministry to tamper any further with the Corn Laws but they could not bring themselves to believe that the crisis was bad enough to make it inevitable. Stanley in particular was so perturbed at the gulf that had suddenly opened up between the prime minister and most of his colleagues that he went to the trouble of writing a formal memorandum. In a covering note to Peel he said it was difficult for him to express the regret he felt at differing so widely from Peel and Graham on the necessity for proposing to parliament a repeal of the Corn Laws. But, he added bluntly, if Peel persisted in his present views, the issue would break up the government. Peel acknowledged the communication in friendly terms but refrained from any comment except to observe that he had not proposed to the cabinet that they should recommend to parliament the repeal of the Corn Laws and still less that they should advise the queen that the Corn Laws should be abandoned.[1] This was factually correct; Peel had said no more in cabinet than that after suspension there would have to be a new law involving a considerable reduction in the existing scale.[2] But Stanley clearly based his words on the unanimous feeling in the cabinet that to open the ports even for a limited period for the free entry of grain would in effect be to repeal the Corn Laws.

The same issue sufficiently weighed on Lord Lincoln's mind to make him, though with the modesty of a junior minister, also put his views in writing. In a letter of 5 November he argued that since suspension, in the opinion of the cabinet, effectively meant repeal, it would be wrong to do it by Order in Council. Parliament could be summoned at two weeks' notice and no real famine conditions yet existed. To meet parliament, however, and propose either the modification or the repeal of the Corn Laws would be to abandon a measure of their own devising at the first real trial of its soundness. Even worse, it would be to repudiate a principle 'which we cannot deny was mainly instrumental in placing us in power'. The alternative of advising the crown that the Corn Laws should be repealed, and resigning in order to allow another set of ministers to put that advice into effect, would on the other hand be mean and cowardly.

---

[1] Peel, *Memoirs*, II, pp. 160–3.
[2] Cf. Herbert's memorandum of Dec. 1845 (*Herbert*, I, 50); Graham to Aberdeen, 20 Dec. 1851 (Graham).

What he suggested as a way out of this intolerable dilemma was to leave the Corn Laws intact during the 1846 sessions (except for the admittance of American maize and possibly Australian wheat), announce in 1847 Peel's intention to get rid of protection either immediately or gradually, and fight the general election on that issue. Whether they won or lost, forfeited or retained the loyalty of their followers, they would at least have done their duty by the queen, given the country the chance to consider their proposals, avoided the imputation of betraying the party, kept their character as public men, and maintained the decencies of constitutional government.[1]

It was a long, well-intentioned, and emotional letter from a man who admired Peel and himself disbelieved that the Corn Laws could be continued much longer. But the advice it proffered was muddled and unrealistic. What Lincoln was in fact asking Peel to do was to defend the Corn Laws for a year after it had been decided to abandon them. Whether the decision was taken by the cabinet collectively or the prime minister personally, it seemed to Peel an impossible course. In any case Lincoln had offered no solution for the immediate problem. A partial lifting of duties on certain food imports would start a fierce public controversy over protection and free trade which a general election would transform into a bitter class conflict. As for personal consistency and party loyalty, this for Peel was a matter of private judgement. In his memorandum he had deliberately confined himself to the abstract issue before the cabinet. He had merely added one brief sentence to indicate that he was fully aware of the political implications for themselves as party men and authors of the existing corn laws. The prime consideration for Peel on that aspect of the question was his duty as minister of the crown; all other interests were subordinate. In the long run he was prepared to argue that party ethics and constitutional government would best be served if public men did what they honestly thought right in the national interest. It was a quixotic, very Peelish doctrine. The principle it enshrines is impeccable; in practice the consequences work out more imperfectly. Few party politicians can work within such simple terms of reference. For them the approval of subsequent generations is an insubstantial reward; posterity has no votes at the ballot-box

[1] 40481 f. 322; cf. the refs. in Peel, *Memoirs*, II, 163; *Peel*, III, 231.

or in the lobbies. It may be observed on the other hand that for a determined and self-willed man the appeal to posterity has one decided advantage; the verdict comes too late to affect his action.

The letters from Stanley and Lincoln at least illustrated the depths of division among his colleagues. On 5 November for the first time Peel advised the queen of the probability of disagreement in the cabinet over the Irish crisis. The meeting next day more than justified his warning. The specific proposals he put before his colleagues were to remit the duty on bonded grain and open the ports to all foreign grain at a reduced rate; to meet parliament on 27 November and ask for a ratification of that action; and to announce their intention of introducing after Christmas a modified corn bill. The modifications would include the admission at a nominal duty of maize and colonial corn, and changes in the existing duties on other cereals within the general framework of the 1842 Act. When he asked his colleagues one by one for their opinion Lincoln, Wellington and two more in succession signified their dissent. This was discouraging and Peel turned abruptly to Aberdeen, on whose free trade views he knew he could rely.[1] But when all the heads were counted only three of his colleagues, Aberdeen, Graham and Herbert, were found to support him. The rest either objected in principle to his plan or thought that its necessity had not yet been proved. The peers on the whole seemed to Peel ready to take action if they could be convinced of the urgency of the crisis; and though Wellington had been unable through deafness to follow all the discussions, he had pronounced in favour of getting more information before taking any final decision.[2] In view of this Peel was prepared to give his colleagues time to reconsider the matter while fresh evidence accumulated on what Sidney Herbert was already calling 'the famine question'.[3] The Playfair–Lindley team had not yet put in their final report and public opinion was still not fully roused to a knowledge of the facts. It was agreed therefore that the cabinet should reassemble at the end of the month. If support was still not forthcoming from his colleagues Peel had made up his mind to resign. In any case he

---

[1] Related by Aberdeen to Gladstone in 1849 (44777 f. 298).
[2] Graham (Peel to Graham, 7 Nov. 1845).
[3] In a letter to Graham, 8 Nov. 1845 (Graham).

was determined not to attempt a settlement of the corn issue unless there was a practical assurance of success.

Meanwhile he continued to take what steps were open to him to meet the inevitable crisis in Ireland. Fremantle had been authorised on 2 November to draw as much as he liked on public funds to buy fuel and chemicals for drying and preserving potatoes in accordance with the recommendations of the Playfair Commission and was told to make full use of the Irish Constabulary for that purpose.[1] Next day Graham instructed the Lord Lieutenant to proceed with the setting up of an emergency relief organisation for the distribution of food, provision of employment, and control of the markets. For this he was to mobilise all the available administrative machinery, police, coastguards, Board of Works and Poor Law Unions.[2] On their own side of the water the ministers moved with equal promptitude. Enquiries about potato supplies had already been set on foot among the British consular authorities in the Mediterranean; the Admiralty was instructed to buy oats privately at the ports; and consideration was given to the possibility of obtaining wheat from Odessa and Danzig. More important still, after consultation with Goulburn and Graham, a large order was placed through the house of Baring for the purchase of maize and meal in the U.S.A. Even without further European supplies, the £100,000 authorised by Peel for the Baring transaction was calculated by Goulburn to provide enough food for one million persons for forty days.[3] It was an impressive contribution; but it had to be set against Kane's estimate that the number of Irish who depended exclusively upon the potato crop was no less than four million and the probability that the famine would last not days but months.

The Baring purchase was carried out with great speed and secrecy. Nothing came out in the press until the food ships arrived in Cork at the end of January. Acting with the same caution the remaining ministers in London agreed on 19 November to continue the prorogation of parliament until 16 December. This would leave open until the middle of that month the decision whether parliament was to meet as usual in February or in early January. But while the ministers were still preparing for a decision, public pressure was

[1] *Peel*, III, 227–8.   [2] Graham.
[3] 40445 fos. 258–66.

steadily mounting. The prospect of a poor wheat harvest had already given a fresh stimulus to the League propagandists in October. The knowledge that in addition the potato crop had failed all over the British Isles made them redouble their exertions the following month. The intense public interest and the attitude of some of the leading newspapers, including *The Times*, were already making it a national rather than a partisan question. The meetings of the cabinet in early November had provoked widespread speculation, not all of which was wide of the mark. In the anticlimax of disappointment which followed petitions and remonstrances began to flow in from all over the kingdom, asking for the ports to be opened. To avoid a fresh outburst of public excitement arrangements were made for the full cabinet to meet unobtrusively on 25 November not in Whitehall Gardens but in Peel's official room in Downing Street.[1] Three days beforehand, however, the threatened Irish famine was turned into a political issue by Lord John Russell. Abnormally sensitive to currents of public opinion, with characteristic impulsiveness he published from Edinburgh on 22 November his famous *Letter to the Electors of the City of London* without consulting his colleagues or indeed without much forethought for his own position. Referring to the rumours which surrounded the meetings of the cabinet earlier in the month, followed by apparent total inaction, he called on the public to consider how they could avert or mitigate the approaching calamity. 'The Government appear to be waiting for some excuse to give up the present Corn Law. Let the people by petition, by address, by remonstrance, afford them the excuse they seek.' For himself he announced his final abandonment of the principle of a fixed duty and his conversion to total repeal. In effect the *de facto* leader of the opposition had gone over to the party of the League and placed himself, as far as words could do so, at the head of a country-wide agitation. No stronger confirmation could have been given for Peel's argument that executive action to meet the crisis in Ireland would inevitably bring into question the future of the Corn Laws in England. Even before the famine had actually started, the cabinet had been overtaken by its political consequences. It was a deeply troubled group of politicians who gathered in Downing Street on 25 November. Since they last met the Playfair commission had sent in its

[1] Graham (Graham to Stanley, 19 Nov. 1845).

final report. But if there had been a chance that this document would alter their opinion, it had been destroyed by Lord John Russell. Public advice from political opponents is rarely acceptable or accepted. Peel undoubtedly felt that the *Edinburgh Letter* had weakened his own position. Executive action, which at the beginning of the month would have seemed a deliberate and timely precaution by the government, would now be interpreted as being forced on the cabinet by public agitation headed by the leader of the Whigs. But it was too late to alter course.

They began soberly with an examination of the detailed instructions to the Commission already appointed to deal with famine relief and the danger of epidemic fever in the wake of famine. Approval of the instructions was a tacit recognition of the probability of a great social disaster and Peel wasted no time in pressing the point home on his reluctant colleagues. 'I cannot consent', he observed in a paper which he read out to them on 26 November, 'to the issue of these instructions, and undertake at the same time to maintain the existing Corn Law.' The fresh information at their disposal would justify them in suspending the law but condemn them if they took no action. The issue of the instructions to the Lord Lieutenant would prove that they themselves were convinced of the existence of a crisis serious enough to warrant suspension. He was therefore prepared either to suspend by Order in Council or to summon parliament and recommend suspension in a speech from the throne. But this in turn would compel a review of the whole question of agricultural protection.

> I firmly believe that it would be better for the country that that review should be undertaken by others. Under ordinary circumstances I should advise that it should be so undertaken; but I look now to the immediate emergency, and to the duties it imposes on a Minister. I am ready to take the responsibility of meeting that emergency, if the opinion of my colleagues as to the extent of the evil and the nature of the remedy concur with mine.[1]

It was a brief document, merely setting out the dilemma confronting them. But it was a dilemma which his colleagues still found it impossible to resolve. All the old differences on the fundamental

[1] Peel, *Memoirs*, II, 184.

issue remained. The lapse of time had merely altered the more mechanical aspects of the situation. There was a general recognition that to open the ports by executive action after so long a delay was now no longer advisable. Any decision would have to be taken by the legislature. It was provisionally agreed therefore to call parliament together about 8 January. In that case the queen would have to be advised not later than 19 December and there was a strong feeling that she would first have to be warned that there was a hopeless division of opinion among ministers over the Corn Laws.

For Peel this was to admit defeat before the parliamentary battle started. As a last resort therefore he put down on paper all the detailed arguments that might be lost sight of in a general discussion and circulated it as a cabinet memorandum three days later. In this, the longest of five memoranda which he placed before the cabinet during that critical autumn, he still ignored all considerations of party policy or cabinet consistency. Instead he concentrated on the facts of the situation: the probability that fresh sources of food would have to be found for three million people in the United Kingdom; the general shortage in Europe; the measures adopted by several other countries to encourage the entry of foreign foodstuffs and prohibit the export of their own; the invariable decision of parliament in former times of scarcity to permit duty-free imports; and the need to make arrangements to meet a crisis which might come on them suddenly in the new year. From all this he extracted his conclusions. Delay in taking precautions would endanger their ability to provide food when the demand arose but would still not allow them to escape political controversy when parliament met. If they did not make proposals, their opponents would. Could they resist those proposals when they knew they might become inevitable a few weeks later? Could they hope to carry a vote of half or a quarter of a million to feed Ireland while leaving the Corn Laws intact? Could the government enter the food market and force up the price of grain by their own action to the disadvantage of the public at large? Time was pressing and some decision had to be reached. Once more he put his inexorable question. Were they to maintain, modify or suspend the existing Corn Laws?[1]

[1] Peel, Memoirs, II, 185–94.

Forced now to a decision which seemed to guarantee either the immediate or ultimate destruction of the ministry, four of his colleagues also placed their views on record. Ripon, taking up some remarks by Peel in cabinet on the possibility of finding compensation for agriculture if protection were removed, thought that there should be more discussion of this point before confessing to the queen that they were unable to agree. The Duke of Wellington sent in a terse memorandum announcing his continued belief in the benefits of the Corn Laws and pointing out that the problem in Ireland would arise not so much from the shortage of food as from the sheer inability to buy food among the mass of Irish peasants living on a subsistence economy. He was against the suspension of Corn Laws until an absolute necessity was proved; but if Peel thought the national interest required it, he would recommend the cabinet to agree. 'A good government for the country is more important than the Corn Laws or any other consideration; and as long as Sir Robert Peel possesses the confidence of the Queen and of the public, and he has strength to perform the duties, his administration of the Government must be supported.' Wharncliffe like Ripon pleaded for delay before admitting an irreconcilable split in the government. He was prepared to wait until after Christmas before taking any irretrievable step. Any resignation of the government before then, he thought, would be regarded as a betrayal of the Conservative Party and as a victory for Russell and the Anti-Corn Law League. Further deliberation on the other hand might lead to agreement on some modification of the Corn Laws which would preserve the principle of protection and be accompanied by compensation to agriculture. With him as with Ripon, however, Peel declined to go into arguments as to future policy. What they had to do, he briefly replied, was to make up their minds individually on the one issue of suspension of duties on foreign corn.

The fourth of his correspondents was the man he had known longer and more closely than anyone else in public life, Henry Goulburn. What troubled him most was the personal and political consequences of what Peel proposed to do. 'Abandonment of your former opinions now would, I think, prejudice your and our characters as public men, and would be fraught with fatal results to the country's best interests.' If the party broke up through lack of confidence in its leader, 'and I cannot but think that an abandonment of the Corn Law would produce that result', the last barrier against the revolutionary effect of the Reform Bill would collapse and he saw nothing left but 'the exasperation of class animosities, a struggle for pre-eminence, and the ultimate triumph of unrestrained democracy'. He did not think that the existing crisis provided any justification for risking these consequences. Repeal of the Corn Laws would not relieve the Irish famine. It could not affect that year's supply or bring in any additional grain that could not reach the country under the law as it stood. Domestic prices were not rising as fast as in previous times of scarcity. To abandon the Corn Laws now would be to surrender to clamour what had been denied to reason. It would convince the public that the government had never seriously intended to maintain them. To reinforce his more human arguments he enclosed a memorandum stating half-heartedly the familiar case for some agricultural protection because of the special burdens on the land and pointing out that only if protection was removed gradually could any adequate scheme of compensation be devised.[1]

Goulburn's was the most, Wellington's the least personal of these four letters. What was unmistakable in all of them was their respect for Peel; their desire that his ministry should continue; and their regret at the course he seemed intent on following. Emotionally if not intellectually he still commanded their allegiance. But what they did not do was to provide a simple answer to Peel's simple question. In a sense, as several of his colleagues had shown, that question had been too simple. If suspension implied a review of the existing law, what kind of review was that to be? The consequential question had to be answered before the initial decision could be taken. It was an achievement for Peel perhaps that with all their doubts they had arrived at a point where an actual revision of the Corn Laws could even be discussed. By merely continuing to talk about the problem the cabinet had already gone further than the great majority of them had seemed prepared to go at the beginning of November. But the debate could not go on indefinitely. The prime minister therefore advanced one more step in the task of converting his colleagues. In a fifth memorandum read to the cabinet on 2 December he placed before them his views on the future of protection in

[1] Peel, *Memoirs*, II, pp. 194 et seq.

terms more explicit than any he had employed before. The argument over personal consistency, which had been brought up time and again by his colleagues, had at last had enough effect to make him begin with a defence of his own record. He had always, he reminded them, refused to pledge himself against any alteration in the 1842 Act. On two occasions during the previous session he had agreed in the House of Commons that agriculture could not be exempt from principles applied to other economic interests. His only reservation had been that caution must be exercised in dealing with such an established and important national interest. Quite independently of the Irish famine, he believed that the right course was gradually to remove agricultural protection. If they were now, because of the famine, to suspend the law, it would be necessary to state their ultimate policy on the law itself. Suspension merely compelled an immediate consideration of a problem which might otherwise have been postponed to a later session. It was difficult at that stage to be armed with all the details of a new corn bill but it would be possible on certain points to come to a decision in principle. He would refuse, for example, to admit American maize and colonial corn free of duty while retaining the existing tariff on oats, barley and wheat from other countries; nor would he introduce any bill guaranteeing permanent protection for British agriculture. The broad choice therefore was between the 1842 Act and a new law embodying a progressive abolition of all protective duties. What he was prepared to do, if the cabinet consented, was to introduce a corn law with a new scale of duties. At the pivot point of 51s a quarter there would be a duty of 8s which would decrease or increase proportionally with rising or falling prices for wheat so that at 58s the duty would be only one shilling. The following year the basic duty would be reduced to 7s and so annually until all duties eventually expired. In effect therefore his proposal was for a gradual reduction of duties on foreign corn until they were extinguished completely within a period of eight years.

In the discussion which followed it seemed to Peel that there was a real chance that his plan would receive the support, however reluctant, of a united cabinet. But no decision was taken that day and when they reassembled on Thursday, 4 December, Stanley and Buccleuch said that on reflection they would prefer to retire from office rather than associate themselves with the new plan. By a singular irony of inspired journalism *The Times* that same morning had come out with a report that the cabinet had unanimously agreed on a total and immediate repeal of the Corn Laws. If, as is probable, the statement was based on a private hint from Aberdeen, anxious to influence American opinion over the Oregon question, it could hardly have been more miscalculated. If it did not precipitate the actual decision of Stanley and Buccleuch, it helped like the *Edinburgh Letter* to worsen the general position of the government. With public speculation on the government's intentions now raised to fever-pitch, almost any action would appear forced on them by external pressure, no action at all like cowardice. The long interval of waiting in November and the inability of the cabinet to agree in December had virtually deprived them of all initiative. To Peel it seemed that they had reached a dead end. Faced with the certain resignation of two of his colleagues, conscious that most of the others had a long and painful struggle before they declared their readiness to support him, he at last recognised defeat. Over the question ⌐his party following in parliament he had not been greatly concerned except for its effect, as the duke had reminded him in his memorandum of 30 November, on the ability of the government to pass their measure. But it was precisely the practical aspect which was now dominant. Success would be difficult enough even with a united cabinet behind him; without it he judged the task impossible. He still believed that the public interest required the ultimate repeal of the Corn Laws; but he also thought that to attempt it and fail would be a disaster. All that was left for him to do therefore was to hand over responsibility to the man who had already publicly announced that the Corn Laws must be repealed.[1] The only remaining question was whether it was better for the depleted ministry to meet parliament and make their proposals, resigning if defeated; or to resign immediately, leaving the field clear for their successors. At the final meeting of the cabinet on 5 December all the House of Common members gave it as their opinion that the government after the loss of Stanley and Buccleuch would be unable to carry its bill. All but Granville Somerset thought that the failure would make matters

[1] The cabinet discussions of Nov.–Dec. are fully documented in Peel, *Memoir* II, Pt. III, supplemented by *Peel*, III, ch. VIII.

worse. Peel said that this was his opinion also and he should feel it his duty therefore to resign.

It was failure; but it had been a near thing and he had come remarkably close to success. It was a sign of his dominance as prime minister that starting with only three on his side in a cabinet of fourteen he had ended with only two against him. Time, the accumulation of evidence, the pressure of public opinion, had no doubt assisted him. The intellectual strength of his patient persistent reasoning had done the rest. It was not easy, then or later, to find flaws in his comprehensive and able advocacy. Certainly none of his colleagues could show comparable skill in the marshalling of their counter-arguments. The two great considerations which sustained their opposition were first that there was no definitive proof that famine would occur in Ireland, and second that it would be politically indecent for a Conservative government to abolish protection for agriculture. One of these was capable of practical verification; the other was a question of moral judgement. Neither was an argument for maintaining the Corn Law on its own merits. One of the most revealing aspects of the cabinet discussions was the comparative lack of any robust belief in the Corn Laws themselves. The debate seemed to revolve for the most part around the time, mode, justification and responsibility of abandoning them. Even in the minds of those ministers who were reluctant to tamper with the 1842 Act it was evident that the principle of protection had worn dangerously thin. The fact that the cabinet were in general agreement that opening the ports for a limited period virtually implied ultimate repeal was the clearest practical demonstration of the state to which protectionism had been reduced in the minds of the Conservative ministers themselves. If the 1842 Act could not survive temporary suspension, it was already half-dead. What Peel had overcome was not so much intellectual conviction as the more imponderable factors of inertia, scruple, uncertainty, concern for past consistency, and fears for future consequences. At the same time what must always remain doubtful in retrospect is the extent to which Peel's arguments represented not the successive steps by which he himself slowly moved towards his final position but a skilful dialectic by which he sought to bring his colleagues to the conclusion at which he had already arrived.

The distinction is perhaps theoretical. In the end it would have been difficult even for Peel to have made any clear separation between them. Yet what was striking, and in the end possibly decisive in the history of the crisis, was the spontaneous reaction of Peel and Graham to the news from Ireland. As soon as they realised, about the middle of October, that the failure of the potato crop would entail government intervention, they took it for granted that the repeal of the Corn Laws must follow. So instantaneous a conviction could only have been possible in men who had long ago ceased to believe in either the desirability or value of the Corn Laws. Certainly Peel had arrived at this state of disbelief by an intellectual process. In the session of 1846 he explained repeatedly and at length the reason which had led him to abandon his earlier view that there should be some protection for corn. A further concise explanation was given in his *Letter to the Electors of Tamworth* at the time of the general election of 1847 which he subsequently inserted in his *Memoirs* as the best available account of the considerations which had converted him to repeal. All retrospective versions of critical events must be treated with caution, particularly from politicians. Yet there seems little cause to doubt that these, as far as they go, offer a reasonable account of the way in which Peel's mind had been moving. Certainly there is an essential consistency running through them; the differences are only those of detail and emphasis. In the first place the free trade policy of 1842 had resulted in a reduction in the cost of living and an increase in national consumption. Secondly there was practical proof that, contrary to the doctrine of many economists, the level of wages did not vary with the price of bread. Successive periods of good and bad harvests had demonstrated that there was no such automatic relationship. On the contrary cheap food and rising consumption went hand in hand with full employment, social stability and a lower crime rate. In these circumstances the argument for applying free trade policy to agriculture became irresistible. The reduction in duties on foreign meat and cattle in 1842 had not been followed by the disastrous consequences prophesied by the critics. There was no reason to assume that corn differed in kind from any other article of production. The key to successful farming as industry generally was to be found in more scientific methods, lower costs, greater productivity and an expanding market. To treat agriculture as a special case merely created political problems. Its deepening isolation as the only important industry still enjoying high protection made it a target not only of economic criticism but of social hostility. A growing weight of public opinion had come to agree with the views of the Anti-Corn Law League. The landed aristocracy were increasingly compromised by the unpopularity of the Corn Laws and the whole governing structure of the country weakened in consequence. Fundamentally, however, Peel's conversion to free trade in corn was a matter of conviction rather than an act of concession. In this there was a profound contrast between 1845 and 1829. He had advised Catholic emancipation as a necessary expedient; he advocated the repeal of the Corn Laws as a desirable principle.

Yet it is obvious that if these were the arguments which had led him to change his mind in the course of his 1841–45 ministry, they had operated not as a single irrefutable demonstration but by a process of continuous erosion. By their nature the validity of some of these arguments could only be proved in the years after 1842. If the success of the 1842 budget was a factor in his calculations, for example, it was not seen to be a success until 1844. Yet well before that date Peel's belief in the case for protective corn laws had virtually disappeared. The critical year had been perhaps not 1844 but 1842. In the thirties he had defended the principle of protection, as distinct from the details of the 1828 Corn Law, on grounds of expediency. In the winter of 1841–42 his critical judgement had suggested a lower tariff than his political caution admitted. After that the atmosphere rapidly changed. Graham's famous remark at the end of 1842, in view of his close relationship with Peel, could hardly have failed to reflect previous discussions between the two men. A few months later, in May 1843, Peel expressed his doubts to Gladstone whether he could in future undertake the defence of the Corn Laws.[1] At the start of the 1844 session he said in cabinet that he saw no choice between the 1842 Act and repeal; and in private that alternative began to take shape in his mind as a practical necessity. Even before the potato blight struck Ireland, it is clear (unless his statement to the prince in December 1845 and his more guarded remarks to the Commons in the debate on the Address in January

[1] *Gladstone*, I, 192.

1846 are to be disbelieved) that Peel had made up his mind to announce his change of policy before the end of the existing parliament and seek support for it in the following general election. Yet if 1842 was the turning point, it is difficult to escape the further inference that it was the state of the country during that year which was the decisive influence on Peel's mind. If so, not Ireland but the Condition of England Question was the underlying motive for the repeal of the Corn Laws. In any case a conviction that the Corn Laws were indefensible made it impossible for him to approach the question of the Irish famine with impartiality. This is not to say that for Peel the famine was merely a pretext. But it did mean that his mind was predisposed to a particular course of action. His arguments may have been right. It is difficult to show that they were wrong. But there was no sign that he considered any method of dealing with the Irish famine that did not involve the ultimate repeal of the Corn Laws. As far as he was concerned by 1845 the Corn Laws were living on borrowed time; the Irish famine merely called in the mortgage.

III

As early as 5 November the queen had been told of disagreements in the cabinet over measures to deal with the potato disease. Victoria nothing if not partisan, wrote strong phrases about the need for unity and invited Peel down to Windsor immediately afterwards. When he arrived, however, the prime minister talked about the general seriousness of the situation rather than specific issues or individual dissentients.[1] Even so the postponement of a decision until further information was available took away the appearance of any real crisis. No great alarm therefore was felt at the court until Peel wrote again on 27 November to warn the queen in more stringent terms that there might be serious differences of opinion in the cabinet. With all the speculation raging in the press it was not difficult for the royal couple at Osborne to guess the root of discord. At a moment of impending calamity, Victoria replied with vigour it was essential that the government should remain strong and united.

[1] Graham (Peel to Graham, 7 Nov. 1845).

The Queen thinks the time is come when a removal of the restrictions upon the importation of food cannot be successfully resisted. Should this be Sir Robert's own opinion, the Queen very much hopes that none of his colleagues will prevent him from doing what is *right* to do.[1]

But the wishes of the sovereign on issues of high policy were now only among the *marginalia* of politics. On 6 December, preceded by a note which threw Victoria and Albert into a state of consternation, Peel arrived at Osborne to offer his resignation. To his two young and sympathetic listeners he related the course of events in the cabinet since the beginning of November and spoke of the growing public concern, the intensification of League agitation, the violent anti-Corn Law attitude of that infallible barometer of public opinion *The Times*, and the culminating blow of Russell's *Edinburgh Letter*. He was obviously much moved and told them that it was one of the most painful moments of his life to have to separate himself from them. But it had become overwhelmingly necessary, he said, and indeed he had probably delayed too long. He should have gone when first left in a minority in his own cabinet. Now the country had made its own decision and Lord John Russell had placed himself at the head of public opinion as a result of his dexterity and the cabinet's lack of unanimity. There was a tinge of resentment underlying his account. He did not take kindly to failure; he had no great liking for Russell; and he was unaccustomed to being outmanœuvred by the leader of the opposition. Mention of Russell, however, brought up the next question. Could not Sir Robert, asked Albert, still carry on the government in view of his large party majority. The prime minister returned an emphatic negative. Buccleuch would carry half Scotland; Stanley would head the protectionist peers; and there would be immediate resignations from the Household. In the Commons Tory agriculturalists would turn on him in a rage; Whigs and radicals would deny his right to carry what they would now consider as their measure. It was better, he concluded, that he should go out while nobody was committed, no violent public declarations made, no factions formed.

In the subsequent discussion there was quick agreement that Russell should be asked to form a government. The only conceivable

[1] *VL*, II, 47.

alternative, a protectionist ministry under Stanley, would at once provoke a class conflict. It was essential, Peel stressed, to prevent a clash between the House of Lords and the House of Commons on such an issue. The aristocracy must be disassociated from the cause of protection. 'I am afraid', he told them, 'of other interests getting damaged in this struggle about the Corn Laws; already the system of promotion in the Army, the Game Laws, the Church, are getting attacked with the aid of the League.' When Victoria asked how Russell could govern when his party was in a minority, Peel admitted that he would have difficulties which perhaps, he added caustically, he did not envisage when he wrote his *Edinburgh Letter*:

> But I will support him. I feel it my duty to your Majesty not to leave you without a Government. Even if Lord John goes to the full extent of his declaration in that letter (which I think goes too far) I will support him in Parliament and use all my influence with the House of Lords to prevent their impeding his progress.

He undertook to put this promise in writing and at the end referred once more in a rush of emotion to his regret at resignation. It was not loss of power, 'for I hate power'; nor of office, which was nothing but a plague; but, recorded Albert, 'the breaking up of those relations in which he stood to the Queen and me, and the loss of our society'.[1] Having carried out his last constitutional duty of assisting Victoria to compose two letters, one a conciliatory message of information to Melbourne, and the other a summons to Russell, he returned to London still prime minister but only until the queen had appointed his successor.

From there on 8 December he wrote the queen a formal letter[2] to be shown to Russell, briefly detailing the reasons for his resignation and stating that his wish had been to recommend a revision of the Corn Laws which should contain a provision for their 'gradual and ultimate removal'. He would, he added, be prepared 'to support in a private capacity measures which may be in general conformity with those which he advised as Minister. It would be unbecoming in Sir Robert Peel to make any reference to the details of such measures.'

---

[1] Memorandum by Prince Albert (RA/C 44/13) written in German except for the quotations from Peel's remarks. Pr. in translation in *VL*, II, 48–51.

[2] Dated 10 Dec. in *VL*, II, 52 but the date is clearly 8 Dec. (see 40440 f. 374); cf. *Memoirs*, II, 223. It was possibly not sent off until after the Council on the 10th.

Nevertheless, the principles on which he had been ready to recommend a review of the Corn Laws were in general accord with those stated in Russell's *Edinburgh Letter*. He had wished to accompany repeal with compensation to agriculture and such other provisions as—and he quoted from Russell's *Letter*—'caution and even scrupulous forbearance may suggest'. He would therefore 'support measures founded on that general principle, and will exercise any influence he may possess to promote their success'. He would in addition take full public responsibility for the additional expenditure on the navy and army should the 1846 estimates be approved by his successor. On 10 December the cabinet went down to Osborne for a final council. Reacting from the tension of the previous weeks, they were in an almost hilarious mood, Peel himself was particularly gay, telling jokes and stories in the train on the way down.[1] To avoid a possibly awkward encounter with Russell he returned immediately to London, though during the next few days he was kept fully informed by Victoria and Albert of the protracted negotiations with the Leader of the Opposition.

Russell had been in distant Edinburgh when the royal summons reached him and did not in fact arrive at Osborne until 11 December. He showed some reluctance to commit himself, wished to consult his colleagues, and spoke with concern of his minority in the Commons, though he was somewhat reassured by Peel's letter which had arrived that morning. He seemed equally alarmed however at the prospect of opposition in the House of Lords, over which the royal pair could offer no such guarantee. Peel at once wrote back to the queen that he did not think that the peers would successfully oppose a settlement of the Corn Laws of the kind Russell contemplated. Neither the Duke of Wellington nor, he believed, Stanley would advise resistance. The Whig leaders whom Russell consulted needed all the assurance they could get and Russell approached Graham privately on 12 December to obtain from him some amplification of Peel's views. Graham discussed the matter with his leader and reported the upshot in a letter which Peel himself was largely responsible for drafting. The gist of the communication was that it would be embarrassing for Peel to suggest the details of a Whig settlement of the Corn Law question. But he had been ready

---

[1] *Greville*, 11 Dec. 1845.

before 22 November to recommend a measure which in outline did not differ very much from that suggested in Russell's *Edinburgh Letter*. He thought it sensible to accompany repeal with some compensation; and he would not make captious objections to any measure framed on these lines. This was as far as any politician could be expected to commit himself; yet the Whigs still hesitated. Russell suggested to the queen that he should draw up a detailed measure and show it to Peel before it was finally adopted. In the meantime he asked her for an assurance that the protectionist members of the late cabinet were themselves unwilling to form a government. Though Peel had little doubt of the answer, he put the question personally to Stanley and Buccleuch. Both assured him that they would not participate in a protectionist ministry and Stanley added that he could not even advise that the attempt to form one should be made.

This information was sent to the queen on 15 December. At the same time Peel protested against Russell's wish, before taking office, to secure a pledge from him of support for a specific measure. Quite apart from the probability that any hastily concocted plan might call for subsequent reconsideration by both sides, he thought the mere knowledge of such a pledge would weaken the chances of its success. It would alienate many potential supporters of the new ministry; it would damage Peel's own influence in promoting a settlement. For him to co-operate in framing a bill or to promise in advance to support it 'would be distasteful to the House of Commons and embarrassing to all parties'. This letter, with his consent, was shown by the queen to Russell. He acquiesced in the arguments but started a fresh hare. Russell, like Peel, had so far been thinking in terms of an immediate suspension of the corn laws followed by their gradual abolition. Under pressure from the rank and file of his party, however, he had come round to the policy of suspension followed by total and immediate repeal. If this would prevent Peel from supporting the Whig measure, he wrote to the queen on 16 December, he would have to withdraw. Informed by Victoria of this latest difficulty Peel replied somewhat tartly on 17 December that Russell, having agreed on the unreasonableness of expecting a detailed pledge from Peel on a series of connected measures, was now in effect asking for a specific pledge on one of them. He had already, he pointed out, given assurances of his earnest desire to assist in the settlement of the question, and he could not undertake to be fettered by a previous engagement of this kind. The frigidity of this statement embarrassed the prince, even though he was sensible enough to know that it implied no change in Peel's attitude. Russell and Lansdowne were shown the letter when they arrived at the Castle that evening and were obviously disappointed at having extracted so little from Peel. On one side or the other it fell short of both their expectations. Russell would have preferred a more distinct declaration of support; Lansdowne hoped to learn more of the kind of compensations Peel had in mind so that he could urge them himself on the Whigs. Victoria and Albert argued that Peel could not have acted otherwise. But after rereading Peel's first memorandum of 8 December to squeeze from it the last drop of meaning, the two Whig leaders would only commit themselves to further consultations with their colleagues the following morning.[1]

According to Russell's subsequent explanation in the House of Commons, he had not wanted a specific pledge from Peel, merely a general assurance that he was not precluded from supporting a measure for immediate repeal. The misunderstanding was perhaps only a verbal one. Victoria's description of the conversation which provoked Peel's acid reply was more emphatic on the question of a specific pledge than Russell's subsequent letter which Peel did not see until later. In any case it was clear that Russell and the majority of his colleagues had no real distrust of Peel's willingness to support them.[2] After a further Whig conference Russell returned to Windsor on 18 December and informed the queen that he was ready to form an administration. Peel breathed more freely at the news. He had been slightly conscience-stricken at the thought that his letter of 17 December might have embarrassed the negotiations and he had already tried to smooth away any unfavourable impression in a second letter to the prince. He now prepared with relief to hand over his caretaker commission. To Fremantle in Dublin he sent off a few lines on the 19th, announcing the dissolution of the administration.

[1] RA/C 44/66 (memorandum by Prince Albert). For the negotiations of 11-20 December see Peel, *Memoirs*, II, 226-47; *VL*, II, 54-62; *Peel*, III, 241-55.
[2] Cf. Russell to his wife (Spencer Walpole, *Life of Lord John Russell* (1891), 426-7).

I heartily rejoice [he added with feeling] at being relieved from the thankless and dangerous post of having the responsibility of conducting public affairs, and being expected to conform not to my own sense of the public necessities, but to certain party doctrines, to be blindly followed whatever new circumstances may arise, or whatever be the information which a Government may receive. . . . Whatever country squires may think, it is not safe to guarantee the continuation of the present Corn Laws.[1]

After the excitement of the past few weeks he was in a noticeably elevated mood.[2] He had made up his mind that the Corn Laws must be abolished, even though he was not the most fitting person to do it. He was now spared the odium of another 1829. Loss of office hardly seemed to trouble him. Perhaps he even welcomed the prospect; or persuaded himself that he did.

But he had not finished yet with the unpredictabilities of Lord John Russell. Later the same evening a hasty note arrived from Prince Albert asking him to postpone his final audience with the queen, fixed for the morning of 20 December. Russell had just written to say that he was not after all certain of being able to carry out his commission. The two exclamation marks with which the prince relieved his feelings were probably only a pale reflection of Peel's mind that night. But he had only a short time to wait. Next morning he received a message from Russell through Graham that the Whig leader was going to Windsor to tell the queen that he had been unable to form a government.[3] Peel's reaction was immediate and characteristic. He summoned his own cabinet to meet him at Downing Street at nine o'clock that evening and wrote a brief note to inform Wellington what had happened. 'I am going to the Queen. I shall tell her at once and without hesitation that I will not abandon her. Whatever may happen, I shall return from Windsor as her Minister.'[4] When he entered the queen's room at two o'clock that afternoon she greeted him with the announcement that though he had come to take leave of her, she was still without a minister and without a government.[5] In proceeding to fill up the posts in his new

[1] *Peel*, III, 254-5.
[2] See Lincoln's account to Gladstone on 18 Dec. (44777 f. 237).
[3] Graham (Russell to Graham, 20 Dec.).
[4] Wellington, Saturday n.d. (20 Dec. 1845).
[5] See Peel's account to Heytesbury (40479 f. 539, written 23 Dec.).

ministry, she explained, Russell had encountered objections by Lord Grey to Palmerston's return to the Foreign Office. Faced with a conflict of personalities at the outset of his administration, Russell's half-hearted resolution had vanished into thin air. His political difficulties were obvious and real; he was conscious of the reluctance and pessimism of many of his colleagues; and he had taken Grey's cantankerous protest as sufficient justification for abandoning his dangerous commission without making any serious attempt to get round the difficulty.

Peel was stirred and excited. He blamed Russell's procrastination as the cause of his failure, compared it unfavourably with his own instant readiness to form a ministry when recalled from Italy in 1834, and expressed some hurt at Russell's lack of confidence in his integrity. As for himself, he declared his determination to stand by the queen whatever the consequences. When Victoria observed that he would probably need time for reflection and consultation, he waved aside any need for delay. He would meet parliament alone, if necessary, and lay his proposals before it. There was no sacrifice he would not make to meet the crisis. Staying only to concoct a draft letter for the queen to send to Russell, he left the Castle at four o'clock to return to his waiting colleagues in London. For the second and last time in his life he drove down the steep hill into Windsor as a newly commissioned minister of the Crown. In his emotional mood the events of the last fortnight seemed already like a dream. He felt, he wrote later to the Princess Lieven, like a man restored to life after his funeral service had been preached. Ahead of him was the most formidable task of his political career. That in itself with a man of his temperament was enough to make him forget the strains and tiredness of the previous summer. His ministry was not over yet.

16

THE REPEAL OF THE
CORN LAWS

The cabinet assembled on the evening of 20 December in a vastly different mood to that of a fortnight earlier. Peel opened the proceedings with the blunt statement that he had called them together not to ask what was to be done but to tell them that he was once again the queen's minister. Whether supported or not he was determined to meet parliament and propose the measures he thought necessary to meet the crisis. The question now was one not of the Corn Laws but of the government itself. With both Whigs and protectionists unable to form a ministry, the choice was between himself or Lord Grey and Cobden.[1] When he finished there was a dead silence. It was finally broken by Stanley who said that he still thought the Corn Laws could and should have been retained. He must therefore persist in his resignation. It was clear that he would have consented to the suspension of the Corn Laws provided Peel would pledge himself to their reimposition after a limited period. But in this intransigent attitude he was alone. Buccleuch was obviously upset and asked for time to reflect. The rest heartily approved of Peel's action. Wellington told them that he had been delighted to receive Peel's note that morning announcing his determination not to abandon the queen. He agreed with Peel that the Corn Laws were now a subordinate consideration. With that the first great obstacle was overcome. The loss of Stanley which had seemed so formidable at the beginning of the month now hardly seemed to matter. Protectionism in the rest of the cabinet had been killed stone-dead by the hapless Lord John Russell.

The first task for the prime minister in the next few days was to

[1] Peel to Heytesbury, 23 Dec. 1845 (40479 f. 538).

fill gaps and obtain reinforcements. Wharncliffe had died suddenly on 19 December. There were thus two cabinet vacancies as well as a need in both Houses to recruit debating strength. As a first step, and partly to please the duke, Dalhousie was promoted to the cabinet. A more important prize was Gladstone. Peel saw him on 21 December, offered him Stanley's post at the Colonial Office, presented him with files of correspondence on the Irish famine and the Russell negotiations, and told him to give his answer when he had read them. Gladstone said he would like to see Stanley before deciding. Peel, slightly uneasy, asked Graham to see that Stanley did not influence Gladstone against joining the government. But Gladstone convinced himself of the need for a final settlement of the Corn Laws and in an affectionate interview with Peel the following afternoon accepted office and a seat in the cabinet. The political embarrassment of a long interval between Stanley's resignation and the announcement of his successor was thus avoided; and a Privy Council was hastily arranged for a transfer of the seals. Peel scored another quick success by persuading Buccleuch to remain in office and take Wharncliffe's post as President of the Council. In a graceful letter Stanley told the prime minister that he had assured Buccleuch that there would be no hard feelings on his part at this decision, even though he was still unconvinced of the advantage it would bring to the government. 'He would do you more good in this crisis, as I think I shall, out of office than in.' The logic of this was not easy to follow but if Stanley meant what he said, the auguries were good. Other past and present members of the administration were equally co-operative. Haddington put his post at the Admiralty at Peel's disposal, and acting on a suggestion of Lincoln's, Peel offered it to Ellenborough. The ex-viceroy had been in the cold of retirement long enough to relish the prospects of power once more. Fired by the memory of his exploits in India, he even volunteered to go to Canada as Governor-General if there was any chance of war with the U.S.A. But Peel pointed out that in such an event there would be, as he expressed it to the queen, 'an ample field for his martial genius at the Admiralty'. Haddington received the Privy Seal given up by Buccleuch; and in a final cabinet change, which had been arranged as far back as October, Lonsdale was at last released from the Post Office, St. Germans taking his place with cabinet rank. Though still over-weighted with peers, the ministry was now perceptibly stronger than in the previous session.

At the Privy Council on 23 December Peel was obviously elated at the rapid progress he had made in reconstructing the government. He showed it by the freedom of his conversation with Victoria and Albert afterwards. He confided to them that he had made up his mind not to go into another general election with the restrictions the last had placed upon him. His intention had been to call the party together sometime during the 1846 session and tell them that the Corn Laws could no longer be maintained and that he was going to make a public announcement to that effect before the next election took place. This decision had been overtaken by events. What he now wanted was to remove the whole Corn Law question from the dangerous situation into which it had got: a battleground with the manufacturers, the working classes and the poor which could only end in the defeat of the landed aristocracy. His plan would be to deal with the Corn Laws as part of a general policy designed to remove all restrictions and monopolies, not to benefit one class and triumph over another, but in the interest of all. There would be compensation to agriculture, not as a bribe but in the form of justifiable social improvements. The cost of rural police, legal administration and poor law was a social responsibility which could legitimately be transferred to the central exchequer; and when the railway boom came to an end, the resultant unemployment might be eased by making state loans to landowners to enable them to create work on their estates.[1] The wide vista he opened up obviously evoked the admiration of the prince. Though many details remained to be settled, it was clear that Peel had already mapped out his strategy for the coming parliamentary campaign.

Before the end of the month this general sketch was being translated into more positive directions to the Exchequer and the Board of Trade. 'My wish', Peel wrote to Goulburn on 27 December 'would be not to give undue prominence to corn, but to cover corn by continued operation on the Customs tariff.' By abolishing all duties not worth retaining and reducing all protection, they would merely be applying to the Corn Laws principles of general application. 'Let us leave the tariff as nearly perfect as we can. . . . I attack

[1] *VL*, II, 65.

great importance to *our doing*, and doing now, what yet remains to be done. Let us put the finishing stroke to this good work.'[1] The possibility of suspending the Corn Laws by Order-in-Council, considerably weakened in Peel's mind by the delays of November, was now discarded. Even his plan for an eight-year progressive reduction of the corn duties was drastically modified. A new policy of wrapping up the repeal of the Corn Laws in one last great tariff reconstruction took its place. For this there were tactical as well as economic arguments. It was, a little ominously, not unlike Peel's attempt in 1835 to cover up the constitutional crisis created by the dismissal of the Whigs by offering his own brand of Conservative reform. But historical precedents apart, the scheme had its own inherent weakness. It obscured the fundamental connection between the Irish potato disease and the abandonment of the Corn Laws; and it linked a professedly emergency measure with a long-term economic policy. If it was accepted at its face value, it would strengthen the impression Goulburn had feared, that the government had never been serious in the defence of the Corn Laws. If on the other hand the protectionist opposition refused to be distracted from the central issue of the Corn Laws, the significance of the promised compensation to agriculture might be slurred over, and the remainder of Peel's economic packet suffer from obstruction and delay. It was one thing to make a virtue of necessity; but the virtue would be less recognisable if the necessity was denied. The great attraction of the new policy for Peel, however, was that it made it possible for him to treat the Corn Laws not as an awkward and anomalous case but as a normal part of the tariff system. The integration of his thinking on social and economic questions would at last be achieved.

This came out clearly in cabinet discussion during the second week of January when, after a short Christmas holiday at Drayton, Peel laid before his colleagues his general plan of tariff changes, emphasising the reduction of duties on articles 'connected with the clothing and subsistence of the People'.[2] Concern for the masses was never far away from his economic philosophy and since 1842 it had been its bedrock. To Arbuthnot he had written only a week earlier that 'the agricultural labourers have been better off this winter and last winter than they were before, and rely upon it that when the work-

<hr>

[1] 40445 f. 286; *Peel*, III, 294.   [2] RA/C 23/1.

ing classes feel convinced that their wages do not rise with the price of food, the worst ground on which we can fight the battle of true Conservatism is *food*'.[1] None of the cabinet raised any objection to the principles of Peel's proposals and though he refrained at that stage from going into details, he anticipated no difficulties there either. Admittedly the acquiescence of the cabinet was not the same as the acquiescence of parliament; but he was now confident of passing his measures. There would inevitably be bitter resistance from the agriculturalists; and the extreme radicals might oppose anything short of total and immediate repeal. But Russell had told the queen that he would do what he could to promote a settlement of the corn question and for a free trade policy in general there was strong support in the Commons, backed by an overwhelming preponderance of public opinion in the country. It would mean that Peel would have to steer his plan between rocks on both sides, relying on the shifting currents of cross-party voting. But that would be no new experience. He had not been in the House of Commons for forty years without acquiring a sense of what could be achieved even in confused and difficult circumstances.

The ultimate fate of the government was a different matter. There was no one in the cabinet who did not realise that what was being proposed would produce a crisis in the party greater even than Maynooth. To some of them it seemed inevitable that the party would break up. Ever since the premature announcement by *The Times* the Tory press had raged against Peel's perfidy. County society in the weeks preceding the start of the session had been thick with abuse and threats. Reading the newspapers and listening to the malicious gossip of visitors Julia Peel, left alone at Drayton during December, had almost lost heart at the vituperation with which her husband was being assailed even in his own neighbourhood. In his letter of acceptance on 22 December Buccleuch had said bluntly that Peel's measure would be repugnant to the great mass of the landed and agricultural interest 'by whose constant support you can alone expect to be able to carry on the government'.[2] Peel himself had no illusions on this score. When accepting his cabinet post St. Germans asked him whether he expected after all that had occurred to be able to continue in office. Peel replied that he did

[1] 40484 f. 263 (7 Jan. 1846); *Peel*, III, 326. [2] Peel, *Memoirs*, II, 256.

not. 'It was therefore under no impression', wrote St. Germans later, 'that I was joining a durable administration that I accepted your offer.'[1] But this was a secondary consideration. All Peel's immediate energies were bent on the task confronting him. It was not his habit to take decisions in advance of the circumstances in which they would have to be made.

Parliament opened on 22 January in an atmosphere of intense excitement. In accordance with Peel's predetermined tactics, no specific mention of the Corn Laws was made in the queen's speech. Instead it recommended an extension of free-trade principles 'to maintain contentment and happiness at home, by increasing the comfort and bettering the condition of the great body of my people'. Corn Laws nevertheless dominated even the debate on the Address. After it had been moved and seconded Peel rose to give the explanation for which not only the House but the whole political world had been waiting. The striking feature of his account of the December cabinet crisis was his frank acknowledgement of a change of opinion on the Corn Laws. The Irish potato disease he described as the immediate cause of the break-up of the government in that it necessitated an ultimate decision on future policy. But, he said, he did not wish to attach too much weight to that cause. 'I will not withhold the homage which is due to the progress of reason and to truth, by denying that my opinions on the subject of protection have undergone a change.'[2] He detailed the reasons which had led to that change. It was not theory but the practical experience of governmental policy during the last three years. He had satisfied himself that the rate of wages did not necessarily vary with the price of food; that the removal of protective duties had generally benefited industry; that heavy taxation was best offset by a reduction in the

[1] St. Germans to Peel, 24 June 1846 (40489 f. 539). The suggestion by Gladstone to the contrary (*Gladstone*, I, 212) does not carry much weight. It was written nearly six years afterwards and what Gladstone quoted from recollection of Peel's language on that occasion is not inconsistent with the interpretation that Peel was speaking of his ability to carry his measures, not to keep the party united. Gladstone's own language at the time about his 'most precarious prospects' (*ibid.*, p. 211) in taking office itself points to this conclusion. If retrospective impressions are to be taken into account Gladstone's later remarks can be balanced by Aberdeen's statement in 1856 that when resuming office in 1845 Peel told the queen that he thought he could form a ministry which would last long enough to carry free trade (*ibid.*, p. 210).

[2] *Speeches*, IV, 568.

cost of living; that crime and social disorder were best countered by employment and cheap food. Agriculture had not suffered from the free trade policy already applied to it. The argument of the peculiar burdens on the land was a matter not of economics but of equity which could be met by some form of compensation. That being so, he concluded he could no longer defend the Corn Laws. He admitted that it would have been better if the whole issue had come before another parliament. But this more agreeable course had been made impossible by the disaster in Ireland.

He then went into detail on the spread of the potato disease, the reports of the scientific commission, and the events of December. Finally he repeated his well-known views on the position of a prime minister and his conviction that the essence of true Conservative policy was to advance the material interests of the country, impose the weight of taxation on the classes best able to bear it, and by so doing discourage agitation and end sedition.

> I have thought it consistent with true Conservative policy, to promote so much of happiness and contentment among the people that the voice of disaffection should be no longer heard, and thoughts of the dissolution of our institutions should be forgotten in the midst of physical enjoyment.

It was a firm, coherent speech, lasting about two hours, and the peroration on his sense of responsibility and insistence on freedom of action was delivered in a tone of concentrated emotion. Greville thought his enunciation of Conservative principles too elaborate and likely to alienate some who also claimed that title. He also gave offence by a reference to the difficulty of reconciling 'an ancient monarchy, a proud aristocracy, and a reformed constituency'. Though he clearly meant no more than a statement of the obvious, many took the reference to the aristocracy as a sarcasm. What was more significant, however, than any minor criticism was the reception he got from the benches behind him. They heard him in a silence that was only broken once, when he referred to Stanley' view that the crisis was exaggerated and suspension of the Corn Laws unnecessary. Then the whole Conservative benches seemed to break out in cheers.[1]

[1] Greville, 23 Jan. 1846; Shelley Diary, II, 271.

If further proof was needed of the sullen feeling of his party it came the same evening from Disraeli and Miles. Rising as soon as Russell had explained his own part in the crisis, Disraeli treated the House to what Greville called 'an hour of gibes and bitterness' delivered in his usual impassive manner. He met with violent applause from the Conservative back-benchers, although the official opposition which in 1844 had cheered him on was now silent. Miles, no orator but a genuine representative of the protectionist country gentlemen, savagely challenged those colleagues of Peel who had changed their views on the Corn Laws to resign their seats and stand the test of re-election. And he warned Peel that every constitutional means would be employed by himself and his friends to prevent his measure from passing into law. Nevertheless, no obvious leader for the dissident Tories had emerged in the Commons and nothing yet was known, though everything was suspected, of Peel's detailed plans. The Duke of Richmond, the most prominent protectionist in parliament, harried Wellington in the Lords for a statement of the government's intentions. All he elicited from the duke was a masterful tribute to Peel's conduct in resuming office which brought a grateful note from the prime minister and a personal call from Lady Peel.[1] But there was not long to wait.

On 27 January Peel brought forward his eagerly awaited proposals on the Corn Laws. He emphasised that what he was doing was not singling out agriculture for special treatment but undertaking a general review of the tariff system in which all protected interests would be asked to make sacrifices. He began in fact with a long and rather dull analysis of a whole list of articles on which he proposed to remove or lower duties: tallow, timber, cloth, paper, carriages, candles and soap, dressed hides, straw hats, sugar and tobacco. Then he began to work slowly towards the issue which for most of his audience was the only one which counted. Maize and buckwheat would be let in at a nominal duty, he announced, stressing their value as cattle-fattening foods. He would make immediate reductions in the duties on butter, cheese, hops and cured fish. He would repeal the duties on all foreign meat. Coming at long last to the Corn Laws he said that he did not suggest immediate repeal though he thought it essential in the public interest to make arrangements

[1] *Wellington and His Friends*, p. 203 (Wellington to Lady Wilton, 27 Jan. 1846).

for a final settlement of the question. To give time for readjustment he proposed to make a reduction in the duties on foreign corn for three years and to provide for the expiry of those duties in February 1849. In detail his scheme would impose a rate of 10s when domestic corn was less than 48s a quarter, diminishing to 4s when the price rose to 53s and above. Other cereals would be treated in a comparable manner while colonial corn would be admitted at a nominal duty as soon as the Act was passed. Having thus disclosed the essence of his plan he moved immediately to the question of compensation. First came a proposal to consolidate local highways administration in order to achieve greater economy and efficiency; next the abolition of the law of settlement which enabled urban authorities to send immigrant poor back to their native rural parishes for maintenance; thirdly public loans for the improvement of agriculture; fourth, the removal from county authorities of the costs of prosecutions and custody of prisoners; and finally a partial or total assumption of financial responsibility for poor-law medical officers and school teachers. These details concluded, he devoted the rest of his speech to the general policy of reducing the cost of living; and emphasised the change of public opinion towards the Corn Laws among the mass of the population during the last few years.

He sat down at last having been on his legs for three and a half hours. The cheers at the end, like the applause which had punctuated his speech, came from in front of him. On the Conservative side there was a gloomy silence. It had not been a great speech; certainly not one which matched the occasion. The House had been crowded and curious. Many peers had come to listen. Prince Albert was present, to mark as the angry protectionists thought, the confidence of the court. But there was little that was dramatic in what Peel had to say. After the high tone he had taken in the debate on the Address, it seemed as if he had deliberately intended to lower the tension. The tactics of burying the Corn Law issue in a general tariff revision virtually required this. But it hardly squared with the feelings of his audience. The absence of a proposal to suspend the Corn Laws and the postponement of complete abolition until 1849 robbed the argument of its crisis atmosphere. The complicated details of tariff changes seemed to many impatient members tedious irrelevancies. The immediate admission of maize and colonial corn was not enough to satisfy the doctrinaire free-traders. The three-year transition period and the miscellaneous compensations, unaccompanied by any detailed estimate of their total financial saving, was not enough for those half-hearted protectionists who had been hoping for some acceptable compromise which they could recommend to their angry constituents. Since Peel had asked the House not to enter at once into a debate on his proposals, only a desultory discussion followed. But when the House broke up and members flocked to the clubs, the extreme protectionists were clearly angry, the moderate Conservatives disappointed, and not many of his party seemed happy at his speech. Though the Whigs gave cool approval, only a few ultra-Liberals were disposed to recognise the largeness of the policy he outlined.[1]

Nevertheless the government had put its cards on the table and individual politicians now had to decide on their own course of action. Some had already done so. Hardwicke and Exeter resigned from the Household and were followed by Lord Granby. Gaskell and McKenzie retired from the Treasury; Gordon from the Admiralty; and rumours of other resignations were flying round the clubs. Pressure was also being brought to bear on Peelite supporters. In the proprietorial spirit of the unreformed era Bentinck tried to make Jocelyn retire from Lynn and Richmond called on his brother Arthur Lennox to withdraw from Chichester. Free trade converts representing protectionist electorates had to struggle with both their consciences and their constituents. Lord Ashley and Sturt retired from Dorset; Henniker from East Suffolk; Dawnay from Rutland; and Charteris from Gloucestershire. Others were clearly wavering. To those who resigned Peel wrote unusually gentle and magnanimous replies. To those who hesitated he sent quiet arguments for delay in coming to a decision. His patience was the more remarkable since he was already seriously embarrassed by the question of by-elections for members of the government. Fremantle, sitting for the protectionist pocket borough of Buckingham, had felt it his duty to take the Chiltern Hundreds and could hardly continue in office. Lincoln, having been elected with his father's support for Nottinghamshire, felt no filial compulsion to resign but he was ready if appointed Chief Secretary in Fremantle's place to fight the battle

[1] Cf. *Greville*, 28 Jan. 1846.

for the government in that largely agricultural county. Gladstone's acceptance of office vacated his seat at Newark and unlike Lincoln he did not feel that he could with propriety contest the constituency against his former patron. Where in the spring of 1846 another constituency could be found for a Peelite minister with Gladstone's eccentric record was a task which defied even Bonham's encyclo-paedic knowledge of the electoral field. For all Peel's justifiable claims of national support it was obvious that the representative system was not designed to translate that support into parliamentary seats. Protectionist feeling in Conservative constituencies, Whig and radical allegiances in the remainder, left the government with remarkably little freedom of manœuvre. To vindicate the popularity of the ministers' policy by winning by-elections in large constituen-cies was an attractive proposition. But in the two cases where it was deliberately attempted it failed disastrously. Captain Rous, who came into the Admiralty largely on the assurance that he could retain his seat at Westminster, was defeated in February by de Lacy Evans; and the fact that both candidates were free-traders hardly compensated for the gross miscalculation. The same month Lin-coln, having taken the Irish Secretaryship, was heavily beaten in Nottinghamshire after a bitter contest in which his father used all his influence against him. Not until May, having scraped home by eleven votes at Falkirk, did the new Chief Secretary make his appear-ance in the Commons.

Nevertheless, for all the turmoil of resignations, vacancies and new appointments, Peel at the end of January was in good heart. The cloud of rumours rising from the Whig camp suggested much doubt and division among the opposition. Some were pressing for immediate repeal; others, disappointed at the failure to form a Whig ministry in December, were urging Russell to oppose. The Whig leader himself was said to be in receipt of overtures from the protectionists and undecided on his future course of action. Yet it was unlikely that either the intransigence of the Leaguers or the jealousy of the Whigs could prevent the mass of free-traders from voting for the government. Young, the Conservative chief whip, having sounded opinion in the first week of the session, reported that there would be a large majority in the House for Peel's measures. In the country at large opinion was rallying to the government in quarters that would never have embraced the simple doctrines of the League. Jocelyn at Lynn, having been petitioned by his constituents to remain, decided to defy Bentinck and support repeal. Lord Glenlyon volunteered for a Household appointment and declared that Peel's policy was generally welcomed in Scotland. In Bedfordshire a move by local protectionists to call a county meeting was abandoned when it was realised that it would only support the government. At a meeting there of Petty Sessions eight out of ten J.P.s approved Peel's proposals 'not so much from a knowledge of their probable effect', one of them wrote to Peel, 'as from their past confidence in your judgement and integrity'.[1] Lord Mahon, who at Christmas had sullenly threatened resignation, altered his views when told by some of his chief supporters at Hertford that they hoped he would support the prime minister.[2]

An unsolicited expression of approval which gave unusual pleasure came from one of Graham's old friends, the celebrated Thomas Assheton Smith of Tidworth. One of the most famous Masters of Hounds of the century, more gentlemanly than Osbaldeston and more accomplished than Bentinck, he was the idol of a society not generally conspicuous for its devotion to the prime minister. His cheering and consoling letter was promptly communicated by Graham to Peel, the duke, and other members of the cabinet.[3] Another independent ally came forward in the person of Greville the diarist who published a pamphlet in defence of Peel, anonymously but making no secret of his authorship. Evidence began to accumulate in fact not merely of many converts to repeal among the landed gentry but of a growing feeling among the tenant farmers in some areas that since repeal was inevitable it would be as well to have it at once. But the prime minister was not to be moved by either friends or foes. To Lord Radnor, who urged immediate repeal, he replied that his main object in returning to office was to settle the corn question and that he did not think he would have had much chance of success if he had proposed immediate or total repeal. 'Many people view that alteration with favour or profess to view it', he added shrewdly, '*because* it was not proposed. . . . You have had

[1] RA/C 23/27, 34.
[2] Stanhope (Mahon to Peel, 29 Jan. 1846).
[3] Graham (Graham to Assheton Smith, 6 Feb. 1846).

experience enough of public life to know that great public measures cannot be carried by the influence of mere reason.'[1]

Whether the Commons would more readily consent to repeal by instalments rather than by a single transaction was a matter of judgement. But having committed himself to the first Peel could not go back; and the prospect of success was reasonably good. It would have been even better had it not been for the widespread organisation of protectionist feeling which had taken place during the two preceding years. Arbuthnot in January had cautiously said that he would have no apprehensions of the result 'were it not for these universal meetings of Protectionist Societies, where men pledge themselves before they can know what measures will be proposed'.[2] It was at that level that the potential parliamentary opposition to Peel was being built up in the winter of 1845. The Anti-Corn Law League itself had largely been responsible for this. The spread of League activities into the counties since 1843 and its venomous attacks on landlords had produced a natural but ominous reaction in the agricultural districts. It was first witnessed in the multiplication of local protection societies. Then in 1844 came the formation of a new and more effective Central Agricultural Protection Society in London under the presidency of the Duke of Richmond and counting among its leading figures protectionist M.P.s like Newdegate, Miles, Heathcote and Stafford O'Brien. The 1845 annual meeting of the society, held during the excitement and speculation of December, had already taken up the challenge offered by the League and Russell's *Edinburgh Letter*. A general alarm was issued to its supporters and in the weeks preceding the opening of parliament meetings of local branches were held all over England to get up petitions to parliament and exert pressure on county members. The Society's rule of non-intervention in politics was dropped and they announced their intention to get voters on the rolls and secure the return of as many protectionist candidates as possible.

To Peel this adoption of demagogic tactics was a foretaste of what would happen if the Corn Laws were ever allowed to become an electoral issue.

I see [he wrote to the duke in January] the Protection Society has repealed its rule which prevents interference in elections and proposes

[1] RA/C 23/50–3.   [2] 40484 f. 265 (to Peel).

to fight the anti-Corn Law League with their own weapons; that is, by multiplying the lower class of country voters. All this will tell ultimately in favour of democracy when the excitement of the moment shall have subsided. The 40/- freeholders in Ireland were an instrument used against the landlords.[1]

Nevertheless anger and despair were making the protectionists a more formidable political force than they had ever been before; and it was not the League but Peel who was now the enemy. In the demoralised state in which the official Conservative Party had been left at the end of the 1845 session they had every chance of making their revolt effective. The chorus of angry protest from gentry, parsons, and farmers heard in the provinces in December and January was evidence not only of widespread but of organised opposition. This was something which the Conservative members sitting for counties and rural boroughs could not ignore even if they did not entirely approve. Among the moderates many were committed to oppose repeal even before coming up to Westminster at the end of January. Others, trying to reconcile party loyalty with constituency demands, had placed their hopes on some large measure of compensation which would placate their agricultural electors. Peel's speech of 27 January had largely destroyed that vague prospect of compromise. Immediately afterwards a special meeting of the Central Society began mobilisation of a parliamentary protectionist opposition. For the first time Peel's control of the party was being threatened not merely by dissident groups or disgruntled individuals but by a large protectionist section supported and to some extent dominated by an outside organisation. So far from converting the country squires and farmers the League had produced an 'anti-League' which seriously endangered Peel's ability to produce an agreed national solution of the Corn Law question.[2]

From the League itself there was paradoxically little to fear. Though inevitably it called for total and immediate repeal, the publication of Peel's comprehensive tariff scheme cut the ground from under its feet. The classes which had given money and votes to the League were not prepared to support a doctrinaire opposition

[1] Peel, *Memoirs*, II, 265 (14 Jan. 1846).
[2] See Miss Lawson-Tancred, 'The Anti-League and the Corn Law crisis of 1846' (*Historical Journal*, III, 162).

to the man who had the will and ability to bring about a final settlement of the issue. The *Manchester Guardian* gave instant support for the government's plan;[1] and all the information coming to Peel confirmed that the League was finding no encouragement in the city of its origin for a renewed political campaign. The great mass of manufacturers approved the prime minister's policy and were tired of agitation.[2] With its general strategy for fighting the 1847 election now largely irrelevant, the League could act only as a deterrent to the potential opponents of the government rather than as an obstacle to the government itself. What the crisis curiously did reveal was the underlying cause of Cobden's inveterate hostility to the prime minister. When the news of the cabinet's resignation was received in December, it was greeted by Cobden with a savage attack on the fallen minister at Stockport followed by even more insulting language at a meeting at Covent Garden. Even in the annals of the League's oratory his abuse was repellent enough to draw remonstrances from friends as diverse as George Combe, Charles Buller, and Harriet Martineau. Cobden's reply to Buller, by a devious route through Bingham Baring and Fremantle, eventually passed into Graham's hands at the start of the session.[3] What it demonstrated was that Cobden's old rancour over the incident in February 1843 was still as keen as ever. When Graham put the letter in his hands Peel was astonished that Cobden was still nursing a three-year-old grudge and hurt that he had never said openly that Peel's disclaimer at the time was unsatisfactory. Whether since then, he observed dryly, he or Cobden had shown more avoidance of personalities in their speeches, he was happy to leave to the judgement of others.

Next month a more adroit peacemaker entered the lists. That redoubtable bluestocking Harriet Martineau wrote to the prime minister on 22 February appealing to him to make some generous allusion to the old quarrel that would conciliate not only Cobden but all the followers of the League. 'Most people would say that it is now impossible for you to set the matter right,' wrote the artful

[1] Cf. D. Read, *Press and the People, 1790–1850* (1961), pp. 150–2.
[2] Memorandum by Prince Albert of conversation with Peel, 30 Jan. 1846 (RA/C 23/27).
[3] 40452 f. 105.

lady, 'Mr. Cobden having insulted you as he has done. But I believe not only that what is just and generous always may be done, but that you are a great doer of the impossible, in the government of yourself, as well as in the government of the country.' Peel replied by return, enclosing an extract from his reply to Graham to show that he had believed at the time that a sufficient reparation had been made to Cobden's feelings. Miss Martineau promised to carry the information to the League leaders; but Peel did not leave it at that. A few nights later, on 27 February, Ferrand made a crude and much-criticised attack in the Commons on another leading member of the League. Disraeli then tried to divert attention by saying that Peel himself once accused Cobden of abetting assassination. Peel promptly rose to explain that it had been his wish in 1843 to remove any such imputation. Much as he deprecated a revival of the incident, he went on to say, he could not be sorry at being given 'an opportunity of fully and unequivocally withdrawing an imputation on the hon. member for Stockport which was thrown out in the heat of debate under an erroneous impression of his meaning'. Cobden, the recent recipient of a message from Miss Martineau asking him not to ignore any gesture of reconciliation from Peel, next rose to express satisfaction at the prime minister's words and regret for the terms in which he himself had alluded to Peel.[1] Two days later the post brought Harriet Martineau two communications: a marked copy of *The Times* from Peel to show her in print the results of her diplomacy, and a note of gratitude from Cobden. It was the end of an unhappy episode in Cobden's career and the start of a new relationship between Peel and one of his ablest opponents in public life.[2]

II

By this time battle had been joined in earnest in the House of Commons. On 9 February Peel formally moved that the House should go into committee on his tariff proposals. Continued by adjournment over twelve nights the debate lasted until 27 February. Miles's promise of sustained opposition was more than fulfilled. Of over a

[1] *Hansard*, LXXXIV, 248–9.
[2] 40452 f. 108; *Peel*, III, 328–32; H. Martineau, *Autobiography* (1877), II, 259 et seq.; V. Wheatley, *Life and Work of Harriet Martineau* (1957), pp. 255–7; *Cobden*, pp. 350–4.

hundred speakers who took part in the violent discussions, more than half were protectionists. The debate was technically on an amendment by Miles to postpone the Committee six months and in his opening speech he set the pattern for the opposition by denying the gravity of the Irish crisis, accusing the prime minister of a long-premeditated intention to repeal the Corn Laws, and rejecting as worthless his proffered compensation. Moderate protectionists like Sir William Heathcote and Sir Thomas Acland, while refusing to change their opinions at a moment's notice, refrained from impugning the prime minister's motives and disclaimed any intention of overthrowing his government. Others were less scrupulous in their personal attacks and demanded an appeal to the electorate before a protectionist leader in a protectionist parliament was allowed to throw over his former professions. Disraeli, dropping his usual vein of sarcasm and invective, experimented not very successfully with a speech full of economic argument. He was quietly cut to pieces a few nights later by Sir George Clerk, the vice-president of the Board of Trade, who was not generally reckoned a gladiator of debate. The autocratic Lord George Bentinck appeared in the unusual role of a parliamentary debater with a long and carefully prepared speech marred by characteristically violent outbursts. The free trade doctrine, he declared, was an absolute delusion; the Irish famine a mere pretence; the potatoes were only rotting because they had been dug up unripe; the government had caused the panic by sending a scientific commission to Ireland. In a debate which was reckoned, apart from a few notable exceptions, to be as dull as it was long, the protectionists provided little of interest other than the strength of their feelings.

Nevertheless the emergence of Bentinck was a portent. A younger son of the fourth duke of Portland, household companion and racing partner of Richmond, fox-hunter, race-horse owner and prominent member of the Jockey Club, he added prestige and energy to the already half-organised protectionist party in the Commons. He had sat for twenty years as a silent member for King's Lynn and had taken little part in the activities of the Central Agricultural Protection Society until the end of January. But from the end of November the growing speculation about Peel's intentions had aroused in him a passionate and obsessive interest. He now brought to the protectionist cause the ruthless determination and single-mindedness which he had previously shown in hunting down dishonest trainers and crooked jockeys on the Turf. Violent and unscrupulous by temperament, he made up for his political naïvety by tenacity and force.

For the government good speeches were made by Herbert, who pleaded for a reconciliation of the landed and manufacturing interests; by Graham who said that what they were doing was not only expedient in the circumstances but right in policy; and by Cardwell who methodically destroyed the claims that protection helped either the farmers or the country labourers. Russell, speaking on behalf of the official Liberals, criticised the details of the government's plans, but said emphatically that he would do nothing to endanger their success. Even more encouraging language came from the League leaders. Bright pronounced a panegyric on the prime minister and declared that Peel had left office in December as minister for a party but returned as minister of his sovereign and the people. Cobden, whose ill-health after his winter campaign of oratory made this his one outstanding contribution to the Corn Law debates, delivered an even more cutting rejoinder to the protectionists. Their attacks on the prime minister, he said scornfully, were merely a cover for the hollowness of their case. All they were doing was to make him the most popular man in the country. The protectionists knew themselves they could place no confidence in an appeal to the electorate; and public opinion at large was even more emphatically against them. They would not get a single candidate returned in any borough with a population of more than 20,000; and as for the feelings of the mass of the people, he defied them to call a meeting of the working classes in any part of the country on the subject of the Corn Laws.

Peel, rising on 16 February, the fifth night of the debate, made what was generally recognised as an unusually good speech. He was crisper and firmer than he had been when introducing the resolution; he showed great confidence and determination; and he analysed much more lucidly the chain of events which led him to his present position. The explanations given by Russell at the start of the session had not entirely satisfied him and he used this opportunity to read out further correspondence with the queen which demonstrated the support he would have given to Russell if the latter had persisted with his efforts to form a ministry. Given the situation created by Russell's failure, he argued, no other course was for himself possible. Supposing he had followed the conventional party line and maintained protection? By May the full extent of the Irish disaster would be known to all and it would be obvious that he had failed in his duty as head of the government. Knowing what they knew, the ministers had to act early.

> We saw, in the distance, the gaunt forms of famine and of disease following in the train of famine. Was it not our duty to the country, aye our duty to the party that supported us, to avert the odious charge of indifference and neglect of timely precautions? It is absolutely necessary before you can come to a final decision on this question that you should understand this Irish case. You must do so.

To ensure that they heard, even if they did not believe, he read out letter after letter on the ravages of the disease in Ireland. Having established his case he then went over the familiar sequence of argument. Supplies of potatoes from Europe were not available; Ireland must be fed; parliament and the public would not tolerate public money being spent on that relief while the Corn Laws were on the statute book; once suspended they could not be restored. A change of conviction in the public, a change of heart among many Conservatives, made further successful defence of the Corn Laws impossible. Next he turned to individual opponents and made some good humoured fun of W. Miles and his plea for 'protection to native grease'. Reverting finally to the general issue he said flatly that for a great commercial country like Britain the choice was to advance or recede in its economic policy. If they chose to end restriction and prohibition, they would have done what they could to ensure not only commercial prosperity but the welfare of the great body of the people. Industrial depressions might return. 'Gloomy winters like those of 1841 and 1842 may again set in. Are those winters effaced from your memory?' he demanded. 'From mine they never can be.' But if they did recur, at least there would be the satisfaction of knowing that the Corn Laws had ceased to exist and that the hardships of the poor were not aggravated by man-made restrictions.[1]

As the end of the debate drew near, speculation on the result

[1] *Speeches*, IV, 605.

intensified. At the start the government whips calculated there would be a majority of over a hundred on their side. But as feeling began to declare itself, it was realised that in the opposition would be found the larger part of the Conservative Party. Peel's information on 11 February was that 197 Conservatives would vote against the government and not more than 123 for it.[1] This was a great though not entirely unexpected blow, not merely for the future of the contest in the Commons but for the encouragement it would give to the protectionist peers in the Lords. The event was even worse than these calculations. When the House divided at three o'clock on the morning of 28 February there was a majority of only 97 for the ministerial motion. The analysis of the division offered even less comfort. Though over 40 Liberals were absent or paired, the rest voted almost solidly for Peel: 227 and only 11 against. Of the Conservatives 28 were absent or paired; only 112 voted with their leader; 231 went into the lobby against him. The dividing line had been drawn at last and two-thirds of Peel's party had turned against him. Indeed, if some forty office-holders were deducted from the 112, only seventy independent Conservatives were still loyal.[2] 'This does not look like a strong government,' was Albert's mournful comment; nor was it in any ordinary parliamentary sense. Though the news of Hardinge's repulse of the Sikh invasion enabled Peel to rally a little of the old patriotic Conservative spirit in a speech of thanks to the Army in India early in March, the protectionists defeated the ministers a few days later on a motion to appoint a select committee to enquire into the poor-law administration. Russell voted with the government but the majority of his party preferred to stay away and let the ministers be beaten. It was an unimportant issue but it showed the writing on the wall. The protectionists in the House of Commons were now well organised, with Bentinck as their acknowledged leader and two properly appointed whips. In the Lords, despite his earlier protestations, Stanley both publicly and privately was using language which suggested that he might take over from Richmond the leadership of the protectionist peers.

Nevertheless, the relative ease with which the tariff scheme went through committee during March was encouraging. Villiers's

---

[1] RA/C 23/59, 67.   [2] ibid., 95-8.

expected motion for immediate repeal drew negligible support and Peel had hopes of raising the majority on the second reading of the corn bill to the symbolic figure of a hundred. But there had been no slackening in the fierceness of protectionist resentment; they were merely biding their time. When Peel rose to speak in the debate on the second reading the protectionists promptly clamoured for one of their own men. It was several minutes before quiet could be restored by the Speaker and even so Peel was continually interrupted throughout his speech. Not surprisingly it was not one of his better performances. Much of what he said was a repetition of circumstances already known, though he emphasised more than ever the danger to the aristocracy of allowing its fate to be linked with the Corn Laws, and the cardinal importance of a change in the law for 'the social condition of the millions in the manufacturing districts who earn their subsistence by the sweat of their brow'.

> You may talk of improving the habits of the working classes, introducing education amongst them, purifying their dwellings, improving their cottages; but believe me, the first step towards improvement of their social condition is an abundance of food.[1]

To his audience perhaps the most striking passage in the speech was his reference to the temporary nature of the assistance he was receiving from the official opposition and his inability to count on any future support from the mass of his own party. When he said defiantly that with only 112 Conservative supporters his tenure of power could only be short, he was answered by savage cheers from the benches behind him. It was not a great debate; the interest was in the division. When it came the government majority was only 88; and though this was due to a decrease in the number of those voting rather than to any shift of opinion, the result could only be to encourage protectionist hopes of defeating the bill in the House of Lords.

This in fact was Peel's main anxiety. In the Commons the ninety odd majority for repeal, however diverse in composition, would see it safely through. The Lords, less amenable to party discipline and less exposed to public pressure, were more evenly divided and more incalculable. The change in protectionist tactics observable in

[1] *Speeches*, IV, 650 (27 March 1846).

March suggested that they were pinning their hopes on the peers. Even if outright rejection was beyond their powers, an amendment in committee would have the same effect since the corn bill was a money bill and must either be accepted or rejected in its entirety. Bessborough was vigorously canvassing for the old Whig policy of a fixed duty and an alliance of Whig and Tory protectionists on this issue might easily produce a majority. April saw a hum of parliamentary activity in the upper chamber as both sides tried to organise support among the somewhat amorphous mass of peers. The government collected proxies and counted heads while a knot of protectionist notabilities, headed by what Peel disrespectfully described to Lincoln as 'that great goose the Duke of Richmond', sought audiences with the queen to present addresses against repeal. Though the constitutional propriety of this was doubtful, the cabinet eventually agreed to allow it, despite the grumbles of Wellington that it was an abuse of the traditional peers' privilege of access to the sovereign.[1]

Meanwhile it was clear to all impartial observers that Peel was merely holding office by favour of the Whigs until he had repealed the Corn Laws. Though his position was demonstrably weak, however, he was too good a tactician not to see the strength he derived from the divisions among his rivals. The protectionists had never stood a chance of forming an alternative government; they had failed to force a dissolution; they could not hope to defeat the corn bill in a straight trial of strength. In the Commons their only hope was to beat the government in alliance with the Whigs on some other issue. Revenge in fact was rapidly becoming Bentinck's sole political objective. But for this he had to strike while the feelings excited by the crisis were still high. Once the Corn Laws were repealed he was under no delusion that many of his more half-hearted followers would not drift back to Peel's leadership. To allow the session to end with the prime minister still in office might prove the end of the protectionist revolt. Meanwhile much information about the position of Lord John Russell was coming through to Peel from a variety of well-informed sources. One of them was Aberdeen who had been the recipient of some frank disclosures from Russell himself. Several overtures had been made to the Whig

[1] RA/C 24/35 (memorandum by Prince Albert, 27 Apr. 1846). Cf. also /38-9 (Graham to Albert and Victoria).

leader by the protectionists for a tacit alliance to overturn the government.[1] Russell was also under pressure from a strong section of his own party which was not yet reconciled to total repeal. But if anything was certain it was that to ally himself with the protectionists on a protectionist issue would split the Liberals and throw away radical support. Russell had too much experience of Whig dependence on extreme groups to relish adding Bentinck and his followers to the miscellaneous props on which any future Whig ministry would have to lean. Faced in Peel, Cobden and Bentinck with three leaders who knew their own mind, Russell was cautious at that stage about committing himself to any long-term strategy.

In reality no strategy was needed. As Albert, busily writing one memorandum after another on the chaotic state of the political field, had concluded for himself, it was ultimately impossible that a ministry commanding the solid allegiance of only one-sixth of the House of Commons could continue in office. Even without the formation of a factious coalition against him, Peel was bound to fall.[2] The prime minister was of much the same mind. Writing to Hardinge on 4 April in the unrestrained style he used with his close friends, he observed:

> I have no doubt that of the 230 or 240 Conservatives—or whatever was their number—who voted against us, many will return to their old standard. But suppose a hundred of them remain inveterate and disposed to mischief, they may find the means of placing us in minority, by a union with the Whigs and Radicals.[3]

In the meantime the news of Hardinge's further victories over the Sikhs at Aliwal and Sobraon provided an ironic counterpoint to the difficulties of the ministers at home, contributing to the moral ascendancy of the government if not to its voting strength in the lobbies.

III

In his conversation with Russell early in April Aberdeen had impressed on his visitor that when he took over the government he could only maintain himself in power with Peelite aid. He had better take care therefore that he did not turn them out in such

[1] RA/C, /27 (memorandum by Prince Albert, 10 Apr. 1846).
[2] ibid., /20 (n.d. but almost certainly written in March 1846).
[3] 40475 f. 199, ptly pr. Peel, III, 308.

fashion as to make it impossible for them to support him afterwards. Russell laughed and said that he had heard that it would take a silver bullet to kill Peel and for his part he did not think that one had yet been cast that would kill him.[1] He was wrong. The silver bullet that was to bring down the prime minister had already been in existence for three months. It had been manufactured with a fine appropriateness in that home of firearms and superstition, Ireland. At the end of March the arrival in the Commons of the Irish protection of life bill introduced a fresh element into an already complicated political situation. As far back as the beginning of December the government had been considering the best method of combating the wave of disorder and violence in Ireland which had marked the onset of winter. The importance attached to the problem had been shown by the fact that when the cabinet resigned, Graham asked the Lord Lieutenant to send over the draft bill already approved so that it could remain in the Home Office as an urgently recommended measure for their successors. On his return to office Peel instructed the Irish government to proceed with the crimes bill, together with other measures based on the report of the Devon Commission, for legislation in the following session.[2] To save time the protection of life bill was introduced by St. Germans in February in the House of Lords where it met with the approval of both parties. The Whig peers, especially those with Irish estates, had reservations about the repeal of the Corn Laws. They had none at this stage about the need for firmer measures to protect life and property in Ireland where offences against the peace had more than doubled in 1845 compared with the previous year.

Peel had been sceptical about the value of a revived Insurrection Act and in accordance with his views the new bill merely relied on the well-tried methods of giving the Lord Lieutenant power to proclaim disturbed districts, employ additional constabulary at the expense of the districts concerned, and enforce a curfew at night. Compensation was to be given in the case of maimed or murdered persons and offences under the Act were to be treated as misdemeanours, though breaking the curfew was to be punishable at the discretion of the courts by sentences of up to seven years' transportation.

[1] RA/C 24/27.
[2] Graham (Peel to Graham, 3, 27 Dec.; Graham to Heytesbury, 8 Dec. 1845).

Though the opposition promptly affixed to the bill the opprobiou
name of coercion it was not in fact by contemporary standards a
particularly drastic measure. Despite its easy passage through the
Lords, however, it was clear when Graham introduced the bill on
30 March that there would be considerable obstruction in the
Commons. The Irish Liberals violently attacked the bill. The Whig
took the more moderate but equally damaging view that it should
not take precedence over the corn bill. The protectionists on the
other hand were ready for obvious reasons to support the Irish bi
provided it was given precedence over all other government legisla
tion. It was Young's opinion in fact that if the Irish bill was pushe
through to a first reading, it was highly unlikely that the corn bi
could be read a third time until after Easter. Nevertheless, on 2
March the cabinet decided that the peculiar circumstances of the
Irish bill made it essential to proceed immediately with a first reading
Once that was done, they would resume with the corn bill and allo
no other measure to take priority. The possibility of reachin
agreement with other sections of the House on the timetable wa
dismissed. Bentinck, taking Young's expression of opinion in
private whips' consultation as constituting a definite bargai
claimed that he had been deceived. But Peel insisted on his right
bring forward the corn bill as soon as possible.[1]

In the event, with all sides of the House against him, he mad
little progress with either measure. The first reading of the Iri
bill had to be postponed until after Easter and even when the deba
was resumed, it was dragged out night after night by repeated a
journments. The Irish members, led by Smith O'Brien and t
Young Ireland faction rather than by the ageing O'Connell, exe
cised all the arts of parliamentary obstruction which was Irelan
gift to nineteenth-century British political life. Aided on occasio
to Peel's great annoyance, by slack attendance on the part of t
weary and depleted ministerial back-benchers, they succeeded agai
all precedent in prolonging the debate on the first reading un
1 May. In this the Young Ireland group was acting a part as cyni
as it was unscrupulous. O'Brien admitted in a private House
Commons conversation with Peel that he recognised the need fo
coercion bill. But, he added cheerfully, it was useless for Peel

[1] See the discussion in the Commons on 26 March (*Hansard*, LXXXV, 136–

point admonishingly to the delay caused to the corn bill since he personally would much prefer a fixed duty even though he had voted with his party for repeal.[1] Such effrontery shocked Albert; but the real danger was that other interested members of the House of Commons would be tempted to take a hand in this subtle Irish game. Coercion, obstruction, talk of a fixed duty, and embarrassment to the government offered an appetising situation to any opponent of Peel; and in the course of April an explicit understanding was reached between Bentinck and O'Brien to waste as much time as possible on the Irish bill debates. Equally ominous for Peel was information reaching him through Arbuthnot and the Duke of Bedford that some of the Irish Whig peers like Clanricarde and Bessborough had changed their minds about coercion and were trying to persuade Russell to oppose the bill in the Commons.

The sharpness of temper provoked by the barren obstructed month of April was shown by an incident in the fourth week. Disraeli, to taunt Peel, first perverted the sense of a passage in a speech of Cobden's and then accused the prime minister of having applauded it. Peel interrupted to deny the imputation. Disraeli declared that he had been given the lie and sat down. There was excitement and confusion for a while until explanations were forthcoming on both sides and order restored. Meanwhile Jonathan Peel, who had his fair share of the family temper, went across to Disraeli and said he should know that one man at any rate was ready to say that his assertion was false. Disraeli was at first silent and then appealed to Bentinck. When Bentinck approached him, Jonathan Peel brought in Captain Rous to act on his behalf. He, however, advised an apology and late that night at White's Club drew up with Bentinck a suitable form of words to end the affair.[2] Peel had a tighter control of his temper than his brother but as the interminable amendments and adjournments dragged on even he became tired and anxious. It was not only the Irish bill that was being obstructed; all government business was suffering from the delay. Not one bill had been passed, not a single vote of supply had been taken. All that could be done, as the prime minister confessed to

[1] RA/D 15/25 (memorandum by Prince Albert n.d. but almost certainly Apr. 1846).

[2] The mild official version of the affair is in *Hansard*, LXXXV, 1010–22. For the rest see *Greville*, 26 Apr. 1846.

Victoria and Albert, was patiently to sit it out.[1] When the Irish bill at last arrived at its first reading at the beginning of May, both Whigs and protectionists voted for it and it went through in the end by a comfortable majority. The second reading was fixed for the end of the month and the House returned to the committee stage of the corn bill. On 11 May came the third reading. The debate was relatively short, extending only over three nights, but made up in bitterness what it lacked in length. The long battle over the Irish issue in April had robbed Peel of much of his energy and elasticity, and the final committee stage of the corn bill had seen a renewal of the personal attacks on him by Disraeli and others. On 15 May, the last evening of the debate, Disraeli renewed the onslaught in a speech of studied and sustained invective. It was a long speech and its concluding section perhaps the most brilliant of all the philippics he had launched against the prime minister.

Fortified as he was by his contempt for Disraeli as a man, it could not have been pleasant for a man as tired and highly-strung as Peel was that evening to receive barb after malevolent barb. For thirty years, declaimed Disraeli, Peel had traded on the ideas and intelligence of others. His life was one long appropriation clause; he was the burglar of others' intellects. No statesman had committed larceny on so great a scale. As the orator continued, with his sallow unmoved countenance and passionless voice, the men around him laughed and cheered and laughed again. When Peel rose at last after midnight to wind up the debate, he was met with screaming and hooting from the protectionist benches and for the first quarter of an hour he was struggling to obtain a hearing. Disraeli he dismissed in three sentences. Turning slightly to his left, where Disraeli sat on one of the higher benches behind him, he said that in taking the course he had done, 'the smallest of all the penalties which I anticipated were the continued venomous attacks of the member for Shrewsbury'; and he pronounced the adjective with contemptuous emphasis.[2] If the hon. gentleman held the views he now professed of Peel's career in the thirty years preceding 1841, he added, it was merely surprising that he had been ready to take office under him in that year. He then

---

[1] RA/C 24/28 (memorandum by Prince Albert, 25 Apr. 1846).

[2] See the description by the Duke of Argyll (*Autobiography and Memoirs of the Eighth Duke of Argyll*, ed. Duchess of Argyll (1906), I, 275–6).

once more briefly reviewed the reasons for his decision to abandon the Corn Laws. While admitting that it might have been possible for him to continue their defence, he insisted that it was in the national interest to make a final settlement. As far as his own career and ambitions were concerned, he started to say—and was at once overwhelmed by the storm of jeers and shouts which this reference to his personal integrity immediately evoked. Peel stopped, tried to resume, stopped once more. His voice failed him, his eyes filled with tears, and for a moment the embarrassed and half-sympathetic Whig front bench across the gangway thought he was going to break down. No one had ever seen Peel beaten in the House of Commons before; but he was not beaten now. With an enormous effort he pulled himself together and though quieter than usual he carried through to the end his fifth and last great speech in the memorable Corn Law debates of 1846. Fighting now with his back to the wall and relieved of any necessity to use sophistry with those whom nothing could now convince or persuade, his language was sharper and more revealing than any he had so far used.

A continuance of the Corn Laws, he said, would have been possible but only at the cost of a desperate conflict of classes. 'It was the foresight of these consequences, it was the belief that you were about to enter into a bitter, and ultimately, an unsuccessful struggle', which convinced him that a settlement was to the benefit of all. The Irish crisis merely made necessary a review of the Corn Laws. What made necessary their repeal was a wider consideration. 'The real question at issue is the improvement of the social and moral condition of the masses of the population.' Now, in a period of relative prosperity, was the time to remove the last barriers to economic expansion. Granted that he had changed his mind over protection for corn; but in his general advocacy of free trade he was acting consistently with his whole public career. When the crisis came in Ireland he had to consider first what must be done to avert a great calamity. Next, what was to be done to remove from the landed and agricultural interest the odium of continuing to defend what had become plainly indefensible. This was his object—not the interests of one particular party. Then, gathering his energies for his final, almost valedictory peroration, he said something which came from the heart of his political philosophy:

If I look to the prerogative of the Crown, if I look to the position of the Church, if I look to the influence of the aristocracy, I cannot charge myself with having taken any course inconsistent with conservative principles, calculated to endanger the privileges of any branch of the legislature, or of any institutions of the country. My earnest wish has been, during my tenure of power, to impress the people of this country with a belief that the legislature was animated with a sincere desire to frame its legislation upon the principles of equity and justice. I have a strong belief that the greatest object which we or any other government can contemplate should be to elevate the social condition of that class of the people with whom we are brought into no direct relationship by the exercise of the elective franchise.

Deprive him of power tomorrow, he finished defiantly, they could never deprive him of the conviction that he had used that power, not selfishly or corruptly, but for these great ends.[1]

After he sat down Disraeli rose to make a personal explanation. Speaking uneasily and obscurely he denied that his opposition to the government was inspired by personal motives. He denied that he had ever asked for office. In 1841 there had been a conversation between himself and another person in the confidence of the prime minister; but not of his seeking, nor of the kind the House might suppose. He had never asked a favour of the government nor, he repeated, had he ever directly or indirectly solicited office. It was a curious lie; indeed it was a compound lie. He had both solicited office in 1841 and twice subsequently applied for patronage.[2] All the prime minister did, however, was to repeat significantly his remark that if Disraeli held in 1841 the opinions he had expressed that night, he was wrong to have told Peel that he would be glad to take office

[1] *Speeches*, IV, 687 et seq. (15 May 1846).

[2] Miss Ramsay's statement (A. A. Ramsay, *Sir Robert Peel*, 1928, p. 344 n.) which has been followed by Robert Blake (R. Blake, *Disraeli*, 1966, p. 239), that Peel actually had with him in the House that evening Disraeli's letter of 1841 asking for office is not substantiated by the authority they quote, Goldwin Smith (*Reminiscences*, 1910, p. 177), who merely records a statement by Lincoln that Peel once showed him the letter. This was more likely to be subsequent to the debate since Disraeli's attack and Peel's reply both took place on the same evening. The point of Lincoln's story was to explain why Peel was so indifferent to Disraeli's attacks. Goldwin Smith adds that it was not unlikely that the letter was in Peel's bag at the time. But that is his surmise and is not based on anything Lincoln said at the time. J. Martineau (*Life of Newcastle*, p. 81) states simply that on one occasion Lincoln dissuaded Peel from reading the letter in the House but gives no date.

under him. With that the matter ended and the House proceeded to divide. With nearly a hundred absent or paired, 327 voted for the bill, 229 against, a majority of 98. Of the Conservatives present 106 voted for the government, 222 against. John Young reported eight Conservative pairs in favour of the bill, and three supporters absent for various reasons, a total of 117 in all who still stood by the prime minister. Though the long-desired majority of a hundred eluded Peel to the last, there was some comfort in the fact that five Conservative M.P.s who had previously voted against repeal, including Sir Thomas Acland and Philip Pusey, deliberately absented themselves because they could no longer bring themselves to oppose the measure.[1]

With the corn and tariff bills safely through the Commons Peel now concentrated on the House of Lords. A timetable for the corn bill was settled with Wellington and the duke outlined his simple battle tactics. He would tell the peers that they must pass the measure since they could not afford to isolate themselves from the Commons and the Crown. Ripon consented to introduce the bill, leaving Dalhousie and Ellenborough as the ministerial reserve. Peel stood ready to prime them with any details which might be needed in the course of debate. The air was thick with rumours of an alliance between the Irish Whig peers led by Bessborough and the Tory protectionists under Richmond on the basis of concessions in Ireland and a small fixed duty on corn. The greatest danger was not defeat on the second reading, where the government could use its battery of proxies, but a successful amendment in committee. A defeat there on a snap vote could produce a constitutional clash with the Commons, would certainly delay the bill, and might enable the protectionist wing of the Whig party in the Commons to persuade Russell to reverse his policy. Many friendly backwoods peers were ready to give the government their support by proxy who would not attend to fight the tedious battle of debate. On 17 May St. Germans reported that Bessborough had said he would oppose the use of proxies to reverse any decision reached in committee;[2] and

---

[1] RA/C 24/53-4 (Peel to Victoria, 16 May; Young to Peel, 15 May 1846). The other three Protectionist abstentions were Sir C. Coote (Q. Co.), Sir E. Hayes (Donegal), and Col. Wyndham (W. Sussex).

[2] 40480 f. 537.

the significance of this was obvious. Peel had already foreseen this hazard and on 10 May had circulated a cabinet memorandum asking his colleagues for their views on the constitutional aspect of the question. All agreed that from past precedent and present necessity it was essential to use proxies on the second reading whatever happened in committee.[1]

Nevertheless the ultimate fate of the bill depended on the other parties. The Peelites could no more command a majority in the Lords than in the Commons. That the Tory protectionists would fight to the end was clear enough. On 21 May there was a great protectionist meeting of peers, M.P.s and tenant farmers sent up from different parts of the country with Richmond in the chair. Bentinck, Disraeli, and Sibthorp made speeches, the first attacking with characteristic abusiveness the base Conservatives who had voted for the traitor Peel. Stanley was triumphantly announced as leader of the opposition and violent resolutions were passed pledging those present to do everything in their power to defeat the bill in the Lords.[2] Bentinck's anger was increased the next day when a ten-hour factory bill introduced by Ashley earlier in the session was defeated in the Commons with over fifty protectionists and half the Whig party voting with the government. There had been confident anticipations that the ministers would be beaten and have to resign. Peel himself had expected defeat.[3] But it was not the ten hours issue which was destined to be Peel's silver bullet. Nor was this the last of the blows to protectionist hopes. On 23 May Russell reasserted leadership over his confused and divided party by summoning a meeting of the Whig peers at Lansdowne House. Clarendon informed them that he had the authority of the Lord Chancellor to say that proxies would be used to strike out any hostile amendment in committee to the corn bill. The two Whig law lords, Cottenham and Campbell, confirmed the constitutionality of that action. The decisive speech, however, was made by Russell, who told the gathering that he could be no party to any alteration in the bill. If the government resigned on the issue, the Whig peers must look elsewhere for a leader. The dissidents bowed to the ultimatum and the

---

[1] The correspondence is in Peel, *Memoirs*, II, 271–81.
[2] RA/C 24/61 (memorandum by Prince Albert); cf. *Broughton*, VI, 172.
[3] *ibid.*, /63 (memorandum by Prince Albert, 24 May).

meeting came to a unanimous agreement to support the bill. With that news Peel's last anxiety vanished. The repeal of the Corn Laws was now virtually accomplished. After all the excitement it was almost an anticlimax when a few days later the bill passed its second reading in the Lords by a majority of forty-seven.

The charmed life which the ministry had been leading since January was now nearly over. The normal machinery of government continued but the only interest now was when the end would come. In discussing the situation with the prince on 27 May Peel observed that although he personally was not depressed, the cabinet was in a very vulnerable position. If the postponed sugar duties, on which the Whigs threatened opposition, were a source of danger, in his view the Irish issue was even more so. Whatever happened, he concluded, the ministry that succeeded him would be an extremely weak one.[1] Just before the Whitsun recess Goulburn made his budget statement. In other circumstances a surplus of over £2½ million might have attracted more than passing comment. But the Chancellor of the Exchequer was not destined to go down in history, as one M.P. waggishly suggested, as 'prosperity Goulburn'. The attention of politicians lay elsewhere. For the protectionists the Lansdowne House meeting had destroyed their last hope of blocking the repeal of the Corn Laws. All that was left for Bentinck now was the satisfaction of revenge; and it was becoming obvious what form it would take. Even before the House adjourned Peel warned the prince that a great effort would be made to defeat the government on the second reading of the Irish protection of life bill.[2] When that long-delayed measure resumed its limping progress after Whitsun the surmise became a certainty. On 6 June the House of Commons Liberals were summoned to a party meeting at Russell's house to decide on their policy towards the bill. With only a few dissentient voices, it was agreed to oppose it on the second reading. Since it was known that many protectionist M.P.s would also vote against the bill, it was taken for granted that this would mean the fall of the government and its replacement by a Whig ministry under Russell. It was settled however that no attempt would be made to kill the Irish bill until the Corn Law repeal was safely through the Lords. In the

[1] RA/Y 154 (Memorandum by Baron Stockmar, 29 May).
[2] RA/C 24/71 (29 May).

meantime the Irish members undertook to keep the debate going night after night until the safe moment arrived. Not all the Irish representatives were happy at the decision to withdraw support from the protection of life bill. But the prospect of office had its usual soothing effect on the whole party from moderate Whig landowners to the extreme metropolitan radicals. Three days later on 9 June there was a similar meeting of protectionist M.P.s at Bankes's house at which a considerable number—reports varied from over seventy to under sixty—pledged themselves to oppose the Irish bill.

The decisions of both meetings were known to Peel within a matter of hours and neither came as much surprise. He was quite certain, he wrote to Anson on 9 June, that enough protectionist members would oppose the second reading to leave little doubt of its fate. His own assessment of the situation was that there would be a majority against the bill and that at least sixty protectionists would be found among them.[1] It was a sober and accurate forecast of what happened sixteen days later. But for the moment Peel's only anxiety was over the corn and tariff bills in the Lords where he was doing his best to secure the attendance of friendly peers in committee. For what happened afterwards he was unconcerned. He was not particularly anxious to remain in office once his major measures were through. He was certainly not disposed to withdraw the Irish bill merely to postpone the inevitable fall of the government by a few weeks or months. To Brougham, who suggested this course, he replied frigidly that to withdraw a bill passed by the Lords at the urgent recommendation of the government would be to sacrifice public interest to the necessities of the ministry. Wellington, whose blood was up, advised action of another kind. 'If I was in your position, I would not allow this blackguard combination to break up the Government.' His plan was to make a recent amendment in the Lords to Hardinge's pension bill into a constitutional issue, and threaten to resign if a new bill was not immediately carried. 'This bold step will certainly carry for you the Corn bill and probably the Assassination bill.' Peel patiently explained to the incensed old duke that resignation on such a point would not be understood. The threat of it would merely embarrass their action on the corn and Irish bills.

[1] RA/C 24/78 (memorandum by Anson), /80–81 (Peel to Anson, 7, 9 June).

The more practical difficulty, he told Arbuthnot a few days later, was the unresolved sugar issue and the government's inability to pass the Irish bill into law even if they won a technical victory on the second reading.[1] No single tactical success in fact could alter the fundamental political weakness of the ministry. He described it to Greville, during a chance conversation one morning in Hyde Park, as similar to that of Shelburne's government before the Fox–North coalition, with the Commons divided into three parties each incapable of standing alone.[2]

Meanwhile, the debate on the second reading of the Irish bill started on 8 June in a thin and apathetic House. It came to life later the same evening when Bentinck rose to speak. His main object in intervening at that early stage was to give notice to the Whigs that he was going to oppose the bill and to invite them to join, as he phrased with his usual elegance, in kicking out both bill and ministers together. He justified his change of front by the delay that had taken place, and more emphatically by the sheer untrustworthiness of the ministers. He asserted that Peel had lost the confidence of every honest man in the House; that he had 'chased and hunted' Canning to death in 1827 while later admitting in the House that he had changed his mind over emancipation as early as 1825; and that he was therefore convicted by his own statement of 'base and dishonest conduct, and conduct inconsistent with the duty of a Minister to his Sovereign'. Then for several more minutes he raved on almost incoherently about Peel's crimes, insult to parliament, treachery, guilt and treason.[3]

The initial effect on the Commons of this charge, dug up from the past of nearly twenty years before, and delivered in Bentinck's customary savage style, was to disgust Whigs, Peelites and many of his own supporters. Nevertheless, there had always been something of a legend about Peel's break with Canning in 1827 and after the lapse of so many years the vagueness of most men's memories merely allowed the legendary aspect to persist. It was not easy to dismiss entirely the idea that there might be something in Bentinck's charge and it was regarded as odd that Peel made no immediate answer. In fact Peel had been so angered at the insult that he felt that there was only one possible reply. At the close of the

[1] 40484 f. 341 (13 June). [2] *Greville*, 7 May 1846. [3] *Hansard*, LXXXVII, 177–84.

debate he asked Lincoln to stay behind while he wrote his customary note for the queen. Then, taking his arm, he walked up Whitehall with him in the stillness of the early morning. On their way he told Lincoln that he regarded Bentinck's language as an aspersion on his honour to which there could only be one form of redress and asked Lincoln to act as his second. When he refused Peel said stubbornly he would ask someone else to act for him. Lincoln remonstrated, Peel persisted, and they walked up and down the empty street arguing until the early-morning workmen began to appear. Peel then consented to go to bed, and Lincoln promised to call on him next day. On his return to Whitehall Gardens he found Peel still determined to challenge Bentinck. Only after much persuasion, including an appeal from the younger man for consideration of the queen's feelings in the matter, did he finally give way.[1]

Instead he made a studiously moderate reply in the Commons a few nights later, amply clearing himself before a sympathetic House but not attempting to retort in kind on the protectionist leader. Disraeli, however, who may well have made the suggestion to Bentinck in the first place, returned to the attack later in the debate. The words on which Bentinck based his accusation were alleged to have occurred in a speech of Peel's in 1829. They did not appear in *Hansard* but were present in the version printed by *The Times* and were apparently confirmed by the *Mirror of Parliament*. What they amounted to was an alleged admission by Peel that he had told Lord Liverpool in 1825 that 'the time was come when something respecting the Catholics ought to be done'. On this slender foundation Disraeli renewed the charge on behalf of his leader who was

---

[1] Goldwin Smith (*op. cit.*, p. 176) had the account of this incident many years later but at first hand from Lincoln. The story given by Martineau (*op. cit.*, p. 80) adds that Lincoln also threatened to go to the police. It is quite possible that both arguments and many others were used. The more important detail is the actual date of the episode. It seems more probable that it occurred on 9 June than on the night of Peel's triumphant vindication on 19 June, though Miss Ramsay places it on the latter date. To have challenged Bentinck after so much delay, when Bentinck had been put so clearly in the wrong, and when most of Peel's speech had been directed against Disraeli, would have been less defensible. Goldwin Smith's account does not make it clear which night it was. Martineau says it was because Peel was so wounded by the aspersion that he left the House without deigning to reply. This seems inherently likely and, if so, fixes the incident on 9 June. Peel's silence on that night is otherwise hard to explain.

precluded by rules of debate from speaking again. The affair now assumed more serious proportions. The protectionists were in high feather and even the Whigs half-shaken in their previous support. Peel rose in considerable temper, promised a full explanation, and asked the House meanwhile to suspend judgement. In the interval he sent down to Drayton where all his old correspondence was stored. Although, since he had to delegate the work to others, not all the relevant letters could be found, enough were turned up to provide him with some of the proof he needed. Numerous friends also rallied to the defence. Liverpool's old crony, Charles Arbuthnot, volunteered advice. George Arbuthnot quoted what Planta, another veteran of the eighteen-twenties, had told him. Edmund Peel from Staffordshire even offered later to write privately to Bentinck with refuting evidence from a letter he had received from his brother in 1827. Even that ageing politician in petticoats the Princess Lieven was so moved by reading in Paris a long report of the affair that she sent an extract from her notes on the ministerial crisis of 1827. This was gratifying but hardly likely to convince the House of Commons. Fortunately more authoritative witnesses were available to supply corroborative information. Greville wrote a sympathetic letter to Graham with a copy of Peel's speech of 1829 published by the office of the *Mirror of Parliament* itself in which the crucial words did not appear and Graham sent along with it the Home Office file of newspapers for the years in question. At Aberdeen's request Delane, the editor of *The Times*, made private enquiries among the surviving reporters of that period. From his researches it was clear that the *Mirror of Parliament*, so far from being an independent authority, was simply a rehash of the daily papers written by professional journalists who earned additional money by providing a slightly vamped-up version for the *Mirror* of what they sent in to their own papers. This was confirmed by Charles Ross who, from his own intimate knowledge of the mechanics of parliamentary reporting in the eighteen-twenties, was able to prove that not only was the *Mirror*'s account a virtual duplicate of *The Times* but the independent reports in the *Post*, *Chronicle*, and *Herald* all agreed with the *Hansard* version and did not support *The Times*.[1] From all

---

[1] 40452 fos. 118 (Graham to Peel with enclosures from Greville), 120 (Ross to Graham); 40455 fos. 361-70.

this it was obvious that *The Times* (of whose six reporters who supplied the *Mirror* with material five, according to Ross, had no knowledge of shorthand) had given an inaccurate account of Peel's words which was not confirmed by any other contemporary source except the suspect *Mirror* which had no reporters of its own in the House.

Armed with this information and his own letters to Liverpool during 1825, Peel on 19 June made a detailed explanation in the Commons, refuting point by point Disraeli's argument but disdaining to take issue with the man himself.

> The hon. gentleman frequently and feelingly complains that I won't condescend to bandy personalities with him. I, Sir, defend myself when defence is necessary. . . . Every man has a right to determine for himself with whom and on what occasion he will descend into the arena of personal contest.[1]

It was a devastating vindication which was cheered enthusiastically all over the House. But Bentinck never knew when he was beaten and could never admit that he was wrong. Rising when the cheers were still echoing round the chamber he tried to renew his charges with an anger and obstinacy which appalled his audience. Greville, who lame with gout had hobbled down to hear Peel and as an ex-racing partner of Bentinck knew better than most his savage inexorable temper, was less surprised at that than by the fluency which the protectionist leader had acquired in his first session as a parliamentary debater.[2] If anything was needed to complete Peel's victory it was the castigation which Bentinck and Disraeli received from speakers all round the House on this occasion. The whole prolonged incident merely degraded the protectionists and ironically, in his last few days of office, added to the moral authority of the prime minister. Peel at least was satisfied. In his note to the queen that night he wrote that 'like every unjust and malignant attack, this according to Sir Robert Peel's impressions, recoiled upon its authors. He thinks the House was completely satisfied.'[3]

So far Peel had been content to wait for events to take their course without trying to make formal decisions before the need arose.

---

[1] *Speeches*, IV, 709.   [2] *Greville*, 20 June 1846.
[3] *VL*, II, 79, misdated 12 June but original in RA/C 24/95 endorsed 19 June.

The time had now come for the final question to be settled. Ellen-borough, with his usual originality and something more than his usual lack of realism, had suggested at the end of May that in order to confound the Whigs and reunite the party, the ministers should resign immediately after the corn and tariff bills were through, and then announce that they would give all possible assistance to the formation of a new Conservative ministry. Peel turned aside this absurdity with the mere statement that he could not be a party to it. First, because it would fetter the queen's freedom of choice; and second, because such a ministry would necessarily be a protectionist one.[1] Now, on 21 June, he put his own very different views on paper. The question he asked was whether it was in the interests of the crown, the country or themselves to stay in office once the corn and tariff bills were passed. 'A government ought to have a *natural* support. A Conservative government should be supported by a Conservative party.' There was no chance, he said bluntly, of their passing the Irish bill. Even if they gained a small majority on the second reading they would still be beaten by obstruction and delay. Meanwhile, the remaining programme of public business would either suffer from neglect or force them in the end to abandon the crimes bill. However effected, the loss of that bill would discredit the government and undermine the administration in Ireland.

The alternative was to dissolve parliament. But on what grounds? To do so over coercion would be the worst and most hazardous course. If *No Popery* was a dangerous cry for a general election, coercion for Ireland would be even more so. To dissolve on any other ground would, or at least should, imply that the government hoped to succeed in the appeal to the electorate. 'I think no Ministers ought to advise the Sovereign to dissolve Parliament without feeling a moral conviction that Dissolution will enable them to carry on the Government of the country.' The dissolution by the Whigs in 1841 had been an unjustifiable act; they must take care not to imitate it. On what grounds then could they appeal to the country? Not on the repeal of the Corn Laws; that would be too personal and retro-spective. On the cry of 'free trade and the destruction of Protection'? This would point to an alliance with free traders of whatever political complexion; logical in theory but impossible in practice.

[1] 40473 fos. 328, 331.

The difference of opinion on sugar alone would destroy such an alliance. But in any event if they did obtain an adventitious majority at a general election, it could only be as the result of 'an unnatural combination with those who agree with us in nothing but the principles of Free Trade'. Such an alliance would be as short in its duration as it would be disastrous in its effects. His own advice was to avoid the mistake of the last government and refuse either to remain in office after they had lost power or to precipitate a general election which they could not win.

This document he sent first to the Duke of Wellington, who replied later that same evening still indomitable and defiant. He admitted that if defeated on a major measure the ministers must dissolve. But the simple question for the electorate would then be whether they wanted Peel to continue at the head of the government or not. In view of all his great services to the state, 'there is no friend of yours who can hesitate in letting this question go to the public'. At a pinch the old duke was prepared to fight even on the straight issue of Irish coercion. Sooner or later, he finished superbly, the people of England must be told what was really going on in Ireland and make up their mind to govern it as a civilised society should be governed. Peel sent both letters in circulation to the cabinet. But whatever disagreement there might have been on the more distant problem, there was general agreement that if defeated on the Irish bill they would have to resign. Though the two recently returned members, Ellenborough and Gladstone, were understandably less enthusiastic at the prospect of so early an end to their official existence, they were in a minority. St. Germans probably spoke for most of them when, in agreeing with his leader's arguments, he wrote:

> The time will come and I do not think that it is far distant when the great body of the Conservatives will acknowledge their error, will once more rally round you as the only leader capable of commanding them, and will again place you in power; but for the moment a large part of them are blind with fury and seek to wreak their vengeance on you. To resist them without allies is impossible; to resist them with such allies as Hume and Roebuck is what I am sure you will not consent to do. You have as it seems to me no alternative but to resign and the sooner you embrace that alternative the better.[1]

[1] 40480 f. 539 (24 June 1846).

The day before a more unexpected correspondent had volunteered advice. In a long cordial letter written on 23 June Cobden urged the prime minister not to resign but to dissolve parliament on a cry of 'Peel and Free Trade'. 'Are you aware of the strength of your position with the country?' he asked, echoing perhaps for the only time in his life the sentiments of the Duke of Wellington. 'Practical reforms are the order of the day, and you are by common consent the practical reformer. The Condition of England question —there is your mission.' But his argument involved two assumptions which Peel could hardly make. That it would be possible to amalgamate Peelites, Liberals and Leaguers in one political party, and that Peel would be ready to drop the Irish bill. In his friendly acknowledgement the prime minister evaded both questions. He referred instead to his weariness with office and merely reminded Cobden in one light sentence that it would be difficult to prevent a dissolution resulting from a defeat on the Irish bill from appearing to be an appeal to the electorate on that issue.[1]

The dilemma was resolved two days later. On 25 June the careful co-ordination of events in the upper and lower Houses, for which both protectionists and Whigs had been working, was brought to its planned termination. The corn bill received its third reading in the House of Lords and a few hours later the government was defeated in the House of Commons on the second reading of the Irish crimes bill. It was the end of an era rather than the beginning of one and the means employed not of a kind to rouse enthusiasm. The House received the announcement of the division in unusual silence. A majority of something like twenty against the bill had been expected and Peel had encouraged free-traders and radicals who thought of abstention to vote in the division on the grounds that nothing they could do would save the ministry. In the event it was a majority of seventy-three. 'A much less emphatic hint', Peel wrote wryly to Hardinge, 'would have sufficed for me.'[2] Of Bentinck's protectionists less than a third followed him into the opposition lobby. Nearly a half of them, refusing to allow their opposition on corn to dictate a factious vote on coercion, voted for the bill. Only some fifty who abstained made the difference between

[1] *Cobden*, pp. 390–401.
[2] Peel, *Memoirs*, II, 309.

the anticipated and the actual margin of defeat.[1] But added to the solid mass of Liberal votes, Bentinck's seventy-four were more than enough. Along with Whigs, Leaguers, Irish and radicals, trooped the hard knot of revengeful Tory members—Bankes, Blackstone, Buller, Burrell, Christopher, Jolliffe, Miles, Neeld, Newdegate, Trollope, Tyrell, Vyvyan, Wodehouse and the rest—to vote the Peelite cabinet out of office and the Conservative party out of power for the next thirty years.

A hasty note scribbled in the House of Commons at half-past one on the morning of Friday, 26 June, was sent off by special train to inform the queen. Twelve hours later the cabinet ministers assembled for the last formal act of their existence. It had come to Peel's knowledge that Ellenborough and Brougham had been talking of recommissioning the cabinet by dropping Peel and Graham, and taking on board some protectionists.[2] If there was ever any substance in this feverish dream, it vanished in the clear light of day. The cabinet meeting was the shortest Gladstone had ever known. Peel told them very simply that he was convinced that the reconstruction of the Conservative party was impossible while he was in office. He had made up his mind to retire and strongly advised the resignation of the entire government. Some spoke in agreement and when he asked them if their decision was unanimous, no one dissented.[3] They then broke up, the departmental ministers to clear up the business of their offices, Peel to make ready for his visit to Osborne.

The following Monday the resignation of the government was announced in both Houses. After Wellington's brief speech in the Lords, Aberdeen in his last utterance as Foreign Secretary had the satisfaction of reporting the acceptance by the United States of the British proposals for a settlement of the Oregon question. Even as it sank the great Conservative ministry of 1841–46 was illumined by the rays of success. The coincidence struck many people, not least the prime minister.[4] His own speech of resignation was made the same day. It was an occasion which few of those present could ever have forgotten. Great crowds had gathered to line the route between

---

[1] For details of voting see W. O. Aydelotte, 'The country gentleman and the repeal of the Corn Laws' (E.H.R., LXXXII, 58–9). In brief, of the 241 Conservative Protectionists, 116 voted for the government; 74 against; and 51 abstained.

[2] VL, II, 81.   [3] 44777 f. 245.   [4] RA/C 25/4 (Peel to Victoria).

Whitehall Gardens and Westminster and when Peel came out of his house he was cheered all the way down to the House of Commons. Inside the chamber was packed with M.P.s, peers and ambassadors. Private business was concluded soon after six and there was a pause of some minutes before Peel arrived, a little breathless with the exertion of walking. His manner was dryer and colder than ever, though any sympathetic observer could guess that this was only a mask for the emotions beneath the surface. He put his box containing the Oregon despatches on the table and sat down for a while until he had recovered himself. Then he rose before a hushed House and began to speak in a quiet voice as though already merely a detached spectator of the political scene.

He observed at the outset that if he had failed to carry the corn and tariff bills, he would have been prepared to dissolve parliament and appeal to the country. That being no longer necessary, the ministers had offered their resignation without advising a dissolution since there was no prospect that a general election would give them the support of a united and powerful party. In what was almost a series of bequests to his successors he reminded them that his fundamental policy towards Ireland was to be found not in the temporary protection of life bill but in the Charitable Bequests Act and the Irish colleges; and in his desire for equality of municipal and political rights, impartial patronage, and reform of the relations between landlord and tenant. He commended a prudent continuation of his commercial policy while regretting that he had left a smaller financial surplus than he would have wished. He made a brief reference to the success of British arms in India and a longer one to Aberdeen's work as Foreign Secretary. This led him to the Oregon settlement, which he explained in detail to the House. Returning for the last time to the repeal of the Corn Laws he said it had been carried by a combination of parties not normally in agreement with each other. Yet neither he nor the Whigs were really entitled to the credit for that measure. The name which ought to be associated with it, he said with deliberate emphasis, was that of Richard Cobden. Then came the famous peroration:

In relinquishing power I shall leave a name severely censured I fear by many who on public grounds deeply regret the severance of party ties, deeply regret that severance, not from interested or personal motives, but from the firm conviction that fidelity to party engagements—the existence and maintenance of a great party—constitutes a powerful instrument of government. I shall surrender power severely censured also by others, who from no interested motives, adhere to the principle of protection, considering the maintenance of it to be essential to the welfare and interests of the country; I shall leave a name execrated by every monopolist who, from less honourable motives, clamours for protection because it conduces to his own individual benefit; but it may be that I shall leave a name sometimes remembered with expressions of good will in the abodes of those whose lot it is to labour, and to earn their daily bread by the sweat of their brow, when they shall recruit their exhausted strength with abundant and untaxed food, the sweeter because it is no longer leavened by a sense of injustice.

He sat down; it was all over. When the cheers subsided he rose again once more, and for the last time as prime minister, to make a formal motion of adjournment. After a few adroit compliments from Palmerston and some honest clumsy praise from Hume, the House broke up. Taking Sir George Clerk's arm Peel left by a side door to avoid the growing crowds outside the main entrance. Once in the street, however, he was immediately recognised. The hats came off and the spectators made a lane along which he passed to continuous cheering which did not cease until long after he had entered his house.[1]

IV

The Corn Laws were repealed and by a parliament which the Whigs had dubbed the Protection Parliament. 'No living soul could have done this but Peel,' wrote Hobhouse.[2] It was a compliment from one who rarely complimented Peel. The repeal of the Corn Laws was in a special sense Peel's own achievement. Not only would it have been impossible without the alliance of Peelite Conservatives and Liberal Whigs in parliament, but Peel's own example brought over many individuals who until 1846 had not

[1] See Jarnac's description of the scene outside the House (*Revue des Deux Mondes*, July 1874, pp. 284 et seq.), and the Bishop of Oxford's of the scene inside (*VL*, II, 82).
[2] *Broughton*, VI, 172.

made up their own minds on the issue. W. S. Dugdale of Warwick-shire, for example, spoke in December at an agricultural association meeting at Rugby in favour of protection but after hearing Peel's proposals in January he changed his mind and voted for repeal.[1] 'Before your speech I was what is termed a protectionist,' wrote a Bedfordshire magistrate, 'your speech and propositions have con-verted me.'[2] In sending his proxy in April Lord Dunraven said that

> I was among that number of your friends, who viewing your corn measures with alarm, could not vote for them, yet the confidence I still feel in your judgement led me to examine the whole subject as fully as I could—certainly dispassionately—and I frankly own the result has been my conversion and conviction that your measures are not only expedient at the present moment but contain principles on which alone the institutions and greatness of England can rest securely.[3]

Outside parliament his influence was even more decisive. There were many unpolitical men who had watched the recovery of the country under Peel's administration, who admired and respected his talents, and were ready to take his advice in the winter of 1845–46 that the time had come to do away with protection. Once he had announced his policy, his immense prestige allowed him to dominate the national scene. One of the less publicised aspects of the repeal of the Corn Laws was that it took place with the Anti-Corn Law League standing by as almost silent spectators. Nobody in 1845 would have thought that possible. But Peel was able to enlist a body of support in the country which outweighed the League. Charles Villiers testified in June that

> no other Minister but Sir Robert Peel could have carried the repeal of the Corn Laws; that half the commercial men in the City would have been against it, had it been attempted by Lord John or anyone else; but their confidence in Sir Robert Peel's knowledge and sagacity is such that they say—'upon a question where so much is said on both sides, upon which our own minds are not made up, we feel that the safest course is to trust to him who has proved himself the greatest financier of the day'.[4]

[1] W. S. Dugdale, Diary.   [2] RA/C 23/34 (T. A. Green to Peel, 31 Jan. 1846).
[3] Wellington (Peel to Wellington, 9 Apr. 1846, encl.).
[4] 40484 f. 321 (Lady Westmoreland to Arbuthnot, 8 June 1846, wrongly ascribed to the Duchess of Northumberland in Peel, III, 352).

Yet for all that, perhaps because of that, it was the most controversial act in the career of a man who seemed deliberately to invite controversy; and has remained controversial ever since.

Even his resignation speech, when words could no longer affect the issue, gave offence. Greville wrote roughly of his 'claptrap about cheap bread'. Hobhouse satirically underlined in his diary the phrase about being remembered by those who earned their living by the sweat of their brows as if it was somehow unworthy of a statesman. Others took violent exception to the remark about selfish monopolists. In the passion of the moment few noticed the careful distinction Peel had made between the monopolists and those who were simply loyal to party engagements or believed conscientiously in the need for protection. Even greater outrage was caused by his tribute to Cobden. The Peelites who risked seats and careers to follow their leader, the Liberals who supplied the massed party vote which carried repeal, both felt that their services had been ignored. The Protectionists took it as one more deliberate insult to themselves. Even Leaguers were jealous that one of their number had been singled out for credit. Irrespective of party there were many old-fashioned people for whom Cobden's coarse and savage attacks on the landed aristocracy were too recent to allow him to be promoted overnight to the status of a great national statesman. Various explanations for Peel's reference were hazarded, most of them ill-natured. Some said it was to divide the Leaguers from the Whigs. Others that it was to make permanent the breach with the Protectionists. When Brougham protested that repeal had been the prime minister's own work and Cobden had nothing to do with it, Peel replied that he had meant his words to apply to Cobden's activity in the House of Commons; but he refused to argue the case. His motives therefore can only be guessed. Part of the explanation lay in the quirks of Peel's temperament. The self-deprecating ascription of credit to another was an old characteristic. Whenever he went through a process of intellectual conversion, a kind of compulsive integrity prompted him to disown any personal claims in favour of those who had arrived earlier at the same conclusions. It was a form of humility that came very close to pride.

But in this case there were more personal reasons. Though he had disliked the provocation offered by the League to the landed classes, he had been increasingly impressed by the talents which the League leader brought to the advocacy of free trade in parliament. It had pained him to discover the continuing animosity of a man against whom he had ceased to feel any hostility. The reconciliation which followed had given him corresponding pleasure which was renewed by the kindness of Cobden's letter to him in June. So far the two had never met privately; but Peel had intended to see Cobden as soon as repeal was through in order to express personally his hope that the hard feelings of the past would be replaced by closer acquaintanceship in the future. But Cobden's health had been overtaxed by his efforts during the previous six years. He had made plans for a holiday abroad and after 26 June ceased to appear in the House. Unable to express his feelings directly to Cobden, Peel deliberately chose to pay a high compliment to him on an occasion which was bound to receive great publicity. Nevertheless, from the narrower aspect of party politics, the reference was a mistake. It widened the breach with the protectionists and fortified Whig suspicions that the danger to their administration would come from an alliance between the Peelites and the middle-class radicals. It is difficult to believe that this was Peel's object. It is unlikely that had he anticipated these reactions, they would have deterred him. Party political considerations had almost ceased to have any weight with him by June 1846.

As for the words about cheap bread and sweaty brows, no dispassionate observer of Peel's later career could have doubted that they came from the heart. Novel as such language was in the mouth of a minister of the crown, it expressed Peel's conviction that the Corn Laws were part of the Condition of England question. Unlike the adherents of both League and Anti-League, he did not fall into the trap of thinking that repeal would confer great economic advantages or bring great economic disadvantages. His earlier defence of the Corn Laws on grounds of utility and expediency was in fact more realistic an appraisal than that offered by either the opponents or supporters of repeal. But by 1845 the significance of the Corn Laws was almost entirely psychological. Peel certainly thought that repeal would do something to alleviate the condition of the masses especially in time of hardship. But more important in his view was that repeal would remove a sense of social injustice, would prove that an aristocratic government was not indifferent to the suffering of the unwashed and unenfranchised, and would draw together the different classes of a divided society. It was not that the League advocated repeal which was the decisive argument; but that the mass of the people had come to accept the rightness of the League's case. He meant repeal to be an act of reconciliation, and the emphasis of his closing words was deliberate. Whatever the aristocratic politicians might think, the effect was dramatically successful. Peel was no phrase-maker like Bright or Disraeli, but his last words as prime minister became the best known and most widely remembered political quotation in Victorian society. In public recollection, in print, in letters cut in stone or cast in metal, they entered into the folk-lore of those classes for whom he had intended them.

Criticisms of another kind were levelled at Peel's tactics in carrying repeal. It was said, for example, that he should have called a party meeting beforehand to explain his policy. Brougham told Aberdeen the following year that had Peel communicated with certain peers and leading Conservatives and held a party conclave, a general agreement might have been reached. This is scarcely plausible. No party meeting could have been held until parliament met and by then the Protectionist Society had already begun the organisation of opinion in the agricultural constituencies which made inevitable the emergence of a secessionist party in the Commons. A party debate would probably have accelerated rather than delayed the split. It would be unrealistic to suppose that in itself it would have solved the crisis within the Conservative Party. Peel subsequently adduced various reasons for not summoning the party to discuss the repeal of the Corn Laws. Before the decision to resign on 5 December any meeting would merely have disclosed the division in the cabinet and decreased the chances of getting agreement. After the resumption of office it was clear in broad terms what the cabinet had decided to do. A meeting would have been pointless unless the ministers had been prepared to give details either of the reasons for their change of policy or of the actual measure they proposed to bring forward. The first would have anticipated the debates in parliament; the second would have led to unfair speculation on the corn market. The decisive reason, however, was probably given in his letter to Aberdeen answering Brougham's criticism. His own mind was made up and he did not think that a meeting would have any other result than to show the strength of the opposition to him within the party. Consultation in those circumstances would have been not only meaningless but positively dangerous.[1] The absence of a party meeting over the repeal of the Corn Laws was in fact the measure of Peel's realisation that it could not be carried by the machinery of party government. Certainly at the time there was no evidence that anyone in the cabinet thought a direct approach to the party worth making or even considering.

From another point of view it was arguable that repeal was unnecessary; that the Irish potato disaster was exaggerated; and that Peel used it as a pretext. This was alleged by protectionist speakers in parliament. It was the basis of Croker's savage attacks on Peel in the *Quarterly* which in January 1847 finally brought their long friendship to a frigid end. It has been repeated since. It was, said Monypenny sixty years later in his *Life of Disraeli*,[2] a crisis in his own mind rather than in the facts. As for the reality of the Irish disaster the facts scarcely need recapitulation. Nobody died of famine in Ireland during Peel's administration; but nobody can say what would have happened but for the £750,000 which was spent in relief, public works and loans, and the shipment of maize which enabled the market price of grain to be kept down. For the rest, by 1847 three million were living on public charity; of a total population in 1845 of 8½ million, between half a million and a million died of hunger and disease; a million and a half emigrated. By the time of the 1851 census the rural population of Ireland had fallen by a quarter; the cottier class was almost extinct. It was the greatest social disaster experienced by any European state in the nineteenth century. Graham's remark to Peel in December 1845 after their return to office that 'we have a Nation to carry, as it were, in our arms' was the sober truth.

There can be little doubt either of the genuineness of Peel's concern. Behind his reasoned arguments to the cabinet in November 1845 was an emotional force. As Chief Secretary in 1817 Peel had seen one Irish famine. He had not forgotten the results: the panic, rioting and crime, the migration of the foodless and unemployable peasants to the towns, the swarming together of beggars and destitute, the choked poor-houses and pestilential slums, the fleas, lice,

---

[1] 43065 f. 322; Peel, *Memoirs*, II, 322.   [2] (1912 edn) II, 346.

typhus, dysentery, the overflowing hospitals, the dying and the dead. The religious-minded Graham enclosed with one batch of Irish correspondence a note to Peel which ended solemnly 'it is awful to observe how the Almighty humbles the pride of nations'. Peel was not given to the biblical language which emotion often induced in his Home Secretary but his sense of the Irish tragedy was no less profound. When it did break out it was all the more impressive for being kept so habitually in check. 'Are you to hesitate in averting famine which may come, because it possibly may not come?' he asked savagely in the Commons during the repeal debates. 'Are you to look to and depend upon chance in such an extremity? Or, Good God, are you to sit in cabinet, and consider and calculate how much diarrhoea, and bloody flux, and dysentery, a people can bear before it becomes necessary for you to provide them with food?'[1] He did not talk much about such matters; and his reticence may have deceived others. Fear, as the Duke of Wellington observed when discussing Peel's motives a few months later with Croker, is a strong emotion. It acts in secret and the evidence for it is not easy to establish. But he added a remark which would have been arresting from anyone, and was doubly so from a man as hard and matter-of-fact as the duke. 'I cannot doubt', he wrote to the sceptical Croker, 'that which passed under my own view and frequent observation day after day. I mean the alarms of the consequences in Ireland of the potato disease. I never witnessed in any case such agony.'[2] Strong emotion is not necessarily a good guide to action; but the emotion was there.

Once the reality of the Irish crisis was admitted, the argument inevitably moved to tactics. Theoretically it was open to Peel to suspend the Corn Laws by Order in Council and defy either the League to repeal or the Protectionists to reimpose. This, to put it moderately, would hardly have been a statesmanlike attitude and would certainly not have been capable of indefinite prolongation. In any case the cabinet was unanimous in November that suspension was virtually equivalent to repeal. Stanley himself was guilty of a shift in opinion if, as Graham said, he was prepared after Russell's failure to agree to suspension provided it was not followed by repeal. If suspension was accepted, the whole train of reasoning which Peel

[1] *Speeches*, IV, 639 (27 March 1846).   [2] *Croker*, III, 65.

put before his colleagues came into operation. It would be difficult to refute his argument, not least because it is impossible to say what would have happened had a different course been followed. But certain facts stand out. The duration of the Irish famine, as Peel suspected would be the case, was considerably longer than one year. The crop failure in 1846 was worse than that of 1845. There was another catastrophic outbreak of the disease in 1848 and again, on a decreased scale, in 1849. Not until 1850 was it clearly beginning to die out. Suspension of the Corn Laws would therefore in all probability have lasted for some three years. Meanwhile a general election would have come and gone. During this period the Corn Laws would have been subjected to continuous attack. The quiescence of the League in the 1846 session gave a misleading impression of its strength and determination.

The situation would have been very different had the government shown no sign of repealing as distinct from suspending the Corn Laws. The brief campaign of December 1845 proved that the crocodile still had sharp teeth. Failure to propose a final settlement would have provoked a sustained campaign, fed by harrowing stories from Ireland, as the first effects of the famine became known, and rising to a violent crescendo in the general election of 1847. Had Peel, as Lincoln suggested, delayed announcing his conversion until the eve of that election, it would hardly have prevented a split in his party and would certainly have precipitated an electoral struggle on the Corn Law issue while the famine was at its height. It was for precisely that reason that Peel had no intention of dissolving unless compelled to do so by a defeat in the House. The 1831 election had been a sufficient experience for one lifetime of a direct appeal to the passions and interests of the population. As it was, repeal took place with the League passive, the country quiet, and farmers enjoying a good price for their products. The end of agricultural protection could hardly have come at a better time. Indeed many observers noted a shift in farming opinion towards repeal during the actual contest in parliament. Politicians are often accused of acting only at the last moment and under pressure of circumstances. But action which averts a threatened crisis exposes them to another charge. Because the danger is averted, it can be argued that it would never have come. The success of preventive action is difficult to estimate, impossible to prove. Only failure provides the necessary evidence.

Yet when all the political and intellectual arguments are weighed, it is also true that for Peel the abolition of the Corn Laws had become a question of time; the declaration of his inability to defend them a question of timing. The Irish crisis made him do hastily and without warning what he intended to do later and after due notice. From a party point of view it was disastrous. It was an accusation against him then and later that though there was a practical justification for his policy when he returned to power at the end of December, he had already betrayed his party by his advice to the cabinet in November. In a sense even this distinction is artificial. If Russell's failure brought Peel back with a clear mandate to settle the Corn Law question, it was Peel's own resignation which had given Russell his opportunity in the first place. The significant issue was not the technical justification of the cabinet for doing something at the end of December which they had refused to do at the beginning of November. It was the attitude which conditioned Peel's actions throughout the crisis. This is the real basis for the charge that Peel 'betrayed' his party. The word itself perhaps obscures rather than clarifies the problem. Peel argued with force that he was serving the true interests of the aristocracy and the landed interest in what he did and that the repeal of the Corn Laws was the most conservative act of his life. His followers could justly complain of desertion, hardly of betrayal. He had warned them before and after taking office that he would be guided only by his sense of what the national interest required. He had always maintained that agriculture must ultimately rely on its own resources. He had never supported the Corn Laws on principle. He had said that he would abandon his support if convinced that repeal would benefit the working classes. Yet he had defended them: he had come into power at the head of a party based on the landed interest; and in 1841 that interest expected protection to continue. What he did in 1846 was to sacrifice not only his consistency but the views and commitments of most of the men who had put him in office. He did so rather than persist in a policy which he had come to believe was politically dangerous and economically unsound. It was a choice of evils and he chose what seemed to be the lesser one. But the consciousness of his action is seen in his refusal to discuss in any of his cabinet memoranda the question which occurred at once to nearly all of them: their party obligations and the effect of his proposals on party unity. With his strong sense of executive responsibility it was not surprising that at the start of the crisis Peel was prepared to do what he thought right rather than escape odium by resigning it to others. For most of November there was nothing to show that the task could be delegated to others. Neither the Whigs collectively nor Russell individually had yet declared in favour of repeal. But the *Edinburgh Letter* cut most of that ground from under him. The argument of executive responsibility began to lose force and the compromise plan of 2 December was designed to bring an increasingly unsatisfactory situation to an end. Its failure made him regret that he had not resigned when first left in a minority in the cabinet.

Obviously the Russell fiasco immensely strengthened Peel's position. The executive argument, tenable in November but crumbling away four weeks later, was now firmer than ever. Nevertheless the emphasis which Peel placed on his changed position after 20 December cannot hide the fact that from the start he took the line that the Irish crisis meant the end of the 1842 Act. It was not unreasonable for colleagues like Stanley to conclude, as Peel himself said in cabinet in 1844, that there was no halfway house between that Act and repeal. It was here that he showed little consideration and perhaps not much sympathy for his party. This was something which even his most loyal supporters found hard to bear. For some, suddenly caught between past professions, obligations to constituents, and loyalty to their leader, it was an almost insoluble predicament. 'My criticism on your present measure', wrote one of the latter, Sturt of Dorset, 'shall be very gentle—whether it might not have been managed without stranding others and myself.'[1] The quietness of the reproach is more telling than the abuse of the protectionists. Peel's action meant not only that he alienated many of his party who did not agree with him but that he sacrificed the political careers of some who did. The 'betrayal' of 1846 was not merely of protectionists but of the Peelites too. In private relationships Peel was loyal almost to excess; but on a public issue he was capable of the hardness without which perhaps no statesman can succeed. When Pusey of

[1] *Peel*, III, 335.

613

Berkshire wrote to Peel in February to explain that he meant to cast one vote against repeal in deference to his constituents and then absent himself in order not to obstruct Peel's policy any further, the prime minister noted caustically on the docket that 'Mr. Pusey's letter is a good specimen of an agricultural leader—I never saw such an avowal under a Senator's own handwriting'.[1] Such men might have been spared a little sympathy, even if they did not rise to Peel's own standards of the duty resting on members of the imperial legislature.

But by that date Peel had few reserves of strength or feeling to devote to others. In 1845 he was already a tired man. Despite the stimulus he received from resuming office in December the personal campaign waged against him by Bentinck and Disraeli in the session of 1846 left him more weary of office and more disillusioned with party politics than ever before. Both publicly and privately, to his colleagues as to the queen, he constantly referred to his physical inability to carry on much longer the burden of government. To the queen he said on taking his leave as prime minister that though he parted from her with the deepest feeling of gratitude and attachment, there was one thing she must not ask of him and that was to place himself in that position again.[2] To a man in Peel's state of mind in the autumn of 1845, weary of office and occasionally wondering how it would all end, there must have been a powerful subconscious attraction in the prospect of one last supreme achievement with which to crown his memorable five years of power. All the evidence suggests not only that he knew repeal would break up the government but that he did what he could to ensure that there would be no evasion of the challenge to his continuance in office. It might not be too extravagant to suggest that Peel wanted his ministry to come to an end, provided he could choose the time and manner. From December 1845 he had only one object in mind: the passing of the corn and tariff bills. The Irish protection of life bill became merely test case for the survival of the government; not a contrived but genuine issue, but a test case all the same. Had the government surmounted this, there would have been others. In making repeal and the tariff his single objective, he was also bringing his ministry to an end. The two events were inseparable and he gave no sign that

[1] RA/C 23/56–7.   [2] 44777 f. 261 (conversation with Gladstone, July 1846).

he regretted their inseparability. It was the achievement which mattered; not the price which had to be paid for it.

Over almost a decade Peel had seen the Corn Laws grow into a bitter social issue. His own mind had hardened towards a solution and events had thrown in his way what seemed to him a great and imperative opportunity for ending the conflict. His sense of timing, which was one of his superlative qualities as a politician, was still faultless. The most striking feature of the repeal of the Corn Laws was the calmness and control with which it was carried through. The crisis, to invert Monypenny's phrase, was in the Conservative Party rather than in parliament and the country. Though there was some talk there was never any real danger of defeat in the legislature; and the country watched quietly and expectantly as the bill slowly but inexorably made its way to the statute book. After all the violent propaganda and massive preparations of the League, the actual repeal of the Corn Laws came almost as an anticlimax. The battle for which they had been arming was never fought. Without a dissolution, without a general election, without any threat of physical force, the issue was finally set at rest. The aristocratic constitution had shown its powers of resilience and statesmanship, and in so doing had strengthened its claims to the confidence of the nation. It was for this in the last analysis for which Peel had been working; and in which, though at great personal cost, he had succeeded.

CHAPTER

17

PEELITES, WHIGS AND PROTECTIONISTS

The day after his speech of resignation Peel slipped quietly away to Staffordshire. Julia, for whom the long battle of the Corn Laws had been a personal anguish, came up to town as soon as she heard the news of the government's defeat and together they travelled back home. There in the summer peace of Drayton Park, far from the last despairing importunities of patronage-hunters, Peel spent his first few days of leisure replying to the letters and addresses of condolence which streamed in from home and abroad. It was many years since he had been able to enjoy such personal freedom. 'I do not know how other men are constituted,' he wrote to Aberdeen in August, 'but I can say with truth that I find the day too short for my present occupations, which chiefly consist in lounging in my library, directing improvements, riding with the boys and my daughter, and pitying Lord John and his colleagues.'[1]

The Whigs were in need of consolation. In the brief remnant of the session they had only brought forward two important pieces of legislation, but both in their different ways gave a foretaste of the new pattern of administration. The first was a doctrinaire free trade measure to admit slave-grown sugar on the same terms as ordinary foreign sugar. It was passed by a substantial majority to which Peel contributed both by his presence and his voice; though he made plain that his motive was simply to support the ministers in their new position. The margin of 130 votes secured by the government against protectionist opposition seemed to Peel handsome enough to guarantee their safety for the rest of the year.[2] But having displayed

[1] 43065 f. 203, ptly pr. *Peel*, III, 458.
[2] *ibid.*, f. 199 (Peel to Aberdeen, 1 Aug. 1846).

their fidelity to party policy on sugar, the ministers proceeded to anger and dismay their Liberal followers by proposing a renewal of the Irish Arms Act which they had opposed in 1843. Confronted by bitter complaints from their own side and a majority of only 33 on the second reading, the ministers capped a lamentable performance by withdrawing the bill eleven days before the end of the session. Such inconsistency and timidity evoked Peel's scorn. It also promised ill for the prospects of strong government under the new prime minister. 'I met Lord John at Windsor Castle,' Peel observed caustically to Lincoln in October, 'and certainly without any feelings of envy at his triumph. He looked miserable enough. Every Irish murder must give him a twinge—a shooting pain under the left ribs.'[1]

Despite this early evidence of the personal and parliamentary deficiencies of the Whig administration, Peel made it excessively clear to his friends that he had no intention of returning to office or leading a party again. The savagery of the protectionist attacks had produced in him an emotional reaction which at one point even made him consider retirement from parliament. Though, possibly out of loyalty to the queen, he had receded from that extreme decision, he was determined to maintain in future a completely independent position. Herbert objected that no politician of his standing had ever done so, except Lord Bute who was hardly a politician and certainly not an example. Peel promptly instanced Lord Grenville. If the analogy was weak, it at least showed that his mind had been revolving the problem. When Gladstone argued in similar vein that it would be impossible for him to remain in the Commons as an isolated figure, he replied that events would answer that question better than any reasoning; and he muttered something to the effect that if necessary he would get out of parliament.[2] Tiredness, pain and resentment all contributed to this intransigency. Writing to Graham on 3 July to thank him for his aid in their last successful campaign together, he added that he could not have sustained the effort much longer. 'Few know what I have been suffering from noises and pains in the head.'[3] Yet in the succeeding months his

---

[1] Newcastle, 26 Oct. (1846).
[2] 44777 f. 245 (9 July), 261 (24 July 1846).
[3] Graham; 40452 f. 143 (copy), ptly pr. Peel, III, 456.

adamant attitude showed no signs of softening. To Hardinge still far away in India he wrote unrestrainedly in September of his joy at being released from the 'painful and thankless' task of averting the dangers threatening 'a set of men with great possessions and little foresight who call themselves Conservatives and Protectionists, and whose only chance of safety is that their counsels shall not be followed'. As for the future, he said stubbornly, he intended to keep aloof from party combinations. As far as a man could be justified in coming to such a decision, he was determined never to take office again. He would only consent to be head of a government and that required more youth, more ambition, more love of power than he could pretend to. The following February he expressed in scarcely less forcible terms to the same sympathetic friend his satisfaction at being able to enjoy not only leisure and family life but political independence and 'freedom from the base servitude to which a minister must submit who is content to sacrifice the interests of a great empire to those of a party'.[1]

For the younger Peelites this was not an inspiring prospect. It might be a source of pride to count themselves as the followers of a man who stood supreme among contemporary politicians and, as Greville more than once observed, would be swept back into power on any popular vote. But it was daunting to be told that he had no intention of ever leading them back to the fleshpots of office. There was of course the alternative of making their own way in the dislocated political world of the post-repeal years. But personal loyalty, intellectual conviction, and recent animosities made this almost impossible. The opportunities were there, but they could not bring themselves to accept them. Before he left town on 30 June Peel had an interview with Lord John Russell on general matters arising out of the transfer of office. Russell, impressed by Peel's cordiality and lack of reserve, asked him whether he would object to the inclusion of some of the younger members of his administration in the new government. Peel said he had no personal objection but added discouragingly that he thought the attempt would be useless and unwise. He was surprised when he learned soon after that invitations to join the Whig cabinet had been sent to Lincoln, Herbert and Dalhousie. All three promptly refused without troubling to refer

[1] Hardinge, 24 Sept. 1846, 7 Feb. 1847, ptly pr. *Peel*, III, 472-6.

to Peel, though Lincoln and Herbert showed their replies to Graham. They based their refusal on public grounds; in fact they were offended at the mere offer. Russell had aggravated the offence by sending all three an identical note. 'A new mode of beating up for a cabinet', Lincoln wrote indignantly to Peel,'—by circular!' Peel, though he thought their decision sensible, took the more charitable if more cynical view that Russell's action had been made less with any real hope of success than to disprove the Whig reputation for exclusiveness and jobbery.[1] He was quite prepared however to advise the acceptance of less ostentatiously political ties with the government, such as Wellington's retention of his post of Commander-in-Chief and membership of the Council for the Duchy of Lancaster by Graham and Lincoln; the more so since he knew that all three offers had the strong support of the queen, if not indeed actually suggested by her.[2]

Peel and his followers were at least on common ground in not wanting a formal alliance with the Whigs. Despite the studied neutrality of their chief, the younger men continued to do what they could to keep his party in being. Though Beresford, the protectionist whip, had set up a rival desk in the Carlton, Bonham professed to be unimpressed by his activities and reported cheerfully to Peel in November that Dalhousie, Mahon, Goulburn, Cardwell and others kept up a strong Peelite presence at the Club.[3] With growing doubts as to the wisdom or effectiveness of the government's handling of the ever worsening Irish situation, the Peelites were disposed to be more openly critical of the ministers than their leader. Though they discounted the influence of Bentinck and Disraeli, they were afraid also that if there was no Peelite opposition in the Commons, many Conservative backbenchers would look to Stanley as the one substantial counterweight to the Whigs. With the new session rapidly approaching Goulburn, Lincoln, Herbert, Dalhousie, Cardwell and Young thought it essential to demonstrate the continued vitality of the Peelite section of the party. It was agreed therefore to send out the

[1] Graham (Peel to Graham, 4 July); 40480 f. 554 (Peel to St. Germans); Newcastle (Lincoln to Peel, 2 July); Wellington (Peel to Wellington, 4 July); 40461 f. 480; *Greville*, 4 July 1846.

[2] Goulburn (Peel to Goulburn, 17 Oct. 1846); Graham (Peel to Graham, 3 July, 2 Sept. 1846).

[3] 40597 f. 273.

customary pre-sessional letters requesting attendance to all known supporters of Peel. The object, as Goulburn explained it to Peel in December, was to keep together a party not so much of opposition as of observation, ready to support the government against the wilder schemes of the protectionists but equally ready to ally with the latter in anything that seemed in the national interest. Peel was not enthusiastic. He replied to Goulburn at considerable length, repeating his determination never to take office or organise a party, and showing clearly how bitterly he still felt about his treatment at the hands of the protectionists. As far as Goulburn's professed object was concerned, he observed with unkind realism,

> A party of *observation* as you call it will not succeed. The adherents of a party must be stimulated by something more exciting than the desire to have a compact body throwing its weight into the scale in favour of national interests. Competition for power and the determination to take every legitimate advantage of your opponents in possession of it, are the indispensable cement of a compact and growing party. As I am not prepared to enter into that competition, as from feelings I cannot control the necessity of resuming power would be perfectly odious to me, I am wholly disqualified for the reorganisation of a party.[1]

On the issue of letters he made various criticisms, some rather captious, forbade the mention of his own name, but said he made no objection to the use of any other. With this lukewarm assent the little knot of Peelites went ahead with their preparations. About two hundred and forty letters were sent out over Young's signature and by the beginning of January nearly a hundred favourable replies had already been received.[2]

At the start of the new session the younger Peelites were in good heart. Their whipping-in activity had at least the advantage of preserving their physical unity in the House of Commons. After the resignation of the government the previous summer the ex-ministers had taken their position on the opposition front bench between the red box and the Speaker's chair. Some disagreeable encroachment on these places was expected from Bentinck and Disraeli, who had descended to the front bench along with some of the leading Pro-

[1] Goulburn (20 Dec. 1846).
[2] 40445 fos. 386, 388, 391; 40481 f. 392; 40452 f. 188.

tectionists. But in the 1847 session the Peelites retained without a challenge their former position and the front-bench protectionists continued to sit below the red box. As a result Peel was assured of supporters seated to his left and rear, the respective buffers between the two groups along the front bench being, as Lincoln wrote light-heartedly, 'the not very thickly wadded forms of Mr. Goulburn and Mr. Bankes'.[1] So distrustful a proximity did not argue much for the prospect of Conservative reunion. Some politicians had been talking of such an event before the Whigs were even warm in office. But those most prominent as advocates of reconciliation did not inspire much trust. Two days after Peel's resignation speech Brougham had suggested that Peel should hold a *conciliabule* to discuss opposition tactics in both Houses. To Graham, who relayed the proposal to Drayton, Peel replied bitingly that 'having escaped from the Frying Pan of office I am little disposed to jump into the Hell Fire of a *conciliabule* of which Lord Brougham and Lord Londonderry would be the leading members'.[2] Lyndhurst, to whom both enmities and principles were largely foreign, next put himself forward as a mediator. He had talks with Wellington, Peel, Stanley and Gladstone, made an overture through a third party to Bentinck, and even enquired from Goulburn whether he would be prepared to lead in the House of Commons. Bentinck, falling foul of Lyndhurst over an absurd charge of corruption against the late administration, subsequently chose to expose these activities in the Commons. In a crushing rejoinder in the upper House Lyndhurst read out a letter from Peel containing an emphatic refusal to enter into any party combination for the purpose of regaining office. Though nobody had much approved of Lyndhurst's manœuvres, Lincoln, Gladstone and probably others regretted this public disclosure of what Lincoln called Peel's 'repudiation of office *in prospectu*'.[3]

Premature as these early efforts had been, some of the Peelites did not rule out the ultimate possibility of reunion. But when in the spring of 1847 Goulburn tentatively raised the question of some communication on tactics between the two wings of the opposition, he received little encouragement from his leader. It was perhaps

[1] 40481 f. 400, cf. 40598 f. 62 (Young to Peel, 28 Jan. 1847).
[2] Graham (2 July 1846).
[3] 40481 f. 354; see also 44777 fos. 245, 261; T. Martin, *Life of Lyndhurst*, pp. 416–26.

unfortunate that at the moment Goulburn's letter arrived, Peel had been going through his 1845 correspondence and all his hurt feelings, never far below the surface, had been revived.

> I do not wish [he replied stiffly on 3 April] to be any impediment whatever to the Reunion of the Conservative Body but I cannot be a party to the attempt at Reunion. There are grounds both public and personal which forbid me from being so. I totally differ from the Protectionists (if their name denotes their opinions) on the principle of Protection, and it would be repugnant to my feelings and indeed inconsistent with my sense of Honour to enter into a Protectionist Confederacy with such of the leaders of that Party as during the last session of Parliament either openly preferred or covertly sanctioned accusations against me that were equally injurious to my Character and destitute of Truth.
>
> I should act thus even if I were (which I am not) a Candidate for Power, or if I were (which also I am not) inclined to undertake the painful and thankless task of reconstructing a party. I quite admit however that my position is a peculiar one, justifying feelings on my part which others perhaps need not, perhaps ought not to entertain, and I repeat with the utmost sincerity that I have not the slightest wish to obstruct or discourage any union into which they may be disposed to enter.[1]

There was possibly in the last sentence some slight softening of attitude. It was something for him to recognise how much his attitude was conditioned by a purely emotional reaction. But he still thought Goulburn optimistic and he still found it easy to conclude when brooding over the events of his ministry, that the root causes of party disunity went far back beyond 1845.[2]

What seemed to Peel of more immediate consequence than plans for Conservative reunion was the plight of the uncertain Whig ministry still wallowing in the trough of the Irish famine. Wheat, which had been 47s in August 1846, had risen to over 70s by January 1847 and went on rising steadily until it topped 100s in May. One of the first acts of the government at the start of the new session was to suspend the Corn Laws and Navigation Acts; and despite the healthy surplus inherited from his predecessor, the new

[1] Goulburn.
[2] Cf. his letter to Graham, written the same day (Graham).

Chancellor of the Exchequer Charles Wood had to obtain sanction for a loan of £8 million to meet the continued distress in Ireland when he brought forward his budget in February. On this he had already taken soundings with the late prime minister. Indeed Wood showed from the start an almost deferential desire to obtain Peel's advice and co-operation. The previous December he had contrived an opportunity to write to Peel about banking policy and the operation of the Bank Charter Act. 'I should be very sorry', he added flatteringly in a second letter, 'that in my hands, you had ever reason to think that your measure was not fully carried out. I never gave a more hearty support to any measure since I have had a seat in parliament.' On the eve of the new session he went a step further by inviting John Young to a private dinner at which he talked about the difficulties of the government in Ireland and the shortcomings of his colleagues in finance. 'I presume, meaning the whole to come to you', reported the sceptical Peelite whip. 'For no other reason could he have sent for me. He praised you very highly, looks on your being Prime Minister again, if in health, as certain.'[1] Then at the beginning of February Edward Ellice, the Whigs' general man of business, called on Peel and asked whether he would have any objection to discussing financial matters and allowing Ellice to report back to Wood. Peel expressed a friendly willingness to assist in matters which he had so much at heart. Ellice then explained that he had advised the government to meet the financial difficulties caused by the general economic situation and the enormous expenditure on Irish relief by raising the income tax to 1s and extending it, for a limited period, to Ireland. While paying a judicious compliment to the honesty and courage of this suggestion, Peel was doubtful of its practicability. But he promised to think about it and talk with Wood whenever the Chancellor expressed a wish to see him.

Encouraged by this Wood made a discreet visit to Peel after church on Sunday, 7 February. Peel assured him that they could depend on his desire to support any bold attempt by the government to meet the revenue deficit by direct taxation. But he put before his visitor various points which he thought would need careful consideration before the government committed themselves. In the first

[1] 40598 fos. 38–41.

place, he observed, it would be worse than useless for ministers to bring forward such proposals without being sure that they had the parliamentary strength to carry them. Defeat would be a blow not only to the stability of the administration but to the whole principle of the income tax. In the second place, the state of Ireland made the extension of the tax to that country a questionable decision at that moment; and the attempt to disarm criticism by imposing a time limit might prove an awkward restriction on future ministerial freedom of action. Since the income tax expired in 1848, he concluded, it might be better to postpone any changes until next session, when the subject would come up for discussion in any case, rather than provoke opposition prematurely. Nevertheless, if Wood and Russell decided to adopt Ellice's proposals in 1847, his inclination would certainly be to assist them. He warned Wood, however, that he could speak only for himself, and not for a party.[1]

His words could hardly have failed to carry weight. No financial heroics were attempted when Wood brought forward his budget statement a fortnight later. But though the cabinet wisely decided not to tempt providence, enough difficulties came their way unasked. Peel himself was critical of the ministerial methods of famine relief and distrustful of Russell's temporising attitude towards Bentinck. Yet he did what he could to assist the government in the Commons. Bentinck's proposal to lend £16 million to railway companies in Ireland, which Russell allowed to go to a second reading, was in the end massively defeated. Peel contributed to the rout with a speech in his best forensic style, dissecting all the protectionist arguments and leaving little of Bentinck's case but the pieces. In March he defended the government against Hume's motion to repudiate the Russian loan in retaliation for the annexation of Cracow by Austria under an agreement between the three eastern powers. He spoke on behalf of the Whig educational scheme introduced in April against much radical and Dissenting opposition; and he came to their rescue once more in May in a debate on financial policy and the Bank of England. In the last the protectionists had indulged in much intemperate abuse of the Bank Charter Act of 1844. Peel had the human satisfaction of following Disraeli

[1] For the relations between Peel and Wood in the winter of 1846–47 see 4059 fos. 346–50 (Dec. 1846); 40598 fos. 72–87.

in debate and methodically exposing all the contradictions and fallacies in the various amateur remedies put forward by the country party. The session, the last of the 1841 parliament, ended in July with the Whig administration still intact but with no appearance of strength either at home or abroad. Talking with Greville in February Peel had observed that he feared Russell did not exert the authority and determination a prime minister should.[1] The remainder of the session, marked by a trail of abandoned bills and endless gossip about Palmerston's headstrong handling of foreign affairs, did nothing to shake this conviction.

The Peelites faced the general election with at least the rudiments of organisation. Bonham busied himself with electoral correspondence and refused an invitation to Drayton early in August because there was nobody in London to whom he could delegate the work. Young kept a record of results and there was a residue of electioneering money at his disposal, even if in the event little call was made upon it. Though some of the rank and file had retired from politics, Bonham was able to report on 9 August that they had more than kept their total of ninety; and apart from Manners Sutton at Cambridge and Sir F. Kelly at Lyme Regis, all their former official men had been successful. This was all the more gratifying since the Protectionists had sustained severe losses, particularly in the boroughs. The appeal to the electorate, of which there had been much talk in 1846, had resulted in fact in an endorsement of Peel and free trade. Not economic but religious policy had been the stumbling-block. 'Maynooth has certainly destroyed several of our friends,' Bonham observed to Peel on 2 August, 'Free Trade hardly any.'[2] The nominal strength of the government had materially increased. But since it included some forty members pledged against Whig educational and religious policy, the increase promised to be as much an embarrassment as an assistance. 'To no party except the extreme Radicals is there any real cause of triumph,' was Bonham's conclusion. In a House of Commons with at least four discernible groupings, the government could regularly depend on less than half of the total number of members.[3]

---

[1] *Greville*, 25 Feb. 1847.
[2] 40599 f. 121.
[3] *English Politics*, p. 192.

Peel, returned for Tamworth for a modest outlay of £70 on election expenses and a conventional canvass of the borough and outlying hamlets, professed little interest in the result of the election as a whole and none in the various estimates of the size of the Peelite party. At Tamworth William Yates Peel, without consulting his brother, also put up as candidate. Though some Conservatives were annoyed at his intervention and suspected protectionist plotting, Peel's former Conservative colleague Captain A'Court finally declined to stand. Peel himself studiously refused to interfere or to express any opinion about the second seat.[1] Even his much publicised *Tamworth Letter* was designed for a general public rather than his Staffordshire constituents. 'Some of whom', he observed lightly to Aberdeen, 'will, I fear, have hardly patience to read it through. I rather wished to have a decent opportunity for putting some things upon record.'[2]

The *Tamworth Letter* in fact attracted considerable attention both among politicians and in the country at large, and was used by at least some Peelites in their election campaigns. But it contained yet another unequivocal statement by Peel that he lacked any desire to return to office or lead a party. As Bonham not unreasonably retorted after receiving a copy:

> As the minor characters of the Play cannot make a House without a good Hamlet, and as I believe that Constituencies have at least as keen a relish for 'favours expected' as their representatives, I am not sure that they will be benefited by an intimation which tho' not new to them will not be particularly agreeable to the Electors whose votes are sought for the Goulburns, Cardwells etc.[3]

Had the obstinate Hamlet of Tamworth wished for a larger stage, he could easily have secured it. He had received invitations to stand for North Lancashire, for the City, and for other large towns. He refused them all, even though he was pressed hard by Brougham to accept nomination for the City of London. But loyalty to his own constituency and, equally cogent perhaps, a reluctance to exchange

---

[1] 40598 fos. 303–49. H. J. Pye on behalf of the local protectionists denied any responsibility for putting up W. Y. Peel in order to annoy Sir Robert and unseat A'Court.

[2] 43065 f. 318.

[3] 40599 f. 45 (17 July).

the unfettered freedom of Tamworth for the more onerous responsibilities of a large electorate, made him deaf to all flattery and solicitation. Yet to others it seemed that the election had created a situation in which the government would either have to become more radical in its policy or be content to rely on the casual support of Peelites and Protectionists. In either case Peel's future parliamentary position would be crucial. Victoria in September tried to elicit from Aberdeen some clear information about the state of the Commons and the strength of Peel's party. Aberdeen made the bleak reply that as the basis of party consisted either in the possession or pursuit of office and Peel was interested in neither, it could hardly be said that he had a party at all. This evidently surprised and discomforted the queen. Why she should be surprised, Peel wrote back to Aberdeen, he could not imagine, since he had lost no opportunity of saying exactly the same thing to her. But he added, with a tartness which suggested a certain sensitivity on the subject, 'I suppose Sovereigns are equally incredulous as to the unwillingness of Laymen and Churchmen for preferment, and give no more credit to the professions of a retired minister than to the *nolo episcopari* of an aspiring Dean'.[1]

Events in the autumn demonstrated, however, that members of the government still looked to him for support in time of trouble. The latter half of 1847 was overshadowed by mounting anxiety in business and commercial circles. Several circumstances contributed to the crisis, including a temporary shortage of American cotton, the raw material of Britain's main export industry, and the characteristic recklessness of early-Victorian business enterprise. But the decisive factor was the incongruous coincidence of railway mania and Irish famine. The boom in railway construction since 1844 had strained the entire economy. The famine had produced high prices, speculation and a worldwide hunt for foodstuffs. Investment in foreign railway schemes and heavy purchases of food abroad together led to a serious drain of gold. The Bank of England, having fed the inflationary market with cheap money for so long, was ill placed to check speculation. In the summer of 1847, with supplies at last beginning to pour into the country and the prospect of a good

[1] 40455 f. 442 (Aberdeen to Peel, 18 Sept.); 43065 f. 327 (Peel to Aberdeen, 22 Sept. 1847).

harvest at home, the corn market collapsed. The shock was felt throughout the commercial world. Credit was restricted; there was a run on gold; and even the solid Scotch bankers added to the general alarm by calling for aid. The growing tale of bankruptcies, headed by the corn-brokers, now included some East and West India houses, nearly a dozen provincial banks, and many small London trading firms. The Bank of England, which had been previously slow to react to the monetary pressure, announced at the start of October that it would make no more advances on public securities and raised the bank rate to the crisis level of 6 per cent. But though the Bank directors were confident of their ability to weather the storm, there was growing public and private pressure on the government to suspend the Bank Charter Act. Following discussions between the Bank and the Chancellor of the Exchequer on 23 October, the government sent a formal letter on 25 October advising the Bank to increase its discounts and advances but at a minimum rate of 8 per cent, promising indemnity if it went beyond the maximum issue of notes allowed by the Act.

That weekend Peel had been invited to Windsor Castle. Reaching Whitehall Gardens late on Friday evening he found an urgent note from Wood asking for a quarter of an hour of Peel's time before he went on to Windsor. Wood came at ten, stayed till midnight, and came back three times the following morning. Talking with un-ministerial frankness, he described to Peel the mounting pressure on the cabinet and made it clear that despite his resistance the Bank Act might have to be suspended. Peel counselled fortitude in the face of the inevitable demands for cheap money which every financial crisis produced and told him to listen to such orthodox experts as Jones Loyd, Cotton and Norman, the governor of the Bank of England, rather than City financiers and frightened northern in-dustrialists. Nevertheless, he added, if after consultation with the Bank Wood decided that there was less danger in intervening than in standing aloof, he would support him in any action he undertook. At one point Wood produced a draft letter to the Bank for his criticism. It was a long letter, giving detailed reasons for suspension and ending with a specific injunction to the Bank to raise the bank rate to 8 per cent. In composing it Wood had been influenced by Jones Loyd who had pressed for a 'reasoned manifesto' and a clear directive about the bank rate since he distrusted the ability of the Bank directors to act with sufficient firmness. Peel told Wood to cut out three-quarters of the document and dictated on the spot the kind of letter he himself would send. On the question of the bank rate he urged Wood to say no more than that the directors should be free to raise it above the market level rather than tie their hands by naming an actual figure.[1]

Wood duly redrafted the note on the lines Peel had indicated and after consulting Russell softened the directive on the bank rate to an expression of opinion that in existing conditions it should be not less than 8 per cent. He also, at Peel's suggestion, secured Russell's permission for the situation to be explained to the prince. Next day at Windsor Peel had a long talk with Albert on the crisis. Finding the prince had some difficulty in grasping the technicalities of the subject, he wrote out for him from memory a paper on the 1844 Act and the extent to which it was proposed to modify it. While he was still at the Castle an official box arrived containing the cabinet's decision to intervene and a request from Russell that all the papers should be shown to Peel. In further conversation with the Duke of Bedford on the Monday Peel assured him of his approval for what had been done and his readiness to support it in parliament. But to dispel any possible suspicion, when he got back to Drayton he wrote to the prince asking him to show his impromptu memorandum to Russell so that the prime minister could see for himself that there was nothing in it that could not have come from the cabinet itself.[2]

Like the cool-headed men in Threadneedle Street, Peel had hoped that the panic would exhaust itself without the need for government interference.[3] In the event there was no need to infringe the 1844 Act. From the end of October the reserve of notes and bullion began to build up and 1848 saw the Bank once more on an even keel. Whether the panic would have subsided without the government's letter was debatable. Many were ready to debate it; and by calling parliament together in November the cabinet clearly thought that

[1] This answers the question asked by Clapham (*Bank of England*, II, 209).

[2] 40599 fos. 293–300 (Wood to Peel), f. 307 (Peel's memorandum of the conversations with Wood on the crisis); RA/C 54/19–27; Goulburn (Peel to Goulburn, 28 Oct. 1847); *Greville*, 1 Nov. 1847.

[3] For the Bank's views see Clapham, *Bank of England*, II, 208–11.

an opportunity for debate should be given. What they anticipated was a grand parliamentary attack from protectionists, private bankers, Scottish members, and in fact from all who had suffered in nerves or pocket from the crisis. What they proposed was a select commission to enquire into the causes of the crisis and in particular the effect of Peel's Act of 1844. This on the face of it seemed a slightly hostile approach. But Peel knew from Wood that it was merely a device suggested by Francis Baring, the former Whig chancellor of the exchequer, to forestall and deflect parliamentary criticism.[1] In the ensuing debate Wood showed himself a staunch defender of the Act and refused to accept that its failure to prevent the crisis was proof of its unsoundness. But there were many M.P.s who, from genuine conviction or a desire to discredit Peel, were anxious to prove the contrary. The long, confused discussion which followed tended to take the form of an inquest not only on the 1844 Act but on the whole commercial and financial policy of the late ministry.

Peel's contribution to the debate on 3 December was therefore awaited with interest, all the keener since he had so far made no public comment on the action of the government. In the peculiar position for an opposition member of virtually winding up the debate on behalf of the government, he achieved the ambidextrous feat of vindicating the 1844 Act, approving its suspension by the cabinet, and supporting the motion for a commission of enquiry. He confessed his disappointment that the Act had not prevented panic and uncertainty but criticised the Bank for not having restricted credit and raised the bank rate at an earlier stage. Nevertheless, he concluded, the other two objects of the Act, to maintain convertibility and prevent unrestricted paper circulation, had been achieved. The main difficulties had arisen from lack of capital which no legislation or government could supply.

The inquest of 1847 showed clearly enough that the Act had not caused the crisis. At most it could be criticised for not having prevented it. The danger that the Bank could not back its note issue with gold had been removed in 1844; but there remained the opposite danger that the banking department would not be able to meet the claims of its depositors in notes. In essence the 1847 crisis was one not of currency but of credit. With larger reserves the banking

[1] 40599 f. 293.

department could have given credit more freely; and the lowness of its reserves had been mainly due to the failure of the Bank between 1845 and 1847 to control the market by a more vigorous use of discount rate and credit restriction. The ministers however were pleased at Peel's speech; the crisis was passing; and the political issue of the 1844 Act relegated to the decent obscurity of a select commission. By the end of the year the Whigs could breathe freely once more. They even took the advantage of the emergency autumn session to bring in an Irish crimes act of the kind they had failed to pass the previous year. Though Peel privately thought they had missed an opportunity to obtain an even stronger measure,[1] he supported them handsomely and the bill went through with little opposition.

II

Gratifying as it was for his opinion to be sought in time of crisis, the confidential relations established between Peel and Charles Wood during 1847 could only circumscribe still further his parliamentary position. In many respects he was disposed to think that the Whigs were not up to their work. This in itself was an argument for giving them assistance. But that meant continually subordinating his own views to the overriding necessity of keeping the ministry in office. The renewed session in 1848 demonstrated more forcibly than ever that Peel was becoming a captive of Whig policy. A feature of that year was the disastrous budget introduced by Russell in February, which dragged on in an atmosphere of indecision, recrimination and hostility for most of the session. Faced with a current deficit of nearly £1 million, and an estimated future deficiency of over £2 million as the result of higher services expenditure, Irish relief, industrial recession, and the Kaffir War, the cabinet had finally braced itself for an increase in the income tax from 7d to 1s and its renewal for a period of five years. The storm of opposition from protectionists and radicals led to a precipitate retreat at the end of the month to the safer ground of 7d for three years. Nevertheless, the drastic pruning of expenditure which this entailed, and the political weakness that made it necessary, exposed the ministers to a running

[1] *Greville*, 7 Dec. 1847.

fusillade from all the opponents of income tax and apostles of cheap government. In effect what Russell had attempted was the application of Peel's fiscal doctrine without Peel's political tact. In private conferences with Goulburn, Gladstone and Cardwell when the budget was first introduced, Peel expressed the view that if he had been responsible, he would have absorbed most of the extraordinary items into the exchequer balance, renewed the income tax at 7*d*, and pledged the government to bring current expenditure into line with revenue. This in the end was exactly what the government decided to do; and in making that decision they must have known, through Graham and Greville, that it was Peel's own advice.[1]

In February and March, when the unhappy Wood was caught in a crossfire from Cobden and Disraeli, time after time Peel came to the government's support. He defended the existing structure of the income tax against both the attempt to reduce the assessment on 'precarious' incomes and Hume's move to reduce the period of renewal to one year. He also put the weight of his authority behind the increased expenditure on the armed forces. Though the references to his own policy when in office enraged the protectionists, this in the opinion of Tufnell, the government chief whip, was more than counterbalanced by the effect he had in rallying free-traders to the government.[2] This was not the sum of his services. In May the ministers belatedly sought to fulfil their pledge of reviewing the Navigation Laws. They were met by a hostile amendment from Herries on behalf of the protectionist party. Once more Peel came to the aid of the government with an impressive speech[3] in which he cut the arguments of Herries and Disraeli to ribbons and left Russell, as he himself confessed, with virtually nothing to do in winding up the debate. In the end lack of time compelled the cabinet to abandon the bill. But even after Peel had departed for Drayton he was twice recalled by an urgent summons from Charles Wood in the dying weeks of the session to help defeat a motion by Herries on the currency question.

It had been a demoralising session for the Whigs. In the spring

---

[1] 40777 f. 275; *Greville*, 7 March 1848.
[2] Russell (P.R.O. 30/22/7, Wood (8, 10 March), Tufnell (7 March 1848) to Russell) *Greville*, 23 Feb. 1848.
[3] 9 June 1848.

Russell's floundering exhibition on the budget and his notorious ill-health had raised the possibility of his resignation. There was a strong feeling in some ministerial circles that the administration could not go on without him and in that case Peel would become a national necessity.[1] No encouragement came from Drayton for this line of thought. When Hatherton, the former Whig Chief Secretary, was visiting there at the end of February, Peel told him that no consideration would induce him to return to office. When Hatherton suggested that circumstances might force him back, Peel merely reiterated his determination to preserve his independence and as far as possible his privacy; and he went out of his way to praise Russell and stress his desire to support him.[2] Greville in March made much the same kind of suggestion to Graham and received much the same reply. Peel was adamant against taking office; he was supported in this by Lady Peel; he had no party; it was an absurdity to think he could ever lead either Whigs or protectionists.

It was a daunting catalogue and yet people still speculated. Graham was notoriously more royalist than his king; and not everybody shared his view that a reunion of the Conservative Party was an absurdity. The division among the protectionists in December over Russell's motion for the admission of Jews to parliament had been followed by Bentinck's eviction from the titular leadership of the party in the Commons. His replacement by the Duke of Rutland's son, Lord Granby, was one of the few comic episodes of the 1848 session. A party patronised by rather than led by Stanley, with a thirty-three year old ducal nonentity as his lieutenant, seventy-year-old Herries as its economic expert, and its one man of talent still disliked and distrusted, seemed to have neither present strength nor future prospects. In January Goulburn was confidentially approached by a protectionist emissary who told him that Bentinck and Disraeli were deposed and asked him whether he would take over the leadership. Goulburn declined this flattering offer and observed guardedly that closer co-operation in the Commons was the only reliable road of reconciliation. Nevertheless, he, Lincoln, Gladstone and Graham were asked soon afterwards whether they would meet Ellenborough

[1] Clarendon (Greville to Clarendon, 6 March 1848).
[2] Russell (P.R.O. 30/22/8 Pt. 1), extract from Lord Hatherton's Journal, 28 Feb. 1848.

and Lyndhurst to prepare the ground for a conference with Bankes and Lord Granby. Graham and Lincoln refused point blank. Goulburn and Gladstone thought that they could not refuse meeting Ellenborough; but in the end they heard nothing more. If the protectionists had little confidence in their old leaders, it seemed that they had even less in any new ones that might be drafted in from the Peelites. As the session wore on, moreover, Goulburn's remark about the need for more harmonious action in the Commons began to take on a slightly ironic appearance. On many points there was still a yawning gulf between Peelites and protectionists; nor was the difference merely one of policy.[1] The personal hatred of Peel was still alive among some of the country members. When he rose to speak in the Navigation Laws debate, a section of the protectionists had exceeded even the normal inelegance of House of Commons manners by setting up a great hooting and bellowing in an effort to close the debate before he could be heard. If these exhibitions were rare, few men who sat daily in the House were unaware of the depth of feeling from which they sprang.

Leaderless or not, the protectionists held together during the 1848 session and at times ran the government close to defeat. The most serious occasion was in June over an issue which seemed fated to embarrass every administration which raised it, the sugar duties. From the start of the session growing economic distress in the West Indies had provided a useful platform for the protectionists from which to fire off shots at the Whig Act of 1846 in particular and free trade policy in general. After fumbling with the problem in the early months Russell finally proposed a relief programme involving a loan of half a million to encourage immigration of labour, a progressive reduction in the duty on colonial sugar, and a special duty on certain kinds of foreign sugar. The plan encountered criticism from all over the House. The evangelicals attacked it as encouraging slavery; the West India lobby as insufficient to rescue the colonial planters from impending ruin; the protectionists because it did not give enough protection; and the free-traders because it gave too much. The Peelites themselves disliked the scheme. But while Peel and Graham were prepared on general principles to support the government against an attack headed by Bentinck and Disraeli

[1] Graham (Peel to Graham, 12 Jan. 1848); 44777 f. 278.

their former colleagues—Goulburn, Gladstone, Lincoln, Cardwell and Herbert—were itching to oppose. The first two had a special interest in the West Indies and all of them were growing restive at Peel's perpetual readiness to allow the exigencies of the Whig parliamentary position to override his real feelings about their policy. It was the most disturbing division that had so far opened up in the Peelite ranks. Ringed with opposition on three sides, the government were for a time in real danger of defeat.

It was true that Bentinck, in his usual rancorous fashion, muddied the issue by charging Grey and Hawes, the secretary and under-secretary of the Colonial Department, with dishonest official conduct. But Russell in turn lost support by a sarcastic reference to Bentinck's race-course habits. The younger Peelites had no intention of entering into a permanent alliance with the protectionists. But they were unmoved by the prospect of the government's resignation. They did not think that the weak and blundering Whig administration could continue much longer; and they calculated that the only possible outcome would be a central coalition under Peel. If their reluctant leader needed to be impelled into office, some of them were ready to give him an unsolicited push. It is unlikely that Peel was blind to these ingenuous stratagems. At the height of the crisis Greville told Graham that if the Whigs were defeated, Russell would probably consult Peel before advising the queen on the choice of a successor. Two days later, probably (as Greville thought) after conferring with Peel, Graham impressed on Greville that it was essential that Stanley be given a fair chance to form an administration. He would doubtless fail, but there must be no previous consultation between Russell and Peel which would give him an excuse to decline.[1] This was duly reported by Greville to the Duke of Bedford; but the turn of the protectionists was not come yet. Peel intervened in the crucial debate on Pakington's hostile amendment with a judicious speech[2] which possibly helped to decide the votes of some wavering Peelites. In the end the government scraped through by fifteen votes, even though Goulburn, Gladstone, Herbert, Lincoln, and Cardwell all persisted in their opposition. The margin was narrower than the whips had expected but it carried the battered Whig administration through to the end of the session.

[1] *Greville*, 26, 30 June 1848.   [2] 29 June 1848.

Nevertheless, their credit as a government had almost disappeared. More than ever they had the appearance of a caretaker cabinet keeping the administration of the country going until some more permanent political combination could replace them. In a year which from March onward had seen a succession of successful revolutions in almost every important state in Europe and one last great Chartist demonstration in England, the need for a strong government seemed more pressing than at any time since 1830. In justice to Russell it could be said that he had persisted in his efforts to recruit individual Peelites. Graham in the summer of 1847 had turned down an offer of the Governor-Generalship of India—as a result, the Whigs thought, of Peel's advice. They had better luck with Dalhousie who consulted not Peel but Wellington and finally accepted the post in August. But this hardly assisted the ministers in their domestic troubles, especially as Dalhousie made it painfully clear that his consent in no way implied an abandonment of his former political connections. In October Russell invited St. Germans to become head of the Poor Law Commission. He declined after sending a draft letter of refusal to Peel and waiting for an answer. In endorsing the wisdom of St. Germans's refusal, Peel was perhaps being more objective than might have been thought. Excellent and honourable a man as St. Germans was, Peel confided to Aberdeen, he was not exactly 'the material of which you could construct a Breakwater between the Executive government and an unpopular Poor Law'.[1] Still Russell struggled on with his dispiriting courtship of the heartless Peelites. In June 1848 Hardinge, now back from India, was invited to go to Ireland as Commander-in-Chief. But Hardinge was reluctant to wound the susceptibilities of his old Peninsular colleague, General Blakeney, who had been in Ireland since 1838. He only offered to go if there was a real emergency and then merely as second-in-command.

Having drawn these outlying coverts with little profit, Russell finally resolved on another attempt at bigger game. The death of Auckland on the first day of 1849 provided him with an occasion and four days later he asked Charles Wood to explain to Peel in confidence what he intended. His wish was to take three of Peel's

[1] 43065 f. 333 (Peel to Aberdeen, 7 Oct. 1847); 40480 fos. 552-4 (corr. between Peel and St. Germans, 2, 3 Oct. 1847); 40475 f. 285.

senior colleagues into the cabinet; and he pointed out that though the Peelites might be asked to form an administration if the Whigs resigned, they could never succeed if they were opposed by the protectionists and detached from the Whigs. The alternative in that case would be a protectionist government under Stanley, an event which he assumed would please neither of the other two parties.[1] But Wood had little opportunity for preliminary diplomacy. Acting with his usual impulsiveness Russell wrote on 10 January directly to Graham asking him to come to London to discuss the possibility of his taking Auckland's former post of First Lord of the Admiralty. It was sensible tactics to begin with Graham. Not only was he emotionally more averse to 'Conservative Reunion' than any of the Peelites, but he had never entirely broken his old Whig contacts. Moreover, since Peel and Graham were, in Greville's phrase, political man and wife, the adhesion of the one would be taken as implying the collaboration of the other. Yet Graham, though he wavered, was unable to bring himself to accept. At an interview with Russell on 12 January he declined answering until he could speak with Peel, whom he expected to intercept at Whitehall Gardens on his way back to Drayton from Windsor. Missing him by a few minutes, Graham first decided to travel down to Tamworth the following day and then changed his mind. Peel's carriage sent to meet him at the railway station returned with a note left by Graham as he went through to the effect that he had refused the offer without implicating Peel in any way.[2]

With that opening defeat Russell's campaign collapsed entirely. He had probably intended, after recruiting Graham, to invite into the cabinet Lincoln and either Cardwell or Herbert. But it would have been useless to have proceeded. As soon as the rumour spread around Lincoln took care to inform Cardwell that he would at once refuse any offer; and to Peel he expressed astonishment that Graham had hesitated to the extent of having two interviews with Russell before making up his mind. To make matters worse the *Morning Chronicle*, which Lincoln and Herbert had acquired as an organ of Peelite opinion in 1848, when commenting on the affair made hostile

[1] *Russell, Later Corr.*, ed. G. P. Gooch (1930), I, 192.
[2] 40452 fos. 305, 315; Graham (Russell to Graham, 10 Jan.; Graham to Russell, 12 Jan.; Peel to Graham, 13, 20 Jan. 1848).

remarks about the government to which the *Globe* retorted with an attack on Peel. In fact Peel had probably been relieved that Graham had not found it necessary to consult him; and he privately deplored the tone which the *Morning Chronicle* adopted towards the Whigs. In all the successive overtures made by Russell to the Peelites since 1846 he had made a point of not expressing an opinion until after the event. Pleased as he was at the loyalty of his old followers, to have offered advice on their political conduct would have implied an assumption of leadership which he was not prepared to make. Nevertheless, some of them had the impression that the events of 1848 had produced a faint softening in his attitude. To the revolutionary movements on the continent, the efforts of Cobden and Bright to revive the old League as a new radical party, and the continued political ineptitude of the Whigs, had been added one more marginal factor. In September Bentinck had died.

The following month the observant Bonham was at Drayton in a party which included Lincoln, Hardinge and Goulburn. It struck him that there was great alteration in Peel's attitude towards the possibility of a return to office, not so much in anything specific which Peel said as in his general criticisms of the ministry and his friendly references to several former followers who had left him in 1846.[1] Goulburn made the same comment to Cardwell.

> Our Host's caution in speaking on political prospects was as great if not greater than ever but I thought I perceived a less repugnance on his part to the idea of a resumption of office as not merely possible but as ultimately not altogether improbable. I could not certainly quote anything which fell from him as justifying that opinion but yet taking the whole tenor of the conversation I drew from it that inference. Undoubtedly the death of Lord George has diminished to a certain extent the difficulties of reuniting the main body of the conservative party as with him will die the most rancorous part of personal hostility; and the difficulty of finding a new leader will mainly operate upon many protectionists to induce a return to their former connexions.[2]

The last consideration was one which occurred to many people, not least that incurable busybody, Lord Londonderry.

[1] Stanhope (Bonham to Mahon, 9 Oct. 1848).
[2] Cardwell (1 Oct. 1848).

A short time before Graham and Hardinge had both been at Wynyard. Their host told them that he had been sounding Aberdeen on the possibility of his becoming prime minister and asked Graham whether he would take part in reorganising and leading the Conservative party in the House of Commons. Disraeli, he was assured, would offer no obstacle as he would fall in with anything which offered him material advantage. Graham was distinctly cool. His principles, he told Londonderry, were incompatible with those of the protectionists and High Tories. With some of them, after all that had happened, personal reconciliation was quite impossible.[1] Peel received full reports of Londonderry's overtures, both by letter from Graham and verbally from Hardinge who came on from Wynyard to join the party at Drayton. There was little in Peel's reply to Graham that justified Bonham's and Goulburn's speculations. Peel too had been asked to Wynyard but had refused partly because he had 'no fancy for being paraded at horticultural breakfasts and Bazaars', and partly because he felt that the invitation had some political object behind it. His own interpretation of the conversations with Graham and Hardinge was somewhat cynical. He suspected that Londonderry had been prompted by Stanley and Disraeli because they were anxious to obtain Aberdeen's support for an attack on Palmerston's foreign policy. Londonderry had professed much disinterested anxiety about what would happen if the government collapsed. What he and his confederates were really anxious for, in Peel's opinion, was some means of overthrowing it. But he kept his own counsel and did not mention his correspondence with Graham to any of the other Peelites at Drayton. Meeting Goulburn in London a month later he enquired whether he knew anything of the state of the protectionists or of any attempt to reconcile the different sections of the Conservative Party; but Goulburn knew nothing.[2] Though in January 1849 Graham received another letter from the indefatigable Londonderry reviving the project of Conservative reunion, these country house cabals seemed to him more unrealistic than ever. In March he confided to Peel that the breach in the old Conservative Party was becoming more and more impossible to bridge. As for himself, he added, 'the divisions between me and the Government

---

[1] 40452 f. 278 (Graham to Peel, 25 Sept. 1848).
[2] Graham (Peel to Graham, 26 Sept., 2 Nov. 1848).

are not so wide as between me and the implacable Protectionists'.[1]

The new session arrived therefore with Peel still aloof and independent, and not even his most intimate friends much wiser about his ultimate views on the fragile political situation. It was not obvious in fact that he had any ultimate views. Everything he said and did suggested that he was content to assist the Whigs as long as they could provide an administration which protected the essentials of Peelite policy. The difficulty, for Peel and still more for his followers, was that only part of the Whig administration could be described in these terms. The recurrent dilemma was to decide how far general support of the government should be allowed to override dislike of particular measures. If Russell's ministry could only be sustained by swallowing all their proposals, it was not a very palatable diet. Gladstone was convinced that Peel would never oppose the ministers on any crucial issue, because he did not want either to risk their resignation or to appear to be seeking office for himself. 'Of all members of Parliament he has the smallest degree of free judgement in regard to the announced measures of the government.'[2] As long as Wood remained at the Exchequer, there was some guarantee of financial orthodoxy, though even in the field of fiscal policy there was room for Peelite criticism of Whig measures. When it came to Irish administration and foreign policy it was not so much a question of criticism as of flat disagreement. There was hardly a feature of Russell's handling of the Irish problem, for example, of which Peel could wholeheartedly approve. He thought the famine relief given by the government inadequate, the machinery unsuitable, and the distribution of loans misguided. In the enforcement of law and order he thought the Whigs too timid; in their larger policy for Ireland too unimaginative. The political and economic paralysis caused by the famine provided in his view an opportunity for carrying through fundamental reforms in Ireland which would have been unthinkable a few years earlier. He was prepared to support land legislation of the type recommended by the Devon Commission and it was an open secret that his views on the religious problem had already travelled far beyond Maynooth. At a party at Vernon Harcourt's house at Nuneham in July 1848 which included Sheil and Bentinck's

[1] 40452 fos. 221, 328, cf. *Graham*, II, 80–2.
[2] 44777 f. 283 (March 1849).

brother-in-law Evelyn Denison, he talked freely about the need for taking advantage of the favourable situation in Ireland to make a final settlement of the relations between the state and the Roman Catholic Church. In their distressed state the Irish priests would accept any reasonable offer and he told Sheil that what he favoured was direct endowment of the clergy by the government. When Sheil told him flatteringly that having solved two great questions, there was no reason why he should not solve this one also, Peel said he was too old. 'It would be impossible for me to do it,' he observed, though sooner or later it would have to be done.[1]

Whether John Russell had the stomach for such a radical programme as this was doubtful. In his interview in January 1849 Graham told him rather harshly that Ireland was being occupied, not governed, and emphasised the need for more constructive policies. Russell, however, seemed to think that as long as Ireland remained peaceful, there was no case for starting anything controversial. In his peculiar parliamentary position this was understandable; but it did not satisfy either Graham or Peel. In the 1849 session Irish affairs continued to absorb parliamentary attention. One of the early measures put forward by the government in fact was a renewal of the Act suspending *Habeas Corpus* passed the previous year. Peel supported it with obvious reluctance. He had been annoyed by Russell's tactlessness in dragging up the old Appropriation dispute earlier in the debate; and while accepting the government's proposal he said pointedly that he had no great confidence in the men by whom the Act was to be administered. When the Whigs opposed his own coercion Act in 1846, he reminded the House, Russell had argued that redress must precede coercion. He would not exact a similar pledge now, he said bitingly, but he hoped the government would take the opportunity of introducing reforms for Ireland on which they could all agree. Something of what he himself had in mind he disclosed at the end of March in one of the most interesting though most neglected of all his speeches on Ireland.

The occasion was a debate on the Irish Poor Law. He used it to discuss with calmness and great perceptivity the true nature of 'the

---

[1] W. T. McCullagh, *Memoirs of R. L. Sheil* (1855), II, 387–8. A report of Peel's conversation was sent to Bentinck by Denison, see Disraeli Papers (Bentinck to Disraeli, 24 Sept. 1848).

evils that afflict that unhappy country' and the possible remedies that a British government might undertake. He pointed out at the start that the famine had not created but merely exposed the realities of the Irish problem. Using the evidence of the Devon Commission he argued that what was wrong with Ireland was its fundamentally defective social and economic structure: the mass of impoverished labourers, the struggling small-holders, and the debt-encumbered, inefficient estates which threw an impossible burden on their more efficient neighbours. What they must ensure was that Ireland should not be dragged down once more into the vicious circle of dearth, debt, disorder, crime and repression. A few good harvests in Ireland might be the worst thing that could happen if they distracted the attention of the legislature from the deep-seated causes of Ireland's ills. The famine had presented them with the opportunity to lay the foundations for a better social order. 'We are now deliberating and acting on one of the most extraordinary crises in the history of a nation.' No single remedy existed, but a start must be made somewhere. They could begin with the distressed areas, appoint a government commission to take over bankrupt poor-law unions and superintend loans for drainage, fisheries, public works, and emigration. But all these devices would be useless unless the landed estates could be improved and until there was a shift from subsistence potato-growing to large-scale cattle and cereal farming. Why should not such a commission, he enquired boldly, take over the encumbered or insolvent estates at present administered by the Court of Chancery and arrange for them to be farmed by men of capital and efficiency? Why not, he proceeded with even greater daring, make the commission not only responsible for managing encumbered estate but 'instrumental in forwarding the transfer of property from on class of proprietors to another'. To those who might be startled a the notion of breaking up landed estates, he offered the reminde that what was done for Ireland was in the end done for the good o Great Britain. A sick Ireland affected the health of the entire com munity. 'It is in the growing conviction that its weakness will b our weakness, its disease our disease, that I see the faint hope of decisive remedy.'[1]

It was a speech of great courage and imagination which evoked

[1] *Speeches*, IV, 788 (30 March 1849).

warm response from many with first-hand knowledge of the Irish scene. But the suggestions it contained were a generation before their time. The Whigs were solidly against them, though Clarendon, the Lord Lieutenant, who was in London at the time, was sufficiently impressed to seek an interview with Peel the following week. It was a friendly and unreserved meeting. They discussed Peel's plan and Clarendon elaborated all the ministerial objections to it. So far from taking offence Peel assured Clarendon of his desire to assist in any policy of improvement and begged him not to leave Ireland until he had done something for the country. Though he provided Clarendon with a long memorandum on his proposals, he said he would willingly abandon his own scheme if Clarendon would take up the question of encumbered estates. Despite Russell's lack of enthusiasm, Clarendon did bring forward an Irish encumbered estates bill later in the session.[1] Peel's suggestion for a special commission to replace the administration of the Court of Chancery was adopted with limited powers to sell to new owners; and though it fell short of the wider policy he had advocated, Peel supported the measure. Between Clarendon and Peel there was a sympathy on Irish problems which the Lord Lieutenant was unable to detect among the grandees of his own party; and at intervals in the next twelve months there were further consultations between the two men on such matters as the constitution of the new Irish university and Russell's plan for abolishing the office of Lord Lieutenant.

Though there seemed little likelihood of any radical Irish measures emerging from Russell's cabinet, it was something that Peel could influence individual members of the administration. A policy of association at least offered more reward than one of opposition; and the 1849 session saw a continuation of his steady support for the government. He helped to deflect a radical attack on colonial administration in British Guiana and Ceylon, and was instrumental in ensuring that the committee to which these questions were referred came to an innocuous conclusion.[2] He supported the Jewish disabilities bill in a debate marked by the maiden speech of his son Frederick which brought the customary compliments to his pleased

[1] *Peel*, III, 509–19, cf. *Greville*, 2, 6 Apr. 1849; 20 Feb. 1850.
[2] See the *Autobiography* of H. Taylor (1885), II, 37–8 for an account of Peel's astute handling of the Guiana committee.

parents. He did not play a prominent part in the debate on the repeal of the Navigation Acts which was one of the major events of the session but he was active behind the scenes in mobilising Peelite support. There was considerable discussion between Peel, Goulburn, Lincoln, Cardwell and Gladstone on the government's bill and not all the Peelites were enamoured of the proposals. After the second reading but before the committee stage Gladstone and Cardwell went to Peel with a forceful representation of their objections. He advised them to communicate their misgivings to the government but made it clear that he could not countenance any attempt to impose changes on the ministers by a factious combination in the House of Commons. He believed, he told his sceptical younger colleagues, that there would soon be an attempt to reimpose protective duties which he would resist with all his powers. He would be sorry therefore to see them involved in any move against a government which after all was acting on Conservative principles and with his general approval. Gladstone duly approached Labouchere who told him that the ministers had made up their minds to resist any amendment. With that the threatened Peelite opposition ended.[1] Though the bill encountered a sharp attack from the protectionists headed by Herries and Granby, the Peelites refrained from any damaging criticisms. Graham took over Peel's usual role in delivering a masterful speech on the third reading which anticipated most of what Russell had to say when winding up for the government; and the bill passed by a majority of over sixty.

The real danger was not in the Commons, however, but in the Lords. There the opposition had declared their intention of defeating the bill regardless of the consequences and it was generally expected that the government would resign if beaten. Before the crucial debate came on Charles Wood sent Peel an analysis of the probable voting of the peers and asked him to use his influence. Peel was not happy at this request. He had always been chary of soliciting political support among members of the upper House. Ellenborough was known to be a strong opponent of the measure; and Ripon preferred to remain silent. Wood's wistful hope that some prominent Peelite like St. Germans would speak early in the debate on the ministerial side was disappointed. When on Peel's advice he approached

[1] 44777 fos. 283, 286 (March 1849).

Ashburton, he only encountered another refusal. The government's anxiety was shown by an unusual request from Albert for Peel's assistance in getting Buccleuch's support. Peel declined to make a direct approach but he impressed on Aberdeen and Hardinge the need to stand by the ministers and he anticipated that Aberdeen's example would tell on Buccleuch.[1] Even this cautious activity was valuable in a debate where every vote might prove significant. On the second reading in the Lords in May the bill passed by only the narrow margin of ten votes. But it was enough and once more the ministers seemed safe for the remainder of the session.

Nevertheless the renewed depression in agriculture, coinciding ominously with the legal expiry of the Corn Laws in 1849, provided the protectionists with both excuse and incentive to continue their attacks on the government. In July Disraeli moved for a select committee on the state of the nation in a speech which contained a general denunciation of free trade policy. Four nights later Peel intervened in the debate with one of the most comprehensive explanations of his concept of free trade that he had ever made. Ignoring all the political topics raised by previous speakers, he concentrated on the one issue of commercial policy and answered Disraeli point by point both on his criticism of the government and on the economic policy he advocated as an alternative. It was an exercise in which Peel excelled: logical, practical and analytic, conducted without passion or personal animosity, as though as he said, it was 'a purely scientific controversy into which party feeling did not enter'—and with a command of knowledge and experience which no other man in parliament could match. Apart from the massive deployment of factual evidence which filled most of the speech, two other features were noticeable. One was the courtesy with which he spoke of his opponents. He complimented Disraeli on his 'very able speech'. As for the protectionists,

> of that party, whatever cause of dissension may have arisen, I shall never speak without sincere respect. I believe them to be in error as to this principle of protection, but that error is influenced by no selfish or interested motive.

The other was his insistence that free trade was not just a matter of money.

[1] 40601 fos. 277–92, ptly pr. *Peel*, III, 504; 40441 f. 394; RA/C 57/21.

It is a question which affects the happiness of the people, which affects their social progress, their progress in morals, in the enjoyment of life, in refinement of taste and civilisation of manners—it concerns these things at least as much as it concerns the accumulation of wealth.

Later in the speech he referred to the effect on Chartism of the confidence inspired by the repeal of the Corn Laws among the working classes.

It was that confidence in the generosity and justice of parliament which in no small degree enabled you to pass triumphantly through that storm which convulsed other nations in 1848.

It was not only London which had presented a 'majestic spectacle' in the critical spring of that year.

You must go to the great seats of manufacturing industry—to Stockport, to Paisley, to Manchester—to the mines—to collieries . . . to places where in former periods—in such times as 1818 and 1819—social order has been shaken to its foundation

to find the most striking examples of the new spirit among the mass of the working classes. 'Surely', he ended, 'these are significant facts—surely these are decisive proofs.' And he asked the House not to throw away these great fruits of their policy for the paltry measures suggested by the opposition.

As a final exposition of the policy he had pursued since 1841 it could hardly have been bettered in either manner or matter. No one could know that they were listening to Peel's swan-song on the work of his last great ministry. But Disraeli's motion was defeated by 140 votes and a few weeks later the session came to an end. All the same, the problem of Whig political weakness and Whig policy uncertainties remained even after members had dispersed. Between protectionist demands for agricultural concessions and radical demands for cheaper government, the ministers' path seemed as faltering as ever. Their only hope, Peel confided to Graham at the end of the session, was to tie the protectionists to their declared policy of restoring protection and rally all free trade forces solidly against them. But this meant that the Whigs would have to forget their past policies and continue to pitch overboard every rash pledge given when in opposition. 'The act of pitching over is not always done very gracefully,' he added satirically, 'though it is so often repeated that one would hope that with practice, there might be at least some dexterity acquired.'[1] The ghosts of the old Whig principle of a fixed duty and the old Whig dislike of the income tax still haunted the political scene in the autumn of 1849. The protectionists were taking up various ideas for relieving agricultural distress and at a meeting in Buckinghamshire in September Disraeli propounded a plan for equalising the land tax at a higher standard rate and creating a sinking fund of £5 million to facilitate agricultural credit. Reading about it up in Scotland Peel was moved to mild scorn. 'Tadpole and Taper', he wrote to Goulburn 'would have devised a better "cry" than this for the great protection interest on the eve of a General Election.'[2] Unlike his ingenious lieutenant in the Commons, however, Stanley was not yet prepared to abandon the principles on which the Conservative Party had split in 1846 and shared Peel's opinion of the futility of the land tax scheme.

As the winter drew nearer there was increasing talk of a move to restore a fixed duty of 5s on foreign corn. Ellice in November mentioned the possibility to Graham in a curious letter which could be interpreted as fishing for the reaction of the Peelites. 'I believe, if the Whigs dare,' Graham observed when forwarding it to Peel, 'their secret desire is to revert to that proposal. It is clear that Cobden's firm resistance alone prevented Ld. John Russell from acceding to it in 1845.' Though less sceptical than Graham about the Whigs' fidelity to free trade, Peel thought there could be no harm in dropping a warning shot across the cabinet's bows. He therefore composed a letter for Graham, ostensibly private but intended to be shown to Ellice. In this, while professing a diplomatic disbelief in the rumours that Russell would propose the restoration of a duty on corn, Peel carefully recorded the occasions since November 1845 on which Russell had pledged himself against such a policy. He ended significantly:

Depend upon it that Lord John and many at least of his colleagues would prefer the alternative of breaking up twenty governments to the alternative of such a fearful struggle as must follow the attempt

[1] Graham, 21 July 1849.
[2] Goulburn, 20 Sept. (1849).

647

by a Government to reimpose duties on the import of food. I know not what the present issue of such a Contest might be, but I do know, that its ultimate issue would be most disastrous.

Graham showed this to Ellice who read it attentively and returned it with the remark that he agreed with every word.

Even so, Graham noted suspiciously, he did not commit himself in any way about the intentions of the government. Rather more assurance came from the Duke of Bedford who met Peel at Windsor about a week later and invited him to go on to Woburn. From the tenor of his conversation, Peel reported to Graham on 27 November, 'I consider the Duke (and I conclude therefore Lord John) to be decidedly adverse to the renewal of Protection'. The ministers themselves were clearly conscious of a sudden cold draught of Peelite distrust. A sympathetic letter from the Duke of Bedford at the end of the month on the follies of the agriculturalists enabled Peel in turn to speak out freely on the danger of any attempt, whatever the pretext, to revive protectionism. Bedford's reply, containing an extract from a recent letter from Lord John Russell giving explicit guarantees about the Corn Laws, convinced even Graham. A few days later Charles Wood in a railway-train conversation with Peel's son-in-law, Villiers, pointedly said to him, 'Tell Sir Robert that we had six cabinets and the Corn Laws never once mentioned in any of them'.[1]

Despite the lingering protectionist proclivities of some of their members the cabinet had no desire for a battle in parliament with an anti-protectionist party headed by Peel. Policy as well as preponderant conviction tied them to a free-trade platform. What they feared was the recurrent threat of a combination of ultra-radical and ultra-Tory forces on some financial question. With Cobden' radical group pressing for retrenchment and the protectionist perceiving in the abolition of the income tax the chance of reverting to a tariff-based revenue, the danger was real enough. In December Tufnell, the government chief whip, sent an urgent plea to Young to muster as many Peelites as possible for the start of the new session Young replied somewhat coolly that he thought the protectionist

[1] Graham (Graham to Peel, 14, 22 Nov.; Peel to Graham, 17 Nov. (two letters 24, 27 Nov., 6, 9 Dec. 1849, ptly pr. *Peel*, III, 523–5); 40452 fos. 412–27; Goulburn (Peel to Goulburn, 14 Dec. 1849).

too weak to embarrass the government except in conjunction with the radicals. Even then there was little likelihood that the Peelites would not follow their leader in assisting the government on any free trade issue.[1] The real question was how much longer the eighty or ninety nominal Peelites in the Commons would continue to be regarded as a coherent party in the face of Peel's studied neutrality as a party leader. Many of them represented rural constituencies; many of them had agricultural sympathies. The continued farming depression made more than a few look with favour at protectionist schemes for compensation who would have rejected a simple return to protective tariffs.

When parliament opened at the end of January 1850 the topic of agricultural distress dominated the debate on the Address; and Disraeli at once gave notice of a motion on the subject. He was well aware of the attraction this would have for the Peelites. A few days before the debate he dropped elaborate hints to Lord Londonderry, whom he knew to be in contact with Aberdeen, about the desirability of Conservative reunion. For himself, he said airily, he realised that a return to protectionism was out of the question. He was looking only at practical measures which might reconcile the two wings of the Conservative party. He knew that he himself could not be minister and he was prepared at the right time to advise his friends to accept Graham as their leader in the House of Commons. Even the jovial and communicative Londonderry found this a trifle hard to swallow but he duly passed on the message. Graham was unimpressed. He was glad to hear, he replied dryly, that Mr. Disraeli was convinced of the futility of protection; but his overtures could lead to no result.[2] Next day Disraeli made his motion in the Commons for a committee of the whole House to consider a revision of the poor rate. The proposal he brought forward, having quietly abandoned his sinking-fund scheme, was to relieve the landed interest of some £2 million of poor-law and other local charges by transferring them to the national exchequer. For the Peelites it was not a happy occasion. Graham, defending the government against the motion, was answered by Gladstone. His arguments in turn were criticised by Peel later in the two-day debate. The

[1] 40602, fos. 399–400.
[2] Graham (Londonderry to Graham and reply, 18 Feb. 1850).

motion was lost by only twenty-one votes. Thirty-five Peelite
voted with Disraeli as against twenty-eight headed by Peel who
supported the ministers.

To Young, who himself had parted company with his leader on
the issue, it seemed as if a crisis had been reached in the history of the
Peelite party; and not only perhaps among them. Writing to Peel
the day after, he pointed out that the result of the division merely
confirmed the impression he had formed in the debate on the
Address that Whigs and radicals were numerically inferior to th
combined forces of Protectionists and Peelites. Without Peelite ai
the previous evening the government would have been defeated b
seven votes. The Peelites, 'mostly men of considerable local influence
good fortune and high character', would stand by free trade. But
'they have no sympathy with and no confidence in the presen
Government. They are with you, not with Lord John Russell
The sixty-three who had taken part in the division, he continued

> about half as many more absent, and nearly an equal number fav
> ourably inclined but generally voting with the Protectionists, sa
> about 160, would rally round you personally, or any organisatio
> distinctly formed under your auspices and guided by your advic
> but they will not make sacrifices and risk their seats night after nig
> and year after year for those whom they cannot help regarding
> political opponents. I do not believe that any active opposition
> contemplated but support will no doubt be withheld, and witho
> such support, the Whigs have no command of a majority.

The small defeats already experienced by the government might I
followed by larger ones. It was rumoured that some thirty radica
were hostile to the ministers, ready to connive at their defeat, an
hoping for an early general election in which they could strength
their own numbers.

> I mention this because so large a number of men have sought con
> munication with me in the course of the last week, probably n
> fewer than 60 or 70, and from all I can gather, if a Protection
> Government is to be averted by any arrangement, and your Comme
> cial policy receive fair play for some years to come during its infan
> and this period of transition, you yourself are the only person a
> or likely to effect these objects.[1]

[1] 40603 f. 92, ptly pr. *Peel*, III, 532.

The problem was not new. But it was the sharpest warning yet given to Peel, from the man in the best position to know, that if he did not soon take the initiative, a solution of a more unwelcome sort might emerge from the sheer pressure of political forces. Young may have exaggerated both the weakness of the government and the strength of the potential support for Peel. But his fundamental diagnosis was clearly right. The difficulty for the Peelites was that their heads took them one way, their hearts another. It was not a situation which could last for ever.

The situation was the more dangerous since the session of 1850 also brought into the open the long-standing dissatisfaction of the Peelites with Palmerston's handling of foreign affairs. The *entente cordiale*, subjected to intolerable strain by the Spanish marriages, had ended abruptly with the fall of the Orléans monarchy and the rise of Louis Napoleon. The aftermath of the 1848 revolutions still convulsed the continental states in 1849; and though the old order had been eventually restored, it was clear that Europe would never be the same again. To Aberdeen and Peel, as to many other British politicians, it seemed that the European states system was facing an era of internal and external strain and that Palmerston, by his encouragement of democratic nationalism, was contributing to the tension. Their dislike of Palmerston was embittered by his popularity with many radicals and by the widespread conviction that his colleagues only acquiesced in his bellicose policy because they feared the trouble he could create in parliament if he were dismissed. Though Peel had been extremely guarded in his public comments on foreign affairs, he was increasingly aware of the feeling both at court and in the House of Lords against the Whig Foreign Secretary. He shared the common opinion that Palmerston represented the one positively harmful and dangerous element in the ministry. Where he stood almost alone was in his view that Palmerston's iniquities were not a sufficient justification for overthrowing the entire government. The previous year Palmerston's support of the rebels in Italy against the Austrian government had brought sharp criticism in the Lords from Stanley, Brougham and Aberdeen. In a virtual censure debate at the end of the session the government had been run close to defeat and had only been saved by their proxies. Aberdeen had tried to persuade Peel then that an attack on Palmerston would only result in his personal resignation and that this in the long run would strengthen rather than weaken the government.[1] But it was noticeable that Peel took no advantage of a subsequent debate in the Commons to join in the attack; and the 1849 session ended with Palmerston still entrenched in office.

Next session the anti-Palmerstonian campaign blazed up more furiously than ever. Early in 1850 the news came that Admiral Parker's fleet, fresh from an anti-Russian demonstration in the Dardanelles, had been used to blockade the Piraeus and seize goods and ships as security for compensation claimed from the Greek government on behalf of certain British subjects. To a large section of public opinion at home the Don Pacifico incident, as it became known, seemed merely a discreditable example of a strong power bullying a weak. Peel in his own circle expressed himself strongly about both the Greek business and the previous naval affront to Russia which he considered even more irresponsible.[2] But what he said in private and what he was prepared to do in parliament were entirely different things. In the Lords Stanley and Aberdeen made various critical speeches. The interest in the Commons at first mainly confined itself to questions which merely allowed Palmerston to vindicate his actions without having to meet a full-scale debate. Throughout these early weeks Peel was silent: a circumstance which enabled the *Globe*, in an article inspired and perhaps partly written by Palmerston, to claim that the absence of Peelite criticism in the Commons indicated that Peel was in sympathy with Palmerston' 'generous and farsighted views' on foreign policy. Graham and Aberdeen at once drew Peel's attention to the article, the latter commenting rather bitterly that he was not surprised at this interpretation but that it was 'unfortunate, and likely to prove injurious in its consequences'.

Peel, who considered Aberdeen ultra-sensitive in everything connected with Palmerston and unduly influenced by his intimacy with Guizot and Princess Lieven, wrote back with more than a shade of severity. He denied that the public, whatever the *Globe* might say, would be misled by his silence, particularly at a time when parliamentary discussions would clearly embarrass negotiations with

[1] *Greville*, 3 June 1849.
[2] *ibid.*, 22 Feb. 1850.

Russia and France, co-guarantors with Britain of the new Greek kingdom. To argue that individuals must at once proclaim their views on the abstract justice of every public action of the ministers might sound plausible, 'but this virtuous theory does not suit the rough practice of what is called parliamentary government'. So far as his own position was concerned:

> I have had no disposition for offensive warfare on any question either of foreign or domestic policy. It neither suits my private inclination, nor the isolated position in which I stand in the House of Commons, nor my views with regard to the policy under present circumstances of a change in the Government and the various consequences which I presume that change would entail.

If there was to be a serious indictment of the government's foreign policy, he continued, it would have to be done as a deliberate and collective action.

> This may be a very good reason for men acting in concert, that is, forming party connections and cooperating in the spirit and with the unity of Party—or for those who have had enough of party connections and are resolved to maintain themselves free from its engagements to retire altogether from an arena only suited to the contentions of party. I shall have no difficulty in making my choice between these alternatives.[1]

Here veiled but unmistakable was the threat that he might even leave politics rather than connive at the fall of the Russell administration. But even this rejoinder did not deter Aberdeen from continuing to argue that the mere knowledge of Peel's condemnation, whether public or private, would have a salutary effect. The difference between the two men was in their assessment of consequences. Aberdeen, in the academic atmosphere of the House of Lords, looked outward to Europe and wanted some demonstration of opinion which would reassure foreign powers and assist the cabinet in restraining Palmerston. Peel, in the mundane House of Commons, looked to the general position of the government and, with Graham, believed that either from choice or necessity the

[1] 43065 f. 420 (2 Apr. 1850), f. 431 (Aberdeen to Peel, 4 Apr.). See also 40452, fos. 431, 434; 40455 f. 490; Graham (Peel to Graham, 2, 4 Apr. 1850), ptly pr. *Peel*, III, 535-41.

cabinet were so chained to Palmerston that his overthrow would
entail the collapse of the whole administration.

Nevertheless, the development of the Greek crisis was not to be
stayed by private letters between the Peelites. Under pressure from
his colleagues Palmerston grudgingly accepted the good offices of
France to end the dispute. But he so arranged matters behind his
colleagues' backs that before any compromise could be reached
Parker resumed his blockade and the Greek government yielded
The French promptly withdrew their ambassador from London; the
court was shocked into strong protest; Russell warned Palmerston
that he contemplated transferring him to another office at the end
of the session; and a full-scale parliamentary inquest was now inevi
table. Twice postponed at Lansdowne's request, Stanley's motion of
censure came before the Lords in June. By this time the Greek affair
had become the topic of the session, with the fate of the govern
ment clearly dependent on the outcome. In the Lords Stanley and
Aberdeen carried their motion by thirty-seven votes, with most of
the Peelite peers joining in the condemnation. To save the govern
ment's position Roebuck was put up to move a resolution in the
House of Commons which would reverse the verdict of the Lords
Peel had given no encouragement to the attack on Palmerston in the
upper House. As late as 11 June Aberdeen had been uncertain in fac
whether Peel would not influence some of the Peelite peers again
Stanley's motion.[1] But in the parliamentary situation created by
Roebuck's sweeping motion of approval for Palmerston's foreig
policy, Peel reluctantly concluded that it was impossible for hin
to remain silent. He had not sought a challenge, but being challenge
he could no longer evade the issue. In the circumstances of a gran
parliamentary set-piece, there was little danger of a ministeri
defeat. It was accepted several days beforehand that the governme
would get a majority. The only question was its size. The mo
optimistic Whigs spoke of fifty; though this was not the gener
view.[2] In the event the four-day debate turned into a triumph f
Palmerston. Even oratorically he took the honours with his gre
civis Romanus speech on the second night. Lasting from just befo
ten o'clock to half-past two it was one of the classic parliamenta

[1] *Aberdeen–Lieven Corr.*, II, 489.
[2] Clarendon (G. C. Lewis to Clarendon, 28 June 1850).

speeches of the century, though Hobhouse noted slyly that in the course of it both Peel and Russell fell asleep for about an hour.

Peel spoke on the last evening.[1] It was the speech of an elder statesman, a speech for all seasons, quiet, reflective, unpartisan, not designed to win votes but the more impressive because of its restraint. He began by repudiating any party collusion, any attempt to condemn the general conduct of the government, any desire to overthrow a ministry which he had consistently supported for four years and with whose general principles he had much in common. He was faced however with a resolution which called on him to agree that the course followed by the government in foreign affairs was best calculated to maintain the honour of Britain and peace with other countries. After detailing various incidents in recent dealings with France, Russia, Spain, and Greece, he concluded regretfully that he could not approve of the British actions. Peace existed, but only at the cost of strained relations with the leading states of Europe. If these were dismissed as mere incidents of diplomatic life, he must ask what diplomacy was for.

It is a costly engine for maintaining peace. It is a remarkable instrument used by civilised nations for the purpose of preventing war. Unless it is used to appease the angry passions of individual men, to check the feelings that rise out of national resentments . . . it is an instrument not only costly but mischievous. If then your application of diplomacy be to fester every wound, to provoke instead of soothing resentments, to place a minister in every court of Europe for the purpose, not of preventing quarrels, or of adjusting quarrels, but for the purpose of continuing an angry correspondence, and for the purpose of promoting what is supposed to be an English interest . . . then I say, that not only is the expenditure upon this costly instrument thrown away, but this great engine, used by civilised society for the purpose of maintaining peace, is perverted into a cause of hostility and war.

He had, he continued, no disposition to enter into controversy on the various matters raised by Palmerston 'in that most able and most temperate speech, which made us proud of the man who delivered it'. But he must take issue with Roebuck's speech introducing the

[1] 28 June 1850 (*Speeches*, IV, 846).

resolution in which he argued that the moral influence of the British
government should be used to support any body of men, anywhere
in the world, who were struggling to achieve self-government
against their legitimate rulers. That was a statement which he could
not accept. It was a statement which ran contrary to the principle
followed by every statesman of eminence in England for the last
half-century—the principle of 'non-interference with the domestic
affairs of other countries, without some clear and undeniable necessity arising from the circumstances affecting the interests of your
own country'. What was the basis of self-government? How was it
to be construed? Was it monarchical or republican? Did it extend to
countries outside Europe? to India? to China? Was it to justify the
interference of other countries with British possessions?

> Which is the wisest policy—to attempt to interfere with the institu-
> tions and measures of other countries not bordering on our own, out
> of an abstract love for constitutional government—or to hold that
> doctrine, maintained by Mr. Fox, Mr. Pitt, Lord Grenville, Mr. Can-
> ning and Lord Castlereagh—that the true policy of this country is
> non-intervention in the affairs of others?

You would not, he argued, advance the cause of constitutional
government by attempting to dictate to other nations. If you failed
you left a feeling of hostility among your opponents, and a sense of
betrayal among those whom you tried to assist. If you succeeded
there was no assurance that your achievement would last. 'Constitutional liberty will be best worked out by those who aspire to freedom
by their own efforts.' For these reasons, he ended, he must give his
dissent, his reluctant dissent, to the resolution.

He was followed by Russell and Disraeli; and after a brief reply
from Roebuck, the House divided, 310 to 264 for the resolution.
A majority for the government of 46 was as much as either side had
expected. As he left the chamber to walk home in the early dawn
of 29 June, Peel was a tired but contented man. The government was
still safe, which was his chief concern. But he told his companion
that he had been glad to have had the opportunity to raise his voice
in favour of peace. Behind him, as members streamed away, were
Roebuck and Sir David Dundas. Looking at Peel's tall figure moving
up Whitehall ahead of them, Dundas remarked that he must be one

of the happiest men in England, having voted with his party and yet in accordance with his own feelings and opinions.[1] It was an irony of history that Peel's last act in the House of Commons was to go into the lobby with a united Conservative opposition.

[1] *Life of J. A. Roebuck*, ed. R. E. Leader (1897), p. 242.

PEEL AND HIS CONTEMPORARIES

Peel in his prime was one of the more conspicuous members in the House of Commons. Even apart from his air of authority and the deference which surrounded him, his purely physical appearance was a dominating one: the big figure in the long blue frock-coat, white waistcoat and drab trousers, the florid complexion and curly reddish hair, and legs that always seemed slightly out of proportion to the rest of the body. One of the first things that struck strangers was his peculiar gait—'his two left legs' as O'Connell satirised it—the stately forward progression with the eyes absorbed in thought, the arms hanging limply down, the feet almost sliding over the floor. Next people noticed the broad countenance with the curved nose and intelligent blue eyes. If not abstracted in some inward contemplation, his look was direct and expressive, sometimes beaming with humour but equally capable of cold austerity. His mouth often twitched with a half-smile either of suppressed amusement at the foibles of others or in ironic deprecation of himself. Though never a fop, he was fastidious in his personal habits. Carlyle noticed his hands at a dinner party in 1850 when Peel was pointing to the detail in Reynold's portrait of Dr. Johnson—'as fine a man's hand as I remember to have seen, strong, delicate and scrupulously clean'.[1] He took care with his clothes and was one of the best-dressed men in public life. The ample white waistcoat was usually adorned with a gold watch–chain and a large bunch of seals with which he would play as he leaned back with legs crossed and big hat tipped over his eyes listening to debates in the House. When he rose to speak he had a variety of gestures well known to his audience. He usually began slowly and quietly, standing erect with hands clasped behind him under his

[1] J. A. Froude, *Thomas Carlyle* (1885), II, 44.

coat-tails. As he warmed to his theme he would lean his left arm on the table and point a single admonitory finger at his critics. During significant passages in his speech he would thump the box in front of him at regular intervals. When he made some deft exposure of the absurdities of a previous speaker or had some congenial party senti-ment to offer, he would turn his back on the Speaker and look half-humorously at the ranks of his supporters as he uttered a sentence which he knew would be followed by laughter and cheers.[1]

As a speaker he had the physical asset of a strong, flexible voice. He could range without effort from soft persuasiveness to sonorous defiance, from sly banter of an opponent to a grave solemnity which hushed the House to silence. Though, like most politicians of the time, he had some provincialisms in his accent, he was singularly clear and precise in his diction. Measured and reasonable in argu-ment, he was rarely aggressive, never ungenerous. His style was conversational and analytical. He appealed to the minds of his audience rather than their hearts. Temperamentally unfitted for oratory in the grand manner, he had no gift for the sublime passage or polished phrase. The set perorations which he occasionally affixed to his major speeches were sometimes laboured. What he had done, however, was to weld his voice and intellect into a superb instru-ment for work in the House of Commons. He never forgot that the purpose of speaking was not to delight posterity or even readers of the morning newspapers, but to have an immediate effect on the men sitting round him. For this what was essential was knowledge of the business in hand, ability to seize on the weakness in the opposing case, skill in marshalling every argument in support of his own, and an awareness of the interests, opinions, and prejudices of his audience. The House had dozens of members who, given due notice, could come down and deliver a glittering speech on a set theme. But these isolated displays of verbal brilliance were of little parliamentary value compared with Peel's more professional qualities: the intuitive sense of the ebb and flow of debate, the reten-tive memory for all that had been said on the other side, the practised

[1] For some contemporary descriptions see *Random Recollections of the House of Commons* (1837), pp. 108–20; *Sir Robert Peel and his Era* (1844), esp. pp. 254–8; H. Martin, *Personal Sketch of Sir Robert Peel* (Hamburg, 1850); *Sir Robert Peel, States-man and Orator* (1846); cf. also Lord Dalling, *Sir Robert Peel* (1874), pp. 84–5.

skill in incorporating new matter into a prepared speech, the instinctive knowledge of the time to intervene, the tactful choice of appeal and argument. There were occasions certainly when Peel misjudged the mood of the House of Commons; mainly when his temperament got the better of his judgement. But for a man who was by nature quick-tempered and impulsive these were remarkably rare. At his best there were few men who could influence the House so expertly as Peel in the period after 1832. Lord John Russell once said that the three best parliamentary speakers he had ever heard were Plunket, Canning and Peel. Plunket was the most persuasive; Canning the most charming; Peel the most formidable in debate.

The compliment would not have displeased Peel. He was perhaps never a natural speaker; hard work and experience alone made him one. As a young man he had studied the art of dialectic[1] and his skill in later life was that of the great craftsman rather than the supreme artist. For parliamentary purposes it was perhaps the more useful talent. It led him for example to master that art of destroying an opponent's case which consists not merely in systematically refuting his argument but in finding the key point which if overturned brings the whole edifice to the ground.[2] In advancing his own arguments it was as though he was addressing himself to the neutral or the wavering. His aim was to convince rather than to captivate; his method a process of intellectual proof. A characteristic speech would begin with a definition of the issues, followed by an enunciation of the various solutions or actions open to the House. Each of these he would then successively examine and discard until only one remained. He was aware himself of the extent to which this had become a Peelite gambit. 'I have more than once excited a smile,' he confessed good-naturedly in a debate in 1847, 'when as first minister of the Crown, I have said that there were three courses which it was open to me to adopt.'[3] The technique of proof by elimination had the advantage of bringing all aspects of the question under consideration and seeming to point to an irresistible conclusion. Peel was one of the greatest special pleaders in parliamentary history. At his best he persuaded because he seemed persuaded himself by the

[1] *Mr. Secretary Peel*, p. 239.
[2] e.g. his speech on the Poor Law debate of 1843 (*Speeches*, IV, 180).
[3] *ibid.*, p. 717 (March 1847).

correctness of his own analysis. At his worst he seemed to be reciting arguments not because he believed in them but because he believed that others might. Much of Peel's reputation in certain quarters for being devious, evasive and plausible, came from this. To argue political propositions as though they were mathematical theorems is a great gift; but it has the defect that politics is not the same as mathematics. To wish to arrive at an irrefutable decision by an intellectual process may in human affairs merge unconsciously into a search for reasons to justify a foregone conclusion. To his exasperated opponents Peel had no equal in the gentle art of dressing up a case. Had he been at the bar, G. C. Lewis once observed, he would have got more verdicts than Scarlett.[1]

If he rarely entranced, he usually interested his audience; and though he hardly ever attempted elaborate ironies or witticisms, he began about 1828, with growing confidence in his mastery of the House, to display a taste for quiet fun. Peel's public humour was of the mild variety which consists in good-natured amusement at the foibles of others and a conscious enjoyment of an occasional verbal pleasantry. Discussing the metropolitan police bill in 1829 he remarked that three angels, let alone three drunken beadles, would be insufficient to protect the streets of Kensington. Of Huskisson in 1830, who had half-heartedly criticised an amendment as being milk-and-water, 'he must say that the smallest possible infusion of milk in the water was precisely that which would suit the rt. hon. gentleman's constitution'. On Poulett Thomson's motion for a select committee on taxation in the same year, 'the hon. member for Dover did not let the cat out of the bag, but he suffered a little kitten to escape'. Of Althorp's abortive 1831 budget, 'the misshapen offspring of financial love fell below the blows of the reformers'. And of the Chancellor of the Exchequer's invitation to the opposition in 1834 to suggest a better subject for tax remission than the house tax, 'there was never so clear an invitation to be ravished'. He could even embark on the hazardous game of teasing the Irish members. 'The hon. and learned gentleman,' he observed once of O'Connell, 'reminded him of the elephant wounded in battle which was often more dangerous to its friends than its foes.' Of Feargus O'Connor, 'the hon. and learned gentleman appeared to take fire

[1] To Graham (Graham, 5 Nov. 1849).

very easily, and boil at a very low temperature'. When Sheil once began a speech by stammering 'necessity—necessity—necessity—', Peel called out across the gangway 'is not always the mother of invention'. Hume was another target. Of the Church Temporalities bill in 1833, Peel said that he 'growled a faint opposition to it'. When over the Stockdale case in 1839 the dissatisfied Hume asserted that the House of Commons had been rolled in the mire, Peel remarked lightly that 'the hon. member having been dragged through the mud, now came forward and shook his muddy locks at him'. Again, in the Afghan debate of 1843, having read out at Hume's request a series of extracts from a previous speech which in fact only demonstrated Hume's earlier support for the war which he now criticised, Peel ended good-humouredly, 'I have struck the hon. gentleman above and below, and in the middle, and I hope he's satisfied'.

To his family and close friends this development in his public manner came as no surprise. From early days he had a taste for quizzical comments on the absurdities of human nature, and residence in Ireland provided him with an inexhaustible fund of anecdotes with which he would in later life when in the mood delight an intimate circle. This characteristic he preserved to the end. Carlyle met him for the first time in 1848 at a dinner at Bath House at which the observant writer sat next to the great man.

> He is towards sixty and, though not broken at all, carries especially in his complexion, when you are *near* him, marks of that age: clear, strong blue eyes which kindle on occasions, voice extremely good, low-toned, something of *cooing* in it, rustic, affectionate, honest, mildly persuasive. . . . Reserved seemingly by nature, obtrudes nothing of *diplomatic* reserve. On the contrary, a vein of mild fun in him, real sensibility to the ludicrous, which feature I liked best of all.[1]

On this occasion Peel told his well-known 'toolip' anecdote, about the London mob who at the time of the reform bill debates gathered outside the House of Lords to howl down the peers as they arrived in their coroneted coaches. 'Why don't you shout?' asked one man in the crowd of his neighbour. 'No', answered the other, nodding to

---

[1] Froude, *op. cit.*, I, 433.

an approaching episcopal carriage displaying the customary mitre as its armorial emblem, 'I reserves myself for the toolip.'

Women as well as men enjoyed his conversation. Georgiana Liddell, then a maid of honour, described 'a most agreeable and entertaining breakfast' at Windsor Castle in October 1844. Ellenborough, just back from India with bleached hair and sun-burned cheeks, was there with the prime minister.

> Sir Robert and Lord Ellenborough have been talking the whole time, telling us all sorts of funny and interesting anecdotes, and sending us all into fits of laughter. I hardly ever saw Sir Robert so well, or in such high spirits, and he was so amusing.[1]

Much of the effect of his stories depended on the skill in telling and the touches of small detail. There was one about the Lord Mayor who, going to meet the queen on her recent visit to the City, decided to wear jackboots over his shoes and stockings to keep off the mud. On arrival at Temple Bar he found himself unable to extricate his leg from one of them and was caught in a frenzy of embarrassment, hopping on one foot with several men tugging at the other, while the noise of the queen's approach grew louder and louder. Another concerned a city alderman sitting next to Canning at a Mansion House Dinner, who praised Lord Chief Justice Ellenborough as a man of uncommon sagacity. Canning courteously agreed but enquired what in particular the alderman had in mind. 'Why Sir,' came the prompt reply, 'had he been here, he would have told me by a single glance of his eye which is the best of those five haunches of venison.' A further set of anecdotes turned on the well-known stinginess of that great lawyer, Lord Stowell, who had been his senior colleague in the old days when Peel was M.P. for Oxford University. One was about Stowell's purchase from Portugal of a large quantity of port which proved on arrival to be acid, or in the language of the trade, 'pricked'. On the advice of a wine-dealer Stowell advertised the whole consignment under the impressive label of 'Lord Stowell's Port' and it was snapped up at a good price without the normal precaution of sampling. Some time later Stowell was travelling through Ramsgate and stopped to dine at the Royal Hotel. The waiter, ignorant of his identity, strongly recommended

---

[1] Lady Bloomfield, *Reminiscences*, p. 66.

him to try a bottle of 'Lord Stowell's Port'—'all the gentlemen of the town drink nothing else'. 'Yes,' said Stowell with great amusement, '—but, waiter,—many bowel complaints in your town?' Peel's impromptu remarks tended to be a shade more malicious than his anecdotes. Stopping in front of his portrait of Croker, a friend of Peel's remarked, 'How wonderfully like! You can see the quiver of his lips.' 'Yes,' said Peel, 'and the arrows coming out of it.' On another occasion, at a meeting of the British Museum Trustees, there was gossip about the extravagances of young Tomline, the spendthrift grandson of Pitt's old tutor, the late bishop of Winchester. Someone exclaimed, 'What would his grandfather say if he could now look up?' 'I observe,' said Peel slyly, 'you don't say look down.'

Not everyone encountered the lighter side to Peel's nature. In large assemblies he was apt by his reticence and formality to add to his widespread reputation for coldness. It was a matter of common observation at Drayton during the autumn round of parties how Peel became more talkative whenever the guests diminished to a small circle of old friends and grew more impersonal and ceremonious when the company was swelled by strangers. Even at his own dinner-table, if there was a large gathering, he rarely took the lead in conversation; and on such occasions few others had the courage to do so. This reserve, which sometimes went further than Peel could have realised, was not a device for concealing opinions or hiding his intentions. Carlyle was right in his observation. It was the result partly of shyness, partly of an incurable distaste for saying more than he felt or believed. Gladstone noted Peel's strict use of words even in small things. He would not, for example, write to a colleague that he had found a memorandum valuable unless he had really done so. In ordinary social conversation this precision was often misunderstood. Unless he was in a friendly atmosphere, he found it difficult to relax. In these circumstances he fell back into the habits of a preoccupied mind too abstracted in his own reflections to realise the effect he was making on others. Years of official life, acting on a temperament that was self-conscious by nature, had made it easier for Peel to deal with problems than with people. Even when giving his full attention to others, his mental absorption could easily be taken the wrong way. There was a story told by Hawes, the radical member for Lambeth, who went to the prime minister with a request from a House of Commons committee of which he was chairman. Hawes was ushered in, received a cordial welcome, and stated his case. When he finished Peel gazed at him without uttering a word. Finally Hawes, growing uncomfortable, picked up his hat and observed, 'I beg your pardon, Sir Robert, I see you think I have been taking too great a liberty in coming to you as I have done. I wish you good morning.' At that Peel started up and exclaimed, 'Good gracious, you are quite mistaken. I was only thinking how best I could comply with your request.' And he added a disarming remark about his unfortunate manner which so often gave people the wrong impression.[1]

A contrast to this in later life was his friendly relations with his younger followers. They included not only Lincoln, Herbert, Eliot, Cardwell and Gladstone but lesser figures like George Smythe, after he became under-secretary at the Foreign Office, and William Gregory, the grandson of Peel's old Irish colleague. Gregory entered parliament as member for Dublin in 1842 at the age of twenty-five. He was at once taken up by Peel who introduced him to the Speaker and gave him an open invitation to drop in at Whitehall Gardens at any time. Gregory soon had the run of the house. If the prime minister was busy, he would silently raise a hand and his visitor would close the door again. If not, he would call young Gregory in for a chat, discuss the political topics of the day, and frequently end up with some racy story 'which he told', recounted Gregory, 'extremely well and with fits of laughter'. With his young men Peel behaved more like an indulgent uncle than a prime minister. On the famous occasion when Ashley beat the government on the factory question in 1844, Gregory leapt up in his place and waved his hat in the air. When the excitement died down Peel who was sitting just below him turned and said laughingly, 'My good fellow, I shall give you a scolding if you wave your hat over my head whenever you beat me; and the Speaker will give you a scolding if you wave it at all.'[2] Gregory, who refused an Irish lordship of the

[1] Related by A. G. Stapleton to whom it was told at the time by George Hamilton who had it direct from Hawes (*Macmillan's Magazine*, XXXI (Nov. 1874), pp. 1–2).
[2] *Sir William Gregory*, ed. Lady Gregory (1894), p. 81; cf. *Nineteenth Century*, XXV (1889), pp. 582 et seq.

Treasury in 1846, proved a disappointment; but it was not for lack of encouragement.

With Lincoln and Sidney Herbert, who fulfilled all Peel's early expectations, his relations were even closer. For Lincoln, estranged from his stiff, melancholy father, he almost took the place of a parent, watching over his political career and advising him on the unhappy personal problems created by his wife's adultery. During the South Nottinghamshire by-election in February 1846 Lincoln sent off almost daily bulletins to Peel on the progress of the campaign. In return light-hearted letters came from Peel written in an easier and more colloquial style than he used with almost any other correspondent. He gave a joking description of St. Germans's wounded dignity at not being told in advance of Lincoln's appointment as Chief Secretary; and talked disrespectfully of 'Sir Gorgeous Provender' when referring to that well-known gastronomic dandy, Sir George Warrender. Reporting a rumour that Collett, the Conservative member for Lincoln, was going to bring the Duke of Newcastle's election letter before the Commons as a breach of privilege, Peel ended with a comical sigh for these unwanted complications. 'These boys will be the death of me.'[1] Writing to Lincoln after Peel's death Herbert recalled that the very last time he was with Peel they were talking about Lincoln and his affairs 'and he gave the attention and the anxious advice which a Father would have given for a son. God knows, we two owe him much.'[2]

The kindness that was one of Peel's basic qualities came out in many ways. In the fact, for example, that with few exceptions he never bore a grudge against past opponents; and in his practical sympathy with personal misfortune or unhappiness. When Maginn, the Irish Tory journalist who had violently attacked him over Catholic emancipation, fell on hard times towards the end of his life, Peel anonymously subscribed £100 to a fund raised on his behalf and sent a further sum before he died.[3] Sydney Smith, the Whig clerical wit who had lampooned Peel on many occasions, was invited by the prime minister in 1843 to a dinner in honour of the

---

[1] Newcastle (Peel to Lincoln, Feb. 1846).

[2] Martineau, *Newcastle*, p. 98.

[3] *N&Q* 1st Ser. V, 433. Maginn's health was ruined after imprisonment for debt.

King of Saxony. When Smith self-consciously declined, Peel got Buckland to make him change his mind. There was a good-humoured exchange of notes between the two men and when Smith arrived at Whitehall Gardens he was received with unusual warmth by his host.[1] Macaulay, whose studied personal attacks on Peel during his last ministry were second only to those of Disraeli, found himself four years later getting on wonderfully well with Peel on the Board of the British Museum. Their acquaintanceship ripened and on 1 June 1850 he found himself dining in Peel's house. 'How odd!' he reflected in his diary.[2] Less sophisticated men than the Whig historian experienced the same surprise. Bernard Barton, the Quaker poet, tried in the spring of 1846 to dissuade Peel from repealing the Corn Laws by the peculiar device of sending him two sonnets, exhorting him to retire to Tamworth. Peel countered this by asking him to dinner. Warned by well-meaning friends of Peel's coldness and lack of sociability, Barton arrived with a plain man's determination not to be overawed by the condescension of the great. In the event he was completely disarmed. Peel welcomed him cordially, introduced him to various eminent guests and despite the novel experience of dining off plate and being waited on by liveried footmen, Barton was soon at ease. After dinner they adjourned to the gallery. Peel noticed his guest's interest in the pictures and walked round with him, pointing out his favourites. As he talked 'little touches of natural feeling occasionally oozed out', which led Barton to conclude with some astonishment that Peel had more of a heart than might be supposed in a man so full of affairs.[3]

Another admirer of Peel's was Frances Braham, Countess Waldegrave, who having married two raffish sons of Lord Waldegrave in quick succession, was left doubly widowed and a dowager countess at the age of twenty-five. After this unconventional beginning she became in 1847 the wife of George Granville Harcourt, a pompous elderly widower of sixty-one who tried to make her conform to his own standard of respectability. Frances, a young, witty, impulsive girl full of vitality, became reserved and nervous in the disapproving

---

[1] S. J. Reid, *Life of Sydney Smith* (1884), p. 369.
[2] G. O. Trevelyan, *Lord Macaulay* (1876), II, 277.
[3] *New Letters of Edward Fitzgerald*, ed. F. R. Barton (1923), pp. 108–15. The date of the dinner was 14 Mar. 1846.

atmosphere of Harcourt's social circle and only relaxed when she could escape to a more friendly environment. She first met the Peels in 1848 when they were guests at her husband's house at Nuneham. Later the same year she visited Drayton. Lincoln and Gladstone were in the same party and there was a general air of constraint because the news had just come that Lady Lincoln who had gone abroad on the pretext of having medical treatment, was in fact travelling round Europe with Lord Walpole. Peel, who was touched by Lady Waldegrave's brave attempts to distract Lincoln, noticed also how much more cheerful and self-confident she was at Drayton than in her own home. When he mentioned this to her, she told him of the misery she endured at the formal dinner parties at her husband's town-house in London where she was terrified by the iciness of the great society matrons. Peel told her to take no notice. 'One of these days you'll find you're a remarkable woman.' His quiet comment, says her biographer, did more for her morale than any of the adulation she was to receive in the rest of her life.[1]

Lady Waldegrave, though Peel did not live to see it, went on to become one of the great social and political hostesses of the Victorian era. With Haydon the painter, another of Peel's protégés, it was a different though no less illuminating story. After Peel had helped to get him out of a debtor's prison in 1830 an intermittent friendship had developed between them. Haydon called on his patron in London and on at least one occasion was invited to Drayton. Peel assisted him in a practical way by commissioning a large portrait of Napoleon, visiting his studio and advising him on small matters. But Haydon, obstinate, egocentric and harassed by poverty, was a difficult acquaintance. His importunity drew from Peel in 1832 the mild protest that it was rather hard, because he had assisted Haydon in the past, that he should be exposed to incessant requests to commission pictures which he really did not require. At the same time Haydon ignored his advice to turn to portrait painting rather than the grand historical themes on which the artist spent so much fruitless time and money. The Napoleon picture itself was a source of heartburning. Having named 100 guineas as his fee, Haydon was immediately sorry he had not asked more. When, six years later, he told Peel that the sum had been too small, Peel added another £30.

[1] O. W. Hewett, *Strawberry Fair* (1956), pp. 64–70.

Not surprisingly he was less than pleased when Haydon wrote from his frequent place of sojourn in a debtor's prison to remind him again that the price was still much too low. Yet Haydon in his candid moments admitted that Peel 'had a tender heart' and had shown patience and kindness in the face of the 'bitter things' Haydon often said to him.

In the spring of 1846 while the great corn and Irish debates raged in parliament, Haydon made one last effort to establish himself with a one-man exhibition in London which proved a complete failure. In June, overwhelmed by innumerable debts, he wrote despairing letters to Peel, Brougham, and the Duke of Beaufort asking for help. Only the previous autumn Peel had obtained a clerkship in the Record Office for Haydon's son. Caught as he was in the thick of the controversy over Bentinck's 'Canning' charges, he might have been excused for ignoring this latest appeal. Yet, 'Who answered first?', demanded Haydon passionately in his diary.

> Tormented by D'Israeli, harrassed by public business, up came the following letter.
>
> Sir, I am sorry to hear of your Continued Embarrassments. From a limited fund which is at my disposal, I send as a Contribution towards your Relief from those embarrassments the sum of £50 . . . I am, Sir, your obedient servant, Robert Peel. . . .
>
> And this Peel is the man who has *no heart*![1]

Six days later Haydon committed suicide before the unfinished canvas of one of those great unwanted epic subjects to which he had sacrificed his career. In his will he twice mentioned Peel. 'I return my gratitude to Sir Robert Peel, always a kind Friend in emergencies'; and again, 'I hope my dear friend Sir Robert Peel will not forget my Widow and family'. Nor did he; almost his last act as prime minister before he left London on 30 June was to transmit for the queen's signature a pension warrant for £50 per annum for Mrs. Haydon.[2]

II

There were other acquaintanceships of a more decorous and elevated nature. Loss of office did not bring to an end, for example, Peel's

[1] *Haydon*, V, 551–2. [2] 40441 f. 296.

close friendship with the royal family. Indeed, between 1846 and 1850 his relations with Victoria and Albert were as close as Melbourne's had been with the queen in the years immediately after 1841. He was a frequent guest at Windsor and Buckingham Palace; and on public as well as private occasions the attention Victoria and Albert paid to him was obvious to all. Albert could almost be included among Peel's band of young men as far as affection and deference were concerned. What set him apart was the constitutional delicacy of the relationship between a parliamentary politician and the queen's husband. It was a situation of which the tutor was more conscious than the pupil. Albert, young, modest and aware of his ignorance, was eager to learn; but his desire for instruction did not always square with the niceties of constitutional procedure.

Even before Peel left office there was an engaging example of the difficulties which Albert could unwittingly create for his mentor. In the spring of 1846 the royal couple were faced with an early and inevitable transfer of power to the Whigs. It was a prospect viewed with some apprehension at Windsor. Like William IV twelve years before Albert was particularly apprehensive of future Whig policy towards the Church. In March Charles Wood had talked somewhat indiscreetly to Anson about the need for the Whigs to tackle the Irish Church question when they came into office. A few days later Albert mentioned this to Peel and spoke of the embarrassment which would be created for the queen if the new administration made an attack on the Establishment. He referred to the coronation oath and confided that he wished to be armed in advance with Peel's views in case he ever had to advise the queen on the issue. Faced with this unexpected recrudescence in a Coburg of the problem of royal conscience with which the last three Hanoverians had plagued their ministers, Peel cautioned the prince against any mention of the topic by himself or the queen. As a salutary warning he recited the long list of ministers—Pitt, Grenville, Grey, Wellington, and himself in 1835—who had come to grief on the Church issue and told the prince that to take a stand on the coronation oath would merely expose the monarchy to a personal conflict with party policy and religious fanaticism. Having delivered this broadside, he relented sufficiently to say that he was quite ready to go into the whole question with Albert if his views were likely to be of any use to the queen. He then, recorded Albert,

> debated the question in all points of view, argued for and against on constitutional grounds, on grounds of expediency, on the principle of equality, of restitution, of national compact, etc. etc. We finally agreed, that he should make out for me a little scheme for a course of studies on this subject.

While the prime minister prepared a curriculum in constitutional history for his royal pupil, Albert painstakingly committed to paper 'all the arguments through which Sir R. Peel went which will be of the greatest use to me'.

When they met again two days later Albert showed Peel the voluminous memorandum, extending to six sheets, which he had made of his conversation. Somewhat taken aback, Peel read the document through twice. Then, with obvious uneasiness, he told the prince that he had no idea that his words were to be taken down and that it could not be allowed to stand as a correct record of his real opinions. What he had done, he explained, was what he often did in cabinet. He had put up various lines of argument not because he necessarily believed in them all but because he wished to ensure that all aspects of the question were thoroughly considered. To leave such a document as this behind, however, might have embarrassing consequences. It would look as though before leaving office he had tried to dissuade the queen from a policy which his successors might propose to her. At this, to Peel's relief, Albert threw the offending document in the fire. In its place the prince had to fall back on the blameless constitutional reading-list which Peel had prepared for him: pamphlets, parliamentary debates, a chapter of Blackstone's *Commentaries*, and an extract from a letter of Burke's, the whole of which, Peel added encouragingly, was well worth reading, 'as indeed is every line which Mr. Burke ever wrote on any subject'.[1]

As it turned out the question of the Irish Church did not emerge as a crucial issue of politics until Albert was dead and Gladstone had replaced Russell as leader of the Liberal Party. The only other important occasion on which Albert tried to elicit Peel's views on

[1] For the whole incident see RA/D 15/9–12; *VL*, II, 76–7.

delicate matters of domestic policy was after the general election of 1847 when he sent Peel a paper on the general state of parties and asked for his comments. Peel returned it with a long covering letter in which he avoided answering any of the prince's specific questions and confined himself to a largely retrospective account of his relations with the Conservative Party and some generalised reflections on the likely course of British political development. If he thus courteously evaded the real object of the prince's communication, he revealed with clarity his attitude towards the disruption of 1846. It was a bleak and unforgiving analysis. The Tory Party had certainly been reconstructed after the Reform Act of 1832 but 'the seeds of its final Dissolution were probably sown at its Birth'. It acquired strength because of the wisdom and moderation with which it first behaved. But with growing power it forgot the source of its influence, 'became impatient of control, and both in civil and ecclesiastical matters was inclined to revert to principles of action incompatible with the political Change effected by the Reform Bill'. He then cited various speeches and statements of his own to justify the claim that 'in any part which I may have taken in laying the foundation of the Conservative Party, I cannot reproach myself with having gained its confidence on false pretences'. Even before taking office in 1841 and long before Maynooth and corn came to divide the party, there had been many instances where he had great difficulty in making his opinion prevail without an open rupture. But, he added defiantly,

> I made as few Concessions to Party as it was possible to make, consistently with the maintenance of Party Connection, and however much I have been blamed for not showing more deference to a great Party, and for not acting more steadily on Party Principles, all I have to regret is that I shewed so much.

As for the future, he thought there were signs of increased democratic tendencies in some of the large urban constituencies. But only a very stupid protectionist could fail to see that the repeal of the Corn Laws had removed the main issue on which this new spirit could be exploited. The next effort would probably be on the question of parliamentary reform. But at the moment there was no immediate topic on which popular feeling could be roused. Before a new reform campaign was feasible, the political demagogues would have weakened themselves by internal rivalries and dissensions. What he hoped would be demonstrated to parliament was that 'the best way of making progress with public Business, and of advancing the Cause of Rational Reformation and improvement, will be to submit to the influence of less turbulent, less noisy but more sagacious Leaders'. Despite the general impression that the new House of Commons had too many men of inferior talents and was dominated by too many sectarian interests, his conclusion was optimistic. 'The quiet good sense and good feeling of the people of this Country will be a powerful instrument on which an Executive government may rely for neutralising the mischievous energies of the House of Commons.'[1] Whatever the truth of this diagnosis, what it implied was that there was little hope of reuniting the Conservative Party and no urgent political danger that would justify a coalition government. If Albert was able to read between the lines of this letter, he would have realised that Peel was not to be easily dislodged from his independent position.

The subject on which the prince more frequently sought and more readily obtained Peel's advice was foreign policy. It was a field of activity to which royalty was traditionally partial and for which Albert believed he had special qualifications. For Peel it was a more congenial because a less partisan aspect of politics. The issue of the Spanish marriages in particular was one which drew together Englishmen of all shades of opinion. At the beginning of September 1846 the British government had been officially informed that simultaneous marriages would take place between Queen Isabella and the reputedly impotent Duke of Cadiz, and between her younger sister and the Duc de Montpensier, younger son of Louis Philippe. Though Guizot tried to enlist the sympathies of Aberdeen, and his royal master those of Victoria, opinion in Britain unanimously condemned their action. The physical deficiencies of the Bourbon candidate, though perhaps less important in French eyes than was commonly supposed, gave a distasteful air to the whole arrangement. 'If Don Francisco is what he is supposed to be, and what the Court of Spain told Bulwer that he is,' Peel wrote to Aberdeen on 22 September, 'the sacrifice of the happiness of the Queen of Spain is a shameful outrage on her sex and station. I am

[1] RA/C 45/23; 40441 f. 370.

utterly ashamed both of the King and Guizot.' He was still more shocked when, on a visit to Windsor a week later, the prince showed him a letter of Louis Philippe's detailing the results of his enquiries into the possible sterility of the Spanish queen and the doubtful virility of her intended husband. He found the royal couple at Windsor angry and depressed at the news from Spain. Though the prince went out shooting with Peel on two mornings, he neglected the birds to talk endlessly about the Spanish affair. At his request Peel undertook a prolonged historical investigation into the Treaty of Utrecht and the renunciation by Philip V for himself and his successors of the crown of France. Having read all the available printed literature on successive eighteenth-century marriage treaties, including works by St. Simon and Bolingbroke, Peel in the end confessed that 'the whole transaction is to me unintelligible'.

This was the more disappointing since Palmerston, to retrieve what he could from this diplomatic disaster, was trying on the basis of the Utrecht treaty nearly a century and a half earlier to obtain a formal renunciation of the Spanish throne for any children of the Montpensier marriage. Peel's opinion was sought by all the parties to the dispute. The prince sent him the correspondence between Palmerston and Guizot; Palmerston sent a batch to Aberdeen with permission to pass it to Peel; Guizot sent him copies of his replies to Palmerston. The advice Peel gave conveyed little consolation to Windsor. He agreed that the double marriage ceremony, which took place with undiplomatic haste in October, was a flagrant breach of faith. But he counselled a protest only against the manner, not the validity, of the marriages. Great care, he warned, should be exercised not to assume a position which would oblige any future British government as a matter of consistency to refuse recognition to a possible succession by a child of the Montpensier marriage to the Spanish throne. With this prudent advice Aberdeen was in complete accord. The queen and prince, momentarily Palmerstonian in outlook, were alarmed that this division of opinion between their past and present ministers might be exploited by the French. When shown some of Palmerston's subsequent despatches on the subject, Peel privately thought their tone unnecessarily angry. But he observed the constitutional proprieties by refraining from any comment except on purely factual details. For the rest, apart from writing to

Brougham in Paris who he knew would pass his strictures on to Louis Philippe and Guizot, he kept silent on the matter. Except for Aberdeen, none of his intimates knew of his correspondence with the palace.[1]

The revolution in Paris the following year destroyed both the dynastic schemes of the Orléans monarchy and the British fears of a renewed Franco-Spanish Family Compact. At the same time it ended the brief honeymoon of sympathy between Windsor and the Foreign Office. In March 1848 the prince asked Peel to call in for a talk on 'the many awful events that are taking place around us'. The spread of revolutionary feeling in Italy and Palmerston's outspoken Italian sympathies brought his first important clash with the monarchy. In October Albert was writing mournfully to Peel that 'it has been a very great satisfaction to me to have been able to converse with you upon subjects which are of such moment to us and with regard to which I have felt very much alone and the want of the opinions of a friend'.[2] The growing rift between Palmerston and the monarchy, however, made it impossible for Peel to be more than a sympathetic but discreet listener to Albert's complaints. Fortunately there were less controversial matters on which he could act as counsellor to the young prince. When Albert was approached to become Chancellor of Cambridge University in the spring of 1847, Peel strongly advised him to accept. The situation became more complicated when a contest first threatened and then materialised, mainly because of an inter-college rivalry between Trinity and St. John's. But even when the election yielded Albert only a narrow victory Peel insisted that he ought to take the office. To reinforce his persuasions he drew up a cogent memorandum listing six reasons why Albert should accept.[3] The prince swallowed his pride, and the Peels were among the guests invited to his inauguration in July, dining in college halls and drinking tea on college lawns with dons, bishops and other academic notabilities.

When in less than six months the industrious Albert took up the question of educational reform at Cambridge he turned almost

[1] 43065 fos. 213, 225–88 (Peel to Aberdeen, Oct. 1846–Jan. 1847); RA/I 46/7–24 (corr. Peel and Prince Albert, Nov. 1846).

[2] 40441 fos. 382, 388.

[3] *ibid.*, fos. 356–60; RA/F 36/35–8; Goulburn (Peel to Goulburn, 15 Feb 1847); Martin, *Prince Consort*, Pt. I, 65–7.

instinctively to Peel for advice. The chief embarrassment was created by the formidable Dr. Whewell of Trinity who had been the prince's chief supporter for the chancellorship but whose views on curricular changes were distinctly limited. He held that in the scientific field mathematics should hold the place of eminence and that new-fangled subjects such as chemistry should not form part of the degree course. There was much doubt and controversy about their principles, he magisterially observed, and their professors would suffer if they could not offer indisputable truths. Peel dealt tartly with this piece of academic obscurantism. Were students at Cambridge, he enquired, to learn nothing about electricity and the speculations about its connection with the nervous system merely because all doubts had not been removed. 'If the principle for which Dr Whewell contends be a sound one,' he observed sardonically, 'it will be difficult to deliver a lecture on Theology.' As for the Master of Trinity's opinion that another hundred years should elapse before new scientific subjects should be admitted to the curriculum, it 'exceeds in absurdity anything which the bitterest enemy of University Education could have imputed to its advocates'. His own view was that more encouragement should be given to lecturers in science; they should have the same prospects of academic promotion as in the more traditional subjects. With characteristic prudence, however, he told the prince to proceed gradually and quietly, obtaining the advice of the more enlightened men at Cambridge and winning their confidence and co-operation in a gradual widening of the degree course.[1]

Peel was also drawn into a project for a great international industrial exhibition which the prince, as President of the Society of Arts, brought forward in 1849. While approving in principle Peel made the cautious proviso that the prince and the government should have nothing to do with the scheme until a large body of manufacturers had agreed to participate. The advice was taken and the preliminary investigation undertaken by the Society later that year was the basis for the ultimate success of the Great Exhibition. When the royal commission was issued in January 1850 Peel's name was on the list and he at once became one of its more active members. In April he suggested to Albert that Lyon Playfair, who had shown

[1] RA/F 32/18–21 (Oct.–Nov. 1847).

considerable interest in the project, should be recruited as an official member, primarily to act as liaison officer between the Society of Arts and the Royal Commission. When Playfair because of his other commitments showed some reluctance to serve, Peel intervened with a reminder of his claims on Playfair's gratitude. The chemist capitulated; Peel took him to the prince; and the invitation was finally accepted with the stipulation that he should be allowed to consult Peel whenever problems arose in the negotiations with the industrial exhibitors. On these occasions Peel and Lord Granville, the young vice-president of the Board of Trade, were usually present and with their experience and authority smoothed over innumerable difficulties.[1]

Peel's friendship with Playfair was an instance of his general encouragement of the small but growing band of scientists and technologists who were beginning to make their mark on early Victorian society. Of all the leading politicians of the day he probably was the most sympathetic to the progress of scientific thought. It was this which brought him in 1848 the offer of the Presidency of the Royal Society, an honour which he refused on the grounds that it should be confined to men of science. It had been information from several of his scientific acquaintances which first brought Playfair to his notice in 1842. Lack of prospects at home had tempted the young chemist to take a chair at Toronto and it was only Peel's timely intervention which kept him in Britain. Though he had nothing to offer at the moment, Peel made what for him was an unusual promise of finding a suitable post as soon as possible. Next year he appointed Playfair to the Royal Commission on large towns and when this came to an end, he secured his appointment as chemist to the Geological Survey undertaken by the Board of Works. From the start Playfair took his place as a regular member of the scientific parties which were becoming a feature of Drayton hospitality. He was invited down in 1842 to meet a distinguished company which included Buckland the geologist, Smith of Deanston, the authority on agricultural drainage, and Pusey the politician, farming expert, and editor of the *Agricultural Society Journal*. When he was appointed to the geological survey in 1843 he was again invited down to meet

[1] RA/F 24/35; *Playfair*, pp. 112–14. See also Yvonne ffrench, *The Great Exhibition*, pp. 56–81.

his future chief, Lord Lincoln. On this occasion a little incident took place which revealed both Peel's scientific interest and his sense of humour. In the party were Buckland, Follett the Solicitor-General, and Stephenson the railway engineer and inventor. In a discussion after dinner Stephenson in his rough Northumbrian accent hazarded the remark that the sun was the original source of power in the steam-engine through the medium of the plant life of which coal was the residue. Buckland laughed at this far-fetched theory and the inarticulate Stephenson was too abashed to elaborate his suggestion. Peel, however, remained silent and next day asked Playfair for his opinion. The chemist agreed that it was not an absurd notion and at Peel's request primed Follett with scientific arguments to support it. After dinner the subject was deliberately raised once more. In the subsequent debate Follett with his forensic skill routed the geologist and left the simple-minded Stephenson entranced at what could be achieved with 'the gift of the gab'.[1]

Playfair, Stephenson and Buckland were again present at a party at Drayton in 1847 which was largely devoted to the cause of scientific farming. Some sixty tenant farmers were invited to dinner in the long portrait gallery and speeches were delivered by Playfair, Buckland, Parkes the drainage expert, and three agricultural writers, Woodward, J. J. Mechi, and Huxtable, on such unwonted after-dinner topics as draining, soil preparation, manuring and cattle-feeding.[2] Peel had been trying for many years, both by public support and personal example, to spread the doctrines of scientific farming on which he believed the future of British agriculture depended. As far back as 1836 he had warned the House of Commons that agriculture must look to self-improvement rather than any external financial or legislative aid, and argued that unless farmers improved their land, they would never be able to compete with the produce of virgin territories overseas which steamships were bringing into the world market.[3] He was an original member of the Royal Agricultural Society founded in 1838 which was a notable advocate of deep draining and he even contributed a note on that subject to the

[1] *Playfair*, pp. 72–87.

[2] *Agricultural Gazette*, 2 Oct. 1847. An account of the proceedings was published as a pamphlet by the office of the *Gardener's Chronicle*, price 2d.

[3] Debate on the Agricultural Committee of 1836, 21 July 1836 (*Speeches*, II 326–7).

Society's *Journal*. After the passing of the 1842 Corn Law he embarked on a systematic education of farming opinion in his own neighbourhood. In October of that year he collected a party of experts including Buckland who addressed an open-air meeting of farmers and tenants in front of Drayton Manor.[1] In 1843 he was subscribing for a course of lectures on agricultural improvement to be delivered at Tamworth Public Library. The same year he addressed the Farmers' Club at Tamworth on the results of experiments with guano and offered to make similar trials on his own land. In December 1844 he assembled another party of scientists at Drayton—Buckland, Playfair, Wheatstone, Stephenson, Pusey, and Smith of Deanston—and for the first time invited his principal tenants to dine before listening to the experts talking on various aspects of scientific farming.

What he supported in public he practised in private. His correspondence with friends like Arbuthnot and Graham, themselves keen agricultural improvers, often strayed into such unpolitical topics as turnips, stock-breeding, manure, and prize cattle. They in turn sometimes acted for him in purchasing pedigree bulls and heifers from Scotland and the north of England. When old General Dyott went to Drayton in 1840 to inspect a famous bull which had just been acquired, Peel told him that he was anxious to farm not to make a profit but to encourage his tenants and neighbours by purchasing high-class breeding animals and the most modern agricultural implements.[2] One of his special interests was draining, which both for pasture and arable land was one of the greatest needs of contemporary British agriculture.[3] Not the least valuable of the legislative measures of his last ministry had been the Public Money Drainage Act of 1846, introduced in May 1846 though not passed until August, which authorised advances to landowners of up to £2 million in Britain and £1 million in Ireland, and played a notable part in the development of Victorian estate administration.[4] Deep draining, as distinct from trenching, had been developed as a science largely by James Smith of Deanston in Perthshire. It was a cardinal

---

[1] *Dyott*, II, 364.   [2] *ibid.*, p. 323.
[3] 'The crying need of the day both for pasture and arable land' (Lord Ernle, *English Farming*, 1936, p. 365).
[4] See D. Spring, *English Landed Estates* (1963), pp. 148–50.

factor in bringing the sour wet lands which characterised much English farming land at that time into a state of fertility; but the great obstacle was expense. In 1840 Peel ordered a new subsoil plough from Scotland and four years later Smith himself was brought down to assist with a preliminary drainage scheme that was being undertaken on the Drayton estate. In the twelve months which followed Smith's visit in April 1844 Peel expended £1,250 on the draining of 150 acres of his own farm land. At over £8 an acre, however, the cost deterred him from embarking on a general drainage scheme for the whole of his property. Like other landowners he found his tenants reluctant to pay more rent on account of improvements carried out by their landlord and he was equally reluctant to use any compulsion.[1]

Nevertheless, the success of his first operation encouraged him to continue. In the autumn of 1845 he was conducting a highly knowledgeable correspondence with Arbuthnot on the improved pipe-draining technique evolved by Josiah Parkes, the consulting engineer to the Royal Agricultural Society. In October that expert was professionally engaged to visit Drayton and give his advice. Under his supervision a large drainage scheme was carried out in the course of the next few years on Peel's estates at Drayton, Kingsbury, Bangley and Tamhorn, and at Oswaldtwistle in Lancashire. Under the stimulus of this activity some of Peel's tenants began to co-operate by paying 4 or 5 per cent of the total outlay on the work done on their farms.[2] Such a contribution Peel judged to be necessary otherwise every tenant would have expected him to undertake these costly operations free of charge. Even so it was a heavy charge on Peel's private budget. 'A great portion of my annual expenditure for some time past', he confessed in December 1849 to his brother Edmund (himself in arrears of rent to the tune of £5,557), 'has been in draining and other improvements upon landed property.'[3] The same month he circulated a letter to all his tenant farmers on the general prospects of agriculture in so far as they affected the relations

[1] 40609 f. 51.

[2] There is a large correspondence (1845–48) between Peel and Josiah Parkes in the Parkes Papers which illustrates in detail Peel's close supervision and wide knowledge of the problems involved in these draining operations. Josiah was the brother of Joseph the radical politician and parliamentary agent.

[3] Goulburn, 28 Dec. (1849).

of landlord and tenant. In this he argued that the effects of the repeal of the Corn Laws would be to maintain low prices in average seasons and prevent very high prices in bad. He followed this with a warning that they should dismiss from their minds the possibility that any future parliament would be likely to reimpose protection. While not committing himself to a general reduction of rents, he offered to make adjustments in particular cases. 'I will make it, and make it with much greater pleasure in favour of an old and improving tenant, than in favour of a stranger.' But he impressed on them that no abatement of rent would enable them to compete with farmers elsewhere who by good management and scientific skill were producing in some cases twice as much from their land. As a practical proposition he offered during the following year to devote 20 per cent of the rent paid by individual tenants for improvements on their farms, preference being given to drainage, consolidation of small fields, and conservation of manure. If further draining was necessary, he was prepared to undertake it if the tenant paid 4 per cent of the cost. If the security of a lease was preferred to an annual tenancy, he would grant it whenever he was satisfied of the ability and capital of the farmer concerned. Alternatively he would give them a legal guarantee of compensation for improvements.[1]

Peel in fact by 1850 had become one of the model agricultural landlords of the time. By that date most of the necessary draining work on his estates had been completed. Parkes alone had drained about 500 acres in Staffordshire and Warwickshire and a further 1,000 acres at Oswaldtwistle. At Drayton there had been spectacular results; in some instances the yield had increased fourfold.[2] A survey undertaken by Caird, as 'Commissioner' for The Times, in 1850 singled out the Peel property as an example of enlightened farming policy. It also refuted the allegations of protectionist speakers about the poor condition of labourers on Peel's estate at Kingsbury. Not only were the farm buildings substantial and in good order, but the labourers themselves were earning 9s to 10s a week. The poor rate was low and the men were fully employed all the year round. Their

[1] Printed letter dated 24 Dec. 1849 (copy in Goulburn), ptly pr. Peel, III, 528. In the following six months the 20 per cent was largely expended on manure, guano and fertilisers such as lime and bones.
[2] Agricultural Gazette, 2 Oct. 1847.

cottages, kept in repair at Peel's expense, were superior to the general run of labourers' dwellings.[1] From other sources less likely to be partial than Caird came similar testimony. The League journalist Somerville, writing under his pseudonym of *Whistler at the Plough*, interviewed old cottagers at Drayton in 1844 and confirmed Peel's reputation as a humane landlord. Retired labourers were given low rents and a grant of land, and there was no recourse to the inhumane but legal practice of sending those who were not natives of the parish back to their original homes.[2]

The condition of the lowest-paid workers had never been overlooked by Peel, despite his absorption in the general economic improvement of his property. On this, as on other matters of social concern, he found a kindred spirit in Prince Albert. In August 1846, for example, the prince gave a banquet followed by music dancing and games, to his estate workers and their families a Osborne. Though nearly five hundred were present, there were happily no irregularities. Describing the event to Peel, he added

> You will remember that we often talked about the use or possibility of giving public entertainments to the working class. I am therefore particularly glad, that this should have succeeded so well. One thing I am sure of, and that is, that the English *people* generally can enjoy themselves with propriety, and are not so dull and cold as the Saint of the day wish to represent and make them.

Peel replied next month that he himself was meditating a holiday for his own labourers on the same plan as that which was such a success a Osborne. The good effects of such festivities, he thought, would not be confined to one day. To be able to look back on past and forward to future entertainments of that kind might cheer many a gloomy day

III

In 1848, when revolutions swept across Europe from the Pyrene to the Carpathians, Britain alone of the great states presented

[1] The report was dated May 1850 but was published just after Peel's death. Peel had encouraged Caird to undertake the task largely to publicise the work done progressive farmers and landowners (see D. Spring, *op. cit.*, pp. 168–9).

[2] *Morning Chronicle*, 8 June 1844, article on 'A day at Tamworth and Drayton Sir Robert Peel as landlord'.

[3] RA/A 83/3; 40441 fos. 316, 323.

spectacle of order and tranquillity. The contrast, which was merely underlined by the fiasco of the Chartist demonstration in April, made many Englishmen ponder on the reasons for their immunity. Peel, calling at the French Embassy to offer his condolences on the collapse of the Orléans monarchy, interrogated Jarnac, the *chargé d'affaires*, on the real nature of the uprising in Paris. When he finally took his leave he observed pensively that the king and Guizot had been in a situation not dissimilar to his own. They had the choice of either parting company with their most devoted political supporters or facing the risks of revolution. The course he had himself taken had been painful, but he still believed it to have been the right one.[1]

As the reports came in during the autumn and winter of the continuing confusion, weakness and anarchy on the continent, his conviction hardened that the moral for Englishmen of all classes was the superiority of their own balanced reforming monarchical constitution over reactionary tyranny on the one hand and democratic excesses on the other. As he wrote to Goulburn in October after the news of the Vienna revolt,

> I hope the people of this country has sense enough to comprehend the lesson which is written for their instruction and will cling the more strongly to their own institutions. Democracy on the continent is teaching us what it can do for the security of Life, Liberty and Property, as compared with Monarchy.[2]

All his instincts, however, inclined him to the side of European conservatism. In November he was welcoming the restoration of governmental authority in Vienna over 'those low demagogues and mad students'; and his first reaction on hearing the proposal to turn the King of Prussia into an Emperor of Germany was one of horror.[3] This was noteworthy since in general Peel was sympathetic towards Germany and its people. He was the only leading British politician with whom the Prussian ambassador Baron Bunsen found he could speak openly on German affairs in the crucial years of 1848–49. He found the Tories hostile, the Whigs apathetic, and in society at large a 'stiff unbelief' in the future of a united nationalist Germany. Even

---

[1] *Revue des Deux Mondes,* July 1874.
[2] Goulburn (16 Oct. 1848).
[3] 43065 fos. 339, 351 (Peel to Aberdeen, Oct., Nov. 1848).

Peel so far reflected the common British attitude as to warn Bunsen in April that it was essential that there should be no German interference in affairs outside Germany until they had settled their constitution. 'You speak', he wrote, 'in the feeling of a future in which we do not believe.' Though the following year he modified his horror at the prospect of a German empire, it was only because by that time he was becoming apprehensive at the continued failure to come to a final decision on the tangled politics of the German Confederation.[1] As for France, he was frankly pessimistic. 'I think', he wrote to Aberdeen on December 1848, 'the French people have pretty well proved themselves to be ungovernable. I am afraid they have too keen a sense of the ridiculous, after all their professions about Republican Liberty and Equality, quietly to submit to the re-establishment of Monarchy *on the basis essential to its stability.*'[2]

Past and present political criticism did nothing, however, to diminish his personal sympathies with the eminent refugees who crowded into London during the spring and summer of 1848. Visiting Louis Philippe and his queen at Claremont he discovered that they were in financial difficulties as a result of the impounding of royal property in France. On his return to Drayton he wrote to Jarnac offering to put a sum of £1,000 secretly at his disposal for the use of the royal couple. Later in the year, when a defective water-supply caused ill-health among the party at Claremont, he wrote again offering the hospitality of Drayton for the king and his entire household. This, like the previous gesture, was declined. But to show his appreciation Louis Philippe paid a formal visit to Drayton in December 1849. Since a rigid sense of protocol apparently prevented the king from passing the night under the roof of a subject of Queen Victoria until he had first been received by her, the visit was uncomfortably brief. Louis Philippe and his younger son the duc d'Aumale were met in London by Peel and Aberdeen, travelled up to Tamworth in the morning, and after an unmodishly early dinner, returned the same evening to London. 'I cannot conjecture', wrote Aberdeen dryly to Princess Lieven, 'the motive of his visit, if indeed he have any except his desire to show regard for Peel.'[3]

---

[1] *Bunsen*, II, 182–9, 214–24.
[2] 43065 f. 359.
[3] *Aberdeen–Lieven Corr.*, II, 353.

Guizot and Jarnac had experienced the hospitality of Drayton in a more leisurely fashion the previous autumn. Both knew Peel well; Jarnac since 1838 and Guizot since 1840. Both had talked with him at length on various occasions about the problems of their two countries and both were left with the enduring impression that Peel's fundamental concern as a statesman was with the social condition of England. 'What struck me above all in the conversation of Sir Robert Peel', Guizot wrote later, 'was his constant and passionate preoccupation with the state of the working classes in England.' To Guizot he described them as 'a disgrace as well as a danger to our civilisation'.[1] The French Revolution of 1789 was a subject in which they had a common absorbing interest; and the Frenchman discovered that his companion was far from sharing the orthodox views of the High Tories on those epoch-making events. For all his moral, political and national prejudices he seemed to Guizot to feel a fascination for the ideas and forces behind the Revolution which sprang directly from his own middle-class origins. The younger and more imaginative Jarnac recorded in somewhat romantic language a similar impression. Sitting over wine after dinner one day in 1847 at Peel's house in Whitehall Gardens, they began to talk about the troubled internal situation in France. Peel asked Jarnac about the writings of the Socialist Louis Blanc, which he had obviously read very carefully, and cross-examined the young Frenchman about the extent of their influence. Jarnac expressed the optimistic belief that such protests against the inevitable conditions of modern society could never have much success in a society as intelligent as that of France. Peel was unconvinced. He put it to Jarnac that the importance of such writings had to be judged by their effects not on the educated and affluent but on the countless masses born to toil, ignorance and undeserved suffering. In their uneducated minds and cankered hearts what upheaval might not be produced by such appeals to their hopes, their greed and their vengeance? The soil of old Europe was already undermined and he could not feel sure that even that of England was unshakeable. Who was to measure the animosities, the envies, the resentments, and the revolutionary feelings at work below the splendid surface of our civilisation? To the startled French diplomat these were new

[1] M. Guizot, *Sir Robert Peel* (Paris, 1856), p. 78.

and disturbing questions. But there was no mistaking the seriousness with which his host put them. 'I understood then for the first time both the precipitate abolition of the corn laws and the dominant characteristic of Sir Robert Peel's peculiar genius.'[1] The events in Europe only a year later could have done nothing to remove either Peel's pessimism or his conviction that in the social problem lay the key to England's future.

Not all Peel's after-dinner conversations however touched on these uncomfortable matters. Freedom from office allowed him greater leisure for the lighter side of life. Throughout these later years he was constantly seen at public and private functions in London and at the innumerable country-house parties that relieved the provincial tedium of the parliamentary vacations. At Drayton Manor itself there was a constant procession of notabilities. In 1847, for example, Peel entertained the Grand Duke Constantine, the second son of the Tsar Nicholas, in June. In July Prince Waldemar of Prussia arrived accompanied by Bunsen. In August he went to Oxford to cast his vote in the general election and was gratifyingly cheered by the crowd of M.A.s outside the Divinity School where the poll was held. Later that month he was shooting grouse with the Duke of Rutland in Derbyshire and in September was invited to stay with Lord Londonderry at Wynyard. Though surrounded by High Tories and Protectionists, and somewhat excessively paraded by his host around the neighbourhood, he was affable to all. His friendliness disarmed any latent hostility and the visit passed off without a discordant note except for some wry faces among his fellow-guests when the Quaker Pease and other radicals came over from Darlington to present an address to the repealer of the Corn Laws.[2] From Wynyard he went on to Cromer to join Lady Peel at the seaside and so back to London. A sociable year ended in December with a literary breakfast at Hallam's where the company included Mahon, Macaulay, Milman, and Bancroft, the American historian. Peel entertained the party with stories about Lord Stowell and got into an argument with Mahon and Macaulay about human sacrifices

[1] *Revue des Deux Mondes, loc cit.* (an extract is printed in translation in Peel, *Letters*, pp. 285–6).

[2] *Letters of C. Greville and H. Reeve*, ed. A. H. Johnston (1924), p. 188 (undated and wrongly assigned to 1849).

among the Romans which was subsequently carried on in a lively and learned correspondence.[1]

With authors and artists Peel was as much at home as with scientists and engineers. In May 1849 he attended the private viewing day at the Royal Academy, where he met Charles Eastlake's young and intelligent wife, the authoress Elizabeth Rigby, and gave an Academy dinner the following evening. Mrs. Eastlake, who had found Peel rather formidable at their first encounter, even though he 'placed himself at my side and spoke nicely about the pictures', soon became an admirer. In March the following year she recorded a party at Lady Peel's—'a magnificent house, and full of distinguished company. Sir Robert Peel was most cordially kind.'[2] Later in the season the Peels were at a reception given by the Water Colour Society and attended as usual the private viewing day of the Royal Academy. In June Peel was entertaining at dinner Passavent the art-historian, Dr. Waagen the director of the Royal Gallery in Berlin, and Rauch the German sculptor. Meanwhile his interest in the growing field of art administration had never slackened. He had been a member of the select committee of the House of Commons appointed in 1835 to promote the principles of design in manufacture. In 1841 a similar committee, set up to consider the place of the fine arts in the rebuilding of the Houses of Parliament, recommended the establishment of a Royal Commission. At Peel's invitation Prince Albert, in one of his first important roles in public life, became President. Peel himself was one of the judges in the competition for frescoes in the new parliamentary building.

Art administration involved art as well as administration; and some of the problems were not easy. When Eastlake, with Peel's backing, was appointed Keeper of the National Gallery, he began a policy of removing the thick varnish with which his predecessor Seguier had protected the paintings in his care. There was an outcry in the press and Eastlake resigned in 1847, though his successor Uwins was also an advocate of cleaning. Peel was concerned at the controversy and went into the subject with care. But by 1850 he

---

[1] Stanhope (Peel to Mahon, Dec. 1847–Jan. 1848, and Mahon's memorandum about the breakfast party, 13 Dec. 1847). See also Stanhope, *Miscellanies*, pp. 112 et seq., for the printed version.

[2] *Journal of Lady Eastlake*, ed. C. Eastlake Smith (1895), I, 227, 243.

had clearly come down on the side of the Eastlake policy.[1] In the selection of paintings, however, he remained conservative, preferring the traditional Dutch, Flemish and English schools to the Italian primitives which were beginning to be the vogue. His invariable expression, according to Eastlake, was 'I think we should not collect curiosities'.[2] Though on this point he found himself out of sympathy with Albert, their disagreement did not prevent him from acting as counsellor to the royal family on aesthetic as well as other matters. In March 1842 he was sending a catalogue of the Strawberry Hill sale in case the queen was interested in purchasing any of the royal portraits and recommending Seguier as the proper person to report on them. In 1846 he intervened to prevent a Velasquez hunting-scene, formerly at the Escurial and belonging to Lord Cowley, from being sold out of the country. He acquired it for £2,200 in the conviction that the trustees of the Royal Gallery, who had once offered to buy it for £3,000, would wish to add it to their collection. Simultaneously he was negotiating with Buchanan, whom he thought 'one of the most slippery of Picture Dealers', for the purchase of three works by Caracci in the Lucca Collection, also apparently for the royal collection. 'The best speculation which the country would engage in', he wrote to Albert, 'would be a Royal Gallery worthy of a National Collection of Pictures.'[3]

He was still adding to his own collection. In June 1845, for example, Haydon noted Peel's secretary Stephenson successfully bidding 510 guineas at Christie's for a portrait of Lord Keppel by Reynolds. He continued to watch the London exhibitions for promising young artists like Buchanan, the Scottish landscape painter, from whom he was said to have purchased two pictures and commissioned three more on his first appearance in London in 1850. Another interest was his collection of contemporary portraits. From 1841 he was commissioning paintings of Graham, Stanley, Hardinge and Gladstone; and by 1844 he was building an extension of the gallery at Drayton to house them all. They included not only politicians but literary figures like Byron, Southey

---

[1] *Journal of Lady Eastlake*, p. 243. See also Peel's interrogation of Eastlake before th Select Committee on the National Gallery in 1850 (*P.P.* 1850, XV).

[2] Cf. T. S. R. Boase, *English Art 1800–1870* (Oxford, 1959), pp. 203–22.

[3] RA/A 83/2.

Wordsworth and Walter Scott; and in 1844 he asked Rogers to allow himself to be added to this distinguished company.[1] Meanwhile, he had rearranged and redecorated his other gallery at Whitehall Gardens and a great concourse of artists, men of letters, peers and politicians was invited in April 1843 to see his Dutch and Flemish masterpieces in their new setting of pale green and gold in place of the former deep crimson. For his commissioned paintings he frequently employed John Lucas. As for himself he submitted less readily to the artist's brush. He sat at the queen's request for the painting by Winterhalter of himself and the Duke of Wellington in 1844. Otherwise he refused to expose himself. There was a belief in art circles that this reluctance was due to Linnell's poorish portrait in 1838 which Peel clearly disliked, though it is possible he may have given some authorisation for it. Another portrait of Peel was later painted by H. W. Pickersgill and offered to the family after Peel's death. It is reasonably certain, however, that Peel did not sit for it even though he had employed Pickersgill for portraits of Wordsworth and others for his Drayton gallery. The vagueness of the Linnell and the woodenness of the Pickersgill portrait may well be explained by their inability to paint directly from their subject. The critics in general agreed that though Winterhalter had caught Peel's general expression and attitude, his best portrait remained that painted by Lawrence in 1825. What the *Examiner* unflatteringly called the 'portly fullness of person' which Peel had in later life was missing; but Lawrence had captured, as no other painter did, a suggestion of the amused and amusing side of Peel's nature which was an essential part of the man.[2] For the actual appearance of Peel in the eighteen-forties, as he was daily seen walking between Westminster and Whitehall, the most faithful impression was recorded not in any painting but in the innumerable sketches of the cartoonist HB.[3]

The mixture of pride and self-consciousness which deterred Peel from exposure to brush and canvas, operated even more puritanically in the matter of personal rewards. Other than the necessary

[1] P. W. Clayden, *Rogers and His Contemporaries* (1889), II, 325.
[2] See the interesting pamphlet published by Messrs Colnaghi (c. 1850) containing press criticisms of the engravings by Samuel Cousins of the Lawrence portrait and by James Faed of the Winterhalter portrait.
[3] This was pointed out as early as 1838, see the review of HB's caricatures in the *Westminster Review*, vol. 28, p. 292.

formality of the Privy Councillorship he accepted no political mark of distinction from the crown throughout his long political career. Wellington in a sensible persuasive letter asked Peel in October 1842 to allow him to propose to the queen the award of the Garter, instancing the precedents of Walpole, North and Castlereagh. Peel replied that his letter was more gratifying than the distinction could ever be. 'So far as private feelings are concerned, I do not desire the Garter. I might indeed say, with perfect truth, I would rather not have it.'[1] How strongly he felt on this point was shown by the note he left behind at his death, desiring that no member of his family should accept any reward or title on behalf of his services in public life. What from pride he rejected for himself, on public principles he distributed only sparingly to others. In his five years as prime minister between 1841 and 1846 he created only five peerages, a record of parsimony unequalled before or since. Three of these went to soldiers; Hardinge, Hill and Gough. Of the remainder, Dunsandle's barony in 1845 was a debt left over from Wellington's ministry of 1828; and the Ellesmere earldom for Francis Egerton in 1846 was as much in recognition of his social position as a duke's son and heir to the great Bridgwater fortune as for his political services. With baronetcies he was only a shade less frugal. 'There would not be a simple squire in the land,' he observed dryly to de Grey in 1841, 'if the fever for honours were not checked.' To R. M. Milnes, who approached him the following year on behalf of his father, he replied discouragingly that 'I advise him to retain the distinction of not being a Baronet'. Of the modest list of seven baronets he created at the end of his ministry, three were exceptions to the usual run of landed gentry. One was J. W. Hogg, an ex-Indian judge and chairman of the East India Company; the second was Gladstone's father, the great Liverpool merchant and plantation owner; the third was Moses Montefiore, the Jewish philanthropist. A baronetcy was also offered to Hallam the historian, who refused. In his civil list awards the outstanding feature was his disinterested promotion of the arts and sciences. Wordsworth was given a pension of £300 in 1842; Tennyson one of £200 in 1845; and Thomas Hood, joking to the last, was twice assisted in the final months of his life against the importunities of his creditors. J. D.

[1] 40459 fos. 303, 307; Wellington (Peel to Wellington, 4 Oct. 1842).

Forbes of Edinburgh, the physicist, Richard Owen the naturalist, Robert Brown the botanist, William Hamilton the astronomer, John Curtis who worked on agricultural insect pests, were among those who had their researches facilitated by a judicious award of pensions. Peel's last civil list recommendations to the Crown in June 1846 were characteristic: £300 to the daughters of Martin Archer Shee, the late president of the Royal Academy; £200 to J. R. McCulloch the economist; £100 to Bernard Barton, his Quaker guest and poetic champion of the Corn Laws; and two sums of £100 and £50 for the sisters and daughter of two officers killed in the fighting on the Sutlej.[1]

IV

Though in his awards to scientists Peel took advice from the leaders in the profession, his literary pensions were backed by his own knowledge. He was surprisingly well-read in the lighter literature of his own day. Tennyson's work he knew well enough by 1845 to have formed a high estimate of his talent. He told Hood in 1844 that there was little he had written which Peel had not read. Increasingly in the latter part of his life he had turned to reading for pleasure and relaxation. It had become his habit when returning from the Commons at night to read for a short time before going to bed to ease his mind from the distractions and irritations of the day.[2] Apart from his special collection of books on Ireland and the French Revolution, his London library had the miscellaneous character that marks the omnivorous reader rather than the bibliophile. The classics were present in force: Cicero, Euripides, Homer, Horace, Lucretius, Ovid, Plautus, Pliny, Sallust, Terence, Thucydides and Virgil. The works of English literature included Shakespeare, Shelley, Southey, Hazlitt, Milton, Pope and Scott; in history Coxe, Dalrymple, Gibbon, Guizot, Hallam and Ranke; in French Molière, Montaigne, Montesquieu, Racine, Voltaire, and St. Simon; in philosophy and political economy Locke, Bentham, Adam Smith and the complete works of McCulloch; and in lighter vein Petronius, Boccaccio and Don Quixote. There were sets of parliamentary debates, legal cases,

[1] RA/A 18/56; *Peel*, III, 430–50.
[2] Cf. *Westminster Review*, N.S. 2 (1852), article on 'Peel and His policy', p. 245 n.

statutes at large, and the *Quarterly Review*, alongside prayer-books and Old and New Testaments in Greek, Latin and English. For the rest his library shelves were full of books that defied categorisation; Jomini on the wars of Frederick the Great, Chambers's *Vestiges of Creation*, Layard's *Remains of Nineveh*, a *Life of Dost Mohammed*, and volumes on such diverse topics as anatomy, physiology, law, banking, botany, medicine, public health, engineering, roman medals, and the Burmese War.[1]

Among the classical authors, to judge from his references in debate and the engaging correspondence between Peel and Russell carried on through the intermediary of the Duke of Bedford in 1849,[2] Peel's favourites were Cicero and Horace. In English literature his most frequently quoted authors were Burke, Shakespeare, Bacon, Pope, and some of the seventeenth-century poets like Dryden, Waller, and Cowley; among the economists Adam Smith, Ricardo and McCulloch whose *Principles of Political Economy* were familiar to him as early as 1830. Literature apart, his bookshelves showed a man interested in the practical side of life—history, law, administration, economics and science—rather than philosophy or theology. Even literature mainly impressed him for the mirror it held up to life. Not many critics would have praised Shakespeare, as Peel did in the House of Commons in 1839, as 'that great poet . . . whose writings are full of more lessons of practical wisdom than the writings of any uninspired writer'. More understandable and orthodox, though still significant. was his admiration for Burke—'that illustrious man who in comprehensive and philosophical views of all public affairs, and of the great principles of social government, surpassed all the statesmen who preceded him, or have followed'.[3]

This practical interest explains his love of history, a subject in which he was more knowledgeable than commonly supposed. His interest in the French Revolution is well known; there were two hundred volumes at Whitehall Gardens on that period alone. But he had read widely in English history at any rate since the sixteenth century. His correspondence with Mahon in 1833 on the latter's *History of the Reign of George I* showed that he was well

---

[1] MS. Catalogue of books, etc., at Whitehall Gardens 1850 (Goulburn).
[2] Walpole, *Russell*, II, 107–8.
[3] *Speeches*, II, 680; III, 622.

acquainted, for example, with eighteenth-century politics and personalities. Mahon was so impressed by his informed and acute observations on Walpole in a chance conversation they had at Hatfield House that he submitted for his comments the draft character-sketch of that minister which he intended for the *History*. In his long critical reply Peel effectively quoted against the young historian such authorities as Pulteney, Bishop Newton, Hardwicke, Onslow and Coxe. Even more impressive than his range of reading was the almost intuitive understanding which his political experience enabled him to bring to this historical problem. Intellectually his assessment of Walpole was in another class from the conventional rhetoric of condemnation which Mahon had inserted in his draft. Perhaps even at that midway point in his career Peel felt an affinity with the great eighteenth-century statesman.

> There must surely have been something very extraordinary [he wrote to Mahon] in the character and powers of that man who, being the son of a private gentleman, without any advantage from a distinguished name, or services of illustrious ancestors, was Prime Minister of England amid great public difficulties for a period of twenty years—who mainly by his personal exertions contributed to establish and confirm without severity, without bloodshed, a new and unpopular dynasty—who tolerated no competitor for power— was emphatically *the Minister* of England—and who seems to have rebuked the genius of every adversary; having had for his adversaries men of the greatest talents and of the highest attainments. Of what public man can it be said with any assurance of certainty, that, placed in the situation of Walpole, he would in the course of an administration of twenty years have committed so few errors, and would have left at the close of it the House of Hanover in equal security, and the finances in equal order?[1]

Whatever comparisons may be made between Walpole and Peel it is difficult to escape the impression that Peel had a keener interest in the career of the great domestic minister of the previous century than in that of Pitt, the conventional idol of the Tory party. His innate sympathy, born of professional understanding, and for that reason profoundly historical, is in illuminating contrast to the superficial literary portrait drawn a few years later by Disraeli of the

[1] Stanhope, *Miscellanies*, pp. 66-80.

'Venetian oligarchy' which ruled England in the eighteenth century.

By 1850 history was beginning to catch up with Peel himself. In June of that year Phipps's *Memoirs of Plumer Ward* appeared, full of reminiscences of the politics of 1810–20 when Peel was first making his mark in parliament. Meeting Herries, an even older survivor of those distant days, Peel told him how pleased he had been to read Phipps's book and be reminded of forgotten but once familiar things.[1] He had used the leisure of retirement to make a contribution himself to the record of his times. He was the last person to write personal memoirs but the same qualities which inhibited him from the vanity of autobiography impelled him with almost painful self-consciousness to set down a justificatory account of the two great controversial episodes of his career—Catholic emancipation in 1829 and the repeal of the Corn Laws in 1846. Though inevitably in form an *apologia*, the two long memoranda he drew up were scarcely apologetic. He had not changed his mind; he still believed he had done right. What he wished to leave behind him was documentary evidence on which posterity could form a considered judgement of these two great crises which had brought him so much obloquy. Although he provided in each case an adequate commentary, the text of both papers was made up of contemporary letters and memoranda. It was an appeal from politics to history; and his supporting evidence was assembled with as much integrity as any man can bring to his own case. The material he used was necessarily a selection; but nothing remained in his correspondence, or indeed in any other collection, to contradict or modify on any essential point the account he gave. When the great mass of Peel papers were put in order at the end of the century and three volumes of letters published by C. S. Parker, there were no secrets to discover. Within their limits Peel's *Memoirs*, as his executors entitled them, still stand as an authentic record of the events with which they are concerned. He wrote them apparently in 1847 and 1848, using his own extensive correspondence as his source, though he had to apply to Graham and Aberdeen for the loan of letters which he had written to them without taking copies. In March 1849 he added a codicil to his will, designating Mahon and Cardwell as his literary executors. He made no reference to any particular set of papers, but he empowered the trustees to

[1] *N&Q*, vol. 190, p. 234, 'Some unpublished letters of J. W. Lockhart'.

publish any part of them and to deposit them ultimately in the State Paper Office, the British Museum or similar repository. It is clear, however, that he indicated privately to Mahon and Cardwell his special wish for the publication after his death of the two memoirs on Catholic emancipation and the Corn Laws.[1] When in due course the executors fulfilled their commission, they added a third paper, drawn up at an earlier date and with a much briefer explanation, on the administration of 1834-45.

The completion of the memoirs and the codicil of 1849 was a curiously valedictory act for a man who had only just completed his sixty-first year, whose health was good, and whose ultimate return to office was thought to be one of the inevitabilities of politics. But Peel was in a nostalgic mood in 1849. In August he, Julia and their youngest child Eliza, now a girl of seventeen, went up to the Highlands where Peel had rented a house from Lord Lovat called Eilean Aigas,[2] about fifteen miles west of Inverness. It was a picturesque stone-built residence, romantically situated on a rocky island formed by two channels of the River Beauly. Some mild historical interest attached to it, since it had been constructed by the self-styled Sobieski brothers whose claims to Stuart blood had entertained Scottish society less than a generation earlier. Despite the dull weather which greeted them Peel was deeply attracted by their island eyrie, perched on a rocky birch-covered cliff and accessible only by a long winding track through the woods and a single wooden bridge spanning the torrent below a foaming cataract. The game was sparse but Peel's interest in shooting had declined noticeably in recent years. It was a lovely, lonely countryside far from the haunts of tourists and he was more than content to while away his days in those idyllic surroundings with only an occasional excursion to nearby beauty-spots. To friends like Prince Albert, Graham, Goulburn and Aberdeen he wrote long pleasant descriptions of the scenery. They in turn repaid him with news of the day. 'It was very kind in you to remind me of the existence of a world from which I am so far removed,' he replied to Goulburn at the end of August, 'I am in a spot well calculated to make one forget it.'[3] With the coming of September the weather

[1] Cf. Guizot, *Sir Robert Peel*, preface, vi–vii.

[2] Pronounced locally Ellen Eggish. The house still stands, probably little changed from the time when Peel was there.

[3] Goulburn (26 Aug. 1849).

set fine and they lingered on in the tranquillity and seclusion as though loath to fix a date for their departure. Lady Peel wrote to Bonham that she had never seen her husband so happy.[1] Not until the second week of October did they finally leave, calling on Aberdeen at Haddo and Graham at Netherby on their leisurely way south. On 17 October they were back at Drayton once more, with the problems of the approaching session already beginning to obtrude into his correspondence. In thanking Aberdeen for his hospitality Peel spoke with unusual affection of their Scottish visit. 'I am sure there is no one, not a Scotchman, who feels a stronger attachment to that country than I do. I know not exactly why and on that very account, the attachment is sincere and lasting.' Then he added an odd sentence. 'It would be painful to me to think, what is very probable, that I shall never see the Highlands again.'[2]

[1] Stanhope (Bonham to Mahon, 21 Sept. 1849).
[2] 43065 f. 391.

EPILOGUE

On Saturday, 29 June 1850, the morning after the great Don Pacifico debate in the House of Commons, Peel rose after a short night to attend a meeting of the Commission on the 1851 Exhibition at eleven. As Julia, who had waited up for him the night before, was feeling tired and unwell, he begged her not to get up to see to his breakfast as she usually did. She remained in bed where she read the newspaper report of his speech and wrote a little note of congratulation to send down to him. At the committee, which lasted until three o'clock, he seemed a little jaded. On his return home he worked for a short time in his study and then went out for his customary ride about five. Passing through the hall he met Julia who reminded him of their dinner engagement that evening with the Jerseys. He promised not to be late, called her back to kiss goodbye, and left the house.

The horse waiting for him outside in the sunshine was a recent acquisition. The bay mare which had been his favourite mount for many years was growing old and he had been advised to get a more sure-footed animal. The new horse was an eight-year-old which had been purchased at Tattersalls the previous April by one of Peel's friends, Becket Denison. It had been hunted regularly and Denison rode it for a time in the London traffic before recommending it to Peel. Lord Villiers also tried the horse and thought it perfectly suitable for his father-in-law. In fact, as transpired afterwards, it had been discarded by Sir Henry Peyton, one of the best riders of the day, because of its trick of kicking and bucking; and it had been unsuccessfully offered round in Berkshire and Hampshire before being sent to Tattersalls for disposal. Paul Hunter of Mortimer had actually recognised the horse in the park and thought of warning Peel but was reluctant to obtrude. Peel's own coachman had his doubts of the animal and advised him not to ride it. But Peel found it hard to disbelieve Denison's assurances and had been riding the horse regularly each evening for about eight weeks without incident.[1]

With his groom in attendance Peel called at Buckingham Palace

[1] A. West, *Recollections*, I, 61; Goldwin Smith, *Reminiscences*, p. 175; Martineau, *Newcastle*, p. 97; *Illustrated London News*, 6 July 1850.

697

and wrote his name in the visitor's book. Then he rode slowly up Constitution Hill towards Hyde Park Corner. Near the top, within sight of St. George's Hospital, he met two daughters of Lady Dover accompanied by a groom on a rather skittish horse. He had barely exchanged salutations before his own horse began to plunge and kick. It then swerved violently and threw Peel over its head. He fell face downward at full length still holding the reins. The horse stumbled on top of him, striking his back with its knees. In the light of what was later discovered, this second impact was probably critical. Two bystanders ran to his assistance. He was raised to a sitting position and one of them went off to seek medical aid at the hospital. Meanwhile, Dr. Foucart, a Glasgow surgeon who had seen the accident, came up and he was joined soon after by Sir James Clark, the royal physician. A Mrs. Lucas of Bryanston Square arrived on the spot in her carriage and offered it to take Peel back to his house. It was obvious that Peel was in great pain. Asked by Foucart whether he was much hurt, he muttered 'yes,—very much' and he was almost unconscious when they lifted him into the carriage. Foucart, Clark, and the other two men accompanied him at a slow pace back to Whitehall Gardens where a message had been sent on to give news of what had happened. As they lifted him out he revived again and walked with assistance to the front door where Julia and other members of the family were anxiously waiting. At the sight of his pale, grazed face Julia almost broke down and Peel, overcome himself by the pain of his effort, fainted once more in Foucart's arms. They carried him into the dining-room which led off from the back of the hall and placed him on a sofa. There, beneath the Wilkies and the Reynolds, in front of the tall windows overlooking the quiet garden by the Thames, the muted activity of the sick-room began.

A distinguished company of medical men quickly assembled: Dr. Hodgson, Peel's family doctor, Sir Benjamin Brodie, the leading surgeon of the day, Dr. Seymour and Mr. Caesar Hawkins, physician and surgeon respectively at St. George's Hospital, together with Clark and Foucart. On examination it was found that there was a comminuted fracture of the left collar-bone with a pronounced swelling of the tissues below the bone and under the pectoral muscles. It was surmised also that one or more ribs at the back were broken, but the acute suffering experienced by the patient made only a perfunctory exploration possible. Some bandages were tied round his chest and arm to prevent movement of the injured part but these so aggravated the pain and restlessness that they were soon removed. A patent water-mattress was procured and with considerable difficulty Peel was placed on a table with his arm supported by pillows. At seven o'clock on Saturday the first bulletin announced to the world that Sir Robert Peel had met with a serious injury. During Saturday evening he was allowed to see Lady Peel but he was in such a state of shock and faintness that it was thought advisable to forbid all other visitors. Peel himself told the surgeons at one point that he thought there was more to his injuries than they could fathom and he would not get over it. Next day there was no sign of improvement. The swelling below the shoulder-blade had enlarged and was pulsating with the action of the heart. It was clear that there was a severe internal haemorrhage which was producing shock not only from loss of blood but also from the intense pain caused by pressure of the haematoma on the large nerves passing through the arm-pit where they are concentrated into a narrow space. A slight improvement in the circulation during the evening allowed the doctors to make an application of leeches to allay the inflammation; but this so exhausted the patient that they had to give him an immediate stimulant. The only other positive measure adopted was mercurial treatment to reduce the inflammation which was continued as long as there seemed any hope of benefit. All Sunday night and Monday Peel remained in the same precarious condition. During the night of Monday, 1 July, he became delirious, frequently attempted to raise himself from the bed, and had such bouts of exhaustion that the doctors thought he would not survive till dawn. During his lapses into unconsciousness he constantly muttered the names of Hardinge and Graham. On Monday evening Hardinge was sent for from next door, came at once, and stayed at Peel's side all night.

Outside the sick-room there was a constant stream of visitors and enquiries. On the first news of the accident the Villiers cancelled their dinner-party and came at once to Whitehall Gardens. Prince Albert accompanied by the Prince of Prussia, Prince George of Cambridge, Wellington and many others called the same evening.

On Sunday the queen sent a messenger round early in the morning and Wellington called a second time in the afternoon as also did Prince George. With Lady Peel almost incapable of any action, the direction of the household was taken over by her two children, William home on leave from the navy and his eighteen-year-old sister Eliza. It was Eliza who summoned her cousin Archibald to see her father and then set off post-haste to Rome to fetch her elder brother Robert, the heir to the baronetcy. Meanwhile, the news had spread all over London. The carriages began to arrive one after the other and a crowd gathered in the street outside. On Monday there was an endless procession of callers from the squares and streets of the fashionable West End from nine o'clock in the morning until past eleven at night. As Monday wore on the crowd at the gates, mainly of working people, began to thicken. They came and went, the men in their labouring clothes and the women in shawls, passing on the latest reports to each other and peering through the railings at the darkened windows; but the numbers never diminished. All night long and all through Tuesday the eddying, whispering crowd filled Whitehall Gardens. When the servant was seen leaving the house at two o'clock with a fresh bulletin there was such a rush to the gates that a policeman had to read it aloud to the crowd. During the afternoon additional police were stationed at each end of Whitehall Gardens to answer enquiries and divert traffic. Outside the gates of Peel's house extra copies of the bulletins were posted up for the information of the constantly growing mass of people. In this intense popular interest there was no doubt an element of morbid curiosity, intensified by the Victorian love of deathbed pathos. But it was not this which impressed contemporary observers as the dominant feeling among these humble watchers in the street. They found the spectacle striking not because it was a conventional but because it was such an unusual and unexpected tribute from the ordinary people of London. 'Unknowing the significance of their own appearance,' wrote one journalist reporting the scene, 'these poor folk were, in reality, the guard of honour accorded to the last hours of Sir Robert Peel—by the People.'[1]

On Tuesday morning, 2 July, there was a gleam of hope. At four o'clock Peel had fallen into a deep sleep which lasted until eight.

[1] *Illustrated London News*, 6 July 1850.

On awaking he said he was in less pain. His pulse had dropped, and he took some tea and broth. It was the first nourishment he had had, other than an egg whipped up in a glass of champagne, since the previous Saturday. Afterwards he walked round the room supported on each side.[1] At noon his condition was still apparently better and Hawkins expressed confidence in his recovery. But within a couple of hours there was a sudden deterioration. His breathing became stertorous and he became unconscious once more. He failed to answer when spoken to and seemed sinking into a coma. Brodie was hastily summoned and for the first time the doctors admitted their fears. The pulse had become more rapid and was growing steadily weaker. His breathing was increasingly difficult and the stimulants administered had no effect. At half-past six they abandoned hope and advised the family that it was unlikely he would live another twenty-four hours. The Bishop of Gibraltar, Dr. Tomlinson, an old friend, was sent for at Peel's wish. He arrived at eight and administered the sacrament. Then members of his family were admitted one by one to take their leave. Peel, though much weaker, was by now in little pain. He revived enough to be able to take each hand in his own and whisper a blessing, his last words being to his youngest child, Eliza. Julia Peel, who had remained kneeling at his side while Tomlinson recited the Communion, was by this time so overcome that she had to be led away shortly afterwards. Hardinge was already present and a little later Graham arrived. By nine o'clock Peel had lapsed into unconsciousness once more. For another two hours the silent company round his bed—his three brothers Lawrence, John and Jonathan, his three sons Frederick, William and Arthur, Lord Villiers, Hardinge, Graham, and the doctors—listened to the painful breathing of the dying man. It ceased at nine minutes past eleven.

II

It was ascertained afterwards that there had been a fracture of one or more ribs underneath the left shoulder-blade. But as the family objected to a *post-mortem*, no final diagnosis of the cause of death was attempted. The subsequent medical accounts by Brodie and Hodgson, however, left little doubt on the salient details of the case.

[1] Graham (Hardinge to Graham, n.d. endorsed 2 July).

Victorian doctors were well accustomed to simple bone-fractures and would have had little difficulty in treating them. The essential feature here was the comminuted, that is to say the fragmented, fracture of the collar-bone accompanied by fractures of the ribs. Fragments of bone undoubtedly pierced a major blood-vessel and may also have introduced through the skin a source of infection. The surgeons believed that it was an injury to the sub-clavian vein which produced the marked haemorrhage and swelling. It is possible that the sub-clavian artery may also have been injured, which would equally explain the pulsation observed in the swelling under the collar-bone. The degree of surgical shock caused by these injuries, arising not only from loss of blood but also from excessive pain, could in itself have produced death. The subsequent symptoms, however, point to the development of broncho-pneumonia. This would explain the relative easing of pain and the growing difficulty of breathing from Monday night onwards. It could have been caused by stasis in the left lung as a result of prolonged pain but might also have been due to direct injury and infection of the lung from the broken ribs. Given the state of medical techniques at the time, it is almost certain that nothing could have saved Peel's life. Chloroform was already being used by Simpson of Edinburgh but its use in this case would have been of no value whatever in allowing a more detailed clinical examination of the injuries. It would merely have killed the patient. Even a century later the exploration of such injuries as Peel sustained would be a hazardous surgical undertaking. The doctors did what their not inconsiderable knowledge and experience suggested. If they failed to prevent a deterioration in the condition of their patient, it is unlikely that their treatment made that condition worse. From the moment Peel was picked up on Constitution Hill he was a mortally injured man. Not the fall in itself perhaps but the knees of a stumbled horse did the irremediable damage.[1]

[1] For the medical history see *The Times*, 4 July, *Lancet*, 6 July 1850. An MS. account drawn up for Peel's executors by Hodgson, dated 2 June 1851, corrected by Brodie and approved by Seymour and Hawkins, is in 40609 fos. 369–77. Cf. the similar account in T. Holmes, *Sir Benjamin Brodie* (1898), Appx M. I am greatly indebted to my friend Mr. John S. G. Blair, F.R.C.S., for putting his professional knowledge at my disposal in dealing with the medical evidence.

Since Peel's death suggestions have occasionally been made both of his morbid

Early on Wednesday morning the postmen and the early newspapers brought the news to countless homes in London. As the day went on flags were flown at half-mast and shops closed all over the country. The House of Commons met at noon and in the absence of Lord John Russell, Hume moved the immediate adjournment of the House. Next day business was again suspended until the evening. Sir George Grey who made the motion could hardly repress his emotions when alluding to Peel's death. When they reassembled Russell paid the formal tribute of the House and was followed by several other members. Many M.P.s were in black, and some took off their hats when Russell began to speak. Graham, incapable of speech, sat there in tears. Goulburn confined himself to a dry statement on behalf of the family rejecting a burial in Westminster Abbey. What was said by others cast light more on the minds of the speakers than on the dead man's political career. Gladstone spoke of the services which he might still have rendered to his country had he been spared. Russell singled out the disinterested support he had given the government in the years immediately after the Reform Act of 1832. In the House of Lords Lansdowne broke with precedent by making a formal reference to the loss sustained by the other House. One tribute at least, he said, was due to the close of such a career: public sympathy, unasked, unsolicited, and unsought, from all quarters and all classes of society. The Duke of Wellington, who could hardly speak for tears, dwelt on Peel's passion for truth as though it was a quality he had not usually encountered among politicians. Throughout their long connection, he told the peers, he had never known Peel say anything which he did not firmly believe to be true. It was left with an odd irony to Stanley to make perhaps the most eloquent and touching tribute to 'a great man and a great statesman'. He spoke of his regret at their past differences of opinion but expressed his conviction that there had never been personal

---

inability to endure physical pain and of his bad horsemanship (e.g. A. West, *Recollections*, I, 61–2). Like any imaginative person he probably disliked the thought of physical pain, but his heroic treatment for sciatica in 1837 and the history of his accident in 1850 do not provide much evidence for his inability to bear it when it came. Similarly, though he had not the build for a good horseman, the observation that he was a bad one would be more convincing had anyone made it before 29 June 1850. As it was, he had been riding regularly for fifty years and this was his first recorded accident.

hostility. He was confident there had been none on his side; equally confident there had been none on the other. Nor had he ever attached unworthy motives to Peel's political conduct. What he had done had always been intended for the public good. Then he added, with a rare glimpse of his inner feelings, 'to promote the welfare of his country he was prepared to make, and did actually make, every sacrifice. In some cases those sacrifices were so extensive that I hardly know whether the great and paramount object of his country's good was a sufficient reason to exact them from any public man.'

During the next few days the newspapers vied in laudatory comment on what *The Times* called, in a leading article on his death, 'the greatest statesman of his time'. Panegyrics, articles, memoirs, biographical accounts, appeared in almost every periodical; cheap pamphlets on his life and work, penny reprints of his last speech, were rushed out from the press. More permanent memorials were also planned. Russell moved an address to the crown for the erection of a monument to Peel in Westminster Abbey. Aberdeen presided over a meeting of political notabilities to raise money for a public statue in London. Hume headed a committee for a Poor Man's Monument to Peel, subscriptions to which were limited to one penny. The Metropolitan Police started a fund for their own memorial to the founder of the force. Similar moves were made in many towns and provinces. What observers noted was the common mood of all classes, from the queen to the humblest labourers. 'Great expressions of national sorrow,' wrote Carlyle, who on the Monday had made a pilgrimage from Chelsea to Whitehall to obtain news and on the Thursday went once more to look at the house where the only politician he respected lay dead. 'Really a serious expression of regret in the public; an affectionate appreciation of this man which he himself was far from being sure of, or aware of, while he lived.'[1] When men searched their memories, they could find

---

[1] J. A. Froude, *Carlyle*, II, 48. Cf. the remark quoted in the *Morning Chronicle*, 20 Jan. 1851, of a man who had worked for forty years in a Birmingham metal factory. 'Nearly every one of us—and, in fact, I believe every one—subscribed towards the monument to the memory of the late Sir Robert Peel. We considered him the working man's best friend for repealing the corn-laws. Our employers did not ask us to subscribe; but we got up the subscription quietly among ourselves. We paid about 30s. or £2 amongst us.' (I owe this reference to the kindness of Mr. B. H. Harrison.)

nothing to equal it since Pitt. But Aberdeen, who could recollect Pitt's death, thought the feeling for Peel was more genuine and widespread.[1] Some of the politicians, circumscribed by their narrow parliamentary world in which the controversies of the past could not so easily be forgotten, were surprised by the outburst of national sentiment. 'I thought he had a great hold on the country,' Greville wrote to Graham, 'but had no idea it was so deep and strong and general as now appears.'[2] The cynical Whig lawyer Campbell made much the same comment and reflected that Peel would probably be thought a greater man by posterity than by his contemporaries.[3] Some surprised even themselves. 'Once,' wrote Macaulay on 4 July, 'I little thought that I should have cried for his death.'[4]

Much of this manifestation of national emotion was coloured by the purely fortuitous circumstances of Peel's death. A great public figure, widely regarded as one of the pillars of the state, had been cut down in his prime by a painful and meaningless accident. For the mass of ordinary people, indifferent to party politics, there had already been a sacrificial element in his resignation in 1846. 'He fell from official power into the arms of the people,' wrote one publication designed for the masses, '. . . for what had he, raised aloft upon the bucklers of a powerful and wealthy party, to gain by stooping from that dazzling height, to raise up the humble and the lowly from the mire into which ignorant and partial legislation had so long trampled them.'[5] The tragic nature of his death four years later irrationally reinforced this popular sense of the great statesman who had deliberately sacrificed the highest rewards of politics for the good of his country. The actions which during his life had made his career so controversial, after his death could be regarded as his greatest merits. In this atmosphere even Catholic emancipation and the vituperation which had accompanied it, could be reckoned to his credit. The justification which Peel had hoped to receive from posterity, he received from his contemporaries while his body still lay at Whitehall Gardens. Nor did those feelings disappear immediately. The statues and monuments that began to appear in parks and public

[1] See his letters to Princess Lieven (*Aberdeen–Lieven Corr.*, II, 500) and Guizot (*Aberdeen*, II, 158).

[2] Graham (n.d. but probably 4 July 1850).

[3] *Campbell*, II, 281. [4] Trevelyan, *Macaulay*, II, 278.

[5] *Chambers' Papers for the People*, IV, 'Sir Robert Peel'.

places all over Britain during the next few years; the cheap prints of his portraits to be found hanging up during the rest of the century in the cottages of agricultural labourers and in the backstreet homes of working-class families; these were mute evidence of the effect of his life on the popular tradition of the nation.

Yet equally permanent and more prominent, as Peel's generation died out, was the record of his inconsistencies and desertions. As emotions receded, the facts became more striking and more inexplicable. In this too there was justice. To make a sudden reversal of previous policy, to desert or betray one's followers, is a decision which any great statesman, and many that are not great, may have to face. To do so twice, as Peel did over Catholic emancipation and the Corn Laws, seemed to indicate something deeper than the chance concurrence of events. To those who put political consistency or party fidelity among the highest political virtues, his offence was unforgivable. Even more dispassionate observers could conclude that he had been either very unfortunate or very careless. Perhaps Peel was in fact prone to political accidents. His pride was too stiff, his temper too authoritative, his readiness to take responsibility too overpowering. His sense of public duty drove him to take up large issues; his intelligence provided him with radical solutions; his integrity denied him ordinary safeguards. He lacked flexibility; he lacked an instinct for political self-preservation; he was not adept at the manipulation of private interest for the public good which is an indispensable feature of representative politics. He tended to overestimate the influence of reason in human affairs; and he sometimes seemed more anxious to win support among his opponents than to make friends among his supporters. With all his understanding and experience he disdained methods which equally upright but more tolerant men employ to obtain their ends. He was always strongwilled, sometimes stubborn. He rarely admitted having made a mistake, never on anything important. Where his actions were most controversial, he was least inclined to concede the possibility of error. When he had made up his mind, nothing could shift him. Retreat did not enter into his vocabulary; compromise seldom. He piqued himself on never having introduced a measure which he did not pass. It was a recipe for success but also for disaster.

As the trusted minister of a powerful monarch he would have

made a great career; and the political world in which he first learnt his trade was not without affinities to this older structure of the European states system. Where it differed was in its parliamentary framework. Power could only be obtained as a constitutional minister; and in the last resort this depended on the House of Commons. To a study of that assembly Peel devoted much talent. In the subtle and intelligent depreciation of Peel which Disraeli inserted into his *Life of Lord George Bentinck*, it was suggested that Peel's one real title to fame was that of being the greatest member of parliament who ever lived. The compliment was ambiguous since it was in lieu of other claims mentioned only to be withheld. But it at least expressed in exaggerated form a truth which no one has seriously challenged. In his knowledge and command of the House, in his prestige and influence with that powerful and critical body, Peel had no equal in the last eighteen years of his life. Yet his stature as a parliamentarian rested on his skill in dealing with the House of Commons as an assembly. He was less happy in dealing with its members as individuals. For that reason he can hardly be said to be among the great House of Commons men. It was the arena of politics, the necessary platform of power. But his fundamental outlook, conditioned by his first twenty years in politics, was executive and governmental. His approach to politics, even in opposition or as a private member, was as a potential minister of the crown. In the two great crises of his career he obtained the consent of parliament to a supreme executive decision; but only at the cost of alienating and affronting many who had been his previous supporters. Peel's intrinsic attitude to politics was exposed in the Catholic emancipation crisis of 1829. It set a precedent not only which his critics did not allow him to forget, but from which his own nature did not allow him to escape. The strengthening of the party system after 1832 made this inherent tendency even more liable to disaster. The man had not altered; and his past record meant that even with his own party he was dealing on a narrow margin of trust. Catholic emancipation scarred him for the rest of his life; but the effect was not to make him more but less amenable to party claims.

Yet the brittleness of his relations with his party back-benchers was in striking contrast to his relations with his cabinet. Against the somewhat slipshod generalisation that Peel was not good at handling

men must be placed his outstanding qualities as head of an administration. The aloofness, the arrogance, the impatience he sometimes
exhibited to the rank and file of his party were singularly absent
when dealing with his official colleagues. In the cabinet, and with
junior ministers, he showed qualities of tact, tolerance, kindness and
loyalty which made his administration one of the most united and
harmonious of the century. He dealt with his colleagues on a basis
of confidence and friendship; he reasoned and persuaded; he tried
to convince rather than command; he never deceived or sacrificed
them. An illuminating comparison could be made, for example,
between Peel's handling of his cabinet in November and December
1845 and Disraeli's dealings with the Conservative cabinet during the
reform bill crisis of 1867. If anything Peel was too loyal to his
ministers; but he had his reward. No other prime minister in the
century, except perhaps Pitt, left behind such a devoted band of
followers. 'My great Master and generous friend', Hardinge called
him when writing to Lady Peel in August 1850. 'He is my leader
still, though invisible', wrote Lincoln sixteen months later. 'I never
take a step in public life without reflecting how would *he* have thought
of it.' Even Gladstone, who of all the younger Peelites had perhaps
least instinctive sympathy with his leader, could still write in 1853
of 'my great teacher and master in public affairs'.[1] It was largely for
this reason that the split in the party, when it came, was of an
unusual nature: as much horizontal as vertical. The cabinet and the
corps of official men, with few exceptions and none of importance
other than Stanley, stayed with Peel. The brains and the experience
of the Conservative Party remained with the Peelites. It was this
which made the disruption of 1846 of such significance for the future
of Victorian party politics.

The same difficulty in generalising is present when assessing Peel
as a party leader. To a large extent his weaknesses were the defects
of his qualities. His profound honesty made him unreasonably
sensitive to any slur on his integrity. His single-mindedness made
him unduly resentful of criticism or opposition from those from
whom he thought he had a right to expect support. His pride
sometimes turned his courage into inflexibility. But his uneasy

[1] Peel MSS. (to Lady Peel from Hardinge, 29 Aug. 1850; from Lincoln (now Duke
of Newcastle), 29 Dec. 1851; from Gladstone, 20 Apr. 1853).

relationship with his party did not spring from temperamental qualities alone. Gladstone once said that Peel's two conspicuous attributes as a statesman were his sense of public duty and his sense of measure.[1] For the latter he instanced his concept of the relations between the leader of a party and his followers. It was not an example which would occur to most critics of Peel's career. Yet Peel was not alone in his balanced attitude towards the claims of party. That the pursuit of party policy is invariably compatible with national interest is one of the engaging assumptions of parliamentary life. It can be less unhesitatingly accepted by men who actually find themselves at the head of affairs. In Peel's day, when the modern party system was in its infancy and the older patrician tradition of government inherited from the eighteenth century still strong, it was even more difficult to accept party as a complete depositary of political wisdom. The narrowness of the representative structure and the abuses of the electoral machinery made a party majority in the House of Commons something less than an adequate register of public feeling. An undue obsession with its own material interests made it even less satisfactory as an arbiter of government policy. If Peel had much to learn about being a party leader, the Conservatives in the 1835–46 period had much to learn about being a national party. Greville summed it up in 1844 when he wrote to Raikes that 'the truth is, Peel had not the qualities requisite for leading a party, though he has all the talents that are necessary; he is too good for his party'.[2] Yet what Peel had done for that party in the ten years that followed the Reform Act was fundamental. He had revived and reformed the scattered forces of the opposition, provided them with a philosophy, recruited fresh sources of strength in the country, and led them to victory in 1841. His place as the founder of modern Conservatism is unchallengeable. Disraeli's subsequent 're-education' of the party in the thirty years which followed the disruption of 1846 was inevitably a return to Peel's principles since only on the basis of those principles could a party of the right in the conditions of Victorian political life obtain and retain power. What Peel gave the Conservative opposition after 1832 was national leadership of a kind which they were not to see again for another generation; and it is a

[1] L. A. Tollemache, *Talks with Mr. Gladstone* (1901), p. 116.
[2] *Corr. of Thomas Raikes*, ed. H. Raikes (1861), p. 372.

paradox of party politics that national leadership is often more effective than party leadership. Peel may not have been a good party leader; there is a case for arguing that he was a great one.

Nevertheless when every allowance is made for the circumstances and traditions which coloured Peel's outlook on party, it remained true that there was a contradiction between his attitude as minister and his position as head of the Conservative Party which he never resolved. He attached primary importance to his responsibilities as a servant of the crown; he valued greatly the confidence of the monarch. Yet the clash of parties and personalities between 1837 and 1841 put both him and his party in an illogical position, claiming to be the party of the constitution but necessarily in an attitude of opposition to the queen. The difficulty with any theory of support for the monarchy was that the institution could not easily be distinguished from the person. It was a party majority gained at a general election which forced Peel against the wishes of Victoria into office. In the old-fashioned language of the eighteenth century, he had 'stormed the closet'. In securing supreme power in 1841 he owed nothing to the crown, everything to party. It could be argued that he made a decisive personal contribution to the great Conservative victory; it is probable, though unprovable, that without him they would never have secured a majority. Even so it was the votes of the Conservative members and the votes of their constituents that put him where he wished to be. The indebtedness he recognised; the obligations which that debt imposed he partly ignored. The limitations of action which party support made necessary he accepted as a matter of parliamentary tactics; though when he thought it feasible he was ready to go beyond those limitations. That they formed a moral frontier which he ought not to transgress he never believed. He conducted himself in office as though the theory of royal confidence and ministerial responsibility to the crown was a reality of political life. Yet if it had been, he would never have come into office. Organised parties after 1832 could not be regarded as a substitute for 'The King's Friends'. Nor did Peel so regard them; but he sometimes acted as though he did. This inherent contradiction was, however, softened by various other features of contemporary political life which later critics often forget. Peel's views accorded with the accepted theory of the constitution even if theory was lagging behind practice. They were shared to a large extent by all the leading politicians of the day even if they never expressed them so explicitly or defiantly as he did. The liberty of action claimed by ministers was matched by the liberty of action claimed by private members of parliament. In the rapid, almost precocious, evolution of party politics in the decade after the Reform Act it was not possible for either party leaders or party followers to make rigid demands on each other. It was not that Peel broke a kind of unwritten party contract, but that he put an excessive strain on a party system which was still gathering experience and evolving its own working rules. His own dominant nature and the difficult age in which he lived in the end made that strain too great.

At the time of his death this failure seemed to most people of little importance compared with his record of public service. It was an impressive catalogue of achievement: the Royal Irish Constabulary, the Bullion Committee and the return to gold, legal and criminal reform, repeal of the Test and Corporation Acts, Catholic emancipation, the Metropolitan Police, the Ecclesiastical Commission, tariff reform and free trade, the income tax, the Bank Charter Act, Maynooth and the Irish colleges, the Devon Commission, the repeal of the Corn Laws. It testified to Peel's master passion in politics: the desire to get things done. The urge towards constructive activity which he first demonstrated as a young Chief Secretary in Ireland never slackened. Moreover, his mind remained fresh and receptive to the end. In some respects indeed he was ahead of his time. In his later Irish policy, for example, where conditions were against him, he could lay only an incomplete foundation for the future. Yet even his unfulfilled plans contained much that was suggestive and useful for a later generation of Victorians. It was said of him, by Disraeli and others, that he lacked originality; that he merely appropriated other men's ideas. The criticism, if intended seriously, betrays a curious misconception. A politician is not a mother but a midwife. Original ideas in themselves are of little practical value. Their importance comes when they are absorbed into a wider stratum of social thought and begin to be part of the process of events. To formulate original ideas is a task for the philosopher; the task of the politician is to translate them into practice. Where the test of statesmanship comes is in choice, timing and execution. Politics is the art of the possible; but to decide what is possible often takes judgement and courage. The measure of Peel's quality is that he did what other politicians thought could not be done. 'A great doer of the impossible', Harriet Martineau had called him. The Whig G. C. Lewis put it more prosaically. 'For concocting, producing, explaining and defending measures he had no equal, or anything like an equal. There was nothing *simile aut secundum*. When a thing was to be done, he did it better than anybody.'[1] Eighteen years later Goldwin Smith, who was so nearly Peel's first real biographer, summed up this view in one lapidary sentence. 'For a quarter of a century, at least, he was without question the first public servant of England.'[2]

To earn such a verdict a man must have several attributes: administrative skill, capacity for work, personal integrity, high standards, a sense of duty. To say that Peel had all these is to utter a commonplace. What is less often remarked on is his sheer intellectual power. It was this above all which enabled him to dominate his political contemporaries both in cabinet and the House of Commons. To read some of his parliamentary speeches, still more some of his cabinet papers, is to be conscious even at this distance of time of an outstanding intellect at work. Few things are more impressive in an examination of Peel's career than the actual quality of mind which he brought to bear on every aspect of administration which came before him. Even in the field of foreign policy, the one most remote from his main interests, the not uncritical Aberdeen confessed in 1850 that 'there is always so much wisdom and prudence in the view he takes of great and difficult affairs, that his opinion cannot but be valuable'.[3] The combination of intellectual ability and wide governmental experience put Peel during the last twenty years of his life in a class by himself. In terms of mental capacity alone he was one of the ablest prime ministers in British history.

Yet a final judgement on Peel would be incomplete if it stopped at that point. Though politics without intellect cannot efficiently be sustained for very long, more intuitive and imaginative qualities are needed to achieve greatness; and Peel after all made his career in politics. It is true that up to 1830 he was primarily an administrator.

---

[1] *Letters of Sir G. C. Lewis*, ed. Sir G. F. Lewis (1870), p. 226
[2] In an article on Peel in *Macmillan's Magazine*, Dec. 1868.
[3] *Aberdeen–Lieven Corr.*, II, 364 (22 Jan. 1850).

His early entry into office and the circumstances of the time made him a natural supporter of government and to that extent a natural conservative. On the one great political issue of the day, Catholic emancipation, his upbringing and his Irish experience placed him without much preliminary reflection in the Protestant camp. The political tie with Oxford University in 1817 fortified that youthful allegiance. But in the course of 1828 his administrative instincts still sufficiently triumphed over his political affinities to produce the first great 'betrayal'. With the Reform Act of 1832, however, his political sense was sharply awakened; and with it his political imagination. His restraint in 1833 and 1834, and his elaboration of a new Conservative philosophy between 1834 and 1841, was a statesmanlike response to a new situation. After he took office in 1841 his outlook on national affairs became increasingly intelligent and farsighted. It had been anticipated by his opponents that Ireland would prove the Achilles heel of the new administration. In fact, once the threat from O'Connell had been countered, his Irish policy displayed a creativity greater than that of the Whigs, the traditional friends of Ireland. But it was not only on Ireland that his mind expanded. The most significant feature of the 1841–46 ministry was his growing concern for the political and social problems of industrial Britain. Whatever Peel lacked, it was not imagination. His rigidity on such secondary matters as poor law and factory reform is unimportant. Indeed it arose logically from his sensible conviction that poverty could only be solved by the production of more wealth. What was important was his assertion that the aristocratic system could only survive if it showed a readiness to promote the welfare of all other classes in the community. It sprang naturally from his concept of the constitution as a mixed and balanced form of government maintaining an equilibrium between monarchy and democracy, and harmonising their conflicting interests.[1] It was given an intense emotional force by his experiences in 1841 and 1842.

The fundamental quality which Peel exhibited after 1841 was his desire to reunite the country.[2] In an age when the executive govern-

---

[1] See e.g. his speech of 27 May 1841 (*Speeches*, III, 760).
[2] Cf. the remarks of Abercromby, the former Whig Speaker of the House of Commons (cr. Lord Dunfermline, 1839), to Baron Stockmar. 'Sir Robert had studied the change which has been progressively taking place in the public mind and, from very close observation, I am *thoroughly* convinced that one of his greatest objects

ment had lost its influence and party was still learning how to govern, he essayed the difficult task of governing according to the ethic of the old system but with the technique of the new. He based his power on party but his policy was neither sectional nor partisan. The events of 1846 were only a supreme example of an attitude which underlay his whole conduct as minister. It is easy now to see how contemporary opinion exaggerated the effects, both baneful and beneficial, of the repeal of the Corn Laws. But the significance of the action taken by Peel in 1846 was symbolic; and as a symbol it was rivalled only by the Reform Act of 1832 as the decisive event in domestic politics in the first half of the nineteenth century. The Reform Act had been a gesture of deference to public opinion and the enhanced stature of new political classes. After 1832 the aristocracy continued to govern the country but it governed on trust. In that situation there were two dangers that might have destroyed the good effects of reform. One was that the aristocracy might be unable to carry out its trust for lack of internal cohesion; the other that it would fail to recognise the terms of its trusteeship. By 1845 the Corn Laws had been elevated in the public mind into a test of governmental integrity. Peel's response and the sacrifice it entailed did more than anything else to heal the social breach and restore public confidence in the good faith of a system which was still essentially oligarchic. By 1850, though Peel could not have known it as he lay dying at Whitehall Gardens, the larger problems of his time had been met and solved. The age of revolt was giving way to the age of stability; and of that age Peel had been the chief architect. The failure of Chartism two years earlier had marked the change that was coming over British society. After his death the transformation continued. The decline in agitation and violence, the softening of class and religious animosities, the growing social reconciliation of which the Great Exhibition was a symbol, the cheapness, prosperity and stability of the mid-Victorian era, the long Indian summer of aristocratic parliamentary rule, all these made England in the twenty years which followed the repeal of the Corn Laws a different world to

was, if possible, to encourage a kind and sympathetic feeling between the different classes and ranks in society, so that each might have adapted itself to a change which is inevitable. This belief is so firmly fixed in my mind, that I have always regarded it as the key by which much of his conduct that has exposed him to obloquy, was to be explained.' (RA/Y 154/49, n.d. but probably 1846.)

the generation of disunity, distress and disorder after Waterloo in which most of Peel's working life had been spent. This, in the last analysis, is the basis on which Peel's claims to greatness must be judged. His allegiance was to an older concept than party loyalty; it was to the service of the state.

III

On the evening of 5 July Peel's body was taken in a plain hearse from Whitehall Gardens to the Euston Square railway terminus. It was accompanied by a mourning coach carrying Frederick Peel, Hardinge, Graham and Goulburn. People gathered along the route and a large number joined behind the little procession on its slow progress to the station. Frederick Peel travelled with the coffin; the others stayed at Euston Square until the train left at quarter to nine. When it arrived at Tamworth at midnight a large number of townspeople were waiting despite the lateness of the hour. Many walked behind the hearse through the summer night all the way to Drayton Manor.

The funeral took place the following Tuesday, 9 July, in the little parish church of Drayton Bassett where not many months earlier Peel had told Julia he wished to be buried beside his mother and father. In accordance with his instructions it was a private ceremony to which outside the family only his oldest and most intimate friends were invited. But all over the country on that day, in great towns like Manchester, Birmingham, Liverpool, Bristol, Leeds, Wolverhampton and Bury, mills stopped work, shops were closed, and in the seaports the flags of the vessels in harbour were lowered to half-mast. It was hay-making season and in the fields between Tamworth and Drayton there were swathes of grass drying in the summer breeze. As the morning wore on, crowds of countrymen, labourers, and estate-workers, with their wives and children, came in from the surrounding district and beyond, from Birmingham, Stafford, Tamworth, Lichfield, Sutton and Coleshill, spreading over the green and wooded expanse of Drayton Park and gathering round the churchyard. Some were in mourning, the humbler folk in their Sunday velveteens with scraps of crape, the women in bonnet and shawl. At midday a special train with the official party from London arrived at Tamworth from where they were conveyed to Drayton in mourning coaches. The Duke of Wellington had been invited but ill-health made it impossible for him to come. Lord Lincoln was abroad; Sidney Herbert, though not in the procession, was inconspicuously present in the church gallery. For the rest the list of pallbearers was like a rollcall of Peel's political career—Aberdeen, Hardinge, Graham, Goulburn, Sir George Clerk, and Bonham.[1]

Shortly before one o'clock, the time fixed for the funeral to begin, the sky became overcast. The wind got up, and a cold rain began to fall. As the church bell commenced to toll, drenching showers swept across the landscape and for a while the park was obscured by driving vapour. The storm lasted about twenty minutes. When it passed, the procession formed up outside the manor. It passed down the drive, in a silence broken only by the hollow sound of the horses' hooves and the grinding of wheels on the wet gravel. At the lodge gates it was joined by the principal tenants on horseback, all in black with crape bands hanging limply from their soaked hats. The long line of coaches and horsemen moved slowly through the little village of Drayton and along the narrow lane skirting the park to the church. As they reached the gate the sky darkened and it began to pour down once more. In the pelting rain the heavy crimson-covered coffin was taken out of the hearse and carried inside.

[1] For descriptions of the funeral see *The Times* and *Morning Chronicle*, 10 July, *London Illustrated News*, 13 July 1850.

SOME MAXIMS AND REFLECTIONS
OF SIR ROBERT PEEL

Speaking with that caution with which I am sometimes taunted but which I find a great convenience.

> H. of C., 1842 (*Speeches*, III, 871)

The longer I live, the more clearly do I see the folly of yielding a rash and precipitate assent to any political measure.

> *ibid.*, 1830 (*Speeches*, II, 231)

I have little confidence in my own infallibility, and as little in the infallibility of others.

> *ibid.*, 1835 (*Speeches*, III, 91)

I see no dignity in persevering in error.

> *ibid.*, 1833 (*Speeches*, II, 684)

A correct arrangement of a few prominent and leading facts is the best foundation for future measures.

> *ibid.*, 1830 (*Speeches*, II, 250)

There seem to me very few facts, at least ascertainable facts, in politics.

> to Lord Brougham, 1846 (*Peel*, III, 357)

Men, and the conduct of men, are much more the creatures of circumstances than they generally appear in history.

> to Mahon, 1833 (Stanhope, *Miscellanies*)

The true policy in Public Life is to act with decision and as far as possible to adhere to what is decided, but not to decide before the time for decision shall have arrived, and carefully to consider in the interval every mode of solving a difficulty.

> to Graham, 30 July 1841 (Graham Papers)

What is right must unavoidably be politic.

> to Goulburn, 23 Sept. 1822 (Goulburn Papers)

The great art of government is to work by such instruments as the world supplies.

> in cabinet, 1844 (44777 f. 172)

If an ancient principle must be abandoned, the new principle ought to be a secure one.

> H. of C., 1835 (*Speeches*, III, 103)

Men, if in office, seemed really to be like the Indians—they inherited all the qualities of those enemies they killed.

> *ibid.*, 1831 (*Speeches*, II, 272)

Whatever party is in, the ministers who sit in the House of Lords will be very different men from those in the House of Commons; will live exclusively among gentlemen, will dine out every day, and pass their time in abusing the House of Commons.

Conversation at Whitehall Gardens, 1837 (44777 f. 40)

Nothing could be more childish than the unbounded confidence which some men had in their infallibility and in the outcry which they raised against any change by others of an opinion once professed.

H. of C., 1833 (*Speeches*, II, 689)

All my experience in public life is in favour of the employment of what the world would call young men instead of old ones.

to Wellington, 1829 (*W.N.D.* VI, 287)

No government can exist which does not control and restrain the popular sentiments.

H. of C., 1832 (*Speeches*, II, 536)

Mixed monarchy is important in respect to the end which is to be achieved rather than in respect to the means by which it is gained.

ibid., 1842 (*Speeches*, IV, 60)

This country has been governed better than any other country on earth.

ibid., 1831 (*Speeches*, II, 330)

We are here to consult the interests and not to obey the will of the people, if we honestly believe that that will conflicts with those interests.

ibid., 1831 (*Speeches*, II, 394)

No man attached to his country could always acquiesce in the opinions of the majority.

ibid., 1831 (*Speeches*, II, 314)

There will always be found a permanent fund of discontent and dissatisfaction in every country.

ibid., 1832 (*Speeches*, II, 511)

I am not sure that those who clamour most, suffer most.

ibid., 1834 (*Speeches*, II, 861)

Gratuitous novelties tended to unsettle men's minds, and engender and foster a desire for innovations.

ibid., 1831 (*Speeches*, II, 368)

That practical problem which in some case or other requires daily solution—to harmonise as far as possible the satisfaction of new wants and necessities with the framework of time-honoured institutions and the social usages and feelings which are closely interwoven with them.

to Graham, 18 Nov. 1842 (Graham Papers)

It is well to make concessions while they yet can be made—many

Sovereigns have had cause to lament having let the hour of concession go by.

>   to Baron Bunsen, 1842 (*Memoirs of Bunsen*, II, 38)

Great public measures cannot be carried by the influence of mere reason.

>   to Lord Radnor, 1846 (RA/C 23/51)

Of all vulgar arts of government, that of solving every difficulty which might arise by thrusting the hand into the public purse is the most delusory and contemptible.

>   H. of C., 1834 (*Speeches*, II, 849)

Do not hastily conclude that everything which a man of science recommends must be advantageous for the public interest.

>   to Haddington, 1842 (40456 f. 98)

Philosophers are very regardless of expense when the public has to bear it.

>   to Haddington, 1844 (40457 f. 306)

General prosperity, and not legal enactments, produce a practical effect upon the rate of wages.

>   H. of C., 1846 (*Speeches*, IV, 653)

There are those who seem to have nothing else to do but to suggest modes of taxation to men in office.

>   *ibid.*, 1842 (*Speeches*, III, 872)

The party interests of a Government are in the long run much better promoted by the honest exercise of patronage than by the *perversion* of it for the purpose of satisfying individual supporters.

>   to Lord de Grey, 1841 (40477 f. 17)

The distinction of being without an honour is becoming a rare and valuable one and should not become extinct.

>   to Graham, 1841 (40446 f. 106)

It seems to me that the distinction of the Peerage, and every other distinction, has been degraded by the profuse and incautious use which has been made of them.

>   to Wellington, 19 Sept. 1841 (Apsley House Papers)

Between the Dissenters and the Established Church there is an enormous neutral ground of infidelity.

>   H. of C., 1835 (*Speeches*, III, 158)

If I can have nothing but improved secular instruction, I would rather have that than ignorance.

>   *ibid.*, 1845 (*Speeches*, IV, 523)

A pamphleteering, letter-writing Bishop ever on the fret is sufficient to throw a Diocese into convulsions.

>to Graham, 24 Dec. 1844 (Graham Papers)

Priests are not above sublunary considerations. Priests have nephews.

>*ibid.*, 13 Aug. 1845

Considering the sanguinary nature of great battles . . . too direct a reference to the special intervention of Almighty God is not very seemly.

>to the Queen, 1846 (RA/A 18/29)

There are many things which I know to be morally wrong, with which neither I nor you can interfere in the way of legislation.

>H. of C., 1844 (*Speeches*, IV, 370)

There is a moral obligation incumbent upon the possessors of property which laws cannot supersede or control.

>*ibid.*, 1846 (*Speeches*, IV, 674)

The sincerity of a man's opinions has nothing whatever to do with the policy or justice of prosecution.

>*ibid.*, 1832 (*Speeches*, II, 545)

Much is said of English severity but not a word about Irish provocation.

>*ibid.*, 1833 (*Speeches*, II, 608)

There is no appetite for truth in Ireland.

>to Leveson Gower, 1828 (40335 f. 77)

I had experience in early life in that country [Ireland] of the danger of saying a civil word, and of the utter uselessness of attempting to coax people out of disappointment at not getting what they wanted.

>to Graham, 15 Oct. 1842 (Graham Papers)

There are many parties in Ireland who desire to have a grievance and prefer the grievance to the Remedy.

>to the Queen, 1844 (RA/A 16/112)

An Irishman has no sense of the ridiculous when office is in question.

>to Graham, 28 Dec. 1845 (Graham Papers)

I have heard of more instances of shots through the hat in Ireland, without the head being affected, than in any other country.

>to Goulburn, 1822 (40328 f. 186)

Every case of firing a bullet through a hat, and not through the head of the wearer is most suspicious.

>to Graham, 14 Sept. 1842 (Graham Papers)

Coercion is not a cure but continued insurrection is positive death.

>H. of C., 1833 (*Speeches*, II, 634)

We stand on the confines of Western Europe: the chief connecting link between the old world and the new.

ibid., 1846 (*Speeches*, IV, 625)

The period in which our lot and the lot of our fathers has been cast—the period which has elapsed since the first outbreak of the first French Revolution—has been one of the most memorable periods that the history of the world will afford.

ibid., 1842 (*Speeches*, III, 886)

Peace . . . is not always to be obtained or preserved at the wish of the government.

ibid., 1830 (*Speeches*, II, 260)

The hasty inordinate demand for peace might be just as dangerous as the clamour for war.

ibid., 1832 (*Speeches*, II, 507)

Nothing is more unfortunate than the course occasionally pursued in this House of loading with personal obloquy and the severest vituperation those who possess the chief authority in countries, whose cordiality it is our interest to cultivate, even though they are governed by institutions less free than our own.

ibid., 1835 (*Speeches*, III, 13)

A cordial and good understanding between France and England is essential to the peace and the welfare of Europe.

ibid., 1841 (*Speeches*, III, 738)

The modern history of France is the substitution of one crisis for another.

to Aberdeen, 1849 (43065 f. 408)

This man [Louis Napoleon] owes his election to the name of another man and probably his best chance of maintaining the Prestige of the name is to imitate the other man as far as the altered circumstances of the Country will permit.

to Aberdeen, 1849 (43065 f. 391)

Infamous as Robespierre and Marat unquestionably are, it would be no easy matter to assign to each their due share of infamy without a very dispassionate enquiry into many minute events which contributed to shape their course, and into the degrees of conflicting dangers between which they had to choose.

to Mahon, 1833 (Stanhope, *Miscellanies*)

Fox was not a man of settled, reasonable, political principles.

Conversation at Drayton, 1836 (44777 f. 23)

Try Walpole and Strafford by the *result* of their counsels, by their result to the Monarchs whom they served, and how powerful would the contrast be in favour of Walpole.

to Mahon, 1833 (Stanhope, *Miscellanies*)

Nothing would surprise me more than to find Walpole convicted of personal dishonesty.

ibid.

So far as the great majority of his [Walpole's] audience was concerned, he had blocks to cut, and he chose a fitter instrument than a razor to cut them with.

ibid.

I know few things more agreeable than the rapid change of scene in such a country as England.

to Goulburn, 22 Aug. 1836 (Goulburn Papers)

English grouse are to Scotch what Scotchmen are to Englishmen. They are much more wary and provident Birds and more given to locomotion.

to Aberdeen, 1836 (43061 f. 193)

[*On the need for a steamer to replace the royal yacht.*] Utilitarianism must prevail on the Romantic and Picturesque even in the case of Royal Voyages. Towing after all is but an ignoble process.

to Haddington, 1842 (40456 f. 160)

[*On the practice of Admirals taking their wives to sea.*] I cannot think that Lady Owen in the 'Formidable' and Lady Seymour in the 'Collingwood' add much to the efficiency of great Line of Battle Ships.

to Haddington, 1844 (40457 f. 161)

I have no wish to withhold justice from writers who give that proof of their sincerity which is implied by the publication of an octavo volume.

H. of C., 1844 (*Speeches*, IV, 352)

BIBLIOGRAPHICAL NOTE

Except where otherwise indicated, quotations from Peel's speeches are taken from the collected *Speeches*. Quotations from the standard collection of correspondence in Parker, *Peel*, are occasionally given without reference where the passage can easily be located under date and subject. Other references are given in footnotes either in full or in abbreviated form. The following lists comprise only manuscript sources and those printed sources for which a shortened title has been used in the footnotes.

A. MANUSCRIPT COLLECTIONS

1. *British Museum Additional Manuscripts*

i. Peel Papers	40181–40617	(see bibliographical note in *Mr. Secretary Peel*)
ii. Aberdeen Papers	43061–43065	correspondence with Peel, 1828–50
iii. Gladstone Papers	44275	correspondence with Peel
	44777	memoranda

2. *Public Record Office, London*

i. Cardwell Papers GD	48/50	correspondence with Goulburn
	48/53	notes on Peel Papers and material for a life of Peel
ii. Ellenborough Papers	30/12/28/5–7	Journal 1834–35, 1837–38, 1841
	30/12/21/1	correspondence with Peel 1829–47
	30/12/29/Pt. 1/18	correspondence with Peel 1834–35
	30/12/29/Pt. 2/9	do.
	30/12/6/6	political correspondence 1835–61
	30/12/4/29	correspondence with Peel 1846
	30/12/37	letters to Ellenborough 1841–44
iii. Russell Papers	30/22/7 and 30/22/8 Pt. 1	correspondence 1848

3. *Royal Archives, Windsor*
   i. Correspondence of Peel with Queen Victoria, Prince Albert and G. Anson 1841–50
   ii. Memoranda by Prince Albert and G. Anson
   iii. Correspondence and Papers on
       a. Change of government 1841
       b. Irish policy 1844–46
       c. Ministerial Crisis Dec. 1845
       d. Peel's policy and change of government 1846
       e. Formation of Russell's administration 1846
   iv. Baron Stockmar's Papers

4. *Other Collections*
   i. *Central Registry of Archives*
       a. Parkes Papers
       b. Hardinge Papers
   ii. *Register House, Edinburgh*
       Clerk of Penicuick Papers
   iii. *Bodleian Library, Oxford*
        Clarendon Papers
   iv. *Nottingham University Library*
       Newcastle Papers
   v. *Surrey Record Office*
      Goulburn Papers (see note in *Mr. Secretary Peel*)
   vi. *Tamworth Public Library*
       Mitchell Collection (see note in *Mr. Secretary Peel*)

5. *Collections in private hands*
   i. Disraeli Papers
   ii. Diary of W. S. Dugdale
   iii. Graham Papers
   vi. Knatchbull Diary and Correspondence
   v. Manners Sutton Papers
   vi. Peel MSS. (see note in *Mr. Secretary Peel*)
   vii. Stanhope Papers
   viii. Wellington Papers

B. CONTEMPORARY PERIODICALS AND NEWSPAPERS

Agricultural Gazette
Annual Register

Chambers' Papers for the People
Christian Observer
Courier
Edinburgh Courant
Farmer's Magazine
Illustrated London News
Lancet
Liverpool Mercury
Macmillan's Magazine
Morning Chronicle
Nineteenth Century
Quarterly Review
Revue des Deux Mondes
Staffordshire Advertiser
The Times
Westminster Review

C. OTHER TITLES ABBREVIATED IN FOOTNOTES

For unspecified five-figure numerals see A, 1.

Aberdeen, Life of the 4th Earl of, by Lady Frances Balfour (2 v., 1923)

Aberdeen–Lieven Corr.: Correspondence of Lord Aberdeen and Princess Lieven, 1832–54, ed. E. Jones Parry (Camden 3rd series, LX, LXII)

Arbuthnot, Correspondence of Charles, ed. A. Aspinall (Camden 3rd. series, LXV)

Arbuthnot, Journal of Mrs., ed. F. Bamford and the Duke of Wellington (2 v., 1950)

Aspinall, Diaries: Three Early Nineteenth Century Diaries, ed. A. Aspinall (1952)

Beaconsfield Letters: Lord Beaconsfield's Letters, 1830–52, ed. R. Disraeli (1887)

Broughton, Lord, Recollections of a Long Life, ed. Lady Dorchester (6 v., 1911)

Bunsen, Memoirs of Baron (2 v., 1868)

Campbell, Life of Lord Chancellor, ed. Mrs. Hardcastle (2 v., 1881)

Cardwell, see A, 2 (i)

Clarendon, see A, 4 (iii)

Clarendon, Life and Letters of the 4th Earl of, by Sir H. Maxwell (2 v., 1913)

Clerk, see A, 4 (ii)

Cobden, Life of Richard, by John Morley (14th ed. 1920)

Croker, Correspondence and Diaries of J. W., ed. L. J. Jennings (3 v., 1884)

Disraeli Papers, see A, 5 (i)

Dugdale, see A, 5 (ii)

Dyott, Diary, ed. R. W. Jeffrey (2 v., 1907)

E.H.R.: English Historical Review

Ellenborough, see A, 2 (ii) journal.

Ellenborough, Corr., see A, 2 (ii) correspondence

English Politics: Reaction and Reconstruction in English Politics, 1832–52, by N. Gash (1965)

Gladstone, Life of, by J. Morley (3 v., 1912)

Goulburn, see A, 4 (v)

Graham, see A, 5 (iii)

Graham, Life and Letters of Sir James, by C. S. Parker (2 v., 1907)

Greville, Memoirs, The. The definitive edition is that ed. by L. Strachey and R. Fulford (7 v., 1938)

H.M.C.: Historical Manuscripts Commission

Hansard, Parliamentary Debates, Third Series

Hardinge, see A, 4 (i)

Haydon, Diary of B. R., ed. W. B. Pope (5 v., Harvard 1960–63)

Herbert, Sidney, A Memoir, by Lord Stanmore (2 v., 1906)

Herries, Memoir of J. C., ed. E. Herries (2 v., 1880)

Hodder; Life of the 7th Earl of Shaftesbury, by E. Hodder (1890)

Hyde, Gladstone: Mr. Gladstone at the Board of Trade, by F. Hyde (1934)

Kitson Clark, G., *Peel and the Conservative Party* (1929)

Knatchbull, see A, 5 (iv)

Knatchbull: Kentish Family, by Sir H. Knatchbull-Hugessen (1960)

McCord: The Anti-Corn Law League, 1838–46, by N. McCord (1958)

Manners Sutton, see A, 5 (v)

Martin, Sir T., *Life of the Prince Consort* (1882)

Martineau, J., *Life of Fifth Duke of Newcastle* (1908)

Mitchell Collection, see A, 4 (vi)

Mr. Secretary Peel, by N. Gash (1961)

N&Q: Notes and Queries

Neumann, Diary of Philipp von, ed. G. Beresford Chancellor (2 v., 1928)

Newcastle, see A, 4 (iv)

P.P.: Parliamentary Papers

Parkes, see A, 4 (i)

Peel MSS., see A, 5 (vi)

Peel: Sir Robert Peel from his Private Papers, ed. C. S. Parker (3 v., 1891–99)

Peel, Letters; The Private Letters of Sir Robert Peel, ed. George Peel (1920)

Peel Memoirs: Memoirs by the Rt. Hon. Sir Robert Peel, ed. Lord Mahon and E. Cardwell (2 v., 1856–57)

Playfair, Memoirs and Correspondence of Lyon, by T. Wemyss Reid (1899)

RA: See A, 3

Raikes: Portion of a Journal kept by T. Raikes esq. 1831–47 (4 v., 1856–58)

Russell, see A, 2 (iii)

Shelley Diary: Diary of Frances, Lady Shelley, ed. R. Edgcumbe (2 v., 1913)

Speeches, of the late Rt. Hon. Sir Robert Peel delivered in the House of Commons (4 v., 1853)

Stanhope, see A, 5 (vii)

Stanhope, Earl: *Miscellanies* (1863)

VL: *The Letters of Queen Victoria, 1837–61,* ed. A. C. Benson and Viscount Esher (3 v., 1908)

Wellington, see A, 5 (viii)

Wellington and His Friends, ed. 7th Duke of Wellington (1965)

Wharncliffe: The First Lady Wharncliffe and Her Family, ed. by C. Grosvenor and Lord Stuart (2 v., 1927)

W.N.D.: *Despatches, Correspondence · and Memoranda of the Duke of Wellington (in continuation of former series), 1819–32,* ed. Duke of Wellington (8 v., 1867–80)

BIBLIOGRAPHICAL NOTE TO NEW EDITION

Of works published since 1971 the following may be suggested as having a bearing on Peel's career, or on aspects of his policy and administration, in the period after 1830. Place of publication is London unless otherwise stated.

A. GENERAL

M. Brock, *The Great Reform Act*, (1973).

Travis L. Crosby, *English Farmers and the Politics of Protection 1815–52*, (Newton Abbot 1976).

G. I. T. Machin, *Politics and the Churches in Great Britain 1832–1867*, (1973).

B. PARTY HISTORY

Lord Butler (ed.) and others, *The Conservatives, A History from the Origins to 1965*, (1977).

J. B. Conacher, *The Peelites and the Party System 1846–52*, (Newton Abbot 1972).

A. Jones and A. B. Erickson, *The Peelites 1846–1857*, (Ohio State University 1972).

D. Southgate (ed.) and others, *The Conservative Leadership 1832–1937*, (1974).

R. Stewart, *Lord Derby and the Protectionist Party 1841–1852*, (Cambridge 1971).

R. Stewart, *The Foundations of the Conservative Party 1830–1867*, (1978).

C. ADMINISTRATION

Sir Norman Chester, *The English Administrative System 1780–1870*, (Oxford 1981).

Fundamental survey of the changes taking place in this period.

W. C. Lubenow, *The Politics of Government Growth, Early Victorian Attitudes towards State Intervention 1833–1848*, (Newton Abbot 1971).

Covers poor laws, public health, railways and industrial legislation.

O. Macdonagh, *Early Victorian Government 1830–1870* (1977).

Covers industrial legislation, poor laws, local government, public health, law and order, and Ireland.

Travis L. Crosby, *Sir Robert Peel's Administration 1841–1846*, (Newton Abbot 1976).

Condensed but useful guide.

D. IRELAND

Robert Kee, *The Green Flag, A History of Irish Nationalism*, (1972).
> Long, evocative narrative account concentrating on the period since the end of the eighteenth century.

Donal A. Kerr, *Peel, Priests and Politics, Sir Robert Peel's Administration and the Roman Catholic Church in Ireland 1841–1846*, (Oxford 1982).
> Skilful and balanced analysis using much new archival material.

G. O'Tuathaigh, *Ireland before the Famine 1798–1848*, (Dublin 1972).

E. BIOGRAPHICAL

Georgina Battiscombe, *Shaftesbury*, (1974).

Muriel Chamberlain, *Lord Aberdeen*, (1983).

E. J. Feuchtwanger, *Gladstone*, (1975).

G. B. A. M. Finlayson, *The Seventh Earl of Shaftesbury*, (1981).

W. E. Gladstone, *I Autobiographica II Autobiographical Memoranda (Prime Ministers' Papers*, 1971–2).

Hermione Hobhouse, *Prince Albert, His Life and Work*, (1983).

R. Rhodes James, *Albert, Prince Consort*, (1983).

Elizabeth Longford, *Wellington*, (2 vols. 1969–72).

John Prest, *Lord John Russell*, (1972).

Richard Shannon, *Gladstone, I 1809–1865*, (1982).

Wellington, The Political Correspondence I 1833–1834 (Prime Ministers' Papers, 1975).

Cecil Woodham-Smith, *Queen Victoria, Her Life and Times I, 1819–1861*, (1972).

F. ARTICLES

N. Gash, 'The Organization of the Conservative Party 1832–1846,', (*Parliamentary History*, vols. I & II, 1982–3).

G. I. T. Machin, 'The Disruption and British Politics 1834–43', (*Scot. Hist. Review*, LI April 1972).
> Examines the schism in the Church of Scotland in the light of the relationship of the Non-Intrusionist Party with the governments of the day.

Ian Newbould, 'Sir Robert Peel and the Conservative Party 1832–1841: A Study in Failure?' (*Eng. Hist. Review*, XCVIII, July 1983).
> Analyses the nature of the Conservative Party in the first decade of its existence.

J. A. Phillips, 'The Many Faces of Reform. The Reform Bill and the Electorate', (*Parliamentary History*, I 1982).
Good review article taking into account views of previous historians.

INDEX

PRINCIPAL ABBREVIATIONS

b.—brother	E.—Earl
Bn.—Baron	Ld.—Lord
Bp.—Bishop	Ly.—Lady
Chan.—Chancellor	M.—Marquess
Ctss.—Countess	Pss.—Princess
Cttee.—Committee	Q.—Queen
d.—daughter	s.—son
D.—Duke	Vt.—Viscount
Dss.—Duchess	w.—wife

INDEX

DATE DUE
